CALIFORNIA

An Interpretive History

EIGHTH EDITION

James J. Rawls

Instructor of History
Diablo Valley College

Walton Bean

Late Professor of History
University of California, Berkeley

Boston   Burr Ridge, IL   Dubuque, IA   Madison, WI   New York   San Francisco   St. Louis
Bangkok   Bogotá   Caracas   Kuala Lumpur   Lisbon   London   Madrid   Mexico City
Milan   Montreal   New Delhi   Santiago   Seoul   Singapore   Sydney   Taipei   Toronto

McGraw-Hill Higher Education ⟨⟩

*A Division of The **McGraw-Hill** Companies*

California: An Interpretive History

Published by McGraw-Hill, an imprint of The McGraw-Hill Companies, Inc., 1221 Avenue of the Americas, New York, NY 10020. Copyright © 2003, 1998, 1993, 1988, 1983, 1978, 1973, 1968 by The McGraw-Hill Companies, Inc. All rights reserved. No part of this publication may be reproduced or distributed in any form on by any means, or stored in a database or retrieval system, without the prior written consent of The McGraw-Hill Companies, Inc., including, but not limited to, in any network or other electronic storage or transmission, or broadcast for distance learning.

This book is printed on acid-free paper.

2 3 4 5 6 7 8 9 0   DOC   DOC   0 9 8 7 6 5 4 3

ISBN 0-07-242438-9

Publisher: Lyn Uhl
Sponsoring editor: Steven Drummond
Developmental editors: Kristen Mellitt and Kate Scheinman
Senior design manager: Jean Mailander
Marketing manager: Janise Fry
Senior project manager: Christina Gimlin
Senior production supervisor: Richard DeVitto
Senior photo researcher: Brian Pecko
Senior supplements producer: Louis Swaim
Art editor: Cristin Yancey
Interior and cover designer: Glenda King
Compositor: Thompson Type
Typeface: Times Roman
Printer: R. R. Donnelley & Sons, Crawfordsville
Cover art: *Swirling Surf, Horseshoe Cove, CA.* © Mark E. Gibson.

Library of Congress Cataloging-in-Publication Data

Rawls, James J.
   California : an interpretive history / James J. Rawls, Walton Bean.—8th ed.
      p.   cm.
   Includes bibliographical references (p.   ) and index.
   ISBN 0-07-242438-9
   1. California—History.   I. Bean, Walton.   II. Title.
F861.R38   2002

                                            2002021272

http://www.mhhe.com

About the Authors

JAMES J. RAWLS, an instructor of history at Diablo Valley College, received his B.A. in history from Stanford University. He was awarded an M.A. and Ph.D. in history from the University of California, Berkeley, completing his doctoral dissertation under the guidance of Walton Bean. Dr. Rawls also has taught California history as a visiting associate professor at the University of California, Berkeley. He serves as the Reviews Editor of *California History,* the journal of the California Historical Society. He is the author of *Indians of California: The Changing Image* and *Chief Red Fox is Dead: A History of Native Americans since 1945,* coauthor of *Land of Liberty: A United States History* and *California: Adventures in Time and Space,* editor of *New Directions in California History: A Book of Readings* and *California History: Teaching with Primary Sources,* and coeditor of *A Golden State: Mining and Economic Development in Gold Rush California* and *California: A Place, A People, A Dream.* His articles and reviews have appeared in such publications as *Journal of American History, Pacific Historical Review,* and *American Indian Quarterly.*

The late WALTON BEAN was, for more than 35 years, a member of the University of California, Berkeley, faculty where he taught undergraduate courses in California history and graduate courses in California and twentieth-century United States history. His highly acclaimed book, *Boss Ruef's San Francisco,* won the Commonwealth Club of California's gold medal and the annual prize of the Pacific Coast Branch of the American Historical Association. Dr. Bean also served as Asia Foundation Professor of American History at the University of Karachi. He received his A.B. and M.A. from the University of Southern California and was awarded his Ph.D. from the University of California, Berkeley.

Crescent City

SISKIYOU MTS.

MT. SHASTA

Klamath R.

Pit River

Trinity R.

Shasta Lake

Eureka

MT. LASSEN

Redding

Susanville

Eel River

Sacramento R.

Red Bluff

Feather R.

Chico

Oroville

Ukiah

Yuba R.

Marysville

Clear Lake

American R.

LAKE TAHOE

FORT ROSS

Santa Rosa

Sacramento

Napa

Mokelumne R.

Stanislaus R.

Mono Lake

San Rafael

Berkeley

Stockton

San Francisco

Oakland

San Mateo

Hayward

Modesto

Merced R.

Redwood City

Palo Alto

San Jose

King's R.

Bishop

Santa Cruz

Merced

OWEN'S VALLEY

San Joaquin R.

Monterey

Salinas

Fresno

Salinas R.

Hanford

DEATH VALLEY

Delano

Kern R.

Needles

San Luis Obispo

Bakersfield

Santa Maria

Barstow

Santa Barbara

MOJAVE DESERT

Ventura

Pasadena

San Bernardino

Los Angeles

Anaheim

Colorado River

Long Beach

Riverside

Palm Springs

Huntington Beach

Santa Ana

Blythe

San Clemente

Salton Sea

Oceanside

IMPERIAL VALLEY

La Jolla

El Centro

San Diego

-N-

SIERRA NEVADA

Contents

Preface xv

Chapter 1   **Introduction: Geography and History**   **1**

The Origins of California   1
Regional Diversity   4
The Climates of California   7

Chapter 2   **The Original Californians**   **10**

Food and Population   11
Aspects of Material Culture   13
Location, Linguistic Groups, Tribes   14
Social Culture   15

Chapter 3   **Discovery, Exploration, and Founding**   **21**

The Finding and Naming of California   21
Cabrillo and the Discovery of Alta California   22
Francis Drake and Nova Albion   24
The Manila Galleon and the California Coast   26
Vizcaíno and Monterey   27
Spain's Indian Policies   28
The Mission as a Frontier Institution   29
Gálvez and the Plan for Alta California   31
The Franciscans and Father Serra   32
The Sacred Expedition   34

Chapter 4   **Outposts of a Dying Empire   40**

Bucareli, Anza, and the Founding of San Francisco   40
Neve and the Pueblos of San José and Los Angeles   44
Native Resistance   46
The Impact of the Missions   48
Attempts at Reinforcement   52
Exploration of the Central Valley   53
The Coming of the Russians   54
The Last Years under the Spanish Flag   55

Chapter 5   **A Marginal Province of a Troubled Republic   58**

Government and Politics in Theory and Practice   58
The Secularization Problem   60
From Echeandía to Figueroa   61
Figueroa and Secularization   62
Alvarado and Provincial Autonomy   64
The Heyday of the Rancheros   66

Chapter 6   **American Infiltration: Traders, Trappers, and Settlers   71**

The Yankee Traders   71
The Beaver Trappers   73
Early Settlers   76
Covered Wagons, 1841 to 1846   79

Chapter 7   **The American Conquest   83**

Overtures, Diplomatic and Undiplomatic   83
Plans of the Polk Administration   85
John Charles Frémont   86
The Bear Flag Revolt   89
The Mexican War and California   91

Chapter 8   **The Gold Rush and Economic Development   97**

Marshall's Discovery at Sutter's Mill   97
The Forty-Eighters   98
The Forty-Niners   101
The Diggings   104
Early Mining Methods   105
Mining Camp Law   107
From an Adventure to a Profession   107
An Economic Multiplier   109
The Historical Significance of the Gold Rush   111

Chapter 9   A New State and Frontier Politics   116

Military Governments   116
The Constitutional Convention and Its Problems   117
The First Legislature   121
The Admission of California to the Union   122
The Feud between Broderick and Gwin   123
Movements for State Division   126
California and the Civil War   126

Chapter 10   Crime and Punishment   130

The Nature of Vigilantism   130
The Hounds in San Francisco   132
The San Francisco Committee of 1851   133
Statewide Vigilance   135
The San Francisco Committee of 1856   136

Chapter 11   Racial Oppression and Conflict   141

Treatment of Mexican Miners   141
Land-Title Troubles   142
The Act of 1851 and the Land Commission   145
Early Discrimination against the Chinese   147
The "Indian Question"   150
Episodes in Extermination   152
Decline and Exploitation   154
Blacks Enslaved and Free   155

Chapter 12   Culture and Anarchy   160

Newspapers and Literary Magazines   160
Writers of the Fifties   161
Bret Harte   163
Mark Twain   164
Joaquin Miller and Other Poets   165
Churches and Schools   166

Chapter 13   Building the Central Pacific Railroad   169

Early Transportation   169
Judah and the Conception of the Central Pacific   170
Enter the Four "Associates"   171
Federal and State Support   173
Difficulties and the Death of Judah   174
Solving the Problems of Construction   175

Chapter 14   The "Terrible Seventies"   179

The Onset of Depression   179
Transportation Monopoly   180
Land Monopoly   184
The Comstock and Overspeculation   186

Chapter 15   Political Turmoil and a New Constitution   191

The Increase of Anti-Chinese Sentiment   191
The Workingmen's Party of California   193
The Constitution of 1879   196
The Frustration of Reform   198
Chinese Exclusion and Segregation   198

Chapter 16   Economic Growth   201

The Wheat Bonanza   201
Wines   203
The Citrus Industry   203
The Rise of Southern California   205
Water and Land   208
Electric Railways and Urbanization   210

Chapter 17   Culture and Oligarchy   215

Henry George   215
Ambrose Bierce   216
Frank Norris   217
Jack London   218
Historiography   220
Lords of the Press   222
The Arts and Architecture   223
Schools, Colleges, and Universities   226

Chapter 18   Politics in the Era of Railroad Domination   231

The Colton Letters   232
The Huntington-Stanford Feud   232
Los Angeles Fights for a Free Harbor   233
The Funding Bill   234
The Southern Pacific Machine   236
William F. Herrin   238
Failure of Nineteenth-Century Reform Movements   239

Chapter 19 Labor and Capital   242

Backgrounds of the California Labor Movement   242
The Rise of Unions in San Francisco   243
The Triumph of the Open Shop in Los Angeles   246
Agricultural Labor: Unorganized and Disfranchised   249
The IWW   250

Chapter 20 The Roots of Reform   254

Boss Ruef and the Union Labor Party   254
The San Francisco Graft Prosecution   256
The Good Government Movement in Los Angeles   259
The Lincoln-Roosevelt League   260

Chapter 21 The Republican Progressives in Power   266

Public Utility Regulation   267
Governmental Efficiency and Finance   267
More Democracy   268
Nonpartisanship and Cross-Filing   269
Woman Suffrage   269
Public Morals   272
The Progressives and Labor   273
The Anti-Japanese Movement   276
The Decline of Progressivism   280

Chapter 22 The Triumph of Conservatism   284

The Rise and Fall of the Socialist Movement   284
The Mooney Case   286
The Criminal Syndicalism Law   288
The Decline of Organized Labor   290
The Collapse of the Democratic Party   291
The Continuing Decline of Republican Progressivism   291
The Federal Plan of Reapportionment   293

Chapter 23 New Industries for Southern California   296

Origins of the Oil Industry   296
The Oil Boom of the Twenties   299
The Automobile Revolution   300
The Movies Discover California   303
The Rise of "The Industry"   304

Chapter 24   Controversies over Land and Water   310

The Yosemite and John Muir   310
The Hetch Hetchy Controversy   313
The Owens Valley–Los Angeles Aqueduct   314
The Boulder Canyon Project   316
The Colorado River Aqueduct   319
The Central Valley Project   321
The 160-Acre Limit   322

Chapter 25   The Great Depression   325

"Sunny Jim"   325
Social Messiahs   327
Depression and Deportation   328
Labor Strife   330
Upton Sinclair and EPIC   333
From Merriam to Olson   336

Chapter 26   Cultural Trends   340

Robinson Jeffers   340
John Steinbeck   342
William Saroyan and Other Writers   344
William Randolph Hearst and Other Journalists   346
The Arts   348
Architecture   349

Chapter 27   Wartime Growth and Problems   354

The Impact of Federal Spending   354
Wartime Shipyards   356
"Americans All"   357
The Rise of the Aircraft Industry   359
The Relocation of Japanese Americans   361

Chapter 28   Politics California Style   369

Nonpartisanship Favors the Republicans   369
Filling the Void   370
The Governorship of Earl Warren   373
The Spurious Issue of "Loyalty"   375
The Governorship of Edmund G. Brown   379
Extremists, Right and Left   381

Chapter 29   Industrialized Agriculture and Disorganized Labor   386

Green Gold   386
The Empire of Agribusiness   387
"Farm Fascism" in the 1930s   388
The Rise and Fall of the Bracero Program   390
Unionization Breaks Through   392
Equal Protection of the Laws   396

Chapter 30   Diversity and Conflict   399

California Indians   399
Asians   402
African Americans   406
Latinos   410
Women   415

Chapter 31   A Season of Discontent   420

The Growth Rate: Peak and Slowdown   420
Transportation   423
Reapportionment   425
Education   426
Campus Turmoil   428
The Hippie Movement   432
Black Radicalism   433
The Decline of Radicalism   434

Chapter 32   Culture and Identity   437

Literature   437
Painting and Sculpture   443
Architecture   449
Music   451

Chapter 33   Recent California Politics   457

The Conservative Revival   457
The Era of Limits and Beyond   461
The Politics of Resentment   467
The Politics of Moderation   472

Chapter 34   The Environment and Energy   482

Regional Protection   482
Biodiversity   485
Growth Control   487

Air Pollution   488
Water Resources   490
Pesticides and Toxic Wastes   493
Renewable Energy   495
Nuclear Power   497
Petroleum Dependency   499
The Electric Energy Crisis   501

Chapter 35   The New California Economy   506

The Sunbelt Shift   506
The Pacific Rim   507
The Post-Industrial Revolution   509
High Technology   510
The Internet Revolution   514
The Arsenal of America   515
Tourism   518
Entertainment   521
Agriculture   525

Chapter 36   Contemporary California Society   529

Transportation   529
Education   532
Health Care   538
Criminal Justice   540
The New Californians   543

Index   554

Appendix   582

Preface

California is more than just another state. It is also a dream, a fantasy, a state of mind. This California of our collective imagination draws its power from universal human needs. Founded on expectation and hope, it promises to fulfill our deepest longings for opportunity and success, sunshine and beauty, health and long life, freedom, and even a foretaste of the future.

Two of the logical consequences of this dreamlike image of California have been growth and diversity. Throughout its history, the Golden State has attracted from across the country and around the world millions of newcomers pursuing the California dream. Today California is by far the most populous state in the union and the most ethnically diverse. The 2000 census revealed that ethnic minorities make up more than half of the state's burgeoning population of nearly 34 million; in other words, every Californian now is a member of one minority group or another.

For many Californians, the dream of a better life has been realized. California is the nation's wealthiest state, ranking first in industrial and agricultural production. It leads in high technology and is home to the nation's entertainment industry. If California were a separate country, it would rank sixth among the nations of the world in gross domestic product.

Other Californians have found the dream denied. Running through the state's history is a bitter strain of conflict. On its way to greatness, California has been burdened by a legacy of racism and nativism, episodes of discrimination and exclusion, a sometimes violent struggle between labor and capital, and an intense contest over the state's land and water resources.

First published 35 years ago, *California: An Interpretive History* has become the standard in the field. The eighth edition retains all the strengths of the earlier editions. It provides a comprehensive survey of the state's cultural and social affairs, along with an account of its political and economic history; it appraises the state's virtues and accomplishments, as well as its faults and failures. Original interpretations are offered of California's most controversial and persistent problems. Each chapter opens with a brief introductory section, previewing the material to be covered.

In the eighth edition, the last several chapters have been substantially revised to reflect the most recent developments in the state's dynamic political, economic, and social history. New sections, for instance, have been added on The Politics of Resentment and The Politics of Moderation in chapter 33; Biodiversity and The Electric Energy Crisis in chapter 34; and The Internet Revolution in chapter 35. New material also has been added throughout the earlier chapters to incorporate the latest scholarship in the field and to highlight the role of ethnic minorities and women. The content of the seventh edition's chapter 13 has been moved to the eighth edition's chapter 8, The Gold Rush, and chapter 13, Building the Central Pacific Railroad. At the suggestion of many readers, the author index and subject index of previous editions have been combined in a single index in this edition. Two new full-color sections have been added, California Visions, as well as a detailed pull-out map and an expanded timeline. A considerable number of new maps, graphs, photographs, and illustrations have been added, and the selected bibliographies at the end of each chapter have been updated. Readers seeking further bibliographical information are referred to Doyce B. Nunis, Jr., and Gloria R. Lothrop (eds.), *A Guide to the History of California* (1989).

Also new to the eighth edition is an official website for students and instructors, *www.mhhe.com/rawls8*. The site includes student quizzes, map activities, interactive exercises, and a set of useful links for each chapter of the textbook. Instructors may download from the site dozens of historic photos, paintings, broadsides, and other documents from the collections of the California Historical Society. These images are in PDF format and are password protected; instructors may use the downloaded images to create Power Point classroom presentations. The site was ably prepared by Marlene Smith-Baranzini, the associate editor of *California History: The Magazine of the California Historical Society*. Other staff members of the California Historical Society prepared a guide to online resources for researchers and students of California history. This guide appears on page 000 of the textbook. I am especially grateful to CHS Executive Director Stephen Becker and his assistant Jennifer Liss.

I have benefited from the advice and assistance of many individuals in the preparation of this book. My greatest debt is to Eugene C. Lee, former director of the Institute of Governmental Studies at the University of California, Berkeley, who generously read and commented on the new material in the latter chapters of this edition. I also acknowledge the assistance of Ted K. Bradshaw, Todd LaPorte, the late James D. Hart, and James J. Parsons, all of the University of California, Berkeley. Special thanks to my father, Jabus W. Rawls, who provided valuable research assistance and helped prepare the new combined index for this edition.

Others who have contributed to the book's improvement are Ricardo Almeraz, Allan Hancock College; Art R. Aurano, Antelope Valley College; Gordon Morris Bakken, California State University, Fullerton; Jacqueline R. Braitman, University of California, Los Angeles; Gregg M. Campbell, California State University, Sacramento; Kathryn Wiler Dabelow, Pasadena City College; Raymond F. Dasmann,

University of California, Santa Cruz; David Eakins, San Jose State University; Robert L. Fricke, West Valley College; Joel Goldman, San Francisco State University; Gerald Haslam, California State University, Sonoma; Robert V. Hine, University of California, Riverside; James D. Houston, University of California, Santa Cruz; Kenneth Kennedy, College of San Mateo; William King, Mt. San Antonio College; Dan Krieger, California Polytechnic State University, San Luis Obispo; Gary F. Kurutz, California State Library; Ward M. McAfee, California State University, San Bernardino; Delores Nason McBroome, Humboldt State University; Shirley Ann Wilson Moore, California State University, Sacramento; Spencer C. Olin, Jr., University of California, Irvine; Donald H. Pflueger, California State Polytechnic University, Pomona; Margaret E. Riley, Las Positas College; Allan Schoenherr, Fullerton College; Mark Sigmon, San Francisco State University; Ray Stafanson, Chabot College; James Steidel, Cañada College; Mark S. Still, College of San Mateo; Gregory H. Tilles, Diablo Valley College; Bonnie N. Trask, Fresno City College; Jules Tygiel, San Francisco State University; James C. Williams, California History Center, DeAnza College; Jerry Williams, California State University, Chico; and Charles Wollenberg, Vista College.

My students at Diablo Valley College have continued to share with me their enthusiasm for California history, and to them I am especially grateful.

James J. Rawls

For Linda

CHAPTER 1

Introduction
Geography and History

California is a notoriously extraordinary place. Its natural charms are of mythic proportions—the grandeur of Yosemite, the dark mystery of the redwoods, the incomparable coastline, the sun-drenched skies. These qualities have contributed mightily to the dreamlike image of California that resides in our collective imagination. Yet these qualities—and many more—also have played an important role in the historical development of California.

The Origins of California

No one knows for sure how California came to be. Stories and theories abound, but there is no consensus about the origins of this remarkable place.

The earliest attempts to account for the origination of California were made by the first peoples to live in the area. The Indians of California developed a wide variety of creation stories, each with its own unique features and cast of characters. Widely differing versions of creation flourished even within individual communities. The native people recognized the unlikelihood of agreement on matters of such importance: "This is how we tell it; they tell it differently."

Likewise, earth scientists today do not agree on the origins of California. The most widely accepted notion is the theory of plate tectonics. Tectonics is the study of forces deep within the earth that give shape to surface features such as mountains and ocean basins. According to this theory, the earth's crust and upper mantle consist of about 20 enormous plates that are in continual motion. The plates lurch and grind against one another, moving at the rate of a few inches a year. (Why the plates are moving is one of the least understood and most debated parts of the theory.) The largest of the plates is the Pacific Plate, underlying about two-thirds of the Pacific Ocean. The Pacific Plate's collision with the North American Plate is at the heart of the plate tectonics theory of the creation of California.

"For an extremely large percentage of the history of the world, there was no California," writes John McPhee, author of *Assembling California* (1993). According to McPhee, the western edge of the North American continent once was far inland, about where the Rocky Mountains are today. California began to emerge as the easternmost part of the state rose out of the primordial sea, carrying upward ancient ocean-floor sediments. Then, over millions of years, other parts of California began to assemble, a piece at a time. Fragments of the earth's crust arrived individually and in massive conglomerates, *docking*, or joining, themselves to the continent and creating what became California.

The main event was the collision of the eastward-moving Pacific Plate and the westward-moving North American Plate. As the plates collided, the Pacific Plate or *subducted*, or descended, beneath the continent's edge. The leading edge of the Pacific Plate plunged deep into the earth and began to melt. The resultant molten rock eventually cooled to form the granite core of the Sierra Nevada mountains. Erosion later removed the surface rock, uncovering the granite below. With the weight of the overburden removed, the mountains became uplifted along *faults*, or deep cracks. In the enormous heat generated by subduction, metal-rich compounds dissolved into solutions and were injected into the fissures of the rocks being formed above. Different combinations of minerals at different levels precipitated to form deposits of copper, lead, tungsten, silver, and gold.

Subsequent dockings of Pacific Plate material doubled the width of California. Geologists have identified rocks in this material that came from the entire Pacific basin, encompassing origins stretching over half the surface of the earth. Thus, embedded in the physical structure of California was a powerful metaphor for the later cultural and ethnic diversity of what became the Golden State.

As the Sierra Nevada rose in the interior, the western edge of the continental plate nosed out along the ocean floor. Sedimentary rocks and ocean-crust material were churned up and piled in great confusion along the continent's edge, forming a low-lying range of mountains along the California coast. Between the newly formed Coast Ranges and the Sierra Nevada lay a deep trough that slowly filled with volcanic debris and sediments eroded from the surrounding mountains. After more than 100 million years of accumulated fill, this intermontane trough became the great Central Valley.

For reasons that are not entirely clear, the relative movements of the Pacific and North American plates changed dramatically about 30 million years ago. The process of collision and subduction ended. Instead, the two plates began sliding past each other in a lateral motion. The boundary between the two plates became a half-mile-wide collection of deep ruptures called the San Andreas Fault zone. Land to the west of the fault began moving northwestward at the rate of a couple inches per year. This lateral motion was smooth and continuous far beneath the surface where the earth was relatively pliable, but the rigid materials near the surface tended to lock and resist the inexorable movement. Whenever a sudden unlocking released accumulated stress along the fault, earthquakes shook the surface.

California has experienced thousands of earthquakes throughout its history. Most have been unremarkable. Accounts of devastating temblors appear in the

The San Andreas Fault cuts through California from Imperial County in the south to Mendocino County in the north. Where streams cross the San Andreas, as here in the Carrizo Plain, their beds have been abruptly displaced by lateral movement along the fault. (*Photograph by R. E. Wallace. Courtesy of the U.S. Geological Survey.*)

stories of California Indians, in the earliest records of European settlers, and in the memories of countless Californians alive today. California falls into the highest seismic risk category in the nation; the frequency of earthquakes in the state is 10 times higher than for the world as a whole.

The lateral movement of the Pacific Plate has been like a conveyor belt through the heartland of California. Much of the land to the west of the San Andreas Fault— including the sites of San Diego, Los Angeles, Santa Barbara, San Luis Obispo, and Monterey—once was located hundreds of miles to the south along the coast of Mexico. In another 30 million years, it will be hundreds of miles to the north. The stresses of this lateral movement have bent entire mountain ranges and opened "pull-apart" depressions such as the Napa and Sonoma valleys.

The final sculpting of California occurred during the Pleistocene Epoch, which began less than 2 million years ago, when great sheets of ice covered much of the northern hemisphere. Changing sea levels altered the Pacific coastline and opened a bridge of land between the continents of Asia and North America. Glaciers in the Sierra Nevada spread and retreated half a dozen times, carving the sheer walls of Yosemite and other U-shaped mountain valleys. Between the succeeding glaciations, freshwater lakes filled the interior valleys and deposited rich layers of fertile soil. Roaming the grassy plains of California were shaggy camels, mastodons, imperial mammoths, and saber-toothed cats (later designated the state fossil, *Smilodon californicus*).

Regional Diversity

California is huge—the third largest of the states, after Alaska and Texas. It extends over nearly 10° of latitude, with a coastline of 1264 miles, and its land surface is almost exactly 100 million acres. Within this vast area are a greater range of landforms, a greater variety of habitats, and more species of plants and animals than in any area of comparable size in all of North America. The profusion of landscapes offers some of the world's most inspiring adventures in scenery and some of its finest opportunities for recreation. Altitudes vary from 14,495 feet at the top of Mount Whitney, the highest point in the United States outside Alaska, to 282 feet below sea level at Badwater in Death Valley, the lowest point in the country, although these two points are only 80 miles apart.

Mountains cover most of the surface of California. The largest range is the Sierra Nevada, occupying one-fifth of the total area of the state. It extends more than 400 miles along California's eastern border and contains many snow-capped peaks over 13,000 feet. This massive barrier isolated the Native American cultures of California for thousands of years; it also impeded European American settlement and posed an immense challenge to the builders of the transcontinental railroad in the nineteenth century. Several modern highways through the range—including those that cross Tioga, Sonora, and Ebbetts passes—are routinely closed in the winter still today.

The eastern side of the Sierra Nevada rises steeply, whereas the western side has a more gentle slope. Forests of pine, fir, and cedar cover the lower elevations. The gold discovered in California in 1848 was eroded from rock outcroppings in the High Sierra and deposited in stream banks and ancient riverbeds of the western foothills.

Beyond the eastern slope of the Sierra is a portion of the Great Basin, a desolate area of mountains and high desert valleys. Here lies Owens Valley, celebrated by author Mary Austin as "the land of little rain" and scene of one of the most bitter water disputes in California history. Farther east are the White Mountains, where grow the bristlecone pines (*Pinus longaeva*), the world's oldest living organisms. Some of these trees have lived for more than 4600 years.

To the north of the Sierra Nevada is a mountainous region that includes the southern tip of the Klamath Mountains and the Cascades. This region's tortured terrain has made it one of the least settled areas of the state. Within the Cascades are Mount Lassen (10,457 feet), a volcanic peak that last erupted in 1921, and Mount Shasta (14,162 feet). To the east of the Cascades lies the rugged Modoc Plateau, a forbidding region almost completely covered with lava flows and igneous rocks extruded through vents in the earth's surface. In the northwest corner of the

The major landform provinces of California. The most striking characteristic of California geography is its diversity.

state are the Klamath Mountains through which the free-flowing waters of the Klamath and Trinity rivers have cut deep and twisting gorges as they rush to the sea.

The Coast Ranges extend from Cape Mendocino in the north to Point Conception in the south. Consisting of uplifted sedimentary material, much of which has been metamorphosed, the Coast Ranges average less than 4000 feet in height.

Most settlement has been in the lowlands between individual ridges, with the greatest concentration of population in the San Francisco Bay area, the only real break in the coastal mountains. Regarded as one of the world's finest natural harbors, San Francisco Bay became the gateway to the state's interior in the nineteenth and twentieth centuries.

On the seaward slopes of the northern Coast Ranges are forests of coast redwoods, the state tree of California, greatly diminished by more than a century of commercial logging. Among the coast redwoods (*Sequoia sempervirens*) are the tallest trees in the world, some having reached a height of more than 360 feet. The Sierra redwoods (*Sequoiadendron giganteum*), also known as *big trees,* have the largest mass of any living thing on earth.

Lying between the Coast Ranges and the Sierra Nevada is the Central Valley, the most productive agricultural region in California. More than 400 miles long and about 50 miles wide, the Central Valley is really two valleys in one. In the north is the Sacramento Valley, drained by the southward-flowing Sacramento River; the San Joaquin Valley lies to the south and is drained by the northward-flowing San Joaquin River. Runoff from the Sierra foothills flows into tributaries of the two river systems, which join in the Sacramento–San Joaquin Delta before reaching San Francisco Bay.

Bunchgrass prairies and oak woodlands once covered the valley floor, and great tule marshes extended over the floodplain. Wetlands, containing the richest of habitats for a wide variety of plants and animals, formerly encompassed perhaps 5 million acres. Beavers in the inland streams first lured European Americans across the continent to California in the 1820s. Overhead is the Pacific flyway, a heavily traveled route for migrating birds. (More than 500 species of birds have been documented in California.) Beneath the surface lie rich deposits of oil and natural gas, created millions of years ago from the remains of marine plants and animals. Irrigated cropland today covers most of the valley and yields more agricultural products than any comparable region in the world.

At the southern end of the Central Valley is yet another group of mountains, the Transverse Ranges, familiar to travelers driving over the "grapevine" along Interstate 5. These ranges stretch along an east-west axis for about 250 miles and extend offshore to form the Santa Barbara Channel Islands. South of the Transverse Ranges lie the Peninsular Ranges, a northern extension of the mountainous spine of the Baja California peninsula. Settlement in the region has centered on the coastal plain at Los Angeles and San Diego. The Los Angeles basin, the largest lowland area in California that directly fronts the ocean, became the most populous region in the state in the early twentieth century. Population spread steadily into the surrounding San Bernardino, San Gabriel, and San Fernando valleys.

The eastern half of southern California is a large desert triangle—a vast expanse of sandy valleys, dried lake beds, and short ranges of rugged mountains. The largest desert in California is the Mojave, covering about 25,000 square miles; the most notorious is Death Valley, an inferno described by one observer as "the very manifestation of a Medieval hell." To the south is the Colorado Desert, a depression that extends to the Gulf of California.

The southern deserts were as much a barrier to overland migration to California in the eighteenth century as the steep eastern face of the Sierra Nevada was in the nineteenth. These formidable obstacles—coupled with California's extreme geographic remoteness from Europe and even from the original Spanish and British colonial settlements in the western hemisphere—meant that European settlement of California began remarkably late. The Spanish founded their first settlement on the Pacific coast in 1519, at Panama. Not until 1769, two and a half centuries later, did they found their first settlement in Alta (Upper) California at San Diego. Throughout the Spanish and Mexican periods, the difficulty of getting to California prevented any substantial numbers of settlers from going there, and despite the American conquest and the tremendous lure of the gold discovery, that difficulty continued to retard its growth until, and even after, the opening of the first transcontinental railroad in 1869.

The Climates of California

Once the barriers of geographic remoteness had been overcome, the unique and gentle climates of California became a greater attraction than gold had been. As geographer James J. Parsons has pointed out, "It so happens that California's arbitrarily conceived boundaries outline the only area of winter rain and summer drought in North America." Except on the northwest coast, where the average annual precipitation ranges up to nearly 110 inches (at Monumental, in Del Norte County), rainfall in California ordinarily occurs only between late October and early May. In the state as a whole, the average yearly precipitation is 23.88 inches; however, throughout the late spring, the entire summer, and the early autumn there is very seldom any precipitation at all.

The dry summers of California made agriculture exceedingly difficult before the development of irrigation on a vast scale in the American period. The uniqueness of the climate then gave the state a virtual monopoly on the production of many valuable agricultural crops, and the invention of the refrigerated railway car made it possible to market them throughout the country. Climate also was a vital factor in the location of other major industries in California, notably the production of motion pictures and aircraft.

Within the common pattern of summer drought, California's climatic conditions vary widely. Indeed, the climates of California are as diverse as those of southern Ireland and the northern Sahara.

California has four of the five major types of climate found around the world (only the hot and rainy tropical climate is not represented). Most common is the Mediterranean climate zone with its relatively warm, dry summers and mild winters. Even within this zone, however, are important variations. Along the coast, marine air and fog keep temperatures more moderate than in the Central Valley, where summers generally are hot and cloudless. An intermediate version of the Mediterranean climate is found in the Coast Ranges and the foothills of the Sierra Nevada. Similar variations are found around the shores of the Mediterranean, in

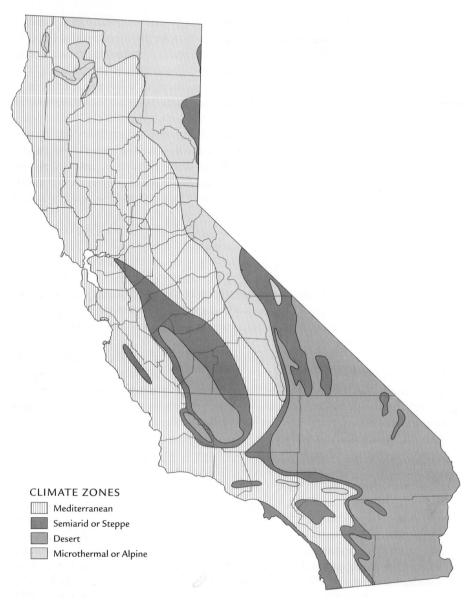

The climates of California. Climatic variations in California are greater than in any comparable area in the United States.

CLIMATE ZONES
- Mediterranean
- Semiarid or Steppe
- Desert
- Microthermal or Alpine

central Chile, on the southern tip of Africa, and in the southern and western parts of Australia.

Semiarid or steppe climates encompass much of the San Joaquin Valley and the fringes of the Mojave Desert. Rainfall here is less than in the Mediterranean zone. A cooler version occurs in a narrow coastal strip from Los Angeles to San Diego.

Notable for its sunny summers, pleasant winters, and little rain, this and the Mediterranean climate zone are what best qualify California for inclusion in the nation's booming sunbelt. The air pollution that has plagued the region since the middle of the twentieth century—casting a noxious pall over sunny California—is the result of a sunlight-activated chemical reaction among pollutants trapped by a combination of onshore winds, interior mountains, and temperature inversions (in which cooler marine air is trapped beneath warmer air above).

Desert climates cover the southeastern third of the state, east of the Sierra Nevada and Peninsular ranges. Cut off by mountains from moisture-laden Pacific storms, this region receives very little rain. Summer temperatures are the highest in the state, averaging over 100°F in July in Death Valley. The southwestern part of the San Joaquin Valley also is in a desert climate zone. Similar climates are found in the Sahara and the deserts of Australia.

The microthermal climates of California are much like those found in the Alps, where summers are short and cool and winters are vigorous. Average temperatures in the coldest month are below freezing at the higher elevations of the Sierra, the Modoc Plateau, and the Klamath Mountains. Most of California's water originates in these higher elevations as winter snowpack and spring runoff. About three-fourths of the annual precipitation occurs in the mountainous northern third of the state, whereas today 80 percent of the water demand (mostly for agriculture) occurs in the southern two-thirds.

California's rich natural resources—its many varieties of forests and soils, its gold, oil, and other minerals—have all contributed vitally to its economic development. So has water for irrigation and power, though moving water from where it naturally occurs to where demand has been created is one of the state's greatest challenges.

Selected Bibliography

On the geologic evolution of California, see John McPhee, *Assembling California* (1993); Rod Redfern, *The Making of a Continent* (1983); and R. M. Norris and R. W. Webb, *Geology of California* (1976). Among the many collections of Native American accounts, see especially Julian Lang (ed.), *Ararapikva: Creation Stories* (1993), and C. Hart Merriam (ed.), *The Dawn of the World* (1993). The definitive guide to California's natural diversity is Allan A. Schoenherr, *A Natural History of California* (1992). See also Philip L. Fradkin, *The Seven States of California* (1995); James Kavanagh, *The Nature of California* (1994); Michael Barbour et al., *California's Changing Landscape* (1993); and Elna Bakker, *An Island Called California* (1984). James J. Parsons's "The Uniqueness of California," *American Quarterly,* VII (Spring 1955), pp. 45–55, is a good introduction to the effects of California's geography on its history. Geographical, historical, and political maps are contained in David Hornbeck, *California Patterns: A Geographical and Historical Atlas* (1983); Crane S. Miller and Richard S. Hyslop, *California: The Geography of Diversity* (1983); Michael W. Donley et al., *Atlas of California* (1979); Warren A. Beck and Ynez D. Haase, *Historical Atlas of California* (1974) and *Historical Atlas of the American West* (1989); and Robert D. Durrenberger, *Patterns on the Land* (1960).

CHAPTER 2

The Original Californians

"In the beginning there was no sun, no moon, no stars. All was dark, and everywhere there was only water." So begins a creation story told by the Maidu Indians of California.

According to the traditional beliefs of many of the state's native people, the California Indians were created and have lived forever in their ancestral homeland. Anthropologists, however, believe that the aboriginal population of California descended from ancient peoples who crossed into North America from Asia over the land bridge connecting the two continents during the glaciations of the late Pleistocene Epoch. Archaeologists estimate that human beings have been living in California for at least 12,000 years—and perhaps for 15,000 years or more.

Whatever the origins of the first Californians, the archaeological record reveals a process of dynamic change and adaptation during thousands of years of human occupation. At the time of first European contact in the sixteenth century, native people were living in each of the diverse regions of California. Every part of the landscape was imbued with human meaning; each mountain and river had a name. What the earliest European explorers labeled "wilderness" was a human homeland—a land abounding with sacred sites, work areas, trails, villages, favored gathering and hunting grounds.

Because their technology did not include metal implements, the California Indians represented a survival of the Stone Age. But the causes and the meaning of this fact have been much misunderstood, largely because of the persistence of rather primitive ideas about the nature of primitive people and, particularly, the persistence of racism—the belief that some races are biologically, morally, and intellectually inferior to others. Among competent ethnologists, the race theories underlying this pattern of thought have long been discredited. Indeed, the very notion of race is now understood to be a social and cultural concept rather than a biological one. Scientists have found that the differences between people of the same racial group are often greater than those between members of different groups. All persons everywhere share 99.9 percent of their genetic code. "Most scholars today would agree that what 'race' signifies is changeable," historian Sucheng Chan has noted, "and is socially constructed and historically determined." Unfortunately, the mistaken belief of racism has been used to justify oppression of some races by others.

The survival of a Stone Age culture in California was not the result of any hereditary biological limitations on the potential of the Indians as a race; rather, they had been geographically and culturally isolated. The vast expanse of oceans, mountains, and deserts had sheltered California from foreign stimulation as well as from foreign conquest, and even within California the Indian groups were so settled that they had little contact with each other. On the positive side, California supported a much larger number of Indians than did any other region of comparable size in North America north of Mexico. The California Indians had made a successful adaptation to their environment, and they had learned to live without destroying each other.

Food and Population

The Indians of California had a vast knowledge and understanding of the natural resources of what later became the Golden State. This knowledge was absolutely essential to the Indians' survival and was passed down, amended, and then passed down again, generation after generation. Each regional economy depended on the use of hundreds of individual species of plants and animals. Coinciding with the seasonal availability of specific resources, the native people followed annual rounds of hunting and gathering.

Until recently, anthropologists tended to categorize the Indians of California as either *hunter-gatherers* or *agriculturalists.* According to this scheme, the Mojaves and the Yumas practiced agriculture to the extent of planting corn, bean, and squash seeds in the mud left by the annual floodwaters of the lower Colorado River; farther west, agriculture also existed among the Cahuilla. All other tribes in California were lumped together as hunter-gatherers. Contemporary scholars have come to understand that both categories are simply opposite ends of a continuum of human interaction with the natural environment.

We now realize that California Indians engaged in a wide variety of practices to manage their land and enhance its yield. They practiced burning of ground cover to replenish the soil, pruned plants and trees, engaged in hand-weeding, and culled animal and insect populations. They amplified the biological diversity of California through various means, including the transplanting of preferred species of animals and plants. Field biologists have noted the repeated appearance of native tobacco plants, elderberry shrubs, jimsonweed, and black walnut trees near ancient village sites. Geographer William Preston recently characterized California as "one of the most altered precolonial landscapes in the Americas."

The natural sources of food in California were remarkably diverse and often ingeniously obtained. The greatest staple was the acorn, which because of its high fat content has a higher caloric value than wheat. When washed free of tannic acid, acorn flour was made into porridge or bread. In many desert areas, mesquite pods took the place of acorns. Deer and small game were generally available. Insects were a widely accepted source of nourishment. Fish were abundant in the streams, notably salmon in the northwest. Fish and meat were often dried. Along the coast, shellfish were consumed in quantities, and many shell mounds as much as 30 feet high, which accumulated as heaps of kitchen refuse over periods of 3000 years, provide important archaeological clues to Indian life.

The most distinctive method used in preparing food was the process of leaching the tannic acid from acorn flour. The flour, produced by pounding husked acorns with a stone mortar and pestle, was winnowed by tossing in a shallow basket. Then it was spread out in a sandy, shallow depression or basin and repeatedly doused with water to wash away the acid. Bread might then be baked in an earthen oven, but much more commonly the flour was placed in a basket with water brought to a boil by hot stones. The stones were heated in a nearby fire, lifted by tongs, dipped in a rinse basket, placed into the cooking basket, and then carefully stirred to ensure that the mixture was evenly cooked. This produced a gruel or porridge, which was eaten either plain or flavored with berries, grass seeds, nuts, or bits of meat or fish.

The cooking basket might be caulked with pitch or tar, but it was often so tightly woven that it would hold boiling water without caulking. As this suggests, the California Indians were remarkably skilled in basketmaking. In this art they had no equals anywhere in the world, either in the utility of the product or in the beauty of the designs. They had developed basketry to such a point that pottery making was hardly necessary and was confined mainly to the southern region, which was influenced by southwestern Indian culture.

Hunting was mainly with the bow, which was often backed with sinew for extra strength. Arrows were cleverly feathered, and the heads were made of obsidian, which is sharper than flint and more readily shaped by flaking. Knives were also of obsidian. Fishing was done with nets or hooks; with harpoons, particularly for salmon; or with poison, accomplished by throwing buckeyes, or horse chestnuts, into small pools at the edge of a stream.

The hunting and fishing were done mainly by men, the gathering of plant foods and the cooking by women. Work activities, however, occasionally overlapped. Men sometimes aided in the collecting of plant foods (such as knocking acorns from oak limbs), and women hunted and trapped small game. In general, everyone worked hard, and the division of labor was fair and effective. The picture of the Indians as lazy is the result of the demoralization that set in after the coming of the white man, who treated Indians as if they were inferior beings and seemed intent on proving that they were.

The term "Digger" as applied to the California Indians is a pejorative misnomer, based on the mistaken idea that they lived largely by grubbing up roots. American pioneer immigrants, seeing Indian women busy with digging sticks, were unaware that they wanted root fibers for basketmaking more often than for food. The diet of the California tribes did include certain roots and bulbs, but perhaps the real reason the Digger legend persisted was that it was easier to deprive the Indians of their lands and their lives if it could be believed that they were only miserable and subhuman creatures anyway.

The actual number of persons supported by the resources of California, before the coming of the Spaniards, can never be precisely determined, but a reasonable

A Pomo gift basket, decorated with shell disks and covered with yellow, green, blue, white, and red feathers in a geometric design. (*Courtesy of the Smithsonian Institution.*)

estimate is that there were at least 300,000 Indians within the present boundaries of the state when the first Spanish settlement was founded in 1769. Some contemporary scholars suggest a population range between 310,000 and 325,000. There have been extremely wide variations among the estimates of the aboriginal population of North America as a whole, but Indian population density in California before European contact was much greater than the average for other areas in what is now the United States.

Aspects of Material Culture

Dwellings were generally simple, often conical or dome shaped, except in the northwest, where they were often solid-frame structures built of redwood planks and in rectangular form. In central California, poles and brush were the most common building materials, and many houses were built partly underground or banked with earth for insulation.

The sweathouse was a distinctive institution, and its use was generally confined to men. (Anthropologists formerly used the term *temescal* for this California institution, but the word is derived from the Náhuatl language, spoken by the Aztecs of central Mexico, and has no association with the Indians of California.) An open fire, not steam, was used to produce heat, and as the upper part of the sweathouse filled with smoke, the men would lie on the floor. Then, while still perspiring freely,

Interior of a sweathouse in central California. (*Courtesy of the Bancroft Library.*)

they would rush to a nearby stream or lake and plunge into the water. In central California this was done as a means of keeping clean as well as healthy—a ritually purifying act. Women and children generally were expected to do their bathing less ceremoniously, and in the early morning before the men were awake. The sweathouse also had some of the aspects of a men's club, and in some tribes the older boys and men customarily gambled, worked, and slept there.

The most common type of boat was the tule balsa, a raft made of reeds bound into a boatlike shape. Seagoing dugout canoes, carved from half a redwood trunk, were used in the northwest; the Chumash of the Santa Barbara Channel region also made seaworthy canoes, though of plank rather than dugout construction.

Men ordinarily wore no clothing at all; the standard garment for women was a knee-length skirt made of plant fibers or skins. In the latter case, the lower part was slit into fringes for decoration and freedom of movement. Women also wore beautifully decorated round basketry caps. When the weather demanded a degree of protection from cold, both sexes wore blankets and robes made of furs. The sea otter was most prized, but deer and rabbit skins were more common. Foul-weather gear also included short trousers, buckskin shirts, and jackets. Ritual costumes, worn only on special occasions, were elaborately constructed and included feather headdresses, feathered capes, shell necklaces, and earrings. Body painting and tattooing also were practiced by many California Indians.

Location, Linguistic Groups, Tribes

The pattern of availability of plant and animal foods, and the complete reliance on them, tended to determine not only the number of people in a community but also its location. The California Indians lived in settled villages of about 100 to

500 inhabitants, usually groups of kindred families; the location of these communities was determined very precisely by the availability of food and water.

Another culture-determining factor was the variety of languages. Language barriers combined with the localized nature of food supplies to intensify isolation and provincialism. Of the five main language stocks in California, four were common to other parts of North America, suggesting that there had been a vast jumble of migrations in very ancient times, before the mixture hardened. These five main stocks were subdivided into 21 language families, which in turn were subdivided into at least 100 mutually unintelligible languages. Indian California was the region of greatest linguistic diversity in the world, excepting, according to some scholars, only the Sudan and New Guinea.

Typically, California Indians knew that they had been born and would die in a little town on the bank of a certain stream and that the land in the immediate vicinity belonged to their people. Just across certain hills, on another stream, were other people whom they might visit and with whom, if they could converse, they might intermarry but on whose proprietary rights they should not infringe. Trade routes crisscrossed California, and the exchange of goods was common. Inland tribes, for instance, traded obsidian and deerskins to coast dwellers for shell beads, dried fish, and sea otter pelts.

Anthropologists have attempted various definitions of the tribe in California. It may be considered a body of people who occupied a distinct territory and shared a similar culture; on this basis there are over 100 such tribes. Anthropologist Lowell J. Bean has described them as "non-political, ethnic nationalities." California tribes did not generally have centralized governmental structures but, rather, consisted of several independent units often identified as "tribelets." Each tribelet included a group of neighboring villages, perhaps with a principal village and three or four smaller ones. Tribelet populations ranged from several hundred to several thousand individuals; territorial boundaries were vigorously defended.

Elsewhere in North America, a tribe was ordinarily a nation with a strong and militant national consciousness. With the exception of the Mojaves and the Yumas on the southeastern margin, no such breadth of organization or political consciousness existed among the California Indians. The village community was usually the highest political unit. Within that unit, the primary duty of the chief or headman was overseeing the production and distribution of resources. Most such leaders were males, but exceptions did occur. "Leadership was primarily local," anthropologist William Simmons has concluded, "without formally structured political alliances like the famous League of the Iroquois." It is easy to see why the California Indians found it difficult to organize a coordinated resistance to a handful of Spaniards, let alone to a horde of Anglo-Americans.

Social Culture

The most extraordinary diversity prevailed not only among the languages spoken but also in nearly all other aspects of culture. Elements of culture occurring only in part of California, most of them only in a small part, greatly outnumbered those that were universal. Scholars have divided California into six major, geographically distinct *culture areas,* within which residents shared common traits, such as dress, housing, manufacturing methods, and other routine activities. (Although culture-area classification has passed out of fashion among contemporary anthropologists, the system remains useful for summarizing the regional diversity of California cultures.) These six areas are commonly identified as the southern, central, northwestern, northeastern, Great Basin, and Colorado River culture areas. The northwest culture area had many of the characteristics of the tribes to the north of it, and the culture patterns of the Colorado River area bore some resemblance to those of tribes to the east. The central culture area was the most distinctively "Californian." Even within these broad subdivisions, there was great diversity. Meaningful generalizations can be made about California Indian culture only if it is understood that there were exceptions to almost every general statement.

Except for the tribes along the Colorado River, the California Indians generally were peaceable and unaggressive. Yet ethnographic and historic resources indicate that tribal groups often viewed one another with suspicion and that wars were not uncommon. The causes of armed conflict included trespass, poaching, the abduction of women, and competition for rare resources. Wars seldom were very lengthy, but they could be deadly. The chief of a tribe was not necessarily the military leader, unless he had given some special evidence of military skill. Feuds involving persons and families were more common than warfare among tribes. Murder was the prime cause, and ordinarily the victim's relatives could be propitiated by some sort of payment for their loss. Even when an intertribal offense led to a small battle, one side would often pay the other to prevent further attacks. If a series of reprisals occurred, it might end with each side compensating the other for the damages.

Social classes hardly existed, except in the northwest, where there was the greatest interest in acquiring wealth and personal property and where slavery, based on debt, was commonly practiced. Indians in other areas were not uninterested in wealth, however. Gambling was widespread. Money was in the form of strings of beads made of dentalia or clam shells.

The family was by far the most important social institution and, in general, a highly effective one. Marriage was a formal and honored institution that established a lifelong relationship of mutual commitment; divorce was often difficult and prostitution was unknown. In the central region a kinship taboo forbade conversation with one's mother-in-law. One interpretation sometimes placed on this custom, however, is erroneous: It actually resulted not from a fear of meddling by the spouse's parents but, rather, from great respect for them.

Women played an essential role in all native cultures. Female elders passed on knowledge, both practical and esoteric, that was necessary for the continued functioning of the tribal unit. In addition to gathering and processing much of the food supply, women were responsible for constructing and maintaining storage facilities. In the central region, women built thatched granaries 15 feet high to store surplus acorns. Women also participated in ritual activities and could gain status through their skill in dancing and singing. Among the Cupeño of the southern

TOLOWA
NW
YUROK
KARUK
SHASTA
MODOC
NE
CHILULA
HUPA
CHIMARIKO
ACHUMAWI
(PIT RIVER)
WHILKUT
WIYOT
WINTU
(NORTHERN
WINTUN)
ATSUGEWI
(HAT CREEK)
PAVIOTSO
(NORTHERN PAIUTE)
MATTOLE
NONGATL
YANA
SINKYONE
LASSIK
WAILAKI
CAHTO
NOMLAKI
(CENTRAL
WINTUN)
MAIDU
YUKI
KONKOW
(NORTHWESTERN
MAIDU)
POMO
PATWIN
(SOUTHERN
WINTUN)
NISENAN
(SOUTHERN MAIDU)
WAPPO
LAKE
MIWOK
COAST MIWOK
WASHO
MIWOK
C
MONO LAKE
NORTHERN PAIUTE
COSTANOAN
(OHLONE)
NORTHERN
VALLEY YOKUTS
OWENS VALLEY
PAIUTE-SHOSHONE
MONACHE
FOOTHILL YOKUTS
WESTERN
SHOSHONE
(PANAMINT/KOSO)
ESSELEN
SALINAN
SOUTHERN
VALLEY
YOKUTS
TUBATULABAL
GB
KAWAIISU
SOUTHERN PAIUTE
CHEMEHUEVI
KITANEMUK
S
CHUMASH
TATAVIAM
SERRANO
MOHAVE
HALCHIDHOMA
CHUMASH
TONGVA
(GABRIELINO)
CAHUILLA
CUPEÑO
GABRIELINO
JUANEÑO
LUISEÑO
CR
KUMEYAAY
(DIEGUEÑO)
YUMA
(QUECHAN)

CULTURE AREAS

S - Southern
C - Central
NW - Northwestern
NE - Northeastern
GB - Great Basin
CR - Colorado River

The tribal boundaries within each of the culture areas changed over time. The boundaries depicted here are based on the earliest evidence available for each group. (*From* Indians of California: The Changing Image, *by James J. Rawls, copyright 1984 by the University of Oklahoma Press; and* Tribal Areas of California *map, copyright 1996 by Pacific Western Traders, Folsom, California.*)

region, women sang "enemy songs" in which they chastised villagers who were not conforming to group norms. Along the southern coast, Chumash women often ruled one or more villages. In the northwestern culture area, women served as spiritual leaders.

A Hupa woman with shell necklace, apron, and basket hat, photographed near the Klamath River in the early 1900s. (*Courtesy of the Huntington Library, San Marino.*)

Religious leadership was combined with the medical profession in the person of the shaman, who was believed to be in direct communication with the supernatural world. Illness was thought to be caused by foreign disease objects in the body, and the shaman claimed the power both to introduce such objects and to remove them, usually by sucking them out. Also included in the religious leadership of most tribes were priests and ritualists. Priests maintained the balanced order of proper behavior and enjoyed considerable political, legal, and economic authority. Ritualists conducted the activities necessary for religious ceremonies. Ceremonial observances were everywhere associated with adolescence and with mourning, and there were many first-fruit, first-salmon, and acorn-harvest festivals.

There were widespread religious cults. The shamans did not usually dominate these loosely organized associations, although they might assume a certain degree of local leadership in explaining their rites. In the southern culture area, the *toloache,* or jimsonweed cult, was prevalent. A drink made from the narcotic jimsonweed was used to induce sacred visions as part of the initiation ceremonies. Among the Gabrielino and Juaneño this cult was much elaborated, and it related to belief in a deity called Chinigchinich. In central California, the Kuksu cult placed more emphasis on esoteric rites that included dancers impersonating several deities. The "world-renewal" cult was a major aspect of religious life on the northwest coast. Its rites were designed to renew abundant food supplies and to prevent calamities.

California Indians believed that all of nature was interconnected and was suffused with a sacred power. Human beings were to respect that power by following carefully prescribed guidelines in even the most routine of daily activities. Killing an animal, drinking from a spring, or entering a cave was to be accompanied by a ritual act, however simple, as a sign of respect and acknowledgment. As Native American historian Edward D. Castillo (Cahuilla/Luiseño) has written, "The religious beliefs and traditions of the Indians of California teach that the blessings of a rich land and a mild climate are gifts from the Creator. The Indians show their love and respect for the Creator—and for all of creation—by carefully managing the land for future generations and by living in harmony with the natural environment."

It is difficult today to appreciate the sense of intimate connection that the ancient peoples of California felt with the natural world. They not only knew the sounds and appearance and habits of the wildlife around them, they also believed they could communicate with animals through speech and dreams. In countless stories, told by elders around flickering campfires on long winter nights, the people were warned of the dire consequences of disrespecting other life-forms. Human greed and wastefulness could cause the world to go out of balance; devastating catastrophes such as droughts and floods would follow.

The religious ideas of the California Indians were, and are, more elaborate than commonly supposed. Their view that the universe is diminishing in quality and quantity bears a striking similarity to the concept of entropy central to modern physics. Likewise, their belief that a prehuman race inhabited the earth is an interesting foreshadowing of the idea of evolution. Some of the beliefs of the Spanish missionaries, such as the idea that human beings were sinful and fallen creatures, were essentially foreign to Indian religious beliefs.

The California Indians had no system of writing, beyond the use of designs and symbols in the decoration of rocks, or in groundpainting as a part of religious ceremony and instruction in the southern region. The highly stylized rock paintings of the Chumash were among the most spectacular and elaborate of any created in the United States. (See Color Plate 1.) Yet the Indians of California were prehistoric in that they left no written records. In this sense, we speak of California as having been first "discovered" by the Spaniards, and of its history as having begun at that time.

Selected Bibliography

For the general reader and student, the best introductory volumes are Joseph L. Chartkoff and Kerry Kona Chartkoff, *The Archaeology of California* (1984); Michael J. Moratto, *California Archaeology* (1984); Robert F. Heizer and Albert B. Elsasser, *The Natural World of the California Indians* (1980); Heizer and Mary Ann Whipple (eds.), *The California Indians, a Source Book* (1971); and Theodora Kroeber, *Ishi in Two Worlds* (1961). The most complete reference is Heizer (ed.), *California* (1978), a volume in the Smithsonian Institution's *Handbook of North American Indians*. A summary account of precontact culture appears in William S. Simmons, "Indian Peoples of California," in Ramón A. Gutiérrez and Richard J. Orsi (eds.), *Contested Eden* (1998), and Lowell J. Bean, "Indians of California," *California History* 71 (Fall 1992), pp. 302–323, part of a special issue devoted to the topic. See also James J. Rawls, *Indians of California* (1984).

The best estimate of the number of Indians in California before the coming of the Spaniards appears in Sherburne F. Cook, *The Population of the California Indians, 1769–1970* (1976). On the proto-agricultural activities of the California Indians, see Thomas C. Blackburn and Marion K. Anderson (eds.), *Before the Wilderness: Environmental Management by Native Californians* (1993), and Henry T. Lewis, *Patterns of Indian Burning in California* (1973). Among the many volumes on the history of individual cultures are William McCawley, *The First Angelinos* (1996); Bean (ed.), *The Ohlone Past and Present* (1995); and Bean, *Mukat's People: The Cahuilla Indians of Southern California* (1972). Other useful volumes include Malcolm Margolin (ed.), *The Way We Lived* (1993); Bean (ed.), *California Indian Shamanism* (1992); Bean and Sylvia Brakke Vane (eds.), *Ethnology of the Alta California Indians* (1991); Heizer and Elsasser (eds.), *A Bibliography of California Indians* (1977); and Campbell Grant, *The Rock Paintings of the Chumash* (1965).

CHAPTER 3

Discovery, Exploration, and Founding

The story of Spanish California is one of great color and fascination, even though the Spaniards themselves were disappointed in it and, in general, regarded it as one of the least important of their colonies.

The Finding and Naming of California

Hernán Cortés, the conqueror of the Aztec empire in central Mexico, was also chiefly responsible for discovering the lower part of what the Spanish ultimately called "the Californias." In his urge to explore northwestward from the lands of the Aztecs, Cortés was following the lure of various tales of magnificent wealth. Spaniards of his time put their trust in the ancient and medieval legends of the Terrestrial Paradise and the Amazon Island, and in such American Indian tales as those of the Seven Cities and of El Dorado, "the Gilded Man," a king whose subjects covered him with gold dust every morning and washed it off every night. In 1533 Cortés dispatched the expedition that discovered lower California, first assumed to be an island rather than a peninsula.

All the early Spanish exploring expeditions involved extreme hardships, and several ended in complete disaster. In some cases only fragmentary records of them exist. Many details are uncertain, and one of these is the identity of the explorer who first applied the name "California."

For centuries the derivation of the name was even more uncertain than the question of who first applied it. In 1862, however, Edward Everett Hale discovered what is undoubtedly the correct explanation. Hale was a Boston Unitarian minister and writer, otherwise best known for his story "The Man without a Country." In the course of his wide readings, he came across an old Spanish novel, *Las Sergas de Esplandián (The Exploits of Esplandián),* written about 1500 by Garcí Ordóñez de Montalvo. In it there were several references to an Amazon island called California.

Montalvo's *Sergas de Esplandián* was a sequel to his translation into Spanish of the Portuguese novel *Amadís de Gaula.* It was an inferior sequel; as Hale remarked, the *Sergas* was deservedly forgotten for 300 years, and its role as the source of the name of California was thus forgotten with it. In the early years of the sixteenth century, however, Montalvo's story went through several editions, and there can be little doubt that Cortés and his captains, if they had not read it, had at least heard it described. In 1524, in a letter to the king, Cortés reported his expectation of finding an island of Amazons a few days' sail to the northwest.

Amadís of Gaul had been the late-medieval ideal of the perfect knight. Montalvo's Esplandián was introduced as the son of Amadís. In the course of a siege of Constantinople in which father and son were leading the defense of the city against an army of pagans, there suddenly appeared among the besiegers a certain Calafía, queen of California. This, wrote Montalvo, was an island "on the right hand of the Indies" and "very near to the terrestrial paradise." It was inhabited by black women "without any men among them, because they were accustomed to live after the manner of Amazons." Their weapons were of gold, "for in all the island there is no other metal." In California "there were many griffins, on account of the great ruggedness of the country." (A griffin is a mythical creature with the body of a lion and the head and wings of an eagle.) When the griffins were young, "the women went out with traps to take them to their caves, and brought them up there. And being themselves quite a match for the griffins, they fed them with the men whom they took prisoners, and with the boys to whom they gave birth." For battle, these monstrous birds were trained to seize men from the ground and drop them from great heights. Later the Amazon queen converted to Christianity, married a relative of Esplandián, and returned with him to California. "What happened after that," wrote Montalvo, "I must be excused from telling." The reader may doubt that the marriage was an entirely happy one.

It may have been in derision that Spanish explorers gave to a barren and hostile place the name of the fabled land of gold they had hoped to find. An alternative explanation is that to Spanish soldiers of the time of Cortés, the "California" of contemporary parlance would in itself have been a highly opprobrious name, directly suitable for a land of desolation and terror—a land in which women were the soldiers and in which women despised men and set griffins on them.

Because California's actual history has so often resembled romantic fiction, it is not entirely inappropriate that it got its name from a novel.

Cabrillo and the Discovery of Alta California

The evidence that Spanish explorers first sighted Alta (Upper) California by land, near its southeast corner, is not quite substantial enough to take the traditional honor of discovery away from Juan Rodríguez Cabrillo, who first sighted it from the sea in 1542. The main purpose of Cabrillo's expedition, sent out under the orders of the viceroy of New Spain, was to search for the long-rumored though mythical Strait of Anián, later sought by the English under the name of the Northwest

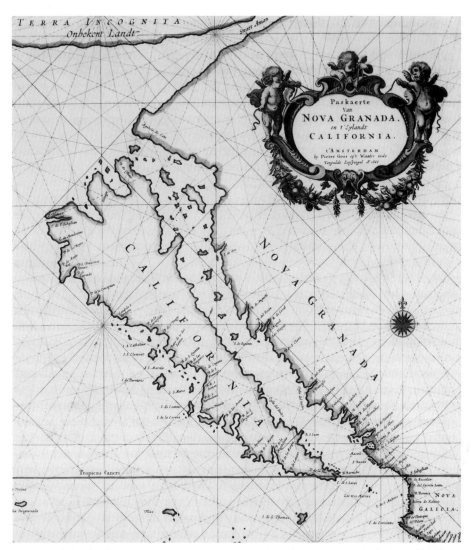

Map of California as an island, drawn by Pietre Koos, 1666. In spite of frequent explorations that proved otherwise, many early maps drawn by Europeans showed California as an island. Note the inclusion of the mythical Strait of Anián to the northeast. (*Courtesy of the California History Room, California State Library, Sacramento.*)

Passage. For more than two centuries, the dream of a water route to Asia through North America would continue to lure the explorers of several nations.

Cabrillo sailed from the port of Navidad on the west coast of Mexico on June 27, 1542. His two small ships, the *San Salvador* and the *Victoria,* were poorly built, manned by conscripts, and wretchedly provisioned. On September 28 he discovered and entered the fine harbor of San Diego. His name for it was San Miguel, but this and the names of all the other points he discovered were changed by later explorers, particularly by Vizcaíno.

After spending 6 days at San Diego, the little vessels made a series of anchorages at Santa Catalina Island, San Pedro, and Santa Monica, and then at Ventura and several other points along the Santa Barbara Channel. They could make no landings north of Point Conception because of the powerful northwest winds. Cabrillo decided to spend the winter in the harbor of an offshore island. Although Cabrillo's men had established generally friendly relations with the Indians on the mainland, they had serious problems with the Indians on the island. On about Christmas Eve, 1542, a shore party was attacked by the islanders. In an attempt to rescue his men, Cabrillo fell and broke his arm or leg. The wound became infected, and the captain died on January 3, 1543.

In obedience to Cabrillo's dying wish, and in spite of their pitiful hardships, his men agreed to continue their explorations under the leadership of the chief pilot, Bartolomé Ferrelo. Before they turned back on March 1, they had actually reached a point off the coast of southern Oregon, but again they could find no new anchorages. In April they reached their home port of Navidad, nearly starved and desperately sick with scurvy. They had found no straits and no rich cities, and they could hardly have appreciated the future value of what they did find. But it is clear that the discoverers of Alta California were men of admirable courage and extraordinary devotion to duty.

Francis Drake and Nova Albion

More than a generation elapsed between the Cabrillo expedition and the next landing by Europeans on the coast of Upper California. This was the visit of Francis Drake and the *Golden Hind* in 1579. It occurred by accident in the course of a 3-year voyage around the world, a voyage intended partly to open up English trade with the Moluccas and partly to "anoy" the king of Spain in "his Indyes" by engaging in what the English regarded as privateering and the Spaniards regarded as piracy. In this period Queen Elizabeth suspected King Philip of complicity in a series of plots on her life, and relations between England and Spain were seldom very far short of outright war. Another and incidental purpose of the voyage was to search for that great "northern mystery," the Northwest Passage.

Nearly a year and a half after he sailed from England, Drake had to make an emergency landing on the coast of California to repair his ship. The *Golden Hind,* originally named the *Pelican,* was a vessel of only 100 tons burden, and by this time it was carrying about 30 tons of captured Spanish treasure, mostly silver. The seams in its hull had begun to open. On June 17, 1579, Drake found "a convenient and fit harborough" where he stayed for 5 weeks. It is probable that this occurred on the Point Reyes Peninsula at what is now called Drake's Bay, although the location of the landing has long been in dispute. Other possible landing sites include an island in the Santa Barbara Channel, a cove inside San Francisco Bay, Bodega Bay in Sonoma County, Trinidad Head in Humboldt County, and places as far north as

An artist's conception of California's Coast Miwok Indians greeting Francis Drake in 1579. Note especially the central figures lacerating their cheeks and, in the background, the setting up of the plate of brass. (*Courtesy of the Bancroft Library.*)

Whale Cove and Coos Bay in Oregon. But only Drake's Bay has the "white bancks and cliffes" whose resemblance to the cliffs on the English Channel contributed to Drake's naming the place Nova Albion, or New England.

The Indians were the most interesting feature of the visit for Drake's men, and they devoted their most detailed accounts of the stop to them. From the descriptions of the houses, the feathered baskets, the ceremonies, and the language of these Indians, anthropologists have clearly identified them as the Coast Miwok, whose country included Point Reyes in present-day Marin County. (See Color Plate 2.) Drake's men assumed, incorrectly, that in placing a feathered crown on Drake's head, the Indians were turning over the sovereignty of their country to him. The Indians also cried pitifully and tore their cheeks with their fingernails until the blood ran, and the English supposed this to be a kind of sacrifice to them as gods. The facts are that these were the mourning practices of the Coast Miwok and that the Indians undoubtedly regarded the Englishmen as relatives who had returned from the dead. Historian Arthur Quinn has interpreted this early encounter as a dark prophecy of the future course of Indian-white relations in California: "It *was* dead generations the natives saw wade onto Point Reyes, dead generations of their people. But it was future death, not past. . . . The mournful wailing of the women held a deeper truth than anyone at that time knew."

In claiming the country for Queen Elizabeth, Drake erected a plate of brass with a chiseled inscription and a hole for a sixpence bearing Her Majesty's picture. In 1937 the University of California announced the finding of this plate and later placed it on display in the Bancroft Library. Experts at Columbia University made tests on the plate in 1938 and pronounced it genuine. However, new tests made in the mid-1970s at the Lawrence Berkeley Laboratory and at Oxford University used the far more sophisticated testing techniques developed in the interim, and the modern researchers concluded that it was "unreasonable to continue to believe in the authenticity of the plate." Analysis of the trace elements found in the metal corresponded to brass of the twentieth century rather than the sixteenth, and X-ray diffraction tests revealed that the brass was produced by a modern rolling process unknown at the time of Drake. Nevertheless, the plate remains on display in the Bancroft, and the controversy over its authenticity continues.

The main significance of the voyage of the *Golden Hind* was that it was the second ship to sail around the world, the first English ship to do so, and the first ship of any nation to make the entire voyage under one commander. (Magellan had been killed in the Philippines.) Drake's title of knighthood, granted after his return, was a modest recognition of so great an achievement. The significance of his landing in California, however, has sometimes been misunderstood and exaggerated.

The Manila Galleon and the California Coast

The Philippine islands were added to the Spanish colonial empire by a gradual process of conquest that began in 1565, and they were governed as a part of the viceroyalty of New Spain until the end of Spanish control in Mexico. By the time of the Drake expedition, the Spaniards had already established a profitable trade route between Mexico and the Philippines, and for many decades Spanish interest in the coast of California was largely the result of the fact that the ships from Manila sailed past it, with their rich cargoes from the Orient, on the last leg of their long trans-Pacific voyage to Acapulco.

Manila was a very convenient gathering point for luxury goods from many parts of east Asia, to be exchanged for silver and gold from the mines of Mexico, and the trade became so large that merchants in Spain were in danger of losing their Mexican markets. The luxury goods from Asia included silks, fine thread, gold and silver brocades, jewelry, perfumes, delicious preserves of peaches and oranges, and treasured spices for the preservation and palatability of meat. Under the prevailing mercantilistic system that discriminated against the colonies in favor of the mother country, the king decreed in 1593 that the Manila galleons must be limited to one a year and their cargoes to a value of 250,000 pesos. Nevertheless the profits were extremely high, and because cargoes were now concentrated in a single annual voyage, there was great temptation to crowd extra goods into space that should have been reserved for food and water.

The voyage from Manila usually took 6 or 7 months, during which the crews suffered horribly from starvation, thirst, and scurvy. The death rate on board the galleons often reached 50 percent. The crews also had to fear English pirates, ever since the forays of Drake. There was, it seemed, a growing need for a port on the California coast where the annual Manila galleon could get fresh food and water and perhaps an escort vessel.

The Spanish authorities entrusted the galleon of 1595 to the Portuguese *adelantado,* or merchant-adventurer, Sebastián Rodríguez Cermeño, on condition that the voyage should include an exploration of the California coast in search of the best site for a port of call. After an especially harrowing passage across the Pacific, Cermeño sighted land somewhere north of Cape Mendocino. There his ship, the *San Agustín,* was nearly wrecked by a storm, and several of the officers took every step short of mutiny in an effort to persuade him to give up the projected explorations. He refused, and on November 6, rounding Point Reyes, he anchored in Drake's Bay, which he called the Bay of San Francisco.

On shore, the Spaniards assembled a launch that had been brought along for use in exploring coastal areas. This little vessel was to be their salvation, for on November 30 a great gale from the southeast, the direction in which the bay is completely exposed, drove the *San Agustín* aground. The breakers pounded it to pieces in a few hours and strewed its cargo, provisions, and timbers along the beach. To the amazement and outrage of his crew, not even this disaster persuaded Cermeño to abandon his interest in exploration. With 70 men crowded into the open launch, the *San Buenaventura,* he found excuses for many landings, and although he sailed past the Golden Gate without seeing it, he described many other points with remarkable accuracy considering his difficulties.

Vizcaíno and Monterey

Cermeño had found no new harbor that was safe, and the viceregal government doubted the thoroughness and accuracy of his charts. The further search for a good harbor in northern California was now entrusted, after long negotiations, to another *adelantado,* Sebastian Vizcaíno. On the understanding that he would be rewarded with various concessions including the future command of one of the Manila ships, Vizcaíno invested a considerable amount of his own capital in an elaborate expedition in 1602. Setting out from Acapulco with two ships and a launch, he permanently renamed many of the places along the California coast, and on December 16 he entered a bay that he named for the viceroy, the conde de Monterey. Vizcaíno announced himself as the discoverer of this bay, although he was not. Cermeño had seen it 7 years earlier, and his description of it, though not detailed, was actually far less misleading than that of Vizcaíno, who made absurdly exaggerated claims for its value as a harbor.

Vizcaíno seems to have feared that if he did not return with a favorable report, he would not receive the rewards he hoped for. The result was that he described the bay to the viceroy not only as having an abundance of fine timber for shipbuilding but also as being "sheltered from all winds"—a claim that can only be described as positively fraudulent, because the bay actually includes no proper harbor at all.

Viceroy Monterey, pleased with the idea that a fine port would bear his name, awarded Vizcaíno the command of the next Manila galleon. Shortly afterward, however, Monterey was promoted to the viceroyalty of Peru. His successor as viceroy of New Spain, the marqué de Montesclaros, completely distrusted Vizcaíno, revoked the award of the galleon, and went so far as to have the expedition's map maker convicted of forgery and hanged.

Montesclaros ridiculed and blocked the whole project of a California port of call. He pointed out, correctly, that when the galleons sighted California, they had only a few days' voyage left because the strong prevailing winds and currents along the coast almost always bore them swiftly southward. In this judgment, history vindicated him, for even after Upper California was finally settled more than a century and a half later, the annual ships from Manila almost never stopped there.

The lapse of 60 years between Cabrillo and Vizcaíno, and of another 167 years between Vizcaíno and actual Spanish settlement of California, emphasizes the utter isolation of California and the low regard in which the Spaniards held it. California was a place that should have contained gold, but apparently did not; a place where a strait should have been, but was not; a barren and dangerous coast that a ship sailed past once a year. Getting to it from Mexico was far more trouble than it was worth. Just as the winds and currents made the southward voyage brief and easy, they made the northward voyage long, difficult, and sometimes impossible. Land travel seemed even more forbidding. Lower California was on the very rim of Christendom during the whole of the Spanish colonial period in America, which lasted more than 3 centuries, and for all but the last half century of that period, Upper California remained beyond the rim.

One can only imagine the thoughts of the native people who lived along the coast of California when they glimpsed the billowing sails of tall ships sailing along the shore of their homeland. Essie Parrish, a twentieth-century Kashaya Pomo Indian, said that when her people first saw a ship on the horizon, they thought it was a giant bird, an omen of the end of their world:

> In the old days, before the white people came up here, there was a boat sailing on the ocean from the south. Because before that they had never seen a boat, they said, "Our world must be coming to an end. Couldn't we do something? This big bird floating on the ocean is from somewhere, probably from on high. Let us plan a feast. Let us have a dance." They followed its course with their eyes . . . saying that destruction was upon them.

Spain's Indian Policies

New Spain lacked the manpower for the settlement of its remote and unprofitable northern frontiers. When the colonization of these areas finally came, it was largely through an ingenious plan intended to transform the Indians into colonists by the use of that remarkable institution, the Spanish mission.

The Spanish attitudes toward the Indians grew from an interesting blend of religious, economic, military, and political motives. The Indians were officially regarded not only as subjects of the Spanish monarchy with rights to its protection, but also as human beings with souls to be saved. Their Most Catholic Majesties, the Spanish monarchs, made frequent references to their duty of Christianization, and the missionaries were untiring in their efforts to carry it out. There were others, however, who were primarily interested in the Indians because they could be made to labor for the profit of their conquerors. In return for the salvation of their souls, the Indians were required to contribute the labor of their bodies.

The most essential key to the Spanish colonial plan, however, was that Indians were to be made Spanish—in religion, in language, and in the gradual intermixture of blood. They were to be required to work; they were also to be permitted to live (if they survived the epidemics of smallpox and typhus). These views were quite different from those of the English colonists; there was no comparable plan for assimilating the Indian into the Anglo-American scheme of things, and displacement or extermination was almost the only alternative. As for intermarriage, the Anglo-Americans were usually intolerant of it. They were generally able to secure wives of English descent, whereas the Spanish American colonies were extremely unattractive to Spanish women.

The Mission as a Frontier Institution

As a method of advancing and consolidating a frontier, the mission had its roots in the long struggle against the Moors in Spain. The cross and the sword had moved forward together, in forcible conversion of the infidel. In Spanish America, each mission had a small guard of soldiers, and there was usually a larger garrison at a *presidio,* or military post, nearby. Cooperation between padres and soldiers was seldom cordial, but it was always indispensable. The missionaries were typically men of tremendous courage and faith, but, with the exception of those who actively sought martyrdom, they were usually aware that the strength of their own personalities had to be supplemented by the soldiers' weapons, even though they were constantly anxious lest the soldiers corrupt the Indian *neophytes,* their apprentices to Christianity. Throughout the Spanish empire, as historian Harry Crosby has observed, "missions were the crux of the conquest." Mission practices were everywhere directed toward the same goal: "the abolition of any pre-Christian practices, religious or secular, that were considered impediments to conversion or to integration with the greater Spanish economy."

The mission, thus, was not only a church but also an agricultural *pueblo,* or town, in which hundreds or even thousands of Indians were concentrated. There were cultivated fields, gardens, orchards, and vineyards, often fenced with nearly impenetrable hedges of prickly pear and watered from irrigation ditches with stone dams. At a little distance, each mission had its *rancho* and, eventually, large herds of cattle.

Theoretically every mission was temporary. If the plan had worked as the Spanish government hoped, each mission would have been "secularized" 10 years after its founding. That is, the pueblo would receive a grant of 4 square leagues of land; the fields, town lots, and other property would be parceled out among the Indians; and community government would pass to native officials who had been trained for the purpose. The mission church would be turned over to parish priests, known as "secular" clergy, as distinct from the missionaries, who were called "regular" clergy because they were under the regulations and vows of a particular order. The missionaries were then supposed to begin their work all over again farther on, in a continuous process of frontier expansion.

In practice, however, the schedule was never met. Most missions continued for decades, and some for more than a century. Although the Laws of the Indies provided that mission Indians should receive real training for self-government, they received little or none. The missionary fathers made the basic mistake of regarding the Indians as children whose minds were incapable of development beyond the child's level. They turned them into helpless dependents and kept them in that condition. Every detail of work, play, clothing, and even the choice of a mate was rigidly controlled. Once Indians joined the missions, they could not change their minds and go back to their old ways of life. They were held by the missionaries in what historian Kevin Starr has called a "churchly captivity." So far as possible the missionaries kept their charges from contact with any Europeans but themselves and did not prepare them to take a place in any kind of society but that of the mission.

There are many viewpoints concerning the effect of mission life itself on Indian morale. The Spanish missionaries often spoke of the "temporal and spiritual conquest" of new provinces. The phrase is apt. Very often, no real conversion took place after the Indians' own gods were destroyed. One skeptical California ranch

Generalized plan of a mission compound on the Spanish colonial frontier. (*Adapted from* California Patterns: A Geographical and Historical Atlas, *by David Hornbeck. Copyright 1983 by the Mayfield Publishing Company.*)

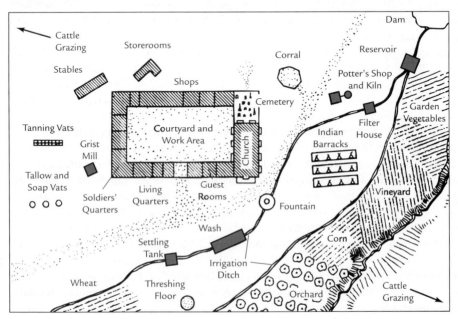

owner, Antonio María Osio, doubted that Indians in the missions ever adopted a true Christianity "simply because they had been sprinkled with baptismal water." Religious instruction consisted primarily of endless repetitions of ritual passages. From the missionaries' point of view, this structured religious activity was part of the transformation of a savage people into industrious Christians. The regimentation of Indian labor, regarded by the Spaniards as "a morally enriching disciplinary activity," completed the process. Anthropologist James Scott has rightly concluded that this imposition of alien ways was an assault on both the dignity and the autonomy of the native people.

Spain had entrusted the frontier regions of northwestern Mexico to the black-robed missionaries of the Society of Jesus in 1591. A century later the Jesuit frontier had been extended northwestward on the mainland as far as the country of the Pimas, and Father Eusebio Kino had begun the building of the missions in Pimería Alta—northern Sonora and southern Arizona. Kino rediscovered the forgotten fact that Baja California was a peninsula and not an island and persuaded his superiors to establish the first of the missions on the peninsula in 1697. But in 1767 the king issued an order expelling the Jesuits from all the Spanish dominions. Charles III of Spain had become convinced that the Jesuits were involved in plots against the interests of the crown.

Gálvez and the Plan for Alta California

The expulsion of the Jesuits from New Spain was entrusted to Visitor-General José de Gálvez, who turned the Baja California missions over to military administrators under Captain Gaspar de Portolá and then to the Franciscans under Father Junípero Serra. The names of these three remarkable men soon became important in the story of the founding of Alta California.

Gálvez was the most effective visitor-general in the history of New Spain, though not the first. The *visita* was a distinctively Spanish administrative technique for investigations and reorganizations, and a *visitador-general* was a special deputy of the king, with extraordinary powers overlapping and sometimes transcending those of the viceroy.

The *visita* of Gálvez, which began in 1765, was primarily intended to reform the finances and increase the revenues of New Spain as a part of the energetic attempts to reorganize the Spanish government under Charles III after the expensive and disastrous Seven Years War. The expulsion of the Jesuits was an added assignment. But the consolidation of the northwestern frontier and its extension to Alta California were Gálvez's own projects and seem to have been the result of his intense personal ambitions. He had risen from rather humble origins, and although he was a brilliant, forceful, and generally successful administrator, he was also unusually vain, selfish, ruthless, deceitful, and unstable. It was, indeed, because of Gálvez's possession of this very combination of qualities that the occupation of San Diego and Monterey, long considered and periodically given up as hopeless, actually materialized. New Spain had been decaying, and Gálvez now made it appear to be flourishing and expanding. This was the sort of achievement which, along with others, later led to his being made Minister of the Indies.

Gálvez proposed a scheme for the consolidation and development of the whole of the far northwest under a vast new governmental unit, to be called a commandancy-general, and to include the areas of Sinaloa, Sonora, Chihuahua, and the Californias. To justify this plan, he made use of the old and perennial fear that some other European power would establish itself on the Pacific coast and menace New Spain from the north. It was long believed that the Spanish colonization of Upper California occurred because of a diplomatic report that Russia was about to move in the direction of Monterey. The truth was that Gálvez's plan was already well advanced when this absurdly exaggerated report reached him, and that he merely added it to the rumors he himself had been spreading about various alleged intentions of the English and the Dutch. Another argument used by Gálvez in support of his plans was that the development of Alta California would ultimately provide a great source of royal revenue, although, as it turned out, the result was an annual deficit during most of the period of Spanish rule.

Gálvez ordered the founding of the new port of San Blas on the coast of Mexico several hundred miles northwest of Acapulco as a naval and supply base for the Californias. In 1768 Gálvez sailed from San Blas for Baja California, where he completed the planning of the "sacred expedition" that would colonize Alta California in the following year. The various divisions of this expedition, two by land and three by sea, were to be launched from the peninsula.

The mainland approach was blocked by Indian rebellions in Sonora. These had been going on unchecked for many years, but Gálvez was sure that a determined military campaign could quickly suppress them. That campaign, however, proved to be as maddeningly unsuccessful and frustrating as a number of its predecessors had been. Once, while visiting Sonora, Gálvez actually suffered a temporary attack of insanity. He had been increasingly given to the belief that he received divine instructions, and now for a brief time he was convinced that he was God himself. At one moment he proposed to reduce the Indians to submission by importing 600 Guatemalan apes as soldiers.

From the viewpoint of the United States, it is fortunate that the Spaniards occupied Alta California when they did. Tenuous as that occupation was, it may ultimately have forestalled the acquisition of the territory by some nation strong enough to have delayed or even prevented its later acquisition by the United States. But at the time and under the circumstances in which it was undertaken, the Spanish occupation of Alta California was impractical and unnecessary and was largely a result of the mental instability of Gálvez, who conceived and ordered it.

The Franciscans and Father Serra

A handful of Spanish officers and missionaries and a scarcely larger number of mestizo and mulatto soldiers and sailors carried out the founding of the colony of Alta California under fantastic difficulties. The military men and the missionaries

Father Junípero Serra
(1713–1784), founder of
the first nine missions in
Alta California. (*Courtesy
of the Bancroft Library.*)

had quite different ideas of what they were doing and why, and they were often at
cross-purposes. But their joint achievement is an impressive tribute to human
courage in the face of adversity.

Saint Francis of Assisi had founded the Order of Friars Minor, oldest and largest
of his orders, in the thirteenth century. The Franciscans were the first missionaries
in the Americas, where their work began with Columbus's second voyage and continued vigorously in many parts of Spanish America through the later period when
the Jesuits and other orders shared the missionary field. The name "Gray Friars"
was sometimes given to the Franciscans because their robes were woven of white
and black wool; the color of their habits was still gray at the time of the founding
of Alta California, though later it was changed to brown.

The decision to entrust the California missions to the Franciscans was the result
of the belief that they were not only more obedient to the vows of poverty than
were the Jesuits but also less disposed to subordinate the interests of their country
to those of their order. This had become the prevailing opinion in the Spanish government. It was inaccurate, and it was unfair to both of the orders concerned. Certainly the relations between the Franciscans and the governmental officials in
California were to include a long series of sharp disputes. Father Junípero Serra, in
particular, vigorously subordinated everything to his conception of religious duty.

Father Junípero, the first and most famous of the missionaries in Alta California,
was a Spanish farmer's son, born in the village of Petra on the island of Majorca in
1713. The family name Serra is the Catalonian form of the Castilian word *sierra*.
Upon joining the Franciscan order, Miguel, as he was originally called, exercised
the privilege of choosing a name by which he wished to be known "in religion."
Junípero had been the name of one of Saint Francis's closest companions, whose

devotion was said to have inspired the founder to wish "that I had a whole forest of such Junipers."

Serra became a professor of philosophy at the University of Majorca, but at the age of 35 he determined to give up this quiet and relatively comfortable position for the strenuous life of a foreign missionary. He also hoped for martyrdom, as had Saint Francis himself, although in neither case was this hope fulfilled. According to Father Francisco Palóu, Serra's former pupil and later companion, assistant, and biographer, Serra once spoke of martyrdom as the true "gold and silver of the Indies" for which they would search.

As prospective missionaries, Serra, Palóu, and Juan Crespí, another of Serra's former students, were first assigned to the apostolic College of San Fernando in Mexico City. This establishment was both a headquarters for Franciscan missionaries in New Spain and a special training center to accustom them to privation, fatigue, mortification, and penance.

In manifestations of zeal, no one excelled Serra. Upon his arrival in Mexico he had chosen to walk all the way from Vera Cruz to the capital. Early in the course of the journey he suffered an insect bite that became infected. He neglected medical care for it, and his leg and foot remained swollen and ulcerous for the rest of his life, a condition that he alternately ignored and regarded as a blessing. While delivering missionary sermons he would sometimes scourge his own shoulders with a chain, or, holding a cross in one hand, beat his breast with a stone held in the other, or burn his bared chest with lighted candles. He slept on a narrow bed made only of hard wooden boards. He kept a thong of sharp-pointed iron links hanging on the wall beside the bed for scourging himself when thoughts that he regarded as sinful came in the night. Serra's strict discipline of his own body provides a context for understanding his conviction that missionaries "should be able to punish their sons, the Indians, with blows." Saint Francis had practiced mortification of the flesh, and it was not uncommon among the missionaries of Serra's time, although regulations of the apostolic college provided that it should never go so far as to be permanently incapacitating.

After an impressive record in missionary work in the Sierra Gorda and other parts of Mexico, Serra became father-president of the missions in Baja California and then of the prospective new missions in Alta California. At the time of his appointment to the latter post, he was 55 years old. He held it until his death in 1784 at the age of 70. As father-president of Alta California, Serra founded the province's first nine missions. Throughout his life he was a vigorous, hard-driving man, never turning back from a task he had begun, always demanding the full measure of work from others as well as from himself. In physical stature, Serra was short, not more than 5 feet 2 or 3 inches in height—but in courage and determination, he was a giant.

The Sacred Expedition

Supplies and men for the first missions and presidios to be founded in Alta California came in part from the peninsula and in part from the mainland by way of San Blas. The Pious Fund of the Californias, transferred from the custody of the Jesuits to that of the Franciscans, was extended to the new ventures in the north, and Gálvez and Serra agreed that church furniture, ornaments, vestments, and utensils, as well as livestock and other supplies, were to be drawn from the Baja California missions.

As was customary in founding new establishments, a number of Christianized Indians from the peninsula were taken along with the expedition in order to serve as, so to speak, bellwethers for the new flock. In addition to soldiers from the garrison at Loreto under Captain Fernando Rivera y Moncada, 25 Catalonian volunteers, light infantry under Lieutenant Pedro Fages, were detached from their previous assignments to the campaign in Sonora. There were also several blacksmiths, cooks, and carpenters, along with Miguel Costansó, military engineer and cartographer, and Dr. Pedro Prat, army surgeon of French ancestry.

The expedition as a whole was under the command of Captain Gaspar de Portolá. When settlements had been established at San Diego and Monterey, Portolá and Rivera were to return to duty on the peninsula, leaving Lieutenant Fages in charge of the military and civil government of the new colony.

Three ships were provided for the expedition, the *San Carlos,* the *San Antonio,* and the *San José,* all less than 200 tons, and all hastily and imperfectly constructed under the difficulties that still hampered shipbuilding on the Pacific coast. All three vessels reached Baja California from San Blas in leaky condition, even before the beginning of the longer voyage, and all three had to be repaired. Visitor-General Gálvez personally superintended the repairs and the loading of the flagship, the *San Carlos,* and carried some of the mission furniture on board with his own hands. When the vessel sailed from La Paz, on January 9, 1769, he accompanied it in a launch to see her round Cape San Lucas. The *San Antonio,* a smaller supply ship, sailed from Cabo San Lucas on February 15. The third vessel, the *San José,* was lost with all on board somewhere on her way toward San Diego.

Of the two land parties, the first was under Captain Rivera, with 27 *cuirassiers.* On the frontier the cuirass was a sleeveless jacket of tough leather, made by quilting several thicknesses of deerskin or sheepskin, and usually arrowproof. Father Crespí, chaplain and diarist of the expedition, noted quite accurately that these *soldados de cuera,* or leather-jacket soldiers, were the best light cavalry in the world and were equally skilled as cowboys. Driving a large herd of cattle, horses, and mules, this party set out from the northernmost Spanish outpost in Baja California on March 24.

The second land contingent, including Portolá and Serra, left the same point on May 15. Following the trail made by Rivera, and less encumbered with livestock, it could move somewhat more rapidly, but the journey over deserts and gullies was a hard one. When Serra's ulcerated leg threatened to disable him completely, he asked a muleteer to treat it as he would a sore foot on one of his animals. The muleteer's poultice of mud and herbs had an almost miraculous effect, and Serra was able to continue, much relieved.

The first objective of the whole expedition was the founding of a presidio and a mission at San Diego as a way station for the journey to Monterey. The *San Antonio* was first to arrive at San Diego, on April 11, after a relatively easy voyage of 54 days.

The *San Carlos,* although she had started a month earlier, did not arrive until nearly 3 weeks later, after 110 days at sea. The effects of scurvy had advanced so far that no one was able to lower a boat, and the men on shore had to board it in order to do so. The first Spanish settlement in Alta California was a sail-tent hospital. Dr. Prat was himself so ill that he could be of little help to the others. He later became insane.

The first land party, under Rivera, arrived on May 14, and Rivera ordered the tents moved several miles northward to the foot of the hill where the presidio would later be built. Portolá rode in a little ahead of his men on June 29, and Serra and the others reached the stricken camp on July 1. Of about 300 men in the various branches of the sacred expedition of 1769, not more than half survived to reach San Diego, many died of scurvy there, and for months half the survivors were too sick to travel farther. All but a handful of the Christianized Indians who had been brought with the land contingents had died or deserted; the military officers had felt compelled to deny them rations from the dwindling food supplies.

Of the sailors, 38 had died. The *San Antonio,* with a truly skeleton crew of eight men, had to be sent back to San Blas to bring new supplies for the whole expedition and new crews for both ships. The *San Carlos* was left at anchor in the bay with two men on board to keep it from being stripped by the Indians. The whole situation was stark and desperate. Nevertheless, 2 weeks after his arrival at San Diego, Portolá set out toward his main objective, the legendary harbor of Monterey, taking with him Rivera, Fages, Costansó, Crespí, and nearly all the others who were still able to travel, leaving Serra at San Diego to care for the more than 50 invalids.

On the way north, the expedition felt several earthquakes near the river called the Santa Ana, or Río de los Temblores. Four days later the Río de Porciúncula, site of the future pueblo of Los Angeles, was named by Crespí for the day of its discovery and crossing, August 2. This was the day of the festival of Our Lady the Queen of the Angels, one of many titles of the Virgin Mary. For Franciscans, in particular, an important shrine of the Virgin was the chapel of Porciúncula, near Assisi, where Saint Francis had worshiped.

Continuing northwestward on a route that would become El Camino Real (The King's Highway), remarkably close at most points to the route of the modern Highway 101, the expedition eventually reached the shore of the Bay at Monterey. Portolá, however, failed to recognize the bay, for he could see nothing resembling the fine harbor praised by Vizcaíno and subjected in the interim to 167 years of idealized imagination. Moreover, Portolá and his half-starved men had managed to convince themselves that they would find the *San José,* with abundant food supplies, riding at anchor in that harbor.

After a few days' search the party pushed on northward along the coast. At the end of October they reached Point San Pedro and looked across the Gulf of the Farallons toward Point Reyes and Drake's Bay, which to them was Cermeño's Bay of San Francisco. Although Point Reyes was 40 miles away and they could not be sure of its identity from that distance, they saw enough to increase their fears that they must have passed Monterey without finding it. Sergeant José Ortega understood some Indians to be trying to tell him that a ship was anchored somewhere to the north. Heading a party of scouts, Ortega found his advance blocked by a vast and unknown bay, which he sighted, probably on November 1, 1769, from the top of the ridge between the present cities of Pacifica and Millbrae. Historians long supposed that he also found the Golden Gate at this time, but this is untrue. It was not until a year later that Pedro Fages, scouting northward along the east bay shore, became the first Spanish explorer to see the narrow gap between the peninsulas. Navigators had failed for centuries to see it from the ocean, if we assume that Drake also did not. Part of the explanation lies in the fogs that so often shroud the Golden Gate, and part in the fact that Angel Island and the Berkeley hills lie behind it in such a position as to give, from any distance at sea, the impression of a continuous coastline.

Neither Portolá nor anyone else in the expedition seems to have regarded the discovery of the great bay as anything but an obstacle, except for Father Crespí, who wrote in his diary: "It is a very large and fine harbor, such that not only all the navy of our Most Catholic Majesty but those of all Europe could take shelter in it."

Considering how long Spaniards had been searching for the Strait of Anián, it is surprising that no one speculated that it might now have been discovered, but for weeks the attention of these men had been desperately concentrated on the search for a harbor with a ship in it, and food on the ship. An attempt was made to get around the bay, and Ortega and his scouts got just around the southern end of it, but on November 11 the whole expedition gave up and turned back the way it had come. The group arrived back in San Diego on January 24, 1770.

Nothing encouraging had happened at San Diego during their absence. Serra had founded the mission of San Diego de Alcalá at a temporary location in a hut on Presidio Hill, on July 16, 1769. In his inaugural sermon, he had prayed fervently for a rich "harvest of souls" among the Kumeyaay Indians of San Diego: "May God give them his grace so that in a short time all will become Christians." But there was not yet a single convert. One Kumeyaay baby was offered for baptism, but Serra's joy turned to grief when the Indians suddenly snatched it from his arms and ran off before the ceremony could be completed. Yet nothing, it seemed, could discourage the indomitable father-president.

On February 10, 1770, Portolá sent Rivera and 40 men on the long journey back to Baja California for supplies. A month later, when there was still no sign of the *San José* or of the return of the *San Antonio,* Portolá announced that if no relief came by March 19, the feast of Saint Joseph, the patron of the expedition, he and his men would march south the next morning. Serra and Crespí protested, refused to turn back, and arranged that they would be taken on board the *San Carlos,* still anchored in the bay, to await the coming of a supply ship. After 9 days of prayer, the *San Antonio* was sighted on the very afternoon of March 19. The danger of abandonment had passed.

Portolá now sent the *San Antonio,* carrying Serra, Costansó, and Fages, on to Monterey. Portolá himself set out for the north again by land, with 12 soldiers, leaving 8 to guard San Diego. This time, at last, Portolá fully realized that what he had previously seen of the harbor of Monterey was all there was of it—at best a roadstead with no shelter from the north wind. But he had his orders, and so a presidio of poles and earth was constructed at Monterey, and a mission, San Carlos Borromeo, was built nearby under the direction of Serra. Both were formally established on June 3, 1770. Leaving Fages in charge of the government of Alta California, Portolá then sailed for Mexico.

There was great formal rejoicing in Mexico City over the establishment of the new province, even though the reports of Portolá to the visitor-general and the viceroy were more candid than they cared to hear. Portolá was of the opinion that if the Russians wanted Alta California, which he doubted, they should be allowed to have it as a punishment for their aggressive designs.

Selected Bibliography

Harry Kelsey is the author of several works on the discovery and early exploration of California: "Mapping the California Coast," *Arizona and the West,* XXVI (Winter 1984), pp. 307–324; "Finding the Way Home," *Western Historical Quarterly,* XVII (April 1986), pp. 145–164; and *Juan Rodríguez Cabrillo* (1986). See also Nancy Lemke, *Cabrillo* (1991). The classics in the field are Henry R. Wagner's *Spanish Voyages to the Northwest Coast of America in the Sixteenth Century* (1929) and *Juan Rodríguez Cabrillo* (1941). See also W. Michael Mathes, "Apocryphal Tales of the Island of California and Strait of Anián," *California History,* LXII (Spring 1983), pp. 52–59, and Jack D. Forbes, "Melchor Díaz and the Discovery of Alta California," *Pacific Historical Review,* XXVII (November 1958), pp. 351–358.

A translation of the parts of Montalvo's *Las Sergas de Esplandián* relating to Queen Calafía, with commentary, may be found in Edward Everett Hale, *The Queen of California* (reprinted in 1945). See also Donald C. Cutter, "Sources of the Name 'California,'" *Arizona and the West,* III (Autumn 1961), pp. 233–243, and Dora B. Polk, *The Island of California* (1991).

Arthur Quinn's *Broken Shore* (1981) includes a lyrical account of the landing of Francis Drake in California. Warren L. Hanna's *Lost Harbour* (1979) is a convenient guide to the maze of arguments over Drake's landing spot. Hanna concludes that the evidence is insufficient to warrant a final judgment. See also Norman J. Thrower (ed.), *Sir Francis Drake and the Famous Voyage, 1577–1580* (1984), and John Sugden, *Sir Francis Drake* (1991). On the controversy over Drake's plate, see James D. Hart, *The Plate of Brass Reexamined* (1977), and the response by Robert H. Power, "A Plate of Brass 'By Me . . . C.G. Francis Drake,'" *California History,* LVII (Summer 1978), pp. 172–185, followed by Hart, *The Plate of Brass Reexamined: A Supplementary Report* (1979).

William L. Schurz chronicled *The Manila Galleon* (1939). On the Cermeño expedition, see Wagner, "The Voyage to California of Sebastián Rodríguez Cermeño in 1595," *California Historical Society Quarterly,* III (April 1924), pp. 3–24. Mathes, *Vizcaíno and Spanish Expansion in the Pacific Ocean, 1580–1630* (1968), considerably enhances Vizcaíno's reputation and the significance of his explorations.

Colin M. MacLachlan, *Spain's Empire in the New World* (1988), offers a new analysis of theory and practice in the Spanish empire. The mission system appears in a favorable light in Herbert E. Bolton, "The Mission as a Frontier Institution in the Spanish American Colonies," in his *Wider Horizons in American History* (1939). For a survey of the literature see John Francis Bannon, "The Mission as a Frontier Institution: Sixty Years of Interest and Research," *Western Historical Quarterly,* X (July 1979), pp. 302–322.

The background of the colonization of Alta California is discussed in Harry W. Crosby, *Antigua California* (1994); Herbert I. Priestly, *José de Gálvez* (1916); and Charles E. Chapman, *The Founding of Spanish California* (1916). Robert Browning (ed.), *The Discovery of San Francisco Bay* (1992), and Frank M. Stanger and Alan K. Brown, *Who Discovered the Golden Gate?* (1969), are illuminating. Accounts of the sacred expedition include Herbert E. Bolton, *Fray Juan Crespí* (1927); Priestley, *Description of California by Pedro Fages* (1937); Douglas S. Watson, *The Spanish Occupation of California* (1934); and two accounts of Gaspar de Portolá by Fernando B. Companys (1983) and Josep Carner-Ribalta (1992).

Maynard Geiger, *The Life and Times of Fray Junípero Serra* (two volumes, 1959), is a work of urbane scholarship, in welcome contrast to the defensive tone of Zephyrin Engelhardt, *The Missions and Missionaries of California* (four volumes, 1908–1915). More recent biographies of Serra include those by Don De Nevi and Noel F. Moholy (1985) and Martin J. Morgado (1991). See also Iris H. W. Engstrand, *Serra's San Diego* (1982), and the startling speculations in Janie L. Gustafson, "Never to Turn Back: Three Years in the Life of Junípero Serra," Ph.D. thesis, Graduate Theological Union, Berkeley (1986).

CHAPTER 4

Outposts of a Dying Empire

The Spanish occupation of Alta California now consisted of two pinpoints on the coast, 450 miles apart. In 1771 Serra moved the mission of San Carlos Borromeo from Monterey to the Carmel River. This mission became Serra's headquarters for the arduous struggle to establish the others. Ultimately, there would be 21 missions in Alta California, 9 of them founded during his lifetime, but at the beginning only Serra himself foresaw such a degree of success. Differences of opinion between Serra and Governor Fages deepened into a feud. Fages repeatedly vetoed Serra's requests for new missions because there were not enough soldiers to protect them.

Bucareli, Anza, and the Founding of San Francisco

Visitor-General Gálvez returned to Spain in 1771, and a new viceroy, Antonio de Bucareli, arrived in the same year. At first Bucareli was too busy with other duties to take much interest in Gálvez's new colony. In 1773, however, he turned his attention to it, and for several years he gave it enough care and support to bring it through its precarious infancy. Again the fear of foreign encroachments reinforced Spanish interest in California, the English now rivaling the Russians as objects of concern. The voyages of Captain James Cook in the 1770s indicated a renewed English interest in the Pacific.

In 1773 Serra made a journey to Mexico City to plead for more support for new missions and the removal of Lieutenant Fages as governor of Alta California. Bucareli replaced Fages with Captain Rivera, although this would soon involve Serra in more disputes with the new governor than with the old one.

About the same time, Captain Juan Bautista de Anza submitted a proposal for an expedition to open a land route from northern Sonora to Monterey. With eager encouragement from Serra, Viceroy Bucareli resolved not only to adopt Anza's project of a new land route to Monterey, but also to empower him to extend Spanish settlement to the strategic Bay of San Francisco. Anza was an ideal leader for the project. The opening of a trail from Sonora to Alta California had been the dream of his family for three generations. He led two expeditions to California, one to explore the trail and the other to bring settlers, including some for the new San Francisco site.

On the first of these expeditions Anza rode out from Tubac, a presidio south of Tucson, in January 1774. One of the men with Anza had already traveled through the Colorado River region and had won the confidence of Salvador Palma, chief of the Yumas. The goodwill of the Yumas was a vital factor in the success of Anza's expeditions. Ferried across the Colorado River with the aid of the Yumas and their tule rafts, Anza and his men struck out westward across the sand dunes of the Colorado Desert, became lost, and finally struggled back to the river after 10 days. After leaving much of their baggage with Chief Palma, they traveled southward to get around the dunes, turned west again, and on March 22, 1774, they reached the Mission of San Gabriel, founded 3 years earlier. Continuing to Monterey, and returning the way he had come, Anza reached Tubac in May, and a few months later went to Mexico City to make a full report to the viceroy.

Encouraged by the opening of the new route from Sonora to California, Bucareli promoted Anza to the rank of lieutenant colonel and planned new expeditions for 1775. An expedition to explore San Francisco Bay began under Captain Miguel Manrique, but this commander lost his mind a few days after leaving San Blas and had to be put ashore. He had left several loaded pistols about his cabin, and one of these accidentally exploded, wounding his successor, Lieutenant Juan Manuel de Ayala. The lateness of Spanish settlement of upper California can be vividly seen in the fact that this unfortunate pistol shot occurred within a few days of "the shot heard round the world," fired at Lexington, Massachusetts, on April 19, 1775, and signaling the beginning of the American Revolutionary War.

On August 5 a launch made at Monterey and piloted by Ayala's sailing master, José Cañizares, became the first Spanish vessel to enter the Golden Gate, known to the Spaniards merely as La Boca, or "the mouth." Ayala's ship, the *San Carlos,* sailed through the next day. His wound confined him to his cabin, but the crew spent several weeks in making a thorough exploration of the arms of the bay with the launch. The names of Angel Island and of Alcatraz (Isla de los Alcatraces, or Island of the Pelicans) date from the Ayala expedition, although the name of Alcatraz was then applied to the island now called Yerba Buena.

The second Anza expedition also began in 1775 and was responsible for the founding of the presidio and mission at San Francisco in the following year. Except for Anza's own small escort, this expedition consisted almost entirely of settlers who would remain in California as *pobladores,* or populators. There were about 30 soldier-colonists and their families and 4 civilian settlers and their families, recruited mainly in Sinaloa. The need for *married* soldiers in California came from both the need for future citizens for the province and the desire to reduce the difficulties with the Indians repeatedly caused by soldiers who were either unmarried or living far from their families in Mexico.

From the beginning of Spanish settlement, Indian women and girls were the target of brutal attacks and sexual violence. Mounted soldiers at the San Gabriel mission raided local Tongva villages, chasing, lassoing, raping, beating, and sometimes killing native women. Three soldiers at San Diego in 1773 were accused of raping two Kumeyaay girls and murdering one of them. Sent to Mexico for trial, the soldiers were spared their lives but were sentenced to spend the rest of their lives as citizens of California, a somewhat paradoxical verdict reflecting the evil reputation the new colony had in Mexico.

The time when people would want to go to California was far in the future; only those in the direst poverty were willing to go, and then only on the promise of the government to outfit them completely and to pay all their expenses for years to come.

With the second Anza expedition went a large herd of cattle and horses to serve as breeding stock. Following his previous route, Anza reached San Gabriel in January 1776. There he learned that the Indians had attacked and destroyed the mission at San Diego in the previous November, killing Father Luis Jayme and two soldiers and mutilating the body of Father Jayme.

Governor Rivera had only 70 soldiers in the whole province, scattered among five missions and two presidios. He was on his way from Monterey to San Diego to punish the offenders, and Anza was induced to join forces with him for that purpose. Their arrival at San Diego, coinciding with those of a supply ship for San Blas and a small land force sent up from the peninsula, completely overawed the Indians; however, Rivera was excommunicated by the padres for entering the improvised church to seize an Indian chief who had sought the right of asylum, but who was suspected of being the main instigator of the revolt.

In March, Anza's party of colonists reached Monterey, and Anza himself proceeded to the San Francisco peninsula to choose the sites for the new presidio and mission. Governor Rivera, in spite of orders from the viceroy, had done nothing to prepare for the founding of San Francisco and was in fact bitterly opposed to it. He was now 65 years old and had repeatedly requested retirement. He was still a captain, and part of his irritation at this time was undoubtedly the result of his belief that Anza, who was only 41, had gained promotion to a higher rank for services no greater than his own. It was Rivera, after all, who had led the first overland party of Spanish colonists into California. A few years later, during the Yuma massacre, he would be killed at the age of 70.

For the site of the new presidio, Anza chose a point near the northernmost tip of the San Francisco peninsula. The whole northern part of the peninsula consisted largely of sand dunes, but about 3 miles to the southeast of the presidio site Anza found a little oasis on a creek, and here, on March 29, 1776, he marked the site of the mission. He named the creek *Laguna de Nuestra Señora de los Dolores* because March 29 in the religious calendar was the Friday of Sorrows, referring to Our Lady of Sorrows, the Virgin Mary. From this there later arose the popular name of Mission Dolores for what was officially the Mission San Francisco de Asís.

Various obstacles, including some set up by Governor Rivera, delayed the actual founding of the new establishments for several months. In the meantime, Anza departed for Mexico and left Lieutenant José Moraga in charge of the new colonists.

○ - Mission
☐ - Pueblo
△ - Presidio

San Francisco Solano de Sonoma (1823) ㉑

San Rafael Arcángel (1817) ⑳
Presidio de San Francisco △⑥ San Francisco de Asís (1776)
⑭ San José de Guadalupe (1797)
⑧ Santa Clara de Asís (1777)
☐ Pueblo de San José (1777)
Santa Cruz (1791) ⑫
Villa de Branciforte (1797)
⑮ San Juan Bautista (1797)
Presidio de Monterey △ ② San Carlos Borromeo (1770)
⑬ Nuestra Señora de la Soledad (1791)
③ San Antonio de Padua (1771)
⑯ San Miguel Arcángel (1797)
⑤ San Luis Obispo de Tolosa (1772)
La Purísima Concepción (1787)
⑪
⑲ Santa Inés (1804)
Presidio de Santa Bárbara △ ⑩ Santa Bárbara (1786)
⑨ San Buenaventura (1782)
⑰ San Fernando Rey de España (1797)
☐ ④ San Gabriel Arcángel (1771)
Pueblo de Nuestra Señora la Reina
de los Ángeles del Río de Porciúncula (1781)
⑦ San Juan Capistrano (1776)
⑱ San Luis Rey de Francia (1798)
① San Diego de Alcalá (1769)
Presidio de San Diego △

Spanish California. (*From* Indians of California: The Changing Image, *by James J. Rawls. Copyright 1984 by the University of Oklahoma Press.*)

On June 27, 1776, a group of 193 persons, mostly soldier-settlers and their families, arrived at the site of the San Francisco mission. The presidio was formally established under the command of Moraga on September 17, and Father Palóu formally opened the mission on October 9.

Neve and the Pueblos of San José and Los Angeles

The year 1776 was a time not only of Spanish colonial expansion but also of reorganization. José de Gálvez, having become Minister of the Indies in the royal government of Madrid, authorized a plan to reorganize the higher administration of the frontiers of New Spain. In 1776 the entire group of frontier provinces, including the Californias, was detached from the control of the viceroy at Mexico City and placed under a commandant-general of the "Interior Provinces" with headquarters at Arispe in Sonora.

Within the Californias there was also bureaucratic change. Alta California was now regarded as more important than Baja California, and this was reflected in the reorganization of their joint government in 1776. Felipe de Neve was now appointed governor of both the Californias, with headquarters at Monterey, where he arrived to replace Rivera early in 1777. Neve was another army officer, and probably the best administrator among the Spanish governors of California. Father-President Serra found Governor Neve even more determined than his predecessors to maintain the authority of the government over that of the missionaries. The governors had been so instructed, because it was the policy of the entire Spanish government at this time to treat the church as essentially an arm of the state.

Neve also had been ordered to try to solve the food supply problems of the presidios by establishing agricultural towns or pueblos. With the establishment of secular farming communities, one in the north and one in the south, Neve hoped that the military and civil establishments would no longer have to depend for food either upon the missions or upon the expensive and hazardous supply line from San Blas. In November 1777 he collected 14 men and their families from the presidios of Monterey and San Francisco and settled them at the new pueblo of San José de Guadalupe, the first town to be founded in Spanish Alta California.

In the same year, Neve made a personal survey of possible locations for a southern pueblo. He chose a point near the Río de Porciúncula, about 9 miles southwest of the mission of San Gabriel. There was no harbor, and no navigable river, but that was of no importance for a small agricultural community. Neve set September 4, 1781, as the date for the founding of the pueblo, and it has served as the official birthday ever since. Its name was to be El Pueblo de Nuestra Señora la Reina de los Angeles del Río de Porciúncula, or the Town of Our Lady the Queen of the Angels by the River of Porciúncula. That this would soon be abbreviated was rather obviously inevitable, but the part of it to be chosen by popular usage was a matter of accident. It might have been "Porciúncula," which, because it means "little portion," would be more than a little incongruous today. It turned out to be "Los Angeles," or rather, in the Spanish and Mexican periods, usually simply "Angeles." The modern American expression, "the City of the Angels," often imagined to be a translation of the name, is inaccurate.

It is ironic that San Francisco and Los Angeles, hardly the least materialistic and self-indulgent of modern cities, were named, respectively, for the ascetic Saint Francis of Assisi and for the Virgin Mary.

Like the San Francisco colonists, the Los Angeles *pobladores* were drawn from the poorest classes of Sinaloa, people to whom any change offered some hope of

Eulalia Arrila de Pérez served as the *llavera,* or keeper of the keys, at Mission San Gabriel in the 1820s and early 1830s. (*Courtesy of the Security Pacific Collection, Los Angeles Public Library.*)

improvement. Neve asked for 24 experienced farmers, but it proved impossible to obtain that many. Early in 1781, 12 settlers and their families were sent north. The Los Angeles settlers and their dependents, 46 persons in all, arrived at San Gabriel mission in August. The overwhelming majority of the settlers were people of mixed racial ancestry, both mestizos and mulattoes. Indeed, about half the founding families were of partial African ancestry; one mulatto settler, Francisco Reyes, served as alcalde (chief administrative and judicial officer) of the pueblo in the 1790s. Indians were the mainstay of the colonial workforce, not only in the missions but also in the pueblos. As historian Steven Hackel has observed, "nearly everything grown or manufactured" at the pueblos "resulted from the labor of Indians."

One of the most persistent problems at these remote outposts of empire was the scarcity of Spanish-speaking women. The few women who were willing to come were the wives of soldiers, government officials, and early pueblo settlers. Women who were widowed often found employment as *llaveras* (keepers of the keys) at the missions. Eulalia Arrila de Pérez, the *llavera* at San Gabriel, supervised the padres' kitchen, oversaw the laundry, and managed the winepresses and other small manufactures. "It was I," she later recalled, "who made the chocolate, the oil, the candy, the lemonade. I made so much lemonade that some of it was even bottled and sent to Spain."

Native Resistance

The Indians of California responded to missionization in a wide variety of ways. Ambivalence was widespread. "Most individuals," according to anthropologist Randall Milliken, "struggled with mixed feelings, hatred and respect, in a terrible, internally destructive attempt to cope with external change beyond their control." Some Indians joined the missions out of curiosity; others came because they viewed the missionaries as shamanlike intermediaries to the spirit world. Many California Indians, however, resisted all efforts at missionization. Historian David Weber, author of *The Spanish Frontier in North America* (1992), has neatly summarized the native response to the missions: "Indians only cooperated when they believed that they had something to gain from the new religion and the material benefits that accompanied it, or too much to lose from resisting it."

When the missionaries first arrived among the Gabrielino Indians, the native people "were sadly afraid" and "the women ran to the brush and hid themselves." Pablo Tac, a Luiseño born at Mission San Luis Rey, recalled how his people had responded to the coming of the Franciscans. The Indians were astonished to see the missionaries, he said, "but they did not run away or seize arms to kill them." Instead, the native people sat down and watched the missionaries come near. A leader then arose and said, in his own language, "What is it that you seek here? Get out of our country!"

Passive resistance in the missions included noncooperation, work slowdowns, and the destruction of tools and equipment. Fugitivism was a constant problem. Thus, one of the principal duties of soldiers garrisoned at the missions was to track down and bring back runaways. Indians also resisted the missionaries' attempts at conversion. According to Antonio María Osio, it was customary at Mission San José for Indians to receive a dozen or more lashes after Sunday mass for any offenses they had committed during the week. Then, as a sign of submission, the chastened Indians were expected to kiss the missionary's hand. Osio reported that one new recruit refused to follow the custom, saying to the startled priest: "Father, take your Christianity. I don't want it anymore because I am returning to my land." Meanwhile, a Chumash Indian at Mission Santa Barbara sparked a widespread clandestine revitalization movement in 1801. She called on her people to return to the worship of Chupu, the Chumash earth goddess. The woman warned that all converted Indians would die if they did not renounce their baptismal vows and wash their heads with a special water she called "tears of the sun."

Active resistance to missionization included short-lived revolts, occasional attempts to murder individual missionaries, and raids on mission herds by mission fugitives and unconverted Indians. The first violent attack occurred at San Diego on August 15, 1769, within a month of the mission's founding. Six years later came the killing of Father Jayme when the Indians again attacked the San Diego mission.

The most successful instance of violent resistance occurred on the California side of the Colorado River where two settlements were founded in Yuma territory in 1780. Over the protests of the padres, both establishments along the Colorado were peculiar mixtures of mission, presidio, and pueblo. In June 1781 Captain Rivera and his party of married soldiers reached the Colorado on their way to

California. Some went ahead to San Gabriel, but about half the party, including Rivera, camped on the eastern bank of the river to rest. Their cattle destroyed part of the Indians' supply of mesquite beans, and Rivera's men generally succeeded in antagonizing the Yumas even more than the Spaniards at the new missions had done. On July 17 the Yumas destroyed both missions and the next day crossed the river to surprise and kill Rivera and all his soldiers. The women and children with Rivera were captured. Altogether, 30 soldiers and 4 padres were put to death. Captain Don Fernando Rivera y Moncada, the weary and irascible old veteran who had felt condemned to interminable service in some of the most difficult roles ever demanded of a soldier or a colonial administrator, was released from duty at last.

From the Spanish point of view, the Yuma massacre was a terrible disaster. Some of the captives were later ransomed, but no serious attempt was made to punish the Yumas or to reopen the Colorado River route. The Anza Trail remained cut off until the 1820s, and in the meantime there was virtually no land communication at all between Mexico and California.

"Californias: Antigua y Nueva," map from Francisco Palou, *Relación Historica,* 1787. Note the inclusion of the two ill-fated mission outposts along the Colorado River. (*Courtesy of the California Historical Society, North Baker Research Library.*)

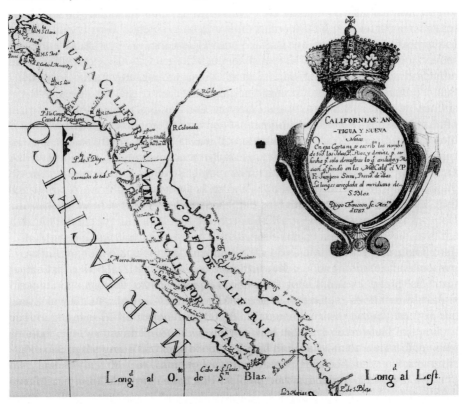

For the next 40 years, from the Yuma massacre in 1781 to the final collapse of Spanish rule over Mexico in 1821, New Spain made little effort to strengthen its outposts in Alta California. There, as elsewhere, the overextended Spanish colonial empire was on the defensive and crumbling. The mission system continued to expand, but it did not succeed in turning the Indians into genuine colonists. Other than the native Indians, there were about 600 persons in Alta California in 1781, and about five times as many in 1821, but the increase was almost entirely from the birth of descendants of the earlier colonists rather than from the arrival of new ones. The numbers of cattle and horses grew much more rapidly, and a fourth institution, the private rancho, began to develop along with the presidios, missions, and pueblos. Nellie Van de Grift Sánchez and other writers have called Spanish California an "Arcadia." Like that isolated mountain kingdom in ancient Greece, it was quiet, simple, and pastoral (at least for the colonial elite). But life for all was by no means as ideal as this analogy would imply.

The Impact of the Missions

Following Serra's death in 1784, his longtime companion Francisco Palóu served briefly as father-president. The following year Fermín Francisco de Lasuén became head of the Alta California missions and served as father-president from 1785 to 1803. It was Lasuén who supervised the building of the beautiful churches, several of which are extant, that replaced the rude structures of Serra's time. Under Lasuén each mission developed into a kind of polytechnical school, teaching the Indians to do fine leather work, operate tile factories and carpentry shops, and even do mural painting. During his tenure as father-president the number of missions doubled, from 9 to 18, and their Indian population more than doubled, rising to about 20,000, nearly as large as it ever became.

Early visitors to Spanish California often described in detail the operations of the missions and their impact on the Indians. In 1786 the comte de La Pérouse, a European nobleman engaged in a global voyage of scientific exploration for the French government, visited Monterey. The two vessels under La Pérouse were the first ships, other than those of the Spanish themselves, to visit Alta California since the voyage of Drake more than two centuries earlier. The French visitor had the highest admiration for the character of the missionaries—"these men, truly apostolic, who have abandoned the idle life of a cloister to give themselves up to fatigues, cares, and anxieties of every kind." But he doubted that they were accomplishing anything of permanent value. Under their theocratic system the Indian was "too much a child, too much a slave, too little a man." In the resorting to stocks, irons, and the lash, and in the use of soldiers to hunt down those who tried to escape, La Pérouse found a distressing resemblance to the slave plantations he had seen in Santo Domingo.

Five years after La Pérouse's visit, Monterey welcomed another scientific exploring expedition, this time Spanish, under the command of Alejandro Malaspina. In the crew of one of Malaspina's ships, incidentally, was the first Anglo-American

Indians at Mission San Carlos Borromeo in Carmel lined up in rigid formation for the visit of La Pérouse in 1786. From a 1791 watercolor copy of the lost original painting made at the occasion. (*Courtesy of the Museo Naval, Madrid.*)

who came to California and stayed—one John Green, a sailor from Boston who died of dropsy a few hours after the expedition arrived at Monterey in 1791. Malaspina's impression of the mission system was in considerable contrast to that of La Pérouse. He denounced the "ridiculous inventions of many foreign authors, who, confusing at times the system with the abuses and ignoring always the primary object of such establishments, have painted all our missions in America as horrible and oppressive." There was no doubt in Malaspina's mind that the missionaries in California had accomplished a great good. The Spanish priests had brought to the Indians "the end of a thousand local wars that were destroying them, social beginnings, a pure and holy religion, safe and healthy foods," and a variety of other blessings.

The question of whether the Indians in the California missions were exploited and wretched or contented and appreciative has long been a matter of debate. It has been said that "the preponderant testimony" describes the mission Indians as happy and well-adjusted, preferring mission life to their previous freedom and grateful for close supervision, hard work, colorful rituals, and the salvation of their souls. This is, to say the least, an extremely questionable conclusion. The bulk of the evidence has been the writings of the missionaries, who naturally tended to believe what they deeply yearned to believe about a matter so vital to their consciences. It is significant that the padres always applied the term "neophytes," by which they meant apprentices in Christianity, even to Indians who had been born in the missions and spent their entire lives there. The belief that any group of human adults could be happy under a system that treated them as if they were hopelessly retarded children is problematic indeed.

The Spanish divided the colonial population, at the missions and elsewhere, into two main groups, the "rationals" and the "irrationals." The *gente de razón,* the people of reason, included all who were not full-blooded Indians. This idea of "civilized" or "rational" persons was synonymous with "whites." Any admixture of white ancestry, mestizo or mulatto, was counted as white and also qualified a person as rational. This distinction was itself irrational. In essence it was a distinction between human and subhuman. Among the rationals, the very few "pure-blooded Spaniards" were at the top of the colonial heap, and degrees of admixture often effectively determined social status.

The best evidence of how the Indians actually felt about the missions would be the testimony of the Indians themselves, but unfortunately very few of them had any opportunity to get their testimony into the historical record. One who did was Bartolomea, an Indian woman who grew up in Mission San Gabriel and later married the "Scotch *paisano,*" Hugo Reid. It should be noted that it was Reid who recorded his wife's recollections and that his non-Catholic background, along with his status as the recipient of a rancho grant carved out of San Gabriel mission lands, gave him a viewpoint that was particularly hostile to the missionaries. The Franciscan historian Father Zephyrin Englehardt described Reid as "that embittered Scotchman" who "lied about religious matters."

Nevertheless, it is clear that Bartolomea (also known as Victoria) regarded life in the mission as a life of misery, humiliation, and terror. The alliance of the padres and the soldiers, she told her husband bitterly, had turned even Indian leaders like her own father into humble, confused, awkward, and shamefaced men. She remembered how the soldiers, armed with muskets, had come to her village when she was 6 years old and taken its people to the mission. At first the Indians had been filled with surprise and astonishment; then a strange lethargy set in. They were told to fear a hell that was lacking in their own religion. Corporal punishment, also, was something that had been unknown to them before.

One stark episode that Bartolomea remembered from her mission childhood occurred when a Gabrielino woman who had a miscarriage was charged with infanticide and punished by having her head shaved, by being flogged every day for 15 days, by wearing irons on her feet for 3 months, and by "having to appear every Sunday in church, on the steps leading up to the altar, with a hideous painted wooden child in her arms." This took place while San Gabriel was under the regime of Father José María Zalvidea, a particularly stern disciplinarian. In Reid's opinion, Zalvidea "must . . . have considered whipping as meat and drink to [the Indians], for they had it morning, noon and night."

Like Serra, Zalvidea was as stern with himself as with his Indian wards. He often lashed his own shoulders and back, and under his coarse robe he always wore a belt with iron points pressing into his flesh. He made San Gabriel "the Pride of the Missions," and yet to a man of his faith, pride was the first of the seven deadly sins. Perhaps this conflict was one of the things that unbalanced his mind; he later suffered a nervous breakdown and was transferred to San Juan Capistrano for hospitalization.

"Habitants de Californie," a poignant and powerful image of five native men at Mission San Francisco, from Louis Choris, *Voyage Pittoresque Autour du Monde,* 1822. Choris was the official artist of a Russian expedition that visited San Francisco in 1816. (*Courtesy of the California Historical Society, FN-30510.*)

As the story of Bartolomea suggests, the impact of the missions on California Indian women was especially severe. The missionaries imposed a system of patriarchy that often undermined the status of women within native society. Women were further degraded by the rapes perpetrated by Spanish-speaking soldiers and civilians. Young unmarried women were required by the missionaries to live in cloistered quarters, locked down at night, to preserve their chastity (and to prevent their escape). "Female separation from the extended family," historian James Sandos has observed, "must have been emotionally painful."

Also from the history of the San Gabriel mission we have the testimony of a 24-year-old shaman named Toypurina. In 1785 she participated in a conspiracy of neophytes and unconverted Indians to destroy the mission. Like other shamans and native leaders, Toypurina likely regarded the missionaries as a threat to her traditional status and authority. When questioned about her role in planning the revolt, Toypurina expressed the anger that she and many of her people felt toward the Spanish colonizers: "I hate the padres and all of you, for living here on my native soil, for trespassing upon the land of my forefathers."

A more positive view of mission life comes from a manuscript written by Pablo Tac, the mission Indian born at San Luis Rey. Tac and another Luiseño youth were taken to Rome by a missionary in 1833. In his manuscript, deposited in the Vatican Library, Tac expressed thanks to God for the coming of the missionaries to California.

He did observe, however, that thousands of his people died as "a result of a sickness that came to California" and that many left "for the woods" rather than submit to Spanish domination.

The most revealing evidence of the impact of the missions on the California Indians was recorded in the mission registers. There one finds a terrifying death rate, caused primarily by diseases for which the Indians lacked immunity. Confinement within the adobe walls of the missions also deprived the Indians of the degree of sanitation they had enjoyed from their sweathouses and their practice of occasionally burning their old dwellings and building new ones. Concentration of Indians in large numbers at the missions, the changes in diet, and the imposition of an alien discipline and regimentation all contributed to the high death rate. The mission registers also reveal a surprising variation in experience from mission to mission. Indians at the Santa Cruz mission, for example, survived an average of 8½ years after conversion, whereas those at San Luis Obispo survived more than twice as long. The infant mortality rate, also erratic, was generally high: more than half the Indians born in the missions died before their fifth birthdays. During the entire mission period, the native population from San Francisco Bay to San Diego fell from 72,000 to 18,000—a decline of over 75 percent.

Although the missions altered many dimensions of native culture—introducing a new language, religion, and economy—the goal of radical transformation was only partially achieved. Historian Lisbeth Haas, author of *Conquests and Historical Identities in California* (1995), has effectively demonstrated the persistence of native ethnic identities and social structures. Preconquest Indian traditions and material cultures were not eradicated by the mission system, in spite of its disruption of virtually every aspect of native life.

The debate over the impact of the missions on the California Indians has been revived in recent years by the movement to have Junípero Serra declared a saint. The canonization process began in 1934 on the 150th anniversary of Serra's death. Thousands of documents on Serra and the missions were assembled by church historians, and in 1985 Pope John Paul II declared Serra to be "venerable," the first step toward sainthood. Three years later the pope elevated Serra to the second step, declaring him "beatific." Supporters of the Serra cause rejoiced that the church at last "recognized the extraordinary holiness of this man who was the founder of civilization in California." Opponents denounced the move. Some described Serra as a sadist and a fanatic, while one critic of the mission system complained that the canonization of Serra "would be another insensitive reminder of past oppression and maltreatment."

Attempts at Reinforcement

At the end of the eighteenth century, Spain began to experience a long series of international difficulties in which it would gradually drift from humiliation into utter disaster. In 1790, in a treaty with England, Spain was forced to give up its claims to exclusive rights on the Pacific coast north of California. George Vancouver was appointed as a British commissioner to work out details of the application of the treaty, and in 1792 and the following year he visited several points in California, with special interest in the presidios. The fourth and last of these, at Santa Barbara, had been established in 1782. Vancouver was amazed at their weakness. At the time of his visits, there were two cannons at the presidio of San Francisco, neither of them serviceable, and three at San Diego, none of them even mounted. Santa Barbara had two cannons, and Monterey eight. The Spanish authorities, worried because the extent of this weakness would now be known to the British government, made plans to try to strengthen their feeble hold on the province.

In 1796 the viceroy, the marqués de Branciforte, and the governor, Diego de Borica, made plans for a new type of pueblo to be colonized by retired soldiers and their families. These ex-soldiers not only would be self-supporting but also would provide a ready reserve in case of foreign incursions. The attempt to carry out this project illustrated the able planning that so often characterized Spanish colonial administration, and the typical frustration of such planning by hopeless difficulties.

The site of the new pueblo, to be called the Villa de Branciforte, adjoined the lands of Mission Santa Cruz—to the bitter objections of the padres. The funds available for founding the new town were sadly inadequate. Not a single ex-soldier could be found in Mexico who would go there voluntarily, and nearly all the colonists who finally arrived in 1797 were men convicted of petty crimes, now sentenced to live in a Spanish version of Botany Bay. It is not surprising that the Villa de Branciforte did not flourish, although it struggled along for many years as a collection of huts. Such was the last attempt under Spanish rule to found any new civil or military establishment in California, with the exception of a few cattle ranchos on lands granted mainly to noncommissioned officers retired from garrison duty.

A dismal impression of Spanish prospects in California must remain, even though Governor Diego de Borica, a jovial Basque who was an early California booster, did his best to brighten the picture in a number of his reports. "This is a great country," he wrote soon after his arrival at Monterey, "the most peaceful and quiet country in the world; one lives better here than in the most cultured court of Europe." Toward the end of his governorship (1794–1800), Borica was still interlarding his reports with such glowing remarks as "To live much, and without care, come to Monterey." But in view of the fact that ill health was causing him to beg for retirement, as Rivera and Neve had done before him, we must suspect that his continued praise of life in California may have been designed to help in finding a willing and competent replacement. This was not easy. The governorship of California was not one of the more desirable posts in the Spanish colonial service.

Exploration of the Central Valley

Spanish settlement in Alta California was confined to a thin coastal strip. Except for the two short-lived establishments on the Colorado, which were wiped out by the Yumas, the farthest-inland Spanish settlement was Mission Soledad—only

30 miles from the sea. Following the discovery of the Central Valley by Pedro Fages during his exploration of the northeastern reaches of San Francisco Bay in 1772, there were periodic efforts to find places suitable for missions in various parts of the great interior region.

No missions were actually founded there, however, and the purposes of most of the Spanish expeditions into the valley were no more than those of pursuing escaped neophytes, punishing occasional raiders, and recovering stolen cattle and horses. The frequent raids on the livestock of the coastal settlements were carried on mainly by Indians who had once lived in the coastal areas but had fled to the interior to avoid missionization.

The outstanding figure among Spanish explorers of the Central Valley was Lieutenant Gabriel Moraga. His father, José, the first commandant of the Presidio of San Francisco, had brought Gabriel to California as a boy with the second Anza expedition. Between 1805 and 1817, the younger Moraga led a large number of expeditions into the great valley. He was responsible for such names as those of El Río de Nuestra Señora de la Merced (the River of Our Lady of Mercy); El Río de Los Santos Reyes (the River of the Holy Kings); the San Joaquin and Sacramento rivers; Mariposa, from the many butterflies seen there in 1806; and Calavares, a place of skulls.

The Coming of the Russians

In the early nineteenth century, the Spanish claim of exclusive rights to settlement in California was challenged by the establishment of a Russian fur-trading outpost north of San Francisco. Count Nikolai Petrovich Rezanov, an official of the Russian-American Fur Company, visited San Francisco in the spring of 1806. He came seeking supplies to relieve the danger of starvation in the Russian colony at Sitka, and incidentally investigating the possibilities of the fur trade in northern California itself. The Spaniards were aware that the Russian position in the Pacific northwest was almost as weak as their own, and they were concerned lest it be strengthened. Trade between Spanish colonies and foreigners was illegal. In the face of such difficulties, Rezanov's mission seemed doomed to failure.

At this point, "seeing that our situation was not getting better," he decided to improve it by a proposal of marriage to Doña Concepción Argüello, the 15-year-old daughter of the commandant of the San Francisco presidio.

Apart from the international political complications, there was a further impediment to granting Rezanov's request for the young woman's hand: he was of the Eastern Orthodox faith, whereas she was Roman Catholic. But her pleas moved the hearts of her father, the governor, and of the padres, and permission was given subject to ultimate approval in Rome. Rezanov then explained that he also would have to secure permission and that this would require him to consult the religious authorities in Saint Petersburg, as well as the czar himself. Thus, the wedding was postponed until his next visit to San Francisco, and in the meantime, he was permitted to gather a cargo of supplies from the missions. Rezanov never returned to

California, having died in the course of his journey to Russia. It was several years before the news of his death reached his fiancée.

Inevitably, accounts of this poignant episode have varied in their estimates of the sincerity of Rezanov's intentions. His own account suggests that he contemplated an honorable marriage, although one of diplomatic convenience. Interpretations of the young woman's feelings have also varied. Bret Harte, in his poem "Concepción Argüello (Presidio de San Francisco, 1800) [sic]," invited his many readers to "listen to the simple story of a woman's love and trust." Others have pointed out that the story was not that simple. In fact it appears that Concepción's youthful love for Nikolai Petrovich, a man 35 years older than herself, was inspired in part by the contrast between the impoverished life of the presidio and her dreams of life at the court of Saint Petersburg. As for Bret Harte's portrait of Concepcíon in her later years as a "trembling, . . . wasted figure" who considered herself to have "died too" when Rezanov did, the actual evidence indicates that in middle age she became a stout and rather jolly woman who found much pleasure in acts of kindness and charity.

Rezanov had secured only a temporary trading concession. In 1812 the Russian-American Fur Company built a fortified village, which it called Ross, a name derived from the same root as the word "Russia." Located on the coast about 18 miles north of Bodega Bay, Fort Ross had several purposes. It was intended to produce food not only for itself but for the company's operation in Alaska, to serve as a headquarters for the hunting of sea otter in northern California waters, and also to serve as a station for the trade that the Russians hoped to open on a regular basis with the Spanish Californian settlements. Though such trade was still forbidden by the Spanish government, locally it was very much needed and wanted, and at this time Spain and Russia were on friendly terms. The Russians insisted that their new settlement carried no hostile intent and professed to have believed that San Francisco was the northernmost limit of Spain's legal possession of the coast. They knew that the Spaniards had no force available that could drive them out, and they politely disregarded the formal Spanish protests. On one occasion the garrison at San Francisco had to borrow powder from a visiting Russian ship in order to fire a salute from the only cannon in the presidio that could still be fired with any safety.

The Last Years under the Spanish Flag

Some of the little scenes that were being enacted in the frontier colony of California during this period were colorful and admirable; others were pitiful and drab. In any case, they received very little attention from the Spanish government, which was in an increasingly tragic situation.

In 1807 Napoleon Bonaparte lured the Spanish royal family to France for a visit, threw them into prison there, and announced that his brother, Joseph Bonaparte, would be the new king of Spain. In the spring of 1808, the Spanish people rebelled against this French regime, and for 5 years Spain was locked in one of the bitterest struggles in history. Meanwhile, Spain had little strength to spare for ruling its colonies, and long and sporadic wars of independence set in. Amid the surging tides of world events, California remained a stagnant backwater.

The Mexican Revolution began in 1810 when the Creole priest, Miguel de Hidalgo, published his famous outcry against tyranny from his parish in the village of Dolores. In all the years until the news of Mexico's final independence reached California in 1822, few people in that isolated colony other than the governors and a few of the padres had any understanding of the issues involved in the terrible internal strife that was taking place in Mexico and Spain. Nor was there much interest in those struggles except for complaints that because of them the supply ships from San Blas came even less often than before, and for several years did not come at all. The people of the presidios and pueblos suffered not only from the absence of all the little extra comforts of life, but even from the absence of clothing other than the crude homemade articles. They became intensely jealous of the self-sustained and growing wealth of the missions. The padres were enjoying the fruits of choice lands and well-irrigated gardens—oranges and grapes, wines and brandies—tended by a large and disciplined force of Indian laborers. Padres, as well as others, were increasingly inclined to engage in contraband trade with foreign vessels, exchanging cowhides and tallow for cloth and other luxuries.

The most sensational events of the period were the looting and burning of Monterey and San Juan Capistrano in 1818 by two privateering vessels sailing under the Argentine flag and commanded by the Frenchman Hippolyte de Bouchard. California was loyal to Spain, hence the military justification for these acts of pseudo-patriotic piracy. Such was California's only participation in the wars of independence. Three years later the tattered flag of Spain was lowered for the last time at Monterey, and the new banner of Mexico, bearing an eagle and a snake, was raised in its place.

Selected Bibliography

David J. Weber's *The Spanish Frontier in North America* (1992) and Peter Gerhard's *The North Frontier of New Spain* (1982) place California in broad context, whereas John A. Schutz's *Spain's Colonial Outpost* (1985) is more narrowly focused. Weber (ed.), *New Spain's Far Northern Frontier* (1979), is an excellent collection of essays. Opportunities for future research are suggested in W. Michael Mathes, "Sources in Mexico for the History of Spanish California," *California History,* LXI (Fall 1982), pp. 223–226. See also Bernard L. Fontana, *Entrada: The Legacy of Spain and Mexico in the United States* (1994), and Doyce B. Nunis, Jr. (ed.), *Southern California's Spanish Heritage* (1992).

Bernard E. Bobb, *The Viceregency of Antonio Maria Bucareli* (1962), includes a description of Bucareli's policies toward California. Herbert E. Bolton, *Anza's California Expeditions* (five volumes, 1930), exhaustively chronicles the two expeditions and the founding of San Francisco; the first volume was published separately as *Outpost of Empire* (1931). See also Harlan Hague, *The Road to California* (1978); Theodore E. Treutlein, *San Francisco Bay* (1968); John Galvin (ed.), *The First Spanish Entry into San Francisco Bay, 1775* (1971); and Edwin A. Beilharz, *Felipe de Neve* (1971).

The first two volumes of *History of California,* written by Henry L. Oak (also included as volumes XVIII [1884] and XIX [1885] of *The Works of Hubert Howe Bancroft*), are a compendium of detailed information. For a demographic analysis of Spanish California, see William Marvin Mason, *The Census of 1790* (1998).

Leon G. Campbell, "The Spanish Presidio in Alta California during the Mission Period, 1769–1784," *Journal of the West,* XVI (October 1977), pp. 63–77, and Richard S. White-head, "Alta California's Four Fortresses," *Southern California Quarterly,* LXV (Spring 1983), pp. 67–94, are brief summaries, while Max L. Moorhead, *The Presidio* (1975), of-fers a more extensive analysis but excludes the Californias. Joseph P. Sánchez, *Spanish Bluecoats* (1991), describes the Catalonian soldiers who served on the northern frontier.

The literature on the impact of the missions on the Indians is extensive. Among the best recent accounts are the articles by Stephen W. Hackel, Michael J. González, James A. San-dos, and Antonia I. Castañeda in Ramón A. Gutiérrez and Richard J. Orsi (eds.), *Contested Eden* (1998); Lisbeth Haas, *Conquests and Historical Identities in California* (1995); Robert H. Jackson and Edward Castillo, *Indians, Franciscans, and Spanish Colonization* (1995); Randall Milliken, *A Time of Little Choice* (1995); Jackson, *Indian Population De-cline* (1994); and Castillo (ed.), *Native American Perspectives on the Hispanic Colonization of Alta California* (1991). The most damning account of the missions appears in Rupert Costo and Jeannette Henry Costo (eds.), *The Missions of California: A Legacy of Genocide* (1987). Earlier critiques appear in Sherburne F. Cook, *The Conflict between the California Indian and White Civilization,* Part II (1943), and "Historical Demography," in Robert F. Heizer (ed.), *California* (1978), pp. 91–98. Francis F. Guest, "An Examination of the Thesis of S. F. Cook on the Forced Conversion of Indians in the California Missions," *Southern California Quarterly,* LXI (Spring 1979), pp. 1–78, and "Cultural Perspectives on Califor-nia Mission Life," ibid., LXV (Spring 1983), pp. 1–66, offer a more positive view. See also Guest, *Hispanic California Revisited* (1996) and *Fermin Francisco de Lasúen* (1973). For an analysis of the importance of Indian labor, see the corresponding chapter in Robert Archibald, *The Economic Aspects of the California Missions* (1978).

George Phillips suggests that the California Indians were far from passive in their re-sponse to the missions; see his *Indians and Intruders in Central California, 1769–1848* (1993). A neglected aspect of the period has been examined by Albert L. Hurtado, *Intimate Frontiers: Sex, Gender, and Culture in Old California* (1999). On the controversy over the missions' founder, see James A. Sandos, "Junípero Serra's Canonization and the Historical Record," *American Historical Review,* XCIII (December 1988), pp. 1253–1269. For the views of foreign visitors, see Malcolm Margolin (ed.), *Monterey in 1786: The Journals of Jean Francois de La Pérouse* (1989); Donald C. Cutter, *Malaspina in California* (1960) and *California in 1792* (1990); and Francis J. Weber, "The California Missions and Their Visi-tors," *The Americas,* XXIV (1968), pp. 319–336.

Accounts of the coming of the Russians include T. C. Russel (ed.), *The Rezanov Voyage to Nueva California in 1806* (1926); *Langsdorff's Narrative of the Rezanov Voyage* (1927); James R. Gibson, *Imperial Russia in Frontier America* (1976); and P. A. Tikhmenev, *A His-tory of the Russian-American Company* (1978).

CHAPTER 5

A Marginal Province
of a Troubled Republic

As one of the most isolated and least valued of all the colonial possessions of Spain, California had grown used to being neglected. The independent nation of Mexico, periodically torn with revolutionary disturbances and established as a republic after a brief and tragic interlude under the "empire" of Agustín Iturbide, was even less able than Spain had been to concern itself seriously or effectively with the distant northern region.

Government and Politics in Theory and Practice

The most influential framers of the Federal Constitution of the United Mexican States, adopted in 1824, were liberal idealists who modeled their country's new organic law in part on that of the United States of America. But there were great differences between the political, economic, and social backgrounds of the two countries. In Mexico, not even the upper class had acquired any substantial experience in self-government under Spanish colonial rule, and only a tiny fraction of the people were literate and prosperous enough to take an informed part in public affairs. Nevertheless, on paper the constitution of 1824 guaranteed both complete political equality and complete racial equality. Not only were Indians entitled to vote and to hold office, but like all other citizens they were supposed to enjoy full freedom of person and property.

The liberal Mexican constitution makers of 1824 dreamed of developing a civil society and a prosperous economy in which republican government and equal rights for all people could become more than empty phrases. As applied to the remote province of California, these vague hopes led to several new policies. Governors of California were now authorized to permit freer trade with foreigners, subject only to import duties, to move toward secularization of the missions, and to increase rancho land grants, including grants to foreigners willing to be naturalized and to accept Roman Catholicism.

Under the first Mexican constitution, California was only a territory, not a state, although it was promoted to the rank of a "department" under the constitution of 1836 and the laws of 1837. Governors were appointed by the government of Mexico. There was a provincial legislative branch, of sorts, in the form of an elected *diputación,* but in practice it functioned only occasionally, when the governor chose to convene it, and then merely as an advisory rather than a legislative body. In effect, the governor not only acted as the civil and military executive but also controlled the provincial lawmaking process, and he exercised nearly all the judicial authority in the more important matters. The general government of California remained what it had been under Spain, a petty military despotism. Control from Mexico City, however, was greatly weakened because the government could provide few soldiers of any sort, and none competent or reliable, for service in California; it lacked the money to pay them.

During California's Mexican period, one important substitute for a system of checks and balances did arise: the comic-opera "revolution," a political device characterized by bombastic pronouncements, chesslike marches and counter-marches, and noisy but bloodless artillery duels, just out of range, in which both sides retrieved each other's cannonballs and fired them back.

As the power of the Mexican governors and the Franciscan missionaries weakened, the real authority in California gravitated into the hands of a small group of ranchero families, mostly California-born. The fact that these families were so closely intermarried was one reason that there was so little actual killing in battles between revolutionary factions. There was too much risk of killing a brother-in-law.

The main political motives of the leaders of this little ranchero oligarchy were, first, the hope of taking over from the missions their lands, their cattle, and their Indian workers and, second, the desire for political power and glory. In their struggles to achieve these objectives, the *Californios,* the Spanish colonists and their descendants, were badly divided by personal, factional, and sectional disputes. In the rivalry between *norteños* and *sureños,* such northern California leaders as Juan Bautista Alvarado, Mariano Guadalupe Vallejo, and José Castro were aligned against southern California politicos like José Antonio Carrillo, Pío Pico, and Juan Bandini. Confronted by the restless ambitions of these volatile native sons of California, governors sent up from Mexico had an increasingly difficult time.

Philosopher Josiah Royce later maintained that the bloodless revolution, given the limitations of its social and historical contexts, was really a comparatively civilized method of settling internal political differences. Government by mock revolution had serious defects, however, and one of these was that the resulting decisions were likely to be temporary. In one 5-year period, from 1831 to 1836, Mexican California had 11 distinct gubernatorial administrations, not counting three men who were appointed to the governorship by Mexico but whom the Californians did not permit to take office. By contrast, there had been only 10 governors in the whole period of more than half a century of Spanish rule.

The Secularization Problem

By far the most important political issue in the province during the 1820s and 1830s was the question of the secularization of the missions, or rather, and more realistically, the question of who was to profit from the acquisition of their lands and herds. This troublesome problem so far overshadowed all others that the whole story of the political and quasi-military events can best be understood in connection with it.

As early as 1749, by royal order, the Spanish government had made an attempt to secularize the missions of Mexico—that is, to turn the properties over to the Indians and replace the missionaries with secular parish clergy. This attempt was abandoned largely because there were not enough secular priests available.

When Mexico gained its independence in 1821, the California missionaries were alarmed. Most of the missionaries were Spaniards, and as such they were targets for the hostility of Mexican revolutionary nationalists. For centuries the Creoles had hated the *gachupines*. A Creole, or *criollo,* was a person who had been born in the Spanish American colonies; sometimes the word meant a person of entirely European ancestry; sometimes it was used without regard to racial origin. The Mexican word *gachupines,* referring to men born in Spain, had originally meant "those who wear spurs," and it implied, usually correctly, that the Spanish-born regarded themselves as superior beings.

For centuries the Spanish church had been an integral part of Spain's authoritarian system of colonial control. Inevitably, republican theories were often anticlerical. Such theories, however, were often rationalizations for avarice. There was rising criticism of the missions for their temporal wealth and for their exploitation of the Indians. Unfortunately these were the same privileges that many an eloquent anticlerical wanted to appropriate for himself. Typical was the complaint of Vallejo that just "twenty-one mission establishments possess all the fertile lands."

The padres argued that the mission Indians were not ready for secularization, and this was certainly true. That the missions had failed to make them ready after more than half a century and showed no signs of ever making them ready were facts that the missionaries blamed on the alleged inherent defects of the Indians rather than on the defects of the mission system or on their own desire to perpetuate it.

Meanwhile, the Indians themselves were becoming increasingly restive. In 1824, during a concerted rebellion, they briefly took over control of the missions at Santa Barbara, Santa Inés, and La Purísima Concepción, with some loss of life and much property damage. Soldiers crushed the insurrection after a battle in which there were many Indian casualties. In 1829 a Lakisamni Yokuts named Estanislao, after the Polish Saint Stanislaus, became the leader of a large pan-Indian band in the San Joaquin Valley. He issued a ringing challenge to the Mexican authorities: "We are rising in revolt. . . . We have no fear of the soldiers, for even now they are very few, mere boys . . . not even sharpshooters." Near the river that was later named after him, "Stanislaus" and his followers fought a battle with 100 soldiers and militiamen under Lieutenant Mariano Vallejo. This and other campaigns completely failed to subjugate Estanislao's band of nearly a thousand ex-neophyte and gentile warriors. Until the end of the Mexican period, they would continue to block Mexican settlement of the San Joaquin Valley.

Valley Yokuts and other Indians also continued to raid coastal settlements, driving livestock deep into the interior. The raids were motivated in part by hunger— Indian consumption of cattle increased as traditional food sources were rendered inaccessible. The raids also were part of a growing Indian commerce with horse traders and New Mexican rustlers from east of the Tehachapis. Historian George Phillips has characterized the raids as evidence of the Indians implementing "strategies of offensive resistance." The Yokuts served as enterprising middlemen in the expanding trade, much to the consternation of the Californios.

From Echeandía to Figueroa

The first governor of California under the Mexican republican constitution, or more precisely and officially the first *jefe político superior* and *comandante general militar,* was José María Echeandía, a lieutenant colonel of engineers. He arrived in 1825 with instructions to proceed cautiously and gradually toward ultimate secularization; however, though he drafted various plans for this eventuality, a number of formidable difficulties stood in the way. The missions were still the chief source of supplies for the presidios. Cash revenues for the territorial government depended on duties levied on the goods imported in exchange for California cowhides and tallow, and the missions were still the chief producers of the hides and tallow.

To add to the governor's troubles, he was in poor health and spent much time in San Diego to escape the fogs of the north. In 1829 the unpaid soldiers at Monterey revolted under the leadership of an ex-convict who had been sent to California as a part of his sentence. The revolt was suppressed after a bloodless "battle" near Santa Barbara, but later in the same year, in deep discouragement, Echeandía submitted his resignation.

Early in 1830 a conservative and proclerical "centralist" faction gained control of the government in Mexico. Its appointee as governor of California was a reactionary politician and army officer, Lieutenant Colonel Manuel Victoria, a vigorous opponent of secularization and a stern believer in the virtues of military authority. Shortly before the centralist coup, the previous Mexican regime had appointed the radical republican José María Padrés as governor, but before he could take office, his appointment was superseded by Victoria's. Padrés remained in California in his earlier position of adjutant inspector of troops. He despised both the personality and the ideas of the man who would now hold the higher office. Padrés was not only a bitter critic of the missions, but also a man of considerable ability and personal magnetism, and several young Californians, including Vallejo and Alvarado, became his disciples. He taught them, as historian Hubert Howe Bancroft put it, "to theorize eloquently on the rights of man, the wrongs of the neophytes, and the tyranny of the missionaries."

Shortly before Victoria arrived at Monterey, Padrés induced the outgoing Governor Echeandía to issue an order for general secularization. When Victoria reached the capital early in 1831, he promptly suspended this decree and soon afterward proclaimed a number of repressive measures. For their opposition to his policies he banished several prominent men, including Padrés, and imprisoned several more. The result was an insurrection in southern California, led by José Antonio Carrillo and ex-governor Echeandía.

When a small force under Governor Victoria met the rebels north of Cahuenga Pass, near Los Angeles, on December 4, 1831, hostilities might have been confined to the verbal level if the governor had not made a disparaging remark about the fighting qualities of his own men. One of his aides, Lieutenant Romualdo Pacheco, was so goaded by this sarcasm that he drew his saber and rode out ahead of the governor's troops. On the rebel side, young José María Ávila was burning with resentment at having been imprisoned in Los Angeles for sedition. He suddenly charged at Pacheco and killed him with a pistol, then spurred toward Victoria and wounded him with a lance thrust. A soldier shot Ávila with a musket, and Victoria, though badly wounded, killed Ávila with his sword. Forty-three years later, a son and namesake of Romualdo Pacheco, born a month before his father's death, would become one of the American governors of California.

By provoking actual bloodshed, Governor Victoria had violated the rules of the California political game. He was packed off to Mexico on the next ship, and there was a chaotic scramble for power. For about a year the south was ruled by Echeandía and the north by Agustín Zamorano. (Zamorano is better known for having imported California's first printing press, used mainly for the publication of official documents.)

The ouster of Governor Victoria was a deathblow to the mission system. Although the conservative faction was still precariously in power in Mexico City, it recognized the need to conciliate the rebellious Californians by permitting secularization of the missions and by appointing a governor who could be trusted to carry it out in the fairest way possible. The man selected was Brevet Brigadier General José Figueroa, governor from early in 1833 until his death in 1835.

Figueroa and Secularization

In terms of both ability and character, Figueroa was by far the best of all the officials sent up by the Mexican republic. The tragedy was that no governor could have arranged the assignments of the mission lands to private ownership in an orderly and satisfactory manner under the conditions that existed.

In August 1833 the Mexican Congress adopted an immediate general secularization law that was extremely vague about procedures for carrying it out. It soon appeared, however, that this law was largely the work of that vocal champion of freedom for the Indians, José María Padrés, and that Padrés had also engineered the Mexican government's approval of an ambitious "colonization" scheme under which he and a group of his Mexican friends were to take over the lands of the missions. His close associate José María Híjar was to be not only the "director of colonization" but also the new governor of the territory.

A substantial number of colonists actually arrived from Mexico to occupy their new estates. Governor Figueroa, however, had already appointed the administrators, or *comisionados,* who were to supervise the disposal of mission lands, and his appointees were all Californians. A notable example was Mariano Guadalupe Vallejo, appointed by Figueroa as not only the administrator of the Sonoma mission and grantee of the Petaluma rancho, but also the military commander of the whole northern frontier district. When Vallejo, Alvarado, and other former Californian admirers of Padrés heard that among his colonists there were 21 prospective mission administrators from Mexico, and when they recalled that there were just 21 missions, their feelings toward their erstwhile intellectual leader underwent a sharp and sudden change. Fortunately, from their point of view, the credentials of Padrés and Híjar were canceled from Mexico City in another of the kaleidoscopic shifts of Mexican politics.

Figueroa's proclamation of August 9, 1834, defined the general terms under which the process of secularization was to be conducted over the next 2 years. Half the property was supposed to go to the Indians, and the law forbade them to dispose of it, but these provisions were not effectively carried out. Some Indians tried to make a living by farming their small allotments of land near the mission buildings, but none of them retained these lands more than a few years. Many never realized that they were supposed to have been given any land at all. (See Color Plate 3.) Former mission neophyte Lorenzo Asisara later recalled what it was like for his Ohlone Indian people when Mission Santa Cruz was secularized in 1834. They were granted a portion of the mission land, he remembered, "but it did not do the Indians any good." The ex-neophytes also received "old mares that were no longer productive [and] very old rams."

The law attempted to limit the killing of cattle at the missions, but as the time of secularization approached, the missionaries slaughtered much of the stock in order to salvage, from the sale of the hides, as much wealth as possible for the Pious Fund. As a result, the missions were surrounded with thousands of skinned carcasses rotting in the sun.

For several years the morale of the padres had been declining. Many of them were old men who had lived so long in the missions that they regarded them as their only homes. Some, on the other hand, looked forward to relief from their responsibilities. Shortly before secularization one padre wrote that there was "hardly anything of the religious left in me. . . . I made the vows of a Friar Minor; instead I must manage temporalities, sow grain, raise sheep, horses, and cows. . . . These things are as disagreeable as thorns . . . , and they rob me of time, tranquility, and health both of soul and body."

Because there were no secular parish priests to replace them, the Franciscans remained at the mission churches to continue their religious duties. For a time many of the neophytes remained huddled around the padres, whereas some left the coastal area to find homes with alien tribes in the interior. Indians who had been trained as *vaqueros,* or cattle wranglers, became laborers on the private ranchos into which the mission lands were gradually subdivided. Still others were able to gain a living as laborers in the towns.

Mounted vaqueros at Mission San José, from Frederick William Beechey, *Narrative of a Voyage to the Pacific,* 1831. (*Courtesy of the California History Room, California State Library, Sacramento.*)

The padres had predicted accurately the fate that was in store for the mission Indians when secularization came. As Father-President Durán pointed out, the Indians living in the pueblo of Los Angeles were forced to labor for the merest pittances and were subjected to frightful punishments for their trivial misdeeds; they were given no security of any kind and were in every way "far more wretched and oppressed than those in the missions."

Alvarado and Provincial Autonomy

Figueroa was deeply disturbed by the failure of his secularization policies to protect the legal and moral rights of the Indians. In any event, his efforts were cut short when, in the fall of 1835, he died of an apoplectic stroke. His passing removed a brake from the rapacity of the mission administrators and their friends and relatives, and again plunged California into noisy "revolutionary" struggles for control of the governorship. After the brief terms of José Castro and Nicolas Gutiérrez as acting governors, Mexico sent up a new champion of centralism, Colonel Mariano Chico, who repeated most of the blunders of Governor Victoria and lasted only 3 months before he too was expelled.

Juan Bautista Alvarado, the clever and eloquent young president of the *diputación,* now emerged as the hero of the Californians, particularly the northerners. With the aid of about 30 riflemen led by Isaac Graham, a Tennessee backwoodsman who had come to California to operate a whiskey distillery, Alvarado seized control of Monterey and deported most of the Mexican officials. On No-

EL C. JUAN B.

ALVARADO GOBERNADOR INTERI-
NO DEL ESTADO LIBRE Y SOBERANO DE LA ALTA CALIFORNIA, Á SUS
HABITANTES·

A broadside from 1837 declaring Juan B. Alvarado to be the governor of the "FREE AND SOVER-
EIGN STATE OF ALTA CALIFORNIA AND ITS INHABITANTS." (*Courtesy of the California Historical
Society, North Baker Research Library, Broadside Collection.*)

vember 7, 1836, California was proclaimed "a free and sovereign State," until Mexico should repudiate centralism and restore the principles of the federalist constitution of 1824. Alvarado became provisional governor, and Vallejo, already in charge
of the northern frontier, now became the military commander of the whole California department. Vallejo was Alvarado's uncle, though only 2 years his senior and
also under 30 years old.

As one of his first official actions, Alvarado proclaimed that the capital of California would continue at his native Monterey. (An act of the Mexican Congress in
1835 had promoted Los Angeles from a pueblo to a city and ordered the capital
transferred there.) Alvarado, however, was forced to placate the southerners by
permitting them to choose a subgovernor with considerable regional authority.
Even if Mexico had not had its hands full with the Texan War of Independence, it
probably would have been disposed to compromise with Alvarado by appointing
him as the legal governor of California under the Mexican republic. He accepted
this arrangement in 1837 and continued to hold the office for 5 years.

In the period before the last fragments of the mission holdings passed into private hands at the end of 1845, the administration of these properties grew steadily
more corrupt, incompetent, and generally disgraceful. In 1839 Alvarado made a
belated and perfunctory effort at reform by appointing a visitor-general of missions, the naturalized Englishman William E. P. Hartnell; however, Hartnell's efforts were futile, partly because mission administrators, such as Vallejo for San
Rafael and Sonoma, and Pío Pico for San Luis Rey, had too much power in their
respective districts. When Hartnell tried to make changes in some of Vallejo's plans
for San Rafael, Vallejo arrested him.

Alvarado and Vallejo soon fell to quarreling with each other, and by 1842 they
were both so disillusioned with the anarchic state of affairs in the province that
they willingly turned over the political and military commands to the last governor
from Mexico, Brigadier General Manuel Micheltorena. He was an amiable man,
but his administration was no better than those of most of his predecessors. The
army of 300 soldiers he brought with him consisted almost entirely of ex-convicts.
Because they failed to receive their pay (as usual), they obtained food and other

items by a highly informal process of foraging, to the outrage of the local population. Alvarado and José Castro led still another revolt, and there was a new "battle of Cahuenga Pass" in February 1845. It was a repetition of the encounter on almost the same spot in 1831, except that this time the only casualties were a horse and a mule, but it was enough to induce Governor Micheltorena to follow the examples of Governors Victoria, Chico, and Gutíerrez by departing for Mexico, along with his ragged and thieving soldiers.

This marked the failure of the last attempt to reestablish any more than nominal Mexican control over California. Pío Pico assumed the governorship with Los Angeles as the capital, but having no influence much farther north than Santa Barbara he had to compromise with the *norteños* by recognizing José Castro as military commandant. This gave Castro the de facto control of the Monterey customs house and consequently of most of the governmental income. This arrangement, made on the eve of the Mexican War, left the province as weak and divided as it had ever been.

The Heyday of the Rancheros

Throughout the Mexican period, the most substantial economic activity was cattle raising, and the chief commercial products were hides and tallow for export. The local processing of these commodities went no further than the staking out of the hides to dry in the sun and rendering of the fat into tallow by melting it in kettles, after which it was poured for storage into bags called *botas,* made out of whole hides.

After the missions disintegrated, there was virtually no manufacturing. Rawhide was used as a local makeshift for all sorts of purposes, but the manufacture of hides into shoes and other leather products was done in New England. Even the simple processes of making soap and candles out of the tallow were done in Chile or Peru. The missions, for their own use, had made such things as coarse woolen blankets, crude shoes, the leather parts of saddles, soap, candles, and coarse pottery. They had also developed irrigated agriculture to the point of producing a remarkable variety of grains, vegetables, and fruits, and some wine and brandy. All these skills disappeared after secularization. The diet of the rancheros and their families consisted largely of fresh or dried beef. Milk was not widely used, and little or no butter or flour was produced. Even such ordinary articles as brooms had to be imported.

There were about 20 private rancho land grants during the Spanish regime, and about 500 during the Mexican period, of which the great majority were made after secularization and especially by Governors Alvarado, Micheltorena, and Pico. Secularization transferred control over the region's most valuable resources—land, livestock, and laborers—from the missionaries to the rancheros. It was, in the words of one historian, "the greatest transfer of land and resources in California since the Spaniards first set foot in the region." Under the liberal Mexican colonization provisions of 1824 and 1828, the maximum legal limit for a private rancho grant in California was 11 square leagues—about 50,000 acres, or 76 square miles.

The Lugo family on their rancho in southern California in the 1880s. (*Courtesy of the Seaver Center for Western History Research, Natural History Museum of Los Angeles County.*)

Not even this generous limit was always applied, because in many cases several different grants were made to the same individuals.

In a ranching country where a dozen acres of grassland might be required to pasture a single cow through the long, dry summer season, such vast grants were not regarded as too large, and minor discrepancies in boundary measurements were of no importance. The boundaries were laid out without the aid of surveying instruments, and the methods of measuring distance ranged from pure guesswork to laying out lengths of a lasso from the back of a horse. As corners of the grant, the *diseño,* or map, might show markers no more permanent than a pile of stones or a clump of cactus. The whole process was accomplished with an easy informality that was very convenient at the time but which would later contribute to the maddening and almost endless confusion of efforts to establish land titles in American courts.

Except for a few grants in the Sacramento Valley, held mainly by naturalized foreigners, the ranchos were located where the missions had been, in a narrow strip along the coast. Cattle were driven on the hoof to the *matanzas,* or slaughterings, as near as possible to the coastal points where the hides and tallow were stored to await the foreign trading ships. Other than the horse and the mule, the only form of land transportation was the lumbering, springless, spine-jarring *carreta,* an oxcart with wheels sliced from a big log. Excellent horses, however, were so numerous that they were allowed to run and graze freely, dragging lassos for easy catching. Walking was a lost art. It was much easier to catch a passing horse, ride it where one wished to go, and turn it loose again. To Richard Henry Dana, author of *Two Years before the Mast* (1840), all Californians in the 1830s seemed to be centaurs.

Some of the most skillful riders were the daughters of the rancheros. California girls usually rode with ease by the time they were 6 to 8 years old. "I never saw ladies in the East," proclaimed one incredulous visitor, "who could approach the poorest of the Spanish ladies whom I have yet seen ride." Women also became landowners and administrators, receiving about 13 percent of the ranchos granted by the Mexican government. Among the ranchera elite was Apolinaria Lorenzano, the unmarried owner of three ranchos. Rancheras supervised their vast estates in a manner similar to that of their male counterparts. They presided over large households and supervised Indian workers who tended their vast herds and fields.

On the typical California rancho there were between 20 and several hundred Indian workers, perhaps 4000 in all. This workforce included former mission Indians and new recruits gathered by the ranch owners. In return for their labor, the Indians usually received nothing more than shelter, food, and clothing. Although the Indian laborers were nominally free, in practice they were bound in a state of peonage for as long as the ranchero cared to hold them. Thus, the rancho economy, like those of the missions and pueblos, contributed to the continuing destruction of California Indian society. As historian Michael González has concluded, the ranchero elite subjected Indian laborers to "routines harsher than any toil at the missions."

The plentitude of cheap Indian labor also contributed to the rancheros' reluctance to work. A recurring phrase in conversation was *"poco tiempo,"* or "too little time," meaning that there was not time enough today to do anything that could be done tomorrow. In the pursuit of pleasure, however, the Californians showed more vigor. There was prodigal hospitality in the entertainment of strangers at fiestas, and singing and dancing were passions with Californians of all ages. Favorite dances were the *fandango,* the *jota,* the *borrego,* the *jarabe,* the *bamba,* and the somewhat more dignified *contradanza.* The *bamba* required a señorita to perform its lively and intricate steps with a full glass of water on her head. In one of the easier variations, while constantly tapping the floor with her feet, she had to step into a silken hobble, raise it to her knees, lower it again, and give two or three whirls, all without spilling the water and all to the accompaniment of swift strumming of the guitar and many shouted comments intended to distract her.

Apart from weddings, which also occasioned 3-day celebrations, the chief social event was the annual *rodeo,* or roundup. Because there were no fences, the cattle that roamed over the myriad hills of several neighboring ranchos had to be annually segregated, and the calves branded. Then the families of the district would gather for days and nights of fiesta, with much dancing, brilliant displays of horsemanship, cockfighting, gambling, and sometimes bull and bear baiting.

Historian Douglas Monroy, author of *Thrown among Strangers: The Making of Mexican Culture in Frontier California* (1990), has interpreted ranchero society as *seigneurial*—signifying the status-conscious activities of a "big" man intent on demonstrating dominance over his family, laborers, and land. Thus it was that the colorful fiestas of the rancheros were more than mere diversions: "These highly ritualized occasions gathered all elements of Californio society into a public spectacle

Fandango, a romanticized view of life on a California rancho, painted by Charles Christian Nahl in 1873. (*Courtesy of the E. B. Crocker Collection, Crocker Art Museum, Sacramento.*)

at which elites wore their finery, supplied abundant food and copious drink, and danced with elegance. In other words, they displayed their wealth and status to their Indian laborers, the common folk, and themselves."

In spite of such displays, the absence of education among the Californio elite was almost incredible. Now and then, for a few days or weeks, a retired soldier with almost no knowledge, and with no idea whatever of how to impart what little he had, would be given a pittance to try to operate a "school" at Monterey or at one of the other towns. Instruction was administered alternately with a cat-o'-nine-tails and a catechism. Vallejo, one of the few literate Californians, recalled with bitterness how one of these incompetent schoolmasters had nearly succeeded in destroying his boyhood interest in learning. For about a year William E. P. Hartnell conducted a boys' school near Monterey under the patronage of Governor Figueroa. These few efforts, except for the teaching of manual arts and church music to the Indians in the missions, represented very nearly the entire history of formal education in California as a Spanish colony and a Mexican province.

California's population in 1845, other than the full-blooded native Indians, was only about 7000. Of these, fewer than 1000 were adult males. The number of native Californians who were literate, even by the loosest definition, was probably no more than 100. Many of the largest landholders could not write their own names. Perhaps no period of history has ever been more extremely romanticized than have "the halcyon days of the dons" in California. The colorfulness of those days was sadly superficial, even for the landed ruling class, in spite of their gay costumes and their desperate attempts to live the good life. (See Color Plates 4 and 5.)

Selected Bibliography

A bold synthesis of this period appears in Douglas Monroy, *Thrown among Strangers: The Making of Mexican Culture in Frontier California* (1990). The best general survey is David J. Weber, *The Mexican Frontier, 1821–1846* (1982). Henry L. Oak's third and fourth volumes of "Bancroft's" *History of California* remain indispensable. Woodrow James Hansen's *The Search for Authority in California* (1960) offers a valuable analysis of political and social problems from about 1820 to 1849.

Gloria E. Miranda provides a useful look at family history in "*Gente de Razon* Marriage Patterns in Spanish and Mexican California: A Case Study of Santa Barbara and Los Angeles," *Southern California Quarterly,* LXIII (Spring 1981), pp. 1–22, and "Hispano-Mexican Child-Bearing Practices in Pre-American Santa Barbara," ibid., LXV (Winter 1983), pp. 307–322. On secularization, see Weber, "Failure of a Frontier Institution: The Secular Church in the Borderlands under Independent Mexico, 1821–1846," *Western Historical Quarterly,* XII (April 1981), pp. 125–144. Gerald J. Geary's *The Secularization of the California Missions* (1934) is useful and enlightening even though consistently biased. For the native response, see Edward D. Castillo, "An Indian Account . . . ," *American Indian Quarterly* (Fall 1989), pp. 391–408, and Michael J. González, "'The Child of the Wilderness Weeps . . . ,'" in Ramón A. Gutiérrez and Richard J. Orsi (eds.), *Contested Eden* (1998).

A Scotch Paisano: Hugo Reid's Life in California, 1832–1853 (1939) and *The Lives of William Hartnell* (1949), both by Susan Bryant Dakin, add notably to the story of secularization and landholding. Other biographical treatments are Robert Ryal Miller, *Juan Alvarado: Governor of California, 1836–1842* (1998), and Alan Rosenus, *General M. G. Vallejo and the Advent of the Americans* (1995). Manuel G. Gonzales, *The Hispanic Elite of the Southwest* (1989), offers an analytical group portrait. For a fascinating memoir of the period, first published in 1851, see Antonio María Osio, *The History of Alta California,* edited by Rose Marie Beebe and Robert M. Senkewicz (1996). Robert G. Cleland, *The Cattle on a Thousand Hills* (1951), provides a good picture of the ranchos, of which a fairly typical example is described in Cleland's *The Irvine Ranch of Orange County* (1962). See also Crisostomo N. Perez, *Land Grants in Alta California* (1996), and David Hornbeck, "Land Tenure and Rancho Expansion in Alta California, 1784–1846," *Journal of Historical Geography,* IV (October 1978).

C. Alan Hutchinson, *Frontier Settlement in Mexican California: The Híjar-Padrés Colony and Its Origins, 1769–1835* (1969), is sympathetic to the colonization scheme and critical of Figueroa.

CHAPTER 6

American Infiltration
Traders, Trappers, and Settlers

The cosmopolitanism of modern California was notable even in the period of tenuous Mexican rule. Of the foreigners who came, the most important historically were the Americans. Very few of these, however, came with any original intention of Americanizing the province.

The Yankee Traders

American interest in California began in the late eighteenth century when New England merchants discovered that there was a lucrative market in China for the fur of the sea otter. These animals flourished, in what were thought to be inexhaustible numbers, along the Pacific coast from the Aleutian Islands to lower California, and particularly along the Alta California shores. The skin of a full-grown sea otter was 5 feet long and more than 2 feet wide, with thick, black, glossy fur, and its value when shipped to the Chinese port of Canton was about $300. The fur seal was more numerous, but less valuable. Although the Spaniards forbade foreigners to obtain furs in California, they could not prevent them from doing so, and ships from New England gained the greatest share of the trade in competition with the British and the Russians.

The first recorded anchorage of an American ship on the coast of California was the result of a bizarre incident in the sea otter trade. In 1796 the ship *Otter,* of Boston, stopped at Monterey on her way to the Hawaiian Islands and China with a cargo of sea otter pelts gathered along the Oregon coast. Her captain, Ebenezer Dorr, asked permission to obtain supplies, which Governor Borica granted. The Yankee captain also asked permission to leave in California several convicts who had escaped from the English penal colony in Australia. Borica refused this request, but Dorr put them ashore at night to get rid of them, even though they had paid him to take them to Boston. Ebenezer Dorr could hardly have been a meaner man if his name had been Ebenezer Scrooge.

Seven years later another voyage for sea otter brought the *Lelia Byrd,* of Salem, into the bay of San Diego on the pretext of needing fresh food. Captain William Shaler and First Mate Richard Cleveland tried to make a clandestine agreement with the port commander for the acquisition of a stock of otter skins, but Cleveland was thrown into jail by the Spanish authorities and had to be forcibly rescued by his shipmates. The *Lelia Byrd* escaped from the harbor only after an exchange of shots with the little battery on Point Loma. Five years later Captain Shaler told his side of the story in an article published in the *American Register.* He regarded the violation of Spanish colonial trade restrictions as a kind of patriotic duty for enter-prising Yankees, and his article not only advertised the possibilities of the Califor-nia fur trade but also advocated American acquisition of the province. "It would be as easy to keep California in spite of the Spaniards," he wrote, "as it would be to win it from them in the first place."

By the end of the Spanish period, both the sea otter and the fur seal had been al-most exterminated along the coast of California. New England whalers began to pay increasingly frequent visits to the coast, but the main American trading interest in the region now shifted to cowhides and tallow. In 1821 the Mexican revolution-ary regime opened the ports of Monterey and San Diego to foreigners, and the spring of 1822 saw the arrival of the *John Begg,* the first foreign ship to be openly welcomed by California port authorities. Among the passengers on this ship was William E. P. Hartnell, newly appointed resident manager of Monterey for the part-nership of Hugh McCulloch and himself, California agents for the British trading firm of John Begg and Company. "Macala and Arnel," in the Hispanicized form of the partners' names, secured a 3-year contract to take all the hides the missions could furnish, at $1 each.

The advantage to the British was short-lived. Within a few weeks of Hartnell's coming, William A. Gale arrived on the *Sachem* from Boston with a cargo of no-tions. By bidding up the price of hides to $2, which was still a remarkable bargain, he seems to have persuaded some of the padres to evade their contract with the British agency. Gale became the resident agent of the Boston firm of Bryant and Sturgis, which soon had such a large share of the hide and tallow trade that for years the United States was commonly known in California as "Boston." During the Mexican period, this one firm was responsible for the export of about half a million hides. Reliable statistics are unavailable, but perhaps 1.25 million hides and 60 million pounds of tallow were loaded on American and British ships be-tween 1826 and 1848. Hides were called "California banknotes" and were, in fact, the province's main form of currency.

Import duties were substantial, ranging at various times from about 25 percent to almost twice that figure. Often these duties were at least partially evaded. Cus-toms officials were paid a commission for keeping their eyes open, but there were Yankee captains who were willing to pay them larger sums to keep their eyes closed. Even if duties were fully paid, however, the profits of bringing out a shipload of New England manufactured goods and returning to Boston with a cargo of hides were as high as 300 percent.

The classic description of the hide and tallow trade was written by Richard Henry Dana in *Two Years before the Mast.* Though it is usually thought of as a portrayal of life at sea and as a tract intended to reform the working conditions of seamen, much of the book was devoted to Dana's observations ashore in California; the crew, in the employ of Bryant and Sturgis, spent most of the 2-year voyage in collecting hides along the California coast.

The Danas of Cambridge were one of the oldest and most distinguished families of New England. As a Harvard undergraduate, Richard Henry had suffered a temporary breakdown of his eyesight, attributed to a case of measles. At the age of 19, in 1834, he signed on as a common sailor for the long voyage to California in the hope that it would improve his health, a purpose which it seems to have accomplished remarkably well almost from the time the ship left Boston harbor.

The outward-bound cargo of "everything under the sun" was quickly disposed of at Monterey, where boatloads of eager purchasers were rowed out to the ship as if it were a floating department store. Dana's pride in his New England heritage was reinforced by what he saw of the Californians, "an idle, thriftless people" who could "make nothing for themselves." The country abounded in grapes, he wrote, "yet they buy, at a great price, bad wine made in Boston and brought round by us, and retail it among themselves at a real (12½ cents) by the small wine glass." Their cowhides, "which they value at two dollars in money, they barter for something which costs seventy-five cents in Boston; and buy shoes (as like as not made from their own hides, which have been carried twice around Cape Horn) at three and four dollars, and 'chicken-skin boots' at fifteen dollars a pair."

Loading the hides was a strenuous operation. Most of the hide depositories had inadequate harbors, and the ship had to be anchored as far as 3 miles offshore. A hide would spoil if it got wet, and each one, stiff and heavy and as broad as the arms could reach, had to be tossed up and balanced on the sailor's head so that he could wade through the surf and put it into a swaying small boat.

The hide and tallow trade was significant not only because it influenced the economic history of New England and of early California, but also because it increased the interest of Americans in a distant region with which for many years it formed almost their only contact. *Two Years before the Mast,* published in 1840, brought Americans the same message that Captain Shaler's journal had carried more than 3 decades earlier, but Dana's message was more substantial and convincing. "In the hands of an enterprising people," he wrote, "what a country this might be!"

The Beaver Trappers

Just as American seagoing commerce with California had begun in the quest for the skin of the sea otter, so the history of overland contact had its beginnings in the search for beaver pelts. The trapper was the spearhead of the American landward advance, particularly in the far west; the first American overland expedition to California was conducted in 1826 by a young beaver hunter named Jedediah Strong Smith. It was he who deserved the title of "the Pathfinder," which was bestowed in later years upon a more publicized and less authentic hero, John C. Frémont. Smith set out with 17 men to traverse the unexplored desert region between the Great Salt

Lake and California. His objectives were the opening of a virgin beaver country and the establishment of a place of deposit on the Pacific for the furs of this new empire. On November 27, 1826, Smith and his men reached Mission San Gabriel, then at the height of its temporal prosperity. From Father José Bernardo Sánchez, the jovial successor of the gloomy Zalvidea, the Americans received a full measure of hospitality, which they remained to enjoy for several weeks.

In the words of his biographer, Dale L. Morgan, Jedediah Smith was "an unlikely sort of hero for the brawling West of his time, that West about which it has been said that God took care to stay on his own side of the Missouri River." The "mountain men" have been portrayed in stereotype as murderous brawlers, given to drunken orgies at their periodic rendezvous. Actually, though there were many such men among them, the personalities and backgrounds of the trappers were remarkably diverse. Smith was a quiet young man who never used tobacco or profanity, partook of wine or brandy only sparingly, and was deeply imbued with a Calvinist religious faith.

In December, Smith journeyed to San Diego in the hope of securing Governor Echeandía's permission to travel in California, but the governor, lacking a full realization of the unlimited energies of American business enterprise, found it difficult to believe that Smith was not a spy. He was inclined to send Smith and his men to Mexico for trial, but he compromised and ordered them to leave California by the way they had come.

Smith chose to define "California" as being merely the coastal strip of missions and presidios. Thus, he felt that he had complied with the governor's orders when, in January 1827, he moved northwestward across the Tehachapis into the San Joaquin Valley. This he found to be a trapper's paradise, and he had accumulated a large number of pelts by the time he reached the river known thereafter as the American. Late in May, apparently by way of the north fork of the Stanislaus River and Ebbetts Pass, Smith accomplished the first recorded crossing of the Sierra and reached his headquarters in northern Utah on July 3.

Within 10 days he was on his way back to California with 18 men, but his situation was worse than it had been in the previous year. At the Colorado crossing, the Mojaves attacked the party and killed 10 of its members. In September the survivors reached the camp of the first expedition in the northern San Joaquin Valley, but when Smith sought assistance at Mission San José, about 15 miles north of the pueblo of the same name, Father Narciso Durán arrested him, and only released him to go to Monterey for another conference with Echeandía. The governor was even more disposed than before to make Smith stand trial for illegal entry into the province, but uncertainty about the consequences of such strong action led to a renewal of permission for the trappers to depart. Early in 1828 they made the first recorded journey by land up to the northwestern coast of California and into Oregon. There the Umpquas killed most of the men. With only two others, Smith finally reached the Hudson's Bay Company headquarters at Fort Vancouver. Three years later he was killed by Comanches on the Sante Fé Trail.

While Smith was pioneering the routes between the Great Salt Lake and California, other adventurous American trappers and traders had been making their way from Missouri into New Mexico. The most notable of these was James Ohio Pattie, who pressed on from Santa Fé to California by way of the Gila Valley. Pattie was a very enterprising but intensely conceited and hot-headed young man. In the fall of 1826 he and a party of other fur hunters trapped along the Gila River to the Colorado. Moving northward, they got into a quarrel and then a bloody battle with the Mojaves. In warfare with the Indians, Pattie and his companions committed atrocities as vicious as those of the so-called savages. It is probable that the reason the Mojaves attacked the 1827 expedition of Jedediah Smith, although they had been peaceful during his previous journey through their country, was that they had had dealings with the Pattie expedition in the meantime.

When Pattie returned to Santa Fé, the governor of New Mexico confiscated all his furs because they had been gathered in Mexican territory without a license. Undaunted, he set out again along the Gila in the fall of 1827. At San Diego, Governor Echeandía, already irritated by the unauthorized incursions of Jedediah Smith, put these new intruders in jail.

At this time an epidemic broke out in the northern missions. According to James Ohio Pattie's own account, he had fortunately brought along a supply of "smallpox vaccine," and he was released in order to undertake a vaccination tour, immunizing more than 20,000 persons, mostly Indians, as far north as Fort Ross. In historical fact the epidemic was of measles, not smallpox, and the vaccination fantasy was one of the many tall tales that later appeared in *The Personal Narrative of James O. Pattie.* The editor of that remarkable volume, and also, to an unknown extent, the writer of it, was Timothy Flint, an author of many works about the west in which fact and fiction were seldom clearly distinguishable. *The Personal Narrative,* first published in 1831, was the original "western," the prototype of uncounted thousands of writings that have since fed the public appetite for the vicarious enjoyment of adventure and violence.

Other trappers soon improved upon the routes of Smith and Pattie. In 1833 Joseph Reddeford Walker, a fur trapper from Tennessee and Missouri, made the first westward crossing through the center of the Sierra Nevada. Walker's expedition from the Rockies to California was a branch of the operations of Captain Benjamin Bonneville, who was on a 2-year furlough from the United States Army. Ostensibly, this leave was granted so that Bonneville could engage in the fur business, but one purpose of it may have been the encouragement of explorations, of potential military value, in Mexican territory. Walker's men discovered what later became the main wagon-train route through central Nevada, along the Humboldt River, which they called more appropriately "the Barren." Though their trail over "the dark and deathlike wall" of the Sierra is partly a matter of speculation, it probably lay somewhere between the headwaters of the East Walker River and those of the Tuolumne. They have often been credited with being the first white people to see the Yosemite Valley. Cold, hunger, and exhaustion dulled their appreciation of it that day in the fall of 1833, and indeed some historians have maintained that what they really saw was Hetch Hetchy Valley.

Early Settlers

The first foreigners to settle permanently in Spanish California did so by accident. In 1814 John Gilroy, a Scottish sailor on an English ship, was left at Monterey because of sickness. He married a daughter of the Ortegas, acquired a part of their lands, and lived to see a flourishing American town, bearing his name, on the site of his rancho. Like so many holders of Mexican titles, however, he would finally lose his property to American land lawyers and squatters.

The first American settler in California, or rather the first one around whose name any substantial body of fact and legend has gathered, was Joseph Chapman, sometimes called "the unwilling pirate." A member of the Bouchard expedition, he was captured at Monterey in 1818 but claimed that Bouchard had shanghaied him in Honolulu. In any case, his skills as a millwright and boatbuilder soon made him a welcome and useful resident.

The next few years saw the arrival of several remarkable Yankees who came as traders and remained to gather a great share of the profits of merchandising into their own hands. William Goodwin Dana and Alfred Robinson at Santa Barbara and Abel Stearns at Los Angeles became the chief merchants of their communities and, partly by marriage, large landowners as well; Thomas O. Larkin became the most important merchant in Monterey.

William G. Dana arrived at Santa Barbara from Boston in 1826. Although he was a relative of the more famous Richard Henry, there was no direct reference to him in *Two Years before the Mast,* and this has given rise to much interesting speculation. It was said that Richard refused to see William at the time of his visit to Santa Barbara. The reason, apparently, lay in William's eager espousal of the Roman Catholic faith and Mexican citizenship and his betrothal to young Josefa Carrillo of Santa Barbara, delayed by nothing more than the formalities of naturalization, which postponed the marriage for 2 years (by which time the bride was 16 years old). It seems probable that Richard, so much more bound to the Calvinist religion, the inherited patriotism, and the racial pride of the family, had his kinsman in mind when he wrote that certain Americans in California had "left their consciences at Cape Horn."

Don Abel Stearns was also the bearer of an old and distinguished Massachusetts family name. He went first to Mexico and had already become naturalized when he arrived in California in 1829. As a prosperous trader in hides and liquors, he was as flagrant a smuggler as were most of his competitors, and yet in 1836 he was appointed *síndico,* or fiscal agent, of the village of Los Angeles. Nicknamed Cara de Caballo, or Horseface, he was a homely man even before he acquired a scar about the mouth, left by the knife of a disgruntled customer in his store. Nevertheless, his appearance did not prevent his marriage to beautiful Doña Maria Francisca Paula Arcadia Bandini, and with the added influence of his wife's relatives he began to acquire the estates that soon made him the largest landowner and cattleman and the wealthiest citizen of southern California. He had no children, which was most unusual among those who married "native daughters." Don Guillermo and Doña Josefa Dana, for example, had 21.

The title *don,* derived from the Latin *dominus,* or "lord," was applied in Mexican California to almost any man of more or less substantial means, particularly a landowner. In baptism and naturalization, a foreign first name was officially changed to its Spanish equivalent. In polite address this might also be done unofficially, as in the case of Don Tomás Larkin, one of the few foreign residents who managed to rise to positions of wealth and importance in California without embracing Roman Catholicism, Mexican nationality, and a native daughter.

Thomas Oliver Larkin, another Massachusetts Yankee, came to Monterey in 1832 at the suggestion of his half brother, John Cooper, who was already engaged in trade there. One of Larkin's fellow passengers on the long voyage around the Horn was Rachel Hobson Holmes, on her way to join her husband at Hilo in the Hawaiian Islands. There she discovered that she was a widow, and a few months later Larkin proposed to her by correspondence. A civil marriage ceremony between two non-Catholic foreigners would have been questioned by the Mexican authorities, and consequently the ceremony was performed on board a ship off the Santa Barbara coast. Mrs. Larkin was the first American woman to live in California.

Larkin opened a general store at Monterey, and his business as an intermediary between ranchers and traders was soon flourishing remarkably. Larkin had, as Bancroft put it, "no inconvenient veneration for the revenue laws," and he offered a tempting charge-account system. The chief officials of the province, among others, became heavily indebted to him. He did a thriving business in redwood lumber, largely for export to the Hawaiian Islands and Mexico. And in his designs for his own home, the customs house, and other buildings, he established the "Monterey style" of architecture.

These early American immigrants had come by sea and taken up residence in the coastal strip. In addition, there were those who came overland and settled mainly in the interior. The first important settler in this American overland migration was "Dr." John Marsh. Still another son of Massachusetts, Marsh had graduated from Harvard with the class of 1823. Later he "read medicine" under an army surgeon stationed in Minnesota, but the surgeon died before Marsh had completed the program of study. Marsh then sold guns to the Sioux in violation of federal law, and in flight from a warrant for his arrest on this charge he emigrated to Los Angeles in 1836. He was destitute, and to earn money he secured permission to practice medicine. For credentials he offered his Harvard bachelor of arts diploma, correctly suspecting that he was the only person in the town who could read the Latin in which the diploma was printed. Because his fees were paid almost entirely in cowhides, his little adobe soon resembled a warehouse rather than a medical office. After a few months, in order to purchase a ranch, he sold his stock of hides for $500 and accepted Roman Catholicism and naturalization.

Marsh was now a morose and greedy man, determined to acquire wealth in compensation for his many disappointments. In 1837 he bought a huge tract near the Sacramento–San Joaquin Delta at the foot of Mount Diablo. Marsh made it the first successful rancho in the great Central Valley. This he accomplished largely by taking payment in cattle for his medical services throughout the northern California settlements. He customarily exacted a fee of 50 head. Marsh also succeeded by

Sutter's Fort. (*Courtesy of the Bancroft Library.*)

adopting the system of Indian labor exploitation that flourished on the ranchos of his Spanish-speaking neighbors. The local Indians, probably Miwoks and Northern Valley Yokuts, made the adobe bricks for Marsh's ranch house and plowed and cultivated his fields. The Indians received no wages for their work, but Marsh fed them beans and beef, gave them a few clothes, and tended to their medical needs.

Two years after Marsh settled in the region of the San Joaquin Delta, John Sutter arrived with his ambitious designs for the Sacramento Valley. Sutter, originally Johann August Suter, was a German Swiss, and in the history of the American movement overland into California he and his New Helvetia were to play a significant role.

Sutter, like Marsh, was a fugitive from tragedy and from justice. In Switzerland he had been married only 1 day before the birth of his first son, and the marriage was unhappy even though it finally produced 5 children. Sutter always lived extravagantly, and in 1834, faced with debtors' prison after the failure of his dry goods business, he deserted his family and absconded to America. After interludes in Saint Louis and Santa Fé, he went with a trapping expedition to Oregon, and then by ship to Honolulu, Sitka, Yerba Buena, and Monterey, where he arrived in July 1839. In the meantime his powers of romantic imagination had made him "Captain" Sutter, formerly of "the Royal Swiss Guard of France." In Oregon he had heard of the Sacramento Valley, and there he now sought the wide-open spaces where people could plan things as they would like them to be.

The quarrel between Governor Alvarado and Comandante Vallejo was at its height, and Alvarado thought he saw a chance to use Sutter, and his grandiose colonization scheme, as a check upon Vallejo's power and pretensions. With the governor's blessing, Sutter selected a tract on the Sacramento River at its junction with the American. After 1 year, the minimum period of legal residence, the glamorous newcomer received not only Mexican citizenship and a grant of 11 square leagues but also the status of a regional official. He was authorized "to represent in the Establishment of New Helvetia all the laws of the country, to function as political authority and dispenser of justice, in order to prevent the robberies committed by adventurers from the United States, to stop the invasion of savage Indians and the hunting and trapping by companies from the Columbia." Beginning with beaver pelts and wild-grape brandy, Sutter went on to establish a cattle ranch and farm, using the labor of Indians. Sutter's herds and fields and vineyards were tended by Indian laborers; all his workshops were staffed by native craftspeople who did the weaving, spinning, tanning, and other tasks. Sutter also succeeded remarkably, for a time, in obtaining credit. In 1841, for example, when the Russian-American Fur Company abandoned Fort Ross, Sutter's note for $30,000 secured the purchase of its implements and livestock with only $2000 paid down. Several cannons from Ross strengthened the defenses of Sutter's own fort. That establishment would soon be a focal point for early American overland migration.

Covered Wagons, 1841 to 1846

The first organized group to cross the Rockies for the purpose of settlement in California was the Bidwell-Bartleson party of 1841. The previous year, John Marsh had written a letter to some friends in the neighborhood of Independence, Missouri, praising the lands and climate of California and minimizing the difficulty of getting there. Lured by this and other rosy testimonials, more than 500 persons organized a Western Emigration Society and pledged to assemble near Independence in the following spring. During the winter, however, Missouri newspapers circulated stories that painted a sharply different picture. One of these concerned the harsh treatment accorded some Americans at Monterey during the "Graham affair" in 1840. Isaac Graham and his band of American riflemen had participated in Alvarado's little revolution of 1836. They later complained that Governor Alvarado was not sufficiently grateful to them. "I was insulted at every turn," Alvarado told Alfred Robinson, "by the drunken followers of Graham." The alcoholic boastings of Graham's men led to rumors that they were plotting a Texan-style revolution. As a result, in April 1840, Graham and 38 other foreigners, mostly Americans, were arrested, packed into Monterey's one-cell jail, and then sent to Mexico. Later they were set free.

In Missouri, however, the news of the episode so discouraged the members of the Western Emigration Society that only one of the original signers appeared at the appointed place in May 1841. This was John Bidwell, a young former schoolteacher. In addition to Bidwell, 68 new prospects appeared. John Bartleson was elected captain, solely because he insisted that otherwise he would not go. As Bidwell later put it, very generously, Bartleson "was not the best man for the position," but "he had seven or eight men with him, and we did not want the party diminished."

No one in the group had ever been west, and their only maps were ridiculously inaccurate. When the time came to leave the Oregon Trail and strike out across the Great Basin for California, about half the emigrants prudently decided to go on to

Oregon, and several others turned back toward Missouri. The rest managed to find the Humboldt River, but had to abandon their wagons. Near the Humboldt Sink, Bartleson and eight other men took the best horses, deserted the party, and rushed on ahead. They failed to find a pass and returned shamefacedly, begging a share of the little food that remained. Bidwell quietly readmitted them to the group. It did not need to be said that he and not Bartleson was now the captain. At the end of October, miraculously, they found their way over the Sierra and down to the Stanislaus, and on November 4, 1841, they arrived at Marsh's ranch.

The miserly Marsh demanded high prices for supplies. By contrast, when Bidwell visited Sutter's Fort a few weeks later, he was cordially welcomed, as nearly all newcomers were. Sutter was the emigrant's benefactor and friend. New Helvetia was to be the headquarters for several rescue parties sent to help stranded travelers over the Sierra. The overland migrants not only received the benefits of Sutter's hospitality, they also witnessed at New Helvetia a working model of what could be accomplished with a labor force of California Indians. Few travelers who visited Sutter failed to be impressed by the apparent ease—and "the occasional exercise of well-timed authority"—with which he had subdued his Indian workers.

In the fall of 1841, an emigrant party including William Workman, John Rowland, and Benjamin D. Wilson traveled from Santa Fé to Los Angeles. In 1843 Lansford W. Hastings, a frontier lawyer with filibustering ambitions, led a group into California from Oregon. Several of its members, including Hastings, had the perverted desire to shoot down an Indian, and the unprovoked murders they committed in the upper Sacramento Valley stored up trouble for them and for future pioneers. The Stephens-Townsend-Murphy party, coming from Missouri in 1844, was the first to succeed in getting wagons over the Sierra, and also the first to make use of what would later be the main route, the Donner Pass, though that name was not acquired until the tragedy that was to follow 2 years later.

The year 1845 saw the beginning of a somewhat more substantial annual migration. Reports from Thomas O. Larkin, John Marsh, and John C. Frémont were stirring up interest in California. Lansford W. Hastings, through speech making and the publication of his dangerously misleading *Emigrant's Guide,* was pursuing his dream of leading hordes of Americans to the western paradise, and hoping that their gratitude would make him a new Sam Houston, president of a Pacific republic or governor of a new American state. The largest emigrant party of 1845, the Grigsby-Ide group, had more than 100 members, and the total for the year was more than 250 persons. More than twice as many came in 1846.

The worse-than-worthless advice of Lansford W. Hastings was a cause of dangerous delays for many of them, and it led the Donner party into the worst disaster in the history of the California Trail. The Donner party was organized at Springfield, Illinois. It passed through Independence on time, in May, but instead of taking the established route by way of Fort Hall, north of the Great Salt Lake, it followed "Hastings' Cutoff" to the south of it. Winter set in early. On November 2 the main party decided to rest overnight only a few miles short of the Sierra summit. That night a snowstorm blocked the pass. Most of the party was snowed in near Donner Lake until February, and many survived only by eating the flesh of the dead. Of 87 persons in the original group, 40 perished. There was heroism as well as horror. James Reed left the party to bring back provisions and returned leading a relief expedition from Sutter's Fort. During his absence, the family of Patrick and Margaret Breen took in two of Reed's children and cared for them along with their own seven children. When rescuers arrived, Tamsen Donner refused to leave her husband, George, who was too weak to travel. Their three daughters were saved, but George and Tamsen died.

Alfred Robinson had written to Larkin urging all possible efforts to publicize California so that "the American population will be sufficiently large to play the Texas game." But California before the gold rush was less attractive to American settlers than either Texas or Oregon; the emigrants to California were primarily interested in trying to advance their own fortunes rather than their country's, and many were so discouraged that they drifted north to Oregon or back to "the States." Nevertheless, overland emigration would undoubtedly have made a change to American sovereignty inevitable in a few years. It had not yet accomplished this by 1846, but other related historical forces had been set in motion.

Selected Bibliography

Adele Ogden's *The California Sea Otter Trade* (1937) is the best treatment of its subject. Significant memoirs are William Shaler, "Journal of a Voyage from China to the North-Western Coast of America Made in 1804," *American Register . . . for 1808,* pp. 136–175, edited and with an introduction by Lindley Bynum (1935), and Richard Cleveland, *Narrative of Voyages and Commercial Enterprises* (1842). See also Magdalen Coughlin, "Boston Smugglers on the Coast," *California Historical Society Quarterly,* XLVI (June 1967), pp. 99–120. The hide and tallow trade is best described in Richard Henry Dana, *Two Years before the Mast* (1840, with many reprintings); Alfred Robinson, *Life in California* (1846); and Doyce B. Nunis, Jr. (ed.), *The California Diary of Faxon Dean Atherton, 1836–1839* (1964).

The story of the beaver trappers and traders is told in Richard Batman, *James Ohio Pattie's West* (1986), and James Clyman, *Journal of a Mountain Man,* edited by Linda M. Hasselstrom (1984). Robert G. Cleland's *This Reckless Breed of Men: The Trappers and Fur Traders of the Southwest* (1952) is readable and reliable. Dale L. Morgan's *Jedediah Smith and the Opening of the West* (1953) is a brilliant biography; see also David J. Weber, *The Californios versus Jedediah Smith* (1990). The Walker expedition is recorded in Bill Gilbert, *Westering Man* (1983); *The Adventures of Zenas Leonard,* edited by John C. Ewers (1959); and *The Life and Adventures of George Nidever,* edited by William H. Ellison (1937). LeRoy R. Hafen (ed.), *The Mountain Men and the Fur Trade of the Far West* (10 volumes, 1971), provides 300 biographical sketches.

On American and other immigrants to California before 1849, both by sea and by land, an indispensable source is the "Pioneer Register," an alphabetical biographical dictionary appended to volumes II–V of the Bancroft *History of California.* A group portrait appears in Charles B. Churchill, *Adventurers and Prophets: American Autobiographers in Mexican California, 1829–1847* (1995). The story of the most prominent Anglo-American in the province is well told in Harlan Hague and David J. Langum, *Thomas O. Larkin* (1990). *The Larkin Papers,* edited by George P. Hammond (10 volumes, 1951–1964), also has references to a remarkable number of persons. *John Marsh, Pioneer* (1930), and his biographer, George D. Lyman, were both medical men with far-ranging interests. James P. Zollinger's *Sutter, the Man and His Empire* (1939) and Richard Dillon's *Fool's Gold: The Decline and Fall of Captain John Sutter of California* (1967) are good biographies. Crucial to an understanding of current scholarship are the critical essays in Kenneth N. Owens (ed.), *John Sutter and a Wider West* (1994), and Allan R. Ottley (ed.), *John A. Sutter's Last Days* (1986).

Good accounts of the overland migration are in John D. Unruh, Jr., *The Plains Across: The Overland Emigrants and the Trans-Mississippi West, 1848–60* (1979); George R. Stewart, *The California Trail* (1962); and Irving Stone, *Men to Match My Mountains* (1956). Rockwell D. Hunt's *John Bidwell* (1942) is a useful biography. There were many memoirs, including Bidwell's *A Journey to California in 1841* (1842) and *Josiah Belden, 1841 California Pioneer,* edited by Doyce B. Nunis, Jr. (1962). For a biography of the founder of Stockton, see James Shebl's lively *Weber!* (1993). On the Donner tragedy, see George R. Stewart, *Ordeal by Hunger* (1936); Jeannette G. Maino, *Left Hand Turn: A Story of the Donner Party Women* (1987); Kristin Johnson, *Unfortunate Emigrants* (1996); Donald L. Hardesty, *The Archaeology of the Donner Party* (1997); and the imaginative reconstruction by James D. Houston in *Snow Mountain Passage* (2001).

A well-balanced view of this period may be found in John A. Hawgood, "The Pattern of Yankee Infiltration in Mexican Alta California, 1821–1846," *Pacific Historical Review,* XXVII (February 1958), pp. 27–38. See also David J. Langum, *Law and Community on the Mexican California Frontier: Anglo-American Expatriates and the Clash of Legal Traditions, 1821–1846* (1987).

CHAPTER 7

The American Conquest

In 1846 the United States declared war on Mexico, and during the course of that war American military forces occupied California. At war's end in 1848, the two nations negotiated a treaty in which Mexico ceded California and other borderland provinces to the United States. These events constitute a watershed in California history: the Mexican War and subsequent transfer of title stand as the great discontinuity in the state's history.

Overtures, Diplomatic and Undiplomatic

Official American efforts to acquire California had an inauspicious beginning in 1835, as an extension of President Andrew Jackson's plans for the purchase of Texas. These schemes originated largely in the fertile brain of Colonel Anthony Butler, an old friend of Jackson, to whom the president had unwisely entrusted the ministry to Mexico. Butler disgraced himself and his government by letting it be known in Mexico City that he expected to purchase the republic's northern territories by buying some of its political leaders. When Butler later tried to implicate Jackson in his schemes for bribery, Old Hickory denounced him as a liar.

President Jackson was interested in California mainly because the acquisition of San Francisco Bay, as a port for American commerce and whaling in the Pacific, might reconcile the north to the annexation of Texas as a slave state. Jackson in 1837 unsuccessfully offered $3.5 million for Mexican recognition of a southwestern boundary of the United States extending along the Rio Grande and thence westward to the Pacific along the 38th parallel. He was unaware that this line would have left the entrance to San Francisco Bay about 12 miles south of the border.

The panic of 1837 began a few weeks after the inauguration of Martin Van Buren, Jackson's chosen successor. Van Buren's single term as president was one long period of depression in which the Treasury was in no condition to provide for purchasing new territory. With economic recovery in the 1840s, the United States began to assert its policy of manifest destiny to extend its borders to the Pacific. Early in the John Tyler administration, Daniel Webster as secretary of state and Waddy Thompson as minister to Mexico advocated a plan to secure California in exchange for cancellation of American financial claims against the Mexican government. But again, as in the Anthony Butler episode, an American blunder raised an outcry in Mexico City that made any peaceful cession of territory to the United States politically impossible.

Early in September 1842, Commodore Thomas ap Catesby Jones, commander of the American Pacific squadron, received a false report at Callao, Peru, that the United States and Mexico were at war and that Mexico intended to cede California to Great Britain rather than see it fall into American hands. Admiral Thomas and his British Pacific squadron had just left Callao, reportedly under sealed orders from England. Jones, who had received instructions in Washington a year earlier to act quickly in just such an eventuality, promptly sailed for California in what he supposed to be a race with Thomas. He anchored at Monterey on October 18 and on the next day demanded the peaceful surrender of the port and the district. This was concluded on the 20th, the American flag was raised, and Jones marched his men ashore six abreast to the tunes of "The Star-Spangled Banner" and "Yankee Doodle." He also proclaimed California under armed but courteous and benevolent American occupation. This proclamation remained in force only 1 day. On the 21st, when Jones landed in person and examined the latest official communications from Mexico, he realized that he had been completely and regrettably misinformed.

Governor Manuel Micheltorena, who was then in Los Angeles, immediately began to organize resistance, urging all Californios to take up arms to defend their territory. When Micheltorena received a letter of explanation and apology from Jones, the governor advised Jones to come to him at Los Angeles. There he received the commodore and his explanations with courtesy and hospitality, but sent reports to Mexico City in an entirely different tone. The Mexican government conveyed an angry protest to Washington demanding extreme punishment for Jones, but although the United States disavowed his actions, he suffered only a temporary removal from his command.

As the Jones incident clearly shows, American suspicions of the designs of Great Britain on California played a large part in American thinking, and incidentally provided a very useful rationalization of American plans. The fact was that Her Majesty's government had no intention whatever of trying to acquire California. There were outward appearances of a designing nature, however, quite sufficient to supply fuel for American fears. In 1839, for example, a London publisher brought out the first book in English entirely devoted to California. This was Alexander Forbes's *History of Upper and Lower California,* which advocated a plan for the British colonization of vast tracts of land in California. In 1841 Sir George Simpson of the Hudson's Bay Company visited California and concluded quite correctly that some native Californians were so afraid of American control that they would welcome a British protectorate. Sir George's enthusiasm for such a development was obvious, and Americans had no way of knowing that the British government did not support his views.

The French, also, had some degree of interest in California dating all the way back to the visit of the comte de La Pérouse. In 1842 the French agent Eugène Duflot de Mofras reported that California was certain to pass to some power other than Mexico, and soon. French hopes were faint, based on little more than the idea that Mexico might prefer to see California in the friendly hands of a Latin and Catholic nation rather than under Anglo-Saxon Protestants. The weakness of Mexican control of California had been so apparent to any observer for so long that a spate of foreign designs was inevitable.

Plans of the Polk Administration

James K. Polk of Tennessee was a political disciple of Andrew Jackson, who lived to congratulate Polk on his inauguration as president in March 1845. Polk, like his mentor, was always ready to believe any rumors of fell designs on the part of the British. Polk also shared some of the anti-British views of Senator Thomas Hart Benton of Missouri, powerful chairman of the Senate military affairs committee. Benton firmly though incorrectly believed that perfidious Albion had intended to acquire California ever since Drake claimed and named New Albion in 1579.

On coming into office, President Polk confided to Secretary of the Navy George Bancroft that the acquisition of California would be one of his most cherished goals. Within the month of Polk's inauguration, Governor Micheltorena and his *cholo* troops were virtually deported from California, and this ended the last desperate effort to assert any effective control over the province from Mexico City. When the news of this development reached the east coast in June 1845, a chorus of newspaper editorials began to call for American acquisition.

During this same period, Polk received reports from Mexico City of the startling proposal of a young Irish priest named Eugene McNamara to bring 2000 families, 10,000 colonists altogether, to a grant of 3000 square leagues in California. McNamara gained the approval of the archbishop of Mexico, and addressed a burning appeal to the Mexican president in which he warned that "before another year the Californias will form a part of the American Nation. Their Catholic institutions will become the prey of the Methodist wolves; and the whole country will be inundated with these cruel invaders." The McNamara scheme was wildly impracticable, but many Americans regarded it with true alarm as being somehow simultaneously a British and a popish plot.

Having determined to acquire California, Polk would have preferred to purchase it. He sent John Slidell on an ill-fated mission to Mexico with an offer of as much as $40 million for Upper California and New Mexico. "Money," said Slidell's instructions, "would be no object when compared with the value of this acquisition." This was Polk's own view, but he was well aware that the prospects of success were dim, and therefore he put an alternative plan into operation simultaneously. This involved secret instructions to Thomas O. Larkin, consul at Monterey since the previous year, to try to persuade the Californians to secede from Mexico and seek American protection.

Larkin had been highly successful in his business pursuits in California, but his sympathies were not with the Californios. He also took great pride in the fact that his were the first children born in California of parents who both had been born in the United States. He had been reporting to Washington every suspicion and rumor of sinister British intentions toward California, and in some instances he seems to have exaggerated his reports beyond what he himself believed, so great was his yearning for American annexation at this time. On October 17, 1845, a secret dispatch signed by James Buchanan, the secretary of state, appointed Larkin "confidential agent in California." He was instructed to warn the Californians against any attempt to bring them under the jurisdiction of "Foreign Governments." Further, he was to "arouse in their bosoms that love of liberty and independence so natural to the American Continent." Should California assert and maintain her independence, Buchanan wrote to Larkin, "we shall render her all the kind offices in our power as a Sister Republic."

The plan had real possibilities. Larkin was on friendly terms with officials at Monterey, whom he had supplied for years with most of their provisions and merchandise. The government had reached a state of truly insufferable confusion, and almost everyone admitted the need for some decisive change. Since the departure of Micheltorena, the capital and the assembly had been at Los Angeles under Don Pío Pico as governor, while the customs and the treasury remained at Monterey, with Colonel José Castro as military commander. Mariano Guadalupe Vallejo was frankly reconciled to American annexation because he considered it both inevitable and preferable to the alternatives. Colonel Castro, though he bristled at any suggestion of American military force, was confidentially circulating a plan for "declaring California independent in 1847–1848, as soon as a sufficient number of foreigners should arrive." Larkin also enlisted the cooperation of Jacob P. Leese of Sonoma, Don Abel Stearns of Los Angeles, and J. J. Warner from near San Diego, and all three became not only active in the scheme, but also convinced that it would work.

The promising Polk-Larkin plan for winning the province by peaceful conciliation of the *paisanos* was impeded by resentment of the blustering actions of Captain John C. Frémont in California in March 1846. A few weeks later, the scheme was entirely nullified by the Bear Flag Revolt—in which Frémont also had a part—and by the outbreak of the Mexican War.

John Charles Frémont

Frémont was one of the most controversial figures not only in the history of California but in the history of the United States as well. His mother, the young wife of a wealthy and elderly citizen of Richmond, had run away with a young French émigré. In Virginia a divorce could be obtained only from the state legislature, which refused to pass the necessary act. Frémont's parents lived together as husband and wife until the death of the father, which occurred when John Charles was 5 years

John Charles Frémont (1813–1890), an impulsive participant in the Bear Flag Revolt. (*Courtesy of the Bancroft Library.*)

old. The circumstances of his birth seem to have given him, as in the analogous case of Alexander Hamilton, a feeling of extraordinary need to establish his place in the world. He was like the young Hamilton, too, in that his promising qualities attracted the sympathy of influential men who helped him gain an education. But there was also a side of Frémont's personality that made him impulsive, unstable, and erratic throughout his life. He was ever the impatient opportunist and adventurer, and there was hardly a single action of his whole career that did not produce some troublesome set of complications—and interminable disagreement among biographers and historians about his motives and conduct.

As a lieutenant in the Corps of Topographical Engineers, Frémont met Senator Thomas Hart Benton, who inspired the younger man with his own fiery enthusiasm for the vast possibilities of westward exploration and expansion and with his dream of extending American territory to the Pacific. At Benton's home Frémont met the senator's daughter Jessie, an extraordinary girl of 16 whose great intellectual gifts had been developed by her father's intensive and devoted tutoring. Frémont and Jessie were secretly married a few months later, and after stormy protests Benton was reconciled to the marriage. Frémont gained a brilliant and beautiful wife and a brilliant and influential father-in-law, and both became his invaluable though highly possessive allies.

Frémont then led a series of western exploring and scientific expeditions, authorized by Congress at the prompting of Senator Benton. The first of these followed the Oregon Trail as far as South Pass in the Rockies. The final report of this expedition—combining Frémont's own genius for publicity with his wife's sparkling literary style—was widely circulated and established Frémont as a national hero.

His second expedition, in 1843–1844, proceeded to Oregon, then south along the eastern side of the Cascade Range and the Sierra Nevada, and across the Sierra into California by way of Carson Pass. There was a temporary flurry over Frémont's setting out with a howitzer, which the War Department had specifically ordered him not to take on the grounds that the expedition was supposed to be scientific and not military. It had to be explained that Jessie Frémont had intercepted this dispatch and had taken it upon herself to suppress it, but her father defended this action successfully in the Senate.

With the second expedition already well publicized, the Frémonts' collaborative prose soon described it in even more fascinating terms than the first. Understandably the report was another best-seller and became the most widely read description of the far west.

In Washington, D.C., in the spring of 1845, Frémont became convinced that war with Mexico was imminent, that his third expedition should be prepared for military rather than merely scientific activities, and that with it he should play an important role in conquering California. In this idea he received some private encouragement from Senator Benton and from Secretary of the Navy Bancroft. There is no evidence, however, that Frémont received authorization for military operations in Mexican territory either from President Polk or from the War Department. Nevertheless, he recruited 60 armed men, all expert marksmen, and arrived in California in December 1845. Early in 1846 Frémont appeared at Monterey. He had come, he said, merely to survey a route to the Pacific, and his men were not soldiers. Colonel Castro, however, peremptorily ordered Frémont and his armed force out of California. In angry and headstrong defiance, Frémont entrenched his men on Hawk's Peak (now Frémont Peak) in the Gabilán Mountains overlooking the Salinas Valley and raised the American flag. Castro called for volunteers and raised a force of about 200. Larkin mediated, and Frémont, after 3 days on his mountaintop, retreated to the Sacramento Valley. Obviously playing for time, he moved slowly northward—"slowly and growlingly," as he put it in a letter to his wife.

On May 9, 1846, he was overtaken near Klamath Lake in southern Oregon by Lieutenant Archibald H. Gillespie of the Marine Corps, who had come to California disguised as a merchant traveling for his health, under instructions from Polk and Buchanan to cooperate as a secret agent with Larkin in the plan of peaceful persuasion. Gillespie, like Frémont, was a rash and high-spirited young man. Arriving in California in April, he had heard reports that war with Mexico was imminent, and these reports he brought to Frémont along with a packet of letters from Senator Benton. The two young officers seem to have convinced each other that the plan for peaceful conciliation was now out of date, that bold initiative was called for, and that Frémont's force should return to California prepared for military action.

Whether Gillespie brought Frémont any secret official authorization to proceed in this way has been hotly debated. There is no reliable documentary evidence for this claim. Frémont probably acted, as he had already acted several weeks earlier at Hawk's Peak, on his own imagination of what the interests of the United States required him to do under particular circumstances. Thus, his own ambitions and impulses had free rein.

The Bear Flag Revolt

In the meantime, a crop of frightening rumors had circulated among the American immigrants recently settled in the Sacramento and Napa valleys. Frémont and his men had spread some of these rumors on their way northward. In particular, it was falsely reported that Colonel Castro would soon follow up his expulsion of Frémont with an expulsion of all the American settlers.

The origins of the Bear Flag Revolt are unclear, and the evidence, especially on Frémont's part in it, is often contradictory. The American settlers in the area were a miscellaneous group of people in a very insecure situation. Nearly all of them were rough pioneers. Some were roving hunters and trappers, or runaway sailors. Most were squatters who probably believed the rumors that they would soon be attacked and driven out of California. Emboldened by the return of Frémont, on June 10 a group under the rough-and-ready Ezekiel Merritt began the revolt by seizing a herd of horses intended for Castro's militia. Some further and more formal action was needed, lest the rebels remain merely horse thieves. Thus, on the morning of Sunday, June 14, a party of more than 30 armed settlers descended on the village of Sonoma.

There were no longer any soldiers at this former military post, and Colonel Vallejo was no longer on active duty, but the filibusters surrounded his home and informed him that he was a prisoner of war. He invited the leaders in to explain what war he was a prisoner of, and when this proved a difficult question, he brought out bottles of *aguardiente,* or brandy, to aid in the discussion. Ezekiel Merritt, William Knight, and Robert Semple had entered first. The rest waited outside for several hours and then elected John Grigsby to go in and investigate. After another interval, they sent in William B. Ide, who, according to his own account, found the previous commissioners befuddled by Vallejo's brandy. Ide, a teetotaler, finally arranged the terms of capitulation, with Jacob P. Leese, Vallejo's brother-in-law, acting as translator. The capitulation was written in English, but Vallejo added a paragraph in Spanish that explained his motives for surrender. Genaro Padilla, author of *My History, Not Yours* (1993), has interpreted this paragraph as a symbol of Vallejo's resistance "within a confined, and dangerous, rhetorical space."

Colonel Vallejo was probably the most widely respected citizen of California. He had no objection to being arrested because, as an advocate of American annexation, he was thus relieved of his embarrassing trust as a Mexican officer. The sensible course would have been to parole him, and he was given some assurance that this would be done, but instead he was taken under arrest to Sutter's Fort. Frémont, who then placed the fort virtually under his own command, committed the foolish outrage of ordering Vallejo into a cell, where he was imprisoned for 2 months. Frémont, feeling that Castro had humiliated him, now acted as if it were Castro and not Vallejo who was his prisoner. He sternly reprimanded Sutter for trying to

Replica of the original Bear Flag, raised over the Sonoma plaza in 1846. Critics later complained that the grizzly looked more like a pig than a bear. (*Courtesy of James Vanderbilt, Sonoma Valley Historical Society.*)

make Vallejo's bare cell more comfortable. The outrageous actions of Frémont and his men deeply embittered the Californios. Vallejo's daughter Rosalía later said that "those hated men" inspired within her "a large dose of hatred" against the Americans.

At Sonoma, Ide and his associates declared themselves a republic and devised a flag. It was a piece of white cotton cloth with a star and a stripe. In the upper left-hand corner, a large lone star, obviously suggesting an analogy with the history of Texas, was painted in red. To the right of the star, and facing it, was what was intended as a grizzly bear, passant. Under these emblems, "CALIFORNIA REPUBLIC." was lettered in black ink. A broad stripe of red flannel, made from an article of used clothing variously recalled as either a petticoat or a man's shirt, was sewn along the bottom of the cotton. This was the original of the banner which the California Legislature adopted in 1911 as the state flag and which since then must be flown over all state buildings.

In later years Ide and Frémont made rival claims, both considerably exaggerated, for credit in the matter of the Bear Flag Revolt. Frémont's connection with its beginning was highly equivocal and opportunistic. He helped to foment the rebellion by encouraging the American settlers to goad the Californios into attacking them so that he and his men could come to their defense. Castro sent about 50 men northward across San Francisco Bay to try to retake Sonoma. On

June 24, there was a skirmish north of San Rafael, later magnified into the "battle of Olompali." In the entire "Bear Flag war," two Americans and five or six Californios were killed.

Frémont, having now assumed command of the Bear Flaggers and having informally merged his force with theirs, crossed from the Marin peninsula on July 1. Entering the long-ungarrisoned little ruin of the San Francisco presidio, he spiked its 10 old Spanish guns. This was a typically Frémontian act—dashing in appearance but superfluous in reality. Those venerable cannons had been cast in Lima about 1625, and for at least 40 years they had been incapable of firing so much as a salute. In a more notable and enduring achievement, described in his *Memoirs,* Frémont gave the entrance to the bay "the name of Chrysopylae, or Golden Gate, for the same reasons that the harbor of Constantinople was called Chryoceros, or Golden Horn."

Frémont joined a Fourth of July celebration at Sonoma, and the next day he more or less formally organized the "California battalion" of American volunteers, with himself in command and Lieutenant Gillespie as adjutant. On the 7th, however, Commodore Sloat raised the American flag at Monterey. It was raised at Yerba Buena and Sonoma on the 9th and replaced the Bear Flag at Sutter's Fort on the 11th. The life of the Bear Flag "republic," a rather romantic and later fantastically romanticized period of a little less than a month, was thus ended.

By instigating the filibustering activities known as the Bear Flag Revolt, and by participating in them, Frémont actually accomplished only two things. One was an unnecessary embitterment of feelings between Americans and Californios, in violation of the United States government's policy and best interests. The other was an enhancement of his own somewhat spurious popular reputation as a patriot and hero.

The Mexican War and California

The causes of the Mexican War were complex and are still disputed. Only a brief sketch of its general background is necessary here. In the 10 years since the establishment of the Republic of Texas in 1836, Mexico had never recognized it as independent. In February 1845 the American Congress passed a joint resolution inviting Texas to join the American Union. Mexico regarded the prospective American annexation of Texas as a hostile act and broke off diplomatic relations with the United States, threatening war but not declaring it. President Herrera prudently feared that a war would not only fail to regain Texas but also lose California and New Mexico. He hinted that he would receive an American minister. After Slidell had reached Mexico City, Herrera changed his mind, but the report that he had even considered receiving an American negotiator led to his overthrow by General Paredes.

Mexico was particularly bitter at the claim of Texas that its southern boundary was the Rio Grande, rather than the Nueces River, some distance to the north. On April 7, 1846, President Polk learned of Mexico's refusal to receive Slidell. The next day General Zachary Taylor was ordered to cross the Nueces and occupy the disputed zone. Soon several Americans were killed in skirmishes with Mexican troops. With this news in hand, Polk asked Congress to declare that a state of war existed by hostile action of Mexico. Congress did so, and Polk signed the declaration on May 13, 1846.

Several months earlier, Secretary of the Navy Bancroft had instructed Commodore John D. Sloat of the Pacific squadron that in the event of war with Mexico he was to occupy such ports in California as he considered necessary for the establishment of American authority in the province. In June, at Mazatlán, Sloat received definite but still unofficial reports that the United States and Mexico were at war. On July 2 he anchored at Monterey but hesitated lest he repeat the embarrassing mistake of Commodore Jones. He offered to fire a salute to the Mexican flag, an honor which the port authorities declined because they lacked the powder to return it. The presidio at Monterey had three guns, all of different caliber, and the California navy consisted of one small vessel with no guns.

After 5 days' delay, Sloat made up for his hesitancy on July 7 by issuing a proclamation that went so far as to declare that "henceforward California will be a portion of the United States." Although he came "in arms with a powerful force," it was not as an enemy to the people of California but "as their best friend." He painted a glowing picture of the benefits that would follow, including greater political freedom and stability, honest and efficient administration, and "a great increase in the value of real estate." Governor Pío Pico responded on July 16 with an order that all citizens of California, both naturalized and native-born, must take up arms against the invaders.

On July 23, Sloat, who had been in ill health for some time, turned over his command to Commodore Robert F. Stockton, and the tone of the occupation changed sharply. Stockton, like Frémont and Gillespie, was eager to distinguish himself by vigorous action. As one of his first acts after assuming command, Stockton mustered the "California Battalion of Mounted Riflemen" into United States service (apparently the naval service, though this has never really been clear), commissioning Frémont as major and Gillespie as captain. Stockton then issued a new, bombastic, and offensive proclamation to the people, drawn up with the advice of Frémont and Gillespie. Colonel Castro at Santa Clara and Governor Pico at Los Angeles concluded that resistance was hopeless, and both left for Mexico. In August, Los Angeles was occupied without resistance. Stockton was now able to announce that California was "entirely free from Mexican dominion," but he irritated the Angeleños by unnecessarily ordering martial law, and then made the further mistake of leaving Gillespie in charge with a small garrison.

The inhabitants of Los Angeles were not accustomed to strict maintenance of order, and Gillespie's rules were oppressive and arbitrary. The order for a curfew, for example, was highly unrealistic. When some of the more disorderly elements behaved with their customary exuberance, Gillespie began to treat them as rebels before they had actually thought of rebellion. They soon thought of it, and Captain José María Flores and several other officers led a revolt that spread rapidly throughout southern California.

On September 24, Gillespie was besieged on Fort Hill near the Los Angeles plaza, but his courier managed to get through to inform Stockton at San Francisco.

Soon afterward Gillespie surrendered under terms that permitted him to march his men to San Pedro for embarkation. At San Pedro, however, they met a relief force of marines and sailors who had arrived from San Francisco and who now joined them for a march back toward Los Angeles. The way was hot and dusty, and the Americans traveled on foot because the rebels had rounded up all the horses in the region.

About 15 miles inland, at Domínguez Rancho on October 8, the Americans encountered a force led by José Antonio Carrillo, well-mounted and equipped with a surprisingly effective cannon. This had long been used to fire salutes at the Los Angeles plaza on festive occasions. Before the town's surrender to Stockton, it had been buried in the garden of Señora Inocencia Reyes. Dug up and lashed to the running gear of a wagon, it proved a deadly weapon, and the "battle of the Old Woman's Gun" was a brilliant victory for the Californios. The Americans suffered a number of casualties and withdrew to San Pedro, leaving Los Angeles in rebel hands for 3 months more. As María de la Guerra observed, "the taking of the country did not please the *Californios* at all, and least of all the women."

In June, at Fort Leavenworth, General Stephen Watts Kearny had received instructions from the secretary of war to occupy New Mexico and then proceed to California to organize a military and civil government there. Kearny occupied Santa Fé without resistance and set out for California with 300 dragoons. On the way, unfortunately, he met Kit Carson, whom Stockton had sent eastward in August with the premature news that California was peacefully and firmly in American hands. Kearny sent most of his force back and continued with only about 100 men. When they reached southern California, they had come 2000 miles in one of the longest and most difficult marches in U.S. Army history. They were exhausted and half-starved, and most of their mounts had been worn out and replaced with mules or unbroken horses.

Several hours before dawn on December 6, Kearny was encamped near the Indian village of San Pasqual, about 35 miles northeast of San Diego, when he learned that a rebel detachment was in the village. Carson assured him that the Californians were cowards who would not and could not fight. Hoping to capture the rebels' horses, Kearny roused his men for an immediate advance in the darkness, cold, and fog. The wretched mounts of the dragoons moved with varying speeds, and the rebels, under Andrés Pico, lured them into a pursuit until they were strung out, then suddenly turned to attack them.

The American cavalry sabers were hopelessly ineffective against the Californian lances, wielded by men whom Kearny well described as "admirably mounted and the very best riders in the world; hardly one that is not fit for the circus." Practically all the casualties were on the American side—22 killed, including several officers, and 16 wounded, among them Kearny himself.

In spite of their impressive achievements on the battlefield, the rebels were weakened by the usual chronic dissensions, by a shortage of powder, and by their gradual abandonment of hope that they could hold out until Mexico should be victorious over the United States in the main theaters of war. A joint force under Stockton and Kearny recaptured Los Angeles on January 10, 1847, after minor skirmishes.

A romanticized depiction of the battle of San Pasqual, 1846. The figure shrouded in smoke beneath the American flag is presumably General Kearny, wounded in battle. Note the lances of the charging Californios. (*Courtesy of the California Historical Society, FN-12646.*)

Flores now fled to Sonora, and Andrés Pico chose to surrender the rebel forces to Frémont, who had reached the San Fernando Valley from the north. Frémont was flattered at being the officer who now received the final surrender, and by the terms of the Capitulation of Cahuenga on January 13, 1847, he extended full pardon to all the rebels. The surrender at Cahuenga ended organized resistance to the American occupation. It also marked the beginning of a series of bitter disputes over the question of who was now in command and who was authorized to act as military and civil governor.

Commodore Stockton still considered himself in charge, and before sailing for further operations on the west coast of Mexico, he appointed Frémont his successor as governor of California. General Kearny refused to recognize this appointment and regarded Frémont as under his own command. Frémont was able to persuade himself that authority he had received from a commodore in the Navy should prevail over the orders of a brigadier general in the Army who was now his own immediate superior. On this basis Frémont rashly assumed the powers of governor and repeatedly defied military orders from General Kearny. Frémont's defiance of authority led to a court-martial in which he was found guilty of disobedience of orders and sentenced to dismissal from the service. President Polk approved the verdict but remitted the penalty. Bitterly, Frémont refused this executive clemency and resigned his commission. Popular opinion generally supported Frémont. In the eyes of the American people in the 1840s, insubordination was not a very serious offense.

Andrés Pico (1810–1876), commander of the Californios at the
battle of San Pasqual. (*Courtesy of
the Seaver Center for Western History
Research, Natural History Museum of
Los Angeles County.*)

The war with Mexico was concluded on February 2, 1848, with the signing of the Treaty of Guadalupe Hidalgo in which Mexico ceded California and other territories to the United States. At the war's end, the land area of Mexico was reduced by half. "The armed conflict occurred for many reasons," historian Manuel Gonzales has concluded, "but mostly because Americans wanted war, or rather what war would provide. The naked truth remains that Mexico had what its northern neighbor craved—land."

Unknown to the signers of the treaty, only 9 days earlier gold had been discovered in the foothills of the Sierra Nevada. Knowledge of the discovery could have made little difference in the negotiations in any event. Mexico had been overrun by American troops and was in no position to quibble over terms of peace, even though California would now be considerably more valuable than it had yet appeared to be.

Selected Bibliography

Neal Harlow, *California Conquered: War and Peace on the Pacific, 1846–1850* (1982), analyzes American interest in California and the reasons for the American victory. Manuel Gonzales, *Mexicanos* (1999), and Norman A. Graebner, "The Mexican War: A Study in Causation," *Pacific Historical Review,* XLIX (August 1980), pp. 405–426, conclude that force was necessary for the United States to accomplish its designs on California. For a broad overview, see Jack K. Bauer, *The Mexican War, 1846–1848* (1993). Genaro Padilla, *My History, Not Yours* (1993), is richly interpretive.

Earlier American projects for peaceful acquisition are described by Robert Glass Cleland in "The Early Sentiment for the Annexation of California," *Southwestern Historical Quarterly,* XVIII (1914–1915), pp. 40, 121–161, 231–260; Harlan Hague and David J. Langum, *Thomas O. Larkin* (1990); Graebner, *Empire on the Pacific* (1955); and Frederick Merk, *Manifest Destiny and Mission in American History* (1963). See especially A. Brooke Caruso, *The Mexican Spy Company: United States Covert Operations in Mexico, 1845–1848* (1991). On rival aspirations, see John Fox, *McNamara's Irish Colony and the United States' Taking of California in 1846* (1999); Merk, *The Monroe Doctrine and American Expansionism, 1843–1849* (1966); Gene A. Smith, "The War That Wasn't: Thomas ap Catesby Jones's Seizure of Monterey," *California History,* LXVI (June 1987), pp. 104–114; and Russell M. Posner, "A British Consular Agent in California: The Reports of James A. Forbes, 1843–1846," *Southern California Quarterly,* LIII (June 1971), pp. 101–112.

The first major biography of Frémont, by Allan Nevins, was generally sympathetic. The first edition of this work bore the title *Frémont, the West's Greatest Adventurer* (two volumes, 1928). Bernard De Voto, in *The Year of Decision, 1846* (1942), deplored all adulation of Frémont, past, present, and future. But Irving Stone, with the license of the novelist, exalted Jessie and her husband in *Immortal Wife* (1944); a more balanced appraisal appears in Pamela Herr, *Jessie Benton Frémont* (1987). See also Herr and Mary Lee Spence (eds.), *The Letters of Jessie Benton Frémont* (1993). Dwight L. Clarke, in *Stephen Watts Kearny, Soldier of the West* (1961), sought to rescue Kearny from the "historical eclipse" to which he was consigned by Frémont and his admirers. See also Kenneth M. Johnson, *The Frémont Court Martial* (1968). Ferol Egan's *Frémont* (1977) is lively and engaging, but Andrew Rolle's *John Charles Frémont* (1991) is more analytical. Mary Lee Spence and Donald Jackson (eds.), *The Expeditions of John Charles Frémont* (three volumes, 1970–1984), make the original documents available.

See also Fred B. Rogers, *William Brown Ide, Bear Flagger* (1962); Werner H. Marti, *Messenger of Destiny* (1960), on Archibald Gillespie; and John A. Hawgood, "John C. Frémont and the Bear Flag Revolution," *Southern California Quarterly,* XLIX (June 1962), pp. 67–96. The conclusion of the war and its continuing legacy are described in Richard Griswold del Castillo, *The Treaty of Guadalupe Hidalgo* (1990), and Iris H. W. Engstrand and Castillo, *Culture y Cultura: Consequences of the U.S.-Mexican War* (1998).

CHAPTER 8

The Gold Rush
and Economic Development

It is ironic but understandable that the Spaniards, who had found so much gold in other parts of the hemisphere, failed entirely to find the vast treasure of the Sierra Nevada. They had seen little reason to explore the approaches to the Sierra, and even less reason to settle there, and the local Indians, if they noticed any gold, had no interest in it. During the Mexican period, a minor discovery was made in 1842 at Placerita Creek, about 35 miles northwest of Los Angeles. The first gold ever sent from California to the United States Mint came from that area, but the placers there were of trifling importance, received little attention, and were soon played out.

The subsequent discovery of gold in the foothills of the Sierra launched the greatest mass migration in the history of the United States up to that time. As news of the discovery spread across the country and around the world, California was transformed. Hundreds of thousands of gold seekers rushed to California, hoping to make their fortunes. Their coming was a foundational event, not only for the economic development of mid-nineteenth-century California, but for much of its political, social, and cultural history as well.

Marshall's Discovery at Sutter's Mill

The crucial discovery was the result, though accidental and indirect, of an American's ingenuity. James Wilson Marshall was a moody and somewhat eccentric master carpenter who had come to California in 1845. In August 1847 Marshall contracted with John A. Sutter to build a sawmill in the foothills in order to provide lumber both for Sutter's own use and for sale to immigrants. Marshall chose a site on the south fork of the American River, where there was an abundance of timber and a flow of water that looked ideal for diversion into a millrace. The site was about 45 travel miles east-northeast of Sutter's Fort, at a place called Coloma, from the Maidu Indian *culloomah,* or "beautiful vale." With a crew including several

Mormons and a number of Indian laborers, construction proceeded remarkably well. In January it appeared that the tailrace needed to be further deepened and its bottom cleared of obstructions. It was while Marshall was inspecting the progress of this work that on January 24, 1848, he saw a glittering particle, caught behind a stone beneath the water. The tailrace was, in effect, a sluice cut through a sandbar at a bend of the river, and if Marshall had actually been searching for placer gold, he could hardly have hit upon a better way of finding it.

With his glittering discovery, Marshall rode down to New Helvetia. There, behind a locked door, Sutter put the samples to several tests in the light of what he knew of the properties of the metal and what he could learn from the *American Encyclopedia.* When Sutter concluded that "it's gold—at least twenty-three-carat gold," Marshall got into such a state of feverish excitement that he insisted on riding back to Coloma in the rain in the middle of the night—the first victim of the gold mania. Sutter's behavior was somewhat less erratic; his primary concern was that the discovery would endanger the completion of his sawmill. At Coloma he persuaded the workers to continue with their task and to confine their prospecting to Sundays.

Efforts to keep the news from spreading were in vain. For example, one of the children of Mrs. Wimmer, the cook at Coloma, talked of the discovery to a teamster; then, to save her boy from being ridiculed as a liar, the good woman showed the teamster some nuggets. Sutter himself made an agreement with some Indians for a lease on the land around Coloma. In dispatching a messenger to Colonel Richard B. Mason, the military governor at Monterey, asking for validation of this agreement, Sutter not only revealed the discovery but also sent along 6 ounces of gold to prove it.

Although the news leaked out quickly enough, it attracted very little attention for several months. There had been idle rumors of gold ever since the expeditions of Drake and Vizcaíno. None had actually been found until the trivial Placerita discovery of 1842, and this suggested that although there was some gold in California, there was not enough to make it worth digging. Brief news reports of gold near New Helvetia, written with obvious lack of conviction, appeared in the two little weekly newspapers of San Francisco—one item in the *Californian* on March 15, 1848, and another in the *California Star* 10 days later—without creating any notable excitement.

The Forty-Eighters

The gold fever did not begin to be epidemic until May 12. On that day, in San Francisco, the mania that would eventually spread over the whole world was touched off deliberately and for purposes of revenue, by the enterprising merchant, manipulator, real estate speculator, and Mormon elder Samuel Brannan.

Brannan had arrived in 1846 as the leader of the California Mormons. A remarkably vigorous young man of Irish ancestry, articulate, ingenious, and highly opportunistic, he began his career as a molder of opinion and emotion by editing a journal published in New York for the Mormons of the Atlantic seaboard. When the lead-

View of San Francisco, 1847. Note that Montgomery Street was then at the bay shore. (*Courtesy of the Bancroft Library.*)

ers at Nauvoo, Illinois, determined in 1845 that the Latter-Day Saints should "flee out of Babylon," Elder Brannan, then 26 years old, was delegated to lead a party of more than 200 by ship around the Horn to California. They sailed from New York in the *Brooklyn* on February 4, 1846. As a flight from the sovereignty of the United States, this migration was frustrated by the Mexican War. When the *Brooklyn* anchored in San Francisco Bay, on July 31, 1846, it found itself alongside the U.S.S. *Portsmouth,* whose commander, Captain John B. Montgomery, had landed on the 9th to raise the American flag over Yerba Buena.

The arrival of the Brannan party tripled the population of that village. The first buildings had been erected there in 1835 when William A. Richardson, an English deserter from a whaler, had put up a shanty of rough boards. Early in 1847 Lieutenant Washington Allon Bartlett of the *Portsmouth* changed the name of Yerba Buena to San Francisco. Otherwise, the town's history had not been very eventful. No one there was as yet especially prosperous, with the exception of Samuel Brannan, who was already its leading citizen.

Brannan engaged in an assortment of business activities and investments, flagrantly putting Mormon funds to his own use and profit. Charged with embezzlement, he was the defendant in one of the first jury trials ever held in California, but the jury disagreed. He continued to gather in the tithes and to decide what should be done with the proceeds. When Brigham Young sent down a deputation from Salt Lake City to bring back "the Lord's money," Brannan said that he would turn over the money when he got a receipt signed by the Lord. Finally, Brannan's superiors in Utah "disfellowshipped," or excommunicated, him, though for some time he denied the validity of this proceeding.

One of Brannan's enterprises was a general store at Sutter's Fort. In March 1848, after customers at this store had begun to offer gold in payment for whiskey and other commodities, Brannan became aware of the reality of the discovery and of the uses to which he could put it. He spent the next several weeks in quietly purchasing every article of merchandise he could get hold of in northern California that would be in demand by gold seekers, then moving these articles to his store at New Helvetia. Then, on May 12, he came down to San Francisco, waved a bottle of gold dust in one hand and his hat in the other, and shouted, "Gold! Gold! Gold from the American River!" When samples of gold reached Monterey, on June 20, Alcalde Colton recorded that "the blacksmith dropped his hammer, the carpenter his plane, the mason his trowel, the baker his loaf, and the tapster his bottle. All were off for the mines, some on horses, some on carts, and some on crutches, and one went on a litter."

The symptoms of the craze which the sight of gold now began to produce in many men have often been described, but perhaps never more vividly than by James H. Carson:

> I looked on for a moment; a frenzy seized my soul; unbidden my legs performed some entirely new movements of polka steps—I took several—houses were too small for me to stay in; I was soon in the street in search of necessary outfits; piles of gold rose up before me at every step; castles of marble dazzling the eye with their rich appliances; thousands of slaves bowing to my beck and call; myriads of fair virgins contending with each other for my love—were among the fancies of my fevered imagination. The Rothschilds, Girards, and Astors appeared to be but poor people; in short, I had a very violent attack of the gold fever.

Within a short time nearly every town in California lost a majority of its population. On May 29 the *San Francisco Californian* complained that "The whole country, from San Francisco to Los Angeles, and from the sea shore to the base of the Sierra Nevadas, resounds with the sordid cry of gold, GOLD, GOLD! while the field is left half-planted, the house half-built, and everything neglected but the manufacture of shovels and pickaxes." The paper also announced that it was suspending publication; it had no choice, in view of the departure of its staff, subscribers, and advertisers. A few days later, the *California Star* also suspended for the same reason.

Even the California Indians did not remain immune to the lure of gold. Colonel Mason estimated in 1848 that more than half the gold diggers in the California mines were Indians. At first, many Indian miners worked as laborers for white Californians, often in a state of peonage similar to their status on the Mexican ranchos. Others labored as independent agents and traded their gold to white merchants for a variety of goods. As hostilities between Indians and whites increased, the number of Indian miners in the goldfields declined rapidly.

Soldiers and sailors deserted by the hundreds. Colonel Mason reported that he was powerless to stop desertions, especially after a soldier on a 3-week furlough found $1500 worth of gold, more than his Army pay for 5 years. Mason toured the diggings in July. Some Mormon miners asked him whether they must turn over to

Sam Brannan the tithes of their findings, which he was soliciting from them, to which the governor replied that they were required to pay as long as they were fools enough to do so.

During the summer months, the contagion began to spread to Hawaii, Oregon, and Utah, and in the fall to Mexico, Peru, and Chile. Altogether probably about 6000 gold seekers came to California from these areas in 1848. The main gold rush from "the States" did not begin until the year of the discovery was almost over.

The Forty-Niners

In September 1848, Lieutenant Edward F. Beale arrived in Washington with reports and also with some actual specimens of gold, sent by Larkin. This led to many newspaper comments and to fairly wide discussion, but as yet few planned to leave for California. The spread of the gold craze over the whole country came after the sending of President Polk's annual message to Congress on December 5. Polk welcomed the news as a justification of his policies in acquiring the Mexican cession. As evidence, the president appended Colonel Mason's report of his personal tour of the diggings, in which Mason asserted that there was enough gold "in the country drained by the Sacramento and San Joaquin Rivers" to pay the cost of the Mexican War "a hundred times over." Two days later Lieutenant Lucien Loeser arrived at the capital with a tea caddy crammed with 230 ounces of gold. Placed on display at the War Department, this soon drew excited crowds.

The mania for sudden wealth now pervaded all classes, and the urge to be off to the goldfields stimulated many related industries. One of these was the hasty publication of alleged guidebooks of varying degrees of fraudulence, most of them derived, at best, largely from Mason's report, along with some fragments of the writings of Larkin, Frémont, and Lansford W. Hastings. One such opus, published in New York in December 1848, was *The Emigrant's Guide to the Gold Mines . . . ,*

Transcontinental air travel existed only in fantasy during the gold rush, but Rufus Porter reported in 1849 that he was "making active progress in the construction of Aerial Transport, for the express purpose of carrying passengers between New York and California." (*Courtesy of the California Historical Society, North Baker Research Library, FN-30706.*)

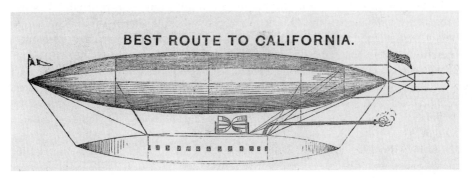

BEST ROUTE TO CALIFORNIA.

30 pages long and selling for 25 cents, or 12½ cents without the map; the latter alternative was the better buy, because the map was entirely worthless. Another item, of 1849 vintage, was *The Digger's Handbook and Truth about California,* by one D. L. Sydney. In penciled insertions on the title page of a surviving copy of this work, some disillusioned purchaser identified the author's initials, D. L., as "Damn Liar."

There were three main routes to the goldfields: by way of the Isthmus of Panama, around Cape Horn, or overland. The sea routes drew the heavy traffic in the first months of the great rush in the winter and early spring of 1849 because they were open all year round, although in the long run more than twice as many gold seekers would go to California by land as by sea. Before 1849 the Cape Horn route had been the most traveled one, but it covered a distance of about 18,000 nautical miles and took 5 to 8 months, and thus the Panama shortcut suddenly became attractive to thousands who feared that all the gold might be gone before they could arrive to claim their share of it.

Moreover, it happened that a new passenger service on the Panama route was just becoming available. Three 1000-ton paddle-wheel steamers were built for the run from Panama to California and Oregon. The first of these, the *California,* left New York in October 1848. When she arrived in Panama in January, she found 700 Americans clamoring to get aboard. They had traveled by ship to Chagres, by small boat up the fever-infested Chagres River, and by mule the rest of the way across the isthmus. The *California*'s rated capacity was not more than 250. After days of intensive ticket scalping, the *California* sailed with about 400 on board. During most of 1849, because of delays at Panama, the average time from New York to San Francisco by this route was 3 to 5 months, though by 1850 increased service in the Pacific had reduced it to 6 to 8 weeks.

Of the Argonauts who chose to travel around the Horn, many were organized in joint-stock companies, both for the voyage and in the expectation of working together in mining operations after their arrival. These companies usually purchased old ships, which they fondly supposed they could sell in California. Actually, most of these vessels joined the fleet of several hundred hulks that were abandoned to settle gradually into the mud along the San Francisco waterfront, and nearly all the companies disintegrated into smaller groups more suitable for prospecting. The removal from service of the hundreds of obsolete old vessels at the same time that the gold rush was stimulating the building of the clipper ships made the early 1850s the golden age of the American merchant marine. The new California clippers were designed to carry premium freight at maximum speed. They were much less important for carrying passengers, who found them highly uncomfortable. In 1851 the maiden voyage of Donald McKay's *Flying Cloud* set a record of 89 days from New York to San Francisco, a record that held for over a century. (The record was beaten in 1989 when an ultralight racing yacht, *Thursday's Child,* using computerized weather maps and high-tech equipment, made the voyage in just under 81 days.)

A majority of the forty-niners traveled overland, especially those from the Ohio and Mississippi valleys. The main route was the California Trail, by way of the

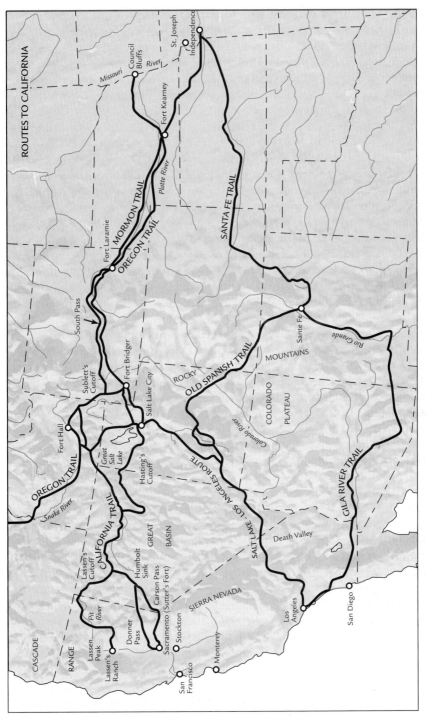

Overland routes to California, 1849. (Adapted from California Patterns: A Geographical and Historical Atlas, by David Hornbeck. Copyright 1983 by the Mayfield Publishing Company.)

Platte, South Pass, and Humboldt. This route was already well-established by the earlier emigrants, but for each person who followed it in 1848 there were 50 in 1849, some of them in wagon trains miles long. Between the Rockies and the Sierra, the loss of oxen and horses was dreadful because the great trek used up all the grass within easy reach of the trail. By the time they reached the 40 miles of unbroken desert southwest of the Humboldt Sink, many were no longer concerned to save their property, but only their lives, and the trail was littered with an almost incredible miscellany of discarded articles. There was very little danger from hostile Indians at this time, but there was a major epidemic of Asiatic cholera. The disease was not only agonizing and usually fatal but also peculiarly terrifying because medical science had not yet discovered that it was transmitted mainly through the contamination of drinking water, and those who tended the sick or came anywhere near them imagined that the ghastly affliction might be spread in various other ways.

Besides the three main arteries of travel, a number of alternate routes attracted smaller contingents. Some crossed the isthmus by way of Nicaragua rather than Panama. There were several fairly important southern trails, not only across Texas and New Mexico but also across old Mexico. A number of forty-niners branched off from the main California Trail by going southwest from Salt Lake to southern California, and, from some who rashly attempted a shortcut from this route, Death Valley earned its name. Others turned north of the Sierra and into the upper end of the Sacramento Valley by way of the Pit River. This roundabout way, known as Lassen's Cutoff, was as outrageously misnamed as Hastings' Cutoff, and in general Peter Lassen and Lansford Hastings were about equally incompetent as guides. The majority chose a direct route through the central Sierra, though many were frightened by the reputation of Donner Pass and instead used Carson Pass about 20 miles south of Lake Tahoe. (See Color Plate 6.)

The Diggings

Before the end of 1849, miners were swarming over the foothill region between the Yuba River in the north and Mariposa in the south, the region now appropriately traversed by California State Highway 49. Within this area lay the *mother lode,* or principal deposit, in a continuous belt extending about 120 miles from a point north of Coloma to a point near Mariposa and varying in width from a few hundred feet to 2 miles. This network of thousands of veins of gold was formed when the Sierra Nevada was being created. In the intense heat generated by subduction, mineral-rich solutions flowed up into fissures in the granitic rock. Erosion then tore loose particles of gold and washed them into the rivers, where they lodged on sandbars, behind stones, or in potholes in the banks or streambeds. These particles were known as *placer* gold, from a Spanish word meaning a place near the bank of a stream where alluvial gold could be found.

The miners spoke loosely of the "mother lode country" as including not only the great vein of ore still embedded in the rocks but also the larger area where placer gold had been deposited. The Mokelumne River, separating Amador and

Calaveras counties, was the approximate boundary between the "northern mines" and the "southern mines." There were also some fairly important gold-bearing areas in other parts of California, particularly in the regions of Mount Shasta and the Trinity and Klamath rivers, where a new rush began in 1850. Lesser discoveries were also made in several isolated parts of southern California.

Early Mining Methods

Very few Americans had any previous experience in gold mining. New Spain had its first major gold rush at Zacatecas in 1548, three full centuries earlier. Spanish miners in Mexico and Peru developed a number of advanced techniques of mining. In fact, there were dozens of Spanish-Mexican mining terms that had no English equivalents and which were soon put to use by the Americans in California. *Placer* was only the most familiar of these; other examples included *bonanza,* or rich ore, and *borrasca,* or barren rock. In the United States, there was a gold mining industry of modest importance in Georgia and the Carolinas during the first half of the nineteenth century, and several veterans of these southern Appalachian diggings brought important knowledge of mining methods to California. The first was Isaac Humphrey, from Georgia, who was at Sutter's Fort at the time of the discovery. Arriving at Coloma a few weeks later and finding the early prospectors still using nothing more than their knives and spoons, he introduced them to the pan and then to the rocker, or cradle.

Of the various devices that used the movement of water to separate particles of gold from sand, gravel, and clay, the simplest was a flat-bottomed pan made of iron or tin. A quantity of what was hoped to be "pay dirt," obtained with the pick and shovel, was tossed into the pan, thoroughly wetted and stirred, and the rocks or pebbles picked out of it. Then the miner held the pan under the surface of a pool or stream and swirled it about with a gently rotating motion for at least 10 minutes, one side of the pan held a little higher than the other, until the clay and nearly all of the sand were washed away. Gold being heavier, particles of it remained in the bottom.

The lure of the gold rush was the prospect of acquiring wealth quickly and easily—by lucky chance rather than hard work. But panning for gold turned out to be one of the most exhausting forms of manual labor ever devised. To the hard work with pick and shovel, panning added the necessity of squatting or stooping in the burning sun, either beside the icy water or in it, for hours, while moving the wrist, arm, and shoulder muscles and concentrating attention very carefully on the overflow.

The first improvement on the pan was the rocker, an oblong box without a top, several feet in length, mounted on rockers like a child's cradle and placed in a sloping position. It was open at the lower end, while above the upper end there was a hopper with a sieve. Three people usually worked together, one shoveling dirt into the hopper, another pouring buckets of water to wash the dirt down through the trough, and a third vigorously rocking the cradle. Thus, the gold was trapped behind the *riffles,* or cleats, nailed at intervals along the bottom. No part of the operation

African American miner with a Long Tom in Auburn Ravine, Placer County, 1852. (*Courtesy of the California Historical Society, FN-13679.*)

of a rocker was as uncomfortable as panning, and some relief from the monotony of the labor could be had by exchanging jobs. Although much of the finer gold slid over the cleats and was lost, the average return was higher than in panning because a much larger quantity of dirt could be processed in a day.

Near the end of 1849, the *Long Tom,* a trough for washing possible pay dirt, appeared as an enlargement and a considerable improvement of the rocker. The tom was usually about 12 feet long, stationary, and placed where a stream of water could be run through it from a ditch or a wooden flume. This eliminated both the pouring of water and the rocking of the cradle. About a year later, the Long Tom evolved into a sluice, a whole series of riffle boxes fitted together into a continuous string, sometimes as much as several hundred feet in length. This device, though commonly employed even in ancient times, seems to have been reinvented in California. In an important related development, a wing dam was built partway across a stream to divert a flow of water into a sluice; sometimes an entire river was dammed and turned aside to expose the pay dirt in a section of the streambed. The reason such relatively efficient methods were so slow in appearing was that they required fairly large groups of men to work together, and in the first 2 years the miners were so intensely individualistic that the industry was still at most a small-business operation.

The final separation of gold from the sand and other dross was often accomplished by the use of mercury, or quicksilver, which has the property of amalgamating with gold. When this amalgam is heated in a closed vessel, the mercury vaporizes. Thus separated from the gold, the mercury can also be recovered, as soon as it cools again from vapor to liquid. Fortunately, quicksilver had been found in 1845 at New Almaden in the hills a few miles south of San José. Unfortunately, many mercury compounds are extremely poisonous and can cause illness or death. Fish and other aquatic organisms were poisoned by unrecovered quicksilver, and later by cyanide, used to separate gold.

Mining Camp Law

The primary concern of the early California miners with legal problems was in the regulation of mining claims. Because the mining camps had sprung up beyond the reach of any established law, they had to adopt their own regulations. Practically none of the land in the gold region had passed into private hands, and the rights of the Indians were ignored. California was in the midst of a peculiarly awkward transition from Mexican to American sovereignty. Congress had not provided for the extension of American territorial government to any part of the Mexican cession, and even if it had, there was no federal mining law that would have been relevant to the California mining camps, because no precious metal had ever been discovered before on public lands of the United States.

In devising their own mining codes, the Argonauts were acting in a tradition of American frontier self-government that went all the way back to the Mayflower Compact. In each camp there was a mass meeting to organize a *mining district* and elect a committee to draw up a set of regulations. Eventually more than 500 camps adopted such codes. Each code defined the permissible size of a claim and required that it be continuously worked if it was to remain valid. Thus, the title was merely usufructuary, not a title to ownership of the land but merely to the use of it for mining purposes. Each district elected a recorder, variously called an "arbitrator" or "chairman," and often its only officer. His duties were to keep the register of claims and to settle disputes arising from charges of claim jumping, sometimes with the assistance of a panel of arbitrators chosen by the contestants.

As described thus far, the plan was highly reasonable and highly democratic. A far less admirable aspect of the codes was that many of them included *restrictive covenants* barring Mexicans, Asians, or other foreigners. Still other problems of the mining camps arose from the extemporized administration of criminal justice, such as lynching and vigilantism. But racial oppression directed against foreigners and Indians in early American California and extralegal methods for the punishment of crime are the subjects of other chapters.

From an Adventure to a Profession

"The miners are beginning to discover," said the *Alta California* in the autumn of 1851, "that they are engaged in a science and a profession, and not in a mere adventure." Within a few years, the gold in the beds and banks of the streams and in surface outcroppings of quartz was inevitably depleted. Rich deposits of the metal lay far below the surface in solid rock or deep in the gravelly hillsides, but mining them required the use of engineering techniques that demanded heavy equipment and substantial amounts of capital.

In extracting gold from solid rock, through processes variously described as quartz, vein, or lode mining, the auriferous rock taken from a mine shaft or tunnel had to be crushed to a fine powder. After an assortment of ingenious contraptions had proved worthless, better results were obtained with more traditional devices, of which the most important was the stamp mill. Dating at least as far back as the sixteenth century in Europe, this was essentially a large mechanized version of the mortar and pestle.

Another machine important in quartz mining was a mule-powered contrivance developed in Latin America and called an *arrastre,* usually anglicized as "arrastra." A mule, plodding around a circular track, moved a horizontal shaft extending from a central post that served as a pivot, and heavy abrasive stones attached to the shaft were thus dragged over the gold-bearing material. It was difficult to grind the ore fine enough, and often less than half the gold actually contained in the crushed rock could be separated from it by quicksilver amalgamation. Sometimes the pulverized rock, mixed with water, was made to flow over coarse blankets so that fine particles of gold were caught in the cloth. The legend of the golden fleece had probably originated in the application of this method to sheepskin in ancient times.

Another major source of gold lay in Tertiary gravels. During the Tertiary geologic era, a great river flowed through the region of the northern mines, laying down an immense bed of gravel containing scattered flakes of gold. Later, when the whole region was thrust up to become part of the Sierra Nevada, new rivers—the Feather, the Yuba, the Bear, and the American—began to flow transversely through the bed of the older one. Much of that bed, however, was now on hilltops and hillsides that had since been gradually covered over with debris. Access to these gravel deposits came with the introduction of hydraulic mining, in which an entire hillside could be washed loose by directing powerful streams of water against it. For this purpose, in 1853, a former sailmaker named Anthony Chabot constructed a canvas hose, and a Connecticut Yankee named Edward E. Matteson invented a tapered nozzle of sheet iron. Thus, "hydraulicking" was born. As the placers gave out and the river-mining communities declined, hydraulic-mining towns like Dutch Flat, Iowa Hill, and Gold Run sprang up and flourished.

Part of the financing required by the expensive quartz and hydraulic operations came from joint-stock companies organized by working miners, but for men of small capital the chances for profit steadily declined. Many of those who remained in the industry were employed by increasingly large corporations, which tended to hire Americans as specialists in management and the handling of equipment and machinery while employing Chinese and Mexicans for less-skilled labor. By 1873 there were fewer than 30,000 individuals engaged in gold mining, of whom three-fifths were Chinese.

Hydraulicking. (*Courtesy of the Bancroft Library.*)

An Economic Multiplier

The impact of the gold rush on other economic activities has long been a subject of speculation and debate among historians. Gerald D. Nash has argued recently that the gold rush helped trigger pivotal economic changes: "In the language of economists, it served as a multiplier—an event that accelerated a chain of interrelated consequences, all of which accelerated economic growth."

Yet the impact of the gold rush on California agriculture was decidedly mixed. The cultivation of crops was brought to a near standstill in the early years of the gold rush as people and capital moved into mining. The insecurity of land titles and the unfamiliarity of such peculiar farming conditions as rainless summers further retarded agricultural development. Fruit and vegetable production in the gold-rush era was significant only in confirming the extraordinary potential of California soils and climate. Cultivation eventually would expand, of course, to meet the needs of a growing population. But the food supply of the Argonauts was largely imported; the main exception was California beef, salted or driven to the mining camps on the hoof.

Cattle ranching boomed temporarily following the gold discovery and then entered a period of steep decline. In 1846 there had been about 400,000 cattle in Alta California, worth about $4 a head. At the end of 1849, the price reached $500 a head at Sacramento, and for years afterward it was more than $50. Large herds were driven overland from the lower Mississippi valley and the southwest, thus increasing the stock and, to a degree, improving the breeds. In 1860 the number of cattle in the state was more than 3 million, but 2 years of disastrous drought, from

1862 to 1864, nearly wiped out the herds and the industry. The great drought marked the transition from the "age of grass" to an age of grain, and wheat then replaced beef as the state's most important agricultural product.

The multiplier effect of the gold rush was more clearly evident in the development of early California manufacturing. The needs of miners for great quantities of lumber made sawmills the foremost branch of manufacturing in the gold-rush era. Wooden sluices and flumes were indispensable in the more advanced states of placer and hydraulic mining, as were heavy timbers in the underground operations of the quartz and silver mines. Moreover, construction in the towns and fencing in the rural areas were generally of wood. Redwood, a raw material of splendid quality and supposedly inexhaustible quantity, was available to meet these demands. In 1860 Mendocino County produced 35 million feet of lumber, mostly redwood, and Humboldt and Santa Cruz counties milled 30 and 10 million feet, respectively.

Flour milling grew and flourished along with the increasing production of wheat. The development of mills for the making of coarse woolen cloth was similarly interrelated with the spread of sheep raising, while tanneries and the making of heavy leather goods were encouraged by the plentiful supply of cowhides. Another important infant industry was the making of wagons and carriages, with the outstanding shops being those of John Studebaker at Placerville and Phineas Banning at Wilmington. Claus Spreckels and William T. Coleman emerged as leaders in the refining of sugarcane from the Pacific islands. In iron manufactures the leading establishment was the Union Iron Works at San Francisco, founded in 1849 and using imported iron. The absence of any important deposits of either iron or coal in California remained a deterrent to the growth of manufacturing.

The development of banking faced serious obstacles during the gold rush. To most Californians, as to most Americans in the years since the disastrous nationwide panic of 1837, "bank" was a hated word, for it seemed to mean primarily a corporation enjoying the special legal privilege of printing and issuing notes that circulated as paper money. This privilege had, indeed, been much abused in the older states. Most of the paper money in circulation throughout the country had been issued by hundreds of separate banking corporations chartered by special acts of state legislatures. The notes of these so-called state banks were unregulated either by government or by specie reserves, and many people had been swindled by receiving payments in such depreciated paper. Every new state constitution, including that of California, which was adopted in the mid-nineteenth century, included a provision prohibiting the legislature from "granting any charter for banking purposes." In California the presence of gold in great quantities made possible its use as the dominant medium of exchange, and for many decades even large financial transactions in California were likely to be conducted in piles of gold coins, especially the $20 gold pieces known as double eagles.

Thus, the state's constitutional ban against the issuance of banknotes as paper money caused relatively little trouble. But in a growing economy the need for savings, lending, and investment institutions was so great that their existence was inevitable. The main effect of the state's provisions against chartering banks was simply to confine the banking business to entirely private concerns, without any particular legal sanction and without any public regulation. In the early mining camps, banking arrangements were often very simple; saloonkeepers frequently doubled as bankers. For many years after the gold rush, a great deal of the banking was done as a sideline by firms engaged in other businesses, notably express companies, real estate brokers, and merchandisers of all sorts.

Under the circumstances, the wonder is that banking failures and defalcations were not more common. In the early 1850s, flush times and fantastic rates of interest made the lending of money immediately profitable. But a panic began in 1855, touched off by the collapse of the San Francisco branch of a Saint Louis express and banking concern. The panic spread quickly, bringing ruin to several other banking agencies. Adams & Company had been weakened by ruthless competition from Wells Fargo, the western branch of the powerful American Express. When Adams & Company went down in the California panic of 1855, there was such a run on the offices of Wells Fargo, that even this giant of early western finance had to resort to a temporary suspension of payments.

The Historical Significance of the Gold Rush

The traditional view of the gold rush describes it as the most fortunate as well as the most significant factor in the whole of California's history. It can be cogently argued, however, that in the long run the state would have been better off if it had contained no gold at all, that because of its other advantages it would eventually have become just as populous and prosperous, and that in the meantime its social evolution would have been not only more gradual, but also far more orderly and civilized.

Obviously the lure of sudden wealth brought an early and rapid influx of population. At the beginning of 1848 California's population other than Indians was less than 15,000. According to the federal census of 1850 it was about 93,000, but this census had a number of notorious defects, the most glaring of which was that all the returns for San Francisco, Contra Costa, and Santa Clara counties were lost. The state took its own census in 1852 and counted 223,856. For 1860 the regular census figure was more than 380,000, and for 1870 more than 560,000. Because the small proportion of women made California's birthrate lower than its death rate, immigration was obviously responsible for the remarkable growth in population. And in these years, the search for economic opportunity was by far the most important force in bringing newcomers to California.

At the end of 1848, about 6000 miners had obtained $10 million worth of gold. In 1849 the amount produced was two or three times as large, but there were more than 40,000 miners to share in it, and thus the individual miner's average daily return declined radically. In 1852, the peak year, the output was close to $80 million and the number of miners about 100,000. The state's gold production then decreased year by year until 1865, when it was less than $18 million. At that point it stabilized, continuing to average about $17 million a year until the turn of the century. During the 100 years after the beginning of the gold rush, the output of California gold totaled approximately $2 billion. All the gold produced in a century was worth less than the value of 1 year's agricultural output of the state in the

1960s, and much of the gold was ultimately destined to be put back into the ground, in the Treasury Department's hoard at Fort Knox.

Meanwhile, much of California was left ravished. Historian Raymond Dasmann has credited the gold rush with accelerating an ongoing process of environmental degradation. Habitats were destroyed; species were depleted. The mania for gold seemed to grant the miners an "unlimited license to create environmental havoc." Hydraulic mining caused the most visible damage, destroying hillsides, streams, rivers, and watersheds. "It was the gold rush," Dasmann has concluded, "that set off the destructive, furious search for the yellow metal that later brought the moving of mountains and filling of valleys." The tortured landscape left behind stands today as "a monument to greed."

It may be granted that if there had been no gold discovery, Oregon would probably have been ready for admission as a state before California was. The first transcontinental railroad might have been built to Oregon. But if California's first transcontinental railroad had been built later, it might have been in the hands of a somewhat less rapacious group of men and it might have obtained less of a stranglehold on the state's economy and politics.

The notion that the Argonauts came to California as pioneers and commonwealth builders is a myth. The great majority of them came in the hope that they could quickly plunder California of its treasure and return to their homes. Many of the forty-niners were young married men hoping to make enough to return to their wives and children with financial security. Most of those who remained in California did so because they failed to accumulate even enough to get them back home. On the whole they were unsuccessful, disillusioned, embittered men.

Women accounted for only about 2 percent of the California-bound Argonauts in 1849, but within a decade they made up half of some wagon trains. Most women on the overland trail maintained traditional roles, doing the "women's work" of cooking and washing and tending the children. Once in California, however, they were able to break the bonds of domesticity and to enjoy a greater freedom than they had known back home. This emerging independence was registered in a divorce rate that was the highest in the nation. Women on the California frontier also became proprietors of a variety of enterprises, and some even adopted unorthodox clothing as a symbol of their liberation from prior constraints. "I commenced my new business in my ordinary long dress," wrote Eliza Farnham about her days as a pioneer farmer in Santa Cruz, "but its extreme inconvenience induced me, after the second day, to try the suit I had worn at home in gymnastic exercises. . . . When I had once put it on, I could never get back into skirts during working hours." Women remained a rarity in most gold-rush communities. They represented about one-twelfth of the state's population according to the census of 1850, increased only to one-third in 1880, and did not equal the number of men until 1900.

The hard labor, the shockingly inflated prices, and the prevalence of sickness and of homesickness all added to the widespread sense of desperation that so many gold-rush diaries record. Often there were efforts to find relief in a desperate kind of humor, as in the naming of such camps as Hell's Delight, Gouge Eye, Poker Flat, Devil's Retreat, Murderers' Bar, Poverty Hill, and Gomorrah, and in the orga-

Hope and grim determination are in evidence in this rare daguerreotype showing a woman in the diggings at Auburn Ravine in 1852. (*Courtesy of the California State Library.*)

nization of the Ancient and Honorable Order of E Clampus Vitus, or "the Clampers." The derivation of the name of this miners' fraternal society is unknown; there are no records of its early meetings, it is said, because they were devoted so largely to hard drinking that no one was ever in condition to keep minutes, or able the next day to recall what had happened. In general, however, there was tragedy rather than humor or romance in the drinking, gambling, and vice in which many miners sought escape from the hardships and anxieties of "seeing the elephant," as the experience of mining came to be called.

Historian Malcolm Rohrbough, author of *Days of Gold* (1997), has captured the essence of the experience in the simplest terms: "The California gold rush was about wealth." Philosopher Josiah Royce, born in the gold-rush town of Grass Valley, earlier had recognized the power of the forces set loose: "All our brutal passions were here to have full sweep, and all our moral strength, all our courage, our patience, our docility, and our social skills were to contend with these our passions." The gold rush was the product of a kind of mass hysteria, and it set a tone for California and created a state of mind in which greed predominated and disorder and violence were all too frequent.

Selected Bibliography

J. S. Holliday's *The World Rushed In: The California Gold Rush Experience* (1981) is a combination of biography and epic narrative. Other good general accounts include Holliday, *Rush for Riches* (1999); Malcolm Rohrbough, *Days of Gold* (1997); Paula Mitchell Marks, *Precious Dust* (1994); Donald Dale Jackson, *Gold Dust* (1980); and John W. Caughey, *The California Gold Rush* (1975). Rodman W. Paul, *California Gold* (1947), stresses the technological, economic, and legal aspects; see also his later work, *Mining Frontiers of the Far West, 1848–1880* (1963). For a comparative analysis of the gold rushes in California and Australia, see David Goodman, *Gold Seeking* (1994).

On the discovery itself, see Theressa Gay, *James Marshall, Discoverer of California Gold* (1967), and Rodman W. Paul (ed.), *The California Gold Discovery* (1966). Paul Bailey, *Sam Brannan and the California Mormons* (1953), deals with Brannan's role. Barry L. Dutka, "New York Discovers Gold in California," *California History,* LXIII (Fall 1984), pp. 313–319, and Ralph P. Bieber, "California Gold Mania," *Mississippi Valley Historical Review,* XXXV (June 1948), pp. 3–28, describe the excitement in the east.

Three useful bibliographical guides are available: Robert L. Santos (ed.), *The Gold Rush of California* (1998); Gary F. Kurutz (ed.), *The California Gold Rush* (1997); and Robert H. Becker (ed.), *The Plains and the Rockies* (1982). The most comprehensive survey is Unruh, cited in Chapter 6, but see also Mary Gordon (ed.), *Overland to California* (1983), and George R. Stewart, *The California Trail* (1962). The diet of the forty-niners is examined in Joseph R. Conlin, *Bacon, Beans, and Galantine Truffles* (1985). David Rich Lewis, "Argonauts and the Overland Trail Experience: Method and Theory," *Western Historical Quarterly,* XVI (July 1985), pp. 285–306, offers a systematic content analysis of diaries kept by men on the way west. Mortality on the overland trail is the subject of Robert W. Carter, "'Sometimes When I Hear the Winds Sigh,'" *California History,* LXXIV (Summer 1995), pp. 146–161.

Several studies have focused on the role of women in the great migration: John Mack Faragher, *Women and Men on the Overland Trail* (1979); Sandra Myers, *Ho for California!* (1980); Lillian Schlissel, *Women's Diaries of the Westward Journey* (1982); Ruth B. Moynihan (ed.), *So Much to Be Done* (1990); and JoAnn Levy, *They Saw the Elephant: Women in the California Gold Rush* (1990). A special issue of the *Pacific Historical Review,* LXI (November 1992), is devoted to western women's history. See also the groundbreaking analysis in Susan Lee Johnson, *Roaring Camp: The Social World of the California Gold Rush* (2000).

The story of the seagoing Argonauts has been told in Charles R. Schultz, *Forty-Niners 'round the Horn* (1999); James P. Delgado, *To California by Sea* (1990); and Oscar Lewis, *Sea Routes to the Gold Fields* (1949).

Some of the best descriptions of life in the diggings are in Marlene Smith-Baranzini (ed.), *The Shirley Letters from the California Mines* (1998); Frank Marryat, *Mountains and Molehills* (1855, 1962); Sarah Royce, *A Frontier Lady* (1932); Josiah Royce, *California . . . A Study of American Character* (1886, 1948); and Charles H. Shinn, *Mining Camps* (1885, 1948). Hubert Howe Bancroft's social history of the gold rush is *California Inter Pocula* (1888). Views of the darker side include George Payson, *Golden Dreams and Leaden Realities* (1853), and Hinton R. Helper, *The Land of Gold: Reality versus Fiction* (1855).

On aspects of legal history, see John P. Reid, *Law for the Elephant: Property and Social Behavior on the Overland Trail* (1980), and John Umbeck, "The California Gold Rush: A Study of Emerging Property Rights," *Explorations in Economic History,* XIV (July 1977), pp. 197–226.

The broader economic aspects are analyzed in several essays in James J. Rawls and Richard J. Orsi (eds.), *A Golden State* (1999); see especially Gerald D. Nash, "A Veritable

Revolution: The Global Economic Significance of the California Gold Rush," and Raymond F. Dasmann, "Environmental Changes before and after the Gold Rush." The rise of hydraulic mining is described in Sherwood D. Burgess, *The Water King, Anthony Chabot* (1992), and in the first chapter of Robert L. Kelley, *Gold vs. Grain* (1959). See also David J. St. Clair, "New Almaden and California Quicksilver in the Pacific Rim Economy," *California History,* LXXIII (Winter 1994/1995), pp. 278–295.

On cattle ranching, see Robert G. Cleland, *The Cattle on a Thousand Hills* (1941); John W. Caughey, "Don Benito Wilson," *Huntington Library Quarterly,* II (April 1939), pp. 285–300; and James M. Jensen, "Cattle Drives from the Ranchos to the Gold Fields of California," *Arizona and the West,* II (Winter 1960), pp. 341–352. On the development of California agriculture, see Lawrence J. Jelinek, *Harvest Empire* (1979); Paul W. Gates, *California Ranchos and Farms, 1846–1862* (1947); and Gerald L. Prescott, "Farm Gentry vs. the Grangers: Conflict in Rural America," *California Historical Quarterly,* LVI (Winter 1977/78), pp. 328–345. Especially useful is Richard J. Orsi (comp.), *A List of References for the History of Agriculture in California* (1974).

Roger Charles Lister, *Bank Behavior, Regulation, and Economic Development: California, 1860–1910* (1993), is an excellent introduction. Ira B. Cross, in *Financing an Empire: History of Banking in California* (4 volumes, 1927) and in "Californians and Hard Money," *California Folklore Quarterly,* IV (July 1945), pp. 270–277, also treats these complex matters with clarity. A special issue of *Journal of the West,* XXIII (April 1984), edited by Larry Schweikart, is devoted to "Banking in the West." See also Lynne P. Doti and Schweikart, *Banking in the American West* (1992).

Social and economic change in the post-gold-rush period is the subject of Ralph Mann, *After the Gold Rush: Society in Grass Valley and Nevada City, 1849–1870* (1982), and Rodman Paul, "After the Gold Rush, San Francisco and Portland," *Pacific Historical Review,* LI (February 1982), pp. 1–22.

CHAPTER 9

A New State and Frontier Politics

The Congress of the United States, deadlocked over the future of slavery in new territories, provided no legal form of government whatever for California from the end of the Mexican War in 1848 until its admission into the Union on September 9, 1850. During this period the confused conditions of the gold rush intensified the disorder that resulted from California's undetermined and very peculiar legal and political status.

Military Governments

From the outbreak of the war until the ratification of the treaty of peace, California was governed under the customs of international law, which provided that in conquered territory under military occupation the previous system of local law remain in effect with such modifications as the military commander considered necessary. Thus, the American commanders were also ex-officio governors; however, there was much uncertainty about their legal status, powers, and responsibilities. Further confusion arose from the changes of personnel. The "governorship" of California passed from Commodore Sloat to Commodore Stockton to Colonel Frémont to General Kearny to Colonel Mason—five governors in the first 10 months of American occupation.

The prevailing system of local government in Mexican California, which the American military governors necessarily adopted, was based on the powers of the alcalde, an office derived from the Arabian and Moorish al-*cadi,* or village judge. The duties of the alcalde were many and remarkably varied, and his jurisdiction was ill-defined and unclear. He performed the functions of mayor, sheriff, and judge, often arresting a person, presiding over the trial, passing sentence, and enforcing the sentence. The partriarchal aspects of the office and the absence of the separation of powers were shocking to many Americans. Walter Colton, appointed and later elected as the first American alcalde of Monterey in 1846, wrote that "such an absolute disposal of questions affecting property and personal liberty never ought to be confided to one man. There is not a judge on the bench in England or the United States whose power is so absolute as that of the alcalde of Monterey."

From the beginning, the American military governors assumed that the ultimate annexation of California to the United States was a foregone conclusion. This view was strengthened in March 1847 by the arrival of Colonel J. D. Stevenson's regiment of New York Volunteers, recruited with the understanding that they would be disbanded in California at the end of the war and would thus provide not merely a garrison but a body of permanent American settlers.

The Treaty of Guadalupe Hidalgo was ratified in May 1848, and the official news of the ratification reached California on August 6. Thereafter, military government had to be continued de facto, with no other legal basis than the law of necessity. Even before the end of the technical state of war, there were many protests against "the inefficient mongrel military rule," as a writer in the *California Star* described it, and against alcalde rule.

The Constitutional Convention and Its Problems

With the news of the ratification of the treaty, the question of how California was supposed to be governed became extraordinarily difficult and embarrassing. Congress could not agree on any system of civil government for California. All such plans bogged down in the national political struggle that had raged since the introduction of Representative David Wilmot's proposal that slavery be forbidden in any territory acquired from Mexico.

General Bennet Riley succeeded Colonel Mason as "civil" governor in April 1849. Late in May he received news that Congress had again adjourned without agreement on a territorial organization for California, and on June 3 he issued a call for a constitutional convention to meet at Monterey on September 1. He had no real authority to do this, but it was a wise and necessary solution of the problem. It was also consistent with the attitude of President Zachary Taylor, a southern Unionist who felt that California might help to break the congressional deadlock over the territorial expansion of slavery if it would confront the rest of the country with an accomplished fact, by drawing up a state constitution that would settle the explosive issue so far as California was concerned.

The president could make this suggestion only informally and unofficially because all the legal authority in the matter lay with Congress. Under the normal procedure, patterned roughly on that of the Northwest Ordinance, Congress would first have established a territorial government; then, when the territory had enough inhabitants, Congress would have passed an *enabling act,* authorizing an elected convention (or sometimes the territorial legislature) to prepare a constitution and submit it for congressional approval with the admission of the state. All but four new states since the original thirteen had evolved through the territorial stage in this way. California would skip that stage entirely—as Vermont, Kentucky, Maine, and Texas had done—but under circumstances that differed from those prevailing in any of them.

President Taylor sent T. Butler King of Georgia as his personal and confidential emissary to California. In the sweltering summer of 1849, King traveled throughout the mining regions, urging the busy miners to take an interest in the forthcoming elections of delegates to the convention. The steamer on which King had arrived from Panama also carried another politician of even greater importance to California's future. This was William M. Gwin of Tennessee, a Democrat who had served one term in Congress. Early in March 1849, after Congress had adjourned with no solution of the California tangle, Gwin realized that California would soon form its own state government. He left Washington with the announced intention of assisting in that process and then of returning as one of the first United States senators from the new state. He achieved both of these ambitions. Obviously, not all of California's golden opportunities were in its mines.

Early in September the convention assembled at Monterey, in Colton Hall, a substantial building that the first American alcalde had erected as a town hall and schoolhouse. Of the 48 delegates who attended, 37 were from the northern districts. The constitutional convention of 1849, however, was not mainly a convention of forty-niners. A large majority of the delegates had been in California more than 3 years. Eight were native Californians, of whom the most important were Mariano Guadalupe Vallejo of Sonoma and José Antonio Carrillo of Los Angeles. Of the Americans, a substantially larger number had come from northern states than from southern. About half the members were under 35 years old. The 14 lawyers formed the largest single occupational group. One delegate, B. F. Moore, from Florida and San Joaquin gave his occupation as "elegant leisure."

General Riley's proclamation had left open the question of whether the new government should be that of a state or of a territory, and this was one of the first questions the convention settled. On a motion introduced by Gwin, who could not become a senator from a territory, the vote was decisively for a state government, even though every southern California delegate who was present voted otherwise. The landowners of what would soon be the southern *cow counties* were well aware that the taxation of ranch land would be the main source of early state revenues, because the miners, though now a large majority of the citizens, generally owned no land on which to pay taxes. The administrative expenses of a territory, on the other hand, would have been paid by the federal government. Naturally the southern Californians would have preferred that alternative, but they were hopelessly outnumbered. Carrillo proposed a compromise by which the part of California north of San Luis Obispo would be a state and the southern part a territory, but the idea was not seriously considered.

To the surprise of many, the question of slavery was easily decided by a unanimous vote. However, the overwhelming sentiment for the exclusion of slavery from California was not based on humanitarian considerations. The question had come to a head in the mines when Colonel Thomas Jefferson Green and a group of other Texans had appeared at Rose's Bar on the Yuba River with a number of black slaves. Green and his fellow Texans appropriated a large number of claims and set their slaves to working them. The Argonauts, whether from the north or from the south, were sensitive on the matter of the dignity of hard manual labor, or rather of their particular form of it; they were outraged at the imputation that gold mining was work appropriate for black slaves. On Sunday, July 29, a mass meeting of miners resolved "that no slave or Negro should own claims or even work in the mines" and served notice that the slaves must be out of the district by the next morning. Three days later the same miners elected William E. Shannon as their delegate to the convention at Monterey. It was Shannon who introduced the provision that "neither slavery nor involuntary servitude, unless for the punishment of crimes, shall ever be tolerated in this state."

A few of the members of the convention held liberal views on racial matters, but the majority did not. This was clear in the debates on a proposal to exclude free blacks, as well as slaves, from California—debates that brought forth angry feelings. The proposal to exclude free blacks was introduced by M. M. McCarver from Kentucky and Sacramento. Many owners of slaves, he said, were planning to bring them to California and free them there on condition that they work in the mines as indentured servants. Moreover, McCarver asserted, free blacks were "idle in their habits, difficult to be governed by laws, thriftless and uneducated," and their presence in California would be an evil "greater than that of slavery itself." At one point the exclusion clause was actually adopted, and it would have remained in the document except for a growing fear that Congress might consider it in violation of the federal Constitution and therefore reject the California constitution as a whole. Blacks were citizens in some of the states in the north, and the federal Constitution declared that citizens of each state should be "entitled to all privileges and immunities of citizens in the several states." The overriding consideration was the fear of anything that might delay the full establishment of "a proper form of state government" and its full national recognition.

At this time the power to deny suffrage on the ground of race was still within the constitutional authority of a state. Here, the chief complication was that the former Mexican citizens of California had the right to become American citizens under the treaty of peace. Most Mexican Californians had some degree of Indian ancestry, and Mexican law had not formally denied suffrage to Indians. In an uneasy compromise the California constitution extended the suffrage only to white male citizens, but authorized the state legislature by a two-thirds vote to extend it to Indians or the descendants of Indians. That the legislature would do this was most unlikely.

The problem that gave the convention most trouble was the question of the eastern boundary. Should this be based on the Sierra Nevada and the Colorado River, or should there be a much larger California extending several hundred miles farther east? The convention, changing its mind repeatedly, almost broke up over this question. As usual, the delegates were primarily concerned with the possible reactions in Washington, D.C. Some argued that Congress might reject the constitution and postpone the admission of California if its boundaries were too large. Others argued the opposite. In the end the decision was for the present boundaries of California: on the north, the 42nd parallel; on the east, the 120th meridian southward to its juncture with the 39th parallel (a point in Lake Tahoe); thence in a straight southeasterly line to the intersection of the 35th parallel and the Colorado River; then down the middle of the channel of that river to the Mexican border, at the point where the Gila flows into the Colorado.

California was the first American state to include in its constitution a provision for the separate property of married women. All property of the wife, owned by her before marriage or acquired afterward by gift or otherwise, should remain her property. Such had been the law in Mexican California, and the Americans were under some obligation to preserve it—but an argument offered by Henry Halleck, a delegate from Monterey, was probably more effective. He advised all his fellow bachelors to vote for this section because it would attract not only prospective wives, but *wealthy* prospective wives, to California. In vain did some of the married delegates protest that nature had made men the protectors of women and that the constitution should not tamper with this relationship.

For public education, California made the usual provisions of a frontier state. That is, it announced its acceptance of the land grants that the federal government customarily made to new states for the support of public schools and for a "seminary of learning," or university. Robert Semple, president of the convention, exuberantly asked his colleagues: "Why should we send our sons to Europe to finish their education? If we have the means here we can procure the necessary talent; we can bring the President of Oxford University here by offering a sufficient salary." But even if Oxford had had an official with the title of president, the University of California could not easily have attracted him, even 20 years later when that institution was opened. Until the twentieth century, it would remain small and isolated.

Some other uninformed statements were also made in the convention, as when a delegate objected to the phrase "a jury of his peers" on the ground that there was no house of peers in democratic America. But in general the convention did a fairly

The great seal of the state of California was adopted at the 1849 constitutional convention in Monterey.

creditable job under difficult circumstances. It is true that not much of the constitution of 1849 was original. A majority of its provisions were taken from the constitution of Iowa; much of the rest of it came from the constitution of New York.

The design accepted for the state seal, on the other hand, was quite original and distinctive, if somewhat cluttered. Minerva, the Roman goddess of political wisdom and of handicrafts and the guardian of cities, appears in the foreground. At her feet crouches a grizzly bear feeding on bunches of grapes. A miner works with rocker and bowl, ships ply San Francisco Bay, and the snowy peaks of the Sierra Nevada are seen in the distance. The Greek motto "Eureka" and 31 stars, the last one for the new state of California, are at the top of the design.

One point of dissension was raised: Mariano Vallejo objected to the bear. It reminded him of the indignities he had suffered in the Bear Flag Revolt, and he proposed that it be removed from the seal unless it were shown as secured by a lasso in the hands of a vaquero. In the end he accepted the assurances of Anglo-American delegates that this particular bear signified no offense to the native Californians.

The First Legislature

A month after the convention adjourned, the first state officials were elected on November 13, 1849, the same day on which the constitution was ratified by a light vote, 12,061 in favor and 811 against. Peter H. Burnett was elected governor, and John McDougal lieutenant governor. On December 15 the legislature began to assemble at the first state capital, San José. In joint session of the two houses, it elected Frémont and Gwin as United States senators; Frémont had the larger number of votes, but a drawing by lot gave him the short term, ending March 3, 1851, whereas Gwin drew the term extending 4 years longer.

The permanent location of the state capital was left open to future bids from rival towns, in order to ensure that land and buildings would be provided without cost to the state government. The fact that California had not yet been admitted to the Union made the prospects for obtaining state funds uncertain, and because the first legislature failed to establish a permanent location, the capital was hawked about in a most undignified manner. Within 5 years the seat of government would be moved from San José to Vallejo, back to San José, back to Vallejo, to Sacramento, back to Vallejo, to Benicia, and at last, in 1854, permanently to Sacramento.

The first state legislature of California, though not a very distinguished body, did not entirely deserve the name that it acquired, "the legislature of a thousand drinks." The appellation seems to have grown out of a phrase repeatedly used by Thomas Jefferson Green. That irrepressible political adventurer from Texas, unabashed when the miners excluded him and his slaves from the Yuba diggings, had secured election as state senator from Sacramento. Moreover, he became chairman of the senate finance committee and was seeking election to one of the four new major-generalcies of the state militia. A number of the candidates for various offices to be filled by the legislature maintained bars from which they dispensed hospitality to the members in the hope of receiving their votes in return. At the end of

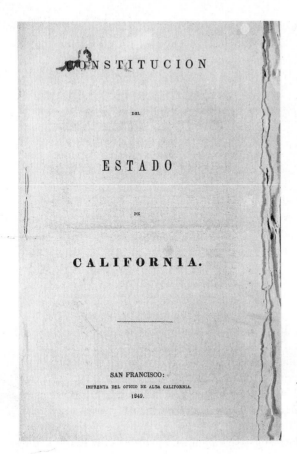

The constitution of 1849, printed in Spanish and English, required public documents to be published in both languages. (*Courtesy of the Huntington Library.*)

each day's session, at least until the one that elected him as a militia commander, Green loudly invited the legislators to have "a thousand drinks" at his expense; journalists could not resist the temptation to apply the phrase as a description of the legislature generally.

The Admission of California to the Union

Congress nearly rejected the new government of California. The new state's admission would upset the equal balance in the number of free and slave states and in the number of their United States senators, a balance that had long given the south a veto against federal laws inimical to its "peculiar institution." In the great debates in the national capital, southern senators demanded an extension of the Missouri Compromise line of 36°30′ to the Pacific coast. This line would have bisected California just south of Monterey, and the portion to the south of it would have been organized as a territory open to slavery. The "great compromise" proposed, instead, that California be admitted as a free state, as its people desired, but that the

On October 29, 1850, San Francisco celebrated the admission of California to the Union. (*Courtesy of the California Historical Society, FN-00616.*)

territories of Utah and New Mexico be organized without the ban of the Wilmot Proviso against slavery. Daniel Webster, in his famous speech in the Senate on March 7, argued for this solution and tried to allay the protests of northern abolitionists and opponents of the expansion of slavery. Slavery, he said, had been perpetuated mainly for its usefulness in the production of cotton. Nature itself had excluded slavery from California and New Mexico by making their lands so arid that cotton could never be grown there, "and I would not take pains uselessly to reaffirm an ordinance of nature nor to re-enact the will of God." Webster could hardly have foreseen that, with the help of irrigation, California would one day produce more cotton than any other state but Texas.

At last, when the south had been further mollified by a stringent new law regulating the return of slaves who had escaped into northern states, the omnibus provisions of the Compromise of 1850 were approved. In addition to the new fugitive-slave law, other provisions of the compromise of 1850 abolished the slave trade (but not slavery) in Washington, D.C. President Millard Fillmore signed the bill for the admission of California on September 9, 1850. The news reached San Francisco on October 18 and was celebrated with colorful parades, but the new state government had already been operating for nearly a year, exactly as if it had been authorized by Congress. Californians were showing a strong disposition to take things into their own hands.

The Feud between Broderick and Gwin

Under the constitution of 1849, elections of governors and other state officials were held every 2 years, in the odd-numbered years. The Democrats won virtually every important election in California in the 1850s except the state elections of 1855, which they lost largely because of the bitter rivalry between the two main Democratic leaders—one of the most sensationally destructive rivalries in American political history.

Apart from the Democratic label, the chief resemblance between David C. Broderick of Tammany Hall and William M. Gwin of Tennessee was that both came to California in 1849 with the announced intention of being elected to the United States Senate. Broderick, who was only 29 at the time of his arrival at San Francisco, had received very little formal education. Gwin, 15 years older, had the advantages of formal training in both law and medicine and also of years of acquaintance with several of the country's leading political figures. Gwin was cool, dignified, and gracious, while Broderick was hot-headed, humorless, stubborn, and domineering.

The son of an immigrant Irish stonemason, Broderick had been a saloonkeeper in New York and a ward boss for Tammany Hall. Once in San Francisco, Broderick formed the nucleus of a Democratic political machine on the Tammany model. He became the first major political boss of San Francisco and soon gained control of the Democratic party machinery throughout the state.

Broderick entered the state senate in 1850 and the next year was elected its presiding officer. By forming an alliance with John Bigler, the speaker of the assembly, and by securing Bigler's election as governor in 1851 and again in 1853, Broderick gained control of the state patronage. He then felt ready to try to replace Gwin in the United States Senate. This, however, was a most formidable undertaking. California Democrats of southern origin, ridiculed by their opponents as the Chivalry or Shiv faction, almost unanimously preferred Gwin to Broderick, although by no means could all of Broderick's Northern or Tammany wing of the party be depended on to support him against Gwin. As senior United States senator, Gwin controlled the federal patronage.

In 1854 Broderick conceived the daring but unsuccessful scheme of trying to compel the state legislature of that year to elect him as Gwin's successor, even though the election would not normally have been held until 1855. In the legislative session of 1855, a deadlock between Gwin and Broderick prevented the election of either, or of anyone else. Consequently one of the United States senatorships remained vacant for 2 years, and the California Democrats were so bitterly divided that the pseudo-patriotic, nativist, self-styled American party, otherwise known as the Know-Nothings, gained control of the state government.

The Know-Nothing Order, nationally consolidated in 1852 out of several secret bodies, was first organized in California in May 1854. It took its name from the fact that originally it required its members to answer all questions by saying that they knew nothing about it. The Know-Nothing movement seemed, for a time, to offer an escape from the frightening national divisions over the slavery issue by promising to unite Americans against foreigners. As a national organization, it was hostile to Roman Catholics because it assumed them to be under allegiance to a foreign power. In California, however, the nativist American movement was much influenced by the local hostility to foreign miners; in particular, racial antipathies were more important than religious or nationalistic ones, and there was much denunciation of the Chinese, while anti-Catholicism was softpedaled. In California, as elsewhere, the identification of candidates with the Know-Nothing party was almost entirely opportunistic. Under J. Neely Johnson, elected governor on the Know-Nothing ticket in 1855, the party offered no serious program of state legislation, nativist or otherwise.

The ambition of Broderick for a United States senatorship grew steadily more obsessive through repeated frustrations. At last, in 1857, he achieved his goal. Both of the Senate seats were to be filled, Gwin's having been vacant for 2 years. By the unscrupulous use of every trick his fertile imagination could conceive, Broderick induced the legislature to elect him to the full 6-year term. Broderick forced Gwin to be content with the 4-year senatorial term, and under the threat of denying him even that, he compelled Gwin to write a letter promising to make no recommendations for the federal patronage. When President Buchanan learned what Broderick had done, he strongly disapproved of it and appointed followers of Gwin to the positions in the customs house, the branch mint, and the Indian agencies in California, and gave none of these appointments to Broderick's supporters.

Broderick was furious. In his one important speech in the United States Senate, he denounced Buchanan and Gwin in terms of the most violent personal vituperation. He did this, he said, because he was opposed to Buchanan's policy of encouraging the formation of a proslavery government in the territory of Kansas. The depth and genuineness of Broderick's convictions on any matter of principle, however, must be very seriously questioned. The extent to which he was willing to injure his party and his friends in order to gratify his personal hatreds became so obvious that it shocked and alienated a number of his former supporters.

In the state elections of 1859 the Gwin group, now known as the Lecompton Democrats because they favored the admission of Kansas to statehood under the proslavery Lecompton constitution, won a sweeping victory over the Broderick men. During the campaign, Chief Justice David S. Terry, a candidate for renomination to the state supreme court, made a speech in which he aligned himself with the Lecompton Democrats—hardly surprising in view of his background and his strongly prosouthern opinions. Broderick, while at breakfast in a hotel dining room in San Francisco, read a newspaper account of Terry's speech and was overheard in an outburst of angry denunciation. Whereas he had believed Terry to be the only honest member of the supreme court, it was now clear that the "d———d miserable wretch" was as corrupt as the other members. Terry waited for an apology until the end of the campaign. He had failed to win renomination, and only a few weeks remained in his term. On election day he resigned from the supreme court and shortly afterward challenged Broderick to a duel. This they fought on September 13, 1859, in a ravine near the ocean, just across the line in San Mateo County. Broderick nervously pulled the trigger of his pistol too soon, and his bullet went wild, but Terry's shot struck his opponent in the breast.

Admirers of Broderick came to believe that his dying words were "They have killed me because I was opposed to a corrupt administration and the extension of slavery." Whether Broderick made this particular statement is doubtful, and in any case it was not an accurate description of the cause of the duel; however, the popular orator Edward D. Baker quoted it in a funeral eulogy and thus launched a myth that ultimately transformed Broderick into a kind of Pacific coast Lincoln.

Movements for State Division

The early historians who believed that Broderick's opposition to the territorial expansion of slavery, rather than his desire for political power, was his most significant motive were probably committing an error of emphasis. The same historians tended to see a proslavery conspiracy in the demands of southern California for separation from the rest of the state during the 1850s. Later historians, such as William Henry Ellison, argued that this was simply and completely an error of fact. It was true that the southern counties of California repeatedly sought permission to secede from the northern ones, Ellison concluded, but the slavery question did not have anything to do with these efforts except that many imagined that it did. The real cause of the movement was the grievance of southern California against too much taxation and too little representation. Recent research by historian Ward McAfee has revealed that the advocates of state division were actually driven by a complex set of motives.

The fears expressed by the southern California delegates in the convention of 1849, to the effect that their part of the state would have to pay an unfair share of taxes, proved to have been extremely well founded. In 1852 Governor McDougal conceded that the 6 cow counties of southern California, with a population of 6000, paid $42,000 in property taxes, while the 12 mining counties, with a population of nearly 120,000, paid only $21,000. A state law exempted from taxation all mining claims on "United States lands," where the great majority of the claims were located. This was one of the innumerable statutes of the 1850s that conferred special favors on the mining interests.

Gradually the justice of southern California's grievance became recognized throughout the state, and in 1859 the legislature approved a plan introduced by Assemblyman Andrés Pico. This provided that the part of California south of 35°45′ (the northern boundary of San Luis Obispo County) should become the territory of Colorado. The voters of that region also approved the plan, but coming as it did on the eve of the Civil War, it had no chance of passage in the national capital. Most members of Congress, ignorant of affairs on the remote Pacific coast, could not be dissuaded from the belief that the measure was simply another dangerous aggravation of the slavery issue.

California and the Civil War

The amount of pro-Confederate sentiment in California was grossly exaggerated during the war—by those who felt and cherished it, by those who feared it, and by those who, for their own political and personal reasons, wished to make it appear greater than it was. Most histories have reflected the contemporary exaggeration.

Actually, less than 7 percent of the population of California in 1860 had come from the seceded states, and there was never any genuine danger that California would desert the Union cause.

Disloyal conspiracies did exist in California, but they were on a small scale. There were clandestine pro-Confederate societies like the Knights of the Golden Circle, the Knights of the Columbian Star, and the Committee of Thirty, but they had only a fraction of the membership that wild rumor attributed to them. There were various dreams of seizing federal arsenals and gold shipments, and there was one romantic but futile attempt to put a conspiracy into actual operation. A group of southern sympathizers secretly armed the small schooner *Chapman* at San Francisco in the hope of capturing a Pacific Mail steamer to use as a privateer under a Confederate letter of marque. Federal authorities knew of the plot almost from its beginning, and they seized the *Chapman* as she was weighing anchor.

The elections and the trends in party politics gave ample evidence that California was safe for the Union. In the state campaigns of 1861, the Republicans and the Union Democrats repudiated the right of secession and pledged the support of California for the war, and their candidates, running on these strongly Unionist platforms, polled together more than two-thirds of the votes. In the California elections of 1861, the continuing Democratic schism enabled the Republicans to elect their first governor, Leland Stanford, by a substantial plurality. By 1864, although the Democrats were reunited in support of the Union, the Republicans had been very successful in branding all Democrats as disloyal, and consequently a large majority of Californians voted for the reelection of Lincoln. The Republicans called themselves the "Union" party from 1863 to 1867.

Because it was never necessary for anyone to "save California for the Union," it is absurd to say that anyone did; however, this honor has been variously claimed for Reverend Thomas Starr King, Colonel Edward D. Baker, Governor Stanford, and others. King was a much beloved Unitarian minister, called to San Francisco from Boston in 1860. He was a captivating orator, and in several lecture tours he spoke for the Union and particularly for contributions to the work of the Sanitary Commission, the "Red Cross of the Civil War." Partly as a result of his efforts, California contributed more than a fourth of the amount that the commission received in the entire country. Colonel Baker, a close personal friend of Abraham Lincoln, was one of the leading organizers of the Republican party in California.

California's military participation in the Civil War was very limited. The federal government did not favor the use of California volunteers in the main theaters of the war because their transportation was too expensive, and the draft was never enforced in California for the same reason. General Don Andrés Pico, victor of San Pasqual and the signer of the Treaty of Cahuenga with Frémont, was deeply hurt by the rejection of his offer to raise a regiment of native Californian cavalry. About 500 young Californians, including several native ones, offered their services to Massachusetts if that state would pay the cost of their organization and transportation. It did so, and the California Battalion, as part of the 2nd Massachusetts Cavalry, took part in more than 50 engagements, mainly in Virginia. About 16,000 volunteers enlisted in California during the war, but they were used mainly for local garrison duty, for guarding the overland mail routes, or for policing Indians in the northwest. A "California Column" was sent to New Mexico in 1862 to repel a Confederate invasion of the territory, but the enemy withdrew before a battle could be fought, and many members of the column left it to join a local mining rush.

Selected Bibliography

A sampling of the latest scholarship is available in John F. Burns and Richard J. Orsi (eds.), *Taming the Elephant: Politics, Government, and Law in Pioneer California* (2002).

Theodore Grivas, *Military Governments in California, 1846–1850* (1962), does much to dispel the confusion that has surrounded that subject. The official *Report of the Debates in the Convention of California* (1850) was well prepared by J. Ross Browne. David Alan Johnson, *Founding the Far West* (1992), analyzes the motives and ideological intentions of the members of the constitutional convention; but see also William H. Ellison, *A Self-Governing Dominion: California, 1849–1860* (1950); Woodrow J. Hansen, *The Search for Authority in California* (1960); and William E. Franklin, "Peter H. Burnett and the Provisional Government Movement," *California Historical Society Quarterly*, XL (June 1961), pp. 123–136. Donald C. Briggs's *Conquer and Colonize: Stevenson's Regiment and California* (1977) is a thorough account that emphasizes the positive contributions of Stevenson's men. Important memoirs are Walter Colton, *Three Years in California* (1850); William H. Ellison (ed.), "Memoirs of Hon. William M. Gwin," *California Historical Society Quarterly*, XXI (1940), pp. 1–26, 157–184, 256–277, 344–367; and Charles A. Barker (ed.), *Memoirs of Elisha Oscar Crosby* (1945).

On the admission of California, see Ronald C. Woolsey, "A Southern Dilemma: Slavery and the California Statehood Issue in 1850—A Reconsideration," *Southern California Quarterly*, LXV (Summer 1983), pp. 123–144. Robert G. Cowan's *The Admission of the 31st State by the 31st Congress* (1962) is an annotated bibliography of the congressional speeches.

The Broderick-Gwin feud may be traced in Arthur Quinn, *The Rivals* (1994); James O'Meara, *Broderick and Gwin* (1881); Thomas, *Between Two Empires . . . William McKendree Gwin* (1969); David A. Williams, *David C. Broderick: A Political Portrait* (1969); and A. Russell Buchanan, *David S. Terry* (1956). See also Mary Jo Ignoffo, *Gold Rush Politics: California's First Legislature* (2000).

The state division movement is covered in W. Ellison, *A Self-Governing Dominion* (1950), and the Pacific Republic idea in Joseph Ellison, *California and the Nation* (1927). For a more recent view, see Ward M. McAfee, "California's House Divided," *Civil War History*, XXXIII (June 1987), pp. 115–130. See also Woolsey, "Disunion or Dissent?" *Southern California Quarterly*, LXVI (Fall 1984), pp. 185–206, and "The Politics of a Lost Cause," *California History*, LXIX (Winter 1991), pp. 372–383.

Gerald Stanley is the author of several important articles on politics before and during the Civil War: "Racism and the Early Republican Party: The 1856 Presidential Election in California," *Pacific Historical Review*, XLIII (May 1974), pp. 171–187; "Slavery and the Origins of the Republican Party in California," *Southern California Quarterly*, LX (Spring 1978), pp. 1–16; "The Slavery Issue and Election in California, 1860," *Mid-America*, LXII (January 1980), pp. 35–46; "Civil War Politics in California," *Southern California Quarterly*, LXIV (Summer 1982), pp. 115–132. See also Robert J. Chandler, "Friends in Time of Need: Republicans and Black Civil Rights in California during the Civil War Era," *Arizona and the West,* XXIV (Winter 1982), pp. 319–340. Older studies include Earl Pomeroy, "California, 1846–1860," *California Historical Society Quarterly,* XXXII (December 1953), pp. 291–302; Benjamin F. Gilbert, *The Governors of California* (1965); Royce D. Delmatier et al., *The Rumble of California Politics* (1965); and Norman E. Tutorow, *Leland Stanford* (1970).

Benjamin F. Gilbert's "California and the Civil War, a Bibliographical Essay," *California Historical Society Quarterly,* XL (December 1961), pp. 289–307, is very useful. See also his "The Confederate Minority in California," ibid., XX (June 1941), pp. 154–170. On California contributions to the war effort, see Tom Generous, "Over the River Jordan: California Volunteers in Utah during the Civil War," *California History,* LXIII (Summer 1984), pp. 200–211; Darlis A. Miller, *The California Column in New Mexico* (1982); Robert Monzingo, *Thomas Starr King* (1991); Richard H. Peterson, "The United States Sanitary Commission and Thomas Starr King in California, 1861–1864," *California History,* LXXII (Winter 1993/1994), pp. 324–337; Aurora Hunt, *The Army of the Pacific* (1951); and Oscar Lewis, *The War in the Far West* (1961).

CHAPTER 10

Crime and Punishment

One of the most striking and significant evidences of the chronic social disorganization in post-gold-rush California was the outbreak of a rash of *vigilance committees.* Most historical treatments of these bodies have condoned their actions, and many have even glorified them. The present account takes a different view.

The Nature of Vigilantism

Richard Henry Dana, in the chapter that he added to his *Two Years before the Mast* after his return visit to California in 1859, described San Francisco as having been rescued from

> its season of heaven-defying crime, violence, and blood . . . and handed back to soberness, morality, and good government, by that peculiar invention of Anglo-Saxon Republican America, the solemn awe-inspiring Vigilance Committee of the most grave and responsible citizens, the last resort of the thinking and the good, taken to only when vice, fraud, and ruffianism have entrenched themselves behind the forms of law, suffrage, and the ballot.

Several historians, writing in the same tone of defensive righteousness, have perpetuated the racist notion that vigilantism was one of the evidences of Anglo-Saxon superiority, a proof of American ingenuity in adapting self-government to the special conditions of the frontier.

The truth is, first, that vigilantism was not a superior institution and, second, that there was nothing exclusively Anglo-Saxon about it, except perhaps the use of the rope instead of the bullet. *Vigilante* is a Spanish word meaning "lookout" or "guard," and the first vigilance committee in California was organized in Los Angeles in 1836. This *junta defensora de la seguridad pública* seized a man and a woman from the custody of the alcaldes and shot them for the murder of the woman's husband.

The true and great contributions of Anglo-Saxon jurisprudence have been on the side of the due process of law, whereas the methods of the vigilance committees were parodies of due process. Their methods were generally more organized and elaborate than those of mere lynch mobs, but the committees did not hold their "trials" in open court. They acted in anger and in haste. They did not consider motions for change of venue. Witnesses for the defendants were usually afraid to testify, or even to appear. Because they had no way of enforcing a sentence of long-term imprisonment, the vigilantes resorted to flogging, ear-cropping, head-shaving, branding, and extralegal hanging (often done so inexpertly as to produce death by strangulation). And there was no provision for appeal or for executive clemency.

Taking the law into one's own hands, particularly after regular courts had been established, was itself a criminal action. Yet, remarkably enough, the early American historians of California almost unanimously applauded it. Even the idealistic philosopher Josiah Royce, in spite of his personal detestation of violence and bullying, strongly praised "popular justice" as exercised by the vigilance committees of San Francisco. Hubert Howe Bancroft indulged in the most elaborate defenses and rationalizations of "popular tribunals" on such grounds as the sacred right of revolution. He maintained that the vigilantes were "the people" and that the people (especially the self-appointed best people) were above all law. These apologistic viewpoints have too often gone unchallenged.

The motives of the vigilantes were complex and remain a matter of dispute. Historian John Boessenecker, author of *Gold Dust and Gunsmoke* (1999), has concluded that vigilantism was used "overwhelmingly for crime control." Boessenecker has calculated that the murder rate in the Golden State in the 1850s was 17 times higher than the national rate of recent years. A resident of Los Angeles was *37 times* more likely to be murdered in 1852 than in 1997. Thus, the 1850s were "a decade of turbulence, violence, and bloodshed that has not been equaled before or since in the history of peacetime America." Earlier studies, such as those by Roger D. McGrath, concluded that lawless behavior affected only a few specialized groups and that the overall crime rate during the gold rush was far lower than that of recent years.

Other historians have emphasized the ulterior motives of the vigilantes. Richard Maxwell Brown, author of *Strain of Violence* (1975), has highlighted the ethnic and class origins of the vigilantes and their victims. Xenophobia and nativism were palpably present in countless episodes of vigilante terrorism throughout the state. In their rhetoric and actions, the vigilance committees in San Francisco revealed an abiding interest in suppressing a feared Irish Catholic presence. Other historians, most notably Peter Decker and Robert Senkewicz, have emphasized the economic motives of the merchant-dominated vigilance committees in San Francisco. Whatever their stated goals, these urban vigilantes clearly were businessmen seeking to bolster their economic position.

Still other historians have stressed the irrational and subconscious motives of the vigilantes. According to this view, people who form lynch mobs and vigilance committees are themselves often inwardly tortured by assorted feelings of guilt. Samuel Brannan, who did more than anyone else to instigate vigilantism in San Francisco, was building the first great California fortune on money that he had diverted from church property and tithes to his personal use and profit. Apostate though he was, he was not unaffected by the knowledge that his former church regarded him as the supreme example of the corrupting influence of money on the human soul. Perhaps Brannan was subconsciously seeking freedom from his own guilt in arrogating to himself the punishment of others.

The Hounds in San Francisco

Congress left California almost literally lawless from 1846 to 1850. Within this vacuum there began to appear, in San Francisco, a form of organized lawlessness and terrorism. When Colonel Stevenson's regiment of New York Volunteers was disbanded, a group of its members led by Lieutenant Sam Roberts formed an organization called the Regulators, or more commonly, the Hounds, allegedly dedicated to maintaining public order, and especially devoted to hounding Latinos and

Hounds attacking Chilenos in San Francisco, July 15, 1849. (*Courtesy of the Bancroft Library.*)

other "foreigners" out of California. Alcalde Leavenworth tried to use them as deputy policemen, but he could not control them. They held drunken parades and levied tribute, bullied merchants by day and looted foreign settlements by night. In the evening of July 15, 1849, they paraded to an attack upon Little Chile, a tent community at the foot of Telegraph Hill, where some of them murdered a mother and criminally assaulted her daughter.

The next morning Sam Brannan addressed a crowd from the roof of the alcalde's little office on the plaza. A counterorganization called the Law and Order party was formed and its members deputized, a charitable fund for the Chilenos was collected, and by sunset Roberts and 18 other Hounds had been caught and imprisoned in a ship in the bay.

Nine men were more or less legally convicted of crimes, but the penalty was banishment, and this proved unenforceable. Many of the Hounds continued their depredations, though no longer openly. In such activities they were joined by some of the Sydney Ducks, ex-convicts or escaped convicts from Australia. The Australian immigrants were thus given a bad name that most of them did not deserve.

The San Francisco Committee of 1851

The beating and robbery of C. J. Jansen, a prominent merchant, in his shop in the heart of town on February 19, 1851, produced another outburst of popular excitement. Two Australians, Berdue and Windred, were arrested and mistakenly identified by Jansen as the men who had assaulted and robbed him. A mob incited by Brannan was preparing to seize and hang the two prisoners without a trial when a young merchant named William Tell Coleman managed to catch the ear of the crowd and persuaded it to organize a "people's court." This procedure, with Coleman acting as prosecutor, resulted in a hung jury. The two men were then returned to the jurisdiction of the regular authorities.

On May 4, 1851, there occurred the fifth and greatest in a series of fires that had repeatedly devastated the city. The fact that this fifth fire happened on the anniversary of the second one intensified the growing suspicion that all the fires had been deliberately set by Hounds and Sydney Ducks in revenge and defiance and to facilitate looting. Loot was found hidden in the Sydney Town district, and criminals were thought to be emboldened by the failure to hang the supposed robbers of Jansen. A volunteer night patrol was organized, and on Sunday, June 8, the *Alta California* published a proposal for a "committee of safety" or "committee of vigilance." That afternoon a meeting in Sam Brannan's office determined to call a larger meeting of other responsible citizens, and on June 9, in Brannan's building, that meeting adopted a constitution for the first San Francisco Committee of Vigilance.

The very next evening, taps on a fire bell summoned the committee to pass judgment on John Jenkins, who had been caught stealing a small safe and was dragged to the committee's headquarters instead of the police station. Jenkins was insolent and threatened that his friends were organizing to rescue him and destroy the committee. The decisive moment came when William A. Howard, a sea captain, cried,

The execution of John Jenkins on the night of June 10, 1851, by the San Francisco Committee of Vigilance. (*Courtesy of the Bancroft Library.*)

"Gentlemen, as I understand it, we came here to hang somebody." Coleman opposed hanging a man at night and suggested waiting until dawn, when Jenkins would "rise with the sun." But Brannan secured the approval of the crowd in the plaza, and there, from a beam at the south end of the "Old Adobe," Jenkins was hanged by moonlight. Thus, the committee began its work by hanging the first criminal it apprehended, within a few hours after his crime, and for a rather petty robbery rather than a murder.

A coroner's inquest into the death of Jenkins identified nine vigilantes as parties to it, but the committee made their arrests impractical by releasing the names of all its other members. In July the committee chanced to apprehend James Stuart, an Australian who had escaped from jail at Marysville while awaiting trial for the murder of a sheriff. After securing a highly picaresque confession from Stuart, the committee hanged him, and in August it also hanged two other Sydney Ducks, McKenzie and Whittaker, whom Stuart's confessions had implicated in various robberies. Before its extrajudicial activities ended in September, the vigilance committee of 1851 had made nearly 90 arrests. Besides its four hangings, it had whipped 1 man, sentenced 28 to deportation, remanded 15 to the authorities for trial, and released 41.

The roster shows that along with Brannan the founders and early members of the vigilance committee of 1851 were predominantly commission merchants and sea captains—two groups that disliked government, courts, lawyers, and politicians as forces that threatened interference with their own freedom of action. It was a peculiar base on which to rest a claim that the leading vigilantes were "the best citizens" of the community, but this claim was made, and has been periodically repeated ever since. It is significant that no lawyers whatever were members of the Committee of Vigilance. The committee would not have welcomed their membership, even had they wished to join it.

Statewide Vigilance

San Francisco's example inspired the formation of several local vigilance committees in other towns and an increase in lynching in the mining communities. Of dozens of such cases, perhaps the most infamous was the hanging of a Mexican woman by a mob of miners at Downieville on July 5, 1851. The woman apparently was named Josefa Segovia but was known as Juanita. The miners had gathered to hear a Fourth of July oration by United States Senator John B. Weller and afterward had celebrated far into the night. In the early hours of the morning, Juanita killed one of them with a knife. The friends of her victim, one Joseph Cannon, asserted the theory that he had not intended to harm her and that his purpose in entering her cabin was only to apologize to her for having broken her door down, which had happened only because he was intoxicated. A witness friendly to Juanita said that Cannon had called her "a whore," and Juanita testified that she feared Cannon "wanted to get into my room and sleep with me."

Within a few hours, Juanita was brought to "trial" by what one observer, David P. Barstow, called "the hungriest, craziest, wildest mob that ever I saw anywhere." After saying that she would defend herself again in the same way under the same circumstances, Juanita adjusted her own noose and stepped from the improvised scaffold. Barstow was certain that "the hanging of the woman was murder. No jury in the world, on any principle of self-defense or protection of life and property, would ever have convicted her." There can be no doubt that ethnicity was the determining factor in her conviction. As historian Manuel Gonzales has concluded, "Juanita was a 'greaser,' her unforgivable sin."

In the riotous cow town of Los Angeles in the 1850s there were more executions, both legal and extralegal, than in the much larger city of San Francisco. It was sometimes difficult to distinguish the legal executions from the lynchings in Los Angeles because of the tendency of the constituted authorities to authorize vigilantism. In 1851, the mayor and the city council created a vigilance committee by formal action. Among those it hanged were three men charged with the murder of Major General J. H. Bean of the California militia. One of the men hanged was later proved innocent. In 1854, Mayor Stephen C. Foster dispersed a mob bent on lynching the gambler and killer Dave Brown by promising that if the regular authorities did not succeed in convicting and executing Brown, he would resign as mayor and join the vigilantes. When Brown's lawyers secured a stay of execution, Mayor Foster kept his promise, directed the lynching, and resumed his office after it was over.

The most famous case in the southern mines occurred at Columbia on October 10, 1855. The drunken viciousness of the mob, the extreme courage of the sheriff in risking his life to try to take the prisoner away from it, and the fact that by that time the legal courts in the area were well-organized, produced some local reaction against lynching in general.

The San Francisco Committee of 1856

The revival of the vigilance committee in San Francisco in 1856 was motivated by a potent mixture of psychological forces, as well as economic, political, ethnic, and religious factors. The committee of 1856 was dominated by the city's leading merchants, who wished to bring about great reductions in their taxes by discrediting the city government as corrupt and wasteful and by taking control of it themselves. The city had been governed mainly by the Democratic organization headed by David C. Broderick. Many of Broderick's followers were Irish Catholics, and many of them were particular objects of vigilante hostility.

The immediate cause of the revival of the vigilance movement was the shooting of James King of William, the anti-Catholic editor of the *Daily Evening Bulletin,* by the politician James P. Casey, on May 14, 1856. James King had added the name of William, his father, to distinguish himself from other James Kings in the District of Columbia, where he was born. His editorship of the *Bulletin* was a sort of journalistic vigilantism. The pen, he felt, could be mightier than the rope or the whip; the printing press, a mightier punisher of evil than the gallows. He denounced the Tammany-style political machine of David C. Broderick and accused him of having imported James P. Casey from New York City as an expert ballot-box stuffer. Casey was elected a county supervisor in an election widely denounced as corrupt. King published in the *Bulletin* the fact that Casey had served a term in the New York state penitentiary at Sing Sing.

A great many people had come from the older parts of the country to escape their pasts, so many that it was often considered a necessary convention in California that a person's past was nobody's business. A popular song of the period was

Oh, what was your name in the States?
Was it Thompson or Johnson or Bates?
Did you murder your wife and flee for your life?
Oh, what was your name in the States?

King's exposure of his prison record deeply disturbed Casey and made him almost incoherent. He threatened King in the *Bulletin* office and shot him on the street an hour later.

The shooting of King became associated in the public mind with the earlier killing of General William H. Richardson by the gambler Charles Cora. Richardson, then serving as United States marshal, had become extremely angry when Cora and his mistress, the wealthy Arabella Ryan, keeper of a notorious house of prostitution, attracted attention by sitting directly behind Richardson and his wife in a box at the opening of a new theater. The next evening Richardson, clearly intoxicated, accosted Cora on the street and drew a derringer, a pocket pistol. Cora drew his own derringer and fired a fatal shot. Cora's first trial ended in a hung jury, and he was in jail awaiting a second trial when the shooting of James King of William occurred.

On the day that King was shot, a group of former members of the vigilance committee of 1851 determined to reactivate the movement, under the leadership of William Tell Coleman, now the most respected of the group. The committee began to collect arms and to form a military unit. On the other hand, a number of prominent citizens formed the Law and Order party, denouncing the vigilantes and adopting the name of the organization of 1849. Among the Law and Order leaders were Mayor Van Ness, Sheriff Scannell, and General William Tecumseh Sherman, whom the governor of the state had recently appointed commander of the San Francisco district of the California militia.

On May 16, Governor J. Neely Johnson came down from Sacramento to confer with Coleman. Few state executives have ever been more bitterly denounced than Johnson was for his role in these conferences and in the events that followed them. He was only 28 years old at the time—California in the 1850s was a young man's country—and he was in an extremely explosive situation. Four days after the shooting of King, 2500 armed vigilantes advanced on the county jail and removed Cora and Casey to the committee's headquarters. The sheriff's 150 deputies made no attempt to resist, and thus a self-appointed committee had virtually taken over the government of San Francisco at a time of almost hysterical public excitement.

Two days later, on the 20th, while Cora was being tried before the vigilance tribunal, word came that James King of William had died. The emotional effect of this announcement ensured the hanging not only of Casey but also of Cora. Both men were hanged with great public ceremony on the 22nd, the day of King's funeral.

The Law and Order leaders had hoped that the committee, having "hanged somebody," would now disband. Instead, it made further arrests and strengthened the defenses of its headquarters building, known as Fort Gunnybags. A Law and Order committee urged Governor Johnson to call out the state militia to suppress insurrection.

Before calling out the militia, Governor Johnson secured a promise of arms from General John E. Wool, commandant of the federal arsenal at Benicia. Justice David S. Terry of the state supreme court issued a writ of habeas corpus for the release of the keeper of the county jail, who was being held prisoner by the vigilance committee. The committee defied the writ. San Francisco Sheriff Scannell telegraphed the governor that a large body of armed men was defying the authority of county and state government and asked for help from the militia. On June 2, Governor Johnson ordered General Sherman to call on "such numbers" of the state militia as he considered necessary, and 2 days later the governor proclaimed San Francisco to be in a state of insurrection.

At this point General Wool reneged on his promise of arms. Sherman, unwilling to command men whom he could not arm, resigned as militia commander. Justice Terry now became the chief adviser of the Law and Order faction, taking time out from his regular judicial duties. He unearthed a statute requiring the federal

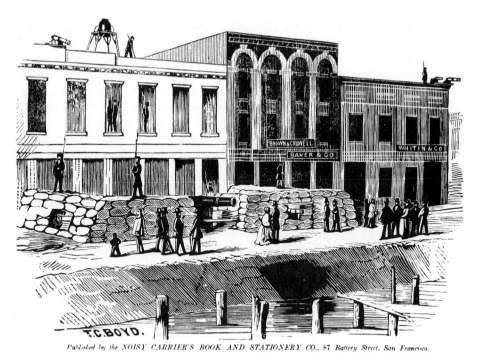

Published by the NOISY CARRIER'S BOOK AND STATIONERY CO., 87 Battery Street, San Francisco.

Fort Gunnybags. From a contemporary letter sheet. (*Courtesy of the California Historical Society, FN-21522.*)

government to furnish a certain allotment of arms to the state militia, and General Wool released 113 muskets. When this shipment was dispatched to San Francisco in a small schooner, the vigilantes intercepted it. Vigilante policeman Steling A. Hopkins then tried to arrest one of the militiamen who had been in charge of the shipment. In the ensuing scuffle, a vigilante accidentally fired a pistol, and Justice Terry stabbed Hopkins with a bowie knife. When Terry sought refuge in a militia armory, a large body of vigilantes forced their way into the building and arrested him.

As one of its members put it, the vigilance committee had organized to hunt coyotes, but in Supreme Court Justice Terry, it had a grizzly bear by the tail. Nevertheless it held a trial, in which Terry brilliantly conducted his own defense. Fortunately, Hopkins did not die. Though Terry was "convicted" of assault with intent to kill, he was released on August 7 after a bitter disagreement among the vigilante leaders. The next day the executive committee decided that although it would remain in existence, the vigilance committee as a whole should disband.

In its 3 months of existence, the committee had hung 4 accused murderers, including Cora and Casey, and had sentenced 30 others to deportation with orders not to return to San Francisco on pain of death. It was claimed that several hundred other bad characters had left the city in fear of the vigilantes.

The San Francisco Committee of Vigilance of 1856 was, as Josiah Royce described it, "a Business Man's Revolution." It was an application of private enterprise to the administration of justice. The philosophy of the vigilante leadership clearly reflected a set of attitudes characteristic of most early California business-people and some later ones—their dislike and distrust of government and their resentment of taxation. After the disbandment of the vigilance committee its leaders formed the People's party, which swept the city elections of November 1856 and won most of the city offices for the next 10 years. Its primary objective was drastic tax reduction; the leadership of both the vigilance committee and the People's party included many of the city's most chronic tax evaders. In 1857, under the People's party administration, San Francisco taxes were slashed so extremely that several of the schools had to be closed and the city could not afford to buy hoses for the volunteer fire companies.

Study of the crime rate before and after the vigilance movement of 1856 does not support the claim of any actual reduction in crime after the vigilantes took over. The charges that the legally constituted courts had been corrupt were in general not true. As for vigilante jurisprudence, its record of violations of due process was appalling.

The leaders of the vigilance committees would have served California far better if they had confined their activities to legal methods and to genuine reforms. It is doubtful that they accomplished anything whatever of real value, and they left a vicious, dangerous, and persistent tradition of contempt for the normal processes of democratic government.

Selected Bibliography

Several studies in recent decades have reassessed the origins of vigilantism. The most important are Richard Maxwell Brown, *Strain of Violence: Historical Studies of American Violence and Vigilantes* (1975); Peter R. Decker, *Fortunes and Failures: White-Collar Mobility in Nineteenth Century San Francisco* (1978); Robert M. Senkewicz, *Vigilantes in Gold Rush San Francisco* (1985); John D. Gordon, *Authorized by No Law* (1987); Kevin J. Mullen, *Let Justice Be Done* (1989); Philip J. Ethington, *The Public City* (1995); and John Boessenecker (ed.), *Against the Vigilantes* (1999) and *Gold Dust and Gunsmoke* (1999).

Roger D. McGrath, *Gunfighters, Highwaymen, and Vigilantes* (1984); Boessenecker, *Badge and Buckshot* (1988); and R. E. Mather and F. E. Boswell, *Gold Camp Desperadoes* (1993), analyze crime on the California frontier. Lawrence M. Friedman and Robert V. Percival, *The Roots of Justice* (1981), and Gordon M. Bakken, *The Development of Law in Frontier California* (1985) and *Practicing Law in Frontier California* (1991), trace the rise of legal institutions.

An account of the first formal organization of vigilantes in California (1836) is in Robert W. Blew, "Vigilantism in Los Angeles, 1835–1874," *Southern California Quarterly,* LIV (Spring 1972), pp. 11–30. The story of Josefa Segovia (Juanita) is told in Manuel Gonzales, *Mexicanos* (1999).

The tone of most earlier historical treatments of the vigilantes was set by three important and influential accounts, all written at about the same time. Charles H. Shinn, in his *Mining Camps* (1885), accepted very uncritically the reminiscences of the participants whom he interviewed. Josiah Royce, in *California, from the Conquest in 1846 to the Second Vigilance Committee in San Francisco* (1886), was more critical of the miners but praised the San

Francisco committees. Hubert Howe Bancroft, in *Popular Tribunals* (two volumes, 1887), defended some of the rural tribunals and was positively worshipful of the urban ones; his views reflected the feelings of most San Francisco businesspeople, of whom Bancroft was one. Mary Floyd Williams, *History of the San Francisco Committee of Vigilance of 1851* (1921), is scholarly in details but generally very admiring. George R. Stewart, *Committee of Vigilance,* (1964), is also sympathetic. The highly laudatory spirit of *"The Lion of the Vigilantes": William T. Coleman and the Life of Old San Francisco* (1939), by James A. B. Scherer, is well suggested by its title. Also generally favorable is Roger Olmsted, "San Francisco and the Vigilante Style," *The American West,* VII (January and March 1972).

Critical early treatments of vigilantism are in William H. Ellison, *A Self-Governing Dominion* (1950); A. Russell Buchanan, *David S. Terry of California* (1959); John W. Caughey, *Their Majesties, the Mob* (1960); and Roger W. Lotchin, *San Francisco, 1846–1856* (1974). Doyce B. Nunis, Jr. (ed.), *The San Francisco Vigilance Committee of 1856: Three Views* (1971), includes an excellent historical introduction and bibliographical essay.

The "official response" to the problem of crime and punishment is described in Shelley Bookspan, *A Germ of Goodness: The California State Prison System, 1851–1944* (1992).

CHAPTER 11

Racial Oppression and Conflict

In the years after the gold rush, a large majority of the American citizens of California cherished a fixed belief in the innate superiority of whites over other races. They also believed that Protestant Christians were better people than were the followers of other religious faiths and that persons of Anglo-American nativity were innately superior to those of other national origins.

Of the fears, the hatreds, and the various kinds of intolerance that accompanied this set of opinions, the deepest were associated with the idea of racial superiority. In part this was because that idea was very closely associated with economic group interest; equally important, however, were the essentially irrational aspects of racial fears and hatreds. The maltreatment of nonwhites and immigrants during the gold rush, historian Kevin Starr has concluded, was "a dark and ominous warning that there was something very wrong in the American national character."

Treatment of Mexican Miners

As Anglo-Americans poured into the mining districts of California in 1849 and 1850, they found themselves in competition with substantial numbers of foreigners. The most numerous of these were Mexicans from the state of Sonora, as the naming of one of the largest towns in the southern mines attested. Others came from Chile, Peru, and elsewhere in Latin America. Feelings of hostility left over from the Mexican War were intensified because many of the Sonorans were experienced miners, skillful in locating good claims. Americans feared that foreigners were removing too much of the readily available gold and that there would soon be none left. Mining-camp codes, enforced by vigilance committees and ratified by the state legislature, excluded Mexicans and Asians from many of the diggings.

Spanish-speaking miners regarded such exclusionary efforts as manifestations of *gringos envidiosos,* or jealous white men, and they took forceful action to defend themselves. When Anglo-Americans attempted to drive a group of Chilenos from their claims in Calaveras County in December 1849, the Spanish-speaking miners attacked the Americans, killing two and wounding four. Several hundred enraged and heavily armed Americans then counterattacked, swearing to "shoot down every one of them on the road." In the ensuing violence, the Americans executed three Chilenos, flogged others, and banished all Spanish-speaking miners from the region.

Further evidence of antiforeign sentiment appeared when the California legislature of 1850 enacted a foreign miners' license tax. Introduced by Senator Thomas Jefferson Green, the act required miners who were not citizens of the United States to pay a fee of $20 a month. This levy was so high that the Mexicans, on whom most of the burden would fall, were unable or unwilling to pay it, and a mass meeting in the town of Sonora announced their refusal. Hundreds of armed American miners, including many veterans wearing their old Mexican War uniforms, then gathered at Sonora to aid the collectors of the tax and to prevent Mexicans from mining without a license.

At this time there were about 15,000 Mexicans in the *southern mines*—in Calaveras, Tuolumne, and Mariposa counties. Under the pressures of the tax and of threats of violence, about 10,000 left the region in the summer of 1850, most of them to return to Mexico. Although the Treaty of Guadalupe Hidalgo provided that Mexican citizens of California who chose to remain there for a year became American citizens automatically, many Americans, in ignorance or defiance of this provision, lumped all Mexicans together, and many native Californians were driven from the mines along with the Mexican nationals, in fear for their lives and with bitterness in their hearts. Their protests had little or no political effect. On the other hand, the protests of American merchants in the mining districts, who had lost so many customers, were strong enough to carry considerable weight in the legislature, especially when it became clear that the nearly prohibitive tax was bringing in only a small amount of revenue. The tax was repealed in 1851, but it was soon reenacted in more moderate form.

Land-Title Troubles

Among the circumstances that made for lawlessness and violence in early American California, one of the most important was the confused condition of the ownership of land. Not until 1851 did the United States government determine its general policy toward the confirmation of titles to the vast lands that had been granted under Mexico; after the determination of the policy, many more years were required to secure actual approval of claims.

American laws required that land titles be defined exactly and clearly, and by American standards the Mexican system was incredibly lax and vague. In California, the Mexican authorities failed to provide the grantees with adequate evidence of their titles or to keep adequate records in the archives. Maps, when there were any, were very sketchy, for professional surveyors were seldom available. The frequent use of the expression "a little more or less" (*poco más ó menos*) after any measure of distance was typical of the Mexican grant system. There were several legal requirements, such as that a grant had to have been approved by the territorial assembly and to have been occupied; very seldom, however, had all the requirements been fulfilled.

There were more than 500 ranchos in Alta California in 1846, but more than 800 claims were filed in the American courts, many of them covering portions of ranchos. The claims covered nearly all the valley lands of the coastal region as far north as the Russian River and a number of large tracts in the Sacramento and northern San Joaquin valleys.

The Treaty of Guadalupe Hidalgo promised that "property of every kind" belonging to Mexicans in the ceded territories should be "inviolably respected," but American settlers generally believed that all the lands in California were now, or ought to be, United States public lands by right of conquest. Americans were accustomed to occupy tracts on the federal public lands before they were surveyed and opened to settlement, and then to be permitted to buy the land at the minimum price. The American settlers of California could not believe that a few hundred Mexican grantees would be permitted to monopolize some 13 million acres of land, little of it visibly improved and much of it entirely unoccupied.

Most of the claims did not represent lands that had been long in the possession of old California families as their homes. In fact a majority of the grants were dated within the last 5 years before the American conquest, and it was accurately suspected that some of those claimed to have been made under Mexican governors had been signed by them after the forced expirations of their terms of office, and antedated. There were many multiple grants. The various claims of the Pico family totaled 532,000 acres, and those of the de la Guerra and Carrillo families more than 300,000 each. Moreover, large-scale speculation had begun. Thomas Larkin, for example, had purchased several claims totaling nearly 200,000 acres.

Governor Richard B. Mason had instructed his secretary of state, Captain Henry Halleck, to make a study of California land titles. In a report completed early in 1849, Halleck pointed out that most of the Mexican claims were imperfect and asserted that many of them were fraudulent. This report had the effect of encouraging the views of those who were known to themselves as "settlers" and less favorably described as "squatters." Their vigorous opinions produced several episodes of violence, of which the most tragic was the *squatter riot* at Sacramento in the summer of 1850.

The town was located on land granted to Sutter by Alvarado, a grant that would eventually be upheld. Several thousand settlers, refusing to recognize the validity of this title, had squatted on vacant lots owned by purchasers from Sutter. After sheriff's deputies began to destroy the squatters' houses and fences, there was a meeting to collect money for a legal defense fund. James McClatchy, later the founder of the city's leading journalistic family, told this meeting that "if the speculators want to fight, I am for giving them battle. . . . Let us put up all the fences pulled down and also put up [hang] all the men who pull them down." He was arrested for trying to carry out at least a part of his threat. On August 13, when an

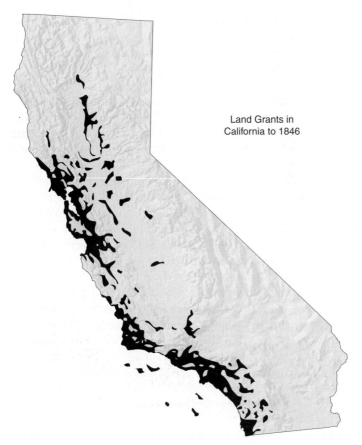

Land Grants in
California to 1846

The dark areas on the map show the grants that were confirmed by the United States. (*From* Land in California, *by W. W. Robinson. Copyright 1948 by the University of California Press.*)

armed band moved to rescue McClatchy from the riverboat that served as a jail, Mayor Harden Bigelow gathered a crowd of citizens, and in a clash at Fourth and J streets the city assessor and three squatters were killed and the mayor was wounded. The next day another battle led to the death of Sheriff Joseph McKinney and several others on both sides.

Meanwhile, the secretary of the interior had appointed a brilliant young attorney, William Carey Jones, to make another investigation. Jones had married a sister of Jessie Benton Frémont, and the views of California land titles embodied in his report in March 1850 coincided with those of his father-in-law, Senator Benton, and of John C. Frémont, his brother-in-law and client, who had had the good fortune to purchase the only Mexican grant on which large amounts of gold were subsequently discovered. The Jones report maintained that the grants were mostly *perfect titles,* that is, formal titles showing evidence of completeness. Thus, Jones recommended a very liberal policy toward the Mexican grants. Naturally the claimants praised this report and the settlers denounced it.

The Act of 1851 and the Land Commission

The act that determined the policy of the United States toward the land claims in California was introduced by Senator William M. Gwin, chief political spokesman for the American settlers. His bill provided for the appointment by the president of a board of three commissioners. This board was to decide the validity of all claims to land under Mexican titles. All the lands of the rejected claims were to be regarded as public lands. Both the claimant and the United States had the right of appeal to the federal district court and then to the United States Supreme Court. Critics of this plan argued that it would have the effect of confiscating the lands of the grantees in California, and thus of violating the treaty with Mexico; every title would be treated as a fraud against the United States until its holder had established it in three different courts, one of them the Supreme Court, located 3000 miles away.

The land commission held its hearings from January 1852 to March 1856. All its sessions were held in San Francisco except for one brief term at Los Angeles. Of the more than 800 cases presented to it, all but a few were appealed to the district court, and 99 were appealed to the Supreme Court. Ultimately, 604 claims, involving nearly 9 million acres, were confirmed, while 209 claims, involving about 4 million acres, were rejected. Some of the cases dragged on in the courts for several decades, and the average length of time required to secure evidence of ownership was *17 years* from the time of submitting a claim to the board.

By the time a grant was confirmed, its original holder was usually bankrupt. The litigation required for an American title under the system established by the Gwin act was long and ruinously expensive. Although the alleged excessiveness of the lawyers' fees has often been exaggerated, there were dozens of instances in which grantees were ruined while their attorneys became rich, especially by taking part of the fees in land, holding the land as a speculation, and eventually winning the case. If grantees tried to sell part of their land to pay the costs of litigation, they could get only a low price because they did not yet have a secure title. If grantees finally managed to establish their title in court, they often found their land occupied by settlers who refused to get off. As historian Lisbeth Haas has concluded, the California newcomers "ended up owning or claiming all or portions of almost every rancho in the state."

The impoverishment of the old landowning families of California evoked expressions of intense bitterness. Apolinaria Lorenzano, once the proud owner of three ranchos, mourned the loss of her lands: "I find myself in the greatest poverty, living by the favor of God and from handouts." Another ranchera, María Amparo Ruiz Burton, traveled to Washington, D.C. to lobby Congress on behalf of the claims of the dispossessed grantees. Burton also attempted to present her case to the general public through *The Squatter and the Don* (1885), a novel filled with a sense of loss and betrayal. "Land is not considered private property until the title to it is confirmed and patented," she wrote. "As the proceedings to obtain a patent might consume years, almost a lifetime, the result is that the [grantees] are virtually despoiled of their lands."

One of the most striking of the land-grant cases was that of John C. Frémont's claim to Las Mariposas, the only Mexican grant in the mother-lode region. Consisting of a sizable part of the present Mariposa County, this grant had been made to Juan B. Alvarado by Governor Micheltorena in 1844. Far from having fulfilled the requirement of occupancy, Alvarado had not even seen the place when in 1847 he sold it to Frémont for $3000. Gold was discovered on it in the spring of 1849—so much gold, in fact, that it became known as the "$10 million" grant. The district court ruled the claim invalid on the ground that the original recipient of the grant had never fulfilled a single one of the several conditions attached to it. The Supreme Court, however, confirmed Frémont's claim, and a patent was issued to him in February 1856, a few months before he became the first Republican nominee for the presidency. Among its many defects, Las Mariposas was an example of the *floating grant,* that is, one in which the total area is stated but the boundaries are not specified. When the official survey was made, the boundaries were swung about in such a way as to include three rich mining districts that Frémont had not previously claimed. Several lives were then lost in attempts to evict miners who had been working in these districts.

In San Francisco, titles were at least as chaotic as in any other part of the state. The pueblo grant of 4 square leagues was not confirmed until 1866, and there were several conflicting claims of private grants, widely and correctly believed to be fraudulent but covering large parts of the area of the city. In this situation squatting was inevitable and rampant, and many a fortune in San Francisco real estate was founded on "shot-gun titles." Squatters fortified the lots they occupied, and one of them tried to fence off Union Square. Landowners had to hire private police.

The entire cities of Oakland, Berkeley, and Alameda were built on the land of a single grant, the Rancho San Antonio, conveyed to Sergeant Luís Peralta in 1820 as a reward for long service in the Spanish army in northern California. Don Luís divided the ranch among his four sons in 1842. For years after 1846, Vicente Peralta stubbornly insisted that he wished no town to be built on his land and refused to sell parts of it for that purpose. Consequently, in 1850 the original street plan of Oakland was laid out as a squatter enterprise. The Peralta grant was recognized in the courts, and several decades passed before the taint of squatting was finally cleared from Oakland titles. It is not surprising that in the twentieth century, the services of title insurance companies were more widely required and used in California than in any other state.

Los Angeles anticipated its later expansive tendencies by claiming that its pueblo grant had been 4 leagues square rather than 4 square leagues. This claim, which would have given the municipality 16 square leagues, was finally reduced to the usual 4.

Many writers have blamed the act of 1851 for the tragic difficulties of early American land problems in California, and Bancroft went so far as to assert that it would have been practically impossible to have devised a worse plan for dealing with them. Yet, even with the advantages of hindsight, no one has convincingly suggested a better one. In any event, the land-title troubles not only caused hardships for the Mexican grantees, they also retarded settlement and damaged the early development of American agriculture in the state. John S. Hittell estimated that during the 1850s, a quarter of a million Americans who would otherwise have settled in California did not do so because of the insecurity of land titles; including all family members, the net loss to California was probably a full million potential residents.

Early Discrimination against the Chinese

At the end of 1849, only a few hundred Chinese had come to seek the gold of California. In 1851, however, the outbreak of the great Taiping Rebellion against the Manchu dynasty plunged China into 15 years of civil war and general disorder that further deepened the poverty of most of its people. For more than two centuries, periods of extraordinary economic depression had induced many thousands of Chinese to emigrate, particularly from south China to several parts of Southeast Asia. Now rumors of easy wealth brought a great stream of Chinese emigrants to Gum San, (Gold Mountain), their name for California. Nearly all of them, like most of the American Argonauts, were young men who dreamed of acquiring a fortune and returning home to enjoy it with the families they had left behind. But whereas most of those Americans who were disappointed in this hope eventually reconciled themselves to becoming permanent residents of California, the Chinese tended to cling for the rest of their lives to the dream of returning to their homeland, even though few of them were ever able to do so.

Many of the Chinese immigrants to California suffered oppression by creditors and other exploiters among their own race. Following a pattern long established in Chinese overseas migration, impoverished young men from Canton, Hong Kong, or the neighboring rural areas made contracts for the payment of their passage under the *credit-ticket system.* In California their labor was sold, through Chinese subcontractors, to Chinese mining companies, which paid them very low wages. The hapless Chinese workers were kept in a state of debt bondage enforced by a Chinese creditor-employer network. This system was reinforced by various types of associations, the most important of which were the district companies, based on the several districts of southeastern China from which nearly all the California Chinese had come.

In 1852 the number of Chinese in California rose to about 25,000. Concentrated in the mining regions and in San Francisco, they were now by far the largest of the foreign minorities. They formed a tenth of the state's population other than Indians, and nearly a third of the population in several of the mining counties. An outburst of agitation against them began when a bill was introduced in the state senate to legalize the enforcement in California of labor contracts made in China. Throughout the mining camps there was such a rash of mass meetings and resolutions denouncing this "coolie bill" that the measure was decisively defeated. "Coolie" was a word around which a great deal of emotion and confusion revolved. Its probable derivation was from *kuli,* meaning "muscle" in Tamil, a language of southern India. The British, using it to mean a hired unskilled laborer or servant, introduced the word into China, where it was approximated by two Chinese characters meaning "bitter strength."

Later, in the legislative session of 1852, the foreign miners' license tax was reenacted with the clear understanding that it would be enforced primarily on the Chinese. The tax was set initially at $3 per month.

The Chinese did not submit passively to such acts of discrimination. In 1852 Har Wa and Long Achik, two Chinese merchants in San Francisco, wrote an elegant letter to Governor Bigler to protest his characterization of all Chinese as "coolies":

> We are good men; we honor our parents; we take care of our children; we are industrious and peaceable; we trade much; we are trusted for small and large sums; we pay our debts and are honest; and, of course, we must tell the truth.

When the legislature in 1853 considered raising the monthly foreign miners' license tax, several Chinese community leaders (aided by white attorneys whom they had hired) lobbied against anything other than a modest increase. The leaders also complained about physical assaults on Chinese miners. Apparently their efforts were successful; the legislature increased the monthly tax by only one dollar.

Much to the irritation of the white miners, but greatly to the benefit of the state treasury, the tax failed to discourage the Chinese, many of whom paid it in the hope that it would reconcile the whites to their continued presence in the mines. Until 1870, when the state supreme court belatedly declared it unconstitutional, this tax, paid by the Chinese almost exclusively, brought in nearly a fourth of the state's entire revenue, even though thieving tax collectors, dissatisfied with the commissions allowed them, often let the Chinese miner off with a payment of $2 if he agreed not to demand a receipt. In addition, many Chinese were victimized by Americans impersonating tax collectors.

The status of the Chinese was undermined further by an infamous decision of the California state supreme court, *People v. Hall* (1854). Four years earlier the legislature had prohibited blacks and Indians from testifying in court, either "in favor of, or against a white man." In *People v. Hall,* Chief Justice Hugh C. Murray (who was 29 years old) pronounced the doctrine that the Chinese were legally Indians, because both were probably descended from the same Asian ancestors. Thus, nonwhites (and whites also) were denied legal protection from any outrage at the hands of a white person if the only witnesses were black, Chinese, or Indian. Leaders of the Chinese community strenuously objected to being grouped together with blacks and Indians. Norman Asing, in a letter to Governor Bigler, argued that the Chinese were "as much allied to the African race and the red man as you are yourself." In a similar vein, San Francisco merchant Lai Chun-chuen wrote to the governor, objecting to the supreme court's decision "that will not allow us to bear witness" based on the erroneous claim "that we Chinese are the same as Indians

Chinese miner panning for gold, 1852. (*Photograph by Eadweard Muybridge. Courtesy of the California Historical Society, FN-04470.*)

and Negroes." In 1869 Fung Tang and other Chinese business leaders met with a congressional delegation to demand relief from California's discriminatory laws: "Most of all—we feel the want of protection to life and property when Courts of Justice refuse our testimony, and thus leave us defenseless and unable to obtain justice for ourselves."

In the meantime, another legal weapon against the Chinese had been found in the federal law which had provided since 1790 that only "free white persons" could be naturalized. This provision was a deep flaw in the application of American ideals of democracy. In California, the provision was used in a remarkable number of laws as an excuse for other forms of discrimination. This shabby device would continue to be employed for nearly 100 years. Its use would end only when discrimination on the ground of race was finally stricken from the federal naturalization statutes in 1952. In California, state laws directed against "aliens ineligible to citizenship," as a euphemism for aliens of nonwhite ancestry, began to appear in 1855 when the legislature sought to impose a head tax of $50 on all immigrants "who cannot become citizens." This was soon declared unconstitutional because the state could not tax immigration, but another state law of 1855 made ineligibility for citizenship the main definition of those to whom the foreign miners' license tax applied, and thus ensured the enforcement of the tax more specifically against the Chinese.

Fortunately, the Chinese were a people who had developed a remarkable adaptability during many centuries of oppression in China itself. Their sufferings, however, and those of all the other racial minorities, were overshadowed by the disasters that befell the California Indians.

The "Indian Question"

Since the 1820s the federal government had followed a *removal policy* as its general solution of "the Indian problem." A *permanent Indian frontier* had been created along the eastern edge of the Great Plains. By a long series of treaties, the Indian nations or tribes of the eastern and central parts of the country had been induced to move west of this line to new lands which the American government promised to reserve for them in perpetuity. But this process had scarcely been completed when, in the 1840s, the extension of the American boundary to the Pacific made the line obsolete. A new federal policy for the Indians of the west had to be devised.

In 1850 Congress passed an act authorizing three Indian agents, or commissioners, to negotiate a series of treaties with the California tribes. The commissioners were Redick McKee, George W. Barbour, and Dr. Oliver M. Wozencraft. They negotiated 18 treaties affecting 139 tribes or bands. Among the Indian signatories were José Jesús (Siakumne), Cornelius (Tuolumne), and Cypriano (Awal). In each of the treaties, the native leaders acknowledged the jurisdiction of the United States, agreed to refrain from hostilities, and ceded to the federal government all claims to the territory they had held. In return the commissioners promised the Indians provisions, cattle, and large tracts of land to be set apart for reservations. The proposed reservations totaled 11,700 square miles, or 7,488,000 acres. This was about 7½ percent of the entire land area of the state. Moreover, although Congress had appropriated only $50,000 for the work of the commissioners, they let contracts totaling nearly $1 million for provisions and cattle, on the theory that, as they reported to Washington, "it is *cheaper* to feed the whole flock for a *year* than to fight them for a *week*."

The federal commissioners overreached themselves, and, unfortunately, their plan failed. Only a small fraction of the California Indians moved even temporarily to the proposed reservations. Opponents of the plan believed it intolerable that vast tracts of rich land within the state should be made the exclusive domain of Indians, and the state legislature recommended that the federal government continue its traditional policy of removing the Indians entirely outside the boundaries of the state. The legislature was careful to distinguish, however, between the "wild" or "hostile" Indians it wanted removed and those it regarded as "tame" or "useful." In the latter category were the Indians who had been influenced by the missions and were now an important source of labor for white farmers and ranchers. The legislature objected to these Indians being placed on the proposed reservations because it would deprive whites of their Indian workers.

When the treaties came up for ratification in 1852, California's United States senators, Gwin and Weller, opposed them so vigorously that the Senate rejected all

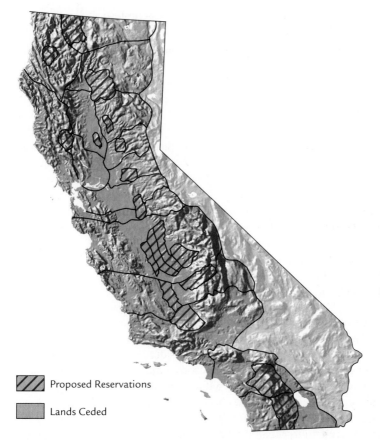

Proposed Reservations

Lands Ceded

Unratified treaty lands, 1851–52. (*From* Indians of California: The Changing Image, *by James J. Rawls. Copyright 1984 by the University of Oklahoma Press.*)

of them. The vast reservations proposed by McKee, Barbour, and Wozencraft thus were aborted. The size of the reservations and the amount of food and supplies the commissioners promised the Indians far exceeded the intentions of Congress, but had their grand design been successful, the history of Indian and white relations in California surely would have been less bloody.

There was widespread fear that the rejection of the treaties would lead the Indians to outbreaks of violence. In 1853, as a palliative, Congress adopted a much more modest plan suggested by Edward F. Beale, the new superintendent of Indian affairs for California. Beale recommended a system of smaller reservations that would also serve as military posts for the United States Army. The Indians would be taught to engage in agriculture and handicrafts, much in the manner of the Spanish missions though without the religious emphasis. Ultimately, it was hoped, the Indians on these reservations might become self-sustaining. Five such establishments, of 25,000 acres each, were authorized under the act of 1853. The first, at Tejon in the Tehachapi foothills, contained about 2500 Indians. Other reservations were soon established in northern California.

Beale pushed his experiment with enthusiasm and vigor, but it had scarcely begun when he was removed from office in 1854. The Office of Indian Affairs in Washington was peculiarly vulnerable to the abuses of the spoils system, and its personnel rotated with every new administration. In general, Beale's successors and their subordinates were incompetent and venal political appointees. In 1858 a federal investigator reported that the reservations were a lamentable failure. In that same year, Indians on the Tejon reservation armed themselves and launched a short-lived strike to protest the intolerable conditions. The *Los Angeles Star* reported that soldiers soon quelled the protest "and the ringleaders were taken out and received from twenty to one hundred lashes."

Unsuccessful as this pitiful system was, however, the federal government failed to devise a better one, and Beale's plan became the model for federal Indian reservations all over the west for many decades afterward.

Episodes in Extermination

The two decades after the gold rush produced dozens of wretched episodes that can best be described as massacres, the great majority of them perpetrated on the Indians by the whites. As the incoming tide of whites drove the Indians from their traditional food-producing areas, many Indians were able to survive only by seizing horses and other livestock belonging to whites, and this led to instant and violent retaliation.

The most terrifying assertions about the California Indians were widely believed. In 1851 Governor John McDougal asserted that 100,000 Indian warriors were in a state of armed rebellion, and the following year one of California's United States senators claimed that only a "master spirit" was needed to "confederate the tribes in a bloody and devastating war." These statements were fantastically false. By this time there were fewer than 100,000 Indians of all ages and both sexes left in the state, and because of their linguistic and cultural differences they were incapable of "confederating" for war or for any other common purpose.

Gripped by fear and convinced of their own racial superiority, whites on the California frontier banded together to exterminate the Indians. Units loosely organized as state militia went on Indian-hunting expeditions. In the process, thousands of Indians were killed. Typical of the extreme anti-Indian sentiment was the demand by the Chico *Courant* in 1866 for vigorous armed action against the Indians. "It has become a question of extermination now," the *Courant* explained. "The man who takes a prisoner should himself be shot. It is a mercy to the red devils to exterminate them, and a saving of many white lives. Treaties are played out. There is only one kind of treaty that is effective—cold lead."

Many of the punitive expeditions launched against the Indians were financed by the state government, and during the 1850s more than $1 million worth of state bonds were issued to pay the expenses of local volunteer campaigns for "the suppression of Indian hostilities." The federal government reimbursed the state for most of these expenditures under congressional appropriation acts of 1854 and 1861. Thus, the actions of the frontier bands took on the aspect of legalized and subsidized murder.

Bret Harte recorded in horrific detail an episode of extermination, as carried out by whites on the northern California frontier in 1860. Harte was working as the junior editor of a local newspaper in the town of Union, now Arcata, in Humboldt County. Before dawn one February morning, a small band of whites attacked a nearby Indian village and perpetrated the most contemptible racist massacre in the history of the state. With axes, hatchets, and knives, the whites killed 60 Indians, mostly women and children. Harte bitterly denounced the murders in an article headlined "Indiscriminate Massacre of Indians":

> A short time after, the writer was upon the ground with feet treading in human blood, horrified with the awful and sickening sights which met the eye wherever it turned. Here was a mother fatally wounded hugging the mutilated carcass of her dying infant to her bosom; there a child of two years old, with its ear and scalp torn from the side of its little head. Here a father frantic with grief over the bloody corpses of his four little children and wife. . . . The wounded, dead, and dying were found all around, and in every lodge the skulls and frames of women and children cleft with axes and hatchets, and stabbed with knives, and the brains of an infant oozing from its broken head to the ground.

Following the article's publication, threats against the life of Bret Harte became so menacing that he left Union for San Francisco. Bearing witness was a courageous—and dangerous—act.

The Indian response to white belligerence involved a wide variety of strategies. As historians James Sandos and George Phillips have demonstrated, the native people of California "played more complex roles than as mere victims of white aggression." Among the coping strategies of the Indians of southern California was the attempt by José Panto (Kumeyaay) to maintain the integrity of his people through negotiation and peaceful relations. Antonio Garra, meanwhile, led his Cupeño followers in a tax revolt against white officials in 1851 and later called for a pan-Indian campaign against the invaders. José Juarez, the highly respected chief of the Chauchila, encouraged Indians in the southern mines to launch an all-out war against the whites. He assured his people that if the whites "follow after us, they cannot find us; none of them will come back; we will kill them with arrows and rocks."

Nevertheless, few of the California Indians were able to offer effective resistance to the military and quasi-military campaigns against them. The main exceptions came in the mountainous northern part of the state. The most famous conflict in that region occurred after a band of Modocs left the reservation which they had been forced to share with the Oregon Klamaths and returned without permission to their former country on Lost River. The conflict could have been prevented by allowing the Modocs to occupy a bit of land that was of very little value to the whites, and which would have been only a tiny fragment of the lands that had once been Modoc territory. In 1873 a force of 400 soldiers, mostly of the regular Army, drove the Modocs to take refuge in the lava beds. There, although heavily outnumbered and fighting only with old muzzle loaders and pistols against rifles and artillery, the Modocs fortified themselves so well that they inflicted many casualties while suffering very few of their own. At a peace conference, where they were offered no better terms than a return to the reservation in Oregon, their chief, Kientipoos ("Captain Jack"), was goaded by some of his warriors into a plot in which they murdered General E. R. S. Canby and a Methodist missionary and wounded an Indian agent. Ultimately, the Modocs were defeated and Kientipoos was hanged, but not until the war had cost the lives of about 75 whites and half a million dollars.

Some of the most geographically isolated of the California tribes, such as the Yahi, tried to continue their ancient manner of life and to avoid all contact with white society. The country of the Yahi was in the Mill Creek region south of Mount Lassen. The gold seekers of the 1850s hunted the Yahi as if they were wild animals, and by 1870 it was supposed that they were extinct. But in 1911 a man who was apparently the last survivor of the tribe was found in a slaughterhouse near Oroville, where he had come in search of food. Professor Alfred L. Kroeber, of the University of California, called him Ishi, the Yahi word for "man." *Yahi* meant simply "the people."

Professor Kroeber and Professor Thomas T. Waterman, also of the University of California, brought Ishi to the university's museum of anthropology, then in San Francisco. There Ishi lived for several years until his death. Middle-aged and in reasonably good health at the time of his "capture" by the sheriff at Oroville, Ishi caught his first cold in San Francisco and later succumbed to tuberculosis. In the meantime, this Stone Age man had adapted himself remarkably well to a twentieth-century environment. Alfred Kroeber believed that Ishi had made the transition from one culture to another more effectively and more quickly than he himself could have done, and the episode became an important example of the kind of evidence that led virtually every competent anthropologist in the world to reject the idea of the biological inferiority of so-called primitive races.

Decline and Exploitation

During the Spanish and Mexican periods, the California Indian population had dropped from at least 300,000 to no more than 150,000 by 1845. With the coming of hundreds of thousands of whites following the American conquest, the Indian death rate tragically accelerated. By 1870 there were only about 30,000 Indians left. In 1900 there were fewer than 16,000. Disease continued to take the largest toll, probably accounting for about 60 percent of the deaths during the second half of the nineteenth century. Starvation and malnutrition probably added about 30 percent to the death toll. Less than 10 percent resulted from purely physical assault through formal military campaigns, informal expeditions, and various other forms of homicide.

In the midst of demographic decline, California Indians were painfully aware of the devastation of their ancestral homelands. Kate Luckie, a Wintun woman, expressed sorrow and anger at what she had seen and heard:

> The white people plow up the ground, pull up the trees, kill everything. The tree says, "Don't. I am sore. Don't hurt me." But they chop it down and cut it up. The spirit of the land hates them. They blast out trees and stir it up to its depths. They saw up the trees. That hurts them. . . . They blast rocks and scatter them on the earth. The rock says, "Don't! You are hurting me." But the white people pay no attention.

Some Indians adapted to the new order by working for whites, often in a state of peonage comparable to that which had existed on the Mexican ranchos. Indian labor was especially prized during the early years of the American period when all other available laborers were making for the goldfields. In those flush times, it was often difficult to procure white labor at any price, and the Indians of California filled the gap. Americans adopted various regulations that continued the Mexican system of Indian labor exploitation. Under an act of the state legislature in 1850, any unemployed Indian could be declared a vagrant and auctioned off to the highest bidder as an indentured servant. A lucrative business of kidnapping Indians, especially children, for sale as household and farm servants flourished. A white person could mistreat and even murder an Indian with virtual impunity. J. Ross Browne, a special agent of the Treasury Department, wrote that "if ever an Indian was fully and honestly paid for his labor by a white settler, it was not my luck to hear it." The treatment of Indian laborers was in general so oppressive that it contributed more to their extinction than to their support, and, particularly in agriculture, the feeling that the landowner had a right to a supply of cheap labor drawn from the people of some supposedly inferior race set an evil precedent for future generations.

As for the alternative of assimilating the Indians into the general population, this was made impossible in the early American period not only by the prejudices of the whites against the Indians but also by the deep resentment which the Indians felt against the whites.

Blacks Enslaved and Free

Although the state constitution prohibited slavery, slaveholders from the south nevertheless brought slaves with them to California. At least 500 enslaved African Americans worked as miners for their white masters; others served as household servants or were hired out as laborers. As historian Shirley Ann Moore has concluded, "slavery remained the most critical issue confronting [African Americans] in the Golden State."

In 1852 the state adopted a harsh fugitive-slave law reflecting the odious federal statute that had been a part of the compromise under which California was admitted to the Union. Only one actual fugitive slave is known to have reached

California, but the law was enforced against a number of blacks whose masters had brought them there and later wished to return them to the south. The last and most famous of these cases, that of Archy Lee, was tried in 1858. The state supreme court ruled that although the master had forfeited his right to the slave by bringing him to a free state after its admission to the Union and by remaining for a substantial time, an exception should be made in this instance because the master was young and in poor health and in need of his slave's services. This decision was widely ridiculed, and Lee was freed shortly afterward by a United States commissioner in San Francisco.

Blacks who came to California from the free states of the north arrived with the same dream of riches that motivated other Argonauts. Although the efforts of Governor Burnett to secure legislation excluding free blacks from California were no more successful than similar efforts in the constitutional convention, the coming of "persons of color" was effectively discouraged in less direct ways. In the late 1850s, there were only 2500 African Americans in California. Several state laws, such as the 1850 ban against their testimony in legal proceedings, infringed on their civil rights and treated them as an inferior people.

The law which most threatened the property and safety of California blacks was the ban on legal testimony. In 1852 African Americans in San Francisco organized a Franchise League to petition the legislature to grant them equal civil rights. Three years later a statewide California Colored Convention was formed in Sacramento, and the petition campaign for the right to testify became more vigorous. James Carter rallied support for the convention among his fellow African Americans:

> Brethren—Your state and condition in California is one of social and political degradation. . . . Since you have . . . migrated to the shores of the Pacific, with the hopes of bettering your condition, you have met with one continued series of outrages, injustices, and unmitigated wrongs unparalleled in the history of nations.

In 1863 the testimony law was finally changed, extending the right of legal testimony to blacks, but Chinese and Indians remained under the ban until 1872, when the testimony law was dropped from the California code in deference to the federal civil rights act. The Colored Convention also actively campaigned for black voting rights, but the legislature refused to extend the franchise to African Americans until 1870 when the Fifteenth Amendment to the United States Constitution was ratified.

In 1858 the state legislature passed the first of several laws that prohibited "Negroes, Mongolians, and Indians" from attending public schools. As the number of children of color increased, the legislature in 1870 ordered the establishment of segregated schools for children of "African or Indian descent." Within two years, more than 20 "colored schools" were established statewide. African Americans protested the segregation. A. J. Ward filed suit in 1874 to win admission of his daughter Mary Frances to a white school in San Francisco when the segregated school in her neighborhood closed. Although the state supreme court rejected the suit, the case of *Ward v. Flood* undermined some of the legal foundations for school segregation. The legislature subsequently modified the school code to permit African American children to attend white schools if no black school was available.

Bridget "Biddy" Mason (1818–1891), an early Los Angeles philanthropist.
"The open hand is blessed," she once said, "for it gives in abundance, even as
it receives." (*Courtesy of UCLA Special Collections.*)

Throughout the remainder of the nineteenth century, the growth of California's African American population was slow but steady. Black Californians accounted for about 1 percent of the state's total population. They remained concentrated in the major cities, where they found their employment opportunities routinely restricted by racial discrimination. Many worked in menial occupations in the lowest ranks of the service and food industries; others were able to overcome discrimination and achieve success as independent business entrepreneurs. Georgia-born Bridget "Biddy" Mason was a black woman who arrived in southern California in 1851 as a slave, obtained her freedom 5 years later, became a successful midwife and nurse, invested in Los Angeles real estate, and established herself as a local philanthropist. Unfortunately, Mason's success was exceptional rather than typical of the experiences of California's earliest black residents.

The issues of diversity that confronted Californians in the mid-nineteenth century are with us still. Historian Kevin Starr, reflecting on the appalling record of racial conflict in the gold-rush era, has reminded his fellow Californians that "we cannot exempt ourselves from continuities and responsibilities of prejudice and racial animosities down to our own time." Although enormous progress has been made in the past century and a half, "the surviving traces of the Forty-niners' disease—hostility to people who are different, who are the Other—[are] as lingering and self-evident as today's headlines."

Selected Bibliography

Practitioners of the "new western history" have emphasized the importance of racial and ethnic minorities. See especially Patricia Nelson Limerick, *Legacy of Conquest* (1987); Richard White, *It's Your Misfortune and None of My Own* (1991); Limerick (ed.), *Trails: Toward a New Western History* (1992); and Sucheng Chan, Douglas Henry Daniels, Mario T. Garcia, and Terry P. Wilson (eds.), *Peoples of Color in the American West* (1994). On the changing status of ethnic minorities in California, see R. F. Heizer and A. J. Almquist, *The Other Californians* (1971); Tomás Almaguer, *Racial Fault Lines: The Historical Origins of White Supremacy in California* (1995); and Lisbeth Haas, *Conquests and Historical Identities in California, 1769–1936* (1995). See also several essays in Kevin Starr and Richard J. Orsi (eds.), *Rooted in Barbarous Soil* (2000), especially Starr's powerful introductory essay as well as those by Sucheng Chan, James A. Sandos, and Nancy J. Taniguchi.

On Mexican Americans, see the special issue of *California History,* LXXIV (Fall 1995), edited by Richard A. Garcia; Leonard M. Pitt, *The Decline of the Californios* (1966); M. Colette Standart, "The Sonoran Migration to California, 1848–1856," *Southern California Quarterly,* LVIII (Fall 1976), pp. 333–358; and R. H. Morefield, "Mexicans in the California Mines, 1848–53," *California Historical Society Quarterly,* XXXV (1956), pp. 37–46. See also Richard H. Peterson, "Anti-Mexican Nativism in California, 1848–1853," *Southern California Quarterly,* LXII (Winter 1980), pp. 309–328.

W. W. Robinson, *Land in California* (1948), and William H. Ellison, *A Self-Governing Dominion* (1950), include well-balanced treatments of the Mexican-grant problems. See also Robert H. Becker, *Diseños of California Ranchos* (1964) and *Designs on the Land* (1969). Paul W. Gates, in "California's Embattled Settlers," *California Historical Society Quarterly,* XLI (June 1962), pp. 99–130, concluded that it was the settlers, rather than the grantees, who were most unfairly treated. Many of Gates's articles have been collected in his *Land and Law in California* (1994).

On the Chinese, see Yong Chen, *Chinese San Francisco* (2001); Madeline Hsu, *Dreaming of Gold, Dreaming of Home* (2000); Chan, *Asian Californians* (1991) and *Asian Americans* (1991); Gunther Barth, *Bitter Strength* (1964); "The Chinese in California," *California History,* LVII (Spring 1978), special issue; S. C. Miller, *The Unwelcome Immigrant* (1970); A. P. Saxton, *The Indispensable Enemy* (1971); Sandy Lydon, *Chinese Gold* (1985); and Stanford M. Lyman, *The Asian in the West* (1970).

On the Indians, see James J. Rawls, *Indians of California* (1984) and "Gold Diggers: Indian Miners in the California Gold Rush," *California Historical Quarterly,* LV (Spring 1976), pp. 28–45; Theodora Kroeber, *Ishi in Two Worlds* (1962); John W. Caughey (ed.),

The Indians of Southern California in 1852 (1952); Richard Dillon, *Burnt-Out Fires* (1973); and George H. Phillips, *Chiefs and Challengers* (1975) and *The Enduring Struggle: Indians in California History* (1981). *The Population of the California Indians, 1769–1970* (1976), by Sherburne F. Cook, deals with the decline in numbers. Two works provide additional insight into Indian-white relations in northern California: Albert L. Hurtado, *Indian Survival on the California Frontier* (1988), and Lynwood Carranco and Estle Beard, *Genocide and Vendetta* (1981). The founder of the reservations, Edward Fitzgerald Beale, is the subject of three biographies: Stephen Bonsal (1912), Carl Briggs and Clyde Trudell (1983), and Gerald Thompson (1983). Thompson's account is the most comprehensive. Recent accounts of the reservation system appear in Ray Raphael, *Little White Father* (1993), and Phillips, *Indians and Indian Agents: The Origins of the Reservation System in California, 1849–1852* (1997). See also Valerie Sherer Mathes, "Indian Philanthropy in California," *Arizona and the West,* XXV (Summer 1983), pp. 153–166; Byron Nelson, *Our Home Forever* (1988); and Todd Benson, "The Consequences of Reservation Life," *Pacific Historical Review,* LX (1991), pp. 221–244.

Rudolph M. Lapp is the author of several important studies of African Americans during this period: *Blacks in Gold Rush California* (1977), *Archy Lee* (1969), and *Afro-Americans in California* (1987). Other general accounts include B. Gordon Wheeler, *Black California* (1993); Taylor Quintard, *In Search of the Racial Frontier* (1998); and Delilah Beasley, *The Negro Trail Blazers of California* (1919). More specialized treatments appear in William E. Franklin, "The Archy Case," *Pacific Historical Review,* XXXII (1963), pp. 137–154; J. A. Fisher, "The Struggle for Negro Testimony," *Southern California Quarterly,* LI (1969), pp. 313–324; Dolores Hayden, "Biddy Mason's Los Angeles, 1856–1891," *California History,* LXVIII (Fall 1989), pp. 100–115; Shirley Ann Wilson Moore (ed.), "African Americans in California," ibid., LXXV (Fall 1996), special issue; and Lawrence B. de Graaf et al. (eds.), *Seeking El Dorado: African Americans in California* (2001).

CHAPTER 12

Culture and Anarchy

The society of gold-rush California was not the typical society of the older American agrarian frontier. The wealth produced by the gold rush meant that there were many who could afford the good things of life. The demand was primarily for material luxuries, but it included cultural satisfactions as well, for the gold rush had drawn a remarkable number of educated men. Moreover, the great distance from the eastern sources of cultural amenities had a hothouse effect on their local production.

Newspapers and Literary Magazines

The most immediate demand of most Americans for the printed word, after, perhaps, their Bibles, was in the form of the newspaper, and the attempt to meet this need had begun soon after the American occupation. The first issue of California's first newspaper, the weekly *Californian,* appeared at Monterey on August 15, 1846, about 5 weeks after Commodore Sloat's landing. To publish it, the naval chaplain Walter Colton went into partnership with the tall frontiersman Robert Semple, whom Colton described as "true with the rifle, ready with his pen and quick at the type case." In a dusty storeroom they found a battered Ramage press, made in Boston many years earlier. Agustín V. Zamorano, a Mexican official, had imported it to Monterey in 1834. There was a barrel of ink but no paper, and the early issues came out on sheets intended for cigar wrappings, about 12 inches by 8 inches. Half in English and half in Spanish, the *Californian* appeared each week until May of 1847 when Semple moved it to San Francisco and sold it. Its first rival, established by Sam Brannan, was the weekly *California Star,* which had been appearing regularly at San Francisco since January 9, 1847. It was printed in a loft above a gristmill.

At that stage in the development of California journalism, it was not surprising that 4 months passed between the great gold discovery and the recognition of its importance by the two tiny newspapers. After their suspension during the early months of the gold mania, the two little San Francisco weeklies merged to become the *Alta California.* First published under that title in January 1849, it became the first California daily a year later and survived for 41 years more. In many respects it was the most important of all of California's early newspapers.

There were soon literally hundreds of newspapers. Throughout the mining districts, almost every boomtown had its paper, some with such names as the *Nevada City Miner's Spy Glass* and the *Downieville Old Oaken Bucket* (though in picturesqueness of title none could match *Satan's Bassoon,* published briefly in San Francisco). Most of the mining-district papers, of course, were ephemeral, partly because of the mobility of their subscribers.

The gold that poured into San Francisco multiplied the wealth of the city in many forms. No one made a fortune in journalism in this period, but that was largely because so many tried. In the 10 years after the gold discovery, 132 periodicals were started in San Francisco alone, and the total number of their proprietors, editors, and reporters was more than 1000. They were printed in six different languages and represented eight religious denominations and seven political parties. In 1859 there were 12 San Francisco dailies, most notably the *Alta,* the *Herald,* the *Call,* and the *Bulletin.*

Poetry, short stories, and other literary pieces often appeared in the early newspapers, for no other frontier has ever inspired so many of its people to write. The scenes of California, and the experiences of getting there and living there, were so often extraordinary and dramatic that they cried out for description. A literary weekly, the *Golden Era,* flourished from the first day of its publication in 1852 and soon had more subscribers than any other paper on the Pacific coast. Much of its success was due to the enthusiasm of one of its young editors, Rollin M. Daggett, who traveled through the mining districts to sell subscriptions and also wrote many of the sketches describing the miners' lives. Though it paid nothing for poetry and only $5 a column for prose, nearly every writer who achieved any reputation in early American California found in it the opportunity for literary apprenticeship. Bret Harte worked on its staff, first as a typesetter and then as a columnist, and it was in the *Era* that he published his first successful story, "M'liss."

The tone of the *Golden Era* was informal to the point of breeziness, and this gave it a popular appeal that enabled it to outlast a number of competitors, including several that aspired to higher literary levels. One of these was *Hutchings' Illustrated California Magazine,* published for 5 years beginning in 1856. Its founder, James M. Hutchings, was an Englishman who had worked in the mines before establishing himself as a writer with his *Miner's Ten Commandments* (leading off with "Thou shalt have no other claim than one"). Printed on a single sheet, this new decalogue sold nearly 100,000 copies.

Writers of the Fifties

Of all the early accounts of life in the mining camps of the gold-rush period, the best were the letters written by a remarkably observant young woman, Louise Amelia Knapp Smith Clappe, who signed herself "Dame Shirley." Her husband practiced medicine in 1851 and 1852 at Rich Bar and then at Indian Bar on the north fork of the Feather River, and while living with him there, she wrote 23 letters to her sister in the east. "I take pains to describe things as I see them," she wrote, "hoping that thus you will obtain an idea of life in the mines *as it is.*" During much of her sojourn she was the only woman in camp, and she invited her sister to imagine spending a winter in a place where there were "no fresh books, no shopping, calling, nor gossiping little tea-drinkings . . . no latest fashions, no daily mail (we have an express once a month), no promenades, no rides or drives; no vegetables but potatoes and onions, no milk, no eggs, no *nothing.*"

The "Shirley letters" were first published in 1854 in *The Pioneer,* a lively but unfortunately short-lived San Francisco literary monthly. This same journal also served to popularize the writings of the first of the far-western humorists, Lieutenant George H. Derby of the U.S. Army topographical engineers, otherwise known as John Phoenix. Assigned to duty in California, Derby wrote humorous sketches for the *Alta* under his alternate pseudonym of Squibob ("a Hebrew word, signifying 'There you go, with your eye out'"). His first really important literary opportunity came when his friend John J. Ames, editor of the weekly *San Diego Herald,* the Democratic organ in the district, left Derby in charge of the paper for several weeks. "John Phoenix" burlesqued everything in the *Herald*'s news and editorial columns and, among other delightful outrages, switched its political support to the Whigs. Then he described editorially, and in advance, the fight that might be expected to occur when the powerfully built and vengeful Ames should return to San Diego: "We held [him] down over the press by our nose (which we had inserted between his teeth for that purpose)" and, "while our hair was engaged in holding one of his hands," struck off a fair copy of the *Herald*'s advertisements on the back of his shirt. Actually, Ames appreciated this most famous joke of early California as much as anyone did, and a few years later he edited the first collection of his friend's *Phoenixiana* in book form. Almost as important as Derby's own writings in the history of American humor were the many stories that were told about him, one being that before introducing his bride to his mother he told each that the other was deaf and then let them shout at each other for half an hour.

Alonzo Delano, or "Old Block," also wrote many humorous sketches, collected into a book called *Chips from the Old Block,* which sold nearly 15,000 copies in California. He was famous for his prodigious nose; in fact, he once asked a passing stranger to brush a mosquito from the end of that protuberance because "you are nearer to it than I am." For eastern readers, on the other hand, he wrote one of the most realistic accounts of the gold rush, *Life on the Plains and among the Diggings.*

It is significant that the best writers of the far west in these years of hazard and hardship were people who had suffered intense personal tragedies in their earlier lives. Shirley was an orphan, Phoenix's father was an eccentric who deserted the family, and Old Block's wife died young, leaving him to care for two invalid children. That Phoenix and Old Block were humorists may be explained in considerable part by the fact that people often laugh because they are afraid they will cry. Mark Twain would write in his old age that "everything human is pathetic. The secret source of humor is not joy but sorrow."

Tragedy also haunted the life of John Rollin Ridge, or "Yellow Bird." That he was half Indian might not in itself have made his life too difficult, for his father was a wealthy Cherokee chief. But when John was 12 years old, he witnessed the bloody knife murder of his father by a group of Cherokees who hated him for signing a treaty under which they had given up their lands. A decade later Ridge appeared in gold-rush San Francisco and began to write poems under the name of Yellow Bird, a literal translation of his Indian name.

Ridge's main literary achievement was the creation of California's greatest legend in his book called *The Life and Adventures of Joaquín Murieta, Celebrated California Bandit,* published in 1854. Of the many crimes committed in various parts of the state in the early fifties, some of the most notorious were attributed to five men, all known as Joaquín. The Joaquíns had five different surnames, one of which was believed to be Murieta. In 1853 the state legislature passed an act authorizing Captain Harry Love, a former Texan, to recruit a band of mounted rangers at state expense for the capture of any or all of the five Joaquíns; Governor Bigler, about to seek reelection, personally offered a $1000 reward for any of them. The rangers returned from their forays with a head pickled in a jar of alcohol and collected the reward, although there was no reliable identification, and one of the rangers later boasted in a saloon that one pickled head was as good as another.

Such was the vague and dubious factual background from which John Rollin Ridge constructed his narrative. One of the threads he wove into it was the Robin Hood legend. Another thread was obviously suggested by one of the "Shirley" letters describing the whipping of a Mexican by the vigilance committee of Indian Bar and the victim's oath of deadly vengeance against his tormenters. This man now became "Joaquín Murieta," and as Joaquín carried out his oath of revenge, always with his knife, Yellow Bird may have been vicariously avenging himself against the murderers of his father. Through Joaquín's guerrilla attacks on the gringos, Ridge may also have vicariously redressed some of the grievances of his own people. (See Color Plate 7.)

Bret Harte

Francis Brett Harte had been sending poems to the papers under the name of Bret for several years before he came to California as a boy of 17, in 1854. Legend has exaggerated his subsequent experience and knowledge of the California mining camps, just as his famous stories created a romanticized picture of mining life that came to be accepted as more genuine than the reality.

Having followed a married sister to the town of Union, now Arcata, Harte became the printer's devil and then the junior editor of the town's weekly paper, the *Northern Californian.* It was there in 1860 that Harte wrote his controversial account of an "Indiscriminate Massacre of Indians." In San Francisco, not long after this episode, Jessie Benton Frémont read some of Harte's work in the *Golden Era,* invited him to her home, and introduced him to her literary and political friends. Frémont also used her influence to get Harte a federal patronage appointment as a clerk in the surveyor general's office and then a better position in the branch mint. These jobs allowed him time for writing while assuring him of an income.

The writing that gave Harte an enduring place in the history of literature was done in less than 3 years while he served as the first editor of and the most important contributor to *The Overland Monthly,* founded in 1868 in San Francisco. Up to this time, Harte had regarded the American period in California with a kind of genteel contempt. In one of his early articles, he had called the 1850s "a hard, ugly, unwashed, vulgar, and lawless era." By 1868, however, Harte was convinced that the time had come to enshrine the gold rush in romantic fiction, and for the early issues of *The Overland* he wrote his best stories. "The Luck of Roaring Camp" is concerned with the death of the camp prostitute in childbirth and the adoption of the baby by the miners. In "The Outcasts of Poker Flat," a gambler and a prostitute sacrifice their own lives in attempts to save their companions, trapped by a snowstorm. In "Tennessee's Partner," after a miner has gone to the dogs and been hanged for robbery, his partner claims the body for burial and soon afterward dies of grief and loneliness.

Harte's most famous poem, usually known as "The Heathen Chinee," though its original title was "Plain Language from Truthful James," appeared in *The Overland* in 1870 and hilariously tells of how a pair of gamblers were outcheated in a card game by the bland and wily Ah Sin. Harte was unhappy when this poem, which he regarded as a trifling little burlesque, became the most widely known of all his writings, and because he detested racial persecution, he was further troubled when the climactic line, "We are ruined by Chinese cheap labor," had the serious side effect of popularizing an anti-Chinese slogan. Unintentionally, he had made a major contribution to the anti-Asian stereotype in America.

Mark Twain

The greatest and the most original literary product of the American west was undoubtedly Mark Twain. Although his writing career began in Virginia City, Nevada, that beginning is a part of the literary history of California, just as the whole history of the Comstock lode was closely interwoven with the economic and social history of San Francisco.

Samuel L. Clemens came to Nevada in 1861, at the age of 25. After trying his hand at mining, in which he was enthusiastic but unsuccessful, he became a reporter for the Virginia City *Territorial Enterprise* in 1862. Early in the following year, he began to sign his articles with what would later be the best known of all American pseudonyms, "Mark Twain," a riverboat leadsman's term meaning 2 fathoms deep. The *Territorial Enterprise* was an offshoot of the San Francisco *Golden Era.* As San Francisco provided most of the financing for the operation of the Comstock silver mines, so it also furnished most of the early Comstock writers. But the journalistic atmosphere of Virginia City was even freer than that of the larger metropolis. It specialized in burlesques and hoaxes, and in this school Mark Twain learned the writing trade. The most popular of Mark Twain's early "scoops" was an account of the discovery of petrified man—petrified in the stance of thumbing his nose at posterity.

Mark Twain (1835–1910) as a young man in San Francisco. (*Courtesy of the Bancroft Library.*)

In 1864 Mark Twain moved to San Francisco, met Bret Harte, and began writing sketches for the *Era*. He spent a visit to the mother lode country mainly in loafing in a saloon at Angel's Camp, listening to tall tales. One of these grew into the story of the celebrated jumping frog of Calaveras County, so larcenously deprived of the laurels of victory when it was weighted down with a belly full of birdshot. Published in a New York paper and promptly reprinted in newspapers all over the country, this story made Mark Twain nationally famous.

In 1867 the *Alta California* sent him on a cruise to the Mediterranean and the Holy Land with a party of culture-hungry American tourists. Two years later he gathered his reports to the *Alta* into *The Innocents Abroad*. Except for a brief visit to San Francisco to arrange for the release of copyright so that this volume could be published in New York, he never returned to California and instead made his home in Hartford, Connecticut. He had had enough of life in the wild west, but in 1872, before turning to other literary themes, he published *Roughing It,* an autobiographical narrative of his western experiences, full of such episodes as his visit to Mono Lake, where, he alleged, it got so cold that the only way to serve a brandy toddy was to chop it off and wrap it in a paper.

Joaquin Miller and Other Poets

The factual details of the life of Cincinnatus H. Miller are often difficult to determine because of the romantic imaginativeness of much of his autobiographical writing. It is probable that he was born in Indiana in 1837, that the family moved to Oregon in 1852, and that he ran away to California in 1854 when he was 17. But whereas, according to his own version, he loved "an Indian princess" who saved his life while he was living near Mount Shasta, another account of the same circumstances had it that he cohabited with an Indian woman who helped him break out of jail when he was arrested for borrowing a horse. In any case, his Indian mistress bore him a daughter named Cali-Shasta.

In 1869 Miller published a long and very bad poem, "Joaquin," glorifying the Murieta legend and describing the bandit's sweetheart as a lineal descendant of Montezuma. Miller's friends, in affection—and his critics, in derision—began to call him "Joaquin," and he adopted this as his pen name. In 1870 he went to England, where he was soon accepted with enthusiasm as "the poet of the Sierras." Always a skillful showman, and quite willing to take advantage of the need of many of the English to regard Americans as eccentric and uncouth, he appeared in London in a red shirt, high boots, and broad sombrero, trying to look as much as possible as if he had stepped straight out of Roaring Camp.

Some of Miller's poems were not entirely without literary merit. This is the most that can reasonably be said for them, but they were probably as important as the poetic efforts of any of his contemporaries on the Pacific coast, even though aspiring poets were very numerous. When Bret Harte compiled an anthology of California poetry in 1866, there were so many outraged protests from poets whose work had not been included that he felt compelled to bring out another volume.

Many of the aspirants were women, and the most talented of these was Ina Coolbirth, California's first poet laureate. She had had a miserable early life, which she seldom talked about. Born Josephine Smith, she was the daughter of a younger brother of the Prophet of the Mormon church. Her father died when she was a child, and her mother left the church when the Prophet announced the doctrine of polygamy. Ina suffered through an unhappy early marriage and a deeply distressing divorce in Los Angeles, and came to San Francisco about 1865. Harte engaged her as one of his coeditors of *The Overland Monthly,* and she became a good friend of several of California's male writers, though the thought of remarriage was too painful for her to consider. Her gentle verses were an escape from sadness through pleasure in such things as flowers, birds, and the wind. For more than 20 years she was a librarian in the Oakland public library, and some of the happiest moments of her life began when a ragged boy named Jack London asked her whether she could suggest anything for him to read. She was also a foster mother, in the more literal sense, to Joaquin Miller's daughter Cali-Shasta and to two nieces.

Quite a different sort of poet was Adah Isaacs Menken, who bared her emotions in her passionate poems as she bared her body on the stage, in flesh-colored tights and strapped onto the back of a horse, in a more or less dramatized version of Byron's "Mazeppa."

Churches and Schools

The first Protestant congregation in San Francisco was organized in November 1848, when it was necessary to include Methodists, Baptists, Presbyterians, Congregationalists, Episcopalians, and Mormons in a community church in order to pay the salary of one chaplain, Timothy Dwight Hunt. "There was sweet pleasure in our unity in diversity," Hunt recalled, with a twinge of regret that the unity could not endure. As wealth rapidly increased and the city's population gradually became a little more settled, eight major Protestant denominations were soon going their separate ways to heaven. By 1852 San Francisco had at least 30 places of worship, including 22 Protestant, 6 Roman Catholic, and 2 Jewish. Throughout the mining-camp towns, earnest evangelists were spreading the gospel, though unfortunately their ministrations were usually least successful with those most obviously in need of redemption.

The Roman Catholic Church in California, which had fallen into utter decay during the last years under Mexico, experienced a remarkable development as a result of the gold rush. In 1846 there were only 13 priests in the whole of Alta California, most of them almost starving. By the early fifties there were more than 100, and their work was being very generously supported. In 1852 it became appropriate to appoint the first archbishop of San Francisco, Joseph S. Alemany.

In contrast with the earnest concern for religious education on the part of the churches, the state government failed miserably to make adequate provision for public schools. Not until 1851 did the legislature pass a law authorizing local communities to establish public schools at their own expense, and not until the following year did it provide any state financial support. California's first public high schools, in San Francisco and Sacramento, were not established until 1856. Superintendent of Public Instruction Andrew Jackson Moulder reported that in the 5 years before 1858, California had spent $754,000 on its prisons and little more than a third of that amount on public education—an expenditure of nearly $2000 for each convict and $9 for each child. Scarcely more than a fourth of the children of school age were attending public schools, usually for less than 6 months of the year. As noted previously, state law initially banned the attendance of nonwhite children from the public schools and later ordered the establishment of schools that were racially segregated.

The gross dereliction on the part of the state government, reflecting the selfishness and irresponsibility of the majority of its citizens and their elected representatives, afforded a special opportunity for the private efforts of a devoted few. Various private schools and academies came into existence, most of them church-supported, but it is doubtful that any real collegiate instruction began before the sixties. By 1866, largely through the efforts of John Swett as state superintendent, several new laws had been passed expanding educational opportunity. For white children, though not for others, something like a decent public elementary school system was established, but even this existed only in the larger towns. Such was the limited state of educational progress a full 20 years after the American occupation of California.

Selected Bibliography

Any account of the subject of this chapter must be indebted to Franklin Walker's excellent volume, *San Francisco's Literary Frontier* (1939). Also useful are Gerald Haslam (ed.), *Many Californias* (1991); Kevin Starr, *Americans and the California Dream* (1973); and the chapter "Culture and Anarchy on the Pacific Coast," in Louis B. Wright's *Culture on the Moving Frontier* (1955). Recent anthologies include Jack Hicks et al. (eds.), *The Literature of California* (2000), and Michael Kowalewski (ed.), *Gold Rush: A Literary Exploration* (1997).

The status of California women is explored in several works: Robert L. Griswold, *Family and Divorce in California, 1850–1890* (1982); Bonnie L. Ford, "Women, Marriage, and Divorce in California, 1849–1872," Ph.D. thesis, University of California, Davis (1985); Jacqueline Barnhart, *The Fair but Frail* (1986); and Ida Rae Igli (ed.), *No Rooms of Their Own* (1991).

On pioneer journalism, see Barbara Cloud, *The Business of Newspapers on the Western Frontier* (1992). *A History of California Newspapers, 1846–1858,* by Edward C. Kemble, first published in 1858 and edited by Helen Harding Bretnor (1962), is still useful. See also John Bruce, *Gaudy Century* (1948), and William B. Rice, *The Los Angeles Star, 1851–1864* (1947).

The best edition of *The Shirley Letters from the California Mines* is by Marlene Smith-Baranzini (1998).

Bret Harte has been the subject of biographies by Gary Scharnhorst (2000), Richard O'Connor (1966), and George R. Stewart (1931). Likewise, Mark Twain's western period has been the subject of numerous studies; see especially those by Nigey Lennon (1982), Bernard Taper (1963), Henry Nash Smith (1957), Edgar M. Branch (1950), and Ivan Benson (1938). George R. Stewart's *John Phoenix, Esq.: The Veritable Squibob* (1937) is an engaging biography, as is James W. Parins's *John Rollin Ridge* (1991). Martin S. Peterson, *Joaquin Miller* (1937), deals with the poet's life, work, and literary reputation; see also M. M. Marberry, *Splendid Poseur: Joaquin Miller* (1953). *Ina Coolbirth* (1973), by Josephine D. Rhodehamel and Raymund F. Wood, is a biography of California's first poet laureate.

On the churches, see Carl Guarneri and David Alvarez (eds.), *Religion and Society in the American West* (1987), and Sandra S. Frankiel, *California's Spiritual Frontiers* (1989). Other recent works include Fred Rosenbaum, *Visions of Reform: Congregation Emanu-El and the Jews of San Francisco* (2000); Laurie F. Maffly-Kipp, *Religion and Society in Frontier California* (1994); Michael Engh, *Frontier Faiths: Church, Temple, and Synagogue in Los Angeles, 1846–1888* (1991); and the multivolume series *The Religious Contours of California,* edited by Phillip E. Hammond and Ninian Smart.

On the schools, see Irving G. Hendrick, *California Education* (1980); David F. Ferris, *Judge Marvin and the Founding of the California Public School System* (1962); and Nicholas C. Polos, *John Swett: California's Frontier Schoolmaster* (1978).

CHAPTER 13

Building the Central Pacific Railroad

For 20 years after the gold rush, Americans in California felt extremely remote from the people of the older states, as indeed they were. For many, the dream of a transcontinental railroad symbolized all sorts of hopes for better things.

Early Transportation

Before the railroad came, the movement of freight and passengers by water was considerably easier than their movement by land. Consequently, the first major arteries of trade and transportation within American California were the routes of the paddle-wheel steamers on San Francisco Bay and on the larger rivers of the Central Valley—between San Francisco and the most important commercial towns of the interior, Sacramento, Stockton, and Marysville. After dozens of small companies had entered the business, overcompetition and rate wars led in 1854 to the consolidation of most of them into the California Steam Navigation Company, which came to enjoy a virtual monopoly of the bay and river traffic. On land, the development of stagecoach lines soon replaced the "pack mule express," and in 1854 five-sixths of the local stage lines were integrated into the California Stage Company, which could then offer regular service over routes totaling more than 1500 miles.

The Overland California Mail Act, passed by Congress in 1857, provided subsidies in the form of mail contracts and thus made possible the opening of overland stagecoach service between Saint Louis and San Francisco in the following year. The postmaster general awarded the contract to the Overland Mail Company, headed by John Butterfield of New York, which was able to establish within 12 months a stage line 2800 miles long, employing nearly 1000 people, and providing 24-day service betweeen San Francisco and the Mississippi River. In the meantime, there had been spectacular but unsuccessful experiments with camel caravans over the southern route to California and with the pony express over the central one. The pony express, though highly colorful, failed to make any substantial profits during its 18 months of operation and came to an end in October 1861 with the opening of the first transcontinental telegraph line.

In the older parts of the country, talk of a transcontinental railroad had begun at least as early as 1832. The first proposal to receive a serious hearing before Congress came in 1845 from Asa Whitney, a New York merchant who had made a large fortune in trade with China and who saw a Pacific railroad as a great new artery of American and European trade with Asia.

Throughout the 1850s, with the intensification of sectional bitterness, southerners feared that a northern or central railroad would develop new free states, and they argued that a southern route, which did not have to cross the great barriers of the Rockies and the Sierra Nevada, could be built much more economically and quickly. Northerners, on the other hand, were adamantly against a railroad that would aid the expansion of slaveholding. Congress could agree only on a provision for surveys of all the possible routes. These surveys, published in 1855 in 13 fat volumes of *Pacific Railroad Reports,* concluded only that five different transcontinental routes were feasible.

Judah and the Conception of the Central Pacific

Credit for the specific plan that led to the building of the first transcontinental railroad belongs mainly to Theodore D. Judah, a brilliant young construction engineer. In his twenties Judah had established a reputation as an engineering genius through such feats as the building of the Niagara Gorge Railroad in New York. In 1854, when he was 28, the promoters of the Sacramento Valley Railroad brought him to California to build their line from Sacramento to Folsom, the first railroad on the Pacific coast.

Judah soon became so fanatically devoted to the idea of a central route for the first transcontinental railroad that a number of his listeners questioned his sanity on the subject, particularly those who had had the experience of crossing the Sierra Nevada. But the idea, with its promise of an end to California's isolation, became increasingly popular, and in 1859 the state legislature approved a Pacific Railroad Convention to drum up interest in the railroad project. When this body met in San Francisco, it delegated Judah to carry its views to Washington, D.C.; however, although he lobbied skillfully and impressively, the sectional deadlock still prevented action.

In 1860 Judah made an intensive search for the best crossing of the Sierra. Daniel W. Strong, a druggist in the prosperous hydraulic-mining town of Dutch Flat, pointed out that Dutch Flat was located on a natural ramp, a long and unbroken ridge extending upward toward Emigrant Gap and Donner Pass. Judah observed that because the slope of this ridge was so gradual and continuous, it would be possible for a railroad to reach the summit elevation of about 7000 feet in a distance of little more than 70 miles from the valley floor with a maximum grade of only 105 feet to a mile. Tremendously excited by this discovery, Judah sat at the counter of Strong's drugstore and drew up tentative articles of association for the Central Pacific Railroad of California.

Judah, Strong, and a number of citizens of Dutch Flat and the neighboring towns were able to muster about a third of the money that would have to be paid down in order to form a corporation. Full of confidence, Judah hurried to San Francisco to secure the remainder, but to his disappointment and disgust not one of the large capitalists in the city would invest in the project. Until Congress acted, they said, construction of the railroad could not begin, and they estimated that after its beginning, 12 to 20 years would pass before its completion. Their money was bringing large and immediate returns in far safer enterprises.

Enter the Four "Associates"

In his appeals to the San Francisco financiers, Judah had made the tactical error of calling upon their public spirit and long-range vision. He turned next to the merchants of Sacramento, and with them he made no such blunder. Instead, he planned his arguments in order to put all the emphasis on the possibilities of large and early returns on very modest initial investments: with a concrete proposal before it, Congress would offer cash subsidies that would pay for the construction; operating income need not wait for completion of the transcontinental line or even of the line within California; the profitable freighting business between Sacramento and new silver mines in Nevada could very soon be captured for the Dutch Flat route simply by building a good wagon road over Donner Pass to the head of construction of the Central Pacific as it advanced into the mountains.

One evening in the autumn of 1860, in a room over the hardware store of Huntington & Hopkins in Sacramento, a group of merchants assembled to hear Judah's plea. Among those present were Collis P. Huntington, Leland Stanford, Charles Crocker, and Mark Hopkins. Because these men were destined to be the *Big Four,* the "railroad kings" of California and of most of the American far west, and thus to acquire not only fantastic wealth but also enormous economic and political power, their backgrounds are of considerable interest.

All of them had come from middle- or lower-middle-class families, and though all were prosperous by 1860, none, as yet, was rich. Collis P. Huntington, the son of a miserly tinker in a small town in Connecticut, had become self-supporting at the age of 14 and a successful traveling salesman a year later. At 21 he was operating his own store at Oneonta, New York. In 1849, with capital of $1200, he joined the gold rush. Buying and selling food and other supplies while waiting for steamer connections in Panama, he tripled his capital. In California, one day's work in the mines convinced him that mining was not his occupation, and instead he opened a store in Sacramento. Leland Stanford, son of an innkeeper in rural New York, had studied law in an office in Albany and practiced in Wisconsin before coming to California to enter the grocery business in partnership with his brothers. He had been the unsuccessful Republican candidate for state treasurer in 1857 and for governor in 1859. Charles Crocker had been a peddler, iron maker, and gold miner,

Left to right, top row: Mark Hopkins, Collis P. Huntington; center: Theodore Judah; bottom row: Leland Stanford, Charles Crocker. (*Courtesy of the Bancroft Library.*)

and was now a Sacramento dry goods merchant. Mark Hopkins, Huntington's partner in the hardware business, was a shrewd and industrious storekeeper, the quietest and least aggressive member of the group; like the rest of them, however, he could be extraordinarily stubborn when he wished to be.

These four—"the associates," as they soon began to call themselves—were tentatively interested in Judah's plan, but cautious. In the spring of 1861, however, the outbreak of the Civil War convinced them that Congress would soon approve the project and subsidize it, and on June 28 the Central Pacific Railroad of California was formally incorporated. Stanford, who had again received the Republican nomination for governor, was elected president of the company, Huntington vice president, and Hopkins treasurer.

Judah was one of the directors and the chief engineer. He was not yet aware of the extent to which he had now lost control of the enterprise or of the difficulties he would soon have with the company's officers. His contributions to the project had thus far been much greater than theirs in every sense except the financial, and their original financial investment was almost incredibly small. The state's railroad incorporation law required stock subscriptions of $1000 per mile of track proposed, in this case $115,000 for 115 miles of track between Sacramento and the state line, but only 10 percent of this amount had to be paid down. Huntington, Stanford, Crocker, Hopkins, and Judah each subscribed for 150 shares of stock at $100 a share; other individuals, most of whom would soon drop out, subscribed for 830 shares more, a total of 1580 shares. But because only 10 percent was paid down, the company started with a mere $15,800 in cash.

In sworn statements made in a legal document filed a few months later, the not-yet-very-Big Four reported that their combined personal assets, mostly tied up in their business firms, totaled about $100,000. This figure is interesting and significant in comparison with the personal fortunes totaling about $200 million that they would ultimately gain from Theodore Judah's project.

Federal and State Support

Judah's next contribution was to secure the indispensable aid of the federal government. In the fall of 1861 he traveled to Washington in the company of the new congressman Aaron A. Sargent, who agreed to sponsor the cause of the Central Pacific in the House of Representatives. Through Senator James A. McDougall of California, Judah also guided the drafting of the corresponding measure in the Senate. Moreover, he was made clerk of the key railroad committees of both houses and was thus in an ideal position to provide arguments for the project at every point in the debates.

In more recent years, for Congress to permit a lobbyist to hold such a position would be grossly improper. In that era, however, the concept of conflict of interest had scarcely begun to develop in the government service. Judah had little difficulty in persuading Congress that the project was of extraordinary importance. He described it as a military necessity in a war that would continue for many years. A railroad would strengthen the bonds that held the far west in the Union and would hasten the flow of much-needed gold from California and silver from Nevada. The withdrawal of the southern senators and representatives from Congress had removed the main opposition to a central route, and Judah's surveys gave assurance that a route directly across the Sierra was entirely feasible.

The result was the Pacific Railroad Act of 1862, which President Lincoln signed on July 1. It was amended 2 years later to make its terms more generous to the railroads, and thus one can conveniently summarize the acts of 1862 and 1864 together. The Central Pacific, a California corporation, was to build eastward from Sacramento. The Union Pacific, a corporation chartered by Congress, was to build westward from Omaha, Nebraska. The federal government would furnish very extensive loans and land grants to both of these companies.

The loans were made in the form of United States 6 percent 30-year bonds, to be issued at the basic rate of $16,000 per mile of track. In the Sierra Nevada and the Rocky Mountains, however, the amount would be $48,000 per mile; for the region between the Sierra and the Rockies, it would be $32,000. As security the act of 1862 gave the government a first mortgage on all property of the railroads. This was changed to a second mortgage in 1864 to enable the companies to market their own bonds more effectively by offering the first-mortgage lien to private investors. But it is entirely clear that the government still expected its loans to be repaid—in spite of the later arguments of the railroads in their efforts to escape this obligation.

In addition to loans, United States public lands were granted to the railroad companies in alternate sections, checkerboard fashion, on both sides of the right-of-way. The practice of making gifts of federal land to encourage the development of railroads had been in use since 1850. Under the act of 1864, the central Pacific and the Union Pacific were given 10 alternate sections (square miles) on each side of the line—that is, half of the land in a strip totaling 40 miles in width. Most of this land would have little value until the railroad was built through it, but its value would then be much increased. The purpose of retaining ownership of the alternate sections for the government was to allow the public treasury to share in the benefits of this increase and at the same time to provide some check on the prices the railroads could eventually have demanded if they had been allowed a monopoly on all the lands in the 40-mile strip.

Leland Stanford was elected governor in September 1861 and took office in January 1862. He did not scruple to advance his own interests as president of the Central Pacific Railroad by using all his influence as governor. In 1863 he induced the state to add further subsidies to those promised by the federal government. The legislature also authorized several counties to issue bonds enabling them to subscribe for large amounts of Central Pacific stock. The constitutionality of some of this legislation was disputed, but in general the state courts upheld it. When a vacancy occurred in the state supreme court, Governor Stanford appointed Charles Crocker's brother, Edwin B. Crocker, to the unexpired term. The new judge was also the Central Pacific's chief legal counsel, and he did not resign from that position while he was serving as a supreme court justice.

Difficulties and the Death of Judah

Actual construction of the railroad began on January 8, 1863, after Governor (and railroad president) Stanford had thrown the first shovelful of earth in the presence of a crowd assembled near the levee at the foot of K Street in Sacramento. (See Color Plate 8.) But in spite of the support already promised by the federal government, a tangle of problems held back the early progress of construction and threatened the very life of the project. Costs were heavy. Iron rails and locomotives had to be bought in the east at wartime prices and transported to Sacramento by sea at wartime freight rates. Cash was short, for each 40-mile unit of construction had to be completed before the federal subsidy on it was forthcoming, and interests hostile to the railroad did everything they could to discourage private investors from lending it money. The Pacific Mail Steamship Company, the California Steam Navigation Company, Wells, Fargo & Company, the California Stage Company, and the Sacramento Valley Railroad, as well as all the California bankers who had money invested in one or more of these enterprises, naturally anticipated that the building of the Central Pacific would injure them, and they joined in denouncing it. A pamphlet called *The Great Dutch Flat Swindle* charged that the promoters were not genuinely interested in a transcontinental railroad at all but merely in the profits of a wagon road to Washoe and in the collection of subsidies.

The Central Pacific's own chief engineer had reason to know that these charges were not entirely unfounded as they applied to the motives of the "associates" at this time. Feeling that his own personal honor was involved, Judah was now bitterly at odds with the four men who were in control. The differences were those between a man primarily interested in the construction of a great railroad and four men primarily concerned with making enormous profits. When the four awarded the construction contracts to Charles Crocker and Company, a dummy concern owned by themselves, Judah protested as strongly as he could. At last he broke with them completely. In October 1863 he sailed for New York, having accepted $100,000 for his interest in the Central Pacific but taking with him options to buy out Huntington, Stanford, Crocker, and Hopkins for $100,000 each if he could persuade the Vanderbilts or other eastern capitalists to back him.

At this point the Sacramento four were discouraged and willing, as Charles Crocker put it, to "take a clean shirt and get out," but Judah contracted yellow fever in Panama and died on November 2, shortly after his arrival in New York. His death was a major tragedy. If he had lived and if his hopes for a reorganization of the Central Pacific under his own leadership had been fulfilled, the history of California might have been very different.

In order to begin collecting the larger subsidies for building in the Sierra Nevada, the Big Four maintained that the western base of the mountains was located only 7 miles east of Sacramento. On the plea that without the higher initial subsidies the whole project might have to be abandoned—and with the aid of some ingenious testimony by the California state geologist and the state surveyor general—the federal government was persuaded to accept this remarkable claim, and the base of the Sierra Nevada was thus moved a considerable distance westward into the Sacramento Valley. The Big Four were now men who could move mountains. They felt no gratitude toward Judah and did not even name a crossroads station in his honor. When at last something like a suitable monument to Judah was erected at Sacramento in 1930, the initiative came not from the railroad's management but from the American Society of Civil Engineers.

Solving the Problems of Construction

By 1865 the initial shortage of cash had been overcome. Federal, state, and county subsidies had built up the Central Pacific's treasury, and freight and passenger revenues began to come in with the completion of the early sections of track. Moreover, the money paid out for construction was being paid to Charles Crocker and

Chinese workers replacing a trestle with earth fill. (*Courtesy of the Bancroft Library.*)

Company on terms that assured very generous profits to that company's backers, the Big Four. At the outset Crocker knew nothing whatever about the building of a railroad, but in view of the remarkable profits to be gained from that activity, under contracts made without the inconvenience of competitive bidding, he was more than willing to learn.

A shortage of labor now replaced the shortage of cash as the most chronic problem holding back the rate of construction. California white workers demanded high wages, and many of them accepted jobs only in order to get a free ride for part of the way to the Comstock mines. In desperation Stanford suggested an experiment with Chinese laborers, even though in his inaugural address as governor in 1862 he had vigorously denounced the immigration of Asians. J. H. Strobridge, superintendent of construction under Crocker, ridiculed the idea on the ground that men whose average weight was only about 110 pounds would be useless for such heavy labor, but Charles Crocker was not so sure, and he decided to give the Chinese a trial. The first experiment, with a crew of 50 Chinese in 1865, was so phenomenally successful that agents were soon recruiting them by the thousands, first in California and then in south China. At the peak of its construction work, the Central Pacific would employ more than 10,000 Chinese laborers, largely brought from China for the purpose.

Labor unions in San Francisco protested, but as the railroad advanced into the mountains and construction continued throughout the year, white workers lost all interest in jobs that required the performance of hard and dangerous labor under the conditions of winter in the Sierra. Determined to accelerate construction, the

California Visions before 1900

COLOR PLATE 1
Unidentified artist, *Painted Cave*, Santa Barbara County, ca. 1000–1870. The meaning of these abstract Chumash designs is unknown today; they may represent spirits or ideas associated with religious ritual. (*Courtesy of the Santa Barbara Museum of Natural History. Photograph by George Stoll.*)

COLOR PLATE 2
Mikhail Tikhanov, *Balthalzar*, 1818. Rich in ethnographic detail, this luminous watercolor by a Russian visitor portrays a young Coast Miwok or Kashaya Pomo in both full-face and profile. (© *The Russian Academy of Fine Arts, St. Petersburg, Russia. Photograph courtesy Anchorage Museum of History and Art.*)

COLOR PLATE 3
Ferdinand Deppe, *Mission San Gabriel*, 1832. Founded in Gabrielino territory in 1771, the mission is shown here just two years before secularization. (*Courtesy of the Santa Barbara Mission-Archive Library.*)

Costume de la Haute Californie

Dame de Monterey.

COLOR PLATES 4 and 5
Unidentified artist, *Costume de la Haute Californie* and *Dame de Monterey*, 1837. These hand-colored lithographs from the voyage of Abel Du Petit-Thouars capture the provincial dress of two proud *Californios*. (*Courtesy of the Bancroft Library, University of California, Berkeley.*)

COLOR PLATE 6
E. Hall Martin, *Mountain Jack and a Wandering Miner*, 1850. With the Land of Promise before him, an archetypal forty-niner gazes dreamily from a lofty precipice in the Sierra Nevada. (*Courtesy of the Oakland Museum of California, gift of Concours d'Antiques, Art Guild. Photo: M. Lee Fatherree.*)

COLOR PLATE 7
Charles Christian Nahl, *Joaquin Murieta*, 1868. This dramatic painting embodies a popular stereotype of the legendary bandido, "rushing along a rough and rocky ravine" moments before his capture and decapitation. (*Courtesy the Collection of Gregory Martin. Photograph © Douglas Sandberg.*)

COLOR PLATE 8
John A. MacQuarrie, *Breaking Ground at Sacramento, January 8, 1863* (detail), 1931. The ground being broken is for the first transcontinental railroad; on hand are the Big Four, with Chinese rail workers standing by to complete the task. (*Courtesy of the California State Railroad Museum Library.*)

COLOR PLATE 9
William Hahn, *Harvest Time*, 1875. This romantic vision of an abundant wheat harvest suggests bucolic tranquility and peaceful egalitarianism; harsher realities often prevailed. (*Courtesy of the Fine Arts Museums of San Francisco, gift of Mrs. Harold R. McKinnon and Mrs. Harry L. Brown, 1962.21.*)

COLOR PLATE 10
California Immigration Commission, *California, The Cornucopia of the World*, 1883. Notice the spigot in the top right corner, releasing a flood of irrigation water for the growing of fruits and vegetables in the bountiful land. (*Reproduced by permission of The Huntington Library, San Marino, California.*)

Central Pacific forced the Chinese to work through the winter months for long hours and low wages. If the company had relied only on white workers, for whom it provided board and lodging, its labor costs would have increased by one-third. Five thousand Chinese rail workers struck "as one man" in the spring of 1867, demanding an 8-hour workday and an increase in wages from $31 to $45 a month. Crocker responded by cutting off their food supply and threatening to discharge them. Within a week the strike was over.

With its labor problem solved, the Central Pacific next confronted some of the world's most extraordinary physical obstacles to the building of a railroad. To get around "Cape Horn," a huge and almost vertical cliff, Chinese workers were suspended along its granite face in wicker baskets, chipping away at the rock with hammers and chisels to create a ledge. Much greater were the difficulties in the building of Summit Tunnel, which had to be drilled through a quarter of a mile of granite so hard that blasts of the black powder then in use merely spurted back through the drill holes. The steam-powered drill had recently been invented, and Stanford purchased one and sent it up to the railhead. Strobridge refused to use it, however, even though Stanford furiously pointed out that the daily progress of the Union Pacific was being measured in miles and that of the Central Pacific in inches. Summit Tunnel took more than a year to complete, beginning in the summer of 1866. It was the last major tunnel in the world to be built with hand tools. On the other hand, the construction of 37 miles of snowsheds did much to redeem the Central Pacific from the charge of backwardness in methods of mountain railroad building.

Charles Crocker and Company did nearly all the original construction work between Sacramento and the Nevada line. To build the remainder of the road the Big Four organized a new corporation in 1867. This was the Contract and Finance Company, in which Huntington, Stanford, Crocker, and Hopkins were practically the only stockholders. In fairness to them it must be said that the Central Pacific was not the only railroad in this period whose chief stockholders were following the practice of letting contracts to themselves. The Union Pacific, for example, was doing the same thing through its dummy organization, the Crédit Mobilier. Because the books of Charles Crocker and Company and the Contract and Finance Company mysteriously disappeared, it has never been possible to determine exactly how large their profits were. But from evidence gathered in later investigations by the federal government, the Big Four probably received twice as much as they had to pay out for the actual costs of construction.

As the tracks advanced across Nevada and into Utah, a spectacular race developed between the Central Pacific's Chinese Americans and the Union Pacific's Irish Americans. At its climax, the workers for the Central Pacific established the record of 10 miles of track laid in a single day, and although the Union Pacific's chief construction engineer, Grenville M. Dodge, pointed out that "they took a week preparing for it, and embedded all their ties beforehand," he could not entirely conceal his admiration. Before Congress fully realized that it had neglected to specify the point where the two railroads should meet, they were building side by side, both anxious to garner the subsidy for every possible mile.

Promontory, Utah, was finally designated as the meeting point, and there in a famous and colorful ceremony on May 10, 1869, the joining of the rails officially
took place. Telegraphers reported each step over wires kept open throughout the
nation. A polished laurel tie was laid down, the last rail was put in place, and several spikes were presented, including one of Comstock silver and two of California
gold. A telegraph line was attached to the last spike and another to a silver sledge-
hammer; Stanford swung to complete the circuit, and missed, but a telegrapher
simulated the blow with his key, and church bells, fire bells, factory whistles, and
cannons announced the news in cities all over the country. Exactly a century after
the founding of the first Spanish settlement in Alta California in 1769, iron rails
linked American California to its kindred states.

Selected Bibliography

The literature on pre-railroad transportation is extensive. See especially Thomas Frederick
Howard, *Sierra Crossing: First Roads to California* (1998); Oscar O. Winther, *Express and
Stagecoach Days in California* (1936); LeRoy R. Hafen, *The Overland Mail, 1849–1869*
(1926); Roscoe P. Conkling and Margaret B. Conkling, *The Butterfield Overland Mail,
1857–1869* (three volumes, 1948); Edward Hungerford, *Wells, Fargo* (1949); W. Turrentine
Jackson, *Wagon Roads West* (1952); Harlan D. Fowler, *Camels to California* (1950); and
Raymond W. Settle and Mary Settle, *Saddle and Spurs: The Pony Express Saga* (1955).

The apparently deliberate destruction of many of the most significant documents by officials of the Central Pacific and its subsidiary companies, and the destruction of the entire
central depository of records of the Southern Pacific by the San Francisco earthquake and
fire of 1906, have placed most unfortunate limits on detailed historical knowledge of the
building and development of the railroad. Nevertheless, several important works have been
written. Bill Yenne's *Southern Pacific* (1985) is a comprehensive account. Oscar Lewis's
The Big Four (1938) is highly readable. *Theodore D. Judah* (1969), by Helen H. Jones, is a
biography; Carl I. Wheat's "A Sketch of the Life of Theodore D. Judah," *California Historical Society Quarterly,* IV (September 1925), pp. 219–271, is more than a mere sketch.
Chapters on the History of the Southern Pacific (1922), by Stuart Daggett, is an intensely
critical study by a professor of transportation economics. On the role of the Chinese laborers, see Paul M. Ong, "The Central Pacific Railroad and Exploitation of Chinese Labor,"
Journal of Ethnic Studies, XIII (Summer 1985).

The heroic prose of Stephen Ambrose, *Nothing Like It in the World: The Men Who Built
the Transcontinental Railroad* (2000), echoes the sympathetic tone of such earlier works as
George T. Clark, *Leland Stanford* (1931); Norman E. Tutorow, *Leland Stanford: Man of
Many Careers* (1970); and David S. Lavender, *The Great Persuader* (1970). *Collis Potter
Huntington* (two volumes, 1954), by Cerinda W. Evans, is extremely, earnestly, and naively
apologistic. The availability of *The Collis P. Huntington Papers, 1856–1901* (1978) on mi-
crofilm is likely to stimulate additional research. See also "Railroads in California and the
Far West," a special issue of *California History,* LXX (Spring 1991), edited by Richard J.
Orsi. Additional sources are listed in the bibliography for Chapter 18.

CHAPTER 14

The "Terrible Seventies"

By a cruel paradox, the completion of the first transcontinental railroad not only failed to bring California the expected surge of prosperity but also marked the beginning of a deep and general depression that continued through the whole of the next decade. A frustrated and embittered populace blamed its disappointments and sufferings on the railroad and on the Chinese. Thus, the difficulties of a long period of economic distress were aggravated by racial antagonism and political upheaval.

The Onset of Depression

One of the many unexpected and unfavorable effects that the completion of the Pacific railroad had on the economy of California was that it suddenly exposed its merchants and manufacturers to intense competition from those of the eastern cities. Until 1869 the bulk of the commerce of California and of most other parts of the far west had come by water to San Francisco. San Francisco merchants, already overstocked in anticipation of new demand, instead found the market glutted with new goods shipped in by rail. As for the hope that the goods exchanged between Europe and Asia would be transshipped by rail across North America and thus help to enrich California's great seaport, most of that trade now passed instead through the Suez Canal, opened in the same year as the Pacific railroad. Nor did land values rise as expected. California speculators had so overinflated the prices of land in anticipation of a boom that the actual completion of the Central Pacific caused a reaction and a decline in real estate values rather than an increase.

After many years of labor shortage, there was now an oversupply and chronic unemployment. In 1868 various labor organizations had been strong enough to secure the passage of a state law providing for an 8-hour day in public works contracts, and unions had been able to persuade many private employers to agree to

the same policy. In order to roll back this advance on the part of labor, certain employers in San Francisco carried on a nationwide propaganda campaign designed
to bring as many new workers as possible to California and thus to weaken labor's
bargaining power. At the same time, Chinese immigration increased sharply, encouraged by the Burlingame Treaty of 1868, and the completion of the railroad released about 12,000 Chinese construction workers, nearly all of whom drifted back
to crowd the California labor market.

When the panic of 1873 struck the national economy as a whole, it intensified
the depression that had begun in California 4 years earlier.

Transportation Monopoly

When the first transcontinental railroad was opened, the Big Four did not believe
that freight and passenger revenues would ever provide the large and guaranteed
profits that they had received from construction subsidies. Thus, they made efforts
to retire from railroading with the fortunes they had already accumulated, but for
several reasons they did not carry out their plans. The original reason was that they
could find no buyer on terms they regarded as favorable, but there were other and
more positive factors, which reconciled them to continuing in the railroad business.
There were more land grants to be had, from further construction within California
and from a new transcontinental line to be built on the southern route. Even more
important, there was the prospect of being able to control rates and ensure profits
by establishing throughout most of the far west a monopoly—of unprecedented
degree and scope—over transportation, the lifeblood of the regional economy.

To ensure its control over the main seaport area, the Central Pacific put together
a network of local rail lines around San Francisco Bay and also gained virtually
complete domination of the bay's strategic waterfronts.

In 1852 the ownership of all the waterfront and tidelands of Oakland had been
granted to that infant community by the state. Oakland, in turn, had promptly
granted the whole of these lands to one of its leading citizens, Horace W. Carpentier, in return for his promise to build three wharves and a schoolhouse. In 1868
Carpentier offered the railroad a controlling interest in the waterfront if it would
make Oakland its main terminus on the east side of the bay. Ownership of the lands
then passed to the Oakland Waterfront Company, a new corporation in which Carpentier and Leland Stanford were the main stockholders. Not until the early twentieth century would the monopoly of Oakland's waterfront be broken.

San Francisco, though it put up a bitter fight, was hardly more successful in escaping from decades of railroad domination. Most of its tidelands had remained
under state ownership. In 1868, at the suggestion of ex-governor Stanford, a state
senate committee recommended that several miles of the San Francisco waterfront,
including all of it that was suitable for railroad terminal facilities, be sold at nominal prices to corporations controlled by the Big Four. The *Bulletin* led other newspapers in denouncing this proposal as a breathtaking outrage, and the railroad had
to be content with a mere 60 acres. But this was enough for a terminal; the Central
Pacific had other means of ensuring that no competing railroad would approach

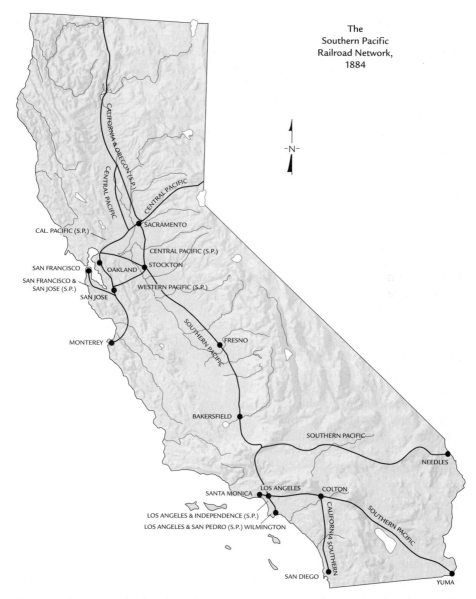

The
Southern Pacific
Railroad Network,
1884

-N-

Transportation monopoly. The principal routes of the Southern Pacific Railroad in California, 1884.

San Francisco for a long time to come, and it had already established political control of the state board of harbor commissioners.

While they were completing their stranglehold on the bay, the Big Four were also making plans to capture the rest of California. They bought out the promoters of the California and Oregon Railroad and began construction of the Shasta route, extending up the Sacramento Valley and eventually to Portland. A line to run southward from the San Francisco Bay region through the coastal counties to Los Angeles and San Diego had been proposed in 1865 as the announced purpose of a Southern Pacific Railroad Company incorporated by a group of San Francisco capitalists. The Big Four acquired control of the Southern Pacific in the late sixties. In the meantime, in 1866, Congress had provided for the first southern transcontinental railroad and authorized the Southern Pacific to build its western link. Thus, by gaining control of the original Southern Pacific, the chief owners of the Central Pacific not only gained control of southern California but also guaranteed themselves a long period of freedom from competition with another transcontinental route.

In 1870 the Big Four were ready to begin construction of the line to southern California—the contracts, of course, being awarded to the Contract and Finance Company. They had already decided not to build along the coast but, rather, through the San Joaquin Valley, because the usable lands in the coastal counties were under private ownership, whereas the San Joaquin Valley was still largely government land where the railroad could locate its grants along its right-of-way.

In its dealings with cities and towns, the railroad was equally ruthless in putting its own interests ahead of the public's. Los Angeles, though it had only about 6000 people, was the largest town in southern California and already had rail connections with the coast at San Pedro and Santa Monica. Crocker threatened to ruin Los Angeles by leaving it off the main line unless it would make the Southern Pacific a present of the Los Angeles and San Pedro Railroad, and pay a further subsidy of $600,000. In an effort to make San Bernardino an example of what could happen to towns that resisted this kind of extortion, the Southern Pacific built its division point a few miles away, thus creating the new town of Colton. For similar reasons the Central Pacific had created the "spite towns" of Lathrop, near Stockton, and Goshen, near Visalia.

By 1882 the Southern Pacific had gained full domination of the southern transcontinental line; its Sunset Route extended all the way from southern California to New Orleans. For many years the Big Four sought to maintain the fiction that the Central Pacific, the Southern Pacific, and a number of other lines were under separate control, but the newspapers and the public became well aware that "the railroad" was a single entity. They began to call it "the Octopus" and to think of its tracks as tentacles reaching from Oregon to Louisiana. Officially, the name "Southern Pacific" emerged as the name of the whole system in 1884, when the Southern Pacific Company of Kentucky was incorporated and took a lease on all property of the Central Pacific. (The name persisted until the late 1990s, when the Southern Pacific was bought by the rival Union Pacific.) Kentucky was chosen for the legal corporate headquarters of the system, not because the Big Four had plans for operating there, but simply because the railroad incorporation laws of that state were among the laxest in the Union.

Monopoly of California rails would not have provided so effective a monopoly of transportation if there had been extensive competition by water. But in 1869 the Big Four bought the California Steam Navigation Company, and with it the control of the bulk of the river traffic. As for ocean commerce, they first made a series of rate-fixing agreements with the Pacific Mail Steamship Company and

The Curse of California. A cartoon from a San Francisco weekly magazine, *The Wasp,* August 19, 1882. (*Courtesy of the Bancroft Library.*)

then, in 1874, organized their own steamship line, the Occidental and Oriental. By 1880 they had so weakened the formerly dominant Pacific Mail that they were able to control ocean transport also.

In no other region of the United States did a railroad enjoy such a degree of freedom from competition. Thus entrenched, the Big Four were free to adopt a system of setting freight rates according to the highest charge that the traffic would bear without completely bankrupting the shipper and thus depriving the railroad of his future business. The railroad could also favor one shipper and ruin another by quoting different rates for the same service. Often its agents would demand to examine the shipper's books and then set the rate according to what they thought the shipper could afford to pay. No railroad system in the world had a greater variety of rates—some high, some low, some published, some secret.

The railroad's power to make or break almost anyone engaged in agriculture, mining, manufacturing, or commerce through its discriminatory freight rates was effectively used in conjunction with the development of its control over politics. Through its rates it could reward its friends and punish its enemies. If politicians did not have economic interests of their own that could be favored or ruined by rate manipulation, their constituents did. The railroad also corrupted politics in a variety of ways and at all levels of government: federal, state, and local. Money was paid to politicians under an assortment of disguises. An officeholder or candidate who was a lawyer might receive a secret fee or salary for unspecified "legal services." For others, there were contributions for "campaign expenses." The Southern Pacific developed a political machine far more powerful than any other in the state. California's government, as well as its economy, became a prisoner of "the railroad."

Land Monopoly

Further public resentment against the railroad grew out of the fact that it had become by far the largest private landowner in the state. Railroads that became parts of the Southern Pacific system received from the federal government a total of 11,588,000 acres in California, about 11½ percent of the entire land area of the state. These railroad land grants, added to various other factors, made the ownership of California's arable land more concentrated than in any other part of the nation. *Land monopoly* was a burning issue.

The general policy of the federal government, under such laws as the Homestead Act of 1862, encouraged the ownership of land in small farm units. But in California the operation of that policy was almost entirely thwarted. According to the theory pronounced in 1893 by Frederick Jackson Turner, "the existence of an area of free land, its continuous recession, and the advance of American settlement westward, explain American development." This "Turner hypothesis" was an oversimplification even as applied to the upper Mississippi valley, the region Turner knew best. As applied to the development of California, the Turner theory of the significance of the frontier is worthless.

If public land in California was fertile or located where transportation facilities would make it possible to market its produce, such land was usually engrossed by speculators before a genuine homesteader had a chance to file on it. The government's retention of alternate sections within the limits of railroad land grants often failed to help the early settler, for by the time they were surveyed and opened the settler typically found himself outbid by a speculator. Government surveyors, private surveyors working under government contracts, and officials of the federal and state land offices acquired advance knowledge of the lands and used this knowledge for speculation on their own behalf or in collusion with others. Many of the most successful California land brokers were also surveying contractors and thus laid the foundations of their prosperous careers.

The federal government granted more than 8 million acres of land to the state—2 million acres as "swamp and overflow" land under an act of 1850 and more than 6 million acres for educational purposes. The state's disposition of these lands was careless, improvident, and in many cases riddled with fraud. Lands in California that had the appearance of swamps in the rainy season might actually be among the richest lands, but they were sold, mostly to large operators, at $1.25 per acre, which was refunded to the purchasers if they swore that they had spent a like amount in reclamation.

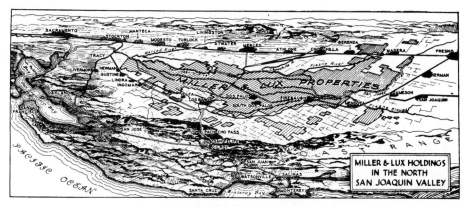

Miller & Lux holdings in the north San Joaquin Valley. (*From* Garden of the Sun, *by Wallace Smith. Copyright 1939 by Lymanhouse, Los Angeles. Courtesy of the Bancroft Library.*)

The possibilities for building up huge landholdings were spectacularly illustrated in the story of Henry Miller, who became the state's leading cattle baron. Born Heinrich Alfred Kreiser, he had arrived in New York from Germany at 19, in 1847, with no resources except his boyhood training in the care of livestock and the cutting of meat. In 1849, with the savings from his wages as a butcher's helper, he bought a ticket to California. From operating a butcher shop in San Francisco, Miller quickly branched out, buying cattle and then buying lands for pasturage. In the San Joaquin Valley, for example, he was so skillful in acquiring swamp and overflow lands that eventually he owned both banks of the San Joaquin River in a solid strip more than 100 miles long, from the area west of Modesto to the region of Madera. Through water monopoly he was able to control much of the land surrounding his own. He formed an effective partnership with Charles Lux, a tall Alsatian who was somewhat more polished than Miller and who often represented the firm's interests in San Francisco while Miller was looking after its ranches in the interior. Ultimately, Miller & Lux owned more than a million acres, and Miller liked to boast that he could ride from Mexico to Oregon and sleep every night in a ranch house of his own.

The engrossment of arable land in advance of agricultural settlement and development was a chronic problem in California and would long have remained so, even if it had not been increased and complicated by the railroad land grants. In general, the question of the wisdom and necessity of granting public lands to railroads in the American west has remained highly debatable. The legal purpose of the grants was to aid the construction of the lines, but the railroads derived their returns from them after the lines were built—often many years afterward. In California, in particular, the grants clearly proved to have been an unwise and unsound policy. They added greatly to the wealth and power of the owners of the Southern Pacific at a time when their wealth and power had already become far too great for the public good.

The expansion of the railroad network in the 1870s did have the desirable effect of encouraging the spread of agricultural settlement in the great Central Valley, but it also created a special set of land-tenure problems. Some of these may be seen in poignantly human terms in the tragic experiences of the settlers of the district of Mussel Slough, near Hanford in what is now Kings County.

The Southern Pacific had published a number of pamphlets inviting settlers to occupy lands within the limits of its grant in the southern counties of the San Joaquin Valley. The railroad had not yet acquired full legal ownership of these lands from the federal government, but its pamphlets promised that as soon as it did so, the settlers would be assured the right to buy the land they had occupied. Prices were predicted in vague and misleading terms, such as "from $2.50 upward" per acre; however, it was very clearly stated that the prices would not include the value of the settler's improvements. Mussel Slough, which carried part of the waters of the Kings River into Tulare Lake, offered possibilities for irrigation, and between 1872 and 1875 the settlers pooled their labor and constructed an elaborate system of irrigation works.

Congress repeatedly failed to appropriate enough money for the effective administration of the land offices, and this delayed the sale of the lands for many years. In 1878, after the railroad had at last acquired the titles, it addressed letters to all settlers informing them of the price of the land they occupied and that it was now for sale "to anyone." These prices ranged from $17 to $40 per acre, and the settlers charged that they included the value of their improvements, in violation of the railroad's published promises. But the federal courts upheld the railroad's contention that it was violating no specific legal contract.

Walter J. Crow and Mills D. Hart now purchased occupied lands from the Southern Pacific at about $25 per acre. The settlers charged that Crow and Hart, whom they denounced as "Buzzard and Gizzard," were dummy purchasers hired by the railroad, although this assumption was based only on the fact that they were willing to pay the railroad's price for the land. On the morning of May 11, 1880, United States Marshal Alonzo W. Poole, acting under federal court orders from San Francisco, drove out in a buggy with Crow and Hart to put them in possession of the lands they had purchased and to evict the occupants. When a group of more than 20 settlers appeared, mounted and armed, the result was the "battle of Mussel Slough," at a point about 5 miles northwest of Hanford. It is impossible to determine who fired first, but seven men were killed, including Crow and Hart. Later, five of the settlers were convicted of resisting a federal officer and served 8-month jail sentences. Because much of the public believed that the railroad had cruelly deceived and robbed the settlers, the prisoners were widely regarded as heroes rather than criminals. More than any other single development, the tragedy at Mussel Slough dramatized the intense popular resentment against large landholders in general and the railroad in particular.

The Comstock and Overspeculation

During the 1870s the mining industry proved to be as great a disappointment as the railroad. The output of gold continued to decline after the peak years of the early 1850s, but the silver mines of the Comstock lode in western Nevada had begun to produce enormous new wealth in 1859. Eventually, $400 million worth of precious metals would be taken from this extraordinary lode. Mushrooming around the entrances to the mine shafts was Virginia City, a metropolis larger than any other in the far west except San Francisco and Salt Lake City. From the beginning, the development of the Comstock was essentially a California enterprise.

The first Comstock boom began in the summer of 1859 when some ore samples taken over the Sierra to Nevada City were assayed at nearly $3200 a ton in silver and about half as much in gold. Soon the great rush of fifty-niners from California to Washoe was on, reversing the direction of the rush of forty-nine. To the amazement of the Comstock miners, one of the hardest problems came from the unprecedented size of the veins. Removal of the ore created chambers too vast to be supported by any known method of timbering, and disastrous cave-ins threatened to shut down one of the richest mines until a young German engineer, Philip Deidesheimer, saved the situation by inventing a process using *square sets.* These sets were made of timbers 4 to 6 feet long framed together in a series of interlocked cribs resembling a honeycomb.

The Comstock soon demanded large aggregations of capital for its mines and ore-processing mills, and San Francisco bankers, along with thousands of small investors, rushed to outbid one another for shares in the bonanza. Virginia City saloons provided not only whiskey but great quantities of oysters and champagne as well, and tickets to see such visiting luminaries as Adah Isaacs Menken were sold for as much as $100.

Several mines paid huge returns for several years, but there were many fraudulent sales of stock in properties with no real access to the lode, and the richer mines became entangled in a maze of litigation. In 1864, when a number of the largest ones had run into *borrascas* and were levying assessments on their stockholders instead of paying dividends, the inflated market collapsed and total value of the silver stocks shrank by more than half. The Comstock had come to the end of its first boom, though it was destined for another and larger one a few years later.

The Comstock experienced its greatest boom in the 1870s. During that decade it produced about three times as much silver as in the previous decade because of the unparalleled richness of the ore at the deeper levels. Yet the effect on California was not to relieve the depressed conditions of the 1870s but to make them worse. The capital of the region, badly needed in other fields, became concentrated in the speculative market for Nevada mining stocks, and the gyrations of these stocks on the San Francisco exchange infected the public with a gambling mania that became one of the most unhappy characteristics of the times. The new bonanza created enormous fortunes for a few men who controlled the richest mines and thus had inside knowledge to use in manipulating the stock market—but by this process they impoverished thousands of other investors.

The first group to attain a degree of power that justified the title of "kings of the Comstock" were certain officials of the Bank of California, who became known as the "bank ring" or "Ralston's ring." A state law of 1862 had permitted the incorporation of banks, and under this law William Chapman Ralston had organized the Bank of California in San Francisco in 1864, just as the first Comstock boom was ending. Most of the mines were in *borrasca,* and several of them were flooded.

Many of the owners were in financial difficulties, and William Sharon, whom Ralston had chosen as the bank's agent in Virginia City, tempted them into heavy borrowing. Then, after a series of foreclosures, the bank came into control of a major portion of the mines and mills. These were consolidated under Sharon's management, deeper deposits of rich ore soon were discovered, and millions of dollars began to pour into the vaults of the bank and the personal accounts of its officials.

With so much of the Comstock's silver behind it, the Bank of California now became and remained for several years the most highly regarded financial institution in the far west, and William Chapman Ralston was generally recognized as the leading citizen of San Francisco. Toward that city, in his own mind, his relationship became that of Lorenzo de Medici to Florence. In his villa at Belmont he provided lavish hospitality for every famous personage who came to San Francisco. For the distinguished tourist in California, an invitation to Belmont became more essential than a trip to Yosemite. When Ambassador Anson Burlingame passed through on his way to China, Ralston named a townsite after him and sold him one of its attractive lots for a future home.

It is interesting to examine the occasion when Ralston had the opportunity to have a town named after himself. The directors of the Central Pacific, in the process of creating a new community on their line in the northern San Joaquin Valley, offered to name it Ralston, partly in gratitude for a loan he had once made to Stanford. Ralston politely declined the honor—but the railroad directors insisted on bestowing it upon him less directly. They named the town Modesto. The idea that modesty was actually one of Ralston's prominent traits can only be regarded, as the directors regarded it, with some hilarity. They were well aware that it was San Francisco, and not a raw new village, which he wished to be considered as his monument.

About the time of the organization of the Bank of California, a self-trained mining engineer named Adolph Sutro conceived a brilliant and daring plan for a revolutionary method of mining the Comstock lode. Sutro proposed digging a tunnel 4 miles long to strike the center of the lode at a depth of about 1650 feet, directly under Virginia City. This was a magnificent plan, but Ralston and Sharon opposed it. If the mines became dependent on the use of his tunnel, then Sutro, not Ralston and Sharon, would rule the Comstock. Other capitalists, following the lead of the mighty Bank of California, refused to invest in the tunnel or to lend money to its promoter.

Not even a beginning was made in the actual construction of the Sutro tunnel until the autumn of 1869. In the meantime the supremacy of Ralston and Sharon was being challenged from another quarter, by the rising fortunes of a group of four Irishmen who would eventually be the wealthiest of the Comstock's kings. John W. Mackay, James G. Fair, James C. Flood, and William S. O'Brien were all sons of poor Irish immigrants. Mackay and Fair were experts on the mines; Flood and O'Brien knew the San Francisco stock market. With inside information, shrewd guesses, and good luck, their fortunes increased steadily. In 1873 they struck the big bonanza, the very "heart of the Comstock," underlying a group of neglected mines that they had bought up and merged under the name of the Consolidated Virginia.

Ralston, whose preeminence was thus threatened, had been overextending himself in imaginative but unsound investments. In 1872 he began construction of the Palace Hotel in San Francisco. With its tier-on-tier balconies around a central garden court, the Palace was a larger luxury hotel than the city could then support, and for many years most of its hundreds of rooms were usually unoccupied.

In an attempt to replenish his wealth, dangerously depleted by such prodigal ventures, Ralston resorted to a desperate gamble. Believing that the Consolidated Virginia's big bonanza must extend into the neighboring Ophir mine, he set out to gain control of the Ophir by buying up a majority of its stock. This drove prices on the San Francisco exchange to ridiculous and unprecedented heights. In January 1875, information that the great bonanza did not actually extend to the Ophir led to the collapse of its stock.

On August 26, 1875, a run on the Bank of California forced Ralston to close the bank's doors. Next morning the directors asked for and received his resignation; then he went for his accustomed swim in the waters of the bay, from which his body was recovered a few hours later. Whether he died by accident or suicide is unknown.

The "Irish four" made Ralston's calamity their own opportunity. Mackay, Fair, Flood, and O'Brien took over several of the bank's mines and mills, consolidated them with their own combine, and established a degree of control over the Comstock that exceeded anything the bank ring had achieved. They also did everything they could to obstruct the completion of Sutro's tunnel, just as Ralston and Sharon had done. By the time the tunnel was completed, in 1879, the richest ore bodies had already been exhausted and the great days of the Comstock were over.

Gripped by panic, depositors descend on the Bank of California to make withdrawals in August 1875. (*Courtesy of the Bancroft Library.*)

Selected Bibliography

"The Terrible Seventies" is the title of a chapter in Gertrude Atherton's *California, an Intimate History* (1914). The volumes by Lewis, Daggett, Tutorow, and Lavender, cited for the previous chapter, are also useful here. See also Henry George. "What the Railroad Will Bring Us," *The Overland Monthly,* I (October 1868), pp. 297–304; John H. Kemble, "The Big Four at Sea; the History of the Occidental and Oriental Steamship Company," *Huntington Library Quarterly,* III (April 1940), pp. 339–358; and Michael Magliari, "Populism, Steamboats, and the Octopus," *Pacific Historical Review,* LVIII (November 1989), pp. 449–470.

On land monopoly, see Chapter 6, "California Latifundia," in Carey McWilliams, *California: The Great Exception* (1949), and Paul W. Gates, "The Homestead Law in an Incongruous Land System," *American Historical Review,* XLI (July 1936), pp. 652–681. Lloyd J. Mercer, "Land Grants to American Railroads: Social Cost or Social Benefit?" *Business History Review,* XLIII (Summer 1969), pp. 134–151, defends the grants. The largest speculator's defense of his own activities may be found in "Henry George Reexamined: William S. Chapman's Views on Land Speculation in Nineteenth Century California," by Gerald D. Nash, in *Agricultural History,* XXXIII (July 1959), pp. 133–137. M. Catherine Miller's *Flooding the Courtrooms: Law and the Far West* (1993) is a legal biography of Miller & Lux, whereas Edward F. Treadwell's *The Cattle King* (1931) is a laudatory "dramatized biography" of Henry Miller by a Miller & Lux attorney. The most comprehensive account is David Igler, *Industrial Cowboys: Miller & Lux and the Transformation of the Far West, 1850–1920* (2001). *The Mussel Slough Tragedy* (1958), by James L. Brown, is a balanced account, as is the chapter on the same subject in Wallace Smith, *Garden of the Sun* (1939); see also John A. Larimore, "Legal Questions Arising from the Mussel Slough Land Dispute," *Southern California Quarterly,* LVIII (Spring 1976), pp. 75–94.

The dramatic story of the Comstock has been told by Remi Nadeau (1999), Ferol Egan (1998), Ronald M. James (1998), Richard H. Peterson (1991, 1979), Oscar Lewis (1986, 1947), Grant H. Smith (1943), George D. Lyman (1937, 1934), and C. B. Glasscock (1931). See also David Lavender, *Nothing Seemed Impossible: William C. Ralston and Early San Francisco* (1975). Marion S. Goldman, *Gold Diggers and Silver Miners* (1981), portrays women on the Comstock as entrepreneurs, not hapless victims.

CHAPTER 15

Political Turmoil and
a New Constitution

During the hard times of the 1870s, class and racial antagonisms in California increased. Opposition to the Chinese intensified, and demands for political and economic reform led to the creation of a new state constitution.

The Increase of Anti-Chinese Sentiment

During most of the 1860s, when jobs were plentiful in California, the flow of Chinese immigration was slight. At the end of that decade, however, when the beginning of a long period of hard times and unemployment coincided with a renewed upsurge of Asian immigration, many Californians demanded ever stronger measures designed not merely to exclude any further Chinese immigrants but to drive out those who had already arrived.

At the same time, the federal government—through the Burlingame Treaty, the Fourteenth Amendment, and the Civil Rights Act of 1870—positively encouraged Chinese immigration and blocked various efforts of state and local authorities to discourage it. Anson Burlingame, American minister to China, had a strong admiration for the Chinese and a great sympathy for the Chinese imperial government. The Burlingame Treaty of 1868 provided for the right of free immigration from China. The Fourteenth Amendment to the federal Constitution, ratified in the same year, forbade any state to "deprive any person of life, liberty, or property, without due process of law" or to "deny to any person within its jurisdiction the equal protection of the laws." The federal Civil Rights Act of 1870 prohibited discrimination in the courts and discriminatory taxes against any particular group of immigrants.

Under these measures the federal courts struck down most of the varied and ingenious anti-Chinese weapons in the arsenals of California state and municipal law. For example, in 1870 when the flow of new arrivals had made the tenements of San Francisco's Chinatown even more than usually overcrowded, a new ordinance made it a misdemeanor to maintain or occupy any sleeping room with less than 500 cubic feet of air per person. But the attempt to enforce this provision soon overcrowded the jails to such a degree that the city was grossly violating its own ordinance. In some of the most important opinions that invalidated this and various other anti-Chinese statutes, Justice Stephen J. Field of the United States Supreme Court wrote masterpieces of refined but scathing sarcasm.

Much of the anti-Chinese feeling was based on essentially irrational fears, directed against an alien people who worshiped strange gods, ate strange foods, and were thought to suffer from strange diseases. But there were more substantial grounds for anxiety about the Chinese, not the least of which was that their low wages tended to depress the wages of American workers. It is significant that Irish Americans were in the vanguard of most of the attacks on the Chinese. A generation earlier, when large numbers of Irish had migrated to the United States after the potato famine of the 1840s, it was they who had been denounced as a menace to the living standards of American labor. Now they could enjoy the position of being the denouncers. In the 1870s the Irish and the Chinese were the two largest foreign-born groups in California, each forming more than a tenth of the population of the state. In San Francisco more than a fifth of the population was Chinese, and the Irish formed almost as large a proportion. The Irish, being white and thus eligible for naturalized citizenship, represented a large bloc of voters, whereas the Chinese had no votes. The Chinese recognized who their opponents were and well understood their motives. Lew Chew recalled that "it was the jealousy of laboring men of other nationalities—especially the Irish—that raised all the outcry against the Chinese." As for the racial ban on their naturalization, Chew believed that most of his fellow Chinese immigrants "would become citizens if allowed to do so, and would be patriotic Americans."

"Anti-coolie clubs" joined with labor unions and "eight-hour leagues" in organizing anti-Chinese parades and other public demonstrations in San Francisco. In the middle of the nineteenth century, a flourishing traffic in the importation of laborers from China into South America became known as the *coolie trade.* Many of these laborers had been kidnapped and were held under "labor contracts" that amounted to slavery. It was often charged that the bulk of Chinese immigration to California was a part of this same infamous system, enforced by the Chinese Six Companies in San Francisco. On the other hand, these companies earnestly denied that any Chinese had come to California involuntarily and earnestly asserted that their own purposes in helping their compatriots to find jobs were wholly benevolent. The truth was somewhere between these two opposite claims.

The strongest defenders of the Chinese, apart from Christian missionary groups, were California employers, whose most common argument was that the Chinese did no harm to American labor because they performed only the hard or menial tasks that white workers did not want, such as the reclamation of tule swamps, seasonal agricultural labor, domestic service, or laundering. The Chinese were also being employed, however, in a growing list of industries in which they were clearly in competition with whites, especially the manufacture of cigars and shoes. Moreover, when Chinese began to be not merely workers in such factories but also owners of them, thus threatening to put white manufacturers out of business, a number

Pacific Chivalry.

This Thomas Nast cartoon first appeared in *Harper's Weekly* in 1879. It illustrates the unsympathetic attitude of many eastern journals toward California's mistreatment of the Chinese. (*Courtesy of the Bancroft Library.*)

of white employers suddenly became as anti-Chinese as the white workers had ever been.

For many Chinese Americans, life in California was marked by daily rounds of humiliation and intimidation. Andrew Kan recalled that his fellow Chinese were vulnerable to frequent racial attacks: "The hoodlums, roughnecks and young boys pull your queue [braid], slap your face, throw all kind of old vegetables and rotten eggs at you." In his poignant account of life in San Francisco's Chinatown in the 1870s, Huie Kin recalled: "We were simply terrified; we kept indoors after dark for fear of being shot in the back. Children spit upon us as we passed by and called us rats."

There were several outbreaks of mob violence. The worst occurred in Los Angeles on the evening of October 24, 1871, after a white man had been killed during a dispute between two Chinese companies. With complete impunity a mob of about 500 people looted and burned the local Chinatown and killed 18 or 19 Chinese, leaving 15 of them hanging from makeshift gallows. Lesser incidents occurred sporadically throughout the 1870s in towns all the way from Chico to San Diego. California newspapers deplored these outbreaks, largely on the ground that they gave California a bad name in the eastern states and made eastern newspapers unsympathetic toward California's demands for Chinese exclusion.

The Workingmen's Party of California

Unemployment, discontent with economic, social, and political conditions in general, and the idea that the Chinese were the prime cause of all difficulties combined to bring about a crisis of unrest in San Francisco in the summer and fall of 1877. The number of Chinese immigrants arriving at San Francisco in the previous year, more than 22,000, had broken all records, and the resulting situation may be compared not to a melting pot but to a pressure cooker.

For several years the unemployed of the whole state had flocked into "the city," where they gathered on street corners and vacant lots to discuss their grievances and to grow bitter at the lavish displays of wealth by some of their more fortunate fellow citizens. In the evening of July 23, 1877, there was a mass meeting on the sandlots in front of the San Francisco city hall. The reasons for this particular meeting had nothing to do with the anti-Chinese movement. Rather, it was called to express sympathy with workers involved in bitter labor struggles in the eastern states. The meeting itself was entirely orderly, but before it was over, an anticoolie club with a band and banners pushed its way into the crowd and called for a resolution against the Chinese. After this demand had been refused, a mob of hoodlums left the outskirts of the meeting, gathered recruits, and wrecked or burned a score of Chinese laundries.

The next day a meeting of business owners organized a Committee of Public Safety, with William T. Coleman, the head of the vigilance committee of 1856, as president. Nearly 6000 men enrolled in this "merchants' militia" within a few hours, and the federal authorities responded to Coleman's requests for aid by placing 1700 rifles from the Benicia arsenal at his personal disposal. Fearing the consequences of the use of firearms, however, Coleman did not issue all of the rifles and armed most of his force with hickory pick handles.

In the evening of July 25, a mob tried to burn the docks of the Pacific Mail Steamship Company. Some such action had been suggested periodically for years, because the Pacific Mail was said to be the largest importer of Chinese laborers. The "pick handle brigade" and the police were able to disperse the mob and prevent the burning of the docks, but in the melee four men were killed and a number wounded. This marked the end of the rioting, and a few days later the Committee of Public Safety was almost entirely disbanded. Some of the money that had been subscribed to it by frightened property owners was given to the city government for the hiring of 150 special police officers.

From these events, many of the city's thousands of unemployed formed the impression that the forces of government were in alliance with the propertied classes against the workingmen. Thus, they were prepared to welcome the idea of a new workers' party that would try to end this injustice by gaining control of the government. Oddly enough, the man who now emerged as the leader of such a movement, a young Irish American named Denis Kearney, was the proprietor of a small business and had himself been a member of the pick-handle brigade. A completely adequate explanation of his motives is probably impossible, but he soon acquired a large following, mainly through his emotional and melodramatic style of oratory.

When the Workingmen's party of California took form, between August and October of 1877, Denis Kearney served as its secretary but soon became its "president." To audiences gathered on the sandlots, Kearney said that workers had as much right as the property owners to be armed and to form militia companies, and to emphasize his point, he shouted that "every workingman should have a musket." In the evening of October 29, Kearney held one of the most dramatic and success-

Denis Kearney (1847–1907), "sandlot orator" and president of the Workingmen's party of California. (*Courtesy of the California Historical Society.*)

ful of his meetings. He gathered more than 1000 of his followers at the top of Nob Hill, where Crocker, Stanford, and Hopkins had built their mansions. It was also the site of Crocker's famous "spite fence," built when a man who owned one small lot with a house on it refused to sell despite Crocker's wish to occupy the entire block between California and Sacramento streets. The board fence, which was 40 feet high, ran along three sides of the lot, almost completely shutting out the view and sunshine from the little home. Pointing to the fence, Kearney cried that if it was not soon taken down, the working people should tear it down. Then he went on to other remarks about the outrages committed by large capitalists, the corruption of incumbent politicians, and the need for his new political party.

Fearing that Kearney's speeches would lead to more riots like those of July, the city government hastily adopted an ordinance against addressing any meeting of more than 25 persons in language suggesting violence or destruction of property. This promptly became known as the *gag law* and served mainly to increase the pressure of the discontent that it sought to repress. Under this ordinance Kearney was arrested, but in his trial in January 1878 he was acquitted on the ground that no violence had actually resulted from his words. In fact, Kearney's speeches and the hope of successful political action through his new party seem to have offered a kind of safety valve. His speeches were generally extemporaneous, and accounts of them differed widely. For example, he was charged with having said that his followers should hold a Thanksgiving Day parade if they had to march "up to their knees in blood," but it was established in court that he had said not "blood" but "mud." Whatever else he may have said, it is certain that he formed the habit of ending his speeches with "And whatever happens, the Chinese must go!"

The Wasp's view of the Workingmen's party parade in San Francisco on Thanksgiving Day, 1877. (*Courtesy of the Bancroft Library.*)

The Constitution of 1879

Demands for a new state constitution had been heard periodically since the 1850s and had increased in volume as the great depression of the 1870s lengthened and deepened. After several defeats at the polls, the calling of a new constitutional convention was finally approved by the voters in the state elections of September 5, 1877. At that time the Workingmen's party of California was still only in its inceptive stage in San Francisco. By the following April, however, when the legislature passed an enabling act setting the elections of delegates to the convention for June 18, 1878, the party under Kearney's leadership was sufficiently well-organized to nominate a full ticket of delegates in every part of the state. Fear that the Workingmen might actually control the convention became so great among conservatives that, in most districts, the Republican and Democratic nominations were fused under the label of "Non-partisan."

The convention, which met at Sacramento in September 1878, was more than three times as large as the Monterey convention of 1849, with 152 delegates as compared with 48. It was in session nearly 6 months, as compared with 6 weeks. In place of an imitative, short, and concise document, it produced one that was much more original, extraordinarily long, and extremely detailed. Yet California's second constitutional convention achieved remarkably little net improvement over the first, and virtually every hope of effective reform was ultimately disappointed.

Of the 152 delegates, 78 were Non-partisans, 51 Workingmen, 11 Republicans, 10 Democrats, and 2 independents. Of the Workingmen, 30 were from San Francisco, and thus the Workingmen carried the city but not the state. By occupation, 57 delegates were lawyers, mostly conservatives; 39 were farmers; 8 were merchants; and the others were scattered over a wide range reflecting the diverse skilled trades of the San Francisco workforce. The conservative delegates, including some of the shrewdest lawyers and politicians in the state, could have controlled the convention easily had it not been that some of the reforms demanded by the Workingmen were also demanded by the farmers and that, on the issues where these two groups could unite, they commanded a majority.

Railroad regulation was one objective that attracted the support not only of workers and farmers but of many business organizations as well. A law of 1876 had defined and prohibited extortion and unjust discrimination in rates and had created a state board of transportation commissioners. The railroad executives had rendered this body powerless simply by refusing to make reports to it. In an effort to make regulation a reality, the new constitution provided for a state railroad commission of three members elected to 4-year terms, with power to establish rates and to set fines and imprisonments for violations.

The farmers also demanded changes in the tax structure to decrease their excessive tax burden. With the help of the workers they secured a provision that mortgage holders must pay the tax on their portion of the equity in a farm. In the hope of fairer assessments of taxes on land, which had fallen very heavily on the farmers and very lightly on the railroad under the system of independent county assessors, a state board of equalization was created.

Corporations and especially banks were the targets of much invective at the convention. Dr. Charles C. O'Donnell, a San Francisco physician who was one of the most vociferous of the Workingmen delegates, defined a corporation as "a corrupt combination of individuals, formed together for the purpose of escaping individual responsibility for their acts." The new constitution included a number of provisions that sought to increase the accountability of bank and other corporation directors and stockholders.

The anti-Chinese article was long, elaborate, and emotional. It authorized the legislature to protect the state from "aliens, who are, or may become . . . dangerous or detrimental"; it forbade the employment of Chinese by corporations or on public works "except in punishment for crime"; it authorized cities to restrict the occupancy of Chinese to certain districts or even to forbid their residence within city limits; and it denounced and prohibited "Asiatic coolieism" as "a form of human slavery."

The result of the convention's labors was almost the longest written constitution in the world, several times as long as the Constitution of the United States. Virtually no one was entirely satisfied with the massive product, and the public debate over its ratification was confused. Conservatives denounced it as communistic and malicious. Workers, on the other hand, were angered because it did so little that was directly in the interest of labor. The strongest sentiment for ratification came from farmers who cherished dreams of lower freight rates and lower taxes. On May 7, 1879, the new constitution was adopted by a majority of less than 11,000 out of a total vote of 145,000.

The Frustration of Reform

The general failure of the constitution of 1879 to produce major improvements in the state's government was most glaringly exemplified in the story of the railroad commission. Instead of establishing new rates, the commission generally adopted the existing ones, except for a lowering of freight rates on certain agricultural products of the northern Sacramento Valley, where a commissioner's farm was located. This same commissioner was permitted to buy lands, which he then sold to the treasurer of the Southern Pacific at a profit of $100,000. Largely by means of such corrupt methods, the railroad's power to control the state would continue to exceed the state's power to regulate the railroad for three decades more.

The constitutional requirement that the creditor rather than the debtor must pay the tax on the mortgaged portion of property was soon easily and almost universally evaded by raising the interest to a rate high enough to include the tax. Equally disappointing to the farmers was the general ineffectiveness of the state board of equalization. The railroad was usually able to escape from higher assessments by contesting them in the courts.

The Workingmen's party began to disintegrate soon after it reached the zenith of its power in the elections of September 3, 1879, in which the Workingmen elected the chief justice of the supreme court, 5 of the 6 associate justices, 11 senators, and 16 members of the assembly. In addition they elected the Rev. Isaac S. Kalloch, a Baptist minister and sensational pulpit orator, as mayor of San Francisco. His administration, however, was stormy, unsuccessful, and discredited. In the course of a lengthy exchange of personal insults, Kalloch was shot and wounded by Charles de Young, publisher of the *Chronicle*. Kalloch's son later shot and killed de Young and was acquitted of murder. Within a year after the adoption of the new constitution, the Workingmen's party had virtually disappeared.

The constitution of 1879, though without substantial reason, was given some of the credit for the upturn in economic conditions in California in 1880, and the return of prosperity reduced the intensity of demands for political and social change.

Chinese Exclusion and Segregation

Another development that reduced public discontent in California was the surrender of the federal government to the state's demands for a ban on Chinese immigration. This occurred because the anti-Chinese vote in California actually came to hold the balance of power between the parties in national as well as in state politics.

Chinese immigration to the United States was so concentrated on the Pacific coast that the other states could not understand California's concern about the problem, but it became clear that California's electoral votes, along with those of Washington and Oregon, could swing the presidency to the party that made the strongest promises to exclude the Chinese. In this situation the national Republican and Democratic platforms began to rival each other in echoing Californian anti-Chinese slogans. The result was a federal law in 1882 that prohibited Chinese immigration for 10 years. In 1892 the Chinese Exclusion Act was extended for 10 years more, and in 1902 the ban was made permanent.

Three years after the passage of the initial Chinese exclusion law, the state legislature ordered the establishment of separate schools for "children of Mongoloid or Chinese descent." This and other official acts of discrimination spurred the California Chinese into renewed action. "Time and again," historian Ronald Takaki has noted, "they took their struggle for civil rights to court." Chinese immigrants Joseph and Mary Tape sued the school board of San Francisco in 1885 because their 8-year-old daughter, Mamie, had been denied admission to a public school. "Will you please tell me," Mary Tape asked the school board, "is it a disgrace to be born a Chinese?" When the board ordered Mamie to attend a racially segregated school, her mother sent an angry letter: *"Mamie Tape will never attend any of the Chinese schools of your making! Never!!!"*

The exclusion law contributed to a general demographic and economic decline among the Chinese in California. Boycotts of Chinese-produced goods by white consumers reduced significantly the economic opportunities for the Chinese. By the early 1900s, there were virtually no Chinese cigarmakers or shoemakers left. Many were relegated to the ranks of common laborers. Others found employment as farm workers. Few Chinese women lived in California at the time of exclusion, and thus the immigrant population faced extraordinary difficulties replenishing itself through natural increase. The exclusion law not only made it nearly impossible for additional Chinese to enter California, it also caused great hardships for those who were already living in the state.

Selected Bibliography

On the Chinese, see Sucheng Chan, *This Bittersweet Soil* (1986) and *Asian Californias* (1991); Judy Yung, *Unbound Feet* (1995) and *Unbound Voices* (1999); Benson Tong, *Unsubmissive Women* (1994); George Anthony Peffer, *If They Don't Bring Women Here* (1999); Charles J. McClain, *In Search of Equality* (1994); Shih-shau Henry Tsai, *The Chinese Experience in America* (1987); Sandy Lydon, *Chinese Gold* (1985); and Chapter 8, "Searching for Gold Mountain," in Ronald Takaki, *A Different Mirror* (1993).

The literature on the opposition to the Chinese is extensive: Alexander P. Saxton, *The Indispensable Enemy* (1971); Stuart C. Miller, *The Unwelcome Immigrant* (1970); Gunther Barth, *Bitter Strength* (1964); Ping Chiu, *Chinese Labor in California* (1963); Elmer C. Sandmeyer, *The Anti-Chinese Movement in California* (1939); and Mary Roberts Coolidge,

Chinese Immigration (1909). The broader context, brilliantly analyzed, is provided by Robert W. Cherny's "Patterns of Toleration and Discrimination in San Francisco," *California History,* LXXIII (Summer 1994), pp. 130–141. On the Los Angeles riot of 1871, consult the articles by Paul M. De Falla, *Historical Society of Southern California Quarterly,* XLII (March and June 1960), pp. 57–88, 161–185, and William R. Locklear, ibid., XLII (September 1960), pp. 239–256.

The best recent study of the Workingmen's party is Neil Larry Shumsky, *The Evolution of Political Protest and the Workingmen's Party of California* (1992). Older accounts include Ralph Kauer, "The Workingmen's Party of California," *Pacific Historical Review,* XII (September 1944), pp. 278–291; James Bryce, *The American Commonwealth,* volume II (1889); and Ira B. Cross, *A History of the Labor Movement in California* (1935). Anti-Chinese action in rural California is described in Daniel Cornford, "To Save the Republic," *California History,* LXVI (June 1987), pp. 130–142, and Michele Shover, "Chico Women," ibid., LXVII (December 1988), pp. 228–243.

James P. Walsh (ed.), *The San Francisco Irish, 1850–1876* (1978), and R. A. Burchell, *The San Francisco Irish, 1848–1880* (1980), are major contributions to our understanding of the role of the Irish in California society. Patrick J. Dowling, *California: The Irish Dream* (1989), offers a series of brief portraits of Irish immigrants.

Debates and Proceedings of the 1879 constitutional convention was published in three volumes (1880). See also Carl B. Swisher, *Motivation and Political Technique in the California Constitutional Convention, 1878–1879* (1930).

On exclusion of the Chinese, see Anthony Gyory, *Closing the Gate* (1998); Lucy E. Salyer, *Laws Harsh as Tigers* (1996); Chan (ed.), *Entry Denied* (1991); and Jules Becker, *The Course of Exclusion, 1882–1924* (1991).

CHAPTER 16

Economic Growth

The increase of wealth in California in the late nineteenth and early twentieth centuries was substantial, but it was far from being an orderly process. Neither the people of California nor those of the United States had yet learned to exert any significant degree of control over the violent fluctuations of the regional and national economies. The 1880s were relatively prosperous, but the panic of 1893 led to another depression so severe that the growth of California's population in the 1890s was a mere 22.4 percent—the lowest rate for any decade between the 1830s and 1930s. The turn of the century, however, coincided with the beginning of a new cycle in which the growth of northern California was impressive and that of southern California truly phenomenal.

The Wheat Bonanza

The droughts that had ruined the cattle industry in the early 1860s were followed by a series of rainy winters, and beginning with the crop year 1866–67, the generous rainfall made possible a full discovery of the potential of the Sacramento and San Joaquin valleys for the growing of wheat without irrigation. It was an ideal crop for the wide, flat valley lands in a time of distant markets and a sparse rural population with limited capital, and for about 30 years, from the early 1860s until the panic of 1893, wheat was California's largest and most profitable agricultural commodity. (See Color Plate 9.)

The largest wheat grower in the state was Dr. Hugh J. Glenn, a physician who occupied himself after 1867 with buying land on credit until he had 55,000 acres, extending for 20 miles along the west bank of the Sacramento River, where he ultimately produced more than half a million bushels a year. His mammoth wheat ranch was in Colusa County; in 1891, after his death, his achievements were memorialized in the creation of Glenn County.

Wheat ranching was a highly speculative enterprise. It also became increasingly mechanized, and one of the most significant aspects of the age of wheat in the great Central Valley of California lay in its contributions to the development of agricultural machinery. The old walking plow known as the "foot burner," with its single plowshare, was replaced by the *Stockton gang plow*, which had several shares attached to a beam, moved on wheels, and was adjustable in width and depth. In a scene made famous in Frank Norris's *The Octopus*, there were 35 such plows in echelon formation, each with 5 plowshares and drawn by 10 horses. At the Glenn Ranch, plowing was often done with as many as 100 gang plows at once, each drawn by an eight-mule team. The Central Valley also produced new machines for planting, pulverizing the earth, and spreading it over the seed in one operation, as well as improvements of the earlier machines to combine the cutting and threshing of the grain. The flat land and dry summers of the valley made it possible to use the largest steam-powered *combined harvesters* in the world, machines so large and heavy that they required 36 horses to move them. The need for mechanical motive power led directly to the invention of the tractor, first used in the San Joaquin Valley with steam power in 1886. Later, Benjamin Holt of Stockton and others would adapt the tractor to the internal combustion engine and develop the "caterpillar" track.

The dry farming of wheat had the peculiar disadvantages of a one-crop agricultural economy. It was a kind of soil mining, ruthlessly carried on year after year without fertilizer or rotation, and inevitably the soil was exhausted and the yields declined. Wheat as a dominant crop began to decline in the middle 1880s under

A steam-powered harvester on a wheat ranch in the San Joaquin Valley. (*Courtesy of the Bancroft Library.*)

competition from the Mississippi valley and from Russia, and it collapsed in the depression of the 1890s. The spread of irrigation had also begun to make wheat less profitable than other California farm products.

One partial compensation for the decline of wheat growing in the 1890s was the rise of sugar-beet production in the same decade, led by Claus Spreckels with his beet fields and refining plants in the Watsonville and Salinas areas and by the Oxnard brothers, Robert and Henry, in southern California.

Wines

The growing of grapes and the manufacture of the fermented juice into wine had their beginnings in California at the missions, for sacramental purposes and for the personal use of the mission fathers, but though the vines were hardy, the mission grapes and the processes of manufacture were of poor quality. Commercial production also began in southern California. Jean Louis Vignes, a most appropriately named vintner from the region of Bordeaux, brought cuttings from France to a vineyard in Los Angeles in the early 1830s, and William Wolfskill established another vineyard nearby a few years later.

After the discovery of gold, the center of grape and wine production shifted to the valleys around San Francisco Bay, and in the 1850s the Hungarian exile Agoston Haraszthy began the work that made him the father of the modern California wine industry, especially at his Buena Vista estate in the Sonoma Valley. In 1861 the state legislature appointed him a commissioner, with responsibility to report on means of improving the industry, and in this capacity he toured the wine regions of Europe and returned with 200,000 cuttings and rooted vines representing 1400 varieties. Meanwhile, the success of the cooperative community at Anaheim, a German wine colony southeast of Los Angeles founded in 1857, had also become an important factor in the industry's growth.

In the 1870s and 1880s, the California vineyards were nearly wiped out by *Phylloxera,* a genus of tiny insects resembling aphids, and the ravages of this pest were brought under control only by gradually replanting the vineyards with resistant stocks. In spite of this and other temporary setbacks, the industry flourished. Vineyards spread through the Sonoma, Napa, Santa Clara, and Livermore valleys. The climate and soils of the Central Valley were also found to be highly favorable, particularly for dessert wines, table grapes, and raisins; ultimately the greatest of all concentrations of vineyards in California would be in Fresno County. In 1900 California produced 19 million gallons of wine, more than 80 percent of the nation's output.

The Citrus Industry

Like the mission grape, the mission orange was not of very good quality. It was thick-skinned, pithy, and often sour. William Wolfskill and a few others operated orange groves in the Los Angeles area during the gold rush, shipping the fruit north to help combat scurvy among the miners. The significant beginnings of the

California orange industry came with three new developments of the 1870s. These were the discovery that oranges grew better on lands that were slightly higher and out of the coastal fog belt, the introduction of the navel orange from Brazil, and the advent of the railroad.

In 1870 J. W. North and his associates purchased the lands of a defunct silk colony on the Rancho Jurupa near what would soon be the town of Riverside, began an irrigation canal from the Santa Ana River, and planted orange groves. Three years later, members of the Riverside group obtained two of the dozen budded trees which the first American Protestant missionary at Bahia, Brazil, had sent to the Department of Agriculture at Washington. Within a remarkably short time the large, sweet, seedless Bahia navels were in production under the name of "Riverside navels." Substantial rail shipments to Saint Louis and Chicago were under way before the end of the 1870s, and in the next decade, with the development of refrigerator cars, rail shipments were increased in volume and extended to the Atlantic coast. The great citrus belt of southern California was in the process of rapid formation.

Use of the summer-ripening Valencia orange along with the winter-ripening Brazilian navels made possible a year-round output. Moreover, the Valencias flourished nearer the coast, and with their increasing introduction in the early twentieth century the citrus belt extended from Santa Barbara to San Diego and from Pasadena to Riverside. Southern California became responsible for more than two-thirds of the nation's production of oranges and more than 90 percent of its lemons.

The early development of the marketing of citrus fruits involved many difficulties. Farmers seldom had enough information about the market to know what a fair price would be, and speculators took every possible advantage of their ignorance. The markets for citrus fruits and other California specialty crops were 2000 to 3000 miles away. Sometimes the anxious shipper of a carload of fruit would receive nothing but a bill and the information that the arrival of other shipments on the same day had so glutted the market that the price received was insufficient to pay the freight and handling charges. The answer was the cooperative marketing organization, in which the California fruit growers eventually achieved considerable success.

In an effort to combat the speculators who controlled the citrus market in the early years, an Orange Growers' Protective Union of Southern California was formed in 1885. Other orange growers' unions formed in the 1890s, the most important of which took the name of the California Fruit Growers' Exchange in 1905. The organization was so successful that its brand name, Sunkist, eventually became almost synonymous with California oranges and lemons in popular usage, and in 1952 its name was officially changed to Sunkist Growers, Inc.

The nonprofit methods of the grower-owned cooperative exposed it to specious charges of being anticapitalistic. As the cooperative system took root in several other fields of agriculture, including deciduous fruits, raisins, walnuts, and dairy and poultry products, many of the private wholesalers frantically denounced the whole cooperative marketing idea as sheer communism.

On the other hand, one of the ablest leaders of the California Fruit Growers' Exchange, Charles C. Teague of Santa Paula, described it as a "federated democ-

Asian workers in the 1890s picking oranges near Santa Ana. (*Courtesy of the California Historical Society, FN-24207.*)

racy." The democracy, of course, extended only to the growers, not to the unorganized and disfranchised people who did the physical work. The citrus industry was built on cheap alien labor, in the beginning mainly Chinese and later Japanese and Mexican.

The remarkable economic achievements of the citrus growers were due in part to the fact that many of them were gentlemen farmers, individuals who had acquired considerable capital before they were attracted to California to enter this particular industry, and therefore could generate sufficient money and credit to ensure success. They called themselves "growers" to dissociate themselves from the rustic clumsiness and ignorance which they felt to be implied by the word "farmer." In later decades, California agriculture in general would become so successfully commercialized that the word "agriculture" itself would begin to be replaced by the new term "agribusiness."

The Rise of Southern California

Through the 1870s the main movement of population into California was confined to its north central parts. From the next decade onward, however, southern California grew at a more rapid rate than did the north.

The first southern California boom, a very modest one, occurred between 1868 and 1876. After the droughts that wiped out the livestock of the region, Abel Stearns narrowly escaped the forced sale of his 200,000 acres of land in the San Gabriel and Santa Ana valleys for $4000 in delinquent taxes. He was saved from utter financial ruin when a group of San Francisco capitalists led by Sam Brannan purchased his ranches and began in 1868 to subdivide them into 40-acre tracts. Having bought the land at distress prices, the Brannan syndicate netted more than $2 million from this investment.

Along with the spread of the citrus industry, a special factor in this early boom was the "health rush" to southern California, which began about 1870. That the climate of the area was helpful in curing tuberculosis was actually a sad delusion, but the physicians of the time encouraged thousands of invalids and their families to believe it, and southern California newspaper editors and other boosters proclaimed its truth. By 1900, after medical theory had generally abandoned the idea, its influence declined, though a myriad of other health fads continued to flourish.

The alleged healthful properties of California's climate led one observer to assert that California was fast becoming "the land of handsome men," and David Starr Jordan pronounced with the scientific authority of a recognized biologist and educator that "California college girls, of the same age, are larger by almost every dimension than are the college girls of Massachusetts. They are taller, broader-shouldered, thicker-chested (with ten cubic inches more lung capacity), have larger biceps and calves, and a superiority of tested strength."

The superior potential of California for agriculture was also widely advertised, though the reports of squashes and melons so large they had to be picked on horseback led to counterpropaganda from other parts of the country to the effect that California farmers spent more time in exaggeration than in cultivation. (See Color Plate 10.) A newspaper editor in Jackson, Mississippi, wrote that "California is a state of mind—exaltation is in the atmosphere. Birds of gorgeous plumage flit through the trees but they have no song. Flowers astound in size, gorgeous color, and infinite variety, but they have little perfume." If this writer had also asserted that the grapes, though beautiful, were sour, it could scarcely have been more obvious that envy was mixed with his derision.

The Southern Pacific Railroad had a vast amount of land to sell, and it took a leading part in the great campaign of advertising California. The railroad's publicity bureau had a number of able popular writers on its payroll, and in a flood of books, both fiction and nonfiction, and of magazine articles and stories, they described California's charms and embellished its romantic heritage. It was the Southern Pacific that began the publication of the phenomenally popular *Sunset,* a magazine of western travel and living. Many independent writers contributed to this outpouring of publicity. The transplanted New Englander Charles F. Lummis, editor of the monthly magazine *Land of Sunshine,* later renamed *Out West,* went so far in romanticizing southern California's past and present that for a time he was the leading cultural chauvinist of the region. Throughout the country the lure of California was becoming so strong that there was an eager market for almost anything that was written or said about it.

A promotional brochure published by the Southern Pacific Railroad in 1907 boosting the attractions of California. (*Courtesy of the California State Library, Sacramento.*)

When the Santa Fe Railroad reached Los Angeles in 1885, it began a rate war with the Southern Pacific. For a brief time, a ticket from Kansas City to Los Angeles could be bought for $1, and the low rates, along with the attendant advertising, launched southern California as a major tourist attraction and contributed to the real estate boom that reached a climax in 1887. Real estate sales in Los Angeles County exceeded $200 million during that year as new lands were settled and brought into profitable use.

The Southern Pacific also played a part in the advertising of California agricultural products, particularly oranges, as a highly successful method of increasing both the railroad's freight business and its land sales at the same time. In 1907 the California Fruit Growers' Exchange, in spite of its constant and bitter denunciations of the Southern Pacific's freight rates, made an agreement with the railroad for a joint advertising experiment using Iowa as a laboratory, billboarding that state with the slogan "Oranges for Health—California for Wealth." The results led the exchange to adopt a large and permanent program of advertising in the same vein, and during the next 7 years orange acreage in California increased by more than 70 percent, mostly in the southern part of the state. (See Color Plates 11 and 12.)

In the early twentieth century, however, the great growth of southern California became increasingly urban rather than rural. In 1920 the population of the Los Angeles metropolitan area was five times as large as in 1900. During the same period the urban population of the San Francisco Bay area did not quite double, and thus by 1920 the populations of the two metropolitan regions were approximately equal, at about a million each.

Water and Land

The peculiar importance of water in the economy of California and the peculiar patterns of its seasonal and regional distribution have made it not only a vital but a perpetually controversial factor in the state's history. Two of the major controversies came to a head in the 1880s, one a struggle of the Sacramento Valley against the hydraulic-mining industry and the other a battle of farmers against *water monopolists* over the control of water for irrigation. Both quarrels were so bitter and destructive that they could be settled only when laissez faire gave way to the intervention of government.

Since the 1850s the hydraulickers had been dumping floods of mud, sand, and gravel into the Yuba, Bear, American, and Feather rivers. Farms were buried by mining debris; Marysville, Yuba City, and other towns were repeatedly flooded; and the rivers, eventually including most of the Sacramento itself, were rendered unnavigable. After many inconclusive legal skirmishes, a decision of the United States circuit court in 1884 outlawed the dumping of debris into rivers, but the hydraulickers had been producing $10 million worth of gold a year, and they did not give up easily. Clandestine operations continued, harried by the "spies" of the farmers' Anti-Debris Association. After many tempestuous and inconclusive wrangles in the state legislature, a federal law in 1893, introduced by Congressman Anthony J. Caminetti of Amador County, finally solved the problem by creating a federal regulatory agency, the California Debris Commission.

The development of irrigation in California in the nineteenth century was slow, in large part because early state policy not only failed to prevent the monopolization of water rights but actually encouraged it. California water law was extremely confused and inadequate during nearly the whole first 40 years of statehood. In 1850 the first legislature simplified its tasks by adopting the common law of England for California. Members of the legislature were not particularly aware that this system included the doctrine of water law known as *riparian rights,* an expression derived from the Latin *ripa,* the bank of a river, and signifying that the owner of land bordering a stream had full rights to a reasonable use of water, whereas the owners of land not contiguous to the stream had no rights to it. Even while the first legislature was in session, the customs and regulations of the mining camps were crystallizing into an opposing system based on the doctrine of *prior appropriation,* which had been used for centuries in Spain, France, and Italy—countries that, like most of California, were considerably drier than England. This concept gave the first user of water the unrestrained right to divert it from the stream and to sell this right to others.

In California the conflicting interests of the advocates of these two legal doctrines led them to fight each other to a political standstill, and consequently California lagged behind almost every other state in the American southwest in adopting a coherent system of water law.

Of the innumerable court battles during this long period of confusion, the most important was fought between two giants, the Miller & Lux Land and Cattle Company and the firm of James B. Haggin and Lloyd Tevis, over water rights in the San Joaquin Valley. Miller and Lux were among the state's most hated water monopolists because of their success in making strategic acquisitions of riverbank lands with an eye to riparian rights. In addition to their landholdings, which gave them control of much of the San Joaquin River area, they had added a 50-mile stretch along the Kern. Haggin and Tevis acquired rights of appropriation farther up the Kern with the intention of diverting water through irrigation canals to lands at some distance from the river. The state supreme court ruled in *Lux v. Haggin* in 1886 that the riparian rights of Miller and Lux made such appropriation illegal.

This decision was hotly denounced as a triumph of the English common law over American common sense, and as a victory for monopoly and speculation over the farmer and agricultural progress. Its intense unpopularity contributed to the calling of a stormy special session of the legislature in the summer of 1886 and finally to the passage of an important new law in the next regular session.

This was the Wright Irrigation Act of 1887, which authorized the establishment of irrigation districts, special units of local government to be formed by more than 50 persons or by a majority of the landowners in the area. These districts were to have the power of eminent domain, the power to overcome riparian rights by condemnation suits, and the right to sell bonds to finance the purchase of water rights and the construction of dams, canals, and other irrigation works. Within the year following the passage of the law, 10 irrigation districts covering more than a million acres were in existence. By 1911, when the fiftieth district was formed, the system had clearly established its vital role in the creation of California's modern agriculture.

The most colorful figure in the history of California irrigation development was Canadian-born George Chaffey, a self-educated engineering genius. The greatest of Chaffey's accomplishments was his development of irrigation in the lower Colorado River area. The region was one of the dreariest desert wastes in the world, though the soil potential was extraordinary. In 1896 the California Development Company was organized, and in 1900 it secured Chaffey's services. Below the Mexican border, he found some ancient dry watercourses through which very economical canals could be built, and within a year he had completed a 70-mile canal through Mexican territory, entering California at the twin border townsites he called Mexicali and Calexico.

One of his greatest inspirations was a new name for the Colorado Desert: the Imperial Valley. This dramatic change of name did much to alter the image that had repelled settlers from the area. They began to move into it in substantial numbers, and the desert did in fact begin to turn into a kind of agricultural empire.

Chaffey left the company in 1905. Not long afterward his successors built a risky bypass canal. After torrential rains the river burst through at this weak point and poured northwestward into the Imperial Valley, turning the dry Salton Sink into the Salton Sea, covering 40 miles of the Southern Pacific's roadbed, and threatening eventually to inundate the whole region. The federal government did not intervene because the break was in Mexican territory, and the flooding continued for nearly 2 years. The Southern Pacific, after taking the opportunity to acquire control of the California Development Company, finally brought the flood under control in 1907 by dumping thousands of carloads of rock and gravel, and the development of the Imperial Valley was resumed.

Electric Railways and Urbanization

The years before and after the turn of the century were the era of the street and interurban electric railway—a development that played a vital part in the urbanization and particularly in the suburbanization of American society. The building of electric railway lines tremendously facilitated the growth of metropolitan areas by making it possible for those who worked in the center of a city to live in its outskirts, or suburbs, in more comfortable homes built on less expensive land. Few workers were willing to spend more than a total of an hour a day in commuting; therefore, in the horse-and-buggy and horsecar era, the practical maximum size of a city was little more than 12 square miles, that is, the area within a radius of 2 miles, the distance that could be traveled in 30 minutes. The trolley car, which could travel at least 5 miles in the same length of time, made it possible for the main residential area of a city to be nearly seven times as large as before—almost 80 square miles. The interurban electric railway also did much to increase mobility and tended to consolidate neighboring towns into a single metropolis.

The cable car had provided a colorful interlude. It was invented in San Francisco by Andrew S. Hallidie, a manufacturer of wire rope, and after the first cable line was built in 1873, on Clay Street, the idea spread to other cities. But the electric trolley introduced in Richmond, Virginia, in 1888 was obviously so much more efficient and economical even on steep hills that cable lines soon disappeared everywhere except in San Francisco, where a few have been retained, largely as tourist attractions and for reasons of local nostalgia.

Street and interurban electric railways reached the height of their importance between the 1890s and the beginning of the automobile age in 1919. The chief opportunities for profits for the promoters of these lines came not from operating revenues but from simultaneous speculation in the real estate that a new line could make suddenly and enormously more valuable.

San Francisco, the city of American California's first half century, was confined to a mere thumbnail of land only 7 miles square at the tip of a peninsula. Most of the space eventually to be occupied by the metropolis of the San Francisco Bay region was in the East Bay. These facts made a strong impression on Francis Marion

Collis P. Huntington (1821–1900), left, with his nephew Henry E. Huntington (1850–1927), right, standing with a newsboy on a San Francisco sidewalk in the 1890s. (*Courtesy of the Huntington Library.*)

"Borax" Smith, a capitalist of large imagination. In 1893 Smith began to reinvest the fortune he had acquired in the borax business in Death Valley in a great scheme to consolidate and expand the street railway lines of the East Bay cities into the Key System and to connect this network with San Francisco by an expanded and consolidated ferry service.

In the southern part of the state, Henry Edwards Huntington was the leading fig-ure in interurban transportation development. Henry was the nephew of Collis P. Huntington, who had no son and who hoped that his nephew would succeed him in

the leadership of the Southern Pacific Railroad. This dynastic plan was strengthened when Collis arranged the marriage of Henry to a sister of Collis's adopted
daughter. In San Francisco in the 1890s, Henry became vice president of the Southern Pacific, but after the death of his uncle in 1900 hopes for his succession to the
presidency of the railroad were frustrated when Edward H. Harriman of New York,
who already controlled the Union Pacific, gained control of the Southern Pacific as
well. This virtual merger continued until 1913 when the federal government dissolved it.

Pacific Electric Railway Company map of the Los Angeles basin, 1907.
(*Courtesy of Andrew Rolle, the Huntington Library, and Security Pacific
National Bank.*)

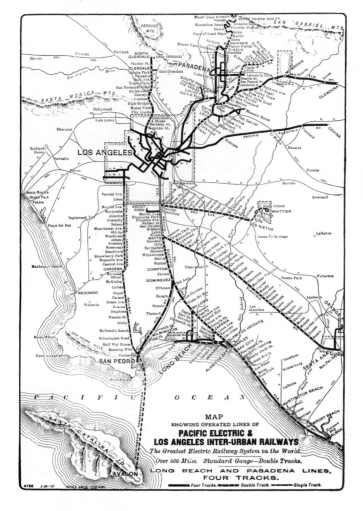

Henry E. Huntington faced the new century by moving most of his own investments and operations to southern California. In 1902 he invested most of his funds in a consolidation and expansion of the street and interurban railways of the region in and around Los Angeles under the name of the Pacific Electric Railway Company. Within a few years, the Pacific Electric (PE) and its "Big Red Cars" welded 42 incorporated cities within a 35-mile radius of Los Angeles into the fastest-growing body in America. The PE became by far the largest network of its kind, with more cars than any five other interurban electric systems, and its transportation of freight as well as passengers cut so heavily into the business of the Southern Pacific in the region that after many efforts Harriman finally succeeded in buying Huntington out, at an enormous price, in 1910.

In less than a decade, Huntington became wealthier than his uncle had ever been, mainly by buying great tracts of land in southern California just before announcing that new branches of the Pacific Electric would be built through them. He had separated from his first wife in the year his uncle died. He was divorced in 1906, and a few years later married his uncle's widow, thus consolidating the entire family fortune. After 1910 he retired from the more active aspects of business and devoted himself to filling his mansion at San Marino with his collection of manuscripts and rare books in the fields of English, colonial, and southwestern American literature and history. After his death in 1927, this was opened to scholars as the Huntington Library. The magnificent grounds of his estate and his great collection of paintings were opened to the public.

Henry E. Huntington shaped the system of transportation that, along with other forces, launched the entire region from Santa Monica to Redlands, and from San Fernando to Santa Ana, on the road to becoming the great city of Southern California.

Selected Bibliography

Various aspects of economic development are treated in Robert G. Cleland and Osgood Hardy, *The March of Industry* (1929); Claude B. Hutchison (ed.), *California Agriculture* (1946); and Gerald D. Nash, *State Government and Economic Development* (1964).

Accounts of wheat ranching are in Wallace Smith, *Garden of the Sun* (1939), and Joseph A. McGowan, *History of the Sacramento Valley,* volumes I, II (1961). The mechanization of California agriculture is described in Walter A. Payne (ed.), *Benjamin Holt* (1983), and Robert E. Ankli and Alan L. Olmstead, "The Adoption of the Gasoline Tractor in California," *Agricultural History,* LV (July 1981), pp. 213–230. On marketing problems, see Rodman W. Paul, "The Great California Grain War, *Pacific Historical Review,* XXVII (November 1958), pp. 331–350, and "The Wheat Trade between California and the United Kingdom," *Mississippi Valley Historical Review,* XLV (December 1958), pp. 391–412. On sugar, see Thomas J. Osborne, "Claus Spreckels and the Oxnard Brothers," *Southern California Quarterly,* LIV (Summer 1972), pp. 117–126.

On wine production, see Charles L. Sullivan, *A Companion to California Wine* (1998); Brian McGinty, *Strong Wine: The Life and Legend of Agoston Haraszthy* (1998); and Vincent P. Carosso, *The California Wine Industry, 1830–1895* (1951).

The rise of the citrus and related industries and of cooperative marketing can be traced in Steven Stoll, *The Fruits of Natural Advantage* (1998). See also a special issue of *California History,* LXXIV (Spring 1995); Richard G. Lillard, "Agricultural Statesman: Charles G. Teague of Santa Paula," ibid., LXV (March 1986), pp. 2–17; Vincent Moses, "Machines in the Garden: A Citrus Monopoly in Riverside, 1900–1936," ibid., LXI (Spring 1982), pp. 26–35; Edward J. Bachus, "Who Took the Oranges Out of Orange County?" *Southern California Quarterly,* LXIII (Summer 1981), pp. 157–174; Walter Reuther, H. J. Webber, and L. D. Batchelor (eds.), *The Citrus Industry* (1967); and Richard J. Orsi, "The Octopus Reconsidered: The Southern Pacific and Agricultural Modernization in California, 1865–1915," *California Historical Quarterly,* LIV (Fall 1975), pp. 197–220.

On the rise of southern California, see Mike Davis, *City of Quartz* (1990); Kevin Starr, *Inventing the Dream* (1985); Remi A. Nadeau, *City-makers* (1948); John E. Baur, *Health Seekers of Southern California* (1959); Glenn S. Dumke, *The Boom of the Eighties in Southern California* (1944); and Carey McWilliams, *Southern California Country* (1946). A thorough account of the promotional literature appears in KD Kurutz and Gary F. Kurutz, *California Calls You* (2000), and Alfred Runte, "Promoting the Golden West," *California History,* LXX (Spring 1991), pp. 62–75. See also Warren Thompson, *Growth and Changes in California's Population* (1955).

Irrigation developments are described in Donald J. Pisani, *To Reclaim a Divided West* (1992) and *From the Family Farm to Agribusiness* (1989); Robert Kelley, *Battling the Inland Sea* (1990); M. Catherine Miller, *Flooding the Courtrooms* (1993); Donald Worster, "Hydraulic Society in California," *Agricultural History,* LVI (July 1982), pp. 503–515; Douglas R. Littlefield, "Water Rights during the California Gold Rush," *Western Historical Quarterly,* XIV (October 1983), pp. 415–434; and Lawrence B. Lee, "William Smythe and the Irrigation Movement: A Reconsideration," *Pacific Historical Review,* XLI (August 1972), pp. 289–311.

George W. Hilton, *The Cable Car in America* (1971), traces the cable car's rise and decline. On the great era of street and interurban electric railways, see George H. Hilton and John F. Due, *The Electric Interurban Railways in America* (1960); William D. Middleton, *The Interurban Era* (1961); Robert M. Fogelson, *The Fragmented Metropolis: Los Angeles, 1850–1930* (1967); William B. Friedricks, *Henry E. Huntington and the Creation of Southern California* (1992); and James Thorpe, *Henry Edwards Huntington* (1994).

CHAPTER 17

Culture and Oligarchy

In the late nineteenth century, a few men with great fortunes dominated California to a degree that justifies the description of its social and political systems as oligarchic. Several of the state's major writers devoted their work largely to protests against this situation. For this as well as other reasons, California was producing a remarkable portion of the country's most significant writing.

Henry George

In the writings of Henry George, California made a striking contribution to the history of ideas. George's theories grew directly out of his personal observation of the California social environment in the late 1860s and the 1870s, and his beliefs were the responses of a sensitive man to conditions and problems that were then more particularly apparent in California than in any other part of the nation. He concluded that monopoly in land, above all, had given oligarchical power to such men as the Big Four, "who a few years ago were selling coal-oil or retailing dry goods, but who now count their fortunes by the scores of millions." George's denunciation of the "unearned increment" from the increase in the value of land and his remedy, a single tax that would confiscate privately owned land, formed a major chapter in the history of native American radicalism.

George was born in 1839 in Philadelphia and came to San Francisco at the age of 19. His writing career began with a series of jobs as reporter or editor for newspapers in San Francisco, Oakland, and Sacramento. One day in 1870, when he was editing the *Oakland Transcript,* he sought relaxation in a ride through the foothills overlooking the bay. A passing teamster told him that the land they were crossing, part of a large unused tract, was being held for a price of $1000 per acre. "Like a flash it came upon me," he recalled in later years; here was the answer to the enigma of why progress had its twin in poverty, of why when wealth increased, poverty increased with it. As land values rose with the growth of population, the person who worked the land had to pay too much for the privilege.

George denounced the railroad as the state's largest private landowner and as the beneficiary of vast subsidies in both land and cash. In a pamphlet titled *The Subsidy Question* (1871), he turned laissez faire theories against big business, reversing the usual line of argument. George pointed out that the railroad, which dominated business in California, had grown not by free competition but by monopoly; that it had been built mainly with government money; and that subsidies were a huge form of governmental intervention in the workings of a free economy.

In 1871, also, George published *Our Land and Land Policy,* a pamphlet in which he first outlined his general doctrine. Stressing the enormous amount of public lands given as grants to the railroads, he proposed that the ownership of these and all other lands should be returned to the people by means of a single massive tax on land. George argued that an end to private rent and to speculation in land would bring an end to industrial depressions and maldistribution of wealth, would free business from all other forms of taxation, and indeed would cure virtually all the ills of society.

George's single-tax doctrine appeared in elaborated form in 1879 in his *Progress and Poverty,* which became one of the phenomenal best-sellers of all time. He popularized what had been well called the "dismal science" of economics in words that often had not only the qualities of poetry but the fervor of religion as well. The single tax, he wrote, would bring "the Golden Age . . . , the culmination of Christianity—the city of God with its walls of jasper and its gates of pearl."

By later standards some of his ideas were illiberal. One of his early editorials justified lynching; he was opposed to labor organizations and to strikes; and he was extremely hostile to the Chinese. George's single-tax dogma was a naive and emotional panacea. Yet the idea and the man who advanced it still command respect for their part in stimulating popular thought about the problems of society.

Ambrose Bierce

Another major literary product of California journalism was Ambrose Gwinett ("Almighty God") Bierce, also known as Bitter Bierce and The Wickedest Man in San Francisco. Though quite as vigorous as Henry George in criticizing things as they were, Bierce claimed to despise reform and reformers—one of the many paradoxes that characterized his personality.

The son of Marcus Aurelius Bierce, an unprosperous farmer who fathered 13 children and gave every one of them a name beginning with A, Ambrose was born in a backwoods portion of southeastern Ohio. The economic and emotional hardships of his early life contributed much to his permanent embitterment.

Bierce welcomed the Civil War as an escape from his family, but 4 years of bloody action did nothing to sweeten his temperament. After the war he came to the far west, and in 1868 he took over the writing of a column called "The Town Crier" in the *San Francisco News Letter.* In later years Bierce became the much-feared literary dictator of the Pacific coast with his columns in the San Francisco *Argonaut,* then in the *Wasp,* and finally, after 1887, in young William Randolph Hearst's *Examiner.* As a Hearst journalist, Bierce frequently unleashed his invective against the leaders of the Southern Pacific and other "malefactors of great wealth."

Bierce's short stories have often been compared to those of Edgar Allan Poe, but whereas Poe often resorted to the supernatural, the weird events in Bierce's narratives always had some sardonic but ostensibly rational explanation at the end. His best stories were those collected in *Tales of Soldiers and Civilians,* later published as *In the Midst of Life.*

In *The Devil's Dictionary,* Bierce defined "birth" as "the first and direst of all disasters," and he often argued that suicide was not only a right but almost a duty. And although the circumstances of Bierce's own demise have remained a mystery, it is clear that in 1913 when he planned to join the army of Pancho Villa as an "observer," he was seeking a death that he did not quite wish to inflict by his own hand. "Goodbye," he wrote to his niece, "if you hear of my being stood up against a Mexican stone wall and shot to rags please know that I think it a pretty good way to depart this life. It beats old age, disease, or falling down the cellar stairs. To be a Gringo in Mexico—ah, that is euthanasia!" Bierce was a deeply tortured man, never fully aware of the causes of his misery.

Frank Norris

In contrast with Bierce, who regarded childhood as a disaster and the rest of life as not much better, Frank Norris attributed to his childhood much of his great enthusiasm for both real and fictional experience. The gifted novelist, Norris once wrote, was the man who retained the dramatizing imagination of a boy.

Benjamin Franklin Norris, Jr., was born in Chicago in 1870 of able and energetic parents. When Frank was 14, the family moved to San Francisco. At 17 he was sent to Paris to study art, but when he began to write stories instead, his father maintained that he was wasting his time and summoned him home. At 20 he enrolled in the University of California and spent 4 years there. Having disliked the stylistic conformity that his English professors at Berkeley demanded, he spent a fifth collegiate year in a creative writing course at Harvard, where he worked on two stories of San Francisco, *McTeague* and *Vandover and the Brute.*

Much influenced by the works of Émile Zola, *McTeague* was the first important contribution to naturalism by an American writer. Its hero is a charlatan dentist, McTeague, who marries Trina, a girl who has won $5000 in a lottery; however, her cousin and jilted suitor takes revenge by informing the authorities that the dentist is practicing without a license. The novel became a study of the degeneration of Trina into miserliness and of McTeague into sadistic brutality. *Vandover and the Brute* has the same basic theme—a man's deterioration into the beast within him. In the end, Vandover's downward path goes so far that he actually becomes a victim of lycanthropy, the delusion that he is a wolf.

Norris soon discovered that the naturalism of these works was too undiluted to permit the publication of either of them as a first novel at a time when the American reading public still demanded that fiction be highly romanticized. In search of further training and experience as a writer, he joined the editorial staff of the San Francisco *Wave,* hoping that some New York publisher might recognize his talent. The hope was fulfilled. S. S. McClure, who kept an eye on the San Francisco journals for new writers, telegraphed an offer to employ Norris as a regular writer. The publication of *McTeague* followed a few months later, in 1899.

Much encouraged, Norris conceived one of the most ambitious projects in the history of American literature, a trilogy to be called *Epic of the Wheat.* The first part would describe the growing of the wheat in California, the second its distribution at the "pit" or board of trade, in Chicago, and the third its consumption in a famine-stricken village in Europe. Each of the three novels would have a central episode based on an actual occurrence, and the first, *The Octopus, a Story of California* (1901), would center on the battle of Mussel Slough. But Norris was not concerned with precise accuracy of historical detail; his intention was to tell the truth in what he regarded as a larger sense, including the greatest possible element of dramatic impact. Although in the course of this research he did apparently visit the town of Tulare, the Bonneville of *The Octopus,* he spent much more time on a 10,000-acre wheat ranch near Hollister, so that the locale described in the novel was not really that of the San Joaquin Valley in 1880 but rather of a coastal valley in 1899, and the wheat growers were not the small farmers of the actual episode but large ranchers. Consolidating his California, Norris also transplanted a mission and a sleepy old Mexican town, based on San Juan Bautista, across the Coast Ranges and into a story in which they had had no actual part.

The Octopus also included a number of more basic inconsistencies. As a "novel with a purpose," *The Octopus* departed from Norris's goal of naturalistic objectivity and became in many of its passages a propagandistic tract for reform of the trusts. Norris was perceptibly influenced by the writers whom he met in the offices of *McClure's Magazine* and who would soon launch the muckraking movement. Theodore Roosevelt read *The Octopus* as a tract and remarked to a friend that apparently "conditions were worse in California than elsewhere." *The Octopus* was and will remain one of the most important of American novels.

Although Norris often wrote mystical praises of "the People," that is, the lower and lower-middle classes, he was a snob, with strong biases of both class and race. He was anti-Asian and anti-Semitic and an admirer of Kipling's Anglo-Saxonism as well as of his literary style. Like most major writers, Norris was as contradictory and complicated as life itself, and he loved life to a degree that made his early death at 32, of appendicitis, peculiarly sad. *The Pit,* based on an actual attempt to corner the wheat market at Chicago, had degenerated into a conventional love story, and was appearing serially in the *Saturday Evening Post* when he died. He had not begun the writing of *The Wolf,* the projected third volume.

Jack London

Few men have risen to success through greater difficulties than did Jack London. He was an unwanted and illegitimate child, born in San Francisco in 1876, presumably the son of an itinerant Irish astrologer who denied paternity and whom he never saw. His mother secured a name for him by marrying John London, a kindly widower who gave his stepson what little feeling of stability there was in his earliest years. The boy grew up on the Oakland waterfront. At 15 he was an oyster pirate, at 17 he went to sea on one of the last seal-hunting voyages out of San Francisco Bay, and at 18, in 1894, he traveled to the east coast and back as a member of the California contingent of Coxey's army of unemployed. One of his hobo acquaintances introduced him to the *Communist Manifesto,* and his left-wing socialist opinions solidified after he returned to Oakland and experienced a series of cruelly hard and low-paying jobs, in which he worked for 60 hours a week in a jute mill, in a hand laundry, and at shoveling coal. For years he signed many of his letters "Yours for the Revolution."

After a few months at Oakland High School and a semester at the University of California, he joined the Klondike gold rush in 1897. He discovered no gold but he collected a great deal of material for the stories through which he hoped to make a living. His first publisher, the *Overland Monthly,* offered him $5 for a story of 5000 words, and when even this small payment was slow in coming, he visited the office of the magazine and collected the amount in small change from the pockets of the assistant editor and the business manager, by threat of physical violence. But success came soon afterward. In 1900 S. S. McClure discovered London, as he had discovered Norris, and published London's first book, a collection of stories called *Son of the Wolf.* Within a few years, London was the highest-paid, best-known, and most popular writer in the world, displacing his hero Rudyard Kipling in the possession of these honors.

The Call of the Wild (1903), the most famous of London's many stories of the far north, concerned a dog that was kidnapped in California and taken to Alaska, where it reverted to savagery and ran with a wolf pack. London wrote several partly autobiographical novels, including *Martin Eden* (1909) and *John Barleycorn* (1913). And there were several novels or other works of socialist propaganda, the most important of which was *The Iron Heel* (1907). This story was especially striking in that it predicted the rise of fascism.

London's social and political ideas were an amalgam of Darwin, Spencer, Marx, and Nietzsche. As his attempt to cross Marx's proletarianism with Nietzsche's Superman suggests, London's professions of socialism were out of tune with his own strongest feelings. His best writing was concerned not with hopes of an idealized collectivist society but, rather, with the opposite theme of the triumph of some individual man or beast over more ordinary members of the respective species in some contest of wild and primordial violence. London's racism, moreover, was more extreme than either Kipling's or Norris's.

London was too emotionally insecure to be capable of happy marriage or of any other stable personal relationship. His second wife, Charmian Kittredge, lived in mortal terror that some other woman would take him away from her as easily as she had seduced him away from his first wife, Bessie Maddern. Hoping to find security in a magnificent house, London spent more than $90,000 on a mansion of stone in Sonoma County, but shortly before he was to have moved into it, the interior of the house was destroyed by fire. The fire may have been set deliberately, and the loss was intensified by the pain of speculating on the identity of the person who had hated him enough to do such a devilish thing to him. The alcoholism that had endangered his health for many years became progressively worse, and in 1916, at 40 and in great pain from uremia, he ended his life, perhaps inadvertently, with an overdose of morphine. His career had symbolized the elemental power of humanity to struggle against tragedy and heartbreak, a struggle that was no less admirable because in his case the odds were too heavy to be overcome.

Historiography

Well before the end of the nineteenth century, California witnessed the carrying out of a truly remarkable project for the writing of its history, a project which in its unbounded ambitiousness was characteristic of the state itself. One day in 1859, Hubert Howe Bancroft, the most successful bookseller in San Francisco and in the whole of the west, happened to place together all the items in his store that dealt with the Pacific coast. Such was the nucleus of the incomparable Bancroft Library. From collecting books, and later manuscripts, Bancroft progressed to the idea of bringing together the history that was in them. Calculating at one point that it would take him 400 years to read the whole of his collection, let alone to write a history from it, and being of a practical turn of mind, he employed a staff of assistants when the actual research and writing project began in 1871. The ablest of these was Henry L. Oak, a young graduate of Dartmouth College who was originally employed as librarian and who had no more formal training as a historian or experience as a writer than did Bancroft himself.

Few things even in California have grown as the Bancroft project grew. *Bancroft's Works,* published between 1882 and 1890, filled 39 fat and closely packed volumes. Bancroft himself was substantially the author of about one-fourth of these books. The others were written, as well as researched, by his assistants. In all these *Works,* however, Bancroft most unwisely and unfortunately represented himself as the sole author; the assistants received no credit except in the thirty-ninth volume, called *Literary Industries,* in which Bancroft described the process of authorship in a most inadequate and misleading way.

The five volumes on the general history of California to 1848 were written by Henry L. Oak. As a whole they were superior to the two volumes on the period 1848 to 1890 written mainly by two of Bancroft's other assistants, William Nemos and Frances Fuller Victor. And a comparison of Oak's writings with the volumes on California that were actually written by Bancroft (*California Pastoral, California Inter Pocula,* and *Popular Tribunals*) makes it clear that Oak was a better historian than his employer. When Henry Oak, having become a brooding invalid after 20 years of hard and anonymous labor, wrote an ineffectual protest, Bancroft replied: "I doubt that authors are in the habit of giving their employees any credit at all." In making this statement, Bancroft was quite unaware of its impropriety and irrelevance. Why later historians have failed to give proper credit to Oak for the authorship of the best volumes in the Bancroft history of California is harder to explain.

Hubert Howe Bancroft
(1832–1918), pioneer California
historian and bibliophile. His
collection of books and manuscripts became the core of the
Bancroft Library at the University
of California, Berkeley. (*Courtesy
of the California Historical Society,
FN-08367.*)

In the process of marketing the mammoth series, also, Bancroft resorted to devices that were highly questionable, though he himself did not consider them so.
Many purchasers of the series, who signed up at the beginning, were not told what
a large number of volumes they were contracting to buy. When the *Works* first
began to appear, Leland Stanford had generously subscribed for 40 sets, under the
impression that a full set would consist of five or six volumes. But after receiving
and paying for 40 copies of each volume of the *Works* through the twenty-third
one, he canceled his subscription in an acid letter.

Finally, when the *Works* were followed in the early 1890s by the *Chronicles of
the Builders of the Commonwealth,* and when it became known that in these enormously expensive vanity publications the length and tone of each biography was
determined by the number of thousands of dollars subscribed by the biographee,
there was a blast of public criticism that damaged Bancroft's reputation. Collis P.
Huntington had subscribed a large sum for the glowing 110-page biography of him
that appeared in the *Chronicles.* On the other hand, the biography of Leland Stanford, which had been fully prepared for publication, was omitted from the set because Stanford refused to make payment.

When the wealthy land-title lawyer Theodore H. Hittell wrote his own *History
of California,* which was published in four volumes between 1885 and 1897, the

extreme public criticisms of a number of Bancroft's methods had misled Hittell into supposing that there could be no value in any of *Bancroft's Works,* and he refused to consult them. Hittell's history was a good one; it could have been still better if he had not made this unfortunate misjudgment.

Not long after Josiah Royce had become a junior member of the philosophy department at Harvard, the publisher of a projected series of volumes on American commonwealths selected him, as one of the most promising young men who had come to the east out of California, to write a volume on his native state. Royce obtained permission to use the Bancroft Library, already by far the largest and best collection of sources in the west. His *California: From the Conquest in 1846 to the Second Vigilance Committee in San Francisco* (1886) took the form of an effort to establish the validity of the Hegelian dialectic of order and disorder, authority and freedom.

Lords of the Press

In the later decades of the nineteenth century and the early years of the twentieth, journalism in California's metropolis of San Francisco differed from that of the frontier days in that there came to be a smaller number of larger newspapers, owned and controlled by a few wealthy men.

Of the major San Francisco dailies destined to survive into the twentieth century, the oldest were the *Evening Bulletin,* founded in 1855, and the *Morning Call,* which dated from 1856. But these were ultimately outstripped in circulation and influence by two morning papers: the *San Francisco Examiner,* which began as the weekly *Democratic Press* in 1863, and the *Chronicle,* founded as the *Daily Dramatic Chronicle* in 1865 by the brothers Charles and M. H. de Young.

One of the most striking developments in the whole colorful history of American newspapers was the rise of William Randolph Hearst, who was born in San Francisco in 1863 and took over the ownership and control of the *Examiner* in 1887, when he was not yet 24 years old. George Hearst, his father, had bought the paper a few years earlier to advance his political ambitions. In January 1887 a Democratic majority in the California legislature elected George Hearst to the United States Senate, and it was on March 4, the day he took his seat in Washington, D.C., that he made the gift of the *Examiner* to his son.

A few months earlier, William Randolph Hearst had been expelled from Harvard at the end of his junior year for indulging in an obscene expression of contempt for his professors. Since then he had worked as a reporter for Joseph Pulitzer's *New York World* in order to study Pulitzer's methods. These he would soon apply to the moribund little *Examiner* with many elaborations of his own and with spectacular results. Young Hearst quickly expanded the *Examiner* from four pages to eight, banished advertising from the front page in favor of headlines followed by sensational stories of crime and corruption, and brought in many special features for the reader's amusement. The term "yellow journalism" has its origin when Hearst hired away from Pulitzer the cartoonist of a popular early comic strip called "The Yellow Kid."

Hearst went to unusual lengths with the *arranged story*: if the news that actually happened was not lively enough, he manufactured news that was. At the *Examiner*'s expense, a young couple was married in a balloon and even, according to the *Examiner,* spent their honeymoon there—"up in the clouds." The real secret of Hearst's success was in his genius for spectacular entertainment. "The public," he wrote in an editorial in 1896, "is even more fond of entertainment than it is of information," and this philosophy of journalism became increasingly important in later years when he acquired an unprecedented number of newspapers in many cities, including the largest cities in the country. He maintained extraordinarily close control over the news and editorial policies of all his papers, and thus he had a greater influence on what was printed and read in America than any other man before or since.

No other California newspaper publisher acquired national influence comparable to Hearst's, but there were several figures of statewide importance. In Sacramento the history of the *Bee* became synonymous with that of the McClatchy family, from the time when James McClatchy became editor in 1857, the year the *Bee* was founded. McClatchy had come from Ireland as a boy, and he brought an Irishman's hatred of land monopoly to his leadership of the squatters in the gold-rush period and then to the *Bee*'s editorial columns. At his death in 1883 the control of the paper passed to his son Charles ("C.K."), who was its fighting editor for nearly 50 years. The most important figure in southern California was Harrison Gray Otis, a native of Ohio who arrived in Los Angeles in 1882 and began his long career as editor and publisher of the *Los Angeles Times.* From the beginning, Otis was an unabashed booster of his adopted city. Praised by some as a visionary and damned by others as a reactionary, Otis's influence on the political, economic, and cultural development of the region was unparalleled.

The Arts and Architecture

The outstanding painter of pioneer life in California was Charles Christian Nahl. Born into a family that had achieved artistic distinction in Germany for six generations, Nahl came to California in 1850 and was soon the leading producer of lithographs for letter sheets, the famous souvenir stationery on which the miners wrote home the news from the goldfields. After Judge E. B. Crocker became his patron in 1867, Nahl was able to devote the greater part of his time to his work in oils, and a number of his paintings were included in the Crocker Art Gallery in Sacramento. Probably the best of these, and certainly the best known, is his *Sunday Morning in the Mines,* which appears badly overcrowded in small reproductions but seems less so in the original, a canvas 9 feet long and 6 feet high.

Thomas A. Ayres became famous as the first artist to portray Yosemite Valley. In 1855 Ayers was a member of the first tourist party ever to enter the valley; in 5 days he produced five drawings, one of which, *The High Falls,* has scarcely been excelled among the thousands of later efforts. Albert Bierstadt and Thomas Hill were among the many who later painted the Yosemite and other California landscapes.

Sunday Morning in the Mines. Painted by Charles Christian Nahl in 1872. (*Courtesy of the E. B. Crocker Collection, Crocker Art Museum, Sacramento.*)

The most intriguing work of Hill, however, was his attempt to provide the ultimate commemoration of the transcontinental railroad in his *Driving the Last Spike.* Leland Stanford had commissioned this painting and promised $50,000 for it; such, at least, was Hill's impression, but after the artist had spent 4 years at work on the huge and elaborate canvas, Stanford refused to buy it and denied that he had ordered it. His most vocal objection was that some 70 officials of the Union and Central Pacific railroads were in the massive picture, very few of whom had actually been present at the scene; even Judah, who had died 6 years previously, was included. In somewhat the same mood in which he broke relations with Hubert Howe Bancroft, Stanford stood foursquare against contractual imposture and in favor of historical accuracy. It was also true, however, that relatives of Charles Crocker strongly objected to the prominent position occupied by Stanford at the center of Hill's picture, and that Stanford's repudiation of the painting tended to restore the peace in the railroad family.

Scottish-born William Keith, whose active career extended from the 1860s until his death in 1911, attained greater prestige than any other California artist. His early paintings of the Sierra country were done with almost photographic realism, but his maturity and his success came when, much to the disappointment of his close friend John Muir, he turned from the high mountains to pastoral landscapes of the foothills, done with a highly mystical quality.

The best California sculptor of the period was probably Ralph Stackpole, whose busts of several well-known San Franciscans were excellent portraits in stone. Greater popular acclaim, however, went to the attitudinized athletic figures by

Driving the Last Spike. This controversial canvas, painted by Thomas Hill between 1887 and 1891, contains over 400 figures, including 70 recognizable portraits. (*Courtesy of the California State Railroad Museum, Sacramento.*)

Douglas Tilden, such as the five men operating an antique drill press in the sculpture created for the Mechanics' Monument at Market and Bush streets in San Francisco.

In the field of music, San Francisco had heard its first grand opera as early as February 12, 1851, when the Pellegrini opera troupe presented Bellini's *La Sonnambula* at the Adelphi Theater. But throughout the nineteenth century, traveling performers from the east continued to outshine the local talent, both in music and in drama.

In architecture, regional developments were somewhat more distinctive. "California mission architecture" has as much interest for the history of mythmaking as for the history of architecture. Charming legends to the contrary, the roof tiles were not shaped on the thighs of Indian women, and the designs for the California mission buildings added little to the older Mexican models. As for the so-called Monterey colonial style, introduced by Thomas Larkin in the 1830s, it was adapted from buildings he had seen in Massachusetts and North Carolina, and nothing about it was either Spanish-colonial or Mexican-republican except the use of adobe as the handiest material for the walls. Nevertheless, in the early twentieth century, mission-revival and Monterey-colonial buildings formed the basis of an important regional architectural tradition.

The availability of redwood in the American period gave San Francisco in the late nineteenth century a larger proportion of wood-frame residential buildings

A photograph by A. J. Russell of the jubilant scene at Promontory, Utah, May 10, 1869. Note the contrast with Hill's idealized painting on the previous page. (*Courtesy of the Oakland Museum.*)

than any other city in the nation. Redwood became so common that there were many attempts to use paint to disguise it as stone, and the wooden house of David D. Colton on Nob Hill was even painted to simulate an Italian marble palace. Even so, the Colton house was a less offensive monument to conspicuous and meretricious waste than were the neighboring mansions of Crocker, Stanford, and the rest. Beauty was regarded as deriving from ornamentation rather than from any genuine architectural function, and there was a profusion of jigsaw carpentry on porches and of ironwork on mansard roofs. In the construction of public buildings, the era is notorious for the tendency of architects to try to build monuments to themselves rather than design structures that would effectively serve the purposes for which they were intended.

Schools, Colleges, and Universities

The development of a sense of public responsibility for education in California in the nineteenth century was slow, lagging far behind the growth of the state's economic resources and population. Not until 1874 did the state adopt compulsory education, and even then, although it applied only to the elementary level, the law was bitterly opposed on the grounds that it was an arrogation of new power by the government. As for public secondary education, there were only 16 high schools in the state in 1879, and several of them were wiped out by the provision of the new constitution that denied state tax funds to high schools because primary and grammar schools were still inadequately supported—which was all too true.

The movement to establish kindergartens in California was led by Emma Marwedel, a German-born educator who opened the state's first kindergarten in Los Angeles in 1870. One of her former pupils, Kate Douglas Wiggin, taught the first free kindergarten classes in a slum district of San Francisco in 1878. To raise money for her school, Wiggin wrote *The Birds' Christmas Carol* (1887), a popular and moving account of an ethereal child. Later she achieved national fame as author of the even more popular *Rebecca of Sunnybrook Farm* (1903).

Teaching was one of the few professions open to women in the late nineteenth century, as men moved on to better-paying positions. Half of all the teachers in Los Angeles in the 1870s were women, and women accounted for over 90 percent of the public school personnel in San Francisco a decade later. Women soon discovered that their pay as teachers and school administrators was less than that of their male colleagues. In San Francisco an Irish immigrant named Kate Kennedy launched a lobbying campaign for "equal pay for equal work." Her efforts were rewarded in 1874 when the state legislature adopted a sweeping reform: "Females employed as teachers in the public schools of this state shall in all cases receive the same compensation as is allowed male teachers for like services."

For many years the private enterprise of religious leaders had taken the responsibility for lighting the torch of higher education. In 1849 a group of Congregational and Presbyterian ministers held a meeting in San Francisco to plan a New England–style college in California. This project first took shape as the Contra Costa Academy, a "family boarding school for boys," which opened in Oakland in 1853. The institution was incorporated as the College of California in 1855, though it continued to function only as a preparatory school until 1860, when it enrolled its first freshman class.

The California legislature assumed some responsibility for higher education in 1866 when it issued a charter for an "Agricultural, Mining, and Mechanic Arts College." The trustees of the College of California then offered to turn over their entire property to the state, to be merged with the proposed agricultural college into a state university. That the private college was dangerously mired in debt was a factor in the trustees' decision, but their offer included a magnificent tract of land north of Oakland to which they had acquired title and to which they had planned to move their own institution. There they had already laid out the adjoining town lots and named the future community for Bishop George Berkeley, the Irish philosopher whose hopes of founding a college in colonial New England had once led him to write a poem, "On the Prospect of Planting Arts and Learning in America," which included the words "Westward the course of empire takes its way. . . ." John W. Dwinelle, one of the college's trustees, was elected to the state legislature and introduced the bill that became the charter of the University of California on March 23, 1868.

Throughout the nineteenth century, it was difficult to attract eminent scholars to the faculty of any institution in the far west, including the University of California. But a few able men did choose to come. Joseph LeConte, biologist and philosopher, won admiration with his writings and lectures on "evolutional ideal-ism," in which he reconciled Darwinian theory with belief in God. Eugene W. Hil-gard began the process of building the college of agriculture into a great institution of applied scientific research. In 1899 the regents brought Benjamin Ide Wheeler to the presidency from a professorship of Greek at Cornell, and for nearly 20 years, in the heyday of the "strong president" system in American higher education, Wheeler was the university's benevolent despot. During this period, Henry Morse Stephens popularized history not only to a generation of students but also in many public lectures throughout the state, and Charles Mills Gayley and his "great books" course drew classes so large that they sometimes had to be held outdoors in the Greek Theater, a gift of William Randolph Hearst.

Leland Stanford, from the time of his rise to affluence, periodically contem-plated the making of some generous gift to the people of California. Leland and Jane Lathrop Stanford had been childless for the first 18 years of their marriage, until the birth of Leland Junior. Their son occupied a very central place in their lives, but in 1884, when he was only 15 years old, he died. The next year the par-ents who had lost their only child founded a university that would bear his name. For the Leland Stanford Junior University, they promised not only their beautiful stock farm at Palo Alto as a campus but also the bulk of their fortune.

After a long and careful search for a president, the Stanfords chose the distin-guished biologist David Starr Jordan, then president of Indiana University. Al-though Jordan had recently stated the opinion that the future of American higher education lay with the state universities, he agreed to come to Stanford, and he set it on its course toward the point at which loyal alumni would describe Stanford as "the Harvard of the West"—and Harvard as "the Stanford of the East."

At the outset there were many expressions of doubt that California needed or could successfully maintain two universities within 50 miles of each other, but in 1891 when Stanford opened, the enrollment was 559 (and included a young man named Herbert Hoover), and there were nearly twice as many at Berkeley. Ten years later the enrollments at both institutions had more than doubled, and nearly 10 percent were graduate students. The 1890s were a turning point. One vital fac-tor was the state law of 1891 that authorized the establishment of a high school by approval of the voters of any city or incorporated town of more than 1500 people, and of a union high school by any two or more districts, the curricula to be such as to prepare the students for the university.

Of the colleges founded by the various Protestant denominations, the majority began as church controlled, and several of them eventually became independent. The University of the Pacific, begun by the Methodists as an academy at San Jose in 1851, was moved to Santa Clara and then reestablished at Stockton in 1924. The Methodists also founded the University of Southern California in 1879. Occidental College was established by the Presbyterians in 1887, and Pomona College by the Congregationalists in the same year. The Quakers founded Whittier College in 1901, and the Baptists established Redlands in 1909.

Of the Catholic institutions, the Jesuit universities of Santa Clara and San Francisco date from schools opened in the 1850s, and Saint Vincent's College in

Los Angeles, chartered in 1869, became Loyola University. Saint Mary's College, growing out of a school established by Archbishop Alemany in San Francisco in 1863, was placed under the administration of the Christian Brothers, moved to Oakland, and relocated in 1928 to the Moraga Valley.

The charter of the University of California required it to admit women, following the lead of several midwestern state universities founded in the previous two decades. California's normal schools—so called after the French term for "teacher's college," *école normale*—began in San Francisco in 1862 and were at first devoted chiefly to the postsecondary training of women as elementary teachers. In 1900 these institutions enrolled about half the women then pursuing higher education. The oldest women's college in the west was opened as a young ladies' seminary in Oakland in 1871 by Dr. and Mrs. Cyrus T. Mills and chartered as Mills College in 1885. Most of the other collegiate institutions in California were coeducational, but the status of women in higher education remained precarious. When enrollment of female undergraduates at Stanford University exceeded expectations, Jane Lathrop Stanford issued an edict in 1899 strictly limiting their admission: "I mean literally *never* in the future history of Leland Stanford Junior University can the number of female students at any one time exceed 500." Several decades would pass before university trustees voted to lift the limit on female admissions.

Selected Bibliography

On several aspects of this chapter, see Kevin Starr, *Americans and the California Dream, 1850–1915* (1973).

Henry George is the subject of biographies by Steven Cord (1965, 1984) and Charles A. Barker (1955). The best treatments of Ambrose Bierce are Paul Fatout (1951), Richard Saunders (1985), and S. T. Joshi and David E. Schultz (1998). Important writings on Frank Norris include the biography by Franklin Walker (1932); the studies by Ernest L. Marchand (1942), Warren French (1962), Donald Pizer (1966); and Robert D. Lundy, "The Making of *McTeague* and *The Octopus*," Ph.D. thesis, University of California, Berkeley (1956). See also Joseph R. McElrath (ed.), *Frank Norris: A Descriptive Bibliography* (1992). On the treatment of the battle of Mussel Slough by Norris and others, see the articles by Irving McKee, *Pacific Historical Review,* XVII (February 1948), pp. 19–28, and James Lorin Brown, ibid., XXVI (November 1957), pp. 373–376.

Jack London has attracted a wealth of biographers: Earle Labor (1994), Carolyn Johnston (1984), Joan Hedrick (1982), John Perry (1981), Andrew Sinclair (1977), Richard O'Connor (1964), Joan London (1939), and Irving Stone (1938).

On historiography, see John W. Caughey, *Hubert Howe Bancroft* (1946); Harry Clark, *A Venture in History* (1973); Robert W. Righter, "Theodore H. Hittell and Hubert H. Bancroft," *California Historical Quarterly,* L (June 1971), pp. 101–110; Robert V. Hine, *Josiah Royce* (1991); and Charles B. Faulhaber, "The Bancroft Library," *Chronicles of California,* IV (Fall 2000), pp. 29–46.

Much information on both major and minor literary figures may be found in Franklin Walker, *San Francisco's Literary Frontier* (1939), *A Literary History of Southern California* (1950), and *The Seacoast of Bohemia* (1966); Lawrence Clark Powell, *California Classics*

(1971); and Jack Hicks et al. (eds.), *The Literature of California* (2000). Robert Louis Stevenson left some lively vignettes of his sojourn in California; all are included in James D. Hart (ed.), *From Scotland to Silverado* (1966).

On the press, see John P. Young, *Journalism in California* (1915); John Roberts Bruce, *Gaudy Century* (1948); and *History of Journalism in San Francisco* (1939–1941), by the California Writers' Program of the WPA. Of the several biographies of Hearst, those by Cora B. Older (1936) and John K. Winkler (1928, 1955) were almost as indulgent toward their subject as were his own parents; the best general treatments are W. A. Swanberg, *Citizen Hearst* (1961), and Judith Robinson, *The Hearsts* (1991). On Los Angeles journalism, see Richard Connelly Miller, "Otis and His *Times,*" Ph.D. thesis, University of California, Berkeley (1961), and Edwin Bingham, *Charles F. Lummis* (1955). See also Sherilyn Cox Bennion, *Equal to the Occasion* (1990), an account of women editors in the nineteenth century.

Edna Milton Hughes, *Artists in California, 1786–1940* (1986), lists over 6000 California artists, while Jeanne Van Nostrand, *The First Hundred Years of Painting in California, 1775–1875* (1980), describes in more depth the work of 80 major artists. See also Birgitta Hjalmarson, *Artful Players* (1999); Nancy Dustin Wall Moure, *California Art* (1998); and Eugene Neuhaus, *William Keith, the Man and the Artist* (1938). A special issue of *California History,* LXXI (Spring 1992), is devoted to California art in the nineteenth century.

Harold Kirker's *California's Architectural Frontier* (1960) and *Old Forms on a New Land* (1991) are important social histories, as is Sally Woodbridge's *California Architecture* (1988).

William Warren Ferrier, *Ninety Years of Education in California, 1846–1936* (1937), is valuable for the early decades, though less so for the period after 1900. See also Judith Rosenberg Raftery, *Land of Fair Promise: Politics and Reform in Los Angeles Schools, 1885–1941* (1992); Irving G. Hendrick, *California Education* (1980); and Doyce B. Nunis, Jr., "Kate Douglas Wiggin: Pioneer in California Kindergarten Education," *California Historical Society Quarterly* (December 1962), pp. 291–307. On higher education, see Gunther Barth, *California's Practical Period* (1994); John R. Thelin, "California and the Colleges," *California Historical Quarterly,* LVI (Summer and Fall 1977), pp. 140–163, 230–249; Verne A. Stadtman, *The University of California, 1868–1968* (1970); Edward M. Burns, *David Starr Jordan* (1953); Gunther W. Nigel, *Iron Will: The Life and Letters of Jane Stanford* (1985); and Andrew Rolle, *Occidental College* (1986).

CHAPTER 18

Politics in the Era of
Railroad Domination

The last third of the nineteenth century was an age of unparalleled corruption in American public life. The leaders of huge corporations dominated not only the American economy but also American politics; and they tended to despise the politicians, many of whom they easily corrupted, and also to feel contempt for government itself. In no state was politics more subservient to big business than in California, for in no other state, as British historian James Bryce remarked, were politics and the economy "so much at the mercy of one powerful corporation." In California the Southern Pacific represented the greatest accumulation of wealth. It was the largest landowner, it was the largest employer of labor, and its rail system was the longest in the nation.

The degree of railroad domination in California has sometimes been exaggerated, and this has led some historians to minimize it to the extent of calling it a mere legend. Historian William Deverell, for instance, recently surveyed a half century of hostility directed at the Southern Pacific and questioned "whether there actually was an all-powerful, monolithic railroad corporation." It is true, of course, that railroad control was far from complete, but in general it was highly effective. The power of the Southern Pacific was not a monolith, nor was it a myth.

When the government of California began its attempts to regulate the Southern Pacific in the 1870s, the railroad responded by intensifying its control of the state government. The more corrupt methods by which the railroad intervened in politics were kept as secret as possible, but the workings of the Southern Pacific's "invisible government" could not always be kept invisible, and they were starkly revealed in such episodes as the publication of the Colton letters and the "Dear Pard" letters, the struggle of Los Angeles for a free harbor, and the railroad's attempt to escape from the payment of its debt to the United States.

The Colton Letters

For 4 years before his sudden death in 1878, David D. Colton had been the confidential manager of the railroad's political interests in California, while Collis P. Huntington was serving the same function in Washington, D.C. Colton was highly skilled in the shadier methods of influencing politicians. He amassed a fortune by performing this type of confidential service in exchange for opportunities to share in the profits of enterprises that would benefit from the special political privileges he could obtain. Collis P. Huntington in 1874 had persuaded his partners to approve an agreement under which Colton was permitted to acquire a large amount of railroad stock on credit. The new associate often used the expression "we five" in his letters to Huntington, though some of the newspapers described the group more accurately as "the Big Four and a Half."

When Colton died, his widow received only a little more than half a million dollars in the settlement of his estate. Not long afterward, when some of the details of the estate of Mark Hopkins were made public and Mrs. Colton noticed that some of Hopkins's shares of stock were quoted as having a far higher cash value than she had been allowed for her husband's identical shares, she concluded that the railroad leaders had cheated her. When they coldly refused a more favorable settlement, she sued the Big Four for $4 million. In 1883, in the course of the trial, her attorneys suddenly introduced as evidence several hundred letters that had been exchanged between Colton and Huntington in the years between 1874 and 1878.

In explicit detail these letters revealed Colton's activities in influencing the elections, reelections, and votes of members of the California legislature and the California congressional delegation and Huntington's similar activities with members of Congress in the east. There were innumerable references to payments of money without vouchers and discussions of the cost of influencing particular legislators and legislative outcomes. In one letter, for example, Huntington had written that "it costs money to fix things . . . I believe with $200,000 I can pass our bill, but that it is not worth this much to us." In another instance he wrote that "the boys are very hungry, and it will cost us considerable to be saved."

The state supreme court, in the case of *Ellen M. Colton v. Leland Stanford et al.,* refused to award Mrs. Colton a larger settlement. But the damage to the Southern Pacific's reputation was far greater than the value of the widow's highest demands. For decades afterward the railroad's opponents could and did cite the Colton letters whenever they wished to denounce the Southern Pacific for corrupting politics. Moreover, a widespread public reaction was that the Big Four were men who would defraud a partner's widow—a more serious moral offense to some people than the payment of money for the votes of politicians.

The Huntington-Stanford Feud

Collis P. Huntington's contempt for people who sought public office, which was extremely apparent throughout his letters to Colton, bore a significant relation to his feelings toward Leland Stanford. For many years Huntington had resented the degree to which Stanford received the lion's share of public attention while he, Huntington, did most of the hard work of managing the railroad's affairs. In 1885, when Stanford secured election to the United States Senate, Huntington was deeply angered. The honor had been promised to Aaron A. Sargent, a close friend of Huntington who had rendered many years of faithful service to the railroad's interests in both houses of Congress.

When the founding of a memorial university was announced, Huntington felt that Stanford's vanity had become completely unendurable, and he made plans to deflate it. At an annual meeting of stockholders in 1890, Huntington announced that he would support Stanford's election to a second term as senator only on condition that he himself be elected to the presidency of the railroad, which Stanford had held for 30 years. Then, after assuming the presidency, Huntington publicly stated that unlike his predecessor he would never "use this great corporation to advance my personal ambition at the expense of its owners, or put my hands in the treasury to defeat the people's choice, and thereby put myself into positions that should be filled by others."

Enemies of the Southern Pacific had often charged that large amounts of railroad money were spent by the railroad to secure Stanford's election and reelection by the California legislature as United States senator. Now the charge was directly corroborated by the president of the railroad itself. Huntington threw his open denunciation in Stanford's face with no more warning than either of them had had from Ellen Colton. In the next few hours, Stanford's friends saw him age 10 years, and his death in 1893 was undoubtedly hastened by Huntington's carefully laid plan to destroy him.

Beginning in 1892 and continuing for several years afterward, Stanford's former private secretary, J. M. Bassett, published in the *San Francisco Report* at weekly intervals a series of letters which he addressed to Huntington. These letters, opening with the salutation "Dear Pard," were intended to injure Huntington as Stanford had been injured. They were filled with charges of the wholesale corruption of national, state, and local officials by the railroad, and though they had little effect in penetrating the thick skin of Collis P. Huntington, they added significantly to a growing mass of public evidence.

Los Angeles Fights for a Free Harbor

In another of his early actions as the new president of the Southern Pacific, Huntington reversed Stanford's policy toward the location of a modern deep-water harbor for Los Angeles. Senator Stanford had supported proposals for federal aid in the construction of a breakwater at San Pedro. Huntington decided that the harbor must be built at Santa Monica because he was able to purchase enough land there to ensure that the Southern Pacific could dominate the harbor by preventing any competing railroad from gaining access to it. Huntington saw no reason why the railroad should have less control over the future port of Los Angeles than it had long exerted over the port of San Francisco. But Los Angeles, though it had only 50,000 people in the early 1890s, felt the stirrings of its future growth and power and determined to fight for a harbor that would be at least relatively free of Southern Pacific control.

In 1891 a board of Army engineers reported that San Pedro Bay was the best site in the region for the construction of a breakwater and thus for the creation of a great harbor. But the next year, Huntington served blunt notice that he would use all his influence in Congress to block any appropriation for the San Pedro project. Los Angeles rebelled, and its chamber of commerce was able to enlist some powerful allies in the fight. Harrison Gray Otis and the *Times,* the owners of the new Terminal Island Railroad, and Democratic Senator Stephen White led the opposition. Huntington's supporters in Congress argued that the government should not spend money for a harbor at San Pedro when "private enterprise"—that is, Mr. Huntington—was willing to undertake the cost of construction nearby; however, it was well known that Huntington expected to persuade Congress to pay for a still larger breakwater at Santa Monica.

In 1896 Congress passed an appropriation for whatever site a new board of engineers should approve. When this report again favored San Pedro, Huntington secured 2 more years of delay. But at last, in April 1899, the first bargeload of rock was dumped to begin construction of the breakwater at San Pedro. In later years the breakwater would be extended eastward to protect the combined harbor of San Pedro and Long Beach; and Los Angeles would become one of the world's great seaports, as well as one of its great cities.

The Funding Bill

The original construction of the Central Pacific had been made possible by federal loans of nearly $28 million payable in 30 years. No payment of interest was required until the full maturity of the loans. Simple interest at 6 percent added more than $50 million to the total obligation, which was legally payable by the year 1899. In the 1870s, though the Big Four began to vote themselves huge dividends, they set aside nothing for payment of the railroad's debt to the government. Instead, they propounded a long series of ingenious and specious arguments for its cancellation.

Congress in 1878 passed a law requiring the Central Pacific to create a sinking fund of 25 percent of the net earnings of the parts of its rail lines that had been built with federal aid. Huntington denounced the legislators who voted for the new law as "communists." But the railroad, by manipulating both traffic and bookkeeping so as to credit as little as possible of its earnings to the original bond-aided portions of the lines, kept the sinking fund to a small fraction of its total debt to the government. In the 1890s Huntington advanced a series of proposals for a funding plan to delay payment for 50 or 100 years, at the extremely low interest rate of ½ of 1 percent. In California this aroused more opposition than any other measure in the long history of public resentment against the railroad, and Adolph Sutro and William Randolph Hearst led a chorus of denunciation of it as a plot to escape the debt entirely.

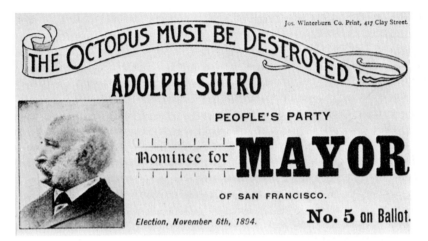

A handbill from Adolph Sutro's antirailroad mayoral campaign in 1894. (*Courtesy of the Sutro Library, San Francisco.*)

Adolph Sutro had sold all his stock in his Comstock tunnel as soon as it was completed. With the million dollars salvaged from that venture, he had moved to San Francisco, and there, by buying land whenever the local market for it reached the bottom of one of its periodic depressions, had become the owner of one-twelfth of the city's entire area. Seal Rocks, the Cliff House, the gardens of his home, and other adjoining portions of his great estate were opened to the public as a park. When the Market Street Railway Company, a Southern Pacific subsidiary, took over the trolley line to this park and refused to continue a low round-trip fare, Sutro built his own parallel line and declared himself the defender of the people against the greed of the Octopus. In 1894 Sutro was elected mayor of San Francisco as the candidate of the People's party. Sutro won the nomination and the election, partly because his many philanthropies had made him a popular figure, but also because he organized a series of mass meetings to denounce Huntington's funding plan.

William Randolph Hearst also threw the full weight of the *San Francisco Examiner* into the battle against the funding plan, and in 1894 the *Examiner* obtained more than 200,000 signatures on petitions against it. In 1896, when the crucial vote in Congress was approaching, Hearst sent Ambrose Bierce and the cartoonist Homer Davenport to Washington, D.C. For more than 20 years, Bierce's opinions of the Southern Pacific leadership had been typified by his frequent printed references to "£eland $tanford," and his articles on the funding bill were as merciless as anything in his long career of journalistic mayhem. His most effective dispatch reported a conversation on the steps of the national Capitol in which Huntington asked him to name his price for stopping his attacks and Bierce replied that his price was the railroad's full debt to the government, payable to the United States Treasury. At the same time, Davenport was making Huntington the villain of some of his most famous cartoons.

HIGHWAYMAN HUNTINGTON TO THE VOTERS OF CALIFORNIA:

"Hand Over Your Honor, Manhood and Independence, and Be Quick About It."

First published in the *San Francisco Examiner* in 1898, this cartoon was typical of Homer Davenport's attacks on the political power of the Southern Pacific. (*Courtesy of the Bancroft Library.*)

In the face of Huntington's claim that failure to adopt his funding plan would bankrupt the whole Southern Pacific system, the rebellious California legislature adopted a resolution urging the federal government not only to foreclose but to assume the ownership and operation of the railroad if necessary. When the funding bill was finally voted down in Congress in January 1897, popular opinion in California was so overjoyed that Democratic Governor James H. Budd proclaimed Saturday, January 16, a public holiday in celebration. Two years later a compromise agreement was reached, and under its terms the railroad completed the payment of its entire debt to the federal government by 1909.

The Southern Pacific Machine

The Los Angeles harbor fight and the funding battle were almost the only major political defeats that the railroad suffered before 1910. These two defeats occurred during the hard times of the 1890s, when public discontent was at a maximum, and they were in considerable part the results of personality conflicts in which the increasing tactlessness and ruthlessness of the aging Collis P. Huntington infuriated other large operators. Moreover, these two issues involved the national government. In purely state and local matters, attempts to break the grip of the railroad's political machine brought only a long succession of humiliating failures for nearly half a century.

By the 1890s the head of the railroad's political department, who was also its chief legal counsel, had become a much more important official than the governor;

in fact, he usually had the power to name the governor or any other public officer in California. Under his direction there was a railroad political manager in every county in the state. This manager might be the Republican boss in a Republican county or the Democratic boss in a Democratic county; in doubtful counties he was merely the railroad boss, with whom both Republican and Democratic bosses had to deal.

A system of political alliance with the other public utility corporations was an important factor in the railroad's power over local political bosses. The railroad itself was then the only statewide public utility, but the political interests of local street railway, gas, light, and telephone companies were similar to those of the railroad if on a smaller scale. The railroad and the other utilities were the private business corporations that could profit most directly from special favors granted by government agencies, and consequently they joined in furnishing the bulk of the money that corrupted state and local politics. This alliance came to be known in California as "the associated villainies."

To place all the blame on the railroad and other utility corporations, however, ignores the fact that they could not have corrupted the state if so many of its citizens had not been corruptible. When lawyers who were not already on the railroad's payroll were elected to the state legislature, they were likely to receive a letter from the law department of the Southern Pacific stating that the railroad wished to retain an outstanding attorney from their region during a period that happened to coincide with that of the coming session at Sacramento. A retainer fee was enclosed, and the privileged nature of the attorney-client relationship protected the secrecy of the transaction.

Of all the agencies of state government, the railroad was most careful to control the bank commission. Bankers who gave aid and comfort to the railroad's enemies could suddenly find themselves in disastrous trouble with this board of commissioners. Consequently, businesspeople or farmers who displeased the railroad by denouncing its rates, or by voting against its candidates, would suddenly find themselves unable to obtain further loans from their banks.

Another effective form of influence was the free pass. It cost relatively little, and it reached people who would have resisted more obvious forms of bribery. Instead of being considered a bribe, the railroad pass was a status symbol. The person who held it felt allied with the successful and powerful leaders of society against the ignorant and envious rabble. The constitution of 1879 specifically forbade free passes for state officeholders, but the provision was never enforced.

Many of the smaller newspapers were subsidized not only with advertising contracts but with regular and secret monthly stipends as well. Larger publishers such as Harrison Gray Otis, M. H. de Young, and John D. Spreckels were far too wealthy to be influenced by trifling financial considerations. But each of these three men had perennial hopes of going to the United States Senate, and though they often joined in attacks on the railroad, there were also many occasions when each of them tempered his criticism of the Southern Pacific because of his own political ambitions.

Not even the courts were immune from the railroad's influence. Justices of the federal and state supreme courts traveled on passes. Most of the judges of the federal district and circuit courts in San Francisco were appointed at the instance of California senators who spoke with the railroad's voice. Justice Stephen J. Field, great and brilliant "craftsman of the law," was a personal associate of the Big Four, owed his position in the United States Supreme Court to their influence, and rendered them invaluable service by writing many of the opinions through which the highest court long protected the railroad and other corporations from effective government regulation.

As for the judiciary at the state level, the machine controlled the election of judges, and one of the regular duties of a county boss was to provide the railroad with secret annotated lists of veniremen, or prospective jurors, to aid its attorneys in impaneling sympathetic juries.

William F. Herrin

Among the important sources of the railroad's power was its ability to enlist the most talented lawyers in its service. One such person was William F. Herrin, who headed the Southern Pacific's legal and political departments from 1893 to 1910. It was under Herrin that the railroad's political machine in California reached its highest level of efficiency.

Herrin in 1889 had won a national reputation when, as special counsel, he aided a United States attorney in defending a federal marshal, David Neagle, against a murder charge. The case grew out of the earlier and equally sensational legal battle in which Sarah Althea Hill had claimed that she was the legal wife of Senator William Sharon under the terms of a "contract marriage" and that she was thus entitled to a large part of his enormous fortune. During the court proceedings, Sharon died, and his alleged widow married one of her attorneys, David S. Terry, former chief justice of the California Supreme Court. United States Justice Stephen J. Field, while on federal circuit court duty in San Francisco, ruled that Mrs. Terry had not been Sharon's wife and had no valid claim on the Sharon estate. Both the Terrys had brought weapons into the courtroom, and both of them threatened Field's life.

At the time of Justice Field's next visit to California, United States Marshal Neagle was assigned as his bodyguard, and when, in a railway station in Lathrop, Terry approached Field and struck him, Neagle shot Terry dead. *In re Neagle* became one of the great cases in the history of American federal-state relations. No federal law had authorized Neagle's assignment as bodyguard or his action in killing Terry; but the United States Supreme Court ruled that these had been "fairly and properly inferable" from the Constitution. It was one of the broadest interpretations yet given to the implied powers of the national government.

Herrin was the attorney who contributed most to the preparation of the case for Neagle in the circuit court proceedings at San Francisco. Collis P. Huntington, deeply impressed with Herrin's talents, chose him, as he had once chosen David D. Colton, to be the railroad's western political manager.

From his office in the Southern Pacific's headquarters at Fourth and Townsend streets in San Francisco, Herrin not only directed all the company's manifold political activities, but grappled with all its complex legal problems as well. Comparison of Herrin with Colton suggests the evolution that occurred between the railroad's first generation and its second in the development of its political techniques.

Failure of Nineteenth-Century Reform Movements

A significant factor in the perpetuation of the railroad's control of California was the widespread sense of futility that followed the many disheartening failures of reform. The railroad always devoted special care to its efforts to gain control of reform movements and leaders. A classic example was Newton Booth, a Republican who was elected governor in 1871 on a platform opposing further state and local subsidies to the railroad. Governor Booth later assumed the leadership of an Independent Taxpayers' reform party and echoed its promises to force the railroad's fares and freight rates down and its tax payments up. But somehow nothing substantial was done toward accomplishing these objectives. The new party secured Booth's election to the United States Senate. A few months later, he was listed in one of Huntington's secret letters to Colton as among the railroad's most important friends.

The last decades of the century in California did bring some valiant struggles for reform. One such crusade induced the state legislature to adopt the Australian, or secret, ballot in 1891. But this applied only to general elections and not to the nominating process. Candidates for state, county, and city offices were nominated by party conventions. There was no effective legal regulation of the party primaries in which the delegates to these conventions were elected. State law still regarded the political party as a kind of private enterprise or private club.

Usually the railroad placed more reliance on Republican candidates and officeholders than on Democrats, but the Democratic party failed dismally to provide an effective vehicle for reform. The railroad was quite willing to make use of Democrats whenever they happened to have a better chance of election, and it often supported the candidates and machines of both parties at once.

The economic distress of the 1890s intensified a growing belief that both major parties were morally bankrupt, and this led to a new flourishing of support for third-party movements. The Nationalist party had a brief but striking career in 1890. Formed by enthusiastic readers of Edward Bellamy's utopian romance, *Looking Backward, 2000–1887,* this movement advocated a gradualist, nonviolent Christian socialism. But its appeal was mainly to urban discontent, and nearly all of its following in California was in San Francisco and Los Angeles.

The Nationalist party soon was overshadowed by the rise of the People's, or Populist, party. The Populist movement was based mainly on the increasingly bitter discontent of the farmers, but it hoped to gain support from city workers as well. At the heart of populism was a distrust of political parties and a firm belief that no important reform could be accomplished until control of the machinery of government was taken out of the hands of party bosses and party conventions and given to the people. Thus, the most enduring contribution of the Populists in California was the spread of public interest in their demands for the direct primary, the initiative, the referendum, and the recall. A few years later this part of the Populist program would play a major role in the progressive movement, the California reform movement that at last brought to an end the era of railroad domination.

Selected Bibliography

Aspects of the railroad's political activities are described in Spencer C. Olin, Jr., *California Politics, 1846–1920* (1981), and George Mowry, *The California Progressives* (1951). The most important of the recent reevaluations of the power of the railroad is William Deverell, *Railroad Crossing: Californians and the Railroad, 1885–1910* (1994). See also Don L. Hofsommer, *The Southern Pacific, 1901–1985* (1986); Bill Yenne, *Southern Pacific* (1985); Stuart Daggett, *Chapters on the History of the Southern Pacific* (1922); Oscar Lewis, *The Big Four* (1938); and Jack W. Bates, "The Southern Pacific Railroad in California Politics," M.A. thesis, University of the Pacific (1942). See also "Railroads in California and the Far West," a special issue of *California History,* LXX (Spring 1991), edited by Richard J. Orsi. The Colton letters are given new voice in Salvador A. Ramierez, *"Free Harbor Fight"* (1992). On the harbor fight, see William F. Deverell, "The Los Angeles 'Free Harbor Fight,'" in *California History,* LXX (Spring 1991), and Willis H. Miller, "The Port of Los Angeles— Long Beach in 1929 and 1979," *Southern California Quarterly,* LXV (Winter 1983), pp. 341–378. Most of the railroad's arguments for cancellation of its debt were brought together by its counsel, Creed Haymond, in *The Central Pacific Railroad and the United States* (3 parts, 1887–1889).

The first volume of the memoirs of Franklin Hichborn, "California Politics, 1891–1939" (reproduced in typewritten copies and available in several libraries including that of the University of California, Los Angeles), provides many insights into the structure and functioning of the Southern Pacific machine. See also William A. Bullough, *The Blind Boss and His City: Christopher Augustine Buckley and Nineteenth Century San Francisco* (1979). Attempts at state regulation are discussed in Gerald D. Nash, "The California Railroad Commission, 1876–1911," *Southern California Quarterly,* XLIV (December 1962), pp. 287–306, and Ward M. McAfee, *California's Railroad Era, 1850–1911* (1973).

R. Hal Williams, *The Democratic Party and California Politics, 1880–1896* (1973), argues that railroad domination of California politics has been so exaggerated that it has become "a legend." Orsi, "The Octopus Reconsidered: The Southern Pacific and Agricultural Modernization in California, 1865–1915," *California Historical Quarterly,* LIV (Fall 1975), pp. 197–220, stresses the positive contributions of the railroad.

On late-nineteenth-century reform efforts, see Curtis E. Grassman, "Prologue to California Reform: The Democratic Impulse, 1886–1898," *Pacific Historical Review,* XLII (November 1973), pp. 518–536, and Eric F. Petersen, "The Struggle for the Australian Ballot in California," *California Historical Quarterly,* LI (Fall 1972), pp. 227–243.

On the case of Sarah Althea Hill and William Sharon, see Paul Kens, *Justice Stephen Field* (1997); Robert H. Kroninger, *Sarah and the Senator* (1964); and Gary L. Roberts, "In Pursuit of Duty," *The American West,* VII (September 1970), pp. 27–33, 62–63.

California populism is discussed in Michael Magliari, "What Happened to the Populist Vote?" *Pacific Historical Review,* LXIV (August 1995), pp. 389–412; Donald E. Walters,

"The Feud between California Populist T. V. Cator and Democrats James Maguire and James Barry," ibid., XXVII (August 1958), pp. 281–298; Eric F. Petersen, "The End of an Era: California's Gubernatorial Election of 1894," ibid., XXXVIII (May 1969), pp. 141–156; John T. McGreevy, "Farmers, Nationalists, and the Origins of California Populism," ibid., LVIII (November 1989), pp. 471–495; David B. Griffiths, "Anti-Monopoly Movements in California, 1873–1898," *Southern California Quarterly,* LII (June 1970), pp. 93–121; and Michael P. Rogin and John L. Shover, *Political Change in California* (1970).

Labor and Capital

The period of the late nineteenth and early twentieth centuries was not only an age of business domination; it was also a time of working-class organization. Unions increased in strength and challenged, often unsuccessfully, the powers of corporate America. Radical organizations appealed to the discontented and called for fundamental economic and political change. In California, as journalist and historian Carey McWilliams once observed, the struggle between labor and capital was one of total engagement.

Backgrounds of the California Labor Movement

The first large-scale labor movement in the state, the Workingmen's party of 1877 to 1880, contributed very little to the development of modern labor organization. Denis Kearney was ignorant of the principles of trade unionism, and with minor exceptions the Workingmen's party received no support from the few small unions then in existence in California. California legislation in the interest of labor also remained very limited. A state bureau of labor statistics was established in 1883, but laws providing on paper for the mechanics' lien and for an 8-hour day on government work lacked provisions essential for their enforcement.

Throughout the country, attempts at effective labor organization suffered from labor's chronic disunity and confusion of aims. One great dispute was over the question of whether labor should avoid organized political action and confine itself to "pure and simple," or "bread-and-butter," unionism—that is, to collective bargaining with employers for strictly economic goals. Another basic disagreement concerned the form of organization. The oldest and most conservative plan was that of craft unionism, in which each skilled trade in a city had its own local union, reaching out toward federation with other locals in the same craft on a state and national basis, and also toward city, state, and national federations of the unions of the various crafts. This idea produced the body that would ultimately evolve into American labor's most important one, the American Federation of Labor.

The Noble Order of the Knights of Labor, on the other hand, stood for a single national union capable of including workers of all crafts or of none. It advocated producers' cooperatives, to be owned by the workers and to take over as many industries as possible. To the left of the Knights of Labor were the Marxists, not yet clearly divided on the issue of peaceful socialism versus communist violence; the anarchists, advocates of the abolition of government; and the syndicalists, who believed that a mighty labor organization should in effect become the government.

Among these alternatives, American labor made an overwhelming choice in favor of craft unionism—collective bargaining for higher wages, shorter hours, and other improved conditions, with political action limited to objectives closely related to these. In other words, American labor decided to seek a fairer share of the benefits of the private system of economic enterprise rather than a replacement of that system by socialized public ownership of the means of production.

The Rise of Unions in San Francisco

It is true that some of the most important leaders of the labor movement in San Francisco in the 1880s were socialists. In 1881 Frank Roney, a member of the Iron Moulders' Union and a former Irish revolutionary, became president of the San Francisco Trades Assembly, then the only citywide federation of unions. A year later Burnette G. Haskell began a lively career as a radical labor organizer.

Haskell was a native Californian, the son of a wealthy pioneer family. Though trained as a lawyer, he was too erratic and visionary to be happy or successful in a routine law practice and instead became the editor of *Truth,* a small weekly paper that his father had founded. One evening in 1882, in search of news, he attended a meeting of the Trades Assembly. Until then he had taken no interest in labor's problems, but from that time onward he threw himself into the cause of socialism. It was typical of him that he tried to reconcile socialism and anarchism, an effort in which, needless to say, he failed. By far the most enduring contribution of his life was his leadership in the founding of the Coast Seamen's Union.

San Francisco's position as the premier seaport of the Pacific coast made it inevitable that the labor problems of the waterfront would play a central part in the history of the city's labor relations as a whole. Moreover, working conditions in the maritime industry were peculiarly atrocious before the development of effective unions. Other workers had the legal right to quit work, but for the sailor this was considered desertion, and under United States law until 1915 it led to arrest and imprisonment. Until 1898 corporal punishment was permitted at sea for "justifiable cause" as interpreted by the captain of the ship. Flogging had been abolished by federal law in 1850 after a long campaign led by Richard Henry Dana and others, but this had merely meant that other forms of physical torture were substituted. The food was vile, and the sleeping quarters were cramped and ill-ventilated "dogholes."

The chief method of hiring seamen which prevailed throughout the world in the nineteenth century was the infamous crimping system. The crimps, keepers of sailors' boardinghouses on the waterfront, served also as the main employment agencies. While in port the sailor lived on credit advances from the crimp for food, clothing, and liquor until the crimp arranged his next voyage. No sailor could get a ship in any other way, and no master could get a crew except by negotiating with the crimp to pay the sailor's wage advance. The master often had to pay the crimp an additional fee, known as "blood money" because drugged and slugged men were frequently shanghaied aboard covered with blood.

Union organization to escape from such conditions began in the coasting trade when Burnette Haskell formed the Coast Seamen's Union in 1885. In the same year, Haskell also formed the Kaweah colony, a utopian cooperative enterprise for timber cutting in what would later be Sequoia National Park. On the theory that this scheme would provide employment for sailors out of work, Haskell gained the support of many union members for the colony and even the investment of some of the union's funds. The Kaweah experiment was unsuccessful, however, and the sailors, perceiving that Haskell was eccentric and undependable, rejected his leadership and with it the socialistic influence in their union. Instead, after merging with a separate union of steamship sailors to form the Sailors' Union of the Pacific in 1891, the coast sailors found their greatest leader for decades to come in Andrew Furuseth, a man who was proud of the sailor's craft and devoted to the philosophy and methods of craft unionism. Furuseth, more than any other individual, was responsible for the reforms of the La Follette Seamen's Act of 1915, which abolished imprisonment for desertion, regulated working conditions, and finally broke the power of the crimps.

In many other industries, also, harsh working conditions still prevailed in the late nineteenth century. San Francisco bakers, for example, worked from 12 to 18 hours a day for 7 days a week, except Sundays, when they worked 6 hours. Conditions showed the greatest improvement in the few occupations in which the bulk of the workers were unionized before 1900, notably the building trades. In general, however, only a small minority of wage earners were union members, and in many occupations there were no unions at all. Formal agreements between employers and unions were rare, and in most cases the employer set the terms and could change them without notice.

In the relatively prosperous years of the early twentieth century, unionism in San Francisco made a remarkable surge forward. There was a great increase in membership, and new unions were successfully established in a number of occupations that had been considered unorganizable in other communities. The often-repeated statement that San Francisco in this period became "the first closed-shop city in the United States" was an exaggeration, however, for except in the building trades the *closed shop,* which meant the employer agreed to hire only members of the union, was actually adopted in very few instances. Indeed, most bargaining agreements were still entirely informal. But in comparison with other American cities, San Francisco did become a stronghold of unionism in about 1900 and remained so until the early 1920s.

In the summer of 1901, the teamsters joined with the sailors and the longshoremen in a waterfront strike that tied up the port for several weeks. Violence between strikers on the one hand and strikebreakers and the police on the other led to hundreds of injuries and four deaths. Again, as in 1877 when the apparent use of the police on the side of the business community had led the workingmen to form a new political party, so in 1901 the assignment of the police to protect strikebreakers led to the organization of the new Union Labor party of San Francisco. For a time that party actually gained control of the city government. During its first 6 years of existence, however, it was controlled by an opportunistic and corrupt political boss, Abraham Ruef, and thus it became significant mainly for its part in the extreme corruption of California party politics, which would at last produce major attempts at political reform in the city and the state.

San Francisco women also participated in union organizing in the early 1900s. Most women workers remained concentrated in low-paying positions, often working in dangerous or unsanitary conditions. In 1901 several hundred waitresses, demanding higher wages, fought a bitter strike that closed nearly 200 San Francisco restaurants. The city's female laundry workers struck 6 years later, as did women who worked at the Ghirardelli chocolate factory. One of the largest strikes came in

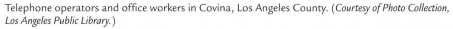

Telephone operators and office workers in Covina, Los Angeles County. (*Courtesy of Photo Collection, Los Angeles Public Library.*)

1919 when 1300 female telephone operators went on strike, demanding and winning the right to bargain collectively.

The Triumph of the Open Shop in Los Angeles

In the same turn-of-the-century period when the idea of the closed shop was coming as near to acceptance in San Francisco as anywhere else in America, Los Angeles was becoming the country's leading citadel of the *open shop,* based on precisely the opposite principle, under which employers refused to make agreements requiring union membership of their employees and even refused to bargain with unions at all.

This remarkable polarization of institutional patterns in the two cities was one of the many extreme contrasts between them. The population of southern California remained relatively sparse and rural before 1900, and because industry was still on a trifling scale in Los Angeles several decades after it had begun to flourish in San Francisco, unions in Los Angeles were less deeply rooted. But of all the factors impeding union growth in southern California, the most remarkable and effective was the personality of Harrison Gray Otis, publisher of the *Los Angeles Times.* With a great fortune built on a highly profitable newspaper and on vast real estate investments in California and Mexico, Otis made himself the leader of the most intransigent group of organized employers to be found anywhere in the United States.

Otis believed that men of wealth, in their wisdom and genius, were the only men to be trusted with economic or political power. A related part of his thinking was that the military plan of social organization was an excellent system. The good soldier never struck and never boycotted. This feeling provided much of the emotional force behind Otis's crusade for the open shop, which he rationalized as "industrial freedom"—the freedom of workers not to join a union and the freedom of employers to discharge them if they did. Otis often said that he favored the closed shop, by what he regarded as the only proper definition of it: closed to union members.

In 1890 Otis precipitated the first major conflict between employers and unions in Los Angeles with the intention of destroying the printers' union, the oldest union in the city. Printers, as Otis pointed out, were the only workers in southern California who were still getting boom-time wages. The boom of the 1880s having collapsed, a wage cut was in order. But instead of negotiating a new agreement, Otis announced a 20 percent cut, locked his union printers out, and refused to discuss a compromise. Before doing this he had formed an association with the publishers of the other three Los Angeles dailies, and had arranged to bring in nonunion printers from San Diego and elsewhere. He paid these strikebreakers the previous union wages—until the strike collapsed. Other unions helped the printers by contributing funds and by joining in a boycott of the *Times* and its advertisers. This boycott was a failure, but it tended to solidify the Los Angeles labor movement for the years of struggle that lay ahead.

The employers who were most antagonistic to unions formed an Employers' Association under the leadership of Otis. They also established an Independent

Labor Bureau to carry on a wide campaign of advertising in the east, promising jobs at high wages for nonunion workers. The Merchants' and Manufacturers' Association (M&M) of Los Angeles, originally formed in the 1890s to promote commercial and industrial enterprise, was at first outwardly neutral in Otis's war with the unions, but in 1903 the M&M announced that it would unite with employers injured by boycotts, which it branded as "unAmerican, unjust, unwarranted, and illegal." Soon afterward, however, it launched a boycott policy of its own—against employers who negotiated with unions. Bank loans were withheld and orders were transferred to other companies. The M&M's boycott was more effective than any that union labor ever attempted.

At this time the drive for the open shop was becoming a national movement. A major slogan of this movement was "The Right to Work," the title of a widely discussed article by Ray Stannard Baker, which expressed sympathy for the *scab,* or strikebreaking, miners in a recent Pennsylvania coal strike. The National Association of Manufacturers declared against recognition of labor unions in 1903, and its president founded a Citizens' Industrial Association of America. This body, in turn, fostered local Citizens' Alliances in which the public was invited to join with employers in fighting organized labor. In Los Angeles the Citizens' Alliance soon recruited the country's largest per capita membership, with heavy financial support from Otis, Henry E. Huntington, and others.

The struggle reached a crisis in 1910, when organized labor took the offensive in a drive for effective unionization of the Los Angeles metal trades. In the spring the metal trades employers of San Francisco agreed to an 8-hour day but warned that they could not long continue it unless their competitors in Los Angeles were unionized and forced to accept the same terms. Consequently, union organizers and funds from San Francisco suddenly strengthened the metal trades unions of Los Angeles to such a degree that they were able to begin a strike of 1500 workers on June 1, 1910, the largest strike the city had ever witnessed. The employers refused to negotiate, and the battle attracted national attention because the whole future of the open shop was clearly at stake in the city where it was strongest. The *Times* outdid itself in denouncing the assault on "the cradle of industrial freedom," and organized labor and its sympathizers throughout the country denounced the *Times* as the nation's leading symbol of union smashing.

Before dawn on the morning of October 1, while the strike was still in full swing, a tremendous explosion destroyed the Times building, killed 20 men, and injured 17 others. Immediately the open-shop forces attributed this "crime of the century," as the *Times* called it, to a dynamite bomb planted by union labor's agents. Labor's partisans, on the other hand, charged that the cause was a leaking gas main, typical of the "fire-trap" in which Otis had compelled his employees to work. Unhappily the truth was that a dynamite bomb had been used and that certain individual union officials were guilty of planning the outrage.

The tragedy of the *Times* was a part of a nationwide struggle between the International Association of Bridge and Structural Iron Workers and the large employers in the field. In 1906 the employers began a belligerent campaign to destroy the power of the Iron Workers and succeeded in establishing the open shop throughout

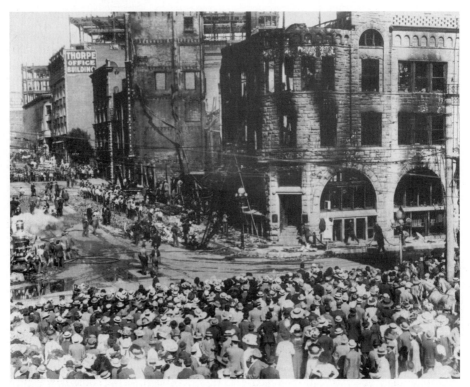

The Los Angeles Times building following the dynamite bombing of October 1, 1910. (*Courtesy of the California Historical Society Ticor Collection, Department of Special Collections, University of Southern California Library.*)

the industry in all large cities except Chicago and San Francisco. Driven to desperation, the union's national leaders secretly resorted to terrorism, and over a period of several years dozens of nonunion construction projects in a number of cities were damaged by explosions of dynamite, though until the *Times* bombing none of these had resulted in loss of life.

William J. Burns, head of a private detective agency, was already investigating some of the lesser incidents when he was employed by the mayor of Los Angeles to investigate the *Times* disaster. In April 1911 Burns arrested Ortie McManigal, a professional dynamiter, who confessed his own part in the bombing campaign and described its planning by officials of the union at their national headquarters in Indianapolis. Union secretary John J. McNamara, his brother James B. McNamara, and McManigal were then brought to Los Angeles to be tried for complicity in the bombing of the *Times.*

Samuel Gompers, president of the American Federation of Labor (AFL), staked his prestige and that of the AFL on the belief that the charges against the McNamara brothers were a frame-up, and Clarence Darrow, one of the country's ablest trial lawyers, was employed for the defense. But on December 1, 1911, the millions of Americans who believed the McNamara brothers to be the innocent victims of an employer conspiracy were stunned by their confession of guilt. The evidence against them was overwhelming, and Darrow advised his clients to plead guilty in order to save their lives.

The McNamaras' confession demoralized American labor, emboldened employers, and intensified the bitterness between the two sides. In Los Angeles the result was 30 more years of dominance for the open shop.

Agricultural Labor: Unorganized and Disfranchised

Historically, the family farm has been the institution most typical of American agriculture. Only a fourth of those gainfully employed in farming in the United States have been wage workers, and these have been hired men attached more or less permanently to one farm and living with the family that owned it. In California, however, more than two-thirds of the total number of persons engaged in agriculture have been wage laborers, the majority of them alien, nonwhite, and migratory. California's "peculiar institution," comparable in some ways to southern black slavery, has been seasonal migratory agricultural labor in which the worker lacked the protections offered in other fields by labor unions and by the right to vote.

Several circumstances contributed to this situation: the persistence of large units of landownership in California, specialization in a particular seasonal crop, as opposed to the year-round operations of the "general farm" more common in the middle west, and the availability, in each successive generation, of some new supply of cheap labor drawn from some supposedly inferior race—first the California Indians, then the Chinese, and later the Japanese, Asian Indians, Mexicans, and Filipinos.

Union organization would have been exceedingly difficult under these circumstances, even if the agricultural employers had not been violently opposed to it. California trade unions were not merely indifferent to the welfare of alien nonwhite workers, but sternly hostile to their presence in the United States. Groups of migratory laborers, white or nonwhite, usually disbanded at the end of the local harvest season, and wages were too low to have permitted the payment of union dues. Even the minority who were citizens of the United States were seldom in any one place long enough to qualify as voters, and because agricultural employers had great influence in the election and reelection of county supervisors and sheriffs, whereas migratory workers had no such influence, local lawmaking and law enforcement weighed heavily on the employer's side.

In the 1880s the majority of seasonal and casual laborers in California agriculture were Chinese, whom the large growers regarded as an ideal labor force. Many of the Chinese immigrants were skilled and experienced farmers with much to teach their American employers about agricultural efficiency, but the exclusion act of 1882 and a steady drift of Chinese from the rural areas to the cities and towns began to deplete this source of labor supply. Moreover, during the depression after the panic of 1893, unemployed whites from the cities, seeking work as "fruit tramps," participated in riots that drove thousands of Chinese laborers from the fields. A few blacks were brought from the southern states, but agricultural wages were so low that they soon found better pay in unskilled labor or domestic service in the cities.

For about a decade, beginning in the late 1890s, the growers found another temporary solution in the Japanese, particularly as field workers in the sugar-beet industry. But the Gentlemen's Agreement of 1907 restricted Japanese immigration, and moreover the Japanese were quick to escape from the role of cheap laborers. Through clubs or associations they began to engage in collective bargaining, and to the pained surprise of the growers they conducted the first successful strikes in the history of California agriculture. When the Japanese began to acquire land, by purchase or lease, white farmers soon joined with city labor unions in anti-Japanese agitation. (See Chapter 21.) In the second decade of the century the growers turned to Asian Indians, especially for labor in the Imperial Valley, and to Mexicans, particularly during and after World War I.

The IWW

The first widespread attempt to organize the migratory workers of California was made by members of a new and radical movement called the Industrial Workers of the World (IWW). The IWW was an anarcho-syndicalist organization formed in Chicago in 1905. The preamble of its constitution denounced craft unionism and called instead for "one great union" made up largely of unskilled workers. The IWW did not exclude any worker because of race, and it condemned the AFL for practicing racial discrimination. The IWW manifesto adopted as its "revolutionary watchword" the "historic mission of the working class to do away with capitalism." Sabotage, sympathetic strikes for the purpose of paralyzing an industry, and "any and all tactics that will get the results sought with the least expenditure of time and energy" were regarded as justified.

The doctrine of the IWW appealed to those whose condition seemed utterly hopeless. Its numerical strength was often exaggerated by the newspapers, and the degree of notoriety it achieved was largely the result of the frightened manner in which many employers and public authorities reacted to it. One tactic of the IWW was the demand for the right of free speech, and when the police and other officials would deny this right, the IWW attracted wide public sympathy. Street-corner gatherings to hear political or religious exhortations were then common occurrences in American cities, and in the early twentieth century many cities adopted ordinances against street speaking—ordinances that were enforced against political radicals but not against such meetings as those of the Salvation Army.

In 1910, when the IWW launched a drive to organize farm laborers in the region of Fresno, several of its members were arrested for speaking on the streets of the town. More than a hundred other members then arrived on freight trains for the purpose of filling the jail, where they attracted so much outraged attention by the mass singing of radical songs that police and firefighters resorted to drenching

IS IT ABOUT TO STRIKE?

An editorial cartoon from the *Industrial Worker,* commenting on the tactics of Fresno authorities in their campaign against the IWW and its "free speech agitation." (*Courtesy of the Bancroft Library.*)

them with firehoses. A mob burned the organization's tent and talked of storming the jail to lynch the prisoners. Chester H. Rowell, progressive editor of the *Fresno Republican,* excoriated the IWW but also denounced the methods being used against it. Instead of giving way to hysterical repression, he advised, Fresno should undercut the IWW by encouraging the growth of normal labor unions. After a stalemate of several months, a compromise freed the men from jail and permitted them to speak in designated areas of the city.

Another and greater free speech fight occurred in 1912 in San Diego, following the adoption of an ordinance that forbade street-corner speaking in the downtown district. This ordinance had been approved after Harrison Gray Otis made a speech to a group of San Diego businesspeople recommending strong measures to suppress radical propaganda. Dozens of Wobblies—a nickname Otis was the first to use in print—then came from other parts of the state to repeat their strategy of overflowing the jails. Business owners formed a vigilance committee, and some of its members inflicted cruel beatings on a number of Wobblies without interference from the police and with open encouragement from the San Diego newspapers, the *Union* and the *Tribune,* both owned by the beet-sugar capitalist John D. Spreckels. Only the police and the vigilantes, not the IWW, resorted to violence. The *San Francisco Bulletin* asked whether it was the "radicals" or the self-styled "good citizens" who had acted as the real anarchists and who had done more to violate the principles of the Constitution of the United States.

In its effort to organize farm labor, the IWW developed methods especially adapted to the conditions of the migratory workers. Giving up the idea of local organizations with permanent dues-paying members, the Wobblies traveled about among the seasonal labor camps, formed temporary organizations on the job, and asked either very small dues or none at all. These tactics were employed among the workers involved in the tragic incident known as the Wheatland riot of August 3, 1913, which occurred on the Durst ranch near the town of Wheatland in Yuba County, a few miles southeast of Marysville.

Ralph Durst, one of the state's largest employers of migratory labor, had collected a surplus of workers for the hop-picking season through alluring advertisements in newspapers in several parts of California and southern Oregon. Needing about 1500 workers, he attracted 2800, mostly aliens. Conditions in his work camp were barbaric. As housing, a few tents were available for rental, but most of the workers built their own rude shelters of gunnysacks and poles, or slept in the open. For 2800 men, women, and children, there were eight outdoor toilets, which also had to serve as the only garbage disposal facilities. The temperature was more than 100°F in the shade. Durst not only refused to provide drinking water in the fields, but also refused the workers permission to rent a water wagon and haul it themselves; a cousin of Durst's had a concession to sell "lemonade," made with citric acid. The "bonus" wage that had been advertised turned out to be nothing more than a device for holding back part of the workers' wages if they left before the end of the picking season.

A mass meeting elected a committee to demand better conditions, with Richard Ford, a member of the IWW better known as "Blackie" Ford, as spokesman. Durst slapped Ford, and the next day, August 3, a posse arrived from Marysville to arrest the agitators. Ford was then addressing another mass meeting, and a deputy fired a shot in the air "to sober the mob." This led to a general melee in which the district attorney, a deputy sheriff, and two workers were killed and many were injured. Governor Johnson sent five companies of the National Guard to Wheatland, and in a trial at Marysville early in 1914, Ford and Herman Suhr, another IWW member, were convicted of second-degree murder on the theory that by leading the strike that resulted in the shooting they were guilty of conspiracy to murder the district attorney. Durst, who was as responsible for the tragedy as any other individual, received no punishment.

Selected Bibliography

Daniel Cornford (ed.), *Working People of California* (1995), contains essays of seminal importance for this chapter. David F. Selvin's *A Place in the Sun* (1982) and *Sky Full of Storm* (1966) are useful surveys of the history of union organization in California. See also Alexander P. Saxton, *The Indispensable Enemy* (1971); Philip Taft, *Labor Politics American Style* (1968); and Ira B. Cross, *History of the Labor Movement in California* (1935).

Jules Tygiel, *Workingmen in San Francisco, 1880–1901* (1992), is a perceptive analysis of the multiple variables at work in late-nineteenth-century labor history. The rise of unionism in San Francisco is also treated in Michael Kazin, *Barons of Labor* (1987); William Issel and Robert W. Cherny, *San Francisco, 1865–1932* (1986); Paul Bullock et al., *Building California* (1982); Robert E. L. Knight, *Industrial Relations in the San Francisco Bay Area* (1960); Paul S. Taylor, *The Sailors' Union of the Pacific* (1923); Hyman G. Weintraub, *Andrew Furuseth* (1959); and Arnold Berwick, *The Abraham Lincoln of the Sea* (1993). See also Jay O'Connell, *Co-Operative Dreams: A History of the Kaweah Colony* (1999).

Grace H. Stimson, *Rise of the Labor Movement in Los Angeles* (1955), and its sequel, Louis B. Perry and Richard S. Perry, *A History of the Los Angeles Labor Movement, 1911–1941* (1963), form the first inclusive account of the history of organized labor in any large American city. See also Robert Phelps, "The Search for a Modern Industrial City," *Pacific Historical Review,* LXIV (November 1995), pp. 503–536. Richard C. Miller, "Otis and His *Times,*" Ph.D. thesis, University of California, Berkeley (1961), is penetrating and critical. For the *Times*'s viewpoint, see *The Forty-Year War for a Free City* (1929). On the McNamara case, see also William J. Burns, *The Masked War* (1913); Louis Adamic, *Dynamite* (1931); Clarence Darrow, *The Story of My Life* (1932); *The Autobiography of Lincoln Steffens* (1931); and Graham Adams, Jr., *The Age of Industrial Violence, 1910–1915* (1966).

On agricultural labor, see Cletus E. Daniel, *Bitter Harvest: A History of California Farmworkers, 1870–1941* (1981); Carey McWilliams, *Factories in the Field* (1939); Paul S. Taylor, "Foundations of California Rural Society," *California Historical Society Quarterly,* XXIV (September 1945), pp. 193–228; and Tomás Almaguer, "Racial Domination and Class Conflict in Capitalist Agriculture," *Labor History,* XXV (Summer 1984), pp. 325–350.

On the IWW, see Dione Miles (comp.), *Something in Common: An IWW Bibliography* (1986). Hyman Weintraub, "The I.W.W. in California, 1905–1931," M.A. thesis, University of California, Los Angeles (1947), is the most detailed account of its subject. Others may be found in Elizabeth Reis, "Cannery Row: The AFL, the IWW and Bay Area Cannery Workers," *California History,* LXIV (Summer 1985), pp. 174–191; Ronald Genini, "Industrial Workers of the World and Their Fresno Free Speech Fight, 1910–1911," *California Historical Quarterly,* LIII (Summer 1974), pp. 100–114; Grace L. Miller, "The I.W.W. Free Speech Fight: San Diego, 1912," *Southern California Quarterly,* LIV (Fall 1972), pp. 211–238; Rosalie Shanks, "The I.W.W. Free Speech Movement, San Diego, 1912," *Journal of San Diego History,* XIX (Winter 1973), pp. 25–33; Cletus E. Daniel, "In Defense of the Wheatland Wobblies," *Labor History,* XIX (Fall 1978), pp. 485–509; Woodrow C. Whitten, "The Wheatland Episode," *Pacific Historical Review,* XVII (February 1948), pp. 37–42; Paul F. Brissenden, *The I.W.W.* (1919, 1957); and Carleton H. Parker, *The Casual Laborer in America* (1920). General accounts of the IWW are Patrick Renshaw, *The Wobblies* (1967); Melvyn Dubofsky, *We Shall Be All* (1969); and Joseph R. Conlin, *Bread and Roses Too* (1969).

Mitchell Slobodek's *A Selective Bibliography of California Labor History* (1964) is thorough and well-annotated.

CHAPTER 20

The Roots of Reform

The forces that contributed to the reform impulse in California in the early twentieth century were many and varied, but the statewide reform coalition that finally achieved a breakthrough in the state elections of 1910 had its immediate origins in developments in the cities of San Francisco and Los Angeles.

Boss Ruef and the Union Labor Party

Throughout the United States, as Lord Bryce remarked in *The American Commonwealth,* the government of cities was a conspicuous failure of American democracy. This had been true in varying degrees since the early days of New York's Tammany Hall, but the problem had become worse in the age of industrialization and urbanization between the Civil War and the rise of the progressive movement in the early twentieth century. Cities, corporations, and labor unions grew so rapidly that government and law could not keep up with them. One result was an increase in the importance of the city boss as an extralegal figure who could furnish a bridge between the lagging institutions of politics and the urgent demands of the expanding conglomerations of economic power. The boss served as a broker in a corrupt system of alliances between big business and politics that menaced democracy in cities throughout the nation.

Cosmopolitan San Francisco might have been expected to produce as the most famous of its bosses a figure as colorful as the city itself. Abraham Ruef was the only son of a moderately wealthy San Francisco family of French Jewish origin. He was a man of unusual culture and brilliant intelligence, heightened by a good university and legal education. After graduating from the University of California in Berkeley and from its law school in San Francisco, he entered politics as an idealistic young reformer. But his ideals began to decline when he attended his first Republican county convention, an experience that impressed him with the apparently hopeless realities of machine rule. Surrendering to opportunism, he became the Republican sub-boss for a district in the northern part of the city. There, at the grassroots level, he learned to bestow the many services and favors that typical nineteenth-century American city bosses and their machines exchanged for the gratitude and the votes of poor and immigrant families—from gifts of turkeys at Christmas to help with naturalization papers.

At the turn of the century, the mayor of San Francisco was the reform Democrat James D. Phelan. Son of one of the city's leading bankers, Phelan was also a millionaire banker in his own right, and as a public officeholder he was above the temptations to corruption that afflicted persons of lesser integrity and inferior financial independence. Ordinarily, Phelan held fairly liberal views on a number of economic and social issues, including the rights of organized labor, but during the great strike in the summer of 1901 his wealthy friends persuaded him to order city police to ride on the drays beside scab teamsters, thus using the police themselves as virtual strikebreakers.

This led to an angry outcry that if the power of government was thus to be used for the destruction of unions, then union members must enter politics and elect a government of their own; with this intention a group calling itself the Union Labor party of San Francisco was organized in September. The philosophy and strategy of American craft unionism were generally opposed to any such movement, and not a single important official of any of the larger San Francisco unions would associate with the new party. It might have died at birth had it not acquired a foster father: Abraham Ruef perceived that he could use it for his own purposes, though he had no genuine interest whatever in labor unions except his interest in their members' votes for candidates he controlled.

Because Mayor Phelan had angered conservatives by refusing to call for state troops to put down the strike almost as much as he had angered labor by his use of city police, his renomination was impossible. The Democratic and Republican nominees for mayor were colorless men. For the Union Labor candidacy, on the other hand, Ruef chose his friend Eugene E. Schmitz, president of the musicians' union. Schmitz was of German-Irish descent and of Roman Catholic faith, and in San Francisco this combination of ethnic and religious factors appealed to such an extraordinarily high percentage of the electorate that it was an essential source of Schmitz's political success, and consequently of Ruef's as well. Schmitz was a tall, handsome, distinguished-looking, commanding figure of a man, and also a model husband and father. "The psychology of the mass of the voters," Ruef told Schmitz, "is like that of a crowd of small boys," to whom such qualities had a deep emotional appeal.

Schmitz was elected mayor in 1901, 1903, and 1905. In the first two of these elections the Union Labor ticket gained only a few seats on the 18-member board of supervisors, the legislative branch of the city-and-county government. But in 1905, to Ruef's own surprise, every one of his 18 Union Labor nominees for the board of supervisors was elected. Voting machines were used for the first time, and nearly all of Schmitz's admirers, fearing to invalidate their votes among the complicated battery of levers, took the easy course of pulling down one lever for the straight party ticket.

Most of the new city fathers were obscure men who knew little about the nature of their office except the popular belief that supervisors customarily received bribes. They suspected, quite accurately, that Ruef received large payments from public utility corporations. In vain he pointed out to them that as a lawyer who held no public office, he could quite legally receive such payments as attorney's fees, but that payments to them, as public officials, would be bribery. The new supervisors concluded that although this fine distinction might be law, it was not justice. They demanded that Ruef share his fees with them if he expected them to vote for the measures his corporate clients desired.

Several transactions of this kind were carried out in 1906. For example, the United Railroads of San Francisco, the largest street railway company, asked for a special ordinance permitting it to convert all its remaining cable car lines to overhead electric trolleys. The company paid an attorney's fee of $200,000 to Ruef; he divided $85,000 among the supervisors, and the ordinance was passed. The Pacific Gas and Electric Company (PG&E) paid Ruef $20,000; of this sum he paid $13,250 to the supervisors and thereby persuaded them not to make a drastic reduction in the gas rate. There were other corrupt arrangements involving telephone and water companies.

The San Francisco Graft Prosecution

Such instances of corruption were by no means unprecedented, either in San Francisco or in other large American cities of the time. What was really extraordinary about them was that through some very unusual circumstances they became known to the public in complete detail. The year 1906 brought two crucial events in San Francisco's history: One was the disastrous earthquake and fire, in April, and the other, in October, was the announcement of the beginning of what turned out to be the most persistent graft prosecution in the history of any city in the United States.

The earthquake that rocked San Francisco at 5:14 in the morning of April 18 was so severe that it caused a number of deaths and injuries within the first few moments. But San Franciscans, anxious to counteract the idea that a similar catastrophe could ever destroy their city again, have always correctly insisted that the greatest damage was done not by the earthquake—over which human beings had no conceivable control—but rather by the subsequent fire, whose recurrence a better-planned water system could render impossible. The initial shock, which started more than 50 separate fires almost immediately by breaking gas connections and chimneys and overturning stoves, also shattered most of the flimsy water mains and left the firefighters helpless. The fires, merging into one vast, continuous conflagration and raging for 3 days and 2 nights, destroyed the greater part of the city. Early estimates of the loss of life put the figure at about 450. More recent research has indicated that as many as 3000 people may have been killed in the disaster and that $1 billion worth of property was destroyed.

The painful difficulties of the struggle to build a new city on the ruins of the old made San Franciscans less tolerant of corruption in their city government and

San Francisco after the 1906 earthquake and fire. The dome is that of the ruined city hall. (*Courtesy of the Bancroft Library.*)

prepared them to welcome an investigation that a small group of reformers had begun to plan, in close secrecy, before the earthquake.

The originator of this plan was Fremont Older, editor of the *San Francisco Bulletin*. Older secured a promise of cooperation from the district attorney, and he induced the reform-minded millionaire capitalist Rudolph Spreckels to pledge his financial support. Spreckels ultimately contributed nearly $250,000 to the prosecution fund, mostly for hiring special detectives. Ex-mayor Phelan also contributed. Older persuaded President Theodore Roosevelt to lend the services of the federal government's ablest special prosecutor, Francis J. Heney, and also of its star detective, William J. Burns, who was then head of the Secret Service of the Treasury Department. Heney was appointed assistant district attorney of San Francisco.

The prosecution's first major move was to secure indictments charging that Ruef and Schmitz had extorted money from the proprietors of several French restaurants under the threat of blocking the renewals of their liquor licenses. The term "French restaurant" then had a special connotation in San Francisco. On the first floor there was a conventional restaurant serving excellent food at moderate prices, but on the second floor there were private supper bedrooms, and the upper floors were houses of prostitution.

The charge that the boss and the mayor had taken money from these establishments was a charge of reprehensible but relatively petty graft, and based on as yet limited evidence. The real breakthrough came when Burns trapped one of the supervisors, Thomas Lonergan, into taking a planted bribe. Heney then offered Lonergan immunity from all prosecution in return for a complete disclosure of every bribery in which he and his colleagues had participated. The other supervisors, confronted with Lonergan's testimony, were also granted immunity and also made complete confessions. With this overwhelming mass of evidence Heney then obtained a full confession from Ruef himself, after promising not to prosecute him if he would testify against the higher-ups—the corporation executives who had made the payments to him as their "attorney." Heney then secured indictments for bribery against Patrick Calhoun, president of the United Railroads, nationally known financier, and grandson of the great statesman John C. Calhoun; against Tirey L. Ford, chief counsel of the United Railroads and former attorney general of California; and against several of the highest executives of the gas and telephone companies.

Heney's strategy was based in part on the ideas of his close friend Lincoln Steffens, the nation's leading journalistic authority on municipal corruption. Both Steffens and Heney had been born in San Francisco, and they shared a deep interest in the future of the city and the state. Steffens had written a famous series of articles brought together in 1904 in his book called *The Shame of the Cities.* The more important source of the massive graft system in America, Steffens concluded, was not the weak little politician who took bribes but the wealthy and powerful business leader who paid them. By 1906, however, Steffens had come to believe that because the blame for corruption was shared by so many the punishment of individuals was useless and inappropriate. Instead, he advocated that after the full shock of publicity of the mass of offenses in San Francisco, there should be a general amnesty so that all could join in the building of a sounder social fabric.

Heney, on the other hand, had no faith in this particular aspect of Steffens's views. Rather, Heney believed that only the exemplary punishment of the greatest offenders could accomplish anything of permanent value. He confided to Steffens that if he should succeed in convicting the general counsel and the president of the United Railroads, Ford and Calhoun, he would then reach for the top and try to send to prison, for bribery, not only the general counsel of the Southern Pacific, William F. Herrin, but also its president, the mighty Edward H. Harriman himself.

But the prosecution fell far short of these objectives. In a series of long trials of Ford and Calhoun, the results were either hung juries or acquittals. To convict the United Railroads executives of bribery, Ruef would have had to testify that they had paid him his attorney's fee in full knowledge that he would use part of the money to bribe public officeholders. Ruef refused to give such testimony. In bitter anger and frustration, Heney revoked the immunity agreement he had made with Ruef and brought him to trial for the trolley bribery. The result was that of all the defendants, Ruef alone was ultimately forced to serve a term in the state prison at San Quentin.

Mayor Schmitz was convicted of extortion in one of the French restaurant cases in June 1907 and automatically removed from office, but his conviction was invalidated by the higher courts.

The San Francisco business community had enthusiastically supported the prosecution at its beginning, when it had appeared to be directed against corrupt politicians, especially Union Labor politicians. But when these men were promised immunity as a reward for furnishing the evidence on which a number of the city's best-known business executives were indicted, the business community's enthusiasm for the prosecution rapidly cooled. In the city elections of 1909 the prosecution was voted out of office in favor of an administration that would discontinue the graft cases.

The San Francisco graft prosecution aroused a deeper and more sustained indignation in the rest of the state than it did in the city itself, and thus it contributed to the growing statewide demands for political reform.

The Good Government Movement in Los Angeles

The Southern Pacific machine dominated Los Angeles politics at the turn of the century, but opposition to it was building up in almost every sector of political opinion, from the right to the left.

Harrison Gray Otis, leader of the city's conservative employers, believed that nothing could possibly contribute as much to the growth, improvement, and prosperity of the community as did the leadership of vigorous individuals like himself. Therefore, as he saw it, the general welfare required that there be no unnecessary restraints on such persons in the free exercise of their talents for acquiring the wealth that was their incentive and reward. But the railroad had become just such a restraint on free enterprise, and Otis opposed its bureaucratic power almost as much as he feared and detested labor unions, or even socialism.

As distinct from the conservatives, like Otis, who had a chronic distrust of government and feared that any political change would open the door to unionism and radicalism, there were various groups of reformers who placed their faith in the improvement and strengthening of government. These groups were divided into political and moral reformers on the one hand, and social and economic reformers on the other.

The political and moral reformers included prominent businesspeople, lawyers, and journalists who shared the conservatives' belief in the supreme importance of business enterprise, but also believed that much could be accomplished by bringing "business efficiency" and "business integrity" into politics. The social and economic reformers believed that government should not merely become more honest and more efficient, but that it should be used to effect deeper and broader improvements in the workings of society. They included socialists and persons impressed by the writings of Henry George and Edward Bellamy or by the social gospel then being preached in many churches. To an extraordinary degree, union labor in Los Angeles had also been driven into alliance with such groups as a result of the extreme tactics of Otis and his associates.

In the face of this diversity among the opponents of the railroad machine in Los Angeles, it was very difficult to assemble a strong coalition of reformers, but this was accomplished, largely through the remarkable talents of Dr. John Randolph Haynes. Since his arrival in 1887, Haynes had combined the most successful medical practice in Los Angeles with the building of a fortune in real estate—a combination of achievements that won him the respect of some of the most conservative of the business community. Largely through Haynes's charm and prestige, and through a Direct Legislation League that he headed, Los Angeles was persuaded to adopt the initiative, the referendum, and the recall in its new charter of 1903.

This was the first provision for the recall in any governmental unit in the world and the first adoption of the initiative and the referendum by a city. In 1904, moreover, Los Angeles put the recall to use for the first time in history. A Good Government League, in which Dr. Haynes was prominent, organized a successful campaign to recall city councilman J. R. Davenport for voting to award the public printing contracts to the *Los Angeles Times* when several other bids had been much lower.

This episode ended any possibility of support from Otis for the political reformers, and thereafter the *Times* never spoke of the Good Government League except to denounce and ridicule its leaders as "the Goo-Goos." But the opposition of the *Times* served to increase the support for reform on the part of Otis's newspaper rival and personal enemy, Edwin T. Earl, publisher of the *Los Angeles Express*. Earl was not only a publisher but also the state's largest lemon grower and consequently an opponent of the Southern Pacific, whose freight rates on lemons were among its most piratical exactions.

In the spring of 1906, Earl hired a young journalist named Edward A. Dickson and authorized him to begin a series of editorials in the *Express* denouncing the railroad machine for its control of the Los Angeles city council. Soon afterward Dickson joined with three young lawyers, Meyer Lissner, Russ Avery, and Marshall Stimson, in organizing a Non-Partisan Committee of One Hundred, and in the city election of 1906 the reform candidates nominated by this group won almost every important office except the mayoralty.

The Lincoln-Roosevelt League

All the leaders and nearly all the members of the Los Angeles Non-Partisan group were in fact Republicans. Many were businesspeople who favored political and moral, as distinct from social and economic, reform. For decades most people in business had been Republicans, whereas city workers had usually been Democrats. In the early twentieth century, reform-minded Republicans in California were deeply concerned lest the Democrats gain leadership of the reform movement in general and thus capture the state government.

The Republican state convention at Santa Cruz in September 1906 made it even more obvious than usual that the California Republican party machinery was subservient to the railroad and its allies. Abe Ruef, who had just reached the height of his power, controlled every member of the large San Francisco delegation and could thus choose the nominee for governor. To secure the nomination of the railroad's candidate, James N. Gillett, William F. Herrin gave Ruef $14,000 "to pay the expenses of the delegates." On the evening after the convention adjourned, there was a testimonial banquet at which a photograph was taken, showing Ruef seated at the

"The Shame of California." Photograph from the *San Francisco Call,* September 10, 1906. Abe Ruef is seated in the center. The future governor, James N. Gillett, stands behind him. Justice Frederick W. Henshaw of the state supreme court stands at the far left. Congressman Joseph R. Knowland is at the far right.

center of a long table with Gillett standing behind him, his hand on Ruef's shoulder in a gesture of affectionate gratitude. Justices of the state supreme and appellate courts, indebted to Ruef for their renominations, were included in the group. Along with such machine stalwarts was Walter Parker, Herrin's lieutenant in Los Angeles. For years afterward this picture was widely reprinted with such captions as "The Shame of California" and "Herrin's Cabinet."

The announcement of the beginning of the San Francisco graft prosecution in October 1906, discrediting Ruef and the nominees of the Santa Cruz convention along with him, gave the Democrats an extraordinary opportunity to win the governorship and most of the other state offices. They had a strong antirailroad platform, and their candidate for governor, Theodore A. Bell, was a vigorous young man with a good reform record as district attorney of Napa County. The Democrats' chances, however, were sabotaged by the ambitious machinations of William Randolph Hearst in his attempts to gain the Democratic nomination for the presidency. In an effort to show the national Democratic party that it could not do without him, Hearst in 1906 was sponsoring a third-party movement called the Independence League, in New York, California, and a few other states. The league's ticket in California, with San Francisco district attorney William H. Langdon as the candidate for governor, took enough votes from Bell and the Democrats to give the election to Gillett and the Republicans.

In December 1906 Dr. Haynes again displayed his talent for encouraging a broad coalition among reformers by organizing a dinner at the California Club in Los Angeles with Lincoln Steffens as the principal speaker and Edward Dickson and Meyer Lissner among the guests. Steffens urged the Los Angeles reformers to extend to the state level the efforts that had brought important successes in the recent city elections.

A few weeks later, Dickson went to Sacramento as correspondent for the *Los Angeles Express* at the session of the state legislature beginning in January 1907. The chance assignment of adjoining desks in the press row to Dickson and to Chester H. Rowell, editor of the *Fresno Morning Republican,* became one of the most important circumstances leading to the movement that would free the Republican party and the state government from the Southern Pacific Railroad.

Dickson and Rowell had never met before, but as they exchanged impressions of the 1907 legislature, which was hardly less subservient to the railroad than the Santa Cruz convention had been, the two journalists discovered that they shared a burning disgust with the condition of California politics. They agreed to join in an attempt to organize a reform movement and sent out the call for a new organization in letters to reform-minded Republicans, especially newspaper publishers and editors, throughout the state.

A southern California group met in Los Angeles on May 21, 1907, adopted Dickson's suggestion of the name "Lincoln Republicans," and drew up an "emancipation proclamation," which announced as its first objective "the emancipation of the Republican Party in California from domination by the Political Bureau of the Southern Pacific Railroad Company and allied interests." Other proposals were the direct primary; the initiative, referendum, and recall; effective regulation of railroad and other utility rates; the outlawing of racetrack gambling; conservation of forests; a workers' compensation act; a minimum wage law for women; and woman suffrage.

On August 1 a larger statewide group met in Oakland and adopted the official name of "the League of Lincoln-Roosevelt Republican Clubs." This hyphenated title was the result of a significant compromise with the desire of Francis J. Heney to change the name to "the Roosevelt League." Heney was an intense admirer of Theodore Roosevelt and particularly of that aspect of his views which led the president to denounce as "malefactors of great wealth" such men as E. H. Harriman, head of the Southern Pacific. Roosevelt's national leadership was an important source of inspiration to progressive Republicans in California, but at Dickson's insistence the name of Lincoln was also retained and included to appeal to Republicans of more traditional views.

In 1908 the reformers were able to elect enough members of the legislature to make possible the enactment of a direct primary law in the 1909 session. It soon became clear that in 1910, with the nominations of party candidates taken away from machine-controlled conventions and given directly to the voters, the league might gain control not only of the state Republican party organization but also of the entire state government, particularly if it could find a very strong candidate for governor to head its ticket.

At first it was supposed that the candidate would be Heney, whose leadership of the San Francisco graft prosecution was making him the state's best-known reformer. But in November 1908, early in the trial of Ruef, Heney was shot and almost fatally wounded by a man whose earlier criminal record Heney had exposed while questioning him as a prospective juror. Whether Heney would make a full recovery was uncertain for several months, and when he did return to the fray, his personality was more extreme and irascible than ever. Many Republicans regarded Heney as "too radical" and particularly resented his open dislike and distrust of all businessmen. Moreover, Heney was a registered Democrat.

During Heney's convalescence his place was taken by Hiram Johnson, who had been one of his special assistants in the district attorney's office. Johnson became chief prosecutor in the trial that ended in the conviction of Ruef, and thus he first

An editorial cartoon from the *Sacramento Bee,* supporting Hiram Johnson's antirailroad gubernatorial campaign in 1910. (*Courtesy of the* Sacramento Bee.)

attracted wide attention as a young man with a potential future as a leader of political reform. In one of those unpredictable circumstances that are such vital ingredients in history, one obscure and demented man had made Theodore Roosevelt president of the United States by pulling the trigger of a pistol. Another, by a similar act, launched Hiram Johnson into state and national politics.

As a courtroom and a platform orator, Johnson rivaled or exceeded the powers of Heney in denouncing evil and in arousing support for reform, and Johnson could appeal to a broader cross section of voters. He did not share Heney's extreme antibusiness bias and would not alienate so many conservative Republicans; at the same time, he could gain support from organized labor. Johnson had been an attorney for the San Francisco Teamsters' Union for 8 years.

He was reluctant to run for governor, however. His father, Grove Johnson, an assemblyman from Sacramento, had long been the principal leader of the Southern Pacific machine in the state legislature. Hiram had first practiced law in partnership with his father in Sacramento, and it was largely to escape their bitter quarreling over differences of political opinion that he had moved to San Francisco. There he had developed a highly lucrative legal practice and had built a delightful home at the top of Russian Hill. To give up these amenities for a return to the scene of his abrasive and torturing conflicts with his father seemed to him, and to his wife, a very poor exchange. He did not consent to run until February 1910, when Heney finally removed himself from the race and joined with Rowell and others in urging

Johnson to become the league's candidate, on the ground that he was the only one who could win and thus free the state from its bondage.

In August, in the first and perhaps the most important statewide direct primary election in California's history, Johnson won the Republican nomination for governor, and the league won control of the Republican party. Johnson's campaign was unique, colorful, and literally hard-driving. He toured the state in an open automobile and, in the smaller towns, announced his arrival by ringing a cowbell. Everywhere he stressed a single theme, his famous "promise to kick the Southern Pacific Railroad out of politics." Among his variations on the theme of the railroad's villainy, he described its practice of secretly charging bribery expenses to operating costs and then charging still higher rates to cover the expenses. "Get us coming and going?" he cried in a speech at Los Angeles. "Why they get us every way, and we foot the bill—we pick our own pockets to bribe ourselves with our own money!"

Actually, in the election in November 1910, the railroad was no longer a genuine issue. The Democratic nominee for governor, Theodore Bell, vied with Johnson in denouncing it. Moreover, he discussed a wider range of reform issues than Johnson did. Anticipating the slogans of future Democrats, Bell said that "California needs a New Deal, a Fair Deal." Unfortunately for the Democrats, and much to their disgust, William F. Herrin concluded that Bell would be the less effective and less dangerous reformer and ordered the railroad's sub-bosses to support him. The support of the railroad, once so crucial in California politics, now cost Bell the votes of thousands who would not credit his outraged disavowals. It was a major factor in giving the governorship to Johnson, who received 177,191 votes to Bell's 154,835. Another factor was the substantial vote of 47,819 for the Socialist candidate, J. Stitt Wilson of Berkeley.

Selected Bibliography

Jules Tygiel, "'Where Unionism Holds Undisputed Sway': A Reappraisal of San Francisco's Union Labor Party," *California History,* LXII (Fall 1983), pp. 196–215, views the ULP as "a legitimate voice of the working class." Earlier accounts of the ULP and the graft trials include Fremont Older, *My Own Story* (1926); Franklin Hichborn, *"The System" as Uncovered by the San Francisco Graft Prosecution* (1915); *The Autobiography of Lincoln Steffens* (1931); Walton Bean, *Boss Ruef's San Francisco* (1952); and James P. Walsh, "Abe Ruef Was No Boss," *California Historical Quarterly,* LI (Spring 1972), pp. 3–16. The story of James D. Phelan is well told in Walsh and Timothy J. O'Keefe, *Legacy of a Native Son* (1993). A reappraisal of the destruction of the San Francisco earthquake and fire of 1906 appears in Gladys Hansen and Emmet Condon, *Denial of Disaster* (1989). On visions for the city reborn and the larger issues of urban planning, see Mansel G. Blackford, *The Lost Dream* (1993), and Robert W. Cherny, "City Commercial, City Beautiful, City Practical," *California History,* LXXIII (Winter 1994/1995), pp. 296–307.

On other roots of reform, see William Issel, "Class and Ethnic Conflict in San Francisco Political History," *Labor History,* XVIII (Summer 1977), pp. 341–359; Tom Sitton, *John Randolph Haynes* (1992); Frederick William Viehe III, "The Los Angeles Progressives,"

Ph.D. thesis, University of California, Santa Barbara (1983); Albert H. Clodius, "The Quest for Good Government in Los Angeles, 1890–1910," Ph.D. thesis, Claremont Graduate School (1953); Donald R. Culton, "Charles Dwight Willard," Ph.D. thesis, University of Southern California (1971); Keith W. Olson, *Biography of a Progressive: Franklin K. Lane, 1864–1921* (1979); and Martin J. Schiesl, "Progressive Reform in Los Angeles under Mayor Alexander, 1909–1913," *California Historical Quarterly,* LIV (Spring 1975), pp. 37–56.

On the rise of the Lincoln-Roosevelt League and its triumph in 1910, see Richard C. Lower, *A Bloc of One: The Political Career of Hiram Johnson* (1993); George E. Mowry, *The California Progressives* (1951); J. Gregg Layne, "The Lincoln-Roosevelt League," *Historical Society of Southern California Quarterly,* XXV (September 1943), pp. 79–101; Grace L. Miller, "The Origins of the San Diego Lincoln-Roosevelt League, 1905–1909," *Southern California Quarterly,* LX (Winter 1978), pp. 421–444; Irving McKee, "The Background and Early Career of Hiram Warren Johnson, 1866–1910," *Pacific Historical Review,* XIX (February 1950), pp. 17–30; Alice M. Rose, "The Rise of California Insurgency," Ph.D. thesis, Stanford University (1942); Spencer C. Olin, Jr., *California's Prodigal Sons: Hiram Johnson and the Progressives, 1911–1917* (1968); Miles C. Everett, "Chester Harvey Rowell," Ph.D. thesis, University of California, Berkeley (1965); and Michael Allen Weatherson, "'A Political Revivalist': The Public Speaking of Hiram W. Johnson, 1866–1945," Ph.D. thesis, Indiana University (1985).

CHAPTER 21

The Republican Progressives in Power

The Californians who organized the Lincoln-Roosevelt Republican movement, which gained control of the state government in the elections of 1910, were primarily individualists. Most of them were young men and women from the urban upper-middle class—lawyers, editors, or independent entrepreneurs. They were highly literate, and three out of four were college educated. Eager to participate in public affairs, and finding that to do so under the old system of machine control would mean the sacrifice of their integrity, they overthrew the old system.

In January 1911, in full control of both houses of the state legislature, the progressives confidently set out to establish a new order of politics in California. They were not, of course, solely responsible for progressive reform in the state. Although the progressives often denounced "the interests," many diverse interest groups and organizations, economic and social as well as political, also played significant parts in the reform process. And the progressives themselves displayed their own class and racial biases in their attitudes toward organized labor and Japanese immigration.

The extent of public support for the work of the legislature of 1911 became clear in the special election of October 10, when the 23 of its measures that required constitutional amendments were submitted to the voters and all but one passed. Theodore Roosevelt described the California program of 1911 as "the beginning of a new era in popular government" and as "the greatest advance ever made by any state for the benefit of its people." The reforms achieved in California in the single year of 1911 were remarkable, but this was partly because no other major state was more critically in need of reform.

Scholars once viewed the California progressives as a case study for political and social reform movements throughout the nation. But such an approach often ignored issues of class, race, and gender—key components that defined the California progressives. As William Deverell and Tom Sitton, editors of *California Progressivism Revisited* (1994), have confirmed, the reform movement in California was a far broader and more complicated phenomenon than sometimes has been understood.

Public Utility Regulation

In the regulation of railroads and other public utilities, the progressives achieved their most unquestionable success. An act drafted largely by John M. Eshleman, who had been elected to the railroad commission in 1910, gave the commission full and effective power to set uniform rates and to end the extortionate and discriminatory practices in which the Southern Pacific had indulged for so many decades. In the vanguard of the demand for this reform were groups of shippers and merchants who wanted to stabilize their businesses. Another measure assigned the commission the power to regulate the rates charged by all other public utilities, except those that were municipally owned. The graft prosecution in San Francisco had more than demonstrated the inadequacy of local regulation of utilities, and officials of several utility corporations favored the new law. The two 1911 laws provided California with what was probably the most comprehensive system of public utility regulation in the country.

Both measures passed by unanimous votes in both houses. Railroad regulation, in particular, was so long overdue in 1911 that not even the railroad attorneys and lobbyists tried to oppose it. Officials of the Southern Pacific found themselves glad to escape from such costly nuisances as the payment of secret rebates to favored shippers within the state, notably several oil companies. After the new system had been in operation a few months, William F. Herrin made a remarkable address to the California Bar Association in which he concluded that "I think no railroad manager would agree to dispense with government regulation at the cost of returning to the old conditions."

Governmental Efficiency and Finance

Many progressive reformers believed that the principles of scientific management, then in vogue in private enterprise, must be introduced into government. They proceeded to develop California's first coherent system of supervision over state finances, largely under the leadership of John Francis Neylan, a dynamic young newspaper reporter who had attracted Johnson's attention while covering the 1910 campaign for the *San Francisco Bulletin*. Neylan proposed the creation of a new agency to be called the State Board of Control, and at the age of 26 he was appointed its first chairman. Under this board California had its first comprehensive budget and its first general inventory of state property. The board exposed graft, regained embezzled money, and secured the removal of 16 corrupt officials.

Taxation in California had undergone a major reorganization in 1910, mainly as a result of the desire of business leaders for a more orderly system. Since 1879 all property taxes had been collected by county boards of assessment under the loose supervision of a state board of equalization. Under the act of 1910, a moderate state tax on the gross incomes of corporations was created, and property taxes were to be paid only to county and local governments.

The Bank Act of 1909 was another example of the influence of private economic groups on reform in the progressive era and of the desire of many such groups to use the power of government to bring greater orderliness into their own activities and thus increase their profits and reduce their losses. The act was drawn up mainly by a committee of the California Bankers Association and would remain the state's fundamental banking law until the 1930s. It created the office of state superintendent of banks, whose duties would include periodic examination of the financial soundness of the banks.

More Democracy

The progressives' view of human nature reflected an Emersonian optimism about humanity's innate capacity for good, and therefore they had a strong faith in the political abilities of "the people." Most of the leading California Republican progressives, though they regarded themselves as patrician reformers, also had a firm belief in democracy as against the conservative emphasis on "representative" government. Thus, the heart of their reform program lay in a group of devices for increasing the power of the voters.

Foremost among these devices was a state constitutional amendment providing two methods of direct participation by the people in the lawmaking process: The initiative enabled the voters to enact laws or constitutional amendments that had presumably been blocked by legislators' unresponsiveness to popular demands; the referendum empowered the people to veto acts of the legislature. A petition signed by 8 percent of the number of voters in an immediately preceding gubernatorial election could place an initiative proposal on the ballot; a referendum required 5 percent. Some of the progressives would have preferred a fixed number of signatures, perhaps 30,000. They pointed out that under the percentage system, with future increases in the state's population, the gathering of an ever-increasing number of signatures would become too difficult and expensive for reform groups and practicable only for large special interests. But this warning, which would prove distressingly valid in later years, went unheeded in 1911.

The recall of public officials, the second major proposal that Governor Hiram Johnson urged upon the legislature, was much more hotly contested, especially because it included the recall of judges. The conservative minority argued that this would interfere with the impartiality of court decisions by requiring judges to "keep their ears to the ground," but Johnson replied that this was better than keeping their ears to the railroad tracks.

Several other measures were also designed to give more power to the voters and to decrease the power of party bosses. For example, the party column and the party circle, which had encouraged voting a straight party ticket, were eliminated from the ballot.

Nonpartisanship and Cross-Filing

The corruption of political parties in California by machine rule had been so extreme that the Johnson progressives mistakenly blamed much of the evil on the party system itself. Consequently, they tried to bring about the virtual destruction of political parties in the state, and although they did not quite succeed in doing this, their efforts had the effect of ensuring that the two-party system would remain extraordinarily weak in California for more than half a century.

The idea of nonpartisan elections was first applied at the level of city government, when the state legislature ratified a new city charter for Berkeley in 1909. Elections of judges and school officials throughout the state were made nonpartisan in 1911, and elections of county officials in 1913.

The *cross-filing* system, which permits a candidate to be the nominee of more than one political party, was adopted for state elections in an amendment of 1913. Under this provision, not only could the name of a candidate appear on the primary election ballot of more than one party, but the candidate's own party affiliations were not identified on the primary ballots.

In arguing that cross-filing was in the interest of the general welfare, the Johnson progressives were rationalizing their need to use it for their own special convenience. In 1912, when the national Progressive or Bull Moose party split off from the Republicans, no Progressive party was formally organized in California even though Governor Johnson was the national third party's nominee for vice president. In 1913 Johnson wished to form a Progressive party in the state, but many of his supporters in the legislature, elected with the Republican label, feared for their reelections if they had to forfeit it. Cross-filing was the solution. It enabled the Progressive party of California to be formed; in December 1913 and in the following year many of the state legislators received both the Republican and the Progressive nominations.

The originators of cross-filing had not realized the full extent of its ultimate effects on the party system. These began to be apparent when one legislator was reelected in the primaries by receiving the nominations of all five parties, the Progressives, the Republicans, the Democrats, the Prohibitionists, and the Socialists.

The cross-filing system reduced the political party system to a shambles and remained in effect for decades, favoring incumbents, encouraging candidates to masquerade as members of parties other than their own, and enabling them to deceive thousands of ill-informed voters.

Woman Suffrage

In 1911 California became the sixth state to adopt woman suffrage, although the all-male voters approved it by less than 2 percent, the smallest margin for any of the state constitutional amendments adopted that year. Hiram Johnson was emotionally opposed to it, though he took no public stand on the issue. Its adoption owed less to support from the progressives as a whole than to the efforts of a number of able and determined women.

For decades such women had struggled against sex discrimination in various fields. California feminists in the 1870s scored an early victory when the state legislature declared women eligible to serve as elected members of school boards and as superintendents. Opponents questioned the constitutionality of allowing non-electors to hold elective office, but effective lobbying by feminists carried the day. Sallie Hart, an energetic public school teacher from San Francisco, spent 6 weeks in Sacramento rallying support for the office-holding bill. One state senator complained of Hart's lobbying methods, "going from seat to seat, like some blazing comet, shaking a kind of fascination from her twirled hair." Likewise, vigorous lobbying by Clara Shortridge Foltz and Laura De Force Gordon, the first women to practice law in California, induced the legislature in 1878 to repeal the law that had denied them admission to the bar. Foltz later recalled that criticism of the repeal

"We have come to the dawn of a glorious tomorrow," said suffragist Caroline Maria Severance (1820–1914), the first woman to register to vote and the first to cast a ballot in Los Angeles. (*Courtesy of the* Sacramento Bee.)

bill was intense: "The bill met with a storm of opposition such as had never been witnessed upon the floor of the California senate. Narrow gauge statesmen grew as red as turkey gobblers mouthing their ignorance against the bill." The bill passed by a mere two-vote majority, and the governor signed it into law only after Foltz visited his office and forcefully but "politely" urged him to do so. The following year, the state constitutional convention approved the text drafted by Foltz and Gordon for Article XX, section 18, of the new state constitution: "No person shall, on account of sex, be disqualified from entering upon or pursuing any lawful business, vocation or profession." Nevertheless, women continued to face barriers of discrimination; not until 1890 did the San Francisco Medical Society admit its first woman member, Lucy Maria Field Wanzer.

The organized suffrage movement in California began in 1869. An early leader of it was Ellen Clark Sargent, whose husband, Senator Aaron A. Sargent, first introduced in Congress the measure that would become the Nineteenth Amendment in 1920. California suffragist Nettie Tator in 1872 argued that it was time "to open the doors to every honorable employment to woman; giving her equal chances with man, and equal pay for the same labor . . . [but] *this will not be done*, until the ballot is put into her hand to *compel it*." The suffragists mounted a strong campaign in the 1890s, and the legislature approved an amendment for submission to the voters, but they rejected it by a wide margin in 1896. The Woman's Christian Temperance Union supported the measure, and many voters feared that woman suffrage would bring prohibition. Overwhelming opposition to votes for women in San Francisco and Oakland outweighed the favorable sentiment in other parts of the state.

Katherine Philips Edson (1870–1933) of Los Angeles, leader of the campaign for woman suffrage and president of the California Federation of Women's Clubs. (*Courtesy of Special Collections, University Research Library, UCLA.*)

In the progressive era, on the other hand, upper-middle-class clubwomen from the cities, including San Francisco and its surrounding towns, as well as Los Angeles, were in the forefront of the campaign. Their statewide organization was called the California Equal Suffrage League, but its most effective subsidiary was the College Equal Suffrage League, an elite intellectual phalanx. These leaders of the suffrage movement formed a coalition with the Republican progressives. Caroline Maria Severance founded the Los Angeles Friday Morning Club and led citywide campaigns for civic reform and woman suffrage. The most politically active member of the club, Katherine Philips Edson, was credited with having induced the Lincoln-Roosevelt League at its first meeting to endorse woman suffrage. Elizabeth Thacker Kent led the California equal suffrage campaign in Marin County and later played a larger role in the nationwide movement when her husband, William, went to Congress.

Public Morals

One factor in the success of woman suffrage in 1911, in contrast with its defeat in 1896, was that temperance was becoming more widely accepted as an important social reform. Much of the support for the Lincoln-Roosevelt League had come from religious and other organizations interested in suppressing the evils of drinking, gambling, and vice. When the league's "emancipation proclamation" of 1907 had promised to free the state from control by the Southern Pacific "and allied interests," many reformers assumed that this expression referred mainly to the various public utility corporations; however, in the eyes of others, it was the liquor, gambling, and prostitution contingents of the "associated villainies" that seemed the most powerful and dangerous of all.

The Lincoln-Roosevelt candidate for lieutenant governor in 1910 was A. J. Wallace, a Los Angeles Methodist minister and oilman who was for many years the president of the Anti-Saloon League of California. Although Johnson privately detested his running mate, Wallace was easily elected and received nearly as many votes as Johnson himself in almost all parts of the state except San Francisco and the wine-producing counties of the bay region.

The leaders of the temperance organizations, though many of them were actually prohibitionists, recognized that outright prohibition was still unacceptable to most of the voters. Therefore they concentrated their attack on the saloon and argued that it was often a center of prostitution as well as of excessive drinking. Since 1874 state law had permitted local areas, at the option of their voters, to ban saloons. In 1911 the legislature passed a much stronger local-option law. In the next 5 years, under this legislation, more than half the districts in the state voted to close all the saloons within their borders.

Under another act of 1911, racetrack gambling was outlawed and remained so for 20 years. Still another measure made slot machines illegal, after a debate in which the decisive factor was the reading of manufacturers' catalogs explaining how easily the machines could be adjusted to guarantee the owner a heavy profit. A

Red Light Abatement Act, declaring houses of prostitution to be public nuisances, was defeated in 1911 but passed in the session of 1913.

The Progressives and Labor

Paradoxically, the Republican progressive leaders had a strong group consciousness along with their feelings of individualism. Their letters to each other often included proud references to "our sort," but they feared and detested "class government" by any class other than themselves, and many of them feared the power of organized labor more than the power of big business. In their view it was the state government, under their own enlightened and humanitarian progressive leadership, that could best protect and guarantee the true interests of labor, and when this had been accomplished, the temporary evil of labor unionism would wither away.

Fortunately for the unions, Governor Hiram Johnson was more sympathetic toward organized labor. His earlier services as attorney for the teamsters' union led many union leaders to support him in 1910, and he appointed several of them to state administrative positions. Studies of voting in San Francisco working-class districts suggest that many union members who had voted Democratic or Socialist in 1910 were persuaded to vote for Johnson in 1914. Organized labor was not unaware that the basic philosophy of many Republican progressives was hostile to important union goals. Yet—and again paradoxically—labor had an important role in California progressivism. By later standards the labor legislation of the Johnson years was not very advanced, but it was more than labor had ever received from Sacramento before.

Workers' compensation, or employer liability for industrial accidents, was one area in which the goals and ideas of the progressives and the labor unions coincided. Some archaic doctrines of common law had long permitted employers to evade financial responsibility for accidental injuries or deaths of their employees in the course of their work. In 1911 a law removed these limits on the employer's legal responsibility and created an industrial accident board to administer the law, but this act included only a voluntary insurance provision. In 1913 a new and broader law made employer participation in the state-operated workers' insurance system compulsory, except in agriculture.

The desire of the progressives to protect the interests of the people as a whole by curbing the power of both labor unions and employers was clearly evident in the struggle in 1911 over the Weinstock arbitration bill. Harris Weinstock, the author of this proposal, was a leading merchant in Sacramento. His bill would have forbade both strikes and lockouts in public utilities until after an impartial board appointed by the governor had recommended terms of settlement. The State Federation of Labor fought this measure bitterly, charging that it was an entering wedge for total compulsory arbitration and the ultimate abolition of the right to strike. Although all five of the Los Angeles progressive senators voted for it, the bill was finally defeated.

"Freak" Legislation?

This cartoon provided editorial support for the minimum wage law and other legislation proposed by the progressives, 1911–13. Note especially the startled reaction of "Plutocracy" in the lower left-hand corner. (*Courtesy of Special Collections, University Research Library, UCLA.*)

A similar battle in 1911 attended the defeat of an anti-injunction bill that labor unions favored and which would greatly have strengthened their position in collective bargaining. Introduced by a Democratic state senator, Anthony Caminetti, this measure would not only have limited the use of court injunctions against strikes; it would also have outlawed the blacklist and the *yellow-dog* contract, in which the employee agreed not to join a union. It also would have legalized secondary boycotts and peaceful picketing.

In the state minimum wage law for women and children, the progressives gave a degree of substance to their claim that they were better protectors of the interests of labor than were the unions themselves. Organized labor at first opposed any minimum wage laws whatever, for the same reason that it opposed compulsory arbitration—that the setting of terms by government boards might weaken and even replace union bargaining. The minimum wage, labor feared, would become the maximum. The 1911 legislature adopted an 8-hour day for women, excluding farm labor and the canning and packing industries, but it did not seriously consider a minimum wage. No state had such a law until Massachusetts adopted the first one in 1912. Katherine Philips Edson of Los Angeles, president of the California Federation of Women's Clubs, led the movement that secured the passage of a California minimum wage law for women and children in 1913.

Records of the Bureau of Labor Statistics showed that a third of the women workers in California were being paid less than 15 cents an hour, and Katherine Edson and other advocates of the new law argued that this condition was a menace to the women's health and morals. An industrial welfare commission was to administer the act, and Governor Johnson, who had joined in pressing for passage of the law, appointed Edson as the commission's executive officer. Edson long had believed that the state should assume a larger responsibility for the welfare of its citizens; now she was in a position to pursue her goals as a progressive and a feminist. As historian Jacqueline R. Braitman has observed, Edson's challenge to traditional attitudes about the role of government "paralleled her belief that women's roles could no longer be determined by nineteenth-century proscriptions that allowed only men to be active in the public sphere while relegating women to the private domestic sphere."

In August 1913 the Wheatland riot suddenly and dramatically awakened public consciousness, and to some extent the public conscience, to the vile and disgraceful conditions in many farm labor camps. (See Chapter 19.) A state-sponsored investigation revealed that the conditions at Durst's hop ranch were typical of those inflicted on migratory workers by many other large agricultural employers throughout the state. The Commission of Immigration and Housing, created by the legislature a few months before, assumed the authority to inspect farm labor camps, and of the 641 that it investigated in 1914, only 195 met its minimum standards, and 188 were branded as dangerously unsanitary. The next year the legislature passed a new labor camp sanitation and housing act, to be enforced by the commission, but though it made admirable efforts at enforcement, its efforts were stubbornly resisted and were never fully effective. Another act, also a product of the Wheatland tragedy, required all employers to provide their workers with drinking water.

The progressives' concern for the welfare of working people produced few improvements in the status of the state's small but growing population of African Americans. Nor were black workers admitted to the ranks of organized labor; nearly all trade unions excluded blacks entirely until World War II. Black Californians responded by organizing their own self-help groups. Two chapters of the National Association for the Advancement of Colored People (NAACP) were formed in the state by 1915. Earlier an all-black town was established in Tulare County by Lieutenant Colonel Allen Allensworth, a former slave and retired army officer. By 1910 the town of Allensworth had several hundred residents, but it failed to achieve economic viability and eventually was abandoned.

Allen Allensworth (1842–1914) was the nation's highest-ranking African American officer when he retired in 1906 as a lieutenant colonel. (*Courtesy of the California Historical Society, FN-32157.*)

The Anti-Japanese Movement

An important area of agreement between organized labor and the California progressives was their shared hostility toward the Japanese. The immigration of Japanese to California had been insignificant until the late 1890s, but it steadily increased in the early twentieth century, and in 1905 San Francisco labor union leaders formed an Asiatic Exclusion League to combat it. Under pressure from this league, the Union Labor city government announced its intention of segregating Japanese public school children along with the Chinese.

California had almost completely excluded Chinese children from its public schools until a court ruling forbade this practice in 1885 and the legislature amended the education code to establish racially segregated schools. In San Francisco a separate public school had then been provided for them in Chinatown. When this Chinese school was rebuilt after the earthquake and fire, its name was changed to "the Oriental School," and on October 11, 1906, the board of education adopted an order requiring Japanese public school children to attend it.

Protests from the Japanese government led to a diplomatic crisis between Japan and the United States, and President Roosevelt ordered an investigation by his secretary of commerce and labor, Victor H. Metcalf, a resident of Oakland and the only Californian in the cabinet. Metcalf reported that there had been only 93 Japanese pupils in the 23 public schools in San Francisco and that many of them had been born in the city. However, 27 had been alien teenagers placed in the elementary grades because of their lack of previous schooling in English. White racists, including Sacramento assemblyman Grove Johnson, declaimed upon the menace to little American schoolgirls who were seated beside older boys with "evil oriental thoughts."

Early in 1907 President Roosevelt invited Mayor Schmitz and the members of the San Francisco Board of Education to Washington, D.C., where they agreed to a compromise. Only overage pupils and those without facility in English might be placed in separate schools, and the new regulations would apply to all children of alien birth, not to Japanese as such.

In return, President Roosevelt promised limits on Japanese immigration and negotiated the Gentlemen's Agreement in which Japan promised not to issue passports good for the continental United States to laborers, whether skilled or unskilled. But parents, wives, or children of Japanese already resident in the United States were not covered by this agreement, and through proxy marriages facilitated by the exchange of photographs, arranged legally and in otherwise traditional fashion by parents or other go-betweens in Japan, thousands of earlier Japanese immigrants brought *picture brides* to America. Many Californians denounced this as "oriental duplicity" and demanded complete Japanese exclusion.

The arrival of the picture brides substantially increased the Japanese American population in California. Fewer than 500 married Japanese women were in California in 1900; 20 years later their number had increased to more than 20,000. Many Japanese American women worked alongside their husbands as farm laborers. Others were employed as domestics in middle-class homes, doing housework and laundering. They worked long hours and encouraged and supported one another. "If you don't talk to anyone," mused one Japanese American woman, "your heart gets heavy. So we told each other things right away."

Many Californians portrayed the Japanese with the same racial stereotypes that had been used against the Chinese in earlier decades, particularly the charges that they were unassimilable and that their low standard of living depressed wages. Soon, however, the Japanese became the object of a new complaint—that their standard of living rapidly became too high. Brought to California to replace the Chinese as cheap farm laborers, some of them began acquiring farmland of their own. Much of this was land that they reclaimed in the Sacramento and San Joaquin valleys and in the San Joaquin delta. They were the first to demonstrate that rice could be grown successfully in California and that potatoes could be grown on a commercial scale. George Shima, known as the "potato king," produced the bulk of the state's crop on his large farm in the delta region.

Bills intended to halt the expansion of the Japanese in California agriculture began to be introduced in every legislative session and were frequently protested by the Japanese ambassador in Washington, D.C.. James D. Phelan, in a statement as near to tolerance of the Japanese as he ever came, once suggested that the United States should say "diplomatically" that it regarded "the Japanese as efficient human

Toki Okamoto, Japanese American picture bride, photographed about 1911. (*Courtesy of the National Archives, Pacific Sierra Region. Record group 85; case file 10448/10-3.*)

machines," but that "as such, they are a menace to our prosperity and happiness. Then the more sensitive citizens of Japan may find some consolation in our confession of economic inferiority." The small farmers of California, who feared the competition of Japanese, reacted with resentment and fury to the idea of making any such humiliating confession.

White supremacy and yellow peril were the watchwords of the overwhelming majority of California voters—progressives and conservatives, Republicans, Democrats, and even Socialists. The leaders of the Republican progressives were with very few exceptions white Anglo-Saxon Protestants of old American stock, a fact that was particularly striking in view of the heavily immigrant character of the state's population. In the spring of 1913, Governor Johnson joined with Francis J. Heney and California Attorney General Ulysses S. Webb in drafting an act that provided that aliens ineligible for American citizenship could not own land in the state or lease it for more than 3 years. Under federal law, all Asians were ineligible for naturalization, but there had been no legal immigrants from China since the federal Exclusion Act of 1882. Thus, the newly passed California law applied almost exclusively to Japanese aliens without openly saying so.

QUICK ACTION NEEDED!

An editorial cartoon calling for "quick action" to protect California farmers from competition from Japanese immigrant landowners, 1913. (*Courtesy of the* Sacramento Bee.)

The device was transparent, and Japan protested so strongly that President Wilson sent Secretary of State William Jennings Bryan to Sacramento to lobby against the bill. Bryan asked that the bill be made applicable to all aliens, but this led to protests from European-owned land and mining interests. Officials of the Panama Pacific International Exposition, to be held in San Francisco, opposed the bill in fear that Japan would boycott the enterprise. Others criticized the bill as unnecessary because the land owned or leased by Japanese was only a tiny fraction of the total acreage, but Chester Rowell replied that the "menace of Japanese ownership" was "not a present fact, but a fear of the future."

Actually, as Johnson was quite aware, the chief effects of the new law were more emotional and political than economic. Although it did have some deterrent effect on Japanese landownership, it also had loopholes. Some Japanese aliens transferred their land titles or leases to their American-born children or to corporations with a majority of the stock entrusted to American-born Japanese.

Hiram Johnson's anti-Asian views were almost as vigorous as those of his father, but his reasons for acting as the behind-the-scenes manager of what was usually called the Heney-Webb alien land bill were primarily reasons of political strategy. The legislature was determined to pass some bill of this kind, and to oppose a measure that was so popular with the state's electorate would have lost him many of his followers. Instead, he won many new ones, particularly in northern California. The alien land measure also served to distract attention from the growing disunity among the progressives and from their increasing disagreements over the nature and limits of reform.

The Decline of Progressivism

In California, as well as in national politics, the extremely individualistic temperaments of the Progressive leaders were sources of weakness as well as of strength. They led inevitably to a series of personal quarrels that played a major part in the disintegration of the progressive movement.

The personality of Hiram Johnson bore some resemblance to that of Theodore Roosevelt, and in the early years of their association Johnson exploited this resemblance to the point of imitating Roosevelt's gestures and exclamations. Both were extraordinarily intelligent and courageous political fighters, but both also had in extraordinary degree the human failing of self-centeredness. It might have been said of Johnson, as it was said of Roosevelt, that he disliked attending weddings and funerals because at a wedding he was not the groom and at a funeral he was

Roosevelt and Johnson

"For there is neither East nor West,
  Border nor Breed nor Birth,
When two strong men stand face to face
  Though they come from the ends of the earth."
—Kipling

A 1912 campaign poster for the Bull Moose ticket. (*Courtesy of the Library of Congress.*)

not the corpse. Both men were prone to impute dishonest motives to anyone who disagreed with them and to attribute to any rival the egotism that was characteristic of themselves. And both were masters of invective.

Johnson's personal letters often included vitriolic opinions of other politicians, and when he lost his temper, he was capable of using the most extreme language, even in a public speech. Harrison Gray Otis's *Los Angeles Times* had touched one of Johnson's most sensitive nerves by referring to his father's record of support for the railroad. Speaking in Los Angeles, Johnson described Otis as "vile, infamous, degraded, and putrescent. Here he sits in senile dementia, with gangrened heart and rotting brain, grimacing at every reform and chattering in impotent rage against decency and morality."

In 1914 Johnson wished to run for the United States Senate and had chosen John M. Eshleman to succeed him as governor, but Francis J. Heney made it known that he would run either for governor or for senator, whichever of the two offices Johnson did not seek. Johnson now regarded Heney as a dangerous rival. He could not break openly with Heney without a disastrous split in the Progressive party, but he solved the problem by running for governor himself, by backing Eshleman for lieutenant governor, and by giving Heney virtually no support in his campaign for senator. The result was that Heney lost the election while Johnson became the first governor of California to be reelected since 1853. He planned to run for the other Senate seat in 1916 and then turn over the governorship to Eshleman.

In June 1916 Roosevelt declined the Progressive party's nomination for the presidency and thus effectively scuttled the party. Returning to the Republican fold, he announced his support for Charles Evans Hughes. In California the old-guard Republicans headed by William H. Crocker, son of Charles Crocker, gleefully assumed that the influence of Hiram Johnson was dead. Hughes made the same miscalculation. In his campaign visit to California in August, Hughes permitted Crocker to plan all his speaking arrangements. They excluded Johnson from every platform where Hughes appeared and did not even arrange a meeting between the two. By chance both stopped at the Virginia Hotel in Long Beach on the afternoon of August 20, but Hughes left for Los Angeles without being informed that Johnson was in the hotel.

The California primaries were held 9 days later. Johnson was still a registered Progressive, but he had cross-filed for the Republican nomination for United States senator. To the horror of the old guard, he won the Republican nomination over their candidate, and the Johnson progressives recaptured control of the Republican state organization.

Under the circumstances, Johnson could hardly have been expected to support Hughes very enthusiastically, and he did not. Hughes lost California, by less than 4000 votes, and the presidency of the United States by losing California. But Johnson, with both Republican and Progressive nominations, won the senatorship by a margin of nearly 300,000.

Once again the California Republican progressives seemed to have triumphed, but the untimely death of Lieutenant Governor Eshleman in February 1916 had reopened the problem of succession and created further disunity. The southern

California leaders insisted on the appointment of Congressman William D. Stephens, former president of the Los Angeles Chamber of Commerce, but Johnson feared Stephens would betray the cause of progressivism. Johnson was so reluctant to have Stephens succeed him that he delayed resigning the governorship until after the beginning of his term as senator and actually held both offices for 2 weeks in March 1917.

Johnson had almost come to believe that he *was* the California progressive movement, and it was true that his personal leadership and popularity had been vital elements in its success. He had built up such a devoted personal following among California voters that they would keep him in the Senate until his death in 1945. But in doing everything he could to discredit Stephens, his successor as governor, he further weakened what remained of California progressivism.

Along with these personal and factional quarrels, larger and deeper forces were also contributing to the decline of the progressive movement. By 1916 many California progressives were satisfied that although they had accomplished little in the way of economic reform, their agenda of political and moral reform had largely been achieved.

Selected Bibliography

A critical reevaluation of the California progressives is under way. For a sampling of the latest scholarship, see William Deverell and Tom Sitton (eds.), *California Progressivism Revisited* (1994). Mowry's *California Progressives,* Olin's *California's Prodigal Sons,* and Everett's "Chester Harvey Rowell," all cited in Chapter 20, remain useful. On direct government, see John M. Allswang, *The Initiative and Referendum in California, 1891–1998* (2001), and David D. Schmidt, *Citizen Lawmakers: The Ballot Initiative Referendum* (1989). On regulation of railroads, other public utilities, banks, and other businesses, see Mansel G. Blackford, *The Politics of Business in California, 1890–1920* (1976), and Roger Charles Lister, "Bank Behavior, Regulation and Economic Development: California, 1860–1910," Ph.D. thesis, University of California, Davis (1982).

The role of California clubwomen is analyzed in Gayle Ann Gullett, "Feminism, Politics, and Voluntary Groups," Ph.D. thesis, University of California, Riverside (1983), and Sara Essa Gallaway, "Pioneering the Woman's Club Movement," Ph.D. thesis, Carnegie-Mellon University (1985). On woman suffrage, see Gayle Gullett, "Constructing the Woman Citizen and Struggling for the Vote in California, 1896–1911," *Pacific Historical Review,* LXIX (November 2000), pp. 573–594; Susan Englander, *Class Conflict and Class Coalition in the California Woman Suffrage Movement, 1907–1911* (1992); and Ronald Schaffer, "The Problem of Consciousness in the Woman Suffrage Movement," *Pacific Historical Review,* XLV (November 1976), pp. 469–494. See also Jacqueline R. Braitman, "A California Stateswoman: The Public Career of Katherine Philips Edson," *California History,* LXV (June 1986), pp. 82–95; Gullett, "Women Progressives and the Politics of Americanization in California, 1915–1920," *Pacific Historical Review,* LXIV (February 1995), pp. 71–94; Judith Rosenberg Raftery, *Land of Fair Promise* (1992); and Sherry J. Katz, "Dual Commitments: Feminism, Socialism, and Women's Political Activism in California, 1890–1920," Ph.D. thesis, University of California, Los Angeles (1991).

Labor measures are treated in Alexander P. Saxton, "San Francisco Labor and the Populist and Progressive Insurgencies," *Pacific Historical Review,* XXXIV (November 1965), pp. 421–438; Gerald D. Nash, "The Influence of Labor on State Policy, 1860–1920," *California Historical Society Quarterly,* XLII (September 1963), pp. 241–257; Norris C. Hundley, Jr., "Katherine Philips Edson and the Fight for the California Minimum Wage, 1912–1923," *Pacific Historical Review,* XXIX (August 1960), pp. 271–286; and Thomas R. Clark, "Labor and Progressivism," *California History,* LXVI (September 1987), pp. 196–207.

Accounts of the anti-Japanese agitation include Frank W. Van Nuys, "A Progressive Confronts the Race Question," *California History,* LXXIII (Spring 1994), pp. 2–13; Roger Daniels, *The Politics of Prejudice* (1962); Herbert P. LePore, "Prelude to Prejudice: Hiram Johnson, Woodrow Wilson, and the California Alien Land Law Controversy of 1913," *Southern California Quarterly,* LXI (Spring 1979), pp. 99–110; Madelon Berkowitz, "The California Progressives and Anti-Japanese Agitation," M.A. thesis, University of California, Berkeley (1966); and Yuji Ichioka, "Japanese Immigrant Response to the 1920 California Alien Land Law," *Agricultural History,* LVIII (April 1984), pp. 157–178. See also the special issue of *California History,* LXXIII (Spring 1994), devoted to Japanese Americans in California.

On state attempts at regulation of agriculture, see Grace H. Larsen, "A Progressive in Agriculture: Harris Weinstock," *Agricultural History,* XXXII (July 1958), pp. 187–193.

The confusion that progressivism brought to the two-party system is described in A. Lincoln, "Theodore Roosevelt, Hiram Johnson, and the Vice-Presidential Nomination of 1912," *Pacific Historical Review,* XXVIII (August 1959), pp. 267–284, and Robert E. Hennings, *James D. Phelan and the Wilson Progressives of California* (1985). The origins of cross-filing are discussed in Franklin Hichborn, "The Party, the Machine, and the Vote: The Story of Cross-Filing in California Politics," *California Historical Society Quarterly,* XXXVIII (December 1959), pp. 349–357, and XXXIX (March 1960), pp. 19–34, and James C. Findley, "Cross-Filing and the Progressive Movement in California Politics," *Western Political Quarterly,* XXII (September 1959), pp. 699–711.

On the campaign of 1916, see Edward A. Dickson, "How Hughes Lost California in 1916," *Congressional Record* (August 19, 1954), and F. M. Davenport, "Did Hughes Snub Johnson?" *American Political Science Review,* XLIII (April 1949), pp. 321–332.

CHAPTER 22

The Triumph of Conservatism

The coming of World War I ushered in an era of renewed conservatism in state and national affairs. During and after the war, there was a strong reaction against radicalism and a further decline of organized labor and the progressive movement. The forces of conservatism were triumphant through the 1920s.

The Rise and Fall of the Socialist Movement

In California, as well as in the United States as a whole, socialism reached its highest point during the progressive era. This not only alarmed conservatives but also gave them an opportunity to attack and weaken progressivism by linking it with socialism.

The beginning of the organized socialist movement in the state went back to the 1880s, when the eccentric millionaire H. Gaylord Wilshire developed a peculiarly American brand of socialism in Los Angeles. Wilshire was an irrepressible and almost incredible figure in the history of southern California. The son of a Cincinnati capitalist, he inherited and lost one fortune and then made and lost a series of others in real estate, orange groves, banks, gold mines, billboards, and even a cure-all electric belt of his own invention. In the boom of the 1880s, he developed and subdivided the Wilshire Tract west of Los Angeles's Westlake Park. Harrison Gray Otis and Edwin T. Earl bought large adjoining lots and built their mansions in this subdivision, through the center of which ran a thoroughfare 120 feet wide named Wilshire Boulevard. But with the collapse of the boom in 1888, Gaylord Wilshire became an avowed socialist, and in 1890 he was the first socialist in the United States to run for Congress. Next he founded *Wilshire's Magazine,* which became the country's most widely circulated socialist journal. Its motto was "Let the Nation Own the Trusts," an idea that would also play a central part in Jack London's novel *The Iron Heel.*

In later years Wilshire Boulevard would be to Los Angeles more or less what the Champs-Élysées was to Paris, and more than 200 enterprises, from a hotel and a country club to a cleaning and dyeing company, would take the name of "Wilshire" because it signified impeccable commercial prestige. Few if any of the proprietors or patrons of these establishments knew the identity of the original bearer of the name.

In the 1890s the leadership of the California socialist movement passed from Wilshire to Job Harriman, a labor union lawyer who came to Los Angeles for his health. The extremely repressive tactics of Harrison Gray Otis and the Merchants' and Manufacturers' Association had driven so much of Los Angeles labor to socialism that Harriman repeatedly came close to being elected mayor of the city. He would almost certainly have been elected mayor in 1911 if he had not committed the socialist cause to the belief that the McNamara brothers were innocent victims of a capitalist frame-up and if the McNamaras had not shattered this faith by confessing their guilt a few days before the city election. (See Chapter 19.) Even after that great setback, Harriman came within 800 votes of being elected mayor 2 years later, but after this final defeat he turned from political activity to the management of a socialist cooperative experiment at Llano del Rio in the Mojave Desert region north of Los Angeles.

In the state election of 1910 more than 12 percent of the vote went to the Socialist candidate for governor, J. Stitt Wilson, a Berkeley Methodist minister who described himself as a "social evangelist." In 1911 Wilson was elected mayor of Berkeley, although in his 2 years in that office he neither attempted nor accomplished anything radical. In 1912 he ran as the Socialist candidate for Congress against Joseph R. Knowland, the impregnable Republican leader of Oakland and dean of the California congressional delegation; although Knowland won 54 percent of the votes, Wilson drew a remarkable 40 percent. In 1912 Socialist congressional nominees in California won 18 percent of the votes, one Socialist assemblyman from Los Angeles was elected, and Eugene V. Debs won nearly 12 percent of the vote for president. The elections of 1914 produced two Socialist assemblymen and one state senator.

Though socialism called in theory for public ownership of all the means of production and distribution, the Socialists in the California Legislature pressed mainly for such limited measures as the 8-hour workday. Most of the legislative proposals of the Socialists were so moderate that they were hardly distinguishable from those advocated by the more liberal of the progressives, but conservative forces formed a Sound Government League in order to fight them, and one of the league's bulletins denounced "creeping socialism," with which conservatives lumped most progressive measures.

The rising tide of socialism in the United States in the first 15 years of the century was a general humanitarian as well as working-class reaction to such prevailing conditions as poverty, long hours and low wages, and the abuse of child labor. The coming of World War I virtually shattered the socialist movement, not only by distracting the country's attention from these conditions but also by creating extreme disunity among the Socialists themselves. In California such prominent

Socialists as Stitt Wilson and Jack London favored the Allied cause and resigned from the Socialist party in 1916 when it opposed American intervention.

The Mooney Case

In northern California, the beginning of a long period of antilabor reaction coincided with the beginning of the war in Europe. In 1914, after several months of economic depression, an "army" of 1500 unemployed under "General" Charles T. Kelley was driven out of Sacramento by a force of deputized citizens armed with clubs. In Stockton, employers formed a merchants' and manufacturers' association in July 1914, imported professional strikebreakers and armed guards, and launched an open-shop drive that produced one of the bitterest labor wars in the state's history.

The San Francisco employers began their drive for the open shop in July 1916, in the midst of a growing national movement for military preparedness. Labor in general opposed the military preparedness movement, whereas most employers favored that movement and seized the opportunity to discredit labor as unpatriotic. San Francisco business and patriotic organizations planned a great Preparedness Day parade on Market Street, in which no labor union participated. The parade was held on July 22. In the midst of it, at 2:06 in the afternoon, a bomb explosion at the corner of Stewart and Market killed 10 persons and wounded 40. Suspicion soon fell upon a radical labor agitator named Thomas J. Mooney.

For several years before the Preparedness Day bombing, Mooney had been active in San Francisco as a left-wing trade union socialist with an aggressive personality and a genius for antagonizing people. An iron molder by trade, he was not a union official. The description of him as a "labor leader" came from opponents of organized labor. He was interested in strike activity for the purposes of social revolution.

In 1913 the electrical workers' union had conducted a long strike against the Pacific Gas and Electric Company (PG&E) throughout northern California during which there were hundreds of depredations against the company's property, 18 of them by dynamite explosions. Warren K. Billings, a young friend of Mooney, had been arrested in Sacramento for the illegal transportation of a suitcase full of dynamite and sentenced to 2 years in prison. Later in 1913, Mooney was arrested for illegal possession of explosives and charged with planning to use them to destroy the PG&E transmission line across Carquinez Straits. He was tried at Martinez, but the evidence was flimsy and he was acquitted.

In the summer of 1916, Mooney was trying unsuccessfully to organize a union among employees of the United Railroads in San Francisco. Within a few days after the Preparedness Day explosion, the police arrested Mooney, Billings, and three others. All five were arrested without evidence, warrants, or formal charges and were denied the right of legal counsel until after they were indicted. From the time of the arrests, the police and the district attorney's office dropped all further search for evidence except that which could be made to point to the defendants'

Thomas Mooney (1882–1942), imprisoned for more than 20 years in San Quentin. (*Courtesy of the Bancroft Library.*)

guilt. Billings was tried for murder in September, convicted, and sentenced to life imprisonment. Mooney was tried in January 1917, convicted, and sentenced to hang. The three others were acquitted or not brought to trial.

The main witnesses for the prosecution testified that they had seen Billings and Mooney at or near the scene of the crime and that Billings was carrying a suitcase presumably containing a time bomb. Overwhelming evidence indicates that these witnesses were perjuring themselves, and it is hard to escape the conclusion that District Attorney Charles M. Fickert was aware of their perjury and encouraged it. Fickert was at best an incompetent lawyer who had always been accustomed to garble or invent facts to suit his purposes. In the Mooney case, he did not prosecute the defendants in good faith but because they were widely hated as radicals and because he believed that to convict them would make him governor of California.

Again, as in the *Times* bombing a few years earlier, millions of people throughout the country believed what their social predilections made them wish to believe about the guilt or innocence of the accused. This time, however, many were afraid of being deceived by the cry of "frame-up" that had been so discredited before, and this made Fickert's work easier. The evidence against the McNamara brothers, so widely disbelieved and denounced, had turned out to be quite genuine. The evidence against Mooney and Billings, so readily believed, was fabricated.

It was apparent to many, however, that there had been an outrageous miscarriage of justice. The case took on international importance in April 1917, with a demonstration outside the American embassy in Petrograd against the execution of a political prisoner named "Muni." President Wilson, concerned both for the interests of justice and for the American image in a war to make the world safe for democracy, asked Governor William D. Stephens to consider a commutation.

In November 1918 Governor Stephens commuted Mooney's sentence to life imprisonment. In the antiradical hysteria of the war and postwar periods, most Californians held to a fixed belief in Mooney's guilt.

The Criminal Syndicalism Law

Throughout World War I, the IWW openly opposed America's participation in it and maintained that the only just war was a class war against capitalism. Long denounced as advocates of industrial sabotage, the Wobblies were now also branded as antipatriotic and often described as "Imperial Wilhelm's Warriors." They were actively involved in many bitter wartime strikes. Late in 1918, 46 IWW members were arrested in Sacramento and tried in the federal courts as seditious conspirators. Most of them were convicted and sentenced to prison.

After the end of the war, the wave of emotional antiradicalism became even greater, for the full force of public hatred was then turned upon "internal enemies." In April 1919 the California legislature passed a criminal syndicalism law. This statute defined *criminal syndicalism* as "any doctrine or precept advocating . . . unlawful acts of force and violence . . . as a means of accomplishing a change in industrial ownership or control, or effecting any political change." Under this law several hundred persons were prosecuted in California during the next 5 years.

One of the first of these trials, and by far the most famous, was that of Charlotte Anita Whitney. Before her arrest in November 1919, when she was 52 years old, Whitney's career had hardly been such as to suggest that she was a dangerous criminal. Rather, she was well known as a philanthropist, social worker, and suffragist. She could trace her descent from five *Mayflower* pilgrims, and her uncle was United States Supreme Court Justice Stephen J. Field. After graduating from Wellesley College, she had served for many years as secretary of the Associated Charities of Oakland. She had joined the Socialist party in 1914, and during the war she was active in the pacifist movement and in the defense of Mooney and Billings. In 1919 Whitney attended in Oakland a convention of left-wing Socialists who had split off to form the Communist Labor party. Whitney worked for a resolution favoring only democratic and peaceful methods, but this resolution was voted down, and instead the convention ratified the national platform of the Communist Labor party.

Whitney's trial for violating the criminal syndicalism law began in January 1920, not long after United States Attorney General A. Mitchell Palmer had launched a series of raids against "Bolshevists, anarchists, and kindred radicals." The proceedings against Whitney were conducted in an atmosphere of hysterical superpatriotism, and they set a pattern for many subsequent prosecutions in which mere membership in an organization advocating violence was interpreted as sufficient evidence of criminal syndicalism under the state law. She was convicted and sentenced to 1 to 14 years in the penitentiary.

Fremont Older, one of the leading critics of the prosecution in the Mooney case, also came vigorously to the defense of Whitney and persuaded his former star

Political activist Charlotte Anita Whitney (1867–1955) and her attorney, John Francis Neylan (1885–1960). (*Courtesy of the Bancroft Library.*)

reporter, John Francis Neylan, to take charge of her appeal. Neylan, who had a highly successful law practice in San Francisco, disagreed sharply with Whitney's political views but believed that she had been unjustly convicted. For 7 years, while she remained free on bail, he fought with all the legal and political resources he could muster to keep her out of prison. The United States Supreme Court finally rendered a decision in the case in May 1927. It unanimously upheld the conviction and also upheld the constitutionality of the California law as being within the state's police power. Neylan was more successful in his fight for a pardon, which Governor Clement C. Young granted in June 1927. In explaining his decision, the governor argued that to imprison Whitney would "revive the waning spirits of radicalism" by making her a martyr. Besides, Young concluded, she was a "lifelong friend of the unfortunate," rather than "in any true sense a 'criminal,'" and "to condemn her at 60 years of age to a felon's cell" was "absolutely unthinkable."

Upton Sinclair and others, observing sardonically that a number of obscure men had been imprisoned for offenses identical in principle with Whitney's, charged that there was one law for the rich and another for the poor. Altogether, there had been 504 arrests and 264 trials under the California criminal syndicalism law, and

128 persons, mostly members of the IWW, had been sent to prison. Twenty-four states had adopted such laws, mostly in 1919, but in all these states except California they were dead letters after 1921. In California, active prosecutions continued until 1924, largely to discourage further attempts by the IWW to organize migratory farmworkers. The law was eventually declared unconstitutional in 1968 by the United States Supreme Court.

The Decline of Organized Labor

In the 1920s the business community had considerable success in branding labor unions as unpatriotic. A large segment of American public opinion believed that the unions had at best been lukewarm in their support of the war and that they had been inclined to defend seditious radicals instead of joining in the national condemnation of them. Adding these widely held beliefs to their arsenal, employer organizations resumed their prewar battles for the open shop, and this time succeeded in establishing it even in what had previously been the union stronghold of San Francisco.

In the summer of 1921, after an unpopular and unsuccessful strike by the building trade unions, the San Francisco Chamber of Commerce created a new Industrial Association to establish and enforce the so-called American plan. This expression had recently received the approval of the National Association of Manufacturers as the official name for the open shop. The drive made such remarkable headway in San Francisco that for the rest of the decade the open shop predominated even in the construction of municipal buildings. The Industrial Association maintained a "permit system" under which it withheld building materials from employers who continued to "discriminate against nonunion men" by making closed-shop contracts with unions. An Impartial Wage Board, established by the association, nearly replaced collective bargaining in the building industry. Representatives of the Industrial Association of San Francisco often argued that it was not a "union-busting" organization, because it forbade employers to discriminate against union members—provided they were willing to work with nonunion people.

In Los Angeles, however, employers were often more candidly eager to destroy unions entirely. The Better America Federation, a new auxiliary of the Merchants' and Manufacturers' Association, was organized in Los Angeles in May 1920 to conduct a lobbying and propaganda battle against organized labor and progressivism. Its drive for members and money made the same sort of patriotic appeals that had been used to sell liberty bonds during the war. It lobbied against higher state taxes on banks and utilities and in favor of proposals to establish the open shop by law and to abolish all the state regulatory boards and commissions that the progressives had created. Its propaganda sought to associate with treason and subversion anyone who disagreed with its objectives.

Throughout the 1920s membership in labor unions steadily declined. In a period of prosperity and high employment, this was remarkable. The prestige of organized labor was low, and that of employer organizations was correspondingly high. Many agreed with the Better America Federation in adopting as mottoes the slogan of President Warren Harding, "Less government in business, more business in the government," and the aphorism of President Calvin Coolidge, "The business of America is business."

The Collapse of the Democratic Party

During the last third of the nineteenth century the balance between the two major parties had been close in California, and Democratic candidates had won five gubernatorial elections to the Republicans' four. After 1900, however, a long series of defeats began to have a cumulative effect on the Democratic party's morale.

In the postwar decade, the Republicans benefited from the general prosperity and from the wholesale migration to California of retired farmers and small businesspeople from the middle west. Throughout the 1920s the Democrats could win no more than 1 of California's 11 congressional seats. Cross-filing Republicans repeatedly won the Democratic nominations for 6 of the seats and were thus elected in the primaries, for which, in several cases, no Democrat even bothered to file. In 1922, of the 80 seats in the state assembly, the Democrats won only 3. Through most of the decade, Republicans outnumbered Democrats in California by four to one in voter registration.

Democratic leadership was uninspiring. When William Gibbs McAdoo transferred his residence from New York to California in 1922, the California Democrats hoped that this acquisition of a leading contender for the presidency of the United States would revive their strength. But McAdoo, who favored strong enforcement of prohibition, made his home in Los Angeles and assumed the leadership of the dry, or prohibitionist, Democrats of southern California, thus deepening the split with the northern California wing of the party, which was decidedly wet. William Randolph Hearst remained a nominal Democrat through the early 1920s but later became a supporter and personal admirer of Republican President Calvin Coolidge. The confused and weakened condition of the California Democratic party was reflected in a contemporary remark by the humorist Will Rogers: "I belong to no organized political party. I am a Democrat."

The Continuing Decline of Republican Progressivism

Senator Hiram Johnson had abandoned the remnants of the Progressive party by 1918, and he campaigned for the Republican presidential nomination in 1920 on a platform of narrowly nationalistic and isolationist "Americanism." His irreconcilable opposition to the League of Nations so far overshadowed his interest in domestic issues that he supported the conservative lawyer Samuel M. Shortridge for the Republican nomination for United States senator, against the distinguished progressive William Kent, largely because Shortridge opposed the league and Kent favored it.

Prohibition was another issue that confused the alignments among progressive and conservative Republicans, as well as among the Democrats. Many of the California progressives were drys, and the disastrous failure of the prohibition experiment accelerated the general decline in the moral fervor of progressivism. Congress had submitted the Eighteenth Amendment to the states in December 1917, in the midst of the war, and California ratified it in the spring of 1919. It proved even less popular and less effective in California than in the rest of the country. Efforts to enforce it were concentrated against small cafés rather than against large distillers and bootleggers, and the Mexican border and long coastline made smuggling easy. The obvious breakdown of prohibition tended to weaken all respect for law and government. One jury had to be admonished for drinking up the liquor that was the chief evidence in the trial.

The continuing crusade against the Japanese, which had never had any genuine connection with progressivism, now became a part of the new wave of superheated patriotic antiforeigner sentiment that was aiding the conservative revival throughout the country. An initiative measure adopted by a vote of three to one in 1920 repealed the provision of the law of 1913 that had permitted Japanese aliens to lease land for 3 years. In the federal immigration act of 1924, California won its long fight for the complete exclusion of "aliens ineligible to citizenship." Without this clause, the quota system finally provided in the act would have permitted only 100 Japanese immigrants per year; but Johnson and Shortridge demanded and secured complete Japanese exclusion. The United States had never before offered Japan so flagrant an insult. The Japanese ambassador's warning of "grave consequences" was interpreted in Congress as a threat, and for this reason it actually contributed to the passage of the exclusion clause.

An unexpected consequence of the exclusion of the Japanese and other Asians was an increase in the immigration of Filipinos. The Philippines were an American possession, and thus Filipinos were not subject to the exclusionary provisions of the 1924 immigration act. Most of the Filipinos who immigrated to California were young and unskilled; they came to fill the farm-labor vacuum created by the exclusion of the Japanese. As their numbers increased, Filipino immigrants provoked a xenophobic reaction similar to the hostility that had greeted earlier newcomers from Asia.

The triumph of conservatism was most apparent in the election of Friend W. Richardson as governor in 1922. A former state treasurer and publisher of the *Berkeley Gazette,* Richardson promised and achieved a program of "sweeping retrenchment." His "economy budget" drastically reduced appropriations, particularly for regulatory boards, humanitarian agencies, and education. "The schools," he told the legislature, "must be put on a business basis. They must not only teach but practice thrift." He chose conservatives to replace the heads of the various regulatory commissions appointed under Johnson and Stephens, and these men often were representatives of the business interests the commissions were supposed to regulate.

For the election of 1926, several leading California progressives formed the Progressive Voters' League and rallied behind the gubernatorial aspirations of Clement

C. Young of Berkeley. Young had been speaker of the assembly during the progressive era and was now lieutenant governor. In his race for the governorship in 1926, he made his progressive followers uneasy by accepting the support of A. P. Giannini and his Bank of Italy. Giannini's swiftly growing institution, soon to be renamed the Bank of America, was well on its way toward the goal of a system of branches to cover the whole of California. Under Governor Richardson the state authorities had yielded to the complaints of independent bankers and had imposed restrictions on the statewide growth of branch banking. Shortly before the primary of 1926, the Bank of Italy contributed generously to the Young campaign fund, and the employees of the bank's branches throughout the state served as volunteer campaigners. By a narrow margin, Young won the Republican nomination from Richardson. At a time when California was almost a one-party state, this assured Young of the governorship. As one member of the Progressive Voters' League put it, he and his fellow progressives had marveled at such a "fortunate acquisition" of support, but when Young became governor, they learned that "we were the acquisition." Early in 1927 Young's new superintendent of banks revoked the restrictions on branch banking. During the remainder of that year, the branches of the Bank of Italy increased from 98 to 289.

Although Young's administration disappointed his most progressive supporters, he did reverse some of the most reactionary policies of Richardson. An act of 1929, with Young's support, made California the first state to require that every county provide old-age pensions. His most substantial achievement was a "businesslike reorganization" of the state government, which inaugurated the cabinet system in the executive branch and improved the budget system.

In the election of 1930, when the main contest was between Young and James Rolph, Jr., for the Republican nomination, Richardson had his revenge. Young was a dry and Rolph was a wet. Richardson encouraged the district attorney of Los Angeles to enter the race and thus divide the dry vote in southern California, so that Rolph narrowly defeated Young in the primary. With Rolph's election as governor, Republican progressivism in California went into an even further decline.

The Federal Plan for Reapportionment

A new system of apportioning the state senate, adopted in 1926, played a little-understood but highly important part in the successful drive of conservative business interests to consolidate their influence upon the state government.

Representation in both houses of the legislature had previously been apportioned according to population, and reapportioned, with considerable gerrymandering, every 10 years. By the early 1920s, however, Los Angeles had grown so enormously that the legislators from San Francisco and Oakland joined with those from the rural northern California counties to block any reapportionment bill that would have given the southern metropolis its full representation.

In 1926 the voters were given a choice between two initiative constitutional amendments. One provided for reapportionment in both houses on the customary basis of population. This was officially called the All Parties proposal, but its main support was in Los Angeles County. Its opponents always called it the "Los Angeles Plan" and thus ensured its unpopularity elsewhere in the state. The alternative proposal, on the other hand, bore the disingenuous but effectively persuasive label of the "Federal Plan." Based on a misleading analogy with the equal representation of the states in the upper house of Congress, this scheme apportioned the seats in the state senate at not more than one to a county and at not more than three counties to a senatorial district. The Federal Plan was approved by a majority of the voters in the 1926 election.

This proposal was advertised as coming from the "dirt farmers" of California, and the four largest agricultural organizations did support it with enthusiasm. Significantly, however, the major financial contribution in aid of its passage came from the San Francisco Chamber of Commerce, though this source was not revealed until after the election. As one progressive observed, the plan was ideally suited to the interests of those special California farmers who labored in the tall buildings on Montgomery Street, the heart of the San Francisco financial district. Over the next several years, the ingenuity of their plan became apparent in the membership of the state senate. Dirt farmers were not in evidence, and a remarkable proportion of the new senators from the rural districts turned out to be attorneys, insurance agents, and others who were local representatives of corporations with headquarters in San Francisco.

California agriculture itself was becoming steadily more industrialized and its interests more and more identified with those of the business community. The new California senate would often be described as "rural-dominated." To put the matter more accurately, it became a stronghold of business conservatism, rural and urban.

Selected Bibliography

Howard Quint, "Gaylord Wilshire and Socialism's First Congressional Campaign," *Pacific Historical Review,* XXVI (November 1957), pp. 327–340, describes the election of 1890. On the career of Job Harriman, see Paul Greenstein, Nigey Lennon, and Lionel Rolfe, *Bread and Hyacinths* (1992); Grace H. Stimson, *Rise of the Labor Movement in Los Angeles* (1955); and Robert V. Hine, *California's Utopian Colonies* (1953). J. Stitt Wilson and the socialist movement in general are treated in Ralph E. Shaffer, "A History of the Socialist Party of California," M.A. thesis, University of California, Berkeley (1955).

The Mooney Case (1968), by Richard H. Frost, is by far the best account. Others are Curt Gentry, *Frame-Up* (1967), and Estolv E. Ward, *The Gentle Dynamiter* (1983). On "Kelley's Army," see Carlos A. Schwantes, *Coxey's Army* (1986). Consult also Thomas G. Paterson, "California Progressives and Foreign Policy," *California Historical Society Quarterly,* XLVII (December 1968), pp. 329–342.

Woodrow C. Whitten's *Criminal Syndicalism and the Law in California, 1919–1927* (1969), is an objective study of the antiradical movement. On Charlotte Anita Whitney, see Lisa Rubens, "The Patrician Radical," *California History,* LXV (September 1986), pp. 158–171, and Al Richmond, *Native Daughter* (1942). See also Ralph E. Shaffer, "Formation of the California Communist Labor Party," *Pacific Historical Review,* XXXVI

(February 1967), pp. 59–78, and "Communism in California, 1919–1924," *Science and Society,* XXXIV (Winter 1970).

On the decline of organized labor, see Issel and Cherny, *San Francisco,* cited in Chapter 19; Stephen C. Levi, *Committee of Vigilance, 1916–1919* (1983); Nelson VanValen, "'Cleaning Up the Harbor': The Suppression of the IWW at San Pedro, 1922–1925," *Southern California Quarterly,* LXVI (Summer 1984), pp. 147–172; and Edwin Layton, "The Better America Federation," *Pacific Historical Review,* XXX (May 1961), pp. 137–148.

On the Democratic debacle, consult H. Brett Melendy, "California's Cross-Filing Nightmare: The 1918 Gubernatorial Election," *Pacific Historical Review,* XXXIII (August 1964), pp. 317–330, and Robert E. Hennings, "California Democratic Politics in the Period of Republican Ascendancy," *Pacific Historical Review,* XXXI (August 1962), pp. 267–280.

On Hiram Johnson's drift away from progressivism, see Richard C. Lower, *A Bloc of One: The Political Career of Hiram Johnson* (1993); Richard D. Batman, "The Road to the Presidency: Hoover, Johnson, and the California Republican Party, 1920–1924," Ph.D. thesis, University of Southern California (1965); Robert E. Burke (ed.), *The Diary Letters of Hiram Johnson* (7 volumes, 1983); and Arlene Lazarowitz, "Hiram W. Johnson: The Old Progressive and New Deal Taxation," *California History,* LXIX (Winter 1990), pp. 342–353.

Political issues of the 1920s are also discussed in Jackson K. Putnam, *Modern California Politics, 1917–1980* (1980); Gilman M. Ostrander, *The Prohibition Movement in California, 1848–1933* (1957); Roger Daniels, *The Politics of Prejudice* (1962); Russell M. Posner, "The Progressive Voters' League, 1923–1926," *California Historical Society Quarterly,* XXXVI (September 1957), pp. 251–261; and Putnam, "The Persistence of Progressivism in the 1920s," *Pacific Historical Review,* XXXV (November 1966), pp. 395–411. See also Joseph Giovinco, "Democracy in Banking: The Bank of Italy and California's Italians," *California Historical Society Quarterly,* XLVII (September 1968), pp. 195–218; Gerald D. Nash, *A. P. Giannini and the Bank of America* (1992); and Felice A. Bonadio, *A. P. Giannini: Banker of America* (1994).

The story of the Filipino immigrants is told in Lorraine Jacobs Crouchett, *Filipinos in California* (1982), and Yen Le Espiritu, *Filipino American Lives* (1994).

On the adoption of the Federal Plan, see George W. Bemis, "Sectionalism and Representation in the California State Legislature, 1911–1931," Ph.D. thesis, University of California, Berkeley (1935); Thomas S. Barclay, "Reapportionment in California," *Pacific Historical Review,* V (June 1936), pp. 93–129; and Bruce E. Cain, *The Reapportionment Puzzle* (1986).

CHAPTER 23

New Industries for
Southern California

In the early twentieth century, California's economy and population expanded with the growth of new industries. Most of the growth occurred in southern California, where the discovery of huge deposits of oil contributed not only to the rise of the petroleum industry but also to the automobile revolution. At the same time, southern California was becoming the capital of the nation's new motion picture industry.

The significance of these changes was clear: the economic and political center of California was shifting southward. Whereas San Francisco had been the great city of the nineteenth century, Los Angeles was emerging as the city of the twentieth.

Origins of the Oil Industry

California's oil industry had its first boom in the 1860s but did not begin to reach major proportions until the 1890s. Its great modern expansion came in the twentieth century.

The boom of the 1860s centered in the area near Ventura, along the southern California coast. In 1861 George S. Gilbert, a whale oil merchant, built a small refinery on the Ojai Ranch north of Ventura. From seepage oil, Gilbert manufactured small quantities of kerosene. In 1864 Thomas A. Scott, vice president of the Pennsylvania Railroad, sent a Yale University chemist, Benjamin Silliman, to evaluate some western mineral properties. In the course of his trip, Silliman investigated the oil resources of the Ventura region. After absorbing the glib optimism of Gilbert, Silliman wrote a number of rosy reports. "California," he predicted, "will be found to have more oil in its soil than all the whales in the Pacific Ocean." In the Ojai region, "the oil is struggling to the surface at every available point and is running away down the river for miles." The first 10 wells drilled on the Ojai property, he estimated, would yield an annual profit of more than $1 million.

Scott placed full faith in Silliman's judgment, for he had already made a large profit by purchasing and developing oil land in Pennsylvania. Scott headed a group of investors who bought the Ojai and several neighboring ranches and sent out the best drilling machinery then in existence. As manager of his California properties Scott chose Thomas R. Bard, a young man from Pennsylvania. In the summer of 1865, Bard began drilling a series of wells, but none of them produced oil in commercial quantities.

Silliman's California reports were quite true, and even understated, as a kind of mystical vision of the ultimate future, but as conclusions from the actual evidence they were fantastically exaggerated and based on a slipshod investigation. Silliman was unaware that California's geology, with its characteristically tilted and folded strata, would make both the finding and the extracting of oil more difficult than in Pennsylvania. California crude oil in the early years was extremely heavy and gummy. Scott refused to finance any further search for oil on his California properties, and the state's first oil boom was over by the end of 1867.

Prospecting continued, however, notably in Pico Canyon, which was still public land and in which oil ventures were conducted under a system of mining claims patterned after those of the mother lode country. Pico Number One, opened in 1875, became the first commercial well in California.

Gradually, deeper drilling began to yield larger quantities and better grades. In 1890 Thomas R. Bard joined with two small operators in organizing the Union Oil Company of California. Bard had turned from oil prospecting to land management in Ventura County and had built a fortune by subdividing Scott's vast lands for ranching purposes, buying lands of his own, and separately leasing the ranches and the oil rights. Bard served as the first president of Union Oil, though he soon relinquished this office and withdrew from active participation in the company's affairs after his election to the United States Senate in 1900.

Silliman's vision began to become a reality in the early 1890s. The Union Oil Company made several substantial discoveries that laid the foundations of its future career as one of the giants of the California industry, and in 1892 Edward L. Doheny made his sensational discovery of a major oil field within the city of Los Angeles. Doheny was a prospector and lawyer who had never hunted oil and had never even seen a derrick. But one day in Los Angeles, when he saw a wagonload of tarry brown dirt being hauled from an excavation to be burned as a substitute for coal, he realized that a mother pool of oil was feeding the pits, the oil thickening to tar as it reached the surface.

In November 1892 Doheny and his partner, Charles A. Canfield, leased a vacant lot near West Second Street and Glendale Boulevard and dug a shaft with pick and shovel, lifting out the dirt with a hand windlass. At a depth of 155 feet, oil began to flow into the shaft. The flow increased rapidly, and the Los Angeles oil boom was on. Hundreds of oil wells mushroomed in front yards and backyards. For the year 1895, the total flow was more than 700,000 barrels, mostly from a strip of land about 600 feet wide and 2 miles long, which overlay a pool of great richness and depth.

Finding a market for this outpouring was an urgent problem. The answer was the substitution of oil for coal. California had produced a little low-grade coal,

Oil wells in Los Angeles transformed residential neighborhoods into oil fields. This crowded scene is on Court Street about 1901. (*Courtesy of the University of Southern California, on behalf of the USC Specialized Libraries and Archival Collections.*)

mainly in the Mount Diablo area, but had imported most of its coal supply at great expense. Now it suddenly had a surplus of a better and much cheaper fuel. Oil burners for locomotives were developed, and by the turn of the century the railroads of the whole southwestern United States were converting to oil. The conversion of the railroads was a turning point, showing the way to the use of oil for powering ships as well as all sorts of stationary engines and ensuring California's future as a major industrial state.

In the years after Doheny's discovery of the Los Angeles City field, other important oil-producing areas were developed in the southern California coastal region, notably in Santa Barbara County and in the Los Angeles basin. But the larger discoveries in the period between 1895 and 1920 came in the San Joaquin Valley. On March 15, 1910, a Union Oil subsidiary company drilling in Kern County brought in one of the world's greatest gushers. The driller, a certain "Dry Hole Charlie" Woods, was instantly renamed "Gusher Charlie." So tremendous was the blast that the derrick disappeared into the crater. Not for several weeks was the gusher brought under control, and then only by building a huge earthen dam around it, high enough to smother it in a lake of its own oil. At last the casing wore out, the hole caved in, and the great gusher was dead, but the surrounding field grew into an oil empire, with its capital in the new town of Taft, named for the incumbent president.

The near monopoly that Standard Oil had established throughout the nation in the last third of the nineteenth century was broken in the early twentieth. As the petroleum industry entered its modern period of enormous growth and passed from its "age of illumination" to its "age of energy," it became highly competitive, although the most important competition was among great corporations.

From the late 1870s to the mid-1890s, Standard had dominated the market in California with oil products imported by rail from its eastern fields and refineries. Standard moved into producing and refining operations in the far west in 1900 when it purchased control of the Pacific Coast Oil Company. This concern had been organized in 1878 by two of San Francisco's leading venture capitalists. In 1906 it was renamed the Standard Oil Company (California). In 1911 an antitrust decision of the United States Supreme Court forced the dissolution of the Standard network into its constituent companies, but Standard of California had already become by far the largest refinery on the Pacific coast.

Another California giant was the Associated Oil Company, originally formed by a number of small producers in the San Joaquin Valley in 1901. The Southern Pacific Railroad purchased control of Associated Oil in 1909, mainly in order to develop its own burgeoning oil interests in the western San Joaquin Valley. By 1919 the Southern Pacific Land Company owned more than 19 percent of all the proved oil land in California, and through its controlling interest in the Associated Oil Company the railroad produced about 18 percent of the state's oil. During the next several years, however, the Southern Pacific gradually divested itself of its direct interests in oil production and refining.

In addition to Standard, Associated, and Union, the major California operators in this period included Shell, Richfield, the General Petroleum Corporation, which was later called the Mobil Oil Corporation, the Texas Company (Texaco), and Edward L. Doheny's Pan-American Petroleum Company.

The Oil Boom of the Twenties

Three tremendous discoveries in the early 1920s, all in the Los Angeles basin area, surpassed all the earlier developments and launched a boom that put oil in the forefront of California's headlong economic expansion in the "prosperity decade." Standard opened the massive new field at Huntington Beach in 1920. The next year, Union brought in the great Santa Fe Springs field south of Whittier, and Shell tapped the still greater bonanza of Signal Hill at Long Beach—richest of all the world's oil deposits in terms of barrels per acre. The value of the California crude oil produced in the decade of the 1920s was more than $2.5 billion. This figure compares very strikingly with the value of all the gold ever mined in the state— about $2 billion. California ranked first among the states in crude oil production for several years in the 1920s.

In 1919 about two-thirds of California's oil came from the San Joaquin Valley, and the major refineries were concentrated in the San Francisco Bay area, but in the 1920s the predominance in all aspects of the oil industry quickly passed to the Los Angeles region. Exports of oil from Los Angeles Harbor made it the largest oil port in the world. Petroleum refining became the state's largest manufacturing industry. In 1925 the value of oil refinery products was twice the value of the output of California's second-largest branch of manufacturing, the canning and preserving of fruits and vegetables.

The most infamous episode in the history of California's great oil boom of the postwar decade was the involvement of Edward L. Doheny in the scandal of the Elk Hills naval oil reserve. Doheny and other oilmen persuaded the federal government that the best way to conserve the oil on western public lands, against the possibility of a future war in the Pacific, was to extract the oil and store it in tanks. With Secretary of the Interior Albert B. Fall, an old friend and a former fellow prospector, Doheny arranged to lease and develop the federal oil lands in the Elk Hills field in western Kern County. A large part of the oil was to be stored in tanks, which Doheny agreed to build for the government on the west coast and at Pearl Harbor.

Fall received a payment of $100,000 in cash, which Doheny's son brought to him in a satchel. Later, Fall was convicted of taking this money as a bribe, but Doheny was acquitted of having bribed him with it. Doheny insisted that in his own view, the payment had been simply a loan to an old friend. To Fall $100,000 was a large sum but it was a trifling amount to Doheny, whose fortune exceeded $100 million. In spite of the legal determination that Doheny was innocent of criminal intent and Fall was guilty of it, the government in a civil suit won a cancellation of Doheny's leases on the ground that they had been obtained through a bribe.

By another irony, the whole Elk Hills affair was regarded at the time as less important than the scandal of the Teapot Dome reserve in Wyoming. For a similar leasing arrangement, operator Harry F. Sinclair paid Fall $300,000, presumably reflecting Teapot Dome's greater richness. But that field proved to be relatively unimportant, whereas Elk Hills proved to be the second-largest field in the nation.

The Automobile Revolution

The vast, deep pools of oil that were discovered in the Los Angeles basin in the early 1920s proved extraordinarily rich in gasoline. Thus, huge quantities of this great source of motive power became available at the very time and in the very region where the use of the automobile was spreading more rapidly than in any other time or place in history. In the early decades of the oil industry, gasoline had been a worse-than-useless by-product of the refineries, important only because of the difficult and dangerous problem of getting rid of it. But in the automobile age, gasoline became the most valuable ingredient in a barrel of oil, and the refineries were completely redesigned to extract as much of it as possible.

At the turn of the century, there were only about 4000 horseless carriages in America, and they were toys of the rich, but major turning points came when Henry Ford introduced his Model T in 1908 and when one of these remarkable cars set a new record for automobile travel a year later by crossing the continent in a mere 22 days, arriving in San Francisco with New York air still in its two front tires. This achievement proved that an inexpensive car could be a good one and that long-distance travel would soon be practical. At the same time, the reports of the primitive road conditions that the Ford had encountered dramatized the need for highways that would "get the country out of the mud."

In nineteenth-century America the counties were responsible for the building and maintenance of roads, but they had notoriously failed to perform this function either efficiently or honestly. In California the Southern Pacific used its control of county government to concentrate road building almost exclusively on feeders for its railroad lines. Some improvement came in the 1880s and 1890s, when bicycling became the rage and when the League of American Wheelmen became important as a better-roads lobby. Demands of farmers for passable roads increased with the establishment of rural free delivery of mail in 1894. Denunciations of glaring waste and corruption on the part of county road overseers led to the creation of a California state bureau of highways in 1895, but it had only research and advisory powers.

Two private organizations of motorists, the Automobile Club of Southern California, with headquarters in Los Angeles, and the California State Automobile Association, with headquarters in San Francisco, were formed in 1900. With many wealthy and influential people on their boards of directors, they soon became major forces in the battle for good roads. In 1909 the California legislature authorized a bond issue of $18 million for the beginning of a system of paved state highways, and the voters approved the bonds in the general election the next year.

Financial support from the national government began with the Highway Aid Act of 1916, which provided dollar-matching grants to the states. Another major source of money was the state gasoline tax. First discovered by the Oregon legislature in 1919, this form of revenue had several outstanding advantages. With obvious fairness, it apportioned the cost of highways among the users of them, and the tax was relatively painless because it was paid in driblets as a part of the price of the commodity. With funds for highways thus ensured, the age of motorization was ready to come into full flower.

Mass motorization transformed California and, most of all, southern California, where climate, scenery, and boosterism combined with low gasoline prices and increasingly good roads to make the region a motorist's paradise. From 1920 to 1930, the population of Los Angeles County more than doubled, from less than a million to 2,208,492. The number of registered private automobiles quintupled, rising to 806,264. By 1925 the city of Los Angeles had one automobile for every three persons—more than twice the national average. Los Angeles became the most thoroughly motorized and motor-conscious city in the world.

It was also the first American metropolis whose major expansion occurred entirely within the automobile era, and the automobile intensified a process that Henry Huntington's Pacific Electric had begun—the freeing of the people of Los Angeles from the urban centralization that the limitations of the streetcar had enforced on other great American cities. With their own cars, people could live at a considerable distance from their work, and could own their homes, with lawns, flowers, and shrubbery. With the coming of the great construction boom of the 1920s, Los Angeles soon had a larger ratio of single-family residences and a lower population density than any other large city in the United States. The modern supermarket, designed for customers who could provide their own transportation for large quantities of groceries, was born in Los Angeles. And Wilshire Boulevard's

The automobile spawned a remarkable tradition of roadside vernacular architecture. Shown here is an early drive-in restaurant in Santa Monica Canyon featuring "service in your car." (*Courtesy of American Stock Photos, Los Angeles.*)

"Miracle Mile" was probably the first large business district in the world to be created especially for the automobile age.

Tourism increased enormously in a great new wave of the American westward movement, and auto camps and tourist cabins sprang up. Service stations became a major new institution. The first of them has been credited to Earl B. Gilmore, whose father had bought land for a dairy farm on a part of the Hancock family's domain, once the Rancho La Brea. A substantial oil field had been opened there in 1901, near the famous pits that had held the bones of prehistoric animals mired in the tar. When Wilshire Boulevard was extended from Los Angeles to the beach at Santa Monica in 1909, Earl Gilmore was just out of Stanford. He put a tank on a farm wagon, painted it red and yellow, parked it at the corner of Wilshire Boulevard at La Brea Avenue, and sold gasoline from his father's nearby refinery—at 10 cents a gallon.

"Our forefathers," said the *Los Angeles Times* in 1926, "in their immortal independence creed set forth 'the pursuit of happiness' as an inalienable right of mankind. And how can one pursue happiness by any swifter and surer means . . . than by the use of the automobile?" Such was the spirit that dominated the prosperous twenties for better and sometimes for worse. The motorcar contributed heavily, for example, to the deterioration of personal morals in the era of jazz, hip flasks, and flappers, for an automobile was a reasonable facsimile of a private room, readily transportable beyond the reach of chaperones.

Quite as revolutionary as the effects of the internal combustion engine on the cities were its effects on agriculture and on rural life. The automobile put an end to the isolation of rural areas and reduced the differences in outlook between the farmer and the city dweller, the truck brought much greater flexibility to agricultural marketing, and the tractor was one of the most crucial laborsaving devices ever invented. Tractor factories had been greatly expanded during their temporary conversion to military purposes during World War I, after the British government had placed huge orders with California's Holt Manufacturing Company for certain vehicles. In a successful effort to surprise the Germans on the western front, the British had circulated the information that the Holt contracts were merely for tanks to carry water for British troops in the deserts of Mesopotamia. In fact, of course, these tanks were armored artillery vehicles with caterpillar treads.

Even during the great depression of the 1930s the use of the automobile continued to increase, particularly in California. Both the city workers and the agricultural migratory laborers kept their cars, even when they were unemployed and on relief.

The Movies Discover California

Of the machines that changed American life in the first half of the twentieth century, the movie camera was as important as the internal combustion engine in the degree of its influence. To comparable degrees, also, the history of the movies and the history of the automobile were especially intertwined with the history of southern California.

At the turn of the century and for several years afterward, most American films were made in New York or New Jersey. The first substantial American narrative film was *The Great Train Robbery,* an 8-minute western made by Edwin E. Porter in the New Jersey countryside in 1903, for Thomas A. Edison's film company. This thrilling production told of a mail train holdup, the formation of a posse, and the pursuit and killing of the desperadoes. By taking the camera outdoors, on location, and by joining together bits of film shot in different places and at different times, Porter pioneered the whole technique of film editing that made possible the development of the motion picture as a truly distinctive art.

At this time Edison and a few others controlled the American patents on cameras and projectors, but a number of pirate film producers sprang up, and a bitter struggle developed. William Selig, who began to make movies in Chicago, was among the many independents who were harrassed by Edison's lawyers. It occurred to Selig that if he made his pictures in a more remote part of the country, it would be harder for Edison's subpoena servers to interfere with his operations. Late in 1907 a director and a cameraman in the employ of Selig arrived in southern California to film the outdoor scenes of a one-reel production of *The Count of Monte Cristo,* and early in 1908 they set up a studio on Main Street in downtown Los Angeles.

Another Chicago producer, George K. Spoor, had recently organized the Essanay Film Manufacturing Company, in partnership with Gilbert M. Anderson (the "A" in Essanay). Anderson, born Max Aronson in Little Rock, Arkansas, was a young ex-vaudevillian who had become famous as the star of *The Great Train Robbery,* and was known as Broncho Billy. Essanay was devoted largely to westerns, for which there was now an insatiable demand, and it obviously made more sense to produce westerns in the far west than in Chicago—not to mention the relatively greater freedom from legal harassment. In 1908 Anderson experimented with various sites in the San Francisco Bay region and finally selected the canyon and ranch area near Niles, a short distance southeast of Oakland. There, during the next 6 years, Essanay ground out 375 one-reel westerns, one a week—all featuring the rugged, valiant, kindly cowboy Broncho Billy. This studio also produced some of the first great comedies of Charlie Chaplin.

In 1909 Edison led seven American film companies and two French ones in pooling their patent claims and forming a group that would often be denounced as "the movie trust" because it claimed the right to deny licenses for filmmaking to all other companies. For several years, until the trust itself was prosecuted and dissolved as a conspiracy in restraint of trade in violation of the Sherman Act, the industry produced almost as many lawsuits as movies. Selig and Essanay, having become members of the trust, were no longer harried by legal charges of patent infringement. But a number of other companies, left outside the favored group and finding themselves more harried than ever, discovered that the Los Angeles suburb of Hollywood offered a very special advantage as a location for independent producers: It was fairly close to the international boundary. When process servers and confiscators of cameras appeared, the precious equipment and film stocks could be hastily packed into automobiles and rushed to safety across the Mexican border.

The environs of Los Angeles also had other and more permanent advantages for moviemaking, and these appealed to members of the trust as well as to independents. Movie cameras had not yet been developed to the point where they functioned reliably with artificial light alone; thus indoor scenes often had to be filmed in sets that were at least partially open to natural light, and there were fewer rainy days in Hollywood than in New York or Chicago. As for outdoor settings, within a few miles of the Hollywood studios were scenes that would substitute for any locale a plot might call for—from the Sahara Desert to the French Riviera, or the battlefield of Gettysburg. Early in 1910 D. W. Griffith brought a company of Biograph players to Los Angeles, where he used Mission San Gabriel for scenes in *The Thread of Destiny: A Story of the Old Southwest,* and a few weeks later he achieved striking new camera effects by photographing the southern California countryside from great distances in a production of *Ramona.*

Eventually the phrase "a Hollywood production" became an even more familiar and valuable asset in the advertising of movies than was the brand name "Sunkist" in the advertising of oranges. Even more than the orange groves, the movies increased southern California's romantic appeal and became a major factor in its burgeoning growth.

The Rise of "The Industry"

A long strike of vaudeville actors in 1900 had led the theater managers, for the first time, to show programs consisting solely of movies. The rental of a series of short films cost less than the wages of a series of vaudeville actors, and the theater owners discovered not only that they could make a profit with an admission charge of only 5 cents, but also that a vast audience, especially of immigrants in the large cities, would flock to see even the crudest films at that modest price. Soon there were thousands of new movie houses called *nickelodeons,* a charming word formed by combining the price of admission and the Greek word for "theater."

Thus, when the movies first came into mass production, they were the poor person's entertainment. Not only the audiences but also the distributors and producers of the early films were drawn very largely from the ranks of people who were struggling to rise from poverty. "Respectable" businesspeople and financiers shunned the infant movie industry as a possible investment. As Polish-born scholar Leo Rosten has put it, "The men who built the motion picture industry . . . were not drawn from the supposedly farsighted ranks of American business," but from "the marginal and shabby zones of enterprise, from vaudeville, nickelodeon parlors, theatrical agencies, flea circuses, petty trade." William Fox, born in Hungary, worked as a cloth sponger in New York before he opened a penny arcade and then a nickelodeon in Brooklyn. Jesse L. Lasky began his working life as a vaudeville cornet player in San Francisco. His brother-in-law, Samuel Goldwyn, was born Schmuel Gelbfisz in Poland, ran away from home in Warsaw, arrived in New York alone as a steerage passenger at 13, and began work as a glove salesman. Louis B. Mayer, born in Russia, spent part of his boyhood as a rag collector in Saint John, New Brunswick. Marcus Loew and Adolph Zukor were small fur dealers before they became partners in the theater business.

All these men were deeply sensitive about their origins. Only one member of the group, Lewis J. Selznick, took public pride in his humble beginnings. Hearing of the abdication of the czar in March 1917, he sent him a famous and fascinating cablegram: "WHEN I WAS POOR BOY IN KIEV YOUR POLICEMEN WERE NOT KIND TO ME STOP I CAME TO AMERICA AND PROSPERED STOP NOW HEAR WITH REGRET YOU ARE OUT OF JOB OVER THERE STOP FEEL NO ILL WILL . . . SO IF YOU WILL COME NEW YORK CAN GIVE YOU FINE POSITION ACTING IN PICTURES STOP SALARY NO OBJECT STOP . . . SELZNICK."

In the early years, the moviemakers, especially the members of the trust, were afraid that their mass audience was not intelligent enough to sit through any one picture longer than one reel (about 12 minutes) and too poor to afford the cost of longer and better pictures. But in 1913 the independent producer Jesse L. Lasky and his director, Cecil B. DeMille, made the first American feature-length movie, *The Squaw Man,* in five reels and proved that longer films could be highly profitable.

Movie patrons had begun to favor certain players by 1910, but the companies in the trust would not advertise the names of actors and actresses lest they demand higher salaries. It was the independents who discovered the star system, through which they could achieve an unbroken succession of hits by featuring personalities so consistently attractive that the patrons would line up at the box office no matter what the quality of the films. Within a few years, salaries of featured players leaped from a maximum of $15 a day to an average of $1500 a week. To the movie audiences, the stars were figures of personified desire or symbols of the great moving forces of comedy or tragedy. Gladys Smith from Canada became better known as Mary Pickford, or "America's Sweetheart," in which capacity she received $500,000 a year by 1915.

Movie audiences, centering their attention on the stars, have never developed an appreciation of the role of directors, but within the industry the vital importance of their function soon came to be recognized. Directors fuse the script, the performers, the camera operators, and the technicians into a single pattern, a motion picture. Ultimately their conception determines the story, what it means, and how it is told.

David Wark Griffith was the first great American director, and his film *The Birth of a Nation* was a remarkable motion picture, especially in such technological achievements as its filming of Civil War battle scenes. But it was also a racist distortion of American history, and because it was more widely shown and left a deeper emotional imprint on its audiences than almost any other film before or since, it stands as a classic example of both the enormous potential power of the art of the cinema and the possibilities for misuse of that power. Griffith was the son of a brigadier general in the Confederate Army, and his film, based on Thomas Dixon's novel *The Clansman,* glorified the role of the Ku Klux Klan in the reconstruction of the south and portrayed black people as an inferior race.

After a special showing of the film at the White House, President Wilson was reported to have said that "it is like writing history with lightning, and my one regret is that it is all so terribly true." Wilson was himself a southerner by birth and early education, and it was during his presidency that lunchrooms, drinking fountains, and lavatories in government buildings in the District of Columbia were racially segregated for the first time since the Civil War. But if President Wilson could see nothing wrong with *The Birth of a Nation,* there were many Americans who could; in the face of a great outcry from critics of the film, Wilson publicly disavowed his endorsement of it. The denunciations, however, merely gave it additional advertising. By 1930 more than 100 million people had seen *The Birth of a Nation,* and by 1948 it had grossed nearly $50 million. It did more to fasten racial stereotypes on the American mind than anything since *Uncle Tom's Cabin,* and it was partly responsible for the great revival of the Ku Klux Klan that reached its height in the 1920s.

A film of special significance in the cultural history of California was *Greed* (1923), based on Frank Norris's novel *McTeague, a Story of San Francisco,* and directed by Erich von Stroheim. It was extravagantly produced and became a financial disaster that led to the decline of its director's career. The novel so fascinated von Stroheim that he filmed it not merely chapter by chapter but line by line, and not on artificial sets but in actual rooms and streets in San Francisco and actual places in Death Valley. After he had spent 6 months in reducing its enormous bulk, the film was still more than 4 hours long. When he refused to edit it further, the Metro-Goldwyn-Mayer executives took it out of his hands and turned it over to a cutter, who reduced it from 24 reels to 11. Von Stroheim refused to look at it again, though even in this mutilated form it was one of the greatest of all motion pictures.

Gradually the movies escaped from their earlier status as an essentially lower-class form of entertainment and began to make a very successful appeal to the middle classes. In the 1920s theater owners in all the larger cities erected huge movie palaces, with lavish ornamentation and regiments of uniformed ushers.

The movies both reflected and accelerated the prevailing trend toward the urbanization of American attitudes and mores. Before 1917 more than half the films made in the United States had portrayed rural scenes and praised the simple values of rural life, but a survey made in the 1920s revealed that even rural audiences had begun to react unfavorably to films with rustic themes and characters, a trend that the theatrical trade paper *Variety* reported under the famous headline "STIX NIX HIX PIX."

Cecil B. DeMille, the leading director for Paramount Pictures, both anticipated and helped create the shift in moral attitudes that occurred in the war and postwar years. Between 1918 and 1921, in such pictures as *Forbidden Fruit, Male and Female, Why Change Your Wife?* and *For Better or For Worse,* DeMille showed movie audiences in intimate detail the things that they should not do, and although these films came around to defending the institution of marriage in the final scenes, they also portrayed human weakness very sympathetically.

Typical of the opulent movie palaces of the 1920s was Grauman's Chinese Theater in Hollywood, here being readied for its first film, the 1927 premier of Cecil B. DeMille's *The King of Kings. (Courtesy of Bison Archives.)*

Some of Hollywood's most famous stars began to set unfortunate examples of flamboyant misconduct in their personal lives, notably Roscoe ("Fatty") Arbuckle, Mary Miles Minter, Mabel Normand, and Wallace Reid. In the face of much criticism, the leaders of the industry persuaded Will H. Hays of Indiana to leave his position of postmaster general in President Harding's cabinet and become the "czar of the movies," with power to draw up a new moral code. The plan of movie self-censorship that emanated from the Hays Office, as it was known, decreed that evil must never be made attractive and must always be punished. The chief result was a series of films that were ostensibly exhortations to repentance and reform, but still managed to include a great deal of sex and violence. DeMille, in particular, was highly successful in adapting to the Hays Office format in his productions of *The Ten Commandments* (1923) and *The King of Kings* (1927).

As the movies became big business, five major and three lesser companies emerged to dominate the film-producing industry. The big five were Loew's (including Metro-Goldwyn-Mayer as its production subsidiary), Warner Brothers, Paramount, Radio-Keith-Orpheum (RKO), and Twentieth Century Fox. The other three were Columbia, Universal, and United Artists.

The introduction of talkies, movies with synchronized sound, pulled the industry out of a temporary slump in 1927, and throughout the great depression of the 1930s it remained more prosperous than most other industries because the public craving for its chief product—escape—was greater than ever. In 1941 there were more moving-picture theaters than banks in the United States. Attendance reached an all-time peak in 1945, but the great period of the movies ended soon after World War II, with the beginning of the rise of television. If the automobile had done much to break up the American family, the television set did just as much to bring it together again, though on a very passive basis.

Selected Bibliography

The emergence of southern California as a distinct regional culture is the subject of Kevin Starr, *Inventing the Dream* (1985) and *Material Dreams: Southern California through the 1920s* (1990). A more popular account may be found in Bruce Henstell, *Sunshine and Wealth: Los Angeles in the Twenties and Thirties* (1984).

The best recent contributions to the history of the California oil industry are Martin R. Answell, *Oil Baron of the Southwest: Edward L. Doheny and the Development of the Petroleum Industry in California* (1998); Margaret Leslie Davis, *The Dark Side of Fortune: Triumph and Scandal in the Life of Oil Tycoon Edward L. Doheny* (1998); Jules Tygiel, *The Great Los Angeles Swindle: The Julian Petroleum Scandal and 1920s America* (1994); and Dan La Botz, *Edward L. Doheny: Petroleum, Power, and Politics in the United States and Mexico* (1991). Gerald T. White, *Formative Years in the Far West: A History of Standard Oil Company of California* (1962), includes excellent material on the background of the industry as a whole. See also his *Scientists in Conflict: The Beginnings of the Oil Industry in California* (1968), and Kenny A. Franks and Paul F. Lambert, *Early California Oil* (1985). Thomas R. Bard's career is the subject of W. H. Hutchinson, *Oil, Land and Politics* (2 volumes, 1965). White's "California's Other Mineral," *Pacific Historical Review,* XXXIX (May 1970), pp. 135–154, is one of several articles in an issue titled "The Petroleum Industry."

On various economic and social aspects, see Scott Lee Bottles, *Los Angeles and the Automobile* (1987); Fred W. Viehe, "Black Gold Suburbs: The Influence of the Extractive Industry on the Suburbanization of Los Angeles, 1890–1930," *Journal of Urban Studies,* VIII (November 1981), pp. 3–26; R. M. Fogelson, *The Fragmented Metropolis: Los Angeles, 1850–1930* (1967); and Ashleigh E. Brilliant, "Social Effects of the Automobile in Southern California during the Nineteen-Twenties," Ph.D. thesis, University of California, Berkeley (1964), and "Some Aspects of Mass Motorization in Southern California, 1919–1929," *Southern California Quarterly,* XLVII (June 1965), pp. 191–208. On tourism, see John F. Sears, *Sacred Places* (1989) and *Motoring Tourists and the Scenic West* (1989).

The coming of the film industry to California is described in Geoffrey Bell, *The Golden Gate and the Silver Screen* (1984), and Donald B. Parkhurst, "Broncho Billy and Niles, California," *Pacific Historian,* XXVI (Winter 1982), pp. 1–22. Major contributions to the history of motion pictures include Tom Gunning, *D. W. Griffith and the Origins of the American Narrative Film* (1991); Bernard F. Dick, *Columbia Pictures* (1991); Arthur Knight, *The Liveliest Art* (1957); and A. R. Fulton, *Motion Pictures* (1960). Leo C. Rosten's *Hollywood* (1939) is a survey of the industry as it was in the late 1930s, written with the aid of a team of social scientists. Hortense Powdermaker, *Hollywood, the Dream Factory* (1950), presents an anthropologist's view. On censorship, see Raymond Moley, *The Hays Office* (1945), and Ruth A. Inglis, *Freedom of the Movies* (1947).

CHAPTER 24

Controversies over Land and Water

Nineteenth-century Americans had regarded their country's natural resources as inexhaustible and had exploited them with the greatest recklessness. In the progressive era, however, interest in conservation greatly increased. California's natural resources were so spectacular and the controversies over their use and development were so complicated and intense that the issues and problems of conservation inevitably became a major theme in the state's history.

The Yosemite and John Muir

One of the many tributes to the incomparable beauty of the Yosemite Valley was the fact that it was the first area in the United States to be designated by the federal government as a park. This action was also one of the first historical landmarks in the growth of the modern sense of public responsibility for conservation in America.

The strongest impetus for creation of a Yosemite Park came from the country's leading landscape architect, Frederick Law Olmsted. In 1864, largely as a result of Olmsted's urging, Congress passed and President Lincoln signed an act granting the Yosemite Valley and the Mariposa Grove of Big Trees to the state of California. Olmsted was then appointed by the governor as the first chairman of the Yosemite State Park Commission. There was no precedent for the idea of a *national* park, but federal grants of land to the states for an assortment of other purposes were so frequent that the proposal for a park met little opposition.

Almost as important in the history of conservation as Yosemite Park itself was the personality of John Muir, who first came to the valley as a young man in 1868 and was never again entirely happy anywhere else. The valley and the mountains around it inspired him to a lifetime of writings and crusades that proclaimed his gospel of humanity's rebirth through the enjoyment of nature's beauty and of humanity's obligation to preserve that beauty as a sacred trust.

Muir had been born in Scotland—"with heather in him," as he said—and had spent his boyhood on a wilderness farm in Wisconsin. Almost from infancy his father forced him to a regimen of memorizing great parts of the Bible, an influence that was very apparent in his later thinking and writing. A good example was his famous description of the Sierra Nevada as he first saw it after he had landed at San Francisco and walked southward from Oakland to Gilroy and thence to the summit of Pacheco Pass. Across the Central Valley on a clear morning, the great range "seemed not clothed with light but wholly composed of it, like the wall of some celestial city. . . . It seemed to me that the Sierra should be called, not the Nevada or Snowy Range, but the Range of Light."

After a short time in the Yosemite region, Muir wrote in his diary that "John the Baptist was not more eager to get all of his fellow sinners into the Jordan than I to baptize all of mine in the beauty of God's mountains." "Climb the mountains and get their good tidings," he wrote in his first book, *The Mountains of California.*

Scottish-born naturalist John Muir (1838–1914) was the founder and first president of the Sierra Club. (*Courtesy of the John Muir Papers, Holt-Atherton Department of Special Collections, University of the Pacific Libraries. Copyright 1984 Muir-Hanna Trust.*)

"Nature's peace will flow into you as sunshine flows into trees. The winds will blow their freshness into you and the storms their energy, while cares will drop off like autumn leaves."

Although Muir had studied geology and botany at the University of Wisconsin, he was not a scientist but rather a brilliant amateur naturalist. His essentially religious approach to nature was a blend of theism and pantheism. God, he felt, was "ensouled as a Principle in all forms of matter." Believing that evolution was not mere chance and survival of the fittest, Muir insisted that humanity, like nature in general, evolved by cooperation rather than competition. Thus, Muir offered a philosophy of society as well as a philosophy of nature. Brought into their true relationship with the wilderness, humanity would see that they were not a separate entity but an integral part of a harmonious whole. Human beings had no right to subdue their fellow creatures or to appropriate and destroy their common heritage; to do so brought unbalance in nature and loss and poverty for all.

In 1889 Muir gained an important ally in Robert Underwood Johnson, one of the editors of the *Century* magazine. On a tour of the central Sierra, Muir convinced Johnson that the Yosemite was being poorly protected under state control and pointed out the devastation that sheep—those "hoofed locusts"—were being allowed to inflict on the mountain valleys of the region. Johnson urged Muir to carry his appeal to the people of the whole nation through articles in the *Century.*

For the next 15 years, the California legislature resisted the demands of Muir and his admirers that the state return the Yosemite Valley to the federal government, but in 1890 the eloquent writings of "great Nature's priest," as Johnson called Muir, aroused so much national emotion that Congress set aside a large area surrounding the valley as a national forest reserve administered by the secretary of the interior, who designated it Yosemite National Park. At the same time, Congress created the Sequoia National Park and the General Grant, which was later incorporated in Kings Canyon. The creation of Sequoia incidentally ensured the final eviction of Burnette Haskell's socialistic Kaweah colony, and the biggest *Sequoiadendron giganteum,* which the Kaweahns had named the "Karl Marx tree," was hastily renamed the "General Sherman."

In 1892 Muir founded the Sierra Club, an organization as enthusiastically devoted to conservationist lobbying as it was to mountaineering.

With Theodore Roosevelt's accession to the presidency in September 1901, conservation gained another ally. Indeed, Roosevelt was soon identifying the whole conservation movement as "my policy." Roosevelt's love of the outdoors was as deep and personal as that of John Muir, but the conservation philosophies of the two men were very different. Muir's views were part of a movement known as *preservationism,* or *aesthetic conservationism.* The preservationists believed that the true object of conservation was to maintain the beauty of the wilderness in its natural state. Roosevelt was more of a *utilitarian conservationist,* in that he supported the techniques of scientific forest management. In spite of their differences, Roosevelt in 1903 requested that Muir serve as his personal guide on a 4-day pack trip in the Yosemite region.

With such powerful allies, it was only a matter of time before Muir and his followers would prevail in their struggle to win federal protection for the Yosemite Valley. At last, in 1905, the California legislature approved the recession of the Yosemite Valley to the federal government. A year later Congress approved the merging of the valley with the surrounding national park. Yosemite National Park today remains a monument to one of the great victories of the California conservation movement.

The Hetch Hetchy Controversy

The city dweller, as well as the farmer, naturally attached great importance to an ensured supply of water. San Francisco was worried by its dependence on the limited nearby resources of the Spring Valley Water Company. In 1900 a new city charter authorized a larger and municipally owned water system. The city engineer reported that the Hetch Hetchy Valley on the Tuolumne River in Yosemite National Park was the ideal site, superior to any of the possible alternatives. Mayor James D. Phelan applied to the secretary of the interior for permission to convert the Hetch Hetchy Valley into a reservoir, but the moment John Muir heard of the plan, he mobilized his forces for battle, and they fought so valiantly that the federal government delayed its final approval of the project for 13 years.

Hetch Hetchy was about 20 miles northwest of its sister valley, the Yosemite. Though only about half as long and half as wide as its much more famous neighbor, it bore a striking and charming resemblance to it and was called by Muir the "other Yosemite." But Hetch Hetchy was so nearly inaccessible that very few people except Muir and some other members of the Sierra Club had ever seen it. Muir called the flooding of Hetch Hetchy as great a sacrilege as the destruction of a cathedral and denounced the proponents of it in the strongest terms he could think of.

James D. Phelan, an outstanding patron of the arts, was outraged at the accusation that he was callously indifferent to beauty. He denounced Muir in return and stoutly asserted that a lake, as well as a valley, could be beautiful.

Phelan and his supporters also argued that while the use of Hetch Hetchy would be granted free of charge, the possible alternative sites not only were inferior and inadequate but also were all controlled by private interests who wished to sell them to the city at exorbitant prices. Considerable weight was given to this argument by sensational revelations concerning the designs of the Bay Cities Water Company. This corporation proposed to construct a water system, which it would sell to the city for $10.5 million, and in 1906 the Union Labor board of supervisors actually voted approval of the project. But this action was hastily reversed in the following year when the confessions of Boss Ruef and the supervisors revealed that the total estimated cost of the project was only $7.5 million; that of the $3 million of estimated profit, the company had promised $1 million as a fee to Ruef; and that Ruef had promised to divide half this money among the supervisors in return for their votes. This project, if it had been consummated, would have been by far the largest of all Ruef's corrupt transactions.

The federal government, sure of being denounced by someone for any action it might take in the Hetch Hetchy matter, vacillated and temporized. The settlement of the long struggle came at last in 1913, essentially because it happened that President Wilson's choice for secretary of the interior was Franklin K. Lane, who had been city attorney of San Francisco under Mayor Phelan and had written many of the city's briefs in the fight. With the weight of the new secretary thrown into the scales, Congress gave final permission for the Hetch Hetchy project. John Muir, defeated by this shift in the sands of politics, was brokenhearted and died a few months later.

The Owens Valley–Los Angeles Aqueduct

San Francisco's chief source of water, the Tuolumne River, begins its flow at the foot of a glacier on Mount Lyell. Only 15 miles eastward across the Sierra divide are the headwaters of the Owens River, the stream to which Los Angeles reached out as the first of the great and distant new sources of water that its phenomenal twentieth-century growth would require. The story of the Owens Valley–Los Angeles Aqueduct involved controversies even more bitter than the struggle over Hetch Hetchy.

The man who conceived the Owens Valley Aqueduct project was Fred Eaton, city engineer of Los Angeles in the 1890s and its mayor from 1899 to 1901. Born in Los Angeles, Eaton had served as superintendent of the city's water system when it was a mere network of open ditches from the Los Angeles River, operated by a private company. For many years Eaton spent his vacations in prospecting for a new water supply. Choosing the Owens River, he recognized that the vital unit in its development would be a storage reservoir near its upper end, in Long Valley, above the main Owens Valley. Hoping for personal enrichment as the just reward of his concern for his native city, he quietly bought the land and the water rights in Long Valley and planned as a private enterprise to sell some of the Owens River water to farmers in Owens Valley and to sell the rest to the city of Los Angeles.

Between 1900 and 1905, the population of that city grew from 102,479 to more than 250,000. Moreover, the rainfall in these years was even less than usual, and in July 1904 Los Angeles came close to the stark terror of a true water famine. The city engineer, William Mulholland, was a former protégé of Eaton's. For years he had responded with friendly ridicule to Eaton's confidential efforts to interest him in the remote Owens Valley. Now, however, Mulholland urgently begged Eaton to "show me this water supply."

In the meantime the United States Reclamation Service had formed a plan to irrigate the Owens Valley. When the federal agency refused to cooperate with Eaton as a private speculator and developer, he agreed to sell his interests to the city of Los Angeles. He also agreed to act as the city's confidential agent in purchasing further lands in Owens Valley necessary for an aqueduct. This he proceeded to do under the guise of buying lands for ranching purposes. The real purpose was to be kept secret as long as possible in order to prevent speculative increases in the price of the land.

The first public knowledge of the aqueduct project came in a long, detailed, and enthusiastic article in the *Los Angeles Times* on July 19, 1905. Not long afterward the *Los Angeles Examiner,* outraged that the *Times* had been permitted to scoop its rivals, published sensational charges of collusion and conspiracy.

Two years before, a syndicate including Harrison Gray Otis, Edwin T. Earl, Henry E. Huntington, and others had acquired options to buy extensive lands in the San Fernando Valley. Under the Owens Valley Aqueduct plan, now revealed, a reservoir just north of Los Angeles would be adjacent to these lands and would provide water for their irrigation as well as for the city's domestic supply. The whole aqueduct project, the *Examiner* charged, had been conceived by the members of this San Fernando land syndicate for their own speculative profit.

This charge, though periodically revived ever since, was based on an erroneous conclusion. The evidence is clear that in 1903 when this group of wealthy men had acquired the San Fernando land options, Eaton's dream of an aqueduct, if they had yet heard of it at all, was not the basis of their plan. Rather, they were acting on inside information from Henry E. Huntington that he was about to build a new line of the Pacific Electric into the San Fernando Valley. The same men were employing this highly profitable technique of group investment in several other prospective suburbs of Los Angeles at this same time.

In a special election in September 1905, the voters of the city overwhelmingly approved an issue of bonds for the beginning of the Owens Valley project. At the end of still another summer of frightening water shortage, the citizens of Los Angeles were in no mood to vote against a plan that promised them an adequate water supply.

The farmers and townspeople of the Owens Valley now began a bitter campaign of denunciation that would continue for decades, charging that the aqueduct was a corrupt scheme to enrich a few of the leading capitalists of Los Angeles by seizing the water that would be needed for the agricultural development of the Owens Valley and using it to irrigate the San Fernando Valley instead. The federal government sided with the city. President Roosevelt was persuaded that the whole future growth of Los Angeles was more important than the interests of "a few settlers in Owens Valley." In 1908, to prevent homestead entries in the path of the proposed aqueduct, Roosevelt ordered the extension of the Sierra National Forest eastward to include the prospective right-of-way, even though the only trees in the region were those planted by the settlers themselves.

Under the direction of City Engineer Mulholland, the construction of the 233-mile aqueduct began in 1908 and ended 5 years later, at a cost within his estimate of $25 million. Unfortunately the aqueduct took its water directly out of the lower Owens River. If a year-to-year storage reservoir in Long Valley had been built when the aqueduct was constructed, or soon afterward, enough water could have been provided to meet the needs of Owens Valley along with those of the city for some time to come, and much bitterness could have been avoided. But Fred Eaton had demanded a price of at least $1 million for his Long Valley land, and Mulholland, breaking his old friendship with Eaton, had condemned the price as too high and advised the city not to pay it. In the early 1920s, a new cycle of dry years and the continuing rapid growth of Los Angeles's population led the city to siphon off

Unidentified saboteurs dynamited the Owens Valley–Los Angeles Aqueduct 14 times in 1927. (*Courtesy of the Bancroft Library.*)

virtually the entire flow of the river, and in 1924 residents of Owens Valley began to dramatize their protests with a campaign of sabotage, which culminated in the dynamiting of several sections of the aqueduct.

Mulholland later succeeded in negotiating a compromise price for Long Valley and a personal reconciliation with Eaton. In 1941, several years after the deaths of Eaton and Mulholland, the dam in Long Valley was completed at last. The volume of water in the Owens River was also increased by extending a long tunnel northward to tap the streams flowing into Mono Lake.

The Boulder Canyon Project

George Chaffey's Imperial Canal and William Mulholland's Owens Valley Aqueduct were temporary and inadequate answers to southern California's insatiable thirst. Seeking access to new sources of water, southern California turned its attention to a vast project for the development of the Colorado River.

Arthur Powell Davis, an engineer for the United States Reclamation Service, had first conceived in 1904 a broad proposal for the development of the lower Colorado under the unified control of the federal government, with a great dam to store the floods and to serve as the heart of the project. The first strong public support for this plan came from the people of the Imperial Valley, who lived in terror of floods. They had not forgotten the catastrophe that began in 1905 when the river burst into the Imperial Canal and created the Salton Sea before it was finally checked in 1907.

The settlers of the valley had many reasons to be dissatisfied with the Imperial Canal, particularly with the fact that its source and the first 50 miles of its flow were in Mexican territory. The Mexican government required that half the canal's water be reserved for the irrigation of Mexican lands, and it held down the price of the water used south of the border so that a much higher price had to be charged on the American side. In 1911 the voters of the Imperial Valley formed the Imperial Irrigation District—the largest of its kind—and approved a bond issue to buy the Imperial Canal. Soon afterward they also began to agitate for an all-American canal, to be built north of the border.

Early in 1922, Secretary of the Interior Fall joined with Arthur Powell Davis, now director of the Reclamation Service, in recommending an extensive plan. Soon afterward their proposals were introduced in Congress in the form of the Swing-Johnson bill. Phil Swing, who had served for several years as chief counsel of the Imperial Irrigation District and had then been elected to Congress, sponsored the bill in the House, and Hiram Johnson gave it his powerful support in the Senate. Six years later it was finally approved as the Boulder Canyon Project Act, but only after a long and bitter struggle in both houses.

Under this plan the federal government was to construct a dam in or near Boulder Canyon, a plant for generating hydroelectric power, and an all-American canal just north of the Mexican border from the river to the Imperial Valley. Leasing of the power to public and private agencies in the region would repay the government for the cost of building the dam, and the Imperial Irrigation District would ultimately repay the cost of building the canal. The city of Los Angeles soon joined with the Imperial Valley in ardent support of the Boulder Canyon project. William Mulholland warned Los Angeles that its growth was outstripping its supply of water from the Owens Valley, and he called for construction of a much larger aqueduct as soon as possible, with the Colorado River as its source.

On the other hand, the federal project aroused tremendous opposition. The first difficulty to be surmounted was a wrangle among the seven states in the Colorado River area. The upper-basin states of Wyoming, Colorado, Utah, and New Mexico complained that all the benefits would go to the lower-basin states of Arizona, Nevada, and California, whose development would be so stimulated that they would gain an unfair share of the water under the laws of prior appropriation. In November 1922 Secretary of Commerce Herbert Hoover persuaded representatives of all seven states to agree to the Colorado River Compact, assuring the upper basin of a permanent claim to about half the flow of the river. Six of the state legislatures ratified the compact, but Arizona balked and began an opposition to the Boulder Canyon project that continued for years and a quarrel with California that continued for decades.

Further opposition came from the American owners of irrigated lands in Mexico, of whom the most notable was Harry Chandler, the son-in-law, heir, and successor of Harrison Gray Otis. Chandler headed a syndicate that owned 862,000 acres of land in Baja California, mainly in the region of the Imperial Canal. Not surprisingly, he and his *Los Angeles Times* denounced the Swing-Johnson bill as a socialistic menace to free American enterprise.

Of all the sources of opposition to the Boulder Canyon project, however, the most formidable were the private power companies. They were then engaged in a national struggle to prevent the federal government from entering the power business. The Swing-Johnson bill provided that the federal government would not act as the distributor of the electric power from the Boulder Canyon project but would lease it to private or municipal corporations, which would build their own transmission lines. Nevertheless, the private companies fought the measure, largely for two reasons. The huge project would reduce the price of power in the southwest by increasing the supply, and much of the power would go to the municipally owned electric system of the city of Los Angeles, thus encouraging its growth at the expense of private companies.

That public ownership and distribution of electric power had come into existence in Los Angeles, a city as passionately committed to private enterprise as any community in the United States, is one of the many striking paradoxes of California history. It was even more remarkable in view of the fact that in northern California the private Pacific Gas and Electric Company (PG&E) achieved an almost complete monopoly over the distribution of power and light. In 1925, after a long controversy, the San Francisco board of supervisors turned over the power from Hetch Hetchy to PG&E. This arrangement was carried out even though Congress in 1913 had flatly forbidden the city to dispose of the power to any private company. Moreover, San Francisco made an almost incredibly bad bargain. PG&E paid the city $2.4 million a year for the Hetch Hetchy power and then retailed the same power for $9 million a year. In sharp contrast the City of Los Angeles Bureau of Power and Light gradually crowded out and acquired the distribution systems of several privately owned electric companies, in a process that those companies regarded as not merely creeping, but galloping, socialism.

Secretary of Commerce Hoover was deeply troubled by the charge that by building a great power plant the federal government would be dealing a heavy blow to a leading American private industry, but he could see no other way to pay for the dam. Hoover's election to the presidency, and the knowledge that he favored the project, finally ended the long battle over its adoption, and the Swing-Johnson bill became law on December 21, 1928.

During the long controversy over the Boulder Canyon project, the name "Boulder Dam" had been unofficially used by both sides of the debate. The official choice of a name for a federal dam, however, was a time-honored prerogative of the secretary of the interior. Dr. Ray Lyman Wilbur, who held that office under President Hoover, chose the name that seemed to him in every way most eminently suitable—Hoover Dam. When the mighty structure was about half finished, Franklin Roosevelt's secretary of the interior, Harold Ickes, declared his intention "to give Boulder dam its original and proper name, which my predecessor in office attempted feloniously to take from it." It was as "Boulder Dam" that President Roosevelt officially dedicated the structure, on September 30, 1935. In 1947 the Republican Eightieth Congress passed a bill to restore the name of "Hoover Dam," and President Truman signed the bill into law. Nevertheless, usage has sometimes continued to vary with partisan preference—or merely with confused recollection.

The building of the dam was a monumental accomplishment. To divert the river from the construction site, four bypass tunnels had to be built through the canyon walls, two on each side. Each of these tunnels was a mile long and 50 feet in diameter with a 3-foot concrete lining. Before any concrete could be poured for the foundation of the dam, the riverbed had to be cleaned down to the bare rock. Then it had to be kept clean and dry during the whole period of construction.

At the base of the dam was the world's largest powerhouse to date, containing the world's largest turbines and generators. They began to operate on September 11, 1936, when President Roosevelt pushed a golden key. Behind the dam was the world's largest reservoir, Lake Mead. Vast as the reservoir was, engineers soberly pointed out that it was doomed to impermanence. They warned that the Colorado would fill Lake Mead with silt within 300 years and that over the next 30 centuries the whole process would have to be repeated 10 times, at each of 10 other possible sites.

The Colorado River Aqueduct

In 1923 Los Angeles and several neighboring communities had begun to plan the formation of a metropolitan water district for the purpose of building the world's longest and largest domestic water supply line, from the Colorado River to the coastal basin. In the discussion of water projects in southern California, it had become impossible to avoid the constant repetition of the phrase "the world's largest."

The Metropolitan Water District of Southern California, officially organized in 1928, originally included Los Angeles and 10 nearby cities. Many others later joined. A $220 million bond issue for the great aqueduct came before the district's voters on September 29, 1931. Although the concern of most of the voters was with water for domestic use, its role in the region's industrial development was equally vital. In 1919, for example, the Goodyear Tire and Rubber Company had become the first major industrial concern to locate a branch plant in Los Angeles because the city could promise the 8 million gallons of water a day that the plant would need. In the crucial petroleum industry, 77,000 gallons of water were required to refine 100 barrels of oil. Later improvements in equipment would enable refineries to recover much of the water and reuse it repeatedly, but in 1930 the Union Oil Company plant at Long Beach was still using more water than all the rest of the city. With such compelling arguments in its favor, the huge bond issue passed by more than five to one. The aqueduct was finished on schedule in 1938, and in 1941 it began to deliver water to the coastal cities.

San Diego remained outside the Metropolitan Water District for several years, partly because it hoped to get water from a branch of the All-American Canal. The city had often shown desperate ingenuity in its long struggle with its water problem. In December 1915, in the midst of a particularly serious drought, it had even signed a contract with a professional rainmaker, Charles M. Hatfield. Promising to fill the Morena reservoir for a fee of $10,000, Hatfield built a number of "evaporating tanks," presumably to send up fumes from some combination of chemicals that remained his professional secret. A few weeks later, a cloudburst caused the

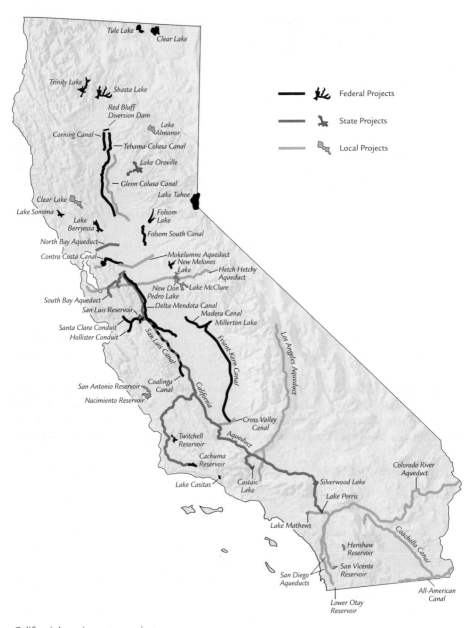

California's major water projects.

reservoir to overflow, washed out a smaller dam below it, and flooded a part of the town. The city council refused to pay Hatfield his fee; they pointed out that he had contracted to fill the reservoir, not to flood the community.

The growth of San Diego during World War II finally compelled the city and its neighbors to form a subgroup of the Metropolitan Water District of Southern

California, and in 1945 construction work began on the first of two branch lines from the Colorado River Aqueduct to the San Diego region.

The Central Valley Project

Proposals for a large government project to aid the advance of irrigation in the great Central Valley were made as early as the 1870s. Strong support for the idea began to crystallize in 1920 when Colonel Robert Bradford Marshall, chief geographer of the United States Geological Survey, but acting in a private capacity, offered the state of California a broad and challenging plan. In its largest features, this was a proposal "to turn the Sacramento River into the San Joaquin Valley" through great canals and to regulate the flow of the upper Sacramento with a high dam near Redding.

On the subject of electric power, the Marshall plan was vague; it said only that "the sale of . . . power at fair rates" would repay much of the cost of the water developments. Many progressives urged that the state government should undertake the public distribution of the power produced by the state-financed water projects, but PG&E was able to block every one of a long series of bills and initiative propositions in the 1920s that would have put the state into the power business. To defeat the proposals for state distribution of water and power, PG&E spent enormous sums through such dummy organizations as the Greater California League. The Greater California League was Eustace Cullinan, a San Francisco attorney for PG&E.

In 1933 the legislature adopted the California Central Valley Project Act. The clinching argument was that California's economy lay prostrate in the grip of the depression and that the Central Valley Project could act as an emergency rescue measure. The state at that time had no real means of being able to pay for the project, and the only hope lay in persuading the federal government to assume the cost. In 1935 the Federal Bureau of Reclamation assumed the responsibility. Construction began in 1937.

The original Central Valley Project, authorized in the 1930s and regarded as the first phase of a much larger program, came into operation as a coordinated system in the 1950s. Its main features were three dams, five canals, and two power transmission lines. The most impressive unit was Shasta Dam, impounding the waters of the Sacramento, McCloud, and Pit rivers in Shasta Lake. Other units were the Friant and Keswick dams and the Friant-Kern, Madera, Delta-Mendota, and Contra Costa canals.

Through all the years when the dams and canals were being built, PG&E managed to block every congressional appropriation for government-owned transmission lines. When the generating plant at Shasta Dam began to produce power in 1944, Secretary of the Interior Ickes had no choice but to negotiate a 5-year agreement for the sale of all this power to PG&E. Repeatedly the company's officials asserted before congressional committees that the Bureau of Reclamation had a "grandiose scheme" for "the socialization of the power industry in northern and central California." As the Southern Pacific had done a few decades earlier, PG&E denounced government infringement on free enterprise, although in both cases it was really monopoly, not free enterprise, which the corporations were fighting to preserve.

At last, through a series of agreements beginning in 1951, PG&E and the federal authorities solved the problem by entering into an uneasy partnership. The Bureau of Reclamation continued to sell power to PG&E; the company agreed, for the first time, to permit the use of its lines for the delivery of federal power from Shasta Dam to the Sacramento Municipal Utility District; and the Bureau of Reclamation was finally able to build its two long-projected transmission lines from Shasta and Keswick dams to its own plant at Tracy for use in pumping water through the Delta-Mendota and Contra Costa canals.

The 160-Acre Limit

Even more controversial than the power question was another issue that involved the federal reclamation laws. The Newlands Reclamation Act of 1902 had provided federal funds for the building of irrigation projects in the arid west. The act limited, however, the amount of water that any one owner of land could obtain from the projects. The maximum was enough water to irrigate 160 acres, or 320 acres in the case of a married couple. The acreage limit was imposed to prevent speculation either by land companies or by the settlers themselves. Family farms, and not large corporate landowners, were to receive the benefits of the irrigation projects.

In California very little was said publicly about this limitation until 1944, and the large landowners indulged in much wishful thinking to the effect that it would never actually be applied to the Central Valley Project. Then, however, the secretary of the interior began to comply with the federal laws that required him to negotiate contracts with irrigation districts, and to include the 160-acre limit in these contracts.

The large landowners of California, including many powerful corporations, now launched a campaign to have the acreage limit set aside. They formed a political coalition with PG&E, supporting that company on power issues in return for its support of their viewpoint on the acreage matter, and this formidable alliance mounted a concerted attack on the Bureau of Reclamation and the Department of the Interior.

In the years of intense debate that followed, much confusion resulted from popular misconceptions, sometimes deliberately fostered. One of these was the widespread and entirely erroneous notion that the 160-acre limit restricted "the amount of land a man could own." What the federal laws actually did was to restrict the amount of federally subsidized water that any one landowner could buy. In 1951, for example, the average price of the best grade of irrigation water from the Central Valley Project was about $2.50 per acre-foot, while the average price for the same grade of water from other sources was $6.77 per acre-foot.

Another misconception was that the owners of land in excess of 160 acres could receive no project water at all unless they contracted to sell the excess land. The truth was that the larger owners were free to buy cheap federal water for a 160-acre *portion* of their land. They could irrigate the rest of it with commercial, or non-project, water. Or they could buy federal water for the larger acreage. It was only if they chose the latter alternative that they were required to sign a contract to sell the excess acres within a certain period of years, at prices that would not allow them an unfair profit from the increase in land values resulting from the federal project.

Congress repeatedly declined to repeal the 160-acre limitation, and the large Central Valley landholders sought relief in the courts. In 1958 the United States Supreme Court unanimously upheld the constitutionality of the acreage limitation. The purpose of the 160-acre limit, the court ruled, was to spread the benefits of federal water projects "in accordance with the greatest good of the greatest number of individuals. This limitation ensures that this enormous expenditure will not go in disproportionate share to a few individuals with large land holdings." The most significant effect of this decision was to convince most of the political leaders of California that any new water projects must be built with state rather than federal funds so that the larger units of land could obtain cheap, publicly subsidized water.

After decades of controversy, California's large landowners scored a partial victory with congressional passage of the Reclamation Reform Act of 1982. This act repealed the 80-year-old 160-acre limit, increasing to 960 acres the amount of land that any one owner could irrigate with water from the federal projects. The act also called for rigorous enforcement of this new, more generous acreage limitation.

Selected Bibliography

Michael Smith, in *Pacific Visions* (1988), gives a masterful account of an emerging environmental consciousness in California. Stephanie S. Pincetl offers a sweeping overview in *Transforming California: A Political History of Land Use in California* (1999). Alfred Runte describes the long-standing struggle over Yosemite in *Yosemite: The Embattled Wilderness* (1990). John Muir is the subject of great and continuing interest. Major works include analyses of Muir and the conservation movement by Steven J. Holmes (1999), Thurman Wilkins (1995), Frederick Turner (1985), Michael P. Cohen (1984), Stephen Fox (1981), Holway R. Jones (1965), and Linnie March Wolfe (1945); an anthology edited by Sally M. Miller (1993); and a bibliography by William E. Kimes and Maymie B. Kimes (1984). See also Susan Schrepfer, *The Fight to Save the Redwoods* (1983), and special issues of *California History,* LXIX (Summer 1990) and LXXI (Summer 1992).

Norris Hundley, *The Great Thirst* (1992), and Sue McClurg, *Water and the Shaping of California* (2000), present comprehensive surveys of California water development. On the Hetch Hetchy controversy, see Kendrick A. Clements, "Politics and the Park," *Pacific Historical Review,* XLVII (May 1979), pp. 185–216, and "Engineers and Conservationists in the Progressive Era," *California History,* LVIII (Winter 1979–1980), pp. 282–303, and Richard Lowitt, "The Hetch Hetchy Controversy," ibid., LXXIV (Summer 1995), pp. 190–203.

The best treatments of the Owens Valley–Los Angeles Aqueduct are in Robert A. Sauder, *Lost Frontier* (1994); Margaret Davis, *River in the Desert* (1993); John Walton, *Western Times and Water Wars* (1992); William L. Kahrl, *Water and Power* (1982); Abraham Hoffman, *Vision or Villainy* (1981); and Remi A. Nadeau, *The Water Seekers* (1950). For a more personal view, see Catherine Mulholland, *William Mulholland and the Rise of Los Angeles*

(2000). Carey McWilliams, *Southern California Country* (1946), revived the syndicate conspiracy version of the Owens Valley project. W. W. Robinson disagreed in "Myth Making in the Los Angeles Area," *Southern California Quarterly,* XLV (March 1963), pp. 83–94.

The Boulder Canyon Project (1941) is a thorough study by economist Paul L. Kleinsorge. Norris Hundley, *Water in the West* (1975), and Beverly B. Moeller, *Phil Swing and Boulder Dam* (1971), discuss the national political problems. See also Joseph E. Stevens, *Hoover Dam* (1988); Mark S. Foster, *Henry J. Kaiser* (1989); Andrew J. Dunbar and Dennie McBride, *Building Hoover Dam* (1993); and Donald E. Wolf, *Big Dams and Other Dreams: The Six Companies Story* (1996).

Donald J. Pisani, *From the Family Farm to Agribusiness* (1984), is a seminal study, as are Donald Worster, *Rivers of Empire* (1985); Marc Reisner, *Cadillac Desert* (1986); Robert Kelley, *Battling the Inland Sea* (1990); and Philip L. Fradkin, *A River No More* (1996). See also the articles in "Water in California," a special issue of *Pacific Historian,* XXVII (Spring 1983), and "Water in the West," a special issue of *Journal of the West,* XXII (April 1983). Useful works on the Central Valley Project are "The Central Valley Project and Related Problems," an edition of the *California Law Review,* XXXVIII (October 1950), and Hugh G. Hansen, *Central Valley Project: Federal or State?* (1955).

Charles M. Coleman, *P.G. and E. of California* (1952), refers to the company's political activities only in very general and favorable terms. A more critical view may be found in Carl D. Thompson, *Confessions of the Power Trust* (1932). See also William A. Myers, *Iron Men and Copper Wires: A Centennial History of the Southern California Edison Company* (1983).

Most of the arguments against the 160-acre limit are collected and elaborated in Sheridan Downey, *They Would Rule the Valley* (1947), "they" being the United States Bureau of Reclamation. The opposite viewpoint is well summarized in Paul S. Taylor, "Excess Land Law: Pressure versus Principle," *California Law Review,* XLVII (August 1959), pp. 499–541, and "Excess Land Law: Calculated Circumvention," ibid., LII (December 1964), pp. 978–1014. See also Clayton R. Koppes, "Public Water, Private Land: Origins of the Acreage Limitation Controversy, 1933–1953," *Pacific Historical Review,* XLVII (November 1978), pp. 607–636, and William D. Rowley, *Reclaiming the Arid West* (1996).

CHAPTER 25

The Great Depression

The prosperity of the 1920s was not well distributed. Proportionally, too much of the national income was in profits and too little in wages, and therefore America's capacity to produce exceeded its capacity to consume. During the 1920s American individualism had too often degenerated into irresponsibility and greed. One manifestation of this trend was the urge to get rich quickly and easily by gambling in the stock market. Millions of speculators bid up the prices of corporate stocks to levels that bore less and less meaningful relation to their true value. The result was the great crash of October 1929, which marked the beginning of the worst and longest depression in American history.

The depression soon spread from Wall Street to San Francisco's Montgomery Street and then to many a small town's Main Street. (See Color Plate 14.) California farm income sank in 1932 to scarcely more than half of what it had been in 1929, and there were thousands of mortgage foreclosures. The number of building permits in 1933 was less than one-ninth the peak figure of 1925. With the spread of mass unemployment in both city and country, the number of Californians dependent on public relief in 1934 was more than 1,250,000—about one-fifth of the whole population of the state. But no mere statistics can convey the real meaning of the great depression. Its meaning was in the suffering, anxiety, and grief of the millions whose lives it blighted.

In California politics, reaction to this disaster came slowly at first. Then it became extreme and frantic. Through the whole decade of depression that followed the crash, politics and government in California remained confused, demoralized, and ineffectual.

"Sunny Jim"

The choice of a governor in 1930, the first year of the depression, represented politics as worse than usual. James Rolph, Jr., had been mayor of San Francisco for

19 years, since his first election in 1911. His early career as mayor was quite cred-itable, but in 1918 he lost the fortune that he had made in the shipping business, and his health and efficiency began to decline. During the 1920s he still com-manded great popular affection, mainly because of the convivial folksiness of his innumerable appearances as the city's official host, greeter, and master of cere-monies. In that "era of wonderful nonsense," he seemed a highly successful large-city mayor, but as governor he was unable to cope with an emergency on the scale of the great depression.

Rolph's most important policy as governor was his opposition to tax reform. His views on taxation were those of the most conservative wing of the business com-munity. Rolph was heavily in debt to one of San Francisco's leading bankers, who was also one of his closest political advisers. The legislature of 1933 adopted a sales tax, with Rolph's approval; but when the legislature also passed an income tax measure, Rolph vetoed it. The burden of the sales tax fell heavily on the poor, and the inclusion of food among the items subject to the tax was especially re-sented. Corner grocers, ringing up small sales, bitterly reminded their customers that they must add "a penny for Jimmy."

In a desperate and deluded attempt to regain his popularity, Rolph made the worst mistake of his career. He openly abetted and defended a lynching. There had been more lynchings in California than in any state outside the south, and more lynchings of white men than in any state whatever. Between 1875 and 1934, Californians participated in 59 lynchings—an average of one per year. At the urging of Delilah Beasley, an African American reporter for the *Oakland Tri-bune,* black assemblyman Fred Roberts sponsored an antilynching bill in the state legislature.

Meanwhile, throughout the country in the early 1930s, there was a wave of kid-nappings, including that of the Lindbergh baby in 1932. At San Jose, on November 26, 1933, two men who had confessed to the kidnapping and murder of the son of a wealthy local merchant were being held in the county jail. When there was talk of mob action, Governor Rolph made a public promise that he would never call out the National Guard "to protect those two fellows." A few hours later, with this open incitement from the governor, a mob broke into the jail, beat the sheriff uncon-scious, and hanged the two prisoners from trees in a nearby park.

Rolph then asserted in another public statement that "this is the best lesson Cali-fornia has ever given the country." He promised to pardon anyone who might be arrested for "the good job" and added that he would like to release all convicted kidnappers from the state prisons into the hands of "those fine, patriotic San Jose citizens who know how to handle such a situation." The lynchers, Rolph theorized, were men with "pioneer blood in their veins," who "were probably reminded of the metage of justice by the vigilantes in the early days of San Francisco's history." As the *New York Times* remarked in a scathing editorial, Judge Lynch had always been a shadowy, unidentified figure. Now there was an actual and visible Governor Lynch.

In 1934 Rolph began another of his picturesque election campaigns. In bur-nished leather boots and a red sash, he inaugurated every fiesta, parade, and rodeo.

An enraged mob batters down the door to the Santa Clara County Jail before pulling two alleged kidnappers from their cells and stringing them up in St. James Park, November 26, 1933. (*Courtesy of the* San Francisco Chronicle.)

But he collapsed during a precampaign tour and died on June 2. Lieutenant Governor Frank Merriam, a Long Beach real estate agent, succeeded him as governor.

Social Messiahs

Californians in the early 1930s were desperately searching for new leadership. It was increasingly clear that they could expect no help from the administrations of President Hoover and Governor Rolph, and the depression was growing steadily worse.

The sufferings of the elderly were especially severe. Thousands of them had come from other parts of the country to retire in Los Angeles or its suburbs. In the 1920s, when they had been able to live fairly comfortably before they lost their savings in the depression, most of them had been conservative in their economic and political ideas, and their interest in colorful leaders had been directed mainly toward religious evangelists. One of these was Sister Aimee Semple McPherson, who preached the "Four Square Gospel" with spectacular theatricality at her Angelus Temple and over her own radio station, KFSG. Sister Aimee also established a relief program for the needy, providing food and clothing for the homeless and destitute of Los Angeles. Another popular southern California evangelist was the Reverend Robert P. Shuler, who operated a rival radio station. In 1926 the

Reverend Mr. Shuler had led the outcry against Sister Aimee when that somewhat tarnished angel was accused of having spent an illicit vacation in Carmel with the director of her radio station during the time when she claimed to have been kidnapped and held for ransom in Mexico. During the early 1930s, Sister Aimee's following declined, not merely because of her personal indiscretions, but because interest was shifting from religious to economic and political evangelism.

Technocracy, which advocated a new society based on scientific management, aroused so much enthusiasm in Los Angeles that chief technocrat Howard Scott moved his headquarters there from the east. In 1933 a group of unemployed businesspeople broke off from the technocratic persuasion to establish the Utopian Society. The utopians drew an overflow crowd for a pageant in the Hollywood Bowl, a spectacle that resembled some of Sister Aimee's productions at Angelus Temple except that it dramatized the triumph not of Good over Evil but of Abundance over Scarcity.

The founder of a much larger and more enduring new movement was Dr. Francis E. Townsend, an unemployed Long Beach physician. At the age of 66, having worked hard all his life, Dr. Townsend was facing destitution. In 1933 he formulated the Townsend Plan and backed it with an organization called Old Age Revolving Pensions, Ltd. All Americans over 60 were to receive pensions of $200 a month, all of which they must spend within 30 days. The money would come from a federal sales tax. This plan, according to Dr. Townsend and his followers, not only would provide a decent living for old people, but also would bring general prosperity by restoring "the proper circulation of money." Though the heart of the movement remained in southern California, Townsend Clubs sprang up all over the nation and soon had a membership of about 1.5 million senior citizens. Their delegates assembled in regional and later in national conventions, where they sang "Onward, Townsend Soldiers." The movement quickly became a powerful force in both state and national politics.

Depression and Deportation

The hard times of the 1930s also contributed to a resurgence of xenophobia and nativism. As in earlier times of crisis, California nativists eagerly sought scapegoats for the state's economic difficulties.

Filipinos were among the first to feel the brunt of antiforeign hostility. White workers complained that recent immigrants from the Philippines were incapable of assimilation and posed an economic threat. Anti-Filipino riots broke out in several rural counties as well as in San Jose and San Francisco. The worst outbreak of violence occurred in 1930, in Watsonville, where one Filipino was killed and several others were badly beaten. "In many ways it was a crime to be a Filipino in California," recalled farmworker and writer Carlos Bulosan.

The hostility culminated in a demand for the deportation of all Filipino workers. In 1935 Congress passed the Filipino Repatriation Act, offering to pay the transportation expenses of any Filipinos who wished to return to their homeland. The

Substantial numbers of Filipinos, such as the asparagus workers pictured here, began arriving in California in the mid-1920s. They suffered sporadic attacks by white farm laborers throughout the following decade. (*Courtesy of the Bank of Stockton Historical Photo Collection.*)

act also prohibited Filipinos thus repatriated from reentering the United States. More than 2000 persons left under the terms of the act.

Far more effective was the move to repatriate aliens from Mexico. California nativists charged that Mexican immigrants were taking much-needed jobs away from American citizens. Nativists also alleged that most Mexicans in California were illegal immigrants and should be barred not only from employment, but also from all public assistance. The solution seemed obvious: deport the undesirable aliens.

The federal government responded with a program of mass repatriation. Between 1931 and 1933, more than 400,000 Spanish-speaking persons were removed from the United States and sent to Mexico; included were Mexican aliens and American citizens of Mexican ancestry. Federal, state, and local authorities at first encouraged a voluntary exodus, but forced deportations also occurred. In California estimates of the number of deportees ranged from 75,000 to 100,000. The government of Mexico protested the indiscriminate apprehension and deportation of any person, regardless of citizenship, who "looked Mexican." And the *repatriados* and their families complained bitterly of mistreatment. As historian Albert Camarillo has observed, "The Chicano community did not passively accept the indignity

upon it by the governmental deportation drives." The pain of repatriation
d expression in a poignant folk ballad:

Goodbye, my good friends,
You are all witnesses
Of the bad payment they give us.

Labor Strife

In the agonies of the depression, California's long tradition of social violence was
reborn in new and bitter struggles between labor and employers.

California labor problems had always been at their worst in agriculture, partly
because the growers had always been able to block the development of collective
bargaining. When the depression turned most of the farm regions into economic disaster areas, labor relations became worse than ever before. Agricultural workers, ill-
fed or unfed, had to suffer the peculiar misery of watching food crops rot because
they could not be sold for enough to pay the costs of harvesting and marketing.

Women performed much of the most arduous work in the canneries—peeling,
cutting, and pitting the fruit. And it was women who often took the lead in mobi-
lizing discontented workers to protest unfair and oppressive conditions. Excluded
from the protection of existing labor laws, women in the canneries worked 16-hour
days for 15 cents an hour. When women cannery workers struck in the Santa Clara
Valley in 1931, police responded by breaking up a mass meeting with tear gas and
fire hoses. About half the officers of the newly organized United Cannery, Agricultural, Packing, and Allied Workers of America (UCAPAWA) were women. Latinas
were among the most effective leaders of the UCAPAWA, including the union's
vice president, Luisa Morena.

Again, as in the days of the IWW, the wretched conditions of the migratory agricultural workers and the general disinterest of conventional labor unions opened
the door to the most extreme radicals, and the radicals played into the hands of the
employers. The Cannery and Agricultural Workers' Industrial Union (CAWIU),
which became active in 1933, was avowedly an arm of the Communist party and
was openly eager to hasten the disintegration of the capitalist system in agriculture.
It provided the leadership for the strikes of the grape pickers at Lodi, the cotton
pickers in the southern San Joaquin Valley in 1933, and the vegetable pickers in the
Imperial Valley in 1934. Employer vigilante groups, sometimes deputized by
county sheriffs, did not hesitate to use violence in crushing these strikes, and the
CAWIU was dissolved when its Communist leaders were arrested and convicted
under the state criminal syndicalism law.

The National Industrial Recovery Act of 1933, in its famous section 7a, recognized the right of employees "to organize and bargain collectively through representatives of their own choosing." In the San Francisco Bay region, where
organized labor had once been strong, the unions took courage from the new federal
law and set out to regain the power they had lost in the 1920s. When the employers

resisted, the struggle became even more violent than in the agricultural regions. Class conflict went to such extremes that police and the National Guard were used to break a strike on the San Francisco waterfront, and in retaliation nearly all the unions in the bay region joined in a general strike in sympathy with the demands of the maritime workers.

The employers in the San Francisco shipping industry had destroyed the power of the International Longshoremen's Association (ILA) in the Bay Area by breaking its strike in 1919. They had used the presence of radicals in several maritime unions as an excuse to destroy unionism itself. From 1919 until 1934, the only longshoremen's union in the San Francisco Bay area was the employer-controlled Blue Book union. Hiring was done under the "shape-up" system. The men gathered on the docks each day, and a hiring boss chose the ones who would get the day's work. The system was riddled with bribery, favoritism, and blacklisting.

A new local of the ILA was formed in San Francisco in the summer of 1933 and soon won practically all the workers away from the employer-controlled union. Within the new local of the ILA, a working longshoreman named Harry R. Bridges led a militant group that persuaded the union to adopt its demands. These included union-controlled hiring halls, better wages and working conditions with extra pay for overtime, and coastwide bargaining so that the facilities in one port could not be used to break a strike or undercut wages in another.

To a group of employers who had enjoyed virtual freedom from any union demands at all for more than a decade, this program seemed "revolutionary." The employers charged that Bridges was a Communist. Bridges, a native of Australia, often said that his ideas were those of militant trade unionism and that he had held these opinions before the Communist party came into existence. In later years the United States government would make long and elaborate efforts to deport Bridges on the ground that he was a Communist, but he always denied the charge, and the government never proved it.

The dock workers in all the Pacific coast ports went on strike on May 9, 1934, and several seafaring unions struck soon afterward. The San Francisco Chamber of Commerce and the San Francisco Industrial Association held a joint meeting and made plans to support the Waterfront Employers' Union in an attempt to open the port with strikebreakers, on the ground that the longshoremen's union was "in the hands of a group of Communists." The business community was confident that it could again break the longshoremen's strike and destroy the union on the radicalism issue, as it had done in 1919.

On the morning of "bloody Thursday," July 5, 1934, 1000 San Francisco police officers tried to clear 5000 pickets from the Embarcadero, the main waterfront street, to enable strikebreakers to work. Pistols were fired on both sides. Sixty-four people were injured (thirty-one of them shot), and two strikers were killed. Governor Frank Merriam sent in the National Guard although Mayor Angelo Rossi had not asked for it. Seventeen hundred National Guard soldiers with fixed bayonets occupied the waterfront.

To this all-out attempt at opening the port, organized labor responded by closing down almost all the economic activity of most of the bay region. Virtually every

Strikers on the San Francisco waterfront flee from police through a cloud of tear gas on "bloody Thursday," July 5, 1934. (*Courtesy of the San Francisco Archives.*)

union in San Francisco and Alameda counties joined in the general strike, which began on the morning of Monday, July 16.

William Randolph Hearst, who was in England, sent instructions to John Francis Neylan, his chief counsel, to unite the major Bay Area newspaper publishers in a strategy of denouncing the general strike as Communist-inspired. News reports, as well as headlines and editorials, gave the impression that the strike was a part of a Communist conspiracy. Bands of vigilantes, with explicit encouragement from the newspapers and from Governor Merriam, broke into several Communist party offices in San Francisco and Oakland, smashed the furniture, and beat up anyone they found on the premises.

The general strike was called off at the end of its fourth day, Thursday, July 19. It had alienated majority public opinion to such a degree that American labor has never attempted a repetition of it. But if the general strike was largely a failure, so was the intransigent effort of the San Francisco employers to retain the open shop. Federal officials, including President Franklin Roosevelt, were now determined to settle the basic issues of the waterfront strike by federal arbitration. Neylan, who had always believed in collective bargaining, now used his influence in persuading the waterfront employers to accept unconditional arbitration. The federal board's ruling, announced on October 12, provided for hiring halls and gave the longshoremen's union almost complete control of them. This was the demand that the union had emphasized most. For years afterward the maritime employers were bitter at what they regarded as a triumph for radicalism, accomplished through federal intervention.

Upton Sinclair and EPIC

At the beginning of the state political campaigns of 1934, it seemed highly probable that California would elect its first Democratic governor in the twentieth century. The blame for the depression had fallen heavily on the Republicans. In the presidential election of 1932, President Hoover had lost not only his home state of California but also his home county of Santa Clara, and Democrat William Gibbs McAdoo was elected United States senator from California in the Roosevelt avalanche. Almost any reasonably presentable New Dealer could probably have been elected governor of California in 1934, but Upton Sinclair, who had been the Socialist candidate for the governorship in 1926 and 1930, threw the whole campaign into a turmoil by announcing in 1933 that he was changing his party registration and would run for governor as a Democrat.

Sinclair had been the country's best-known pamphleteer and propaganda novelist since 1906 when he had published *The Jungle,* a melodramatic story of the heartbreaking conditions of life among the immigrant packinghouse workers of Chicago. Sinclair moved to California in 1915 and made his home in Pasadena. In the middle of the waterfront strike at San Pedro in 1923, he was arrested for trying to read the Constitution of the United States to a meeting of strikers on a vacant lot, and this episode led him to found the southern California branch of the American Civil Liberties Union.

By 1933 he had written 47 books (about half his ultimate output), and there was hardly an aspect of capitalistic society in America that had not received unfavorable attention in one or another of his writings. On the other hand, he regarded Marx as a rigid doctrinaire. Sinclair's own brand of socialism was of the romantic, Americanized sort that had produced the nineteenth-century utopian colonies.

It was characteristic of Sinclair that when he decided to run for governor as a Democrat, he began his campaign by writing a utopian novel about it. *I, Governor of California, and How I Ended Poverty: A True Story of the Future* (1933) was an imaginative history of California from 1933 to 1938. In lively fiction it told how Sinclair was elected governor after a campaign of unprecedented bitterness and how he then put all the unemployed to work in state-aided cooperative enterprises. Through this catchy, quasi-literary device Sinclair set forth his program to End Poverty in California (EPIC). If the voters should decide to let him make his novel come true, a California Authority for Land (CAL) would purchase all the farms that were sold for taxes and establish cooperative agricultural colonies on them, with cooperative stores for the members. A California Authority for Production (CAP) would acquire thousands of factories that had been idle or only partially in use, and a California Authority for Money (CAM) would issue bonds to finance the purchases of the lands and factories and scrip to serve as the medium of exchange among the members of the cooperatives.

The national Democratic administration regarded Sinclair's candidacy as extremely unfortunate and unwelcome. The goal of the New Deal was not to undermine the capitalist system but to save that system by reforming it. Yet not even a statement from President Roosevelt opposing Sinclair could have prevented him from winning the Democratic nomination. Under these circumstances the president adopted a policy of making no public comment whatever about the campaign in California.

The depression was still raging, and thousands of people still lived in terror of being unable to provide food for their families. Wherever Sinclair went, these people crowded around him to wring his hand and promise him their support. In August 1934 he won the nomination with the highest vote that a Democratic candidate for governor had ever received in a California primary. More than two-thirds of his total vote came from southern California. Fifty-four percent of it came from Los Angeles County, where unemployment and other forms of economic hardship were even worse than in the state as a whole.

In the Republican primary, the extremely conservative Governor Merriam won by a plurality over three relatively progressive candidates. As Democrat George Creel remarked, this left the voters of California with "a choice between epilepsy and catalepsy. Sinclair has a fantastic, impossible plan, and Merriam is as modern as the dinosaur age."

Upton Sinclair's campaign weekly, *EPIC News,* featured this editorial cartoon on June 9, 1934. (*Courtesy of the California Historical Society.*)

The California Republicans, now thoroughly frightened, organized an attack against Sinclair on a scale so elaborate and intensive that it marked the beginning of a whole new era in the history of American political campaign techniques. Louis B. Mayer, head of Metro-Goldwyn-Mayer studios and chairman of the Republican state central committee, mobilized the resources of the public relations, advertising, and movie industries.

Sinclair's own writings over the previous 30 years provided his opponents with much of their ammunition. He had denounced and antagonized a remarkable number of groups and institutions: the clergy, in his book *The Profits of Religion;* American colleges and universities, in *The Goose Step;* public schools and schoolteachers, in *The Goslings;* and the press, in *The Brass Check.* But his opponents did not content themselves with reprinting passages from these works; they also indulged in outright fabrications and distortions. In a faked newsreel, a group of tramps, who were actually movie extras made up for the part, were shown debarking from a freight train and telling an interviewer that they were the first of an army of hoboes from the east who were on their way to California because they had heard that as soon as Sinclair was elected there would be a general sharing of the wealth.

Sinclair's opponents falsely charged that he was an atheist, a believer in free love, and a Communist. The Communist party, in fact, denounced Sinclair as a "social fascist"—its current term for anyone who advocated compromise with capitalism. Even the Socialist party of California repudiated him, although in somewhat milder language than the Communists. Sinclair also lost the support of Dr.

Typical of the ridicule heaped on Upton Sinclair during his 1934 gubernatorial campaign was this political cartoon by Fred Korburg in the *San Francisco Call-Bulletin.* (*Courtesy of the* San Francisco Examiner.)

Townsend and his followers by criticizing the Old Age Revolving Pensions plan as "a mere money scheme." Merriam, on the other hand, won an endorsement from Townsend by promising to recommend his plan to the national Congress.

In the November election, Merriam won with a vote of 1,138,620 to 879,557 for Sinclair. A vote of 302,519 went to Raymond L. Haight, a Los Angeles Republican lawyer who had won the nominations of the Commonwealth and Progressive parties.

From Merriam to Olson

Governor Merriam realized and acknowledged that he could not have been elected without the support of many relatively conservative New Deal Democrats, and in 1935 he signed a number of bills that brought the state into conformity with some of the New Deal's policies and measures. The most active Democratic leader in the legislature was Culbert L. Olson, who had been elected state senator from Los Angeles County as a supporter of Sinclair. Though the senate was still predominantly conservative, Olson secured its approval of new laws that repealed the sales tax on food and established a moderate state income tax. Another measure slightly increased the provisions for assistance to the indigent aged.

In the New Deal's Social Security Act of 1935, and in the corresponding Old Age Security program adopted by California in the same year, the use of the word "security" was a gross exaggeration of the benefits actually provided for old people. For state-sponsored old-age pensions, the federal government contributed four-fifths of the first $25 per month and half of any further amount up to $55. California set its maximum figure at $35, which was higher than in many other states, but to receive this maximum pension, old people had to be not only without income but also without relatives who could contribute to their support. These provisions were inadequate, and they required humiliating investigations of personal finances and family relationships.

The way was thus open for a new pension scheme for the state of California alone, and the result was the aberration known as Ham 'n' Eggs. Robert Noble, a Los Angeles radio commentator, formed an organization called California Revolving Pensions and summarized its plan with the slogan "twenty-five dollars every Monday morning." Noble entrusted some of his advertising to an agency operated by the brothers Willis and Lawrence Allen, whose chief client up to that time had been the manufacturer of Grey-Gone, a hair tonic. The Allen brothers then formed their own pension organization, excluding Noble. They shifted his slogan to "thirty dollars every Thursday," and one of their campaign orators hit upon the motto "Ham 'n' Eggs for California," by which the plan came to be commonly known.

In the California elections of 1938, pensions were the most important single issue. William McAdoo's denunciation of the Ham 'n' Eggs movement cost him his seat in the United States Senate. Sheridan Downey, who had won an endorsement from the Allen brothers by enthusiastically endorsing their plan, defeated McAdoo in the Democratic primary. Downey, a Sacramento lawyer, had been the

WARNING!

Retail Stores
Can Not and Will Not Accept
"Retirement
Life Payment Warrants"
(Ham and Eggs—30-Thursday)

A broadside from the campaign against the "Ham 'n' Eggs" initiative of 1938. (*Courtesy of the California Historical Society, North Baker Research Library, Broadside Collection.*)

EPIC candidate for lieutenant governor as Upton Sinclair's running mate in 1934 (opponents had disparaged the ticket as "Uppey and Downey").

If Governor Merriam had flirted with the Ham 'n' Eggers in 1938 as he had flirted with the Townsendites in 1934, he would probably have been reelected. But he openly opposed Ham 'n' Eggs, while Culbert L. Olson won the Democratic nomination and the governorship largely by avoiding a clear stand on the issue. The Ham 'n' Eggs initiative was defeated in the 1938 election, but the vote in its favor, more than 1,143,000, was shockingly large. It might have passed had it not been for the exposure, during the last days of the campaign, of some of the corrupt practices of the Allen brothers, its cynical and irresponsible promoters.

One of Olson's first acts as governor was to carry out his campaign pledge of a pardon for Tom Mooney. Warren K. Billings, Mooney's codefendant, had also been convicted on perjured evidence, but because Billings had previously been convicted of a felony, his pardon would have required a recommendation by the state supreme court. The court recommended only a commutation of sentence to time served, and this Olson granted. Billings would finally receive his full pardon from another Democratic governor, Edmund G. Brown, in 1961.

At the end of his first week in office, Governor Olson collapsed from exhaustion, and a month passed before he was able to resume his duties. This left the new administration without leadership at the most crucial time, and it never fully recovered from this demoralizing blow. But Olson could have accomplished little at best. Conservative Republicans still controlled the state senate, and although the Democrats had a small majority in the assembly, they were split into factions. Olson had almost no previous experience as an administrator. Tactless and quick-tempered, he often antagonized people whose support would have been essential to his success. The main accomplishments of his governorship were a few modest reforms in the state's penal system and in its provisions for the care of the mentally ill.

Throughout the country the reformist enthusiasm of the New Deal was waning. The number of liberal Democrats in Congress was sharply reduced in the 1938 elections, and as war clouds gathered in Europe and Asia, President Roosevelt turned most of his attention to the problems of foreign affairs and national defense. Olson's chance of bringing a New Deal to California was both too little and too late.

Selected Bibliography

General surveys of the period are in Kevin Starr, *Endangered Dreams: The Great Depression in California* (1995); Leonard Leader, *Los Angeles and the Great Depression* (1991); William H. Mullins, *The Depression and the Urban West Coast* (1991); and "The Great Depression and the West," a special issue of *Journal of the West*, XXIV (October 1985). Richard Lowitt, *The New Deal and the West* (1984), describes the effects of federal policy. See also Ronald L. Feinman, *Twilight of Progressivism* (1981).

Gubernatorial administrations during the depression are described in Jackson K. Putnam, *Modern California Politics* (1980), and H. Brett Melendy and Benjamin F. Gilbert, *The Governors of California* (1965). Brian McGinty, "Shadows in St. James Park," *California History*, LVII (Winter 1978–79), pp. 290–307, describes the lynching in San Jose. The earlier and happier years of James Rolph, Jr., are described in Morley Segal, "James Rolph, Jr., and the Early Days of the San Francisco Municipal Railway," *California Historical Society Quarterly*, XLIII (March 1964), pp. 3–18, and Moses Rischin, "Sunny Jim Rolph," ibid., LIII (Summer 1974), pp. 165–172. See also Royce D. Delmatier et al., *The Rumble of California Politics* (1970), and Michael P. Rogin and John L. Shover, *Political Change in California* (1970).

Arthur M. Schlesinger, Jr., *The Politics of Upheaval* (1960), includes excellent accounts of some of the major political developments in California in 1933 and 1934. Luther Whiteman and Samuel L. Lewis, *Glory Roads* (1936), describe technocracy, the Utopian Society, and other proposed roads to the millennium. William E. Akin, *Technocracy and the American Dream* (1977), is a thorough analysis. Biographies of Aimee Semple McPherson are by Nancy Barr Mavity (1931) and Lately Thomas (1959, 1970). On the Townsend Plan, see Abraham Holtzman, *The Townsend Movement* (1963), and J. D. Gaydowski, "The Genesis of the Townsend Plan," *Southern California Quarterly*, LII (December 1970), pp. 365–382.

For the resurgence of nativism in the 1930s, see Francisco E. Balderrama and Raymond Rodríguez, *Decade of Betrayal* (1995); Camille Guerin-Gonzales, *Mexican Workers and American Dreams* (1994); Albert Camarillo, *Chicanos in California* (1984); and Douglas Monroy, *Rebirth: Mexican Los Angeles from the Great Migration to the Great Depression* (1999).

On the agricultural labor strikes, see Eiichiro Azuma, "Racial Struggle, Immigrant Nationalism, and Ethnic Identity: Japanese and Filipinos in the California Delta, 1930–1941," *Pacific Historical Review*, LXVII (May 1998), pp. 163–200; Devra Weber, *Dark Sweat, White Gold* (1995); Vicki Ruiz, *Cannery Women, Cannery Lives* (1987); Clarke A. Chambers, *California Farm Organizations* (1952); and Glenna Matthews, "Fruit Workers of the Santa Clara Valley," *Pacific Historical Review*, LIV (February 1985), pp. 51–70. On the

1934 strike, see David F. Selvin, *A Terrible Anger: The 1934 Waterfront and General Strikes in San Francisco* (1996); Ottilie Markholt, *Maritime Solidarity* (1998); John Kagel, "The Day the City Stopped," *California History,* LXIII (Summer 1984), pp. 212–223; and Bruce Nelson, *Workers on the Waterfront* (1988). On Harry Bridges, see Robert W. Cherny, "The Making of a Labor Radical," *Pacific Historical Review,* LXIV (August 1995), pp. 363–388; Harvey Schwartz, "Harry Bridges and the Scholars," *California History,* LIX (Spring 1980), pp. 66–79; and Charles P. Larrowe, *Harry Bridges* (1972).

Upton Sinclair's temporary capture of the Democratic party is described in Gregg Mitchell, *The Campaign of the Century* (1992); Charles E. Larsen, "The EPIC Campaign of 1934," *Pacific Historical Review,* XXVII (May 1958), pp. 127–148; Leon Harris, *Upton Sinclair, American Rebel* (1975); Leonard Leader. "Upton Sinclair's EPIC Switch: A Dilemma for American Socialists," *Southern California Quarterly,* LXII (Winter 1980), pp. 361–385; Judson A. Grenier, "Upton Sinclair: A Remembrance," *California Historical Society Quarterly,* XLVIII (June 1969), pp. 165–169; and Walton Bean, "Ideas of Reform in California," in George H. Knoles (ed.), *Essays and Assays: California History Reappraised* (1973), pp. 13–26.

An informal history of the rise of the Ham 'n' Eggs movement is Winston Moore and Marian Moore, *Out of the Frying Pan* (1939). See also Tom Zimmerman, "Ham and Eggs Everybody!" *Southern California Quarterly,* LXII (Spring 1980), pp. 1–48, and Carey McWilliams, "Pension Politics in California," in David Farrelly and Ivan Hinderaker (eds.), *The Politics of California* (1951). Jackson K. Putnam, *Old-Age Politics in California* (1970), is a major contribution.

An excellent study of the Olson administration is Robert E. Burke, *Olson's New Deal for California* (1953).

CHAPTER 26

Cultural Trends

The cultural history of California during the early decades of the twentieth century was distinguished by several writers of great scope and power. As a cultural region, California was fast becoming one of the most dynamic and promising of any area in the United States.

Robinson Jeffers

California's greatest poet was born in 1887 in Pittsburgh, Pennsylvania, where his father, William Hamilton Jeffers, was a distinguished professor of biblical literature in a Presbyterian theological seminary. At the age of 5, Robinson Jeffers began to learn Greek and Hebrew. His father was a liberal theologian who taught him to read the Bible as literature rather than divine revelation.

When the boy was 16, the family moved to Pasadena. He attended Occidental College and then began graduate work at the University of Southern California, where he fell in love with Una Call Kuster, a student who was 2 years older than he and who was the wife of another man. Eight years later Una Kuster finally obtained a divorce, and she and Jeffers were married. At about the same time, the young couple chanced to discover Carmel.

Jeffers immediately recognized the place where he would do his life's work. In the mountains of the Carmel coast, he saw "people living amid magnificent unspoiled scenery essentially as they did in the Idyls or the Sagas, or in Homer's Ithaca. Here was life purged of its ephemeral accretions. Men were riding after cattle, or plowing the headland, hovered by white sea-gulls, as they have done for thousands of years." On the point of land between the lovely little bay and the mouth of the river, with granite carried up from the beach with his own hands, he built Tor House and Hawk Tower, a separate study.

In 1916 he published *Californians,* a volume of poems written in conventional poetic forms, but soon afterward, instead of rhyme and meter, Jeffers developed forms directly imitating nature. Also unconventional were the starkly tragic themes of the long narrative poems that began with *Tamar* (1924) and *Roan Stallion* (1925). Tamar Cauldwell, daughter of a rancher at Point Lobos, commits incest with her brother, and the whole family perishes when an insane aunt sets fire to the house. In *Roan Stallion* a part-Indian woman named California transfers her affections from her white husband to her horse. When her husband is being trampled by the stallion in the corral, though she could save his life by killing the horse with a rifle, she deliberately holds her fire until after her husband is dead.

With the publication of these poems in the middle of the 1920s, the work of Jeffers immediately found a place in the upper levels of American literary reputation. *The Women at Point Sur* (1927) was much less enthusiastically received, for its theme was even more shocking to most readers than were the themes of the earlier narratives, though its story was told with equally compelling power and beauty of poetic form and metaphor. Barclay, a minister, after losing his son in World War I, denounces his church, becomes insane, goes to live as a boarder on an isolated ranch, and founds a new religion in which he is God. Then he rapes his own daughter. In addition, the plot includes episodes of child murder and suicide.

Jeffers described his own philosophy as "inhumanism," though he used the term in his own very special sense. He rejected humanism because it overemphasized the rational, the urbane, and the civilized and because it attached too much importance to human consciousness—the characteristic of human beings that seemed to set them apart from nature. Jeffers's poems sought to explore the unconscious, the realm of humanity's "felt nature." But though he read Freud and Jung, Jeffers never sought the aid of a psychotherapist for himself, and both the poet and his wife denied that the circumstances of their own lives had anything to do with his choice of tragic themes.

It seemed, indeed, that no man could have asked more of fortune than to live with a beautiful, talented, and devoted wife in a place that looked north on Carmel Bay and south on Point Lobos, and there to write some of the most unforgettable of modern poetry. But if Jeffers had no conscious feeling of self-blame for loving the wife of another man and taking her to live in these isolated and beautiful surroundings, the subconscious fear of punishment must have been there nevertheless. Perhaps the "imagined victims" in his poems suffered horrible punishments so that Jeffers and his wife need not suffer them.

During the depression of the 1930s, Jeffers's popularity and reputation sharply declined. The themes of his long poems, however, continued to be unrelentingly harsh. They dealt with adultery, murder, madness, and suicide. Jeffers had no sympathy with the complaint that his poems were full of tragedy and violence. These were the themes of Sophocles and Shakespeare, he pointed out, and they were not out of place in a century in which two world wars had killed 100 million people, and a third threatened to exterminate all the rest. "The Inquisitors," published in *The Double Axe and Other Poems* (1948), described three hills in the coast range, squatting like giant Indians to examine the pitiful remnants of human beings after an atomic holocaust.

Robinson Jeffers died in 1962, at 75. He has not had, and is not likely to have, any successful imitators.

John Steinbeck

As clearly as Robinson Jeffers was California's most important poet, John Steinbeck might be said to be its most important novelist. Steinbeck's early writing had as distinctive a relation to the Salinas Valley and Monterey as did Jeffers's poems to the Carmel coast. Indeed, Steinbeck portrayed the Salinas Valley with a thoroughness not given to any other American region in modern fiction, except perhaps William Faulkner's Mississippi.

Steinbeck was born in Salinas in 1902, the year Frank Norris died. He graduated from Salinas High School in 1919 and studied at Stanford University, but, like Norris at Berkeley, he never completed the requirements for a degree.

His first novel, *Cup of Gold* (1929), was an allegorical romance about Sir Henry Morgan, the pirate-governor of Jamaica. From this, Steinbeck turned to the California scene, which would provide the locales for most of his best writing. *The Pastures of Heaven* (1932) was set in a lovely, secluded, fictional valley somewhere near the Salinas Valley. Its unifying theme was the Munroe family, their thoughtless, vicious mediocrity, and the series of episodes in which they ruined the lives of their neighbors by trying to force them into conformity with their own notions of what was proper and respectable.

Steinbeck's satirizing of pretentious middle-class values was also apparent in *Tortilla Flat* (1935), which won him the beginnings of financial success and critical notice. Although several publishers had rejected this droll account of some Mexican American idlers in Monterey on the ground that it was too frivolous for the hard times of the depression, the book sold quite well to readers who enjoyed its supposed praise of a group of irresponsible people who were living on next to nothing. Steinbeck himself had been getting along on very little. His earlier novels brought him only a few hundred dollars in royalties, and when he was writing *Tortilla Flat,* he would have been destitute if his father had not provided him with a small house in Pacific Grove and an allowance of $25 a month.

In Dubious Battle, published early in 1936, took its title from a line in Milton's *Paradise Lost* but dealt with the intensely contemporary and controversial theme of a strike of migratory agricultural laborers organized and led by Communists. The episodes were largely drawn from an actual strike in the cotton fields of the San Joaquin Valley 2 years earlier, though the Torgas Valley of the novel was a composite locale. It resembled the Pajaro Valley, north of Salinas, but there had been no strike there, and the crop in the novel was apples rather than cotton.

The main characters were also composites, partly drawn, like all of Steinbeck's characters, from persons he had known, including in this case two actual Communists. But the widespread charge that *In Dubious Battle* was communistic propaganda ignored the fact that its picture of the leading Communist organizer of the strike is extremely critical. Mac cares nothing for the fate of the workers and wishes only to use them for the destruction of private ownership. Steinbeck had as deep a dislike for communism as he had for any system that subordinated the spirit and dignity of the individual to a cause.

The strike is not yet over at the end of the novel, but it is obviously doomed, and the battle is dubious not in its outcome but in the merits of both sides. Steinbeck was equally critical of the radical leadership of the strike and the ruthlessness of the growers and their vigilante supporters. His most extreme contempt was reserved for the vigilantes. For once he was in full agreement with Mac: "They're the dirtiest guys in any town. . . . They like to hurt people, and they always give it a nice name, patriotism or protecting the constitution."

Steinbeck made an intensive personal investigation of migratory labor conditions in the mid-1930s and summarized his conclusions in a series of articles in the *San Francisco News* in October 1936, later reprinted as a pamphlet under the title *Their Blood Is Strong.* As background he sketched the history of California's importation of foreign labor, which he called "a disgraceful picture of greed and cruelty." Then he described the new agricultural labor supply, the impoverished native American migrants from the Dust Bowl area. For the solution of the desperate and dangerous problem, he recommended that a new state agricultural labor board help to allot labor and determine fair wages and that the workers be helped to form union organizations. Finally, he insisted that vigilantism be drastically punished. It was, Steinbeck wrote, "a system of terrorism that would be unusual in the Fascist nations of the world," and its methods were being "more powerfully and more openly practiced in California than in any other place in the United States."

Of Mice and Men (1938) was a touching allegory of the life of California ranch hands. Made into a successful motion picture, it further increased Steinbeck's reputation. His masterpiece, however, was *The Grapes of Wrath,* published the following year and narrating the experiences of the Joad family, who were evicted from their farm in the Oklahoma Dust Bowl, journeyed to California in an ancient automobile, and suffered the miseries of migratory laborers in the San Joaquin Valley. It was "a crime . . . that goes beyond denunciation," Steinbeck wrote, that children were being allowed to die of starvation in the midst of rotting plenty.

The Kern County Board of Supervisors banned *The Grapes of Wrath* from the public schools and libraries under its jurisdiction, and the Associated Farmers launched an unsuccessful campaign to extend the ban to other counties, but the novel won the Pulitzer Prize and was a runaway best-seller. During the next 15 years, it was reprinted nearly 50 times in 16 editions in English and translated into a dozen other languages. Darryl Zanuck of Twentieth Century–Fox made it into a film while it was still at the top of the national best-seller list. He had taken the precaution of sending private detectives to determine the accuracy of the novel, and they had reported that actual conditions were even worse than the ones Steinbeck described.

The financial success of *The Grapes of Wrath* enabled Steinbeck to take an extended vacation, which also served as the basis for his next book. He accompanied

The Hollywood version of John Steinbeck's *The Grapes of Wrath* was playing at theaters in towns across the Central Valley by 1940. (*Photograph by Dorothea Lange. Courtesy of the Oakland Museum.*)

his friend Edward F. Ricketts, the proprietor of a laboratory of marine biology at Monterey, on an expedition to collect biological specimens in the Gulf of California and described this experience in *The Sea of Cortez* (1941). The mysteries of biology had always fascinated Steinbeck and had given him a love and respect for life in all its forms. Steinbeck immortalized Ed Ricketts, who deeply shared this feeling, in the character of Doc, the hero of *Cannery Row* (1945).

East of Eden (1952) was a powerful novel on which Steinbeck worked with intense labor for 4 years. He began it in order to record for the two small sons of his second marriage the story of his maternal ancestors, the Hamiltons, following their migration to the Salinas Valley after the Civil War. But the fictional family of Adam Trask entered the story and ultimately dominated it. As the final title suggests, the novel became an allegorical reworking of the story of Cain and Abel.

In 1962 Steinbeck's name was added to those of Sinclair Lewis, Ernest Hemingway, and William Faulkner among the very small group of American novelists to win the Nobel Prize for Literature. He died 6 years later.

William Saroyan and Other Writers

Like Steinbeck's Salinas, William Saroyan's native town of Fresno provided much of the best material for his writing career. When Saroyan was 3 years old, his Armenian-born father died, leaving the family in poverty. From the age of 7, Saroyan sold newspapers on the streets of Fresno and later worked as a telegraph messenger and grape picker. He left school at 15, never received a high school diploma, and never went to college.

His first book, *The Daring Young Man on the Flying Trapeze,* consisted of 26 short stories, written at the rate of one a day in a furnished room in San Francisco in January 1934, when he was 25 years old. The title story describes the thoughts and fantasies of a young writer on a day when he has nothing to eat and is completely destitute except for one penny that he finds on the sidewalk.

To Saroyan the vital ingredient in literary style was creative spontaneity, and he worked to establish what he called a "tradition of carelessness," or a "jump in the river and start swimming immediately" style of writing. His most famous novel, and probably his best, was *The Human Comedy* (1943). It dealt mostly with the alternately touching and delightful experiences of two boys who were called Ulysses and Homer Macauley, but were obviously William Saroyan and his older brother, in a town that was called Ithaca, California, but was obviously Fresno.

He wrote several plays, including *My Heart's in the Highlands, The Time of Your Life,* and *Love's Old Sweet Song,* all produced in 1939. In *The Time of Your Life,* the characters are the habitués of a San Francisco waterfront bar who are able to find their inherent virtue when a wealthy drunk gives them money to pursue their aspirations. This play won a Pulitzer Prize in 1940, but Saroyan declined to accept the $1000 award because he believed that "any material or official patronage . . . vitiates and embarrasses art at its source."

Louis B. Mayer brought Saroyan to Hollywood, but Saroyan detested Mayer and he disliked Hollywood. Nevertheless, *The Human Comedy* and *The Time of Your Life* were made into successful films in 1943 and 1948. Following World War II, Saroyan shunned the public limelight, saying that creativity required isolation. He divided his later years between Paris and Fresno and died in his hometown in 1981.

Saroyan was only one of several major novelists and playwrights who were attracted, however briefly, to southern California in the late 1930s and 1940s by the film industry. Two of the most important of these writers were Nathanael West, a native of New York who came to Hollywood as an aspiring scriptwriter, and the English novelist Aldous Huxley, who moved to Los Angeles in 1937. Both West and Huxley were powerfully struck by the contrast between the grim reality of depression-era southern California and the fanciful image of the region presented in the movies.

The Los Angeles of Nathanael West was a city built of illusion and artifice. In *The Day of the Locust* (1939), West describes the desperate quest of people who have been attracted by the California dream of opportunity and romance, but who find themselves impoverished and defeated. The dream becomes a nightmare, and in their desperation the people turn to violence. West's novel ends with an apocalyptic vision of Los Angeles in flames. Huxley shared West's distaste for southern California, regarding Los Angeles as a symbol for corrupt values and deception. In *After Many a Summer Dies the Swan* (1939), Huxley satirized the excesses of southern California's architecture and its religious and scientific cults. The major focus of the novel is a California tycoon, modeled on William Randolph Hearst, whose opulent mansion became for Huxley a bizarre Los Angeles in miniature.

Willaim Randolph Hearst and Other Journalists

Until his death in 1951, at 88, William Randolph Hearst continued to exert a powerful influence on California journalism and on several other aspects of California
society and culture. His publishing empire, at its peak in 1932, included 26 newspapers in cities from Boston to Seattle and from Baltimore to Los Angeles. In California, he owned and controlled the *San Francisco Examiner* and *Call-Bulletin,* the
Los Angeles Examiner and *Herald-Express,* and the *Oakland Post-Enquirer.* In
total circulation of California newspapers in 1932, Hearst papers ranked first, second, third, and fifth, with Harry Chandler's *Los Angeles Times* ranking fourth. Thus,
a fantastic amount of power and influence was attached to the whims of one man
who had never entirely ceased to be a spoiled child.

In 1919 Hearst had begun the building of his "castle" at San Simeon, which ultimately cost at least $30 million and was one of the most expensive and lavish resi-
dences, either private or royal, in the world. On one of his father's ranches was a
2000-foot eminence overlooking the Pacific. There during family camping trips
and picnics in his childhood, Hearst had experienced the happiest moments of his
life. He called it La Cuesta Encantada, The Enchanted Hill, and on its summit, with
the aid of architect Julia Morgan of Berkeley, he built three palatial guest houses

Hearst Castle, the fabulous residence of William Randolph Hearst at San Simeon. (*Courtesy of the
California Department of Transportation.*)

and a fourth and much larger structure called La Casa Grande. This central castle had 100 rooms, many of them transported from Europe with all their paneling, ceilings, and furniture. The rooms were filled with art objects and antiques, and the gardens and terraces with statuary. A huge, rocky hillside was planted with hundreds of full-grown trees at enormous expense because Hearst found its bareness unpleasant. The grounds were stocked with his own private zoo.

In his will Hearst expressed the wish that his castle should go to the University of California as a memorial to his mother, but the university felt that it lacked the funds to maintain the site. Hearst's sons then persuaded the state of California to accept it as a gift in 1957. The fears that it would prove a massive and costly white elephant were not borne out. Half a million people visited it within the first 2 years after its opening as a state monument. Among the attractions of the place, along with its art treasures, was the chance to participate vicariously in the life of a man who had made such a determined attempt to have everything in the world that he wanted.

Even before his death, however, Hearst's newspaper chain had entered a gradual but steady decline, and by 1965 sales and consolidations had reduced the number of Hearst papers to about a third of what it had once been. In California's two principal cities, the Hearst *Examiner*s, after years of losing money, were forced to surrender the entire daily morning field to the *Los Angeles Times* and the *San Francisco Chronicle*. In the Sunday field, a new and strange alliance produced the *San Francisco Sunday Examiner & Chronicle,* with sections independently edited by the *Examiner* and by the *Chronicle.*

For newspapers as well as for nations, hereditary monarchy has always been a notoriously risky method of choosing top-management personnel. Hearst's sons did not approach the journalistic pace that their father had set. The *Times* and the *Chronicle* were also family concerns. Their founders had no sons, but they were able to pass on their power effectively through the female line.

Harry Chandler, who succeeded his father-in-law Harrison Gray Otis as publisher of the *Times* in 1917, was even more energetic than Otis himself. Harry's son Norman, who became the publisher in 1945, improved the quality of the paper in some respects. And Norman's son Otis Chandler, who succeeded his father in 1960, improved it considerably more.

The *San Francisco Chronicle* passed from M. H. de Young to his son-in-law George T. Cameron in 1925, and to de Young's grandson Charles de Young Thieriot 30 years later. Under Cameron and his general manager, Paul C. Smith, the *Chronicle* made a valiant though generally thankless effort to be a west coast *New York Times.* But under Thieriot the *Chronicle* launched a much more successful drive to out-Hearst the *Examiner* in entertainment.

Meanwhile, big city newspapers throughout the state were challenged by several nationwide trends. From 1945 to 1965, the cost of newspaper production in large cities increased twice as fast as the income from advertising. At the same time, there was an enormous increase in the number of suburban dailies. Both circulation and advertising followed the bulk of the population increase into the suburbs. Still further competition came from television advertising and newscasting.

The Arts

San Francisco maintained its reputation as the cultural capital of California without effective challenge until World War II, after which Los Angeles became a serious rival for cultural leadership.

For many years after its founding in the middle 1920s, the M. H. de Young Memorial Museum in San Francisco's Golden Gate Park remained the principal art gallery on the Pacific coast. By 1960 its attendance exceeded 1 million persons a year, and on Sundays it often had more visitors than even the Metropolitan Museum of Art in New York City. The California Palace of the Legion of Honor was established in 1924 in San Francisco's Lincoln Park. It attracted almost as large an attendance as the de Young. These two museums were heavily committed to the time-tested and accepted art of the past. The San Francisco Museum of Art, on the other hand, attempted the more difficult role of educating the public in the appreciation of contemporary painting and sculpture.

During the early decades of the twentieth century, several public and private institutions for the promotion of the arts were established in southern California, laying the ground for the eventual preeminence of Los Angeles as a cultural center. In 1917 the Otis Art Institute was founded in the former home of Harrison Gray Otis, and 4 years later the Chouinard Art Institute, a school of art and design, was estab-

Migrant Mother. Dorothea Lange took this famous photograph in 1936 at Nipomo, on Highway 101, south of San Luis Obispo. She reported that this family of Dust Bowl refugees had just sold the tires from their car to buy food. (*Courtesy of the Library of Congress.*)

lished by Nelbert Chouinard. The richly endowed Henry E. Huntington Library and Art Gallery in San Marino continued to expand its collection; in 1922 it purchased Gainsborough's *Blue Boy* for $620,000.

By the 1920s photography had come to be accepted as an art form rather than as just a medium of documentation. Among California's leading photographers were two remarkable women, Imogen Cunningham and Dorothea Lange. Cunningham began her career early in the twentieth century with soft-focus portraits of people, plants, and objects, but later she specialized in producing sharply focused and exquisitely detailed pictures. Lange established a studio in San Francisco in 1918 and married the local artist Maynard Dixon. Her most famous work was a series of photographs capturing the plight of the Dust Bowl refugees of the 1930s, first published as *An American Exodus* (1940). Later she recorded the tragedy of Japanese American relocation during World War II. (See page 365.)

In the field of music, California's chief distinction was the rise of the San Francisco Opera Company. Founded in 1923, it was the second-oldest continuous opera group in the United States, after New York's Metropolitan. Nine years later its history entered a new phase with the opening of the War Memorial Opera House—the first municipally owned opera house in the nation. Among the state's symphony orchestras there was no serious attempt to rival the leadership of the San Francisco Symphony until 1919, when William Andrews Clark, Jr., became the first outstanding patron of music in southern California by endowing the Los Angeles Philharmonic. In 1922 this orchestra began to present its famous summer concerts under the stars in the new Hollywood Bowl. With 22,000 seats, the Bowl was the world's largest natural amphitheater.

Architecture

At several periods in the twentieth century, California produced or attracted some of the most talented architects in America. Of these, Willis Polk, Bernard Maybeck, and John Galen Howard in the San Francisco Bay area, the Greene brothers in Pasadena, and Irving Gill in San Diego and Los Angeles had begun their work before the turn of the century, though their most notable achievements came after 1900.

Willis Polk was trained in the offices of A. Page Brown in San Francisco and Daniel Hudson Burnham in Chicago. Polk collaborated with Brown in the design of San Francisco's Ferry Building in 1896 and assisted Burnham in 1903 in drafting the elaborate and ill-fated San Francisco master plan, of which the Civic Center was the only major feature actually adopted. After the earthquake and fire, Polk became known as "the man who rebuilt San Francisco," an exaggerated description that he himself did not hesitate to endorse. The Chronicle Building, the Mills Building, the Pacific Union Club, and the restoration of Mission Dolores, as well as many of the finest residences in the city, were among his more famous assignments.

Most of Polk's downtown commercial buildings were of a monumental and conservative style, with much neoclassical ornamentation, but in 1918 he produced the world's first "glass skyscraper." This was the Hallidie Building on Sutter near Montgomery, appropriately named for another local pioneer, the inventor of the cable car. Polk could not entirely forgo the use of decoration, in the form of lacy ironwork that contrasted oddly with the great glass facade, but his Hallidie Building was the first really outstanding architectural innovation ever attempted in San Francisco.

Bernard Maybeck, too, had his own special genius for the new as well as for the old in architecture. To Maybeck all ages were the present. He was equally interested in the industrial environment of the twentieth century and in the Romanesque and gothic structures he had admired as a student in Paris, and these interests combined to produce a remarkably freewheeling eclecticism.

In 1896, when Phoebe Apperson Hearst visited the campus of the University of California with an offer to endow a mining building as a memorial to her late husband, Maybeck was a young man holding a bread-and-butter job as a teacher of descriptive geometry. He was also the university's nearest approach to a professor of architecture, and as such he was delegated to encourage Mrs. Hearst's tentative interest in providing future buildings for the campus. To his own amazement, he succeeded in persuading her to endow a lavish international architectural competition for a master plan. Emile Benard of Paris, who won the prize, refused to come to Berkeley in order to put his own plan into practice. Instead, John Galen Howard of New York was brought to Berkeley in 1901 to supervise the plan's execution.

During the next few years, Maybeck designed many residences in Berkeley and San Francisco, most of them immediately recognizable as "Maybecks" because of his distinctive blend of gothic revival with Bay region redwood shingle. His most famous building was San Francisco's Palace of Fine Arts, with its delightful lagoon, designed for the Panama Pacific International Exposition of 1915. The resulting structure became such a beloved part of the San Francisco landscape that when its temporary materials eventually crumbled, it was rebuilt in permanent form.

Among Bernard Maybeck's pupils was Julia Morgan, the first woman to graduate from the University of California with a degree in mechanical engineering and the first to receive a diploma in architecture from the École des Beaux-Arts in Paris. Morgan began her career as an architect working for Maybeck but soon opened her own office in San Francisco. Among her major commissions was the rebuilding of the neoclassical interior of the Fairmont Hotel after the earthquake and fire of 1906. She also enjoyed the patronage of Phoebe Apperson Hearst and her family. In addition to the famous castle at San Simeon, Morgan designed 700 other structures throughout California and the nation. "My buildings will be my legacy," she once remarked. "They will speak for me long after I'm gone."

In Pasadena the brothers Charles and Henry Greene created the California bungalow style, which not only dominated residential architecture in southern California in the early twentieth century but also was widely imitated in other states. "Bungalow" was originally a British-Indian corruption of the word *bengali,* and referred to a single-storied house or cottage designed for English civil servants during short terms of residence. Pasadena attracted many wealthy people who also wanted fairly simple dwellings for part-time occupancy.

Postcard view of an early-twentieth-century bungalow in Los Angeles. (*Courtesy of the California State Library, Sacramento.*)

In 1903 the Greene brothers designed for Arturo Bandini a bungalow modeled on the plan of the early California adobes, though built of redwood. The rooms were grouped around three sides of a patio or central court, enclosed on the fourth side by a wooden, flower-covered pergola. The patio was an outdoor living room, and there was great freedom of movement between the indoor and outdoor parts of the house. The Greenes acquired so many wealthy clients that virtually all of their later houses were large and expensive, but their many imitators designed thousands of modest bungalows that were pleasant, practical, and enormously popular as homes, though they lacked the quality of the Greene brothers' fine woodcrafting.

The first California architect to be deeply committed to modernism was Irving Gill. Like Frank Lloyd Wright, Gill was trained as a drafter under Louis H. Sullivan in Chicago. Sullivan's motto was that "Form follows function." Poor health brought Gill to San Diego in 1893, and there he developed a highly original style, using plaster-coated reinforced concrete walls, flat roofs, and simple windows, all with an austere complete absence of ornament.

When planning began for San Diego's Panama Pacific Exposition, to be held in 1915, Gill was the city's best-known architect, but the local authorities entrusted the control of the building plans for the fair to Bertram Goodhue of New York, who had written a book on Spanish colonial architecture. Goodhue, in his buildings for the San Diego exposition, revived the extravagant and sometimes capricious ornamentation that had been the dominant style of architecture in Spain and Mexico in the late seventeenth and early eighteenth centuries. For many years after the San Diego fair, there was a great vogue for elaborate Spanish ornamentation in California.

Nothing could have been in more extreme contrast with the work of Irving Gill. The San Diego exposition disheartened Gill and set back the public acceptance of modernism. Gill gave up his practice in San Diego and moved his office to Los Angeles, where he received only a few commissions.

When modernism finally began to achieve genuine acceptance in California, it was largely through the work of Richard Neutra, an Austrian architect who settled in Los Angeles in 1926. Neutra was one of the small international group, including Adolf Loos and Frank Lloyd Wright, who achieved an early realization that the machine was at the base of the new architecture and not an evil spirit to be feared and exorcised. Neutra and other architects of the International Style made use of many of the new materials and methods that machine production made possible. Examples were their uses of plate glass or prefabricated structural parts and of reinforced concrete as a self-supporting slab. Employing such modern materials and taking particular advantage of the mild climate to make the fullest use of sliding glass doors (or rather walls), Neutra designed some of the most delightful and beautiful homes, schools, and commercial buildings in southern California.

Selected Bibliography

Robinson Jeffers is the subject of important studies by James Karman (1995), Louis Adamic (1983), Melba Berry Bennett (1966), Frederic I. Carpenter (1962), Radcliffe Squires (1956), Lawrence Clark Powell (1932, 1934, 1940), and George Sterling (1926). See also the bibliography compiled by S. S. Alberts (1933).

The best biography of John Steinbeck is Jackson J. Benson, *The True Adventures of John Steinbeck* (1984). More specialized is Brian St. Pierre, *John Steinbeck: The California Years* (1984). Other major works on Steinbeck are by David Wyatt (1990), Joseph J. Frontenrose (1964), Warren French (1961), and Peter Lisca (1958). Important articles include Tim Kappel, "Trampling Out the Vineyards: Kern County's Ban on *The Grapes of Wrath*," *California History*, LXI (Fall 1982), pp. 210–222, and Benson Loftis and Anne Loftis, "John Steinbeck and Farm Labor Unionization," *American Literature*, LII (May 1980), pp. 194–223. On William Saroyan, see the biography by Lawrence Lee and Barry Gifford (1998).

Valuable commentaries on California writers are Gerald Haslam, "Literary California," *California History*, LXVIII (Winter 1989), pp. 188–195, and David Wyatt, *The Fall into Eden* (1987). General anthologies of California literature include Jack Hicks et al. (eds.), *The Literature of California* (2000), Haslam (ed.), *Many Californias* (1991), and John Caughey and LaRee Caughey (eds.), *California Heritage* (1971). Several hundred novels about California are listed and briefly described in Alice K. Melton, *California in Fiction* (1961). See also Newton D. Baird and Robert Greenwood, *An Annotated Bibliography of California Fiction, 1664–1970* (1971).

W. A. Swanberg's *Citizen Hearst* (1961) is the best biography. Several of the other works previously cited in Chapter 17 for the earlier part of Hearst's long career are relevant for the later part of it as well. See also Judith Robinson, *The Hearsts* (1991); Winifred Black Bonfils, *The Life and Personality of Phoebe Apperson Hearst* (1927, 1991); Lindsay Chaney, *The Hearsts* (1981); Richard H. Peterson, "Philanthropic Phoebe," *California History*, LXIV (Fall 1985), pp. 284–289; Oscar Lewis, *Fabulous San Simeon* (1958); Robert Gottlieb and Irene Wolt, *Thinking Big: The Story of the Los Angeles Times* (1977); and William Rivers and David Rubin, *A Region's Press: Anatomy of Newspapers in the San Francisco Bay Area* (1971).

On the arts, see Edan Milton Hughes, *Artists in California* (1986); Nancy D.W. Moure, *Painting and Sculpture in Los Angeles, 1900–1945* (1980); Stephen M. Fry (ed.), *California's Musical Wealth* (1988); Howard Swan, *History of Music in the Southwest 1825–1950* (1952); Ronald L. Davis, *A History of Opera in the American West* (1965); and José Rodriguez (ed.), *Music and Dance in California* (1940).

Harold Kirker, *Old Forms on a New Land* (1991), offers an interpretive survey of California architecture. Studies of individual architects include Ginger Wadsworth, *Julia Morgan* (1990); Taylor Coffman, *The Builders behind the Castles* (1990); Richard Longstreth, *On the Edge of the World* (1982); Kenneth H. Cardwell, *Bernard Maybeck* (1977); Randell L. Makinson, *Greene and Greene* (1977); and Esther McCoy, *Five California Architects* (1960). On the architecture of southern California, see the studies by David Gebhard and Hariette Von Breton (1989), Paul Gleye (1981), Reyner Banham (1971), and Douglas Honnold (1956). The career of Richard Neutra can be traced in works by W. Dione Neutra (comp., 1986) and Esther McCoy (1960). Karen J. Weitze, *California's Mission Revival* (1984), describes the provincial forces opposed to modernism.

CHAPTER 27

Wartime Growth and Problems

From 1919 to 1941, the strongest feeling of the majority of Americans toward world affairs was their determination that the United States must never be involved in another world war. Senator Hiram Johnson of California was in the forefront of those who were called "isolationists" in this sense. But the raid on Pearl Harbor on December 7, 1941, left the American people no further choice. The Japanese attack, which came without warning and destroyed or crippled most of the American Pacific fleet with bombs and aerial torpedoes, immediately produced more support for an all-out military and industrial effort than Americans had shown in any previous war.

The Impact of Federal Spending

In the period including the fiscal years from 1940 to 1946, the federal government spent $360 billion within the continental United States. Of this sum, it spent about $35 billion in the state of California. It would be almost impossible to exaggerate and it is difficult even to comprehend the full effects of these unprecedented expenditures in stimulating economic expansion. Every previous element in the state's economic history was dwarfed in comparison. In the fiscal year ending June 30, 1930, the federal government's total expenditures had been less than $3 billion, of which it had spent only $191 million in California. In fiscal 1940 federal spending in the state had risen to $728 million, much of it for relief and old-age pensions. But in the single wartime fiscal year 1945, the federal government spent more than $8.5 billion in California.

When the Nazis began the war with their invasion of Poland in September 1939, neither California nor the rest of the country had fully recovered from the depression that had begun with the crash nearly 10 full years before. The state's population had increased 21.7 percent during the depressed 1930s (the lowest percentage

Fear of enemy bombardment prompted the sandbagging of this building on Grant Avenue in San Francisco, 1941. The words were painted on by a newspaper artist when the photo first ran. (*Courtesy of the* San Francisco Chronicle.)

increase recorded for any decade since American acquisition). But the total personal income of California in 1939 barely exceeded the 1930 figure of $5 billion, which meant that per capita income in 1939 had not yet climbed back to the level of 1930.

In 1945, however, the personal income of Californians was $15 billion. In other words, the war and the increase in federal spending raised total personal income in California to more than *three times* its prewar figure. This meant an enormous increase in per capita wealth, even allowing for inflation and for a state population growth of 30 percent between 1940 and 1945.

Federally financed activities took many forms, of which the most obvious were new or expanded military installations and new defense industries. In 1930 there had been only a handful of military installations in California, including the San Francisco Presidio, Fort Ord, the Mare Island Naval Shipyard, some naval facilities at San Diego, and March Field. By the end of the war all of these had been enormously expanded, and the list had grown to include camps Beale, Cooke, Pendleton, Roberts, and Stoneman; the Oakland Army Base and the Oakland Naval Supply Center; the Alameda Naval Air Station, the San Francisco Naval Shipyard, and the Treasure Island Naval Station; and several major Air Force bases—Castle, McClellan, Parks, and Travis.

Government money poured out through wage and salary payments to civilian and military personnel, investments in public and private facilities, purchases of supplies, and payments in the form of grants, subsidies, and interest. California received a disproportionate share of all these federal expenditures at a time when they had grown enormously.

The most apparent effect on California's economy, apart from the general increase in its size, was the wartime expansion of manufacturing. Under government contracts, American private industry produced a great variety of the sinews of war. In California, almost overnight, ships and airplanes became the most important of all the state's products.

Wartime Shipyards

With the government providing the bulk of the capital, Henry J. Kaiser of Oakland became the chief private entrepreneur of California's wartime shipbuilding industry. Kaiser's reputation as an engineering and industrial genius had begun with the construction of Hoover and Parker dams and had continued to grow with his major role in the building of the San Francisco Bay Bridge and the dams at Bonneville and Grand Coulee. In order to produce his own cement, Kaiser had built Permanente, the largest cement plant in the world. Before the United States entered the war, he had projected the first steel mill on the Pacific coast, at Fontana, 50 miles east of Los Angeles.

New shipyards sprang up in 1942 at Richmond, Oakland, Sausalito, Vallejo, and San Pedro. In full operation for 24 hours a day in three shifts, they were soon building "liberty ships" in 25 days, and in 1943 a new freighter was launched every 10 hours at one or another of the Kaiser shipyards.

At the peak of production in July 1943, civilian employment in the shipbuilding industry in California was nearly 300,000. Instead of the mass unemployment of the 1930s there was now a desperate shortage of labor. To one sign that read "Help Wanted!!! Male or Female, Young or Old, Experienced or Inexperienced," someone added "Dead or Alive!!!" Kaiser advertised for workers in every part of the country, and, in addition to the climate, he offered such inducements as high wages, on-the-job training, a subsidized plan for group medical care, and exemption from the draft by virtue of employment in an essential war industry.

The mushrooming growth of the shipyards put heavy strains on the surrounding communities, and every facility from schools to sewers was stretched to the breaking point or beyond it. Thousands of families lived in "temporary" wartime housing projects that would remain as slums for decades afterward. The most severe growing pains were probably those of the cities of Richmond and Vallejo. In each, the population increased from about 20,000 in 1940 to more than 100,000 in 1945, and the nonwhite population rose from less than 2 percent to nearly 14 percent.

"Americans All"

Because the shipyards could not afford to exclude anyone from their desperately short supply of labor, they offered extraordinary opportunities for women and members of minority races, whose previous chance for good pay in skilled occupations had been limited. Thousands of women were hired to work in the shipyards as electricians, steamfitters, and welders. But the disunity within American life was painfully evident in the intense prejudices of male shipyard workers against women and of whites against nonwhites. Black shipyard workers organized the United Negro Labor Committee to demand equal insurance benefits and voting privileges denied them by racially discriminatory unions. African American women were especially active in the fight for equal rights. When Frances Albrier completed twice the required number of hours of training for being a welder and was denied employment at the Kaiser shipyards in Richmond, she successfully campaigned to change the company's hiring practices. Tarea Hall Pittman helped newly arrived southern blacks understand the urgency of the challenge

Workers at the Kaiser shipyard in San Pedro raise their hats in a victory salute during the spring of 1945. Note especially the presence of women in the workforce. (*Courtesy of Special Collections, San Francisco Public Library.*)

they faced: "They could see the vestiges of discrimination here, that California was going to be exactly like Texas, Arkansas, Alabama, and Georgia and every place else if we didn't do something."

Racial divisions also were evident in the worst stateside disaster during the war. On July 17, 1944, two ammunition ships and a train exploded in a horrendous blast at the Port Chicago Naval Magazine on the south shore of Suisun Bay. Killed in the blast were 320 men, two-thirds of whom were African American sailors serving in a segregated unit assigned the unenviable task of loading ammunition. After the disaster, 50 of the surviving members of the unit refused to return to duty, citing unsafe working conditions and a lack of proper training. All the sailors were convicted of mutiny and sentenced to military prison. Later efforts to have their convictions overturned failed, even though the Navy admitted "there can be no doubt that racial prejudice was responsible for the posting of African Americans to the loading divisions at Port Chicago." On the fiftieth anniversary of the incident, a memorial containing the names of the victims of the blast was dedicated at the site.

Americans of Japanese descent also served in racially segregated military units during the war. California-born Japanese Americans enlisted in the 442d Regimental Combat Team. They distinguished themselves and suffered heavy losses in the Allied invasion of Italy in the autumn of 1943. The 442d became the most decorated regiment in the annals of the American Army. Their service was later recognized by a monument of a phoenix rising from barbed wire, dedicated in the nation's capital in 2001. "Japanese Americans came here with a promise, and the promise was broken," commented Democratic Congressman Mike Honda. "But they held true to the promise; their spirit and patriotism never wavered."

Among the wartime contributions of Native Americans, a select unit of Marines at Camp Pendleton in San Diego County developed a secret battlefield code based on the Navajo language. Hundreds of Indian "code talkers" served with distinction in the Central and South Pacific. When necessary, the code talkers fought alongside their fellow Leathernecks and risked their lives as troubleshooters and stretcher bearers.

Welcoming the chance to demonstrate their loyalty, Latinos enlisted in the armed forces in record numbers. One of the wartime slogans of Mexican American servicemen was "Americans All." As the war progressed, it became evident that some of the heaviest battlefront casualties were being suffered by infantry divisions containing a disproportionate share of Mexican Americans. Representing just a tenth of the population of Los Angeles during the war, Latinos accounted for a fifth of all casualties. California Congressman Jerry Voorhis, a Democrat from Orange County, observed:

> As I read the casualty lists from my state, I find anywhere from one-fourth to one-third of those names are names such as Gonzales or Sanchez, names indicating that the very lifeblood of our citizens of Latin-American descent in the uniform of the armed forces of the United States is being poured out to win victory in the war. We ought not to forget that.

The Rise of the Aircraft Industry

The importance of shipbuilding was doomed to end with the war, but the wartime expansion in the manufacturing of aircraft and in the industries closely related to it became a much more enduring and ultimately a much larger factor in California's growth.

Before the 1930s aircraft manufacturing in the United States was a small industry in which skilled artisans engaged in the leisurely production of custom-built planes. The more substantial factories were then in the east. Glenn L. Martin, who had established one of the first airplane factories in America in 1909, built some of his early planes in southern California, but he later moved his operations to Cleveland and then to Baltimore. In 1916 the brothers Allen and Malcolm Loughead set up a shop in Santa Barbara in association with John K. Northrop. During World War I, they won a contract to build seaplanes for the Navy, but the war ended before they could begin production. Refusing to be discouraged, the three men moved their little factory to Burbank and dispelled the previously hopeless confusion over the pronunciation of "Loughead" by adopting Lockheed as their company name.

In 1920 young Donald Douglas left a job as chief engineer and vice president of Martin's company in Cleveland to go into business for himself in southern California. With an initial capital of $600, Douglas set up his drafting room in the rear half of a barber shop on Pico Boulevard in Los Angeles. No banker would lend him a cent, but he attracted the interest of Harry Chandler, publisher of the *Times* and perpetual booster of new industry for the Los Angeles area. On the strength of an order for three Navy torpedo planes, Chandler and nine other southern California businesspeople loaned Douglas a total of $15,000, enabling him to establish a factory in an abandoned motion picture studio in Santa Monica. That factory succeeded so well that in 1924 two Douglas-built Army planes made the first flight around the world, though they took several months to complete it.

T. Claude Ryan, a former Army flyer, established the first daily scheduled airline passenger service in the United States in 1922 between San Diego and Los Angeles, and the next year he began to manufacture planes at San Diego. There his small company achieved a national reputation by building the *Spirit of St. Louis,* in which Charles A. Lindbergh made his spectacular flight from New York to Paris in 1927.

The depression was particularly hard on the aircraft industry. In 1932 Douglas went for 4 months without an order and kept his workers employed at gardening and plant maintenance, whereas the Lockheed company, whose general manager had mortgaged his house and car to meet a payroll during the previous Christmas week, went into bankruptcy.

Even in the period between the two world wars, more than half the country's airplane production was done under government contract, and no company survived without a share of military orders. Nevertheless, the military air forces of the United States in the late 1930s were alarmingly unprepared for war. As late as 1939, the entire output of the American aircraft industry was less than 6000 planes of all types—the full capacity of the factories then in existence. In May 1940, when

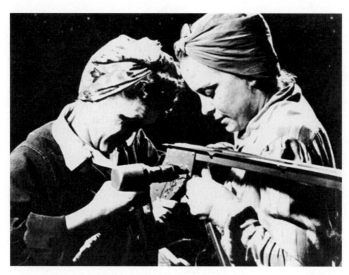

Women assembly workers rivet a gusset to a wing rib at the Long Beach plant of the Douglas Aircraft Company in October 1943. (*Courtesy of The Life and Times of Rosie the Riveter, Clarity Productions documentary. Contact: ConField@aol.com.*)

the Nazis invaded France, President Roosevelt called for an output of 50,000 planes a year, and although this figure was then regarded as shocking and impossible, actual production would more than double it by 1944.

The wartime expansion of aircraft manufacturing compressed 40 years of normal industrial progress into 40 months. In 1933 all the airframe factories in southern California together employed only about 1000 people. In November 1943 they employed 280,300.

As in the shipyards, the airframe plants actively recruited women to fill jobs previously held by men. Women made up over 40 percent of the workforce of the aircraft industry in southern California and thus made a major contribution to the war effort. The new employment opportunities also had a significant impact on the attitudes of the women workers. One female airframe worker later recalled, "All my life, I sorta had an inferiority complex and that was gone—completely—'cause I found out I could do a lot of things that I didn't know I could do."

Airframe plants, which made up the bulk of the aircraft industry in California, were only a part of the total process of aircraft production, but they were the largest part. They built the fuselage, wings, and tail; the engines, propellers, and other equipment were made in separate factories. During the war much of the automobile industry in Detroit was converted to making aircraft engines, but it was the airframe plants that assembled all the parts into the finished plane.

Aircraft accounted for nearly 60 percent of the money that the federal government spent under prime contracts for goods manufactured in California during World War II, but the profits of the aircraft companies were small. The great bulk of the expansion was accomplished with federal funds, through contracts under which the government guaranteed the entire cost and the companies received only a fixed fee in addition.

Four of the country's leading aircraft producers, Douglas, Lockheed, North American, and Northrop, had their main plants in the Los Angeles area, and two, Convair and Ryan, were in San Diego. Because clear, mild, and consistent weather offered great advantages for the production and testing of aircraft, climate became one of the principal factors in the location of airframe plants, and southern California therefore received a large share of the industry's wartime expansion. That share would have been even larger had it not been for the memory of Pearl Harbor and the fear that Japanese carrier-based bombers might attack the Pacific coast. The gigantic Douglas factory of Santa Monica was hidden under a camouflage cover, with dummy houses, streets, and trees, so that from the air and even from the ground it was almost impossible to distinguish the plant from its suburban residential surroundings.

The Relocation of Japanese Americans

The elaborate and expensive camouflaging of southern California aircraft factories, though it proved unnecessary, did no great harm, but the fear of Japanese attack also led the government of the United States into a massive, tragic, and needless blunder. This was the evacuation from the west coast of all persons of Japanese ancestry and the imprisonment of most of them, citizens and aliens alike, without trial, behind barbed wire, under armed guard, in so-called relocation camps in desert areas in the interior.

The attack on Pearl Harbor and false rumors of sabotage and other treasonable acts by Japanese Americans reactivated all the stereotyped racist delusions that had long formed the beliefs of many Californians about the Japanese. Since the early years of the century a number of the state's most influential newspapers, politicians, and organizations had frequently portrayed all persons of Japanese extraction as sly, sinister, ruthless, and incapable of loyalty to any country but Japan.

For the more effective dissemination of such ideas, Valentine S. McClatchy, publisher of the *Sacramento Bee,* had formed the California Joint Immigration Committee in 1921. This body coordinated the propaganda activities of four existing anti-Japanese organizations. Among its members were the secretary-treasurer of the state Federation of Labor, the master of the state Grange, the grand president of the Native Sons of the Golden West, the deputy adjutant of the California Department of the American Legion, and the attorney general of California. Attorney General Ulysses S. Webb, one of the principal authors of the state's alien land law, often asserted in public speeches that persons of Japanese origin had inherent racial traits that rendered them unassimilable and untrustworthy as Americans. Earl Warren, when he succeeded Webb as attorney general of California in 1939, held similar views.

Immediately after the raid on Pearl Harbor, rumors of treacherous acts by Japanese Americans in Hawaii began to circulate both in the islands and on the mainland. Rumormongers claimed to know on the best authority that Japanese vegetable trucks had blocked roads, or that one truck had rushed across Hickham Field and knocked the tails off a line of fighter planes, or that a huge arrow cut in a field of sugarcane the night before the raid had guided the Japanese bombers to this or that important target.

For the first several weeks after the Pearl Harbor raid, the gradually increasing demands for some sort of mass action against the Japanese Americans on the west coast received little support from Lieutenant General John L. DeWitt, head of the Western Defense Command. On December 26, DeWitt telephoned from his headquarters at the San Francisco Presidio to the provost marshal general in Washington, D.C., to report that he had just received a visit from a representative of the Los Angeles Chamber of Commerce who demanded the internment of all the Japanese in the Los Angeles area, regardless of whether they were citizens of the United States. DeWitt was opposed. "I'm very doubtful that it would be a commonsense procedure," he told the provost marshal general. It would be "likely to alienate the loyal Japanese," and "an American citizen, after all, is an American citizen."

A month later, however, General DeWitt changed his mind, largely as a result of the sensational publicity given to the report of the Pearl Harbor investigating commission under Supreme Court Justice Owen J. Roberts. That report, published on January 25, 1942, laid the blame for the disaster mainly on the Army and Navy commanders in Hawaii, Lieutenant General Walter C. Short and Admiral Husband E. Kimmel, respectively, and charged these two officers with "dereliction of duty" in having failed to take adequate precautions for the defense of the islands. Short and Kimmel had already been removed from their commands, but several congressional leaders now demanded that they suffer the further disgrace of being court-martialed. The Roberts Report also asserted that the "Japanese spies on the Island of Oahu" had included "persons having no open relations with the Japanese Foreign Service." Many Americans interpreted this statement as new and official evidence of widespread Japanese American disloyalty.

The truth was that there was not a scrap of valid evidence to connect any Japanese American resident of Hawaii with any act of espionage or sabotage. But this would not be widely known until after the war. The Roberts Report, at the time it was published, had an enormous and inflammatory effect on public opinion, especially in California.

On January 27 DeWitt had a long conference with Governor Culbert L. Olson. A few weeks before, Olson had pleaded for tolerance of Japanese Americans and for confidence in their loyalty, but now, DeWitt informed the War Department, the governor had joined those who were "bringing pressure to move all the Japanese out." Attorney General Earl Warren, Mayor Fletcher Bowron of Los Angeles, and many others were making this demand, DeWitt reported, and the agitation for it came from "the best people of California. Since the publication of the Roberts Report they feel that they are living in the midst of a lot of enemies." In a conference a few days later, DeWitt remarked with intense emotion that "I am not going to be a second General Short."

DeWitt was now in a state of suppressed terror, brought on by fear of the disgrace that had befallen Short and Kimmel, and it was in this state of mind that he prepared a report to the secretary of war on the "Evacuation of Japanese and other Subversive Persons from the Pacific Coast." Among other remarkable statements, this document asserted that "the Japanese race is an enemy race" and that "along the vital Pacific Coast over 112,000 potential enemies, of Japanese extraction, are at large today. There are indications that these are organized and ready for concerted action at a favorable opportunity. The very fact that no sabotage has taken place to date is a disturbing and confirming indication that such action will be taken."

This fantastic line of reasoning was very widely accepted. On February 13 the entire west coast congressional delegation sent a letter to President Roosevelt demanding the "immediate evacuation of all persons of Japanese lineage . . . aliens and citizens alike" from "the entire strategic area" of California, Oregon, and Washington.

Secretary of War Henry L. Stimson and Assistant Secretary John J. McCloy, in a conference with President Roosevelt at the White House on February 11, had already asked the president for authorization to move Japanese American citizens as well as aliens from "restricted areas" on the west coast. There would "probably be repercussions," Roosevelt replied, but they must act from their judgment of military necessity. McCloy informed DeWitt by telephone that the president had given the War Department "carte blanche."

Meanwhile, Attorney General Francis Biddle and his assistants in the Department of Justice had prepared a battery of arguments opposing the mass evacuation of American citizens as unconstitutional and the evacuation of the enemy aliens as unnecessary and unwise. Before they could present these arguments, the president informed Biddle that the question would be decided entirely on military grounds.

On February 19, President Roosevelt signed a most extraordinary document. This was Executive Order 9066, authorizing the secretary of war "whenever he or any designated Commander deems such action necessary or desirable, to prescribe military areas . . . from which any or all persons may be excluded."

On March 2, the Western Defense Command issued its Public Proclamation No. 1. All persons of Japanese ancestry were, in effect, *ordered* to migrate *voluntarily* from Military Area No. 1—the western halves of California, Oregon, and Washington and the southern half of Arizona. But this led to bitter protests from communities and states in the interior against being "used as a dumping ground" for the presumably disloyal and dangerous Japanese, and on March 27 another proclamation ordered the coast Japanese to cease voluntary migration and instead to await controlled evacuation and internment. Soon afterward this order was extended to include Military Area No. 2—the other halves of the west coast states and Arizona.

There were then more than 93,000 Japanese Americans in California, 14,000 in Washington, and 4000 in Oregon, or a total of about 112,000 in the three coastal states. Of these more than 71,000 were *Nisei* and about 41,000 *Issei*. Nisei were American-born citizens, of whom only a few hundred were more than 35 years old; a large majority were under 21. Issei were Japanese immigrants, nearly all of whom were adults, because Japanese immigration had virtually ceased when Congress banned it in 1924. Because the Issei were Asians, they had never been eligible for naturalization, and their legal status was now that of enemy aliens. In any case, the proclamations of the Western Defense Command generally used the word "Japanese" without making a distinction in the matter of citizenship.

During the spring of 1942, under Army supervision, nearly all the west coast Japanese Americans were confined in improvised *assembly centers* at racetracks, fairgrounds, or livestock exhibition halls. (See Color Plate 15.) During the summer and fall, they were evacuated to more permanent *relocation camps*. There were 10 of these, located in some of the bleakest parts of the continent. Two were in California—at Manzanar in the Owens Valley and at Tule Lake near the Oregon border. Most of the camps were in desert regions, intensely hot in summer and bitterly cold in winter. The buildings were made of wood frame and tar paper.

These barracks cities were called relocation camps or centers rather than concentration camps, and they were under the control of a civilian agency, the War Relocation Authority (WRA). The administrators of the WRA were carefully chosen, mostly from the permanent staffs of the federal departments of Agriculture and the Interior, and in general they were able and understanding persons who wished to allow the internees the maximum of self-government that was possible under the circumstances. But the camps were essentially prisons, surrounded by tall barbed-wire fences and guarded by soldiers.

Relocation had a devastating effect on Japanese American families. The residents of the camps did their best to maintain traditional family structures, but disintegration was a constant threat. The stress hit many Japanese American women particularly hard. "Our family unit had been very strong until that time," Kimiko Kitamaya later recalled. "It broke down a little bit in the camps because the younger kids were running around and being very independent. So the family unit that we always considered as very strong, slowly disintegrated."

The evacuation was based on the argument of "military necessity," but this argument was untenable. The Japanese never contemplated an invasion of the mainland of the United States, and moreover neither General DeWitt nor any other commander ever maintained that such a landing might be attempted. As for the possibility of air raids, the Japanese lost one of their carriers in the Battle of the Coral Sea, May 4–8, 1942; in the Battle of Midway, June 4–6, they lost four more—all the carriers they could have committed to any further action in the central Pacific, let alone in the eastern Pacific. Any possibility of an air attack on the American mainland ended with the Battle of Midway. Yet the movement of Japanese American internees from the local assembly centers on the west coast to the relocation centers in the interior took place *after* that battle.

The logic behind the claim of military necessity becomes even more puzzling when the evacuation of Japanese Americans from the west coast is contrasted with the government's policy toward Italian Americans and German Americans. The United States was at war with Japan, Germany, and Italy, but only Americans of Japanese ancestry were subject to mass evacuation. Individual aliens from

A former landscape gardener from southern California demonstrated his skill and ingenuity by creating a rock garden alongside his tar paper–covered barrack at the Manzanar relocation center in 1942. (*Photograph by Dorothea Lange. Courtesy of the Bancroft Library.*)

Germany and Italy—including some who were naturalized citizens—endured wartime internment and exclusion. But these actions affected only those aliens declared "dangerous" by various intelligence agencies. It was a small group. Out of the several hundred thousand German and Italian aliens living in the United States, about 2000 were placed in wartime internment camps and 250 naturalized citizens were ordered to move from coastal states.

The argument of military necessity appears even more contrived when one considers what happened to the Japanese Americans living in the Hawaiian Islands. There were about 160,000 persons of Japanese ancestry in the islands, one-third more than the number on the mainland. Not only did thousands of them live in close proximity to military and naval installations on Oahu, but they actually worked in them and continued to do so after Pearl Harbor, simply because they formed the bulk of the skilled labor on the island and could not have been replaced for months. Furthermore, the military government that ruled the islands during most of the war argued that there was no need to relocate the Japanese Americans because they were already effectively controlled. All major "Japanese relocation" plans for Hawaii were thus abandoned. As an Army spokesman explained to the Honolulu press, "The shipping situation and the labor shortage make it a *military necessity* to keep most of the people of Japanese blood on the island." [The italics are added.]

It was not only the labor force of Hawaii that was dependent on the Japanese Americans at the outbreak of the war. The two Hawaiian National Guard regiments that shared in the task of guarding the islands included many men of Japanese descent. They were not withdrawn from the Guard regiments until May 1942, when sufficient replacements had finally arrived from the west coast. Then they were formed into the 100th Infantry Battalion. Later, mainland Japanese Americans recruited from relocation camps were enlisted in the heavily decorated all-Nisei 442d Regimental Combat Team.

In the words of the official history of *The United States Army in World War II,* "little support for the argument that military necessity required a mass evacuation of the Japanese can be found in contemporary evidence." Instead, in defense of the Army, its official history makes the remarkable suggestion that "the cooperation of the white population of the Pacific states in the national defense effort could not have been . . . assured" if the government and the military had not bowed to "formidable pressure" from west coast civilians for Japanese American removal.

On the other hand, the United States Supreme Court, in upholding the evacuation, maintained that the Army had acted from military necessity and that in time of war it was not the prerogative of any civilians, even the members of that Court itself, to attempt to evaluate the decisions of the military on military matters.

In the Hirabayashi case in 1943 and the Korematsu and Endo cases in 1944, the Supreme Court drastically weakened the constitutional rights of all Americans in wartime by condoning a massive injustice that had been inflicted on a particular group of Americans because of their race. As Justice Frank Murphy put it in his dissent in the case of Korematsu, the majority of the Court upheld the government and the military in an action that went "over the . . . brink of constitutional power and . . . into the ugly abyss of racism." Justice Robert H. Jackson, in his separate dissent, pointed out that the principle approved by the majority decision would thereafter lie about "like a loaded weapon ready for the hand of any authority that can bring forward a plausible claim of an urgent need."

Most of the evacuees were held in the relocation camps for more than 2 years until after the War Department revoked the west coast exclusion orders in December 1944. About half of them returned to the west coast during 1945 and 1946. In many cases their return was greeted with threats and acts of terrorism, but strong voices were also raised in their behalf. General Joseph W. Stilwell, in particular, denounced the terrorists as "barfly commandos." Mary Masuda, a young woman who had spent 2½ years at the Gila River relocation center, received threats of violence from a group of vigilantes when she returned to her home near Santa Ana. Her brother, a war hero who had been killed in Italy, was posthumously awarded the Distinguished Service Cross. On December 8, 1945, General Stilwell presented Sergeant Masuda's medal to his sister in her home, and this sobering incident received wide publicity.

In the postwar years, many Californians gradually came to realize the enormity of the mistake that had been made. Many could accept the view of the War Relocation Authority in its final report (1946): "Since we are continually striving, with the better part of our minds, to be a united people, it becomes important for us to

understand and evaluate what we did, both officially and unofficially, to this particular racial segment of our population in time of global war."

Selected Bibliography

Roger W. Lotchin (ed.), *The Way We Really Were: The Golden State in the Second Great War* (2000), and Kevin Starr, *The Dream Endures: California Enters the 1940s* (1997), are excellent introductions. The best general surveys are Gerald D. Nash, *The American West Transformed* (1985) and *World War II and the West* (1990). Nash analyzes the impact of the war on California's economy, urban development, ethnic minorities, and cultural life. More localized studies include Marilynn S. Johnson, *The Second Gold Rush: Oakland and the East Bay in World War II* (1993), and Arthur C. Verge, *Paradise Transformed: Los Angeles during the Second World War* (1993).

On the relationship between urban development and defense spending, see Lotchin, *Fortress California 1910–1961* (1992), and a special issue of *Pacific Historical Review*, LXIII (August 1994), edited by Lotchin. See also Martin J. Schiesl, "City Planning and the Federal Government in World War II: The Los Angeles Experience," *California History*, LIX (Summer 1980), pp. 126–143, and Mark S. Foster, *Henry J. Kaiser* (1989).

Charles Wollenberg's *Marinship at War: Shipbuilding and Social Change in Wartime Sausalito* (1990) is a penetrating analysis. Dorothea Lange's wartime photos of the East Bay are available in Wollenberg (ed.), *Photographing the Second Gold Rush* (1995). See also Shirley Ann Wilson Moore, *To Place Our Deeds: The African American Community in Richmond, California, 1910–1930* (2000); Katherine Archibald, *Wartime Shipyard* (1947); "Richmond Took a Beating," *Fortune*, XXXI (February 1945), pp. 262–269; and Sally M. Miller and Daniel A. Cornford (eds.), *American Labor in the Era of World War II* (1995).

John B. Rae's *Climb to Greatness: The American Aircraft Industry, 1920–1960* (1968) is the standard short account. Others are William A. Schoneberger and Paul Sonnenburg, *California Wings* (1987); Arlene Elliott, "The Rise of Aeronautics in California, 1849–1940," *Southern California Quarterly*, LII (March 1970), pp. 1–32; and Arthur P. Allen and Betty V. H. Schneider, *Industrial Relations in the California Aircraft Industry* (1956).

Jacobus tenBroek, Edward N. Barnhart, and Floyd W. Matson, *Prejudice, War, and the Constitution* (1954); U.S. Department of the Interior, War Relocation Authority, *WRA: A Story of Human Conservation* (1946); Allan R. Bosworth, *America's Concentration Camps* (1967); and Roger Daniels, *Concentration Camps* (1981), are general accounts of the causes, events, and historical and legal significance of the Japanese American evacuation.

Morton Grodzins, *Americans Betrayed* (1949), stresses the influence of California pressure groups and politicians on the making of the decision. U.S. Army, Western Defense Command, *Final Report: Japanese Evacuation from the West Coast, 1942* (1943), is a distressingly unreliable and misleading apologia, written largely by Colonel Karl R. Bendetsen and submitted over the signature of General DeWitt. Compare with Stetson Conn et al., *Guarding the United States and Its Outposts* (1964), a volume in the official history *The United States Army in World War II*. Roger Daniels, "The Decisions to Relocate the North American Japanese: Another Look," *Pacific Historical Review*, LI (February 1982), pp. 71–77, stresses the underlying racist motivations for relocation. On the Supreme Court decisions, see Peter Irons, *Justice at War* (1983) and *Justice Delayed* (1989). See also Lawrence DiStasi (ed.), *Una Storia Segreta: The World War II Evacuation and Internment of Italian Americans* (2001).

The impact of relocation on Japanese Americans is described in Dorothy S. Thomas et al., *The Spoilage* (1946) and *The Salvage* (1952); Mine Okubo, *Citizen 13660* (1946), an enlightening memoir; Harry H. L. Kitano, *Japanese Americans* (1969); Bill Hosokawa, *Nisei* (1969); Audrie Girdner and Anne Loftis, *The Great Betrayal* (1969); Edison Uno, *Japanese Americans* (1971); and Maisie Conrat and Richard Conrat, *Executive Order 9066* (1972), with photographs by Dorothea Lange and others. Roger Daniels has compiled a documentary history in *American Concentration Camps* (1989) and a collection of interpretive essays in *Japanese Americans: From Relocation to Redress* (1986).

CHAPTER 28

Politics California Style

The middle decades of the twentieth century were a crucial period in the political history of California. Both major parties remained extraordinarily weak, and new institutions emerged to fill the void. In the free-for-all of California politics, spurious issues and a galaxy of political exotics created an impression of political fervor. Pundits marveled at the anomalous spectacle of the state's Democratic majority consistently electing Republicans to office. The tide turned in 1958 when the Democrats at last managed to gain control of the state government.

Meanwhile, California's political leaders were capturing the national limelight. The state was on its way to becoming a training ground for national leadership.

Nonpartisanship Favors the Republicans

The rolls of registered voters show that the great depression of the 1930s had converted California from an overwhelmingly Republican to a heavily Democratic state. In 1930 the number of Californians registered as Democrats had been only 22 percent of the two-party registration. In 1936 it had risen to 60 percent, and this three-to-two superiority of Democratic over Republican voters continued with little variation for decades afterward. Yet from 1942 until 1958, the preponderantly Democratic voters of California elected heavy majorities of Republicans to state offices.

More than ever before, the political conditions of the depressed 1930s had identified the Republicans as the party of the haves and the Democrats as the party of the have-nots. A large majority of the business community continued to be Republican. So did a substantial proportion of white Anglo-Saxon Protestants. The Democrats, on the other hand, drew the bulk of their following from labor, the unemployed, and ethnic and religious minority groups. Most of the huge increase in Democratic registration in the early 1930s was made up of citizens who had never taken the trouble to register before and who did so now out of a desire to vote for a government that would take a greater interest in the less advantaged members of society.

All this meant, however, that most Democratic voters were less educated and less informed than most Republican voters. In this situation California's peculiar cross-filing law tended to keep Republican incumbents in office. Under that law the party affiliations of candidates did not appear on the primary election ballot, but a candidate running for reelection was listed first and identified as the incumbent. Hundreds of thousands of Democratic voters were quite unaware that the incumbent whose name appeared on the Democratic primary ballot could be and in fact usually was a Republican. Under this system, three-fourths of the elections to state offices were won in the primaries by incumbents who won the nominations of both major parties. In the legislative session of 1945, for example, 36 of the 40 state senators were elected in the primaries, and most of them were Republican incumbents.

In other respects, also, the Republicans were in a much better position than the Democrats to cope with the "nonpartisan" system (or rather the antiparty system), which the Republican progressives under Hiram Johnson had introduced. The Republicans not only had most of the experienced and successful candidates; they also had far more money for political campaigning, and they had the support of a great majority of the newspapers, including the three most influential ones, the *Los Angeles Times,* the *San Francisco Chronicle,* and the *Oakland Tribune.*

A newspaper is ordinarily a business enterprise, dependent for the bulk of its income on the advertising of other business enterprises. Consequently, most newspaper publishers preferred the Republican party, with its orientation toward business interests, low taxes, and a minimum of governmental control. Remembering the preponderance of Democratic voters, however, California newspapers tended to support Republican candidates as individuals without overstressing their party affiliation.

Filling the Void

Cross-filing and the other antiparty laws of the progressives had been designed to destroy the power of corrupt political machines in California. By weakening the traditional party organizations, these laws opened the way for alternative institutions to fill the power vacuum. These institutions included special-interest lobbyists, professional campaign-management firms, and informal party organizations.

Lobbying has often been known as "the fourth branch of government" or as "the third house" of a legislature. In fact, the lawmaking process in any democratic government would be crippled if the legislative body tried to operate without the constant flow of information from representatives of interested groups. But the corrupt use of power, and especially the power of money to influence legislation and the elections of legislators, has always been a menace to democracy.

Arthur H. Samish, king of the California lobbyists, represented a coalition of liquor, oil, bus, trucking, mining, banking, billboard, theatrical, racetrack, and other

Arthur H. Samish (1899–1974) and "Mr. Legislature." Taking pictures for *Collier's,* photographer Fred Lyon caught Samish in this remarkable pose in his suite at the Senator Hotel in Sacramento. (© Bettman/Corbis.)

interests. He came to have almost as much power in the 1930s and 1940s as William F. Herrin had exercised at the turn of the century. Samish organized the state's brewers, distillers, and tavernkeepers into a kind of pro-saloon league, and in 1935 he made a contract with the California State Brewers' Association providing an assessment of 5 cents on every barrel of beer for a political fund to be dispensed by Samish with no accounting. In later years he often reminded his clients in the liquor industry that as a result of his efforts California had the lowest liquor taxes in the nation. He also reminded the oil companies that retained him as a lobbyist that oil severance taxes in Louisiana and Texas were about 100 times as high as in California.

In 1938 the Sacramento grand jury employed a private detective to investigate charges that Samish had attempted to bribe members of the state senate. The detective reported finding "ample evidence that corruption, direct and indirect, has influenced the course of legislation." Samish, it was discovered, had received from his clients about $500,000 during the previous 3 years. The basis of Samish's method was "to acquire influence with a group of Legislators through campaign contributions or other favors and then to sell that influence to industries concerned with legislation."

Ten years later, in 1949, *Collier's* magazine published an exposé called "The Secret Boss of California." Forgetting, for once, the importance of secrecy in his operations, and giving way to the most blatant braggadocio, Samish posed for a color photograph in his hotel suite at the state capital. On his knee he held a ventriloquist's dummy, which he addressed as "Mr. Legislature." The appearance of such an article and especially of such a picture in a national magazine finally compelled the California legislature to take some sort of action. It passed a law requiring lobbyists to register and to file monthly financial statements, but these statements usually proved to be so vague that they were meaningless.

The downfall of Samish finally resulted from his failure to report his income and expenditures to the federal government. In 1953 he was convicted of income tax evasion and later served 2 years in a federal penitentiary. The state assembly reorganized its committee system in 1953 to eliminate Samish's influence. The next year, one former speaker of the assembly was convicted of bribery in liquor license transactions and another was indicted but released after two hung juries.

In addition to lobbying, which gained such a dangerous degree of influence over the legislature, another institution that emerged in California politics was the professional campaign-management firm—a distinctive contribution of California to American politics. In the 1930s an organization called Campaigns, Inc., founded by Californians Clem Whitaker and Leone Baxter, revolutionized political campaigning by making carefully planned use of the mass media and the commercial techniques of the advertising industry. It was natural that the first full-fledged professional campaign-management firm in the United States should have developed in California because of the state's lack of party organization, its constant influx of new voters, and its extraordinarily frequent use of the initiative and the referendum.

Clem Whitaker was a reporter in Sacramento at the age of 17. Within a few years, he was operating his own Capitol News Bureau, furnishing syndicated news on state politics to more than 80 California papers. In 1933 he met Leone Baxter, an articulate young widow who worked for the Redding Chamber of Commerce. Joining forces, Whitaker and Baxter in 1934 managed the Republican campaign against Upton Sinclair, and though they later expressed regret at some of the shabbier devices they felt compelled to use against him, this campaign firmly established their reputation. The partners were married in 1938.

For the next 20 years their support decided many of the key issues of California politics. They usually managed the campaigns for or against five or six initiative or referendum propositions in every state election. Whitaker and Baxter would accept no campaign that was not in accord with their own political views, and as their financial success increased, their views became more and more conservative. The purposes of their clients, Baxter wrote, must be consistent with "individual initiative and personal responsibility; the free operation of our economic society; reasonable freedom from government control and direction." In 1945 Whitaker and Baxter took over the campaign of the California Medical Association to brand a state health plan as "socialized medicine." Their success led the American Medical Association (AMA) to employ them in 1949 for its drive to block President Harry Truman's federal health insurance proposals. The multimillion-dollar campaign fund was drawn largely from special compulsory assessments on the doctor members of the AMA. This was the largest cause that Whitaker and Baxter had ever served, but it was not the most meritorious. Their tactics created so much resentment that they ultimately did almost as much to advance as to retard the movement toward nationwide health insurance, which finally went into effect in 1966 in spite of their efforts.

Dozens of other professional campaign-management firms followed in the success of Whitaker and Baxter. Some firms specialized in boosting candidates, others in gathering the signatures needed to place propositions on the ballot. The influence of such firms in California politics was enormous. "If you give me $500,000," one professional campaign manager told author Gladwin Hill, "I'll guarantee to get on the ballot a measure to execute the governor by Christmas."

The third institution to emerge as a consequence of California's nonpartisan politics was the informal party organization. The Republicans had formed the first such body, the California Republican Assembly (CRA), at a low point in their party's fortunes in 1933, but the Democrats had been unable to follow suit because of the lack of comparable dedication and enthusiasm among their grassroots volunteer workers. In 1952, however, Adlai E. Stevenson became a kind of patron saint for liberal Democrats, and hundreds of new Democratic clubs sprang up in support of his presidential candidacy. Intense disappointment at his defeat played a part in bringing these clubs together in a statewide federation the next year, the California Democratic Council (CDC).

State conventions of the unofficial California Republican Assembly had contributed heavily to Republican successes by making preprimary endorsements of candidates. On the other hand, extreme confusion and division had continued to weaken the Democratic aspirants in the primaries until their party acquired its own informal nominating machinery in the state conventions of the California Democratic Council. For some years after this system was established, few candidates of either party could win nomination without the endorsement of the CRA or the CDC. Some protested that these endorsements defeated the whole purpose of the direct primary and essentially returned the nominating function to the party convention system, but the informal organizations were much more democratic and less subject to boss control than the old party conventions had been, and to the degree that they could unite each party behind one candidate, they reduced the costs of preprimary campaigning and the excessive role of money in elections.

The Governorship of Earl Warren

The California Republicans found in Earl Warren a leader who was ideally qualified to turn the state's nonpartisan tradition to Republican advantage. Warren did this so successfully that when he was elected to his second term as governor in 1946, he won the Democratic as well as the Republican nomination and became the only California governor ever elected in the primary.

Warren was born in Los Angeles in 1891 and grew up in Kern City, a railroad town near Bakersfield. His father, who had come from Norway, was a master car mechanic for the Southern Pacific and later a real estate broker. Like Hiram Johnson, his political hero, Warren studied at the University of California in Berkeley and made his early political reputation as a public prosecutor. But the personalities of the two men were very different. Johnson was emotional and volatile; Warren was calm and almost stolid.

After a term as state attorney general, Warren easily defeated Culbert L. Olson for the governorship in 1942. During the war years when California enjoyed the unprecedented blessing of a large surplus of revenue from the wartime boom, Warren became a very popular governor. He sponsored reductions in taxes and still was able to preserve a surplus in the treasury for the postwar expansion of such services as highways and public higher education to keep up with the state's tremendous growth.

In 1945 Warren alarmed his conservative supporters by recommending a state compulsory health insurance law. Some of the more advanced Republican progressives had advocated state health insurance as early as 1916, but this, along with many other social reforms, had been a casualty of World War I. Governor Olson had revived the proposal, but the opposition of the California Medical Association and the private insurance companies, in alliance with conservative interests in general, had always defeated it. The same alliance now defeated Warren's proposals also, and the experience did much to disillusion him with the conservative elements in the Republican party.

The oil and trucking lobbies disillusioned him further by their resistance to an increase in the gasoline tax, which Warren requested in 1947 in order to pay for a great expansion of state highways and freeways. Sam Collins, speaker of the assembly, permitted an oil lobbyist to use the speaker's office as a command post for the battle against the tax bill, though a compromise increase was finally agreed upon. As Warren pointed out, the oil and trucking interests were remarkably shortsighted in their opposition to the measure, because it made possible a new statewide network of freeways that increased the sale of gasoline and greatly aided the growth of the trucking industry.

In Warren's election to an unprecedented third term as governor of California in 1950, he did not quite repeat his triumph of 1946 by winning the Democratic as well as the Republican nomination in the primary, but in the general election in November he received a million votes more than the Democratic nominee, Congressman James Roosevelt of Los Angeles.

Democrats often complained that Warren represented himself as nonpartisan whenever he ran for governor, but that in presidential years he was strictly a Republican. As temporary chairman and keynote speaker of the Republican national convention in 1944, he delivered an intensely partisan address. In 1948—the only election he ever lost—he was the Republican nominee for vice president, as the running mate of Governor Thomas E. Dewey of New York. In 1952 Warren was an important contender for the Republican presidential nomination, which he would probably have received as the compromise candidate if the convention had not managed to break the deadlock between Senator Robert A. Taft and General Dwight D. Eisenhower.

In September 1953 President Eisenhower appointed Governor Warren as Chief Justice of the United States.

When Warren left the governorship, his successor was Lieutenant Governor Goodwin J. Knight, a Republican from Los Angeles. Although he strenuously opposed the liberal policies of Warren on such issues as state health insurance, Knight recognized that Warren's remarkable successes in gaining reelection as a Republican governor were based on his ability to capture Democratic votes, and particularly labor votes. Therefore, Knight made and kept a promise that as governor he would veto all antilabor measures. Thus, he received the formal endorsement of the California Federation of Labor, and in his campaign in 1954 he easily defeated his Democratic opponent, who had little political experience and was virtually unknown to most of the voters.

The Spurious Issue of "Loyalty"

The Republican ascendancy in state politics during the late 1940s and 1950s was aided by the anticommunist enthusiasm of the cold war. Cold war tensions also led to bitter division and recrimination in the state's film industry, and propelled the University of California into a storm of controversy that lasted for years.

Congress in 1938 created the House Un-American Activities Committee (HUAC), chaired by a conservative Democrat from Texas, Congressman Martin Dies. One of the early targets of HUAC's anticommunist investigations was the film industry in Hollywood. In 1947 a list was issued of suspected Communists in

Film stars such as Lauren Bacall and Humphrey Bogart went to Washington, D.C., in 1947 to protest the HUAC investigation of communism in Hollywood. (© UPI/Bettmann/Corbis.)

the industry, and eventually 250 actors, writers, and directors were barred from further employment. Testimony against the "Red Menace in Hollywood" came from such industry leaders as Jack Warner, Louis B. Mayer, and Gary Cooper. Ronald Reagan, president of the Screen Actors Guild from 1947 to 1952, cooperated fully in the effort to rid the studios of suspected Communists. Walt Disney testified before Congress that the Screen Cartoonists Guild was Communist controlled and had plotted to make Mickey Mouse follow the party line. Other film leaders— including Humphrey Bogart, Gene Kelly, Judy Garland, and Katharine Hepburn— risked their careers by speaking out against the anticommunist hysteria.

The impact of anticommunism was also soon apparent in state and national politics. With the defeat of Germany and Japan in World War II, the Soviet Union secured an enormous expansion of its military power, and of communist influence, in eastern Europe and eastern Asia. In the United States, the Republican party had considerable success in blaming these menacing developments on the policies of the Democratic national administration. By charging that the liberal Democratic leadership was "soft on Communism," the Republicans had their revenge for all the years when they had been branded unfairly but effectively as the party of depression: They now branded the Democrats unfairly but effectively as the party of treason.

In the congressional elections of 1946, the Republicans gained control of both houses of Congress, and in California seven Democratic incumbents lost their seats in the House to Republicans. One of the victorious Republicans was Richard M. Nixon of Whittier, a political newcomer who defeated Jerry Voorhis, the liberal Democrat who had represented the district for 10 years and had been one of the most effective supporters of the New Deal.

Richard Nixon would later become the first native son of California to win the presidency of the United States. He was born in 1913 to Quaker parents at Yorba Linda in Orange County. In 1922 the family acquired a general store and gasoline station in Whittier, and there Nixon and his brothers worked long hours after school. He worked his way through Whittier College, won a scholarship that enabled him to attend and graduate with honors from the law school of Duke University, practiced law in his hometown, and served during the war as a Naval Reserve officer.

In his campaign against Voorhis in 1946, Nixon followed a strategy of innuendo that the Republican National Committee had recommended to the party's candidates. He accused his Democratic opponent of disloyalty to America, not directly but through guilt by association. He charged that Voorhis was "one of those who front for un-American elements, wittingly or otherwise, by advocating increased federal controls over the lives of the people"; that Voorhis had the endorsement of the CIO Political Action Committee; and that the CIO-PAC was Communist-infiltrated. "Of course I knew that Jerry Voorhis wasn't a Communist," Nixon remarked afterward, "but I had to win. . . . Nice guys and sissies don't win many elections." Adlai Stevenson, a later victim of similar attacks, would describe them more harshly: "Nixonland, a land of slander and scare, of sly innuendo, of a poison pen, the anonymous phone call, and hustling, pushing, shoving—the land of smash and grab and anything to win."

As a member of HUAC during his first term in Congress, Nixon rendered a service of enormous practical value to his party. He discovered convincing evidence that Alger Hiss, a Democrat who had served in the State Department during the war, had been a secret Communist during the 1930s, when he had engaged in an espionage scheme to transmit government documents to the Russians. Eventually, on January 21, 1950, Hiss was convicted of perjury for denying these charges. Republicans now argued that under the Democrats, a one-time Communist spy had been able to infiltrate the upper levels of the federal government, even the Department of State, and that therefore the Democratic party in general must be tainted with communism.

The nation's fear of world communism intensified with the explosion of the first Russian atomic bomb in 1949 and the outbreak of the Korean War in 1950. In this period many Americans were even willing to credit the wild charges of Senator Joseph McCarthy of Wisconsin, who made a series of speeches in which he "held in his hand a list" alleged to contain the names of "card-carrying Communists now employed in the State Department." McCarthy never turned up a single person who was or ever had been a Communist in the government service. Nixon, on the other hand, had actually uncovered one such person, according to the verdict of a jury.

In 1950 Nixon won the election to the United States Senate over the Democratic nominee Congresswoman Helen Gahagan Douglas, a former Broadway actress. Nixon's most effective campaign weapon against Douglas was the charge that her voting record in the House of Representatives corresponded with the Communist party line. Nixon had chanced on the most rapid political escalator that the times provided. In 1951, after his election as senator, and again in 1953 after his further elevation to the vice presidency, nearly every Republican member of the House of Representatives applied for a seat on the committee on un-American activities.

The California legislature established its own joint Fact-Finding Committee on Un-American Activities in 1941, with Jack B. Tenney of Los Angeles as chairman. Tenney was a piano player and songwriter whose first widely known achievement was the composing of a popular song called "Mexicali Rose." As chairman of California's un-American activities committee, Tenney set himself up as prosecutor, judge, and jury. He bullied witnesses and denied them the rights of due process that they would have had in a normal legal proceeding. He bracketed the innocent with the guilty, convicted by accusation, punished by publicity, and tried to silence criticism by directing these methods against every critic.

The reports of the Tenney committee often included charges of communist influence in the University of California. Early in 1949 Tenney introduced a proposal for a state constitutional amendment to take from the regents and give to the legislature the power to ensure the loyalty of the university's employees. The university's lobbyist and comptroller, James H. Corley, considered this a dangerous political interference in university affairs. He persuaded Tenney not to push his constitutional amendment in return for a promise that the university itself would take some sort of action. This led the regents to adopt the famous loyalty oath, which embroiled the University of California in the bitterest controversy in the history of American higher education up to that time. The new oath required the professor or other university employee to swear that he or she did "not believe in," was "not a member of," and did "not support any party or organization that believes in, advocates, or teaches the overthrow of the United States Government, by force or by any illegal or unconstitutional methods." The faculty rebelled. Many distinguished scholars whose loyalty was beyond question refused to sign, and the university was thrown into an uproar that continued for nearly 3 years.

Ironically, the state supreme court eventually ruled that Tenney's proposed constitutional amendment would have been meaningless because the legislature had always had, and the regents had never had, the authority to ensure the loyalty of university employees. Another irony was that shortly after the proposed university oath was made public, Tenney was discredited and deprived of all his power in the legislature. In June 1949 he was forced to resign the chairmanship of the un-American activities committee because he had begun to accuse fellow members of the legislature of being Communist sympathizers.

In the face of the faculty rebellion against the special oath, university president Robert Gordon Sproul asked the regents to repeal it. But regent John Francis Neylan led a majority of the board in refusing to do so and in clinging to the refusal during a year of bitter debate. This was the same Neylan who had once accepted the case of Charlotte Anita Whitney and appealed her conviction for criminal syndicalism all the way to the United States Supreme Court—this fighting liberal of earlier years was still fighting but no longer liberal. He was, in fact, a strong admirer of Senator McCarthy.

Governor Warren, as an ex officio member of the board of regents, favored repeal of the special oath. It was, he argued, not only harmful to the university and to academic freedom; it was also completely worthless. A Communist, he pointed out, "would take the oath and laugh." No one who was plotting to commit treason would cavil at mere perjury. But these arguments did not prevail. Regent Lawrence Mario Giannini, son and successor of the founder of the Bank of America, said that if the board rescinded the oath, "flags would fly in the Kremlin" in celebration and he himself would feel compelled to "organize twentieth-century vigilantes" against the subsequent wave of communism in California. Other regents argued that "insubordination" not "disloyalty" was the issue. In August 1950, by a vote of 12 to 10, the board voted to dismiss 32 nonsigning professors. In September the academic senate at Berkeley voted to "condemn" this action of "a bare majority" of the regents. Thus, for the first time in history, an American university faculty adopted a formal resolution of censure against a university governing board.

Professor Edward C. Tolman, previously chair of the Berkeley psychology department, led the nonsigners in bringing suit against the board as represented by its secretary and treasurer, Robert M. Underhill. In 1951 a state district court of appeals ruled that the special oath violated the state constitutional provision protecting the freedom of the university against political influence. The state supreme court disagreed with this interpretation in its final ruling in *Tolman v. Underhill* in 1952, but it also invalidated the oath and ordered the professors reinstated, on the narrower ground that the requirement of a loyalty oath was within the power of the legislature and not of the regents. The legislature, in a special session called after the beginning of the Korean War in 1950, had adopted the Levering Act requiring an elaborate nondisloyalty oath of all state employees, including those of the university, and the state supreme court upheld this requirement. In doing so it was following the current doctrines of the United States Supreme Court; however, under Warren as chief justice that body became more liberal. In the 1960s it struck down similar oath laws in several other states and thus enabled the supreme court of California to declare the Levering oath unconstitutional in 1967, largely on the ground that mere membership in an organization was not evidence of disloyalty.

The state committee on un-American activities was dissolved in 1971, after the senate's new president pro tem, James R. Mills, a liberal Democrat from San Diego, discovered that it had established "subversive" files on several senators because they had voted against its appropriations.

The Governorship of Edmund G. Brown

The year 1958 was a turning point in California politics. Before that year, the Republicans held five of the six statewide executive offices that were filled by partisan elections, both of the United States senatorships, nearly two-thirds of the seats in the House of Representatives, and more than two-thirds of the seats in the state legislature. After 1958 these proportions were almost exactly reversed. Through a combination of Democratic efforts and Republican blunders, the latent Democratic majority was at last able to assert itself.

A key factor in the Democratic resurgence was the decision by Republican senator William F. Knowland to run for governor in 1958 on a platform openly antagonistic to organized labor. Knowland's decision was based on a combination of personal and political factors, not the least of which was his desire to reverse Governor Knight's prolabor policies by securing passage of a state right-to-work law. The phrase "right to work," based on the idea that a worker should not have to join a union in order to hold a job, was a code name for an assault on the union shop. Following passage of the Taft-Hartley labor relations act of 1947, several states had adopted right-to-work laws forbidding union-shop contracts. Knowland hoped to consolidate his position as a leader of American conservatism, lead the large California delegation to the Republican national convention in 1960, and thus secure for himself the presidential nomination.

Knowland succeeded in winning the Republican nomination for governor, and Edmund G. Brown emerged as the victor in the Democratic primary. Voters in the November election were thus faced with a sharp choice between candidates and philosophies. Knowland endorsed a right-to-work ballot proposal, Initiative Proposition 18, and Brown campaigned against it.

In the campaign of 1958, organized labor achieved the greatest degree of unity that it had shown in the whole history of California politics, in support of Brown and in opposition to Knowland and the open shop. There were about 1.5 million union members in California, and with their close relatives they constituted more than a third of the eligible voters. Against Proposition 18, labor collected a campaign fund in excess of $2.5 million, more than twice the total funds contributed in the proposition's favor. Labor also sponsored a huge campaign of billboard, television, and newspaper advertising, stressing the argument that the "so-called right to work means the right to work for less and less and less."

In the election of November 1958, Brown won nearly 60 percent of the votes and Proposition 18 lost by almost exactly the same percentage. The vote for Brown was 3,140,176; for Knowland, 2,110,911. Brown carried 54 of the state's 58 counties. The Democrats won margins of 27 seats to 13 in the state senate and 47 to 33 in the assembly.

Edmund G. Brown, who now emerged as the leader of the California Democrats, was a native San Franciscan, born in 1905. When he was in the seventh grade at Fremont Grammar School, a ringing patriotic speech for the sale of liberty bonds had earned him the nickname of "Patrick Henry" Brown, and he continued to be known as Pat throughout his later career. He graduated from the San Francisco College of Law, became district attorney of San Francisco in 1944, and was elected state attorney general in 1950.

When Brown was inaugurated as governor in January 1959, the Democrats were in control of both houses of the California legislature for the first time in 80 years. In his inaugural address, Governor Brown promised to follow "the path of responsible liberalism . . . , in the giant footsteps of such memorable governors as Hughes and Roosevelt in New York, Wilson in New Jersey, La Follette in Wisconsin, Altgeld and Stevenson in Illinois, and Johnson and Warren in California."

Brown proposed a number of liberal measures, and the legislature enacted most of them. He recommended a law against racial discrimination by employers and labor unions, and the legislature responded with a fair employment practices act. Maximum payments for unemployment insurance, disability, and workers' compensation were substantially increased. For the protection of consumers, a state office of consumers' counsel was created, with authority to act against false or misleading practices in labeling and packaging and deceptive carrying charges on installment credit purchases. A state economic development agency was established to attract new industries and aid long-range planning.

Tax increases were adopted to meet a deficit left over from the previous year and to enable the state government to keep up with the swift growth of the state's population by expanding its programs of highways, aid to local school districts, and crime control. At the governor's urging, the legislature authorized studies that led to a master plan for higher education and to plans for the reorganization of many state offices under centralized departments. Cross-filing in elections was abolished. The legislature, however, in 1959 defeated Brown's request for a minimum wage of $1.25 an hour for workers not covered by federal law. Abolition of capital punishment, which he urged in 1960, was also rejected.

Probably Brown's greatest single achievement as governor was the adoption of the huge bond issue that enabled the state to proceed with its master plan for water development.

Most of California's water was in the northern half of the state, whereas most of the need for water was in the southern half. The Los Angeles basin, for example, had only 0.06 percent of California's natural stream flow of water. Under Governor Earl Warren, the legislature had authorized studies for a statewide water program that would ultimately be much larger than the federal Central Valley Project, but organized labor, conservative bankers, and majority opinion in northern California were strongly opposed to the state plan. Labor leaders argued that because the state program would not come under the federal limitation of 160 acres on the size of farms eligible to receive publicly subsidized water, the plan would result in the "unjust enrichment" of huge landowning corporations that were already too rich and too powerful. Major beneficiaries, labor pointed out, would include the Southern Pacific, Standard Oil, the Kern County Land Company, the Los Angeles Times Corporation, and other groups that held vast tracts in the southwestern San Joaquin Valley.

In the face of this opposition Governor Knight refused to become involved in the battle, but Governor Brown believed that the water plan was indispensable for California's future growth, and he threw all his political weight behind it. In 1959, at his insistence, the legislature authorized the submission to the voters of a bond issue of $1.75 billion. This was the largest issue of bonds ever adopted by any state for any purpose. Most of the money would be used for the Feather River Project, the first phase of a much larger long-range plan. The voters of California approved "Brown's water bonds" in November 1960 after he had urged them to do so in speeches throughout the state.

The heart of the Feather River Project was Oroville Dam, 735 feet high, the tallest in the United States, which ensured a controlled flow of water to the San Joaquin Delta region. From the delta, as Brown said at the groundbreaking ceremonies in October 1961, "we are going to build a river 500 miles long" in order "to correct an accident of people and geography." He was referring to the aqueduct that would carry water along the western side of the San Joaquin Valley and into southern California.

Extremists, Right and Left

One of the key factors in California politics in the 1960s was the emergence of vividly colorful but startlingly eccentric new varieties of fanaticism at both ends of the political spectrum. On the far right, the John Birch Society became a ludicrous parody of the conservatism of the Republicans, and thus contributed substantially to their defeats in the state election of 1962 and the national election of 1964. At the other extreme, an anarchistic student wing of the New Left parodied the liberalism of the Democrats and contributed to the defeat of Governor Brown in the election of 1966.

The tendency to polarization in philosophical and political opinions has always characterized the discussion of human affairs. Medieval philosophers asserted that every human being was born either a Platonist or an Aristotelian. Environment is a more probable explanation than heredity, though Gilbert and Sullivan, in the context of English party politics in the nineteenth century, maintained that

Every boy and every gal
That's born into the world alive
Is either a little Liberal
Or else a little Conservative.

In twentieth-century American politics, especially after the 1930s, liberalism was the belief that government should take positive actions in the interests of the greater welfare and greater liberties of the whole people and that it should also take negative, regulatory actions to protect the public from abuses of freedom by private business. Most American conservatives, during the same period, regarded their doctrine as an alternative and superior theory of progress. They argued not merely for the need to conserve what was good in the past, but also for the related belief that the best way to ensure the continued progress and improvement of American society was to leave the fullest possible freedom to the operations of private enterprise. The mainstream of American politics was a constant process of compromise between these two philosophies. But to the extremists of both the radical right and the radical left, compromise was unendurable.

The John Birch Society was founded in 1958 by Robert Welch, a retired candy manufacturer who had been defeated for the Republican nomination for lieutenant governor of Massachusetts and who suspected that communist infiltration of the Republican party had been responsible for his defeat. Welch and many of his followers believed that the graduated income tax, social security, the United Nations, and racial integration in the public schools were communist plots; that the fluoridation of water was a communist conspiracy to weaken the American people by slow poison; and that President Harry S. Truman, President Dwight D. Eisenhower, and Chief Justice Earl Warren were communist agents.

Most Birchers concealed their membership, and the general public first became aware of the society's existence in January 1961, when Thomas M. Storke, veteran publisher of the *Santa Barbara News-Press,* exposed some of its activities in his newspaper. In 1962 Storke received a Pulitzer Prize for distinguished achievement in journalism "for calling public attention to the efforts of the semisecret John Birch Society to wage a campaign of hate and vilification." The *Los Angeles Times* published its own attack on the Birchers in March 1961. Nevertheless, the organization continued to grow in several parts of the country, and most of all in southern California. Wealthy businesspeople and retired military officers joined it in considerable numbers. Two Republican members of the House of Representatives from southern California avowed their membership in the Birch Society.

To Richard Nixon, who was planning to run for governor of California in 1962, the fantastic doctrines of Welch and his followers were a serious embarrassment. Nixon felt that the Birch Society was "the monkey on the elephant's back" and that if he accepted its support, the result would be the best-financed but most disastrous campaign in the state's political history. Therefore, he publicly repudiated the Birchers and stated that there was no place in the Republican party for anyone who charged that Eisenhower was a Communist. Nixon could hardly have done otherwise. He was indebted to Eisenhower for two terms as vice president and for the

Republican presidential nomination in 1960. Nixon's attempt to dissociate himself from right-wing extremism cost him some of his right-wing support. Nixon then made a desperate effort to use his old issue of left-wing extremism against Governor Edmund G. Brown. But his campaign charge that Brown, a Roman Catholic, was "soft on communism" was absurdly unconvincing.

Another discreditable tactic backfired when Leone Baxter concocted a scheme, approved by Nixon and his campaign manager H. R. Haldeman, for a postcard poll pretending to come from an actually nonexistent group of Democrats and condemning the California Democratic Council as pro-Communist. Democratic leaders discovered and denounced this fraud, and 10 years later would recall it as a "warm-up for Watergate."

Throughout the 1962 campaign, Nixon gave an irritating impression of arrogance and overconfidence that disenchanted many who had once voted for him.

California Republicans were badly split in the 1962 gubernatorial campaign. The bitter loser, Richard Nixon, vowed never to be a candidate again. (*Courtesy of the* Sacramento Bee.)

Many also disliked his apparent intention to serve only 2 years as governor and then use the office as a stepping-stone to the presidency in 1964. In the election on November 6, 1962, Brown defeated Nixon by nearly 300,000 votes. On the morning after the election, Nixon appeared at a press conference, unshaven and distraught, and delivered a rambling attack on the press, blaming his defeat on unfair reporting of his campaign. A few weeks later, he announced that he would leave California to become a partner in a law firm in New York City.

The split between the moderates and the right-wing extremists continued to bedevil the Republicans in 1964. At the Republican national convention in San Francisco, the large California delegation, headed by ex-senator William F. Knowland, clinched the nomination for ultraconservative senator Barry Goldwater of Arizona. It was widely reported that at least a hundred of Goldwater's delegates were Birchers. In an apparent reference to the Birch Society, Goldwater included in his acceptance speech a statement that "extremism in the defense of liberty is no vice" and that "moderation in the pursuit of justice is not a virtue." His supporters at the convention cheered wildly, but the words had an opposite effect on millions of voters in the television audience. In the election in November, President Lyndon B. Johnson defeated Goldwater, both in California and in the nation, by the widest margins given to a presidential candidate since 1936.

Thus, in 1964 the Democrats seemed firmly entrenched both in Washington, D.C., and in Sacramento, but the political sands were soon to shift again. Lyndon Johnson was about to ruin his presidency with a disastrous war in Southeast Asia. And the screen and television actor Ronald Reagan had attracted considerable interest with a widely televised fund-raising address that was the highlight of the campaign for Goldwater.

Selected Bibliography

Jackson K. Putnam, *Modern California Politics, 1917–1980* (1980), provides a useful overview of the gubernatorial administrations of the period. See also his interpretive article "The Pattern of Modern California Politics," *Pacific Historical Review,* LXI (February 1992), pp. 23–52. Kurt Schuparra, *Triumph of the Right: The Rise of the California Conservative Movement, 1945–1966* (1998), offers a perceptive account. Eugene C. Lee, *California Votes* (1963), gives a review and analysis of registration and voting from 1928 to 1962.

On the effects of cross-filing, see Dean E. McHenry, "Cross Filing of Political Candidates in California," *Annals of the American Academy of Political and Social Science,* CCXLVIII (November 1946), pp. 226–231; Robert J. Pitchell, "The Electoral System and Voting Behavior: The Case of California's Cross-Filing," *Western Political Quarterly,* XII (June 1959), pp. 459–484; and Dean R. Cresap, *Party Politics in the Golden State* (1954).

The most detailed treatment of lobbying activities is Elmer R. Rusco, "Machine Politics, California Model," Ph.D. thesis, University of California, Berkeley (1960). For the principal exposés, see Howard R. Philbrick, *Legislative Investigative Report* (1939), and Lester Velie, "The Secret Boss of California," *Collier's,* CXXIV (August 13 and 20, 1949). Arthur H. Samish and Bob Thomas, *The Secret Boss of California* (1971), presents a lively memoir.

Important accounts of the rise of campaign-management firms are Carey McWilliams, "Government by Whitaker and Baxter," *The Nation,* CLXXII (April 14 and 21 and May 5, 1951), and Robert J. Pitchell, "The Influence of Professional Campaign Management Firms in Partisan Elections in California," *Western Political Quarterly,* XI (June 1958), pp. 278–300. The rise of informal party organizations is described in Leonard C. Rowe, *Pre-primary Endorsements in California Politics* (1962); Markell C. Bear, *Story of the California Republican Assembly* (1955); Francis Carney, *The Rise of the Democratic Clubs in California* (1958); and James Q. Wilson, *The Amateur Democrat* (1962).

The career of Earl Warren is described in biographies by Irving Stone (1948), Luther A. Huston (1966), Leo Katcher (1967), John D. Weaver (1967), Bill Severn (1968), Richard B. Harvey (1969), Jack Harrison Pollack (1979), G. Edward White (1982), and Bernard Schwartz (1983). More specialized studies include Edward R. Long, "Earl Warren and the Politics of Anti-Communism," *Pacific Historical Review,* LI (February 1982), pp. 51–70. See also *The Memoirs of Earl Warren* (1977) and James J. Rawls, "The Earl Warren Oral History Project," *Pacific Historical Review,* LVI (February 1987), pp. 87–97.

On the loyalty issue in California, consult Larry Ceplair and Steven Englund, *The Inquisition in Hollywood* (1983); Jerold Simmons, "The Origin of the Campaign to Abolish HUAC," *Southern California Quarterly,* LXIV (Summer 1982), pp. 141–157; Edward L. Barrett, Jr., *The Tenney Committee* (1951); David P. Gardner, *The California Oath Controversy* (1967); George R. Stewart, *The Year of the Oath* (1950); and R. L. Pritchard, "California Un-American Activities Investigations," *California Historical Society Quarterly,* XLIX (December 1970), pp. 309–327. On Jerry Voorhis, see his autobiography (1947) and Paul Bullock's biography (1978). Helen Gahagan Douglas is the subject of two articles in the *Southern California Quarterly:* Ingrid W. Scobie, LVIII (Spring 1976), and Colleen M. O'Connor, LXVII (Spring 1985). See also Scobie, *Center Stage: Helen Gahagan Douglas, A Life* (1992). The early career of Richard Nixon is covered in biographies by Earl Mazo (1960) and William Costello (1960). See also Richard M. Nixon, *Six Crises* (1962) and *RN: The Memoirs of Richard Nixon* (1978).

On the sweeping Democratic victory of 1958, see Gayle B. Montgomery and James W. Johnson, *One Step from the White House: The Rise and Fall of Senator William F. Knowland* (1998). Analyses of the governorship of Edmund G. Brown include Martin Schiesl (ed.), *The California of the Pat Brown Years* (1997); Roger Rapoport, *California Dreaming: The Political Odyssey of Pat and Jerry Brown* (1982); and Gary G. Hamilton and Nicole W. Biggart, *Governor Reagan, Governor Brown* (1984).

Industrialized Agriculture
and Disorganized Labor

The evolution of modern agriculture in California is a story of great complexity, marked by occasional moments of high drama. Through the middle of the twentieth century, agriculture remained California's largest single industry. The value of the state's farm products exceeded the value of the output of any branch of manufacturing in the state—or rather of any *other* branch of manufacturing. California farms themselves, in the words of Carey McWilliams, had long been "factories in the field."

The structure of agriculture in the state was not only extraordinarily complex in itself; it was also closely interrelated with other industries, especially the canning, packing, processing, transportation, and marketing of food and kindred products.

Green Gold

Among the states, California had ranked first in farm income since the 1930s, and its lead was steadily widening. Several of its climates permitted year-round growing and favored the production of fruit and truck crops for luxury markets at seasons when other states could offer little or no competition. California's unmatched level of farm capitalization permitted the greatest use of scientific techniques and resulted in the nation's highest level of farm productivity.

California's agriculture was not only the most prosperous in the country but far and away the most diversified. Because of the variety of its soils and climates it had 118 different types of farms, according to the United States census classification, whereas Pennsylvania, which ranked second in this respect, had only 25 types. Thanks in part to the genius of Luther Burbank of Santa Rosa, nearly 300 different agricultural commodities were produced in California, including all of the nation's commercial supply of almonds, artichokes, figs, nectarines, and olives; a third of the nation's fruit, including most of the apricots, grapes, pears, plums, and prunes;

and more than a fourth of the nation's vegetables, including most of the asparagus, broccoli, carrots, celery, and lettuce.

Although California agriculture as a whole was remarkably diversified, the great majority of the farms were extremely specialized. Specialization even within a crop was common. For example, many farms produced peaches exclusively for canning or for drying, and many produced grapes only for the table or for raisins or for wine.

The Empire of Agribusiness

Throughout the twentieth century, successful farming in California was becoming a business organized in larger and larger units. This process of consolidation was occurring not only through *horizontal integration,* or the merging of farm units into larger ones, but also through the still more revolutionary process of *vertical integration,* in which a large company operated at every level from the field to the supermarket. The men who had pioneered in the formation of these vertically integrated agricultural corporations were two Italian immigrants, Mark J. Fontana and Joseph Di Giorgio.

Fontana had created the California Fruit Canners' Association in 1899 and in 1916 had been instrumental in merging four large packing concerns into the California Packing Corporation (CalPac), which became the world's largest canner of fruits and vegetables. CalPac was the grower as well as the packer of many of the goods that were sold under its Del Monte label. Joseph Di Giorgio had become a large grower in the southern San Joaquin Valley early in the century and had bought the marketing and shipping interests of the Earl Fruit Company in 1910. The canned goods produced by the Di Giorgio Corporation were known to consumers through its S&W label.

Another integrated farmer was Schenley Industries, which raised many of the grapes that went into its wines. Hunt Foods and Industries, headed by Norton Simon, did not operate as a grower but was important as the world's largest processor and distributor of tomato products and as a major producer of salad and cooking oils.

The backing of such large aggregations of capital facilitated the constant development of new technological advances in all of the complex operations of agribusiness. An indispensable ally in this process was the University of California's college of agriculture, an outgrowth of the Morrill Land Grant College Act, adopted a century earlier for the purpose of aiding the country's millions of small farmers. The federal and state funds that supported the college's tremendously successful research program were augmented by contributions from the Giannini Foundation of Agricultural Economics. A. P. Giannini, founder of the Bank of America, was also a regent of the university. His son, Lawrence Mario Giannini, succeeded him both as a regent and as head of the bank.

The impact of science and technology on California agriculture was astounding. In 1961 university agricultural engineers devised a mechanical tomato picker so efficient and gentle that when they ran a fresh egg through it, the egg was deposited

Cotton harvesting in the San Joaquin Valley. The plants had been defoliated by aerial spraying. (*Courtesy of Agricultural Publications, University of California, Berkeley.*)

in the box uncracked. Soon afterward they developed a mechanical thumb that could press down on the top of each head of lettuce, decide electronically whether it was ready to be picked, and signal another part of the machine to pick it. Nine-tenths of California's cotton was being picked by machinery before the rate reached one-tenth in the southern states. Agricultural scientists developed mechanical tree shakers for fruits and nuts. For the more delicate fruits there were machines that could lift a human picker into the branches of the tree and swing him or her rapidly among them.

A major factor encouraging the further advance of a mechanized, highly capital-ized agriculture, concentrated in high-income-per-acre crops, was the growth of the income of the average American family. With this increase came ever-greater demand for fruits, vegetables, dairy products, poultry, and eggs—all California specialties.

"Farm Fascism" in the 1930s

California growers had discovered very early that the cost of labor was the only cost of production that they could usually keep down, and they had kept it down, with all the economic and political power at their command.

Since the early American period, farmland values in California had been capi-talized on the basis of the availability of cheap, unorganized migratory labor, much of it alien and nonwhite—Chinese, then Japanese, and later Mexican and Filipino. Thus, the historic cheap-labor surplus, by helping to keep land prices high and farm mortgages heavy, had kept the small farmers' return on their own labor to a low level while maintaining the profits of the large farms that employed the bulk of the hired workers.

In 1933 and 1934, when the Communist party organized a series of agricultural strikes and made a determined effort to unionize migratory farm labor, the forces of agribusiness launched an all-out countercampaign through a new organization called the Associated Farmers of California. The funds for its support came largely from the California Packing Corporation; the Southern Pacific Railroad; the Industrial Association of San Francisco; Southern Californians, Inc., a group of industrial employers; the Holly Sugar Corporation; and the Spreckels Investment Company. The Pacific Gas and Electric Company also made common cause with the large growers because their needs for power to pump irrigation water made them some of its best customers. Most of these big-business concerns tried to keep their contributions to the Associated Farmers confidential in order to maintain the image of a "farmers' organization."

Throughout the state, units of the Associated Farmers worked in intimate cooperation with local law enforcement officials. Most county sheriffs were allied with agribusiness interests. In some counties, migratory workers could not be employed unless they were registered with the sheriff's office, and the Associated Farmers provided the sheriff with lists of "agitators" and "dangerous radicals," including all persons known to have been members of unions. Such people not only were denied employment but were frequently ordered out of the county as well.

When a strike threatened, growers or their managerial employees were often made special deputies, though they did not always wait for this legal authorization and often acted simply as armed vigilantes. In the strike of the AFL lettuce packers' union at Salinas in 1936, agribusiness groups recruited a "general staff," which supplanted the sheriff and the chief of police. Colonel Henry Sanborn, an Army Reserve officer and publisher of an anticommunist journal, was employed as coordinator of all antistrike forces, including the local law enforcement officers as well as a so-called citizens' army armed with shotguns and pick handles. The chief of the state highway patrol and a representative of the state attorney general's office gave their approval to this arrangement.

The Associated Farmers also aided in many prosecutions not only of Communists but of almost any other agricultural strike leaders under the state criminal syndicalism law.

Among the justifications used by the embattled growers in their extreme resistance to any form of labor unionism were two arguments that had some color of validity during the darkest years of the great depression in 1933 and 1934. At that time it was often true that growers could not have paid higher wages without raising the cost of production above the prices that the crops could be sold for; it was also true that the main attempts to organize migratory farm laborers were then in the hands of the Communist party. But agribusiness interests continued to repeat these arguments in later years when prices and profits had risen greatly and when radical influence was no longer substantially involved.

In the middle and later years of the 1930s, dispossessed families from the Dust Bowl region came into California at the rate of more than 100,000 persons a year, most of them to swell the supply of migratory farm labor. People of Anglo-American stock, working in family groups, now made up the bulk of the state's migratory labor force for the first time, and as a result, the public interest in the plight of farm laborers increased somewhat, though only temporarily. Carey McWilliams's *Factories in the Field* and John Steinbeck's *The Grapes of Wrath,* both published in 1939, helped to stimulate this interest. McWilliams's book included a chapter on the activities of the Associated Farmers and their allies entitled "The Rise of Farm Fascism."

In the administration of Governor Culbert L. Olson, McWilliams was chief of the state division of immigration and housing, and in that capacity he made himself a thorn in the flesh of agribusiness by inspecting private farm-labor camps and denouncing their vile conditions. The annual convention of the Associated Farmers passed a resolution describing McWilliams as "California's Agricultural Pest Number One, outranking pear blight and the boll weevil." The state legislature, under agribusiness influence, passed a bill to abolish McWilliams's position, but Governor Olson pocket vetoed this proposed "anti-McWilliams act."

In 1939 and 1940 the La Follette committee, a subcommittee of the United States Senate Committee on Education and Labor under the chairmanship of Senator Robert M. La Follette, Jr., of Wisconsin, held extensive hearings in California to investigate "violations of free speech and rights of labor." But most of its recommendations for reform, introduced in 1942, produced no action in Congress. With the coming of World War II, the Dust Bowl migrants flocked to the shipyards; Mexicans and Mexican Americans again became the majority of the California farm labor force; and the public lost interest in the whole matter.

The Rise and Fall of the Bracero Program

The demands of World War II produced a sudden, genuine, and desperate shortage of farm labor. A partial solution to the problem was provided by the use of German prisoners of war as farm laborers. Research by historian Bonnie Trask has found that more than 15,000 German prisoners were working in California cotton fields in 1945. President Truman halted the program the following year when all prisoners of war were repatriated.

Far more numerous were the wartime workers imported from Mexico. In 1942, under an act of Congress and an agreement with Mexico, the United States Department of Agriculture assumed the responsibility for recruiting, contracting, transporting, housing, and feeding these temporary immigrant farm workers. In a formal sense, this was the beginning of the *bracero program.* The meaning of the word "bracero" (strong-armed one), from the Spanish *brazo* (arm), bears a striking resemblance to the meaning of the Tamil word *kuli.*

There had been an informal bracero program 25 years earlier during World War I, when private labor contractors supplied California growers with seasonal workers from Mexico. Thousands of peons, or landless laborers, had been eager for the opportunity; the Mexican Revolution had turned many of them into displaced persons, much as the Taiping Rebellion had nudged thousands of destitute Chinese toward California in the 1850s.

The growers were able to persuade Congress not to include Mexico in the postwar quota system of immigration restrictions, and the surge of Mexicans into California had continued through the 1920s. Each year an average of 58,000 Mexicans came northward to work in the cotton fields of the Central Valley, where they accounted for more than 75 percent of the harvest workforce. This immigration was reversed in the depression decade of the 1930s as federal and state authorities deported Mexicans. The Mexican *campesinos,* or farm workers, who remained during the depression participated in several strikes, most notably in the strawberry fields around El Monte in the San Gabriel Valley and in the cotton fields near Corcoran in the San Joaquin Valley.

The Mexican government in the 1930s found itself forced to pay the costs of repatriating many of its impoverished nationals who could no longer obtain work in California and who were not eligible for relief there. In 1942 the Mexican government feared that this experience would be repeated, and it therefore demanded that the United States government, rather than private labor contractors, must take responsibility for the immigrant workers.

After World War II the bracero program continued in force with the enthusiastic support of California growers, though President Truman, to their irritation, removed the program from the grower-oriented Department of Agriculture and assigned it to the Department of Labor by executive order in 1948.

More numerous than the braceros in the years after the end of World War II were the illegal undocumented workers. Although their exact numbers could not be known, it was estimated that more than half a million of these illegal immigrants crossed and recrossed the international boundary each year, most of them to work in the fields of California and other states in the southwest.

In 1951 Congress adopted the famous Public Law 78 (P.L. 78) and also gave special legislative recognition to a new agreement with Mexico. Together these measures provided the most elaborate plan of importing contract workers in which the United States had ever engaged, and although the plan was approved as a "Korean War emergency" measure, it ultimately provided the basis for continuing the bracero program until 1964, 11 years after the Korean War had ended.

Under this system, Mexican officials assembled the braceros and the United States Department of Labor provided for their transportation to reception centers north of the border. There they were turned over to labor contractors representing the growers' associations. At the insistence of the Mexican government, there were standard contracts covering wages, hours, transportation, housing, and working conditions. The American government guaranteed the provision of emergency medical care, workers' compensation, disability and death benefits, and burial expenses. Though such provisions were minimal, they were far superior to the benefits available to American farm laborers, who enjoyed no legal protection at all. Opponents of the program, meanwhile, complained that the system was rife with abuses. "Although the bracero agreement contained stipulations with regard to health, housing, food, wages, and working hours," one critic charged, "most were disregarded by both the U.S. government and the growers." Housing was often substandard, wages were universally low, and racial discrimination was severe.

In 1957, the peak year, California imported 192,438 braceros. In 1960 about 100,000 of them were at work in the state at the peak season in early September, and they formed about a quarter of the seasonal farm labor force. Most of them worked on the larger farms; about 5.2 percent of the farms in California employed 60 percent of the total number of seasonal hired workers—including more than 80 percent of the braceros.

As Congress continued to grant extensions of the program, it became increasingly hard to disguise the fact that the bracero system perpetuated the tragic poverty of the American migratory laborers. It depressed wages, destroyed the bargaining power of the domestic worker, and drove away local labor. There were many incidents in which braceros were used as strikebreakers with the connivance of government officials. Ostensibly, P.L. 78 allowed the importation of braceros only when it would "not adversely affect the wages and working conditions of domestic agricultural workers," when "sufficient domestic workers . . . [were] not available," and when "reasonable efforts [had] been made to attract domestic workers at wages . . . comparable to those offered foreign workers." This last provision would have tended to freeze farm wages at the wretched levels of the early 1950s, even if the rest of the provisions of P.L. 78 had been effectively enforced—which they were not. In effect, the system encouraged the growers to offer the lowest possible wages and the worst possible conditions to domestic workers, not merely because this practice saved money for the growers, as it always had, but also because it reduced the "availability" of domestic laborers and thus maximized the growers' legal eligibility to hire braceros.

To employers of seasonal farm workers, the braceros represented a supply of cheap and dependable labor—guaranteed to arrive and to vanish exactly when the employers wanted it to. California growers continued to rationalize such motives on the basis of race, as they had done for more than a century. Anglo-Americans, the growers constantly assured themselves and the public, simply could not perform stoop labor as well as nonwhites, who were equipped by racial heredity with stronger backs. There was no scientific basis for this assumption, and Californians who knew their state's history should not have had to be reminded that Anglo-Americans with gold pans had not only performed the most backbreaking form of stoop labor ever invented, but had also insisted that *only* whites were suited for it.

As agribusiness clung to the braceros, public criticism slowly intensified. Agriculture was in the untenable position of being the only private industry insisting that the government was obligated to provide it with a labor supply, and a cheap one at that. At last, in 1963, Congress refused to approve the customary 2-year extension of the bracero program and instead ordered its termination at the end of the following year, with a few minor exceptions. The growers predicted disastrous shortages of harvest labor and warned consumers of food scarcities and drastic price increases. These predictions proved baseless; 1965 was another record year in California agricultural output, and food prices rose insignificantly or not at all. By offering better wages and working conditions, the growers were able to attract enough domestic labor and thus to refute their own perennial claims that it would be impossible to do so.

Unionization Breaks Through

Though the growers often denied that their desire for braceros was in any way related to their desire to block the organization of labor unions by domestic farm workers, the connection was inescapable and the growers used many of the same arguments for both purposes. Most of these arguments were variations on the traditional American political theme that farming was different from all other business enterprises.

Because the harvesting of perishable crops was intensely seasonal, one argument ran, growers required a "dependable" labor force and were uniquely vulnerable to strikes and therefore could never tolerate unions. This contention ignored a number of facts. Canning was equally seasonal, yet it had long been unionized with great advantage to the employers rather than any undue hardship to them. The marketing of perishable crops was as dependent on transportation workers as it was on harvest and cannery workers, yet the industries involved in the transportation of food had been entirely unionized for decades. Most of the employers in the canning, trucking, railroad, and shipping industries had long since tacitly conceded that union contracts were the best method of ensuring a dependable labor supply. A contention of California growers was that, like other "American farmers," they had always maintained a personal solicitude toward their hired hands and that this would be sacrificed in the "impersonal" process of union bargaining. This contention never had any validity as applied to the typical employer-employee relationships in the state's agriculture, where wage rates were set by growers' associations and where hiring was usually done through labor contractors who performed the functions of company unions.

Growers also declared that they believed in collective bargaining, but only with persons who actually worked for them, not with labor union officials, whom they almost invariably described as "outside agitators." But this was the same claim that employers in virtually every other industry had used in earlier times in efforts to block the beginnings of unions. It ignored the fact that collective bargaining could not be genuine if workers were denied the right to choose experienced representatives as their bargaining agents. The growers wished to continue to hire such representatives of their own—the labor contractors—while continuing to deny any effective representation to the workers.

The most genuine objection of the growers to collective bargaining was that it was sure to raise costs. But not even this objection was valid, even on a strictly economic level. Higher wages would enable hundreds of thousands of American migrant-worker families to buy more food and at the same time would lower the costs of welfare and many other costs of poverty.

Extreme poverty and the disorganization that accompanied it had always been a major obstacle to organizing farm workers, who were generally regarded as too demoralized to be even potential union material. But in 1959 the nation's largest labor organization, the AFL-CIO, opened an offensive on the farm-labor front with a new Agricultural Workers Organizing Committee (AWOC). The nucleus of the AWOC was the Filipino Farm Labor Union, organized 3 years earlier and led by Larry Dulay Itliong. Itliong now spearheaded the effort to recruit members for the newly formed AWOC.

Soon afterward, César Chávez left a secure and comfortable job as an official of a Mexican American community service society to begin the hard and hazardous task of organizing a new and independent union called the National Farm Workers Association (NFWA), at a salary of $50 a week. A cofounder of the union was

Dolores Huerta, a labor organizer and community activist who was born in New Mexico and grew up in Stockton. Chávez had been born near Yuma, Arizona, on a small homestead near the Colorado River. This family farm was lost through unpaid taxes in the depression of the 1930s. He had worked as a migrant farm laborer from early childhood and consequently had obtained his 8 years of formal education with difficulty in nearly 40 different California public schools.

Chávez conceived the new NFWA as a labor organization that would offer its members the benefits of a credit union and other services while it offered employers a stable and dependable workforce made up of skillful and well-organized crews of NFWA members working with no-strike contracts. At that time he placed no hope in agricultural strikes, having seen too many disheartening examples of them, but in September 1965 AWOC members began a strike against 33 grape growers in the district around Delano in northern Kern County, and 2 weeks later Chávez's NFWA decided to join it. For the first several months there seemed to be no chance that the strike could win. So many strikebreakers were brought in that the grape harvest in the district was larger than in the previous year. Yet the strike continued until, in the spring and summer of 1966, it won a series of brilliant victories that set a precedent for ultimate unionization of at least the larger farms throughout California.

If the Delano strike had been attempted a few years earlier, it would have met the fate of every previous attempt to organize farm labor. But now a new force was at work—the strong and increasing sympathy of a part of the Anglo-American public for the civil rights of ethnic minorities in general and farm workers in particular. The AWOC local in Delano, under Larry Itliong as regional director, consisted mainly of Filipino Americans, whereas most of the members of Chávez's NFWA were Mexican Americans. Gifts of money and food for the embattled strikers poured into Delano from several other labor unions, from church groups throughout California, and from many other sympathizers with the civil rights movement.

The dock workers in the San Francisco Bay area refused to load grapes from the struck vineyards, of which the largest were owned by Schenley Industries and the Di Giorgio Corporation. Nationwide boycotts were launched against Schenley wines and liquors, against Di Giorgio's S&W canned goods, and against stores that sold them. In the spring of 1966, executives of Schenley concluded that the adverse publicity was counteracting the effects of the large sums the company spent to advertise its products. In this light, the much smaller amounts the company saved by refusing to raise wages in its vineyards were obviously poor economy. On April 6, 1966, Schenley Industries made the historic announcement that it had agreed to recognize the National Farm Workers' Association as the sole bargaining representative for its field-workers—the first recognition of a farm workers' union by a major California grower.

The next day the Di Giorgio Corporation announced that it would permit its workers to decide by ballot whether they wished to be represented by a union, and if so, what union. The victorious allies, Itliong's AWOC and Chávez's NFWA, merged to form the United Farm Workers Organizing Committee. In the election in August 1966, although the Di Giorgio Corporation had always insisted that its

Union organizers César Chávez (1927–1993) and Dolores Huerta at a meeting of the United Farm Workers (UFW) in 1969. (*Courtesy of the Archives of Labor and Urban Affairs, Wayne State University.*)

employees did not want to be unionized, its field-workers voted overwhelmingly for the United Farm Workers (UFW).

Several northern California growers of wine grapes then signed contracts with the UFW, but the great majority of California producers of table grapes held out. They were encouraged by the election of Ronald Reagan, a vigorous opponent of farm unions, to the governorship in 1966. In 1968 the UFW launched a national boycott of all California table grapes. This move captured the attention of the whole country and became a burning social issue. Although Governor Reagan and presidential candidate Richard Nixon condemned the boycott, the mayors of San Francisco, New York, Chicago, and several other large cities announced their approval of it. The boycott became so effective that the growers were threatened with ruin. At last, in July 1970, most of the large California table grape growers agreed to union contracts with the United Farm Workers.

Dolores Huerta, who served as vice president of the UFW from 1970 to 1973, played an important role in the successful negotiations that ended the grape boycott. She came from a middle-class background but had devoted herself to improving the lives of the underprivileged. As her biographer Richard García has noted, Huerta consistently followed "a pragmatic non-ideological approach to life and change." In later years she became an outspoken critic of the "feminization of poverty" among California farm workers. Mechanization in the fields increasingly allowed growers to reduce the number of their male workers and to employ women at lower wages. Women became the majority of the labor force in the tomato harvest, for instance, working at the bottom of the wage scale.

Chávez's next move was against the lettuce growers of the Salinas Valley, but as soon as those growers learned that the grape producers were about to surrender, they hurriedly negotiated contracts with the Teamsters Union in order to forestall the UFW drive. One maverick Salinas lettuce grower, Bud Antle, had included his field-workers in his contracts with the Teamsters since 1961. Now there was a rush to imitate him because, said a Salinas growers' representative, "the Teamsters are a trade union; Chávez's union is a civil rights movement." Chávez denounced the Teamsters' agreements as *sweetheart contracts,* privately arranged between employers and union officials to benefit themselves at the expense of workers.

In March 1977, after several years of struggle and periodic negotiation, Chávez and the Teamster executives signed a 5-year jurisdictional agreement. The UFW was to represent all field-workers in future contracts with the growers, leaving all cannery workers and some truck drivers to the Teamsters.

Equal Protection of the Laws

Until 1966 agricultural labor was specifically excluded from the provisions of virtually every federal and state law that protected the rights of other workers. Minimum wages, unemployment insurance, social security, collective bargaining— all were guaranteed to others and specifically denied to farm labor. The rationalization for this was always that "farmers had special problems." The truth was that they had special political power. Agricultural employers were heavily overrepresented in Congress and in almost every state legislature, whereas the interests of farm workers were almost totally unrepresented until the 1960s.

The ending of the bracero program had been an important preliminary to reform, but only a negative one. At long last, in 1964, Congress made its first positive moves toward correcting a shameful set of conditions. The Economic Opportunity Act of 1964 included grants to agencies aiding migrant workers, and an amendment to the National Housing Act provided direct loans for construction of farm-labor housing. In September 1966, Congress took the historic step of extending the protection of a new federal minimum wage law to farm workers. This was only a token beginning. Whereas the minimum wage for most other workers was raised to $1.60 an hour, effective in 1968, the national minimum for farm labor was set at only $1, and not even this would apply to small employers.

These new federal laws were merely an entering wedge. More subsidies to help provide decent housing for migrant workers were essential in order to eradicate the rural slums that were far worse than anything in the cities. For migrant workers and their families the conditions of recruitment, transportation, health, sanitation, workers' compensation, child labor, education, and civil and political rights were disgracefully and incredibly substandard.

Of central importance was the right of collective bargaining and the guarantee of this right through extension to agriculture of laws governing election of union representatives. At the federal level, attempts to extend the provisions of the National Labor Relations Act (NLRA) to farm workers remained deadlocked, partly because Chávez did not wish to give up the weapon of the secondary boycott, which was illegal for workers covered by the NLRA.

But in California the replacement of Governor Ronald Reagan by Edmund G. Brown, Jr., made possible a landmark law providing for state-supervised secret-ballot elections in which California's 250,000 farm workers could pick a union to represent them, or reject unionization. Brown personally hammered out the compromise that was adopted in May 1975. The new law created a state Agricultural Labor Relations Board (ALRB) with quasi-judicial powers to oversee elections. The act allowed harvest-time strikes and permitted secondary boycotts in some limited circumstances.

In subsequent years, the makeup of the ALRB would become a matter of great controversy and remain subject to changes in the state's political leadership. Nevertheless, it was clear that the passage of the new federal and state labor laws marked the beginning of a new era for California's agricultural workers.

Selected Bibliography

Two works that analyze the rise of California agribusiness are Donald J. Pisani, *From the Family Farm to Agribusiness* (1984), which views the 1920s as the critical decade of transformation, and Theodore Saloutos, *The American Farm and the New Deal* (1982), which follows the story through the 1930s. On the role of public policy, see Dennis Nodín Valdés, "Machine Politics in California Agriculture," *Pacific Historical Review,* LXIII (May 1994), pp. 203–224; Ellen Liebman, *California Farmland* (1983); and Lawrence J. Jelinek, *Harvest Empire* (1979). Also useful are James H. Shideler (ed.), *Agriculture in the Development of the Far West* (1975), and Richard J. Orsi (comp.), *A List of References for the History of Agriculture in California* (1974).

Major works on the history of California's peculiar farm-labor problems are David Vaught, *Cultivating California* (1999); Cletus E. Daniel, *Bitter Harvest* (1981); Ernesto Galarza, *Farm Workers and Agri-Business in California* (1977); and Carey McWilliams, *Ill Fares the Land* (1942) and *Factories in the Field* (1939).

James N. Gregory has written the definitive study of migration to California during the great depression in *American Exodus: The Dust Bowl Migration and Okie Culture in California* (1989). See also Dorothea Lange and Paul S. Taylor, *An American Exodus* (1939), and Walter J. Stein, *California and the Dust Bowl Migration* (1973).

Bonnie Trask has illuminated an often overlooked part of the story. See her "German Prisoners of War in California Agriculture, 1943–1946," M.A. thesis (1971), and (with Mary Graham) "Agitation in the Fields," in Charles Clough (ed.), *Fresno County in the Twentieth Century* (1986).

On the use of Mexican and other immigrant labor, see Don Mitchell, *The Lie of the Land* (1996); Gilbert G. Gonzalez, *Labor and Community* (1992); Vicki Ruiz, *Cannery Women, Cannery Lives* (1987) and *From Out of the Shadows* (1998); George C. Kiser and Martha Woody Kiser, *Mexican Workers in the United States* (1979); Mark Reisler, *By the Sweat of Their Brow* (1976); Charles Wollenberg, *"Huelga,* 1928 Style: The Imperial Valley Cantaloupe Workers' Strike," *Pacific Historical Review,* XXXVIII (February 1969), pp. 45–58;

Leo Grebler, *Mexican Immigration to the United States* (1966); and R. K. Das, *Hindustani Workers on the Pacific Coast* (1923). On the Filipino farm laborers, see Craig Scharlin and Lilia V. Villanueva, *Philip Vera Cruz* (1992), and Lorraine Jacobs Crouchett, *Filipinos in California* (1982).

Important studies of the bracero program are Henry P. Anderson, *The Bracero Program in California* (1976); Ernesto Galarza, *Merchants of Labor* (1964); Otey M. Scruggs, "The Evolution of the Mexican Farm Labor Agreement of 1942," *Agricultural History,* XXXIV (July 1960), pp. 140–149; N. Ray Gilmore and Gladys Gilmore, "The Bracero in California," *Pacific Historical Review,* XXXII (August 1963), pp. 265–282; and Truman E. Moore, *The Slaves We Rent* (1965).

On the movement led by César Chávez, see Richard Griswold del Castillo and Richard A. García, *César Chávez* (1995); García, "Dolores Huerta," *California History,* LXXII (Spring 1993), pp. 56–72; Peter Matthiessen, *Sal Si Puedes,* (1969); John G. Dunne, *Delano* (1971); Joan London and Henry Anderson, *So Shall Ye Reap* (1970); Ronald B. Taylor, *Chávez and the Farm Workers* (1975); and J. Craig Jenkins, *The Politics of Insurgency* (1985). Linda Majka and Theodore Majka, *Farm Workers, Agribusiness, and the State* (1982), includes a legislative history of the ALRB, while Rex L. Cottle et al., *Labor and Property Rights in California Agriculture* (1982), offers a highly critical view of the board.

CHAPTER 30

Diversity and Conflict

One of the most deplorable aspects of the history of California has been the persistence of discrimination directed against the state's diverse ethnic and racial groups. During the twentieth century, progress was made in overcoming the burden of past discrimination, but the legacy of hostility remained. This chapter traces the story of diversity and conflict roughly through the first three-quarters of the century. More recent developments are covered in Chapter 36.

California Indians

All the nonwhite minorities in American California suffered from various kinds of discrimination, but the mistreatment of the Indians began earliest and was by far the worst. In California, as in other parts of the United States, the history of American treatment of the Indians in the nineteenth century was too often a sickening record of racist murder and sanctimonious fraud.

The problems of the Indians in California were different from those of most other American Indian tribes in that only a minority of the California Indians were ever placed on reservations. The treaties of the early 1850s, providing for large reservations in California, were never ratified, and most of the attempts to provide small reservations were unsuccessful. The California Indians were left to survive as best they might on the fringes of white settlement; most of them did not survive. Of those who did, the majority became agricultural laborers.

Several idealistic individuals tried to improve the situation. In the early 1880s the New England author Helen Hunt Jackson sent copies of her critique of American Indian policy, *A Century of Dishonor* (1881), to all members of Congress. At Jackson's request, Congress then made her a member of a special commission to report on the Indians of southern California. Although the commission's report had little effect on federal policy, Jackson's research for it aided the writing of *Ramona*

(1884), a novel she intended to be the *Uncle Tom's Cabin* of Indian reform. *Ramona* powerfully portrayed the destitution of the homeless Indians of southern California and also, quite unintentionally, created a collection of regional myths that stimulated the tourist trade.

In 1901 Charles F. Lummis organized the Sequoya League with the aid of Thomas R. Bard, David Starr Jordan, and others. Its main object was better treatment of the Indians, and its main accomplishment was an act of Congress that provided money to purchase a tract of land near Pala for the Cupeño Indians who were evicted from Warner's Ranch in San Diego County.

During World War I, a number of Indians served in the armed forces, and in 1924, partly in recognition of that service, Congress gave American Indians the rights of citizenship in the United States and in the states of their residence. Congress also recognized that an injustice had been done to the California Indians, in particular, by the failure to ratify the reservation treaties of the early 1850s, which had promised them more than 7 million acres of land. In 1928 Congress authorized the attorney general of California to bring suit against the United States on behalf of the California Indians to determine what financial compensation should be made to them. A special census provided by the act of 1928 enumerated 23,585 persons as living descendants of nineteenth-century California Indians, and thus entitled to compensation. But the case dragged on until 1944, and when the federal court of claims finally made its award, it was only for a little more than $5 million, or about $200 per person.

In the special case of the survivors of the Cahuilla tribe, also known as the Palm Springs Indians, the results of litigation were startlingly different. In the 1870s the federal government had granted the odd-numbered sections of desert land in the Palm Springs area to the Southern Pacific Railroad and the even-numbered sections, checkerboard-fashion, to the Cahuilla Indians. When Palm Springs became a booming resort town in the 1920s, the surviving Cahuilla, numbering about 100, tried to persuade the federal government to permit the leasing of some of their lands to the eager hotel promoters, but the government refused. Lee Arenas, one of the Cahuilla, managed to interest a former justice of the California Supreme Court, John W. Preston, in taking the case to the Supreme Court of the United States. In 1944 the Court ruled that each of the Cahuilla should receive the rental from $350,000 worth of individually allotted tribal land, as well as a share of the income from 30,000 acres of communal tribal land.

The contrast between the ridiculously inadequate award by the federal court of claims to the California Indians in 1944 and the lucrative award by the Supreme Court to the Palm Springs Indians in the same year was so striking that it helped persuade Congress to pass the Indian Claims Commission Act of 1946. This law entitled Native Americans to payments from the federal government equivalent to the original value of the lands their ancestors had once occupied. The determination of the amounts was a fantastically complex matter, but in 1965, after many years of hearings, the descendants of the nineteenth-century California Indians finally received and voted to accept an award of a little more than $29 million. This was about 45 cents an acre for 64 million acres of land, nearly two-thirds the total area of California.

California Visions since 1900

COLOR PLATE 11
Southern Pacific Railroad, *California for the Settler*,
1911. As the largest private landowner in the state,
the Southern Pacific had good reason to be a
California booster. (*Courtesy of the Seaver Center for
Western History Research, Los Angeles County Museum
of Natural History.*)

COLOR PLATE 12
Union Pacific Railroad, *California Calls You*, 1913. The
Golden State has it all—sunshine, natural beauty, an
epic antiquity (symbolized by a barely discernible distant mission), and a wistful "California girl" shaded by
her poppy-colored umbrella. (*Courtesy of the California
State Railroad Museum.*)

COLOR PLATE 13
Yun Gee, *Where Is My Mother*, 1926–27. Echoing the theme of longing for a faraway homeland, the California artist remembers his mother in China: "That mother of mine, how it tore my heart / To leave her across the sea, / I who was part of her— / She became all of me." (*Courtesy Collection of Li-lan. Photograph © Kevin Ryan.*)

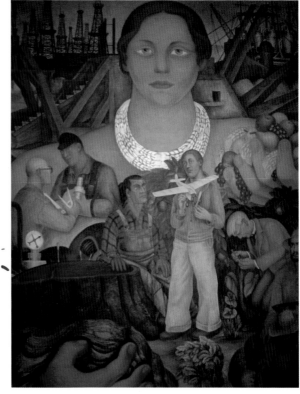

COLOR PLATE 14
Diego Rivera, *Allegory of California* (detail), 1931. The preeminent muralist of Mexico created this richly suggestive tribute for the Stock Exchange Building in San Francisco during the early days of the great depression. (*Photograph by R. J. Bellanca, The City Club of San Francisco. © 2001 Banco de México. Diego Rivera and Frida Kahlo Museums Trust. Av. Cinco de Mayo No. 2, Col. Centro, Del. Cuauhtémoc 06059, Mexico, D. F.*)

COLOR PLATE 15.
Chiura Obata, *Farewell Picture of the Bay Bridge, April 30, 1942*, 1942. A poignant and evocative *sumi*, painted on the day this renowned *Issei* artist began his wartime internment. (*Courtesy of Fine Arts Museums of San Francisco, Gift of the Obata Family, 1996.10.*)

COLOR PLATE 16
Milton Glaser, *California: Here It Comes!*, 1969. Published during the tumultuous decade when California emerged as the nation's most populous state, *Time*'s cover story described the Golden State as "the mirror of America as it will become, or at least as the hothouse for its most rousing fads, fashions, trends and ideas." (© *Timepix.*)

COLOR PLATE 17
Roger Minick, *Woman with Scarf at Inspiration Point, Yosemite National Park,* 1980. The relentless human encroachment onto the California landscape poses a challenge: Can a proper balance be found between economic development and environmental protection? (© *Roger Minick.*)

COLOR PLATE 18
Linden Keiffer, *Balance,* 1996. The works of this African American artist, a native of San Bernardino County, often comment on racial diversity and the need for harmony. (© *Linden Keiffer.*)

During the 1950s, the Native Americans who remained on reservations were subjected to a new federal policy known as *termination.* The policy had many parts, but essentially it was a withdrawal by the federal government from all its relations with the Indian tribes. Federal trust protection of Indian lands was to be removed and the lands sold. As Native American historian Donald Fixico has concluded, "termination essentially implied the ultimate destruction of tribal cultures and native lifestyles, as withdrawal of federal services was intended to desegregate Indian communities and to integrate them with the rest of society." In 1958 Congress passed the rancheria bill, terminating 41 California reservations with a single blow. Complementing termination was the federal government's transfer of Native Americans from reservations to the nation's cities, thus further promoting assimilation. The Bureau of Indian Affairs opened field relocation offices in Los Angeles, San Francisco, Oakland, and San Jose. Finally, in the 1960s, the policies of termination and relocation were replaced by a policy of self-determination, a continuance of federal relationships with the tribes, and handover of responsibility for administering federal programs to tribal governments.

The long and tragic decline in Indian population was reversed in the twentieth century, and the number of persons of Indian ancestry in the state began to rise steadily. The growth in population was due to natural increase and to migration to California of Indians from other states, aided by the relocation program of the federal government. In 1965 the number of Indians living in California had risen to 75,000, less than 10 percent of whom were living on the remaining 82 federal reservations. Only three reservations, at Hoopa Valley, Fort Yuma, and Bishop, had more than 500 residents, and only 18 reservations had more than 100. During the 1970s the Indian population in the state more than doubled, and in 1980 the Census Bureau reported that California, with more than 198,000 Indians, had the largest Indian population of any state in the nation.

Throughout the twentieth century, both the United States and the state of California demonstrated awakenings of conscience in their treatment of Indian people. California abolished all legal distinctions between persons of Indian ancestry and other citizens and led the states in making Indians fully eligible to receive the benefits of the public schools, welfare assistance, old-age and survivor payments, and other public services. In spite of these gains, the Indians of California remained the state's most economically depressed minority group. The rate of unemployment among California Indians was more than three times as high as the rate for whites and somewhat above the rate for blacks. The California State Advisory Commission on Indian Affairs reported in 1966 that the median annual income for reservation Indians was $2268 per family. More than 40 percent of all rural and reservation Indians in the state had not gone beyond the eighth grade, and the school dropout rate for Indians was three times that of the general population.

During the 1960s, California Indians increased their level of political involvement and established several pantribal organizations. The American Indian Historical Society, organized in 1964 by Cahuilla tribal chair Rupert Costo, established an active publication program and called for the revision of textbooks that contained negative stereotypes of Indians. In 1967 concern over the inadequacy of primary and secondary education for Indian youth led to the formation of the

Pomo basketmaker Elsie Allen (1899–1990) practiced and preserved aspects of traditional Califor-nia Indian culture. (*Photo by Scott Patterson. Courtesy of Heyday Books and Victoria D. Patterson.*)

California Indian Education Association, and on many college campuses Native American Studies departments were formed. Four years later a unique Native American institution of higher learning opened its doors in Yolo County. D-Q University, drawing "upon the strength of Native American culture," began offering a full range of academic courses on campus and providing educational programs on reservations throughout the state.

The occupation of Alcatraz Island in San Francisco Bay by a group called Indians of All Tribes from 1969 to 1971 ushered in a period of increased activism among California Indians. The occupiers of Alcatraz hoped to establish an Indian culture center and to encourage Indians everywhere to bolder and more effective action. In northeastern California, members of the Achumawi (Pit River) tribe engaged in sit-ins and took legal action to regain forest lands acquired by the Pacific Gas and Electric Company. "The Earth is our mother," the Achumawis proclaimed, "and we cannot sell her." In the northwestern part of the state, Yurok Indian fishermen clashed with law enforcement officers over fishing rights along the Klamath

River. In 1978 and 1979, Chumash Indians in the Santa Barbara area occupied the site of a proposed supertanker terminal to protest the destruction of what they called Humqaq or Tolakwe, the "Western Gate," through which all new life came into the world and the spirits of the dead departed. "If that place were destroyed tomorrow," said Chumash spiritual leader Kote Lotah, "I feel so strongly about it, I would want to die today so that I could pass through the Western Gate."

California Indians also demonstrated a growing interest in the preservation and revival of their native cultures. This resurgence of interest produced some remarkable results. In 1974 the Cupeño, whose plight had spurred the Sequoya League to action in 1901, dedicated the Cupa Cultural Center at the Pala reservation and offered classes in Cupeño language, culture, and history. In neighboring Riverside County the Cahuilla founded the Malki Museum, offering native-language classes and establishing a repository for Cahuilla artifacts and ethnographic information.

One of the most serious problems facing California's Indian population was inadequate health care. The federal government reported in 1992 that California Indians had significantly higher rates of mortality than the population as a whole. Only 43 percent of Indians in California lived beyond the age of 65, whereas 68 percent of non-Indians lived that long. The mortality rate was higher for Indians at all ages, including infants, and was accompanied by a lower incidence of prenatal and early childhood health care. "It's not surprising that there's a severe problem," commented the director of the California Rural Indian Health Board. "But the extent of the problem is astonishing."

Asians

If the worst racial persecutions in American history were those inflicted on the Indians before 1900, the most obvious and flagrant racist abuse in the United States in the twentieth century was that suffered by Japanese Americans when they were deprived of their liberty and placed in relocation camps during World War II. But that abuse was a temporary one, and the very extremity of the blundering injustice of it ultimately helped enable the people of the United States and the people of California to learn a lesson from it.

Even during the war itself, some Californians had opposed the anti-Japanese hysteria. The Pacific Coast Committee on American Principles and Fair Play, organized in December 1941 with President Robert Gordon Sproul and several members of the faculty of the University of California among its leaders, carried on a valiant campaign in defense of the rights of the Japanese Americans. The heroism of Nisei soldiers was a reproach to anti-Japanese racism, and after the end of the war the memory of Hiroshima and Nagasaki neutralized the memory of Pearl Harbor.

As the War Relocation Authority pointed out in the concluding sentence of its final report in 1946, "Although there is undoubtedly a marked xenophobic tendency in the United States, there is also a strong and stubborn potential for fair-mindedness among the American people—a potential which should be carefully studied, fostered, and brought to the highest degree of assertiveness in the interest of greater racial tolerance and a richer realization of democratic values."

Congress recognized in 1948 that Japanese Americans were entitled to financial compensation. Families had sold their homes and businesses in frantic haste. Some lost everything they had, and many lost most of what they had. Claims totaling $400 million were filed by 44,000 Japanese Americans, who ultimately received settlements totaling $38 million, less than 10 cents on every dollar of estimated loss in real and personal property. Congress also provided for the return of confiscated bank deposits, though the legal process was difficult and the recovery was slow and incomplete.

A major step toward financial resolution of the wartime issue was taken by Congress in 1980 with the formation of the United States Commission on Wartime Relocation and Internment of Civilians. Following 18 months of investigation and hearings, the commission concluded that the wartime internment was a "grave injustice" motivated by "race prejudice, war hysteria and a failure of political leadership." In 1988 Congress approved legislation authorizing payments of $20,000 to each of the 65,000 surviving citizens and resident aliens interned during the war. In addition, both San Francisco and Los Angeles approved reparation payments to Japanese Americans who had lost city jobs when they were interned.

Progress was also made in resolving other long-standing restrictions on Japanese Americans. In 1952, after California's Alien Land Law had been in effect for 39 years, the state supreme court struck it down as unconstitutional. At about the same time, Congress entirely abandoned the racial definition of aliens ineligible for citizenship. Very few nations had ever withheld the privilege of naturalization on racial grounds, and in doing so, the United States had been in the company of Nazi Germany and the Union of South Africa. In 1952 the McCarran-Walter Immigration and Nationality Act provided that "the right of a person to become a naturalized citizen of the United States shall not be denied or abridged because of race."

An important factor in turning the tide of public feeling in favor of Japanese Americans was that they reacted to mistreatment in an extraordinary way—by establishing an unrivaled record of good citizenship. They ranked higher in education and lower in crime and juvenile delinquency than any other ethnic group in the United States, including the native whites. In 1960 they averaged 12 years of schooling, as against 11 for whites and 8.6 for blacks. By the 1970s the difference in educational attainment among the three groups had narrowed considerably, but the Japanese Americans retained a slight edge over the others. In impressive numbers they obtained advanced degrees and jobs in such professional fields as business administration, engineering, and optometry; by 1970 their median family income was $3000 higher than the national median. Their record of physical and mental health was almost incredible. The average longevity of Japanese Americans was 74.5 years for men and 81.2 years for women—nearly 7 years above the figures for California whites and well above the record of any other group in human history. Three Japanese traditions—the strength of the family, the belief in the value of education, and the belief in the virtue of hard work—did most to account for this unparalleled triumph over adversity.

The decline of anti-Japanese sentiment after World War II was foreshadowed during the war years by the federal government's removal of legal discrimination against the Chinese. Congress repealed the Chinese Exclusion Act in 1943 in order, as President Roosevelt put it, to "correct a historic mistake and silence the distorted Japanese propaganda." The results were more important in principle, however, than in practice. Although China was now permitted to have an immigration quota, it was so low that only about 10,000 Chinese were admitted under it in the next 20 years. In 1965, however, Congress abolished the national-origins quota system. Under the new law, total annual immigration remained about the same, but admission was on the basis of skills or family relationships. This permitted a substantial increase in Chinese immigration, much of it from Hong Kong to California.

Chinese Americans in the postwar period established a high rate of achievement grounded in traditional values similar to those underlying the success of Japanese Americans. By the 1970s their average length of school attendance, for instance, surpassed that of whites but did not quite equal the record of the Japanese. For Chinese Americans the educational picture was one of extremes: a very high proportion of them had gone to college, but many had not gone beyond the eighth grade. The wartime shortages of engineers, scientists, doctors, and nurses opened thousands of professional jobs to educated Chinese Americans; this began to occur before the end of World War II, rather than after it, as in the case of the Japanese.

As with other minorities, Chinese and Japanese Americans also increased their political activity. In 1974 March Fong Eu was elected secretary of state, becoming the first person of Asian ancestry to hold statewide office in California. She easily won reelection in four subsequent campaigns. In San Francisco, where Asian Americans made up nearly one-fourth the city's population, five Chinese Americans held elective office by 1980, whereas a decade earlier there had been none. Only about 6 percent of the population of Los Angeles was of Asian ancestry, and in 1985 Michael Woo became the first Asian American ever elected to the city council.

S. I. Hayakawa, the controversial president of San Francisco State University, became in 1976 the first Californian of Japanese ancestry to be elected to the United States Senate. He was defeated for reelection in 1982. In the 1980s Japanese Americans were elected to a host of local offices throughout the state, and Robert Matsui of Sacramento and Norman Mineta of Santa Clara were elected to the House of Representatives.

Filipino Americans in the years after World War II became one of the fastest-growing minority groups in the state. During the early decades of the twentieth century, most Filipinos drawn to California were farm laborers, but under the 1965 immigration law the majority of Filipino immigrants were accountants, nurses, and other skilled professionals. By 1980 Filipino Americans were the largest Asian group in California and were expected to outnumber second-place Chinese Americans by almost two to one in the middle of the next century. A similar upsurge was also seen in the number of Korean Americans, especially in southern California. By 1980 there were some 200,000 Koreans in the Los Angeles area alone, a 500 percent increase since 1976.

Following the American withdrawal from Vietnam in the early 1970s, the escalating turmoil in Southeast Asia led to a mass exodus of refugees. In desperation tens of thousands of Vietnamese, Laotians, and Cambodians fled by sea, and eventually many of these boat people were resettled in the United States. California received about 40 percent of the nation's total Indo-Chinese refugee population, and state officials petitioned the federal government for additional aid in handling the influx. By the mid-1980s an estimated 200,000 refugees were in the state, the majority of whom were on public welfare. Volunteer agencies, including many church-related organizations, assisted in the resettlement effort by sponsoring individual refugee families.

African Americans

Of all the racial minorities, African Americans attracted the largest share of public attention in the decades after World War II. They became more active than other groups in openly protesting racial discrimination, and their protests, both peaceful and violent, received wide coverage in the national news media.

African Americans formed about 11 percent of the total population of the United States in 1940. Their major migration to California began in 1942 with the sudden demand for labor in the shipyards and other war industries, and thereafter the percentage of blacks in the state's population, which had been only 1.8 in 1940, rose to 4.3 in 1950 and 7.7 in 1980. But their presence was even more apparent because most of them became concentrated in all-black neighborhoods in the cities of Los Angeles, San Francisco, Oakland, Berkeley, and Richmond.

In the long struggle for equality, African Americans had to overcome major obstacles in three closely related areas: housing, employment, and education.

California was the first state to attempt a legal sanction promoting segregated housing when the constitution of 1879 authorized cities and towns to restrict the occupancy of Chinese and even to forbid their residence within the city limits. In 1890 the United States Supreme Court struck down this provision in the case of a San Francisco ordinance purporting to define the "boundaries" of Chinatown. In the twentieth century, real estate interests, wishing to maintain the racial integrity of all-white neighborhoods, often relied on the right of contract. Deeds for the sale of residential property included *restrictive covenants* in which the buyer promised not to sell to anyone other than Caucasians. But in 1948, in *Shelley v. Kraemer,* the Supreme Court refused to permit the continued enforcement of these contracts by the courts, on the ground that such enforcement by agencies of state government violated the Fourteenth Amendment guarantee of the equal protection of the laws. The Los Angeles Board of Realtors and the California Real Estate Association launched a campaign to reverse the Court's ruling, but this project failed.

In 1959 the heavily Democratic California legislature adopted the Unruh Civil Rights Act, named for Jesse Unruh, the speaker of the assembly. This law forbade racial discrimination by anyone engaged in business (including real estate brokers) and permitted anyone who suffered such discrimination to recover damages in the

Restrictive covenants barred African Americans from purchasing homes in new housing tracts in Los Angeles in the 1940s. (*Courtesy of the Southern California Library for Social Studies and Research.*)

courts. In 1963 the legislature passed the Rumford Act, named for black assembly-man W. Byron Rumford of Berkeley, which declared racial discrimination in hous-ing to be against public policy and forbade owners of residential property including more than four units, or owners of any publicly assisted residential property, to en-gage in racial discrimination in its rental or sale.

Not long after the passage of the Rumford fair housing or open occupancy law, the California Real Estate Association began a campaign not only against this par-ticular act but also against every form of what the association denounced as "forced housing." This led to the drafting of Initiative Proposition 14, a state constitutional amendment that would have effectively repealed the Rumford Act. In November 1964 the voters of California approved Proposition 14 by more than two to one, and thus most of the white voters demonstrated that they were bitterly opposed to residential desegregation and deeply frightened by it.

The passage of Proposition 14 was among the many grievances that contributed to the massive and tragic Watts riot in Los Angeles in 1965. The number of African Americans in Los Angeles County had grown from about 25,000 before World War II to nearly 650,000 in 1965, and most of them were crowded into the south central part of the city, including the Watts district. Housing in Los Angeles, as the county commission on human relations pointed out, was more strictly segregated than in any city in the southern states. The riot in the "palm tree ghetto" of Watts began on the sweltering and smoggy evening of August 11, 1965, following the arrest of a young black man for drunken driving and the spread of a rumor that two black women had been victims of police brutality. The ensuing riot lasted for several days and was brought under control only by the intervention of the National Guard. At least 34 persons were killed, 31 of them blacks. In terms of loss of life, this did not equal the record of the East Saint Louis riot of 1917, but in terms of property losses, amounting to more than $40 million, the Los Angeles riot was the most destructive in American history. More than 600 buildings were damaged, including more than 200 completely destroyed by fire.

In May 1966 the state supreme court struck down Proposition 14 as an unconstitutional denial of the equal protection of the laws. There were many protests that the court had "violated the will of the people," but the following year the United States Supreme Court confirmed the unconstitutionality of the initiative.

Decisions by state and federal courts also played a central role in the movement to achieve equality of educational opportunity. The most important of these decisions was *Brown v. Board of Education of Topeka* in 1954, in which the Supreme Court forbade racial segregation in the public schools. It was written by Chief Justice Earl Warren for a unanimous court. Reversing the decision of the Court in *Plessy v. Ferguson* in 1896, which had permitted so-called separate but equal facilities, the Court now ruled that public school segregation was a denial of the equal protection of the laws. To segregate black children solely on the ground of their race, said Chief Justice Warren, "generates a feeling of inferiority as to their status in the community that may affect their hearts and minds in a way unlikely ever to be undone." Warren had learned a great deal about racism from his own mistake in advocating Japanese evacuation.

Formal segregation of pupils by race had been abolished in most of the public school districts of California for many years, and the state law that had permitted local districts to continue the practice had been repealed in 1946. Yet *de facto* (without lawful authority) school segregation continued and even increased mainly because of continued residential segregation.

During the 1960s several communities in the state, most notably Riverside and Berkeley, began voluntarily to end segregation of their schools. More typical, however, was the case of Los Angeles in which the school board began the task of desegregation only when under direct court order to do so. The sprawling Los Angeles Unified School District was the nation's second-largest school system. By 1970 about one-quarter of the district's 700,000 students were black, 90 percent of whom attended predominantly black schools, and another 23 percent were of Mexican ancestry, two-thirds of whom attended predominantly Mexican schools. In 1970 superior court judge Alfred Gitelson ruled that the district was guilty of unconstitutional segregation and ordered the school board to implement a desegregation plan. Governor Ronald Reagan labeled the ruling "utterly ridiculous," and the school board took no action pending an appeal of the desegregation order. Judge Gitelson was defeated for reelection, but the state supreme court in 1976 upheld his ruling and ordered the board to prepare a desegregation plan. The following year the board designed a plan that included several voluntary programs and the mandatory busing of some 40,000 students in the fourth through eighth grades. The plan went into effect in the fall of 1978 with considerable confusion, but few disruptive incidents.

In ordering the desegregation of Los Angeles schools, the state supreme court went beyond existing federal desegregation decisions. The federal courts had held that mandatory busing was required only in cases of *de jure* (by law) segregation, where it could be shown that a school district had deliberately segregated its schools in the past. The state court, however, ruled that busing was also a proper remedy for de facto segregation, where segregated schools were the result of established residential patterns.

The greatest threat to the success of school desegregation in Los Angeles, as in cities around the country, was the decline of white enrollment. In the first year of court-ordered busing, one-third of the white students assigned to new schools under the desegregation plan left the Los Angeles school district. Although the rate of *white flight* slowed the following year, the proportion of white students in the district declined from 56 percent in 1966 to 24 percent by 1980. The decline of white enrollment was part of a nationwide population shift from the central cities to the suburbs, a movement caused only partly by the controversy over desegregation. Nevertheless, the prospects for effective desegregation were considerably dimmed by the abandonment of the city schools by white students. As one school integration specialist commented, "There are simply not enough white children to go around."

At least as important as the political and social resistance to black penetration of white neighborhoods and schools was the economic discrimination that kept African Americans in menial jobs, or kept them from getting any jobs at all. In California, as in most other states, nearly all labor unions in fields involving skilled workers had excluded blacks entirely until World War II. As the number of blacks in the California workforce increased dramatically during the war, many unions established all-black *auxiliaries.* Black workers in the auxiliaries were required to pay full union dues but were barred from voting in union elections and received unequal union benefits. In January 1945 the California Supreme Court ruled, in *James v. Marinship,* that the auxiliary practice was "contrary to public policy." This ruling produced important changes in union membership practices, but few blacks actually benefited from the decision. As the war ended, the number of blacks in the skilled workforce began to decline rapidly. In San Francisco, 75 percent of black heads of households had been skilled industrial workers during the war; by 1948, only 25 percent still held skilled jobs, and the black unemployment rate was nearly three times that for all other persons combined.

Thirty years after the end of World War II, the unemployment rate for African Americans in the state was about twice that for the general population, and unemployment among black youths averaged nearly 40 percent. Almost a quarter of all black families in California lived in poverty in 1975, compared with less than 8 percent of whites. By 1980 the income of the typical black family was still less than 60 percent that of the average white family.

In spite of such continuing problems, a substantial black middle class was also emerging in the state. California in the 1980s led the nation in the number of businesses owned by black entrepreneurs. For every 1000 blacks in the state, there were 25 black-owned firms, almost double the national average. By 1985 California had more than 44,000 black-owned businesses, with a total payroll of $217 million.

The number of blacks elected to political office also increased steadily. In 1970 Wilson Riles was elected superintendent of public instruction over the archconservative Max Rafferty, becoming the first African American to win statewide office.

Three years later former police officer and city councilman Thomas Bradley was elected mayor of Los Angeles, receiving the largest white vote for a black candidate in any American city. Also, by 1973 California had three black representatives in Congress—Yvonne Brathwaite Burke, Ronald V. Dellums, and Augustus Hawkins—and the following year black state senator Mervyn Dymally was elected lieutenant governor. In 1978 Dymally failed to win reelection, and Burke was defeated in the race for attorney general by veteran Republican state senator George Deukmejian. Dymally and Maxine Waters of Los Angeles later joined Dellums as members of California's congressional delegation. By 1992 two black senators and six black assembly members, including Assembly Speaker Willie L. Brown, Jr., of San Francisco, were serving in the state legislature. Probably the most popular black official holding partisan office was Los Angeles Mayor Bradley. He served an unprecedented five terms as chief executive of the state's largest city, and in both 1982 and 1986 he won the Democratic nomination for governor.

Latinos

By far the largest ethnic minority in California in the late twentieth century was the group that the census once listed as of "Spanish origin," most of whom, in California, were Mexican Americans.

In 1910, the census had enumerated only 51,000 persons of Mexican ancestry in California, but the Mexican revolution of 1910–20 combined with World War I to begin a long process of mass immigration from Mexico to the American southwest. By 1930, only Mexico City had a larger Mexican population than Los Angeles. The result, however, was what George I. Sánchez has called "cultural indigestion." Most of the immigrants were laborers. Barriers of prejudice and of language blocked their economic advancement and their social assimilation. In Los Angeles, they were concentrated in the eastern part of the city almost to the degree that blacks were concentrated in the southern part of it. East Los Angeles, the collective name for the eastside *barrios,* or neighborhoods, was marred by dilapidated housing and deficient sanitation. But it also was a place where a vibrant community life flourished. As Ricardo Romo, author of *East Los Angeles: History of a Barrio* (1983), has concluded, "the majority of Mexican immigrants, for reasons of language, kinship, and folk customs, chose to live together in barrios. These barrios provided a sense of identity with the homeland and a transition into American society."

Latinas took an active role in community organizing during the 1930s. In 1938 Luisa Moreno, vice president of a newly formed cannery and agricultural workers union, organized El Congreso del Pueblo de Habla Española (The Congress of Spanish-Speaking People). The congress was a coalition of middle- and working-class associations in Los Angeles, dedicated to protecting civil liberties and bettering the lives of Hispanic Californians. Among its supporters were such Hollywood luminaries as Anthony Quinn and Delores del Rio. Elected the first president of the congress was Mexican-born activist Josefina Fierro de Bright. Under her leader-

Josefina Fierro de Bright, first president of El Congreso del Pueblo de Habla Española, estimated that 30 percent of the organization's activists were women. (*Courtesy of the Department of Special Collections, University of Southern California Library.*)

ship, the congress fought discrimination and worked for better housing and health care for Mexican Americans.

World War II brought limited progress. Paradoxically, some of this resulted from uneasy afterthoughts about two glaring wartime episodes of Anglo-American bigotry—the Sleepy Lagoon murder trial and the zoot-suit riots.

On August 2, 1942, in East Los Angeles, the body of a Mexican American boy with a fractured skull was found beside a germ-infested old reservoir used as a swimming hole, which the newspapers dubbed the "Sleepy Lagoon." There had been some scuffling the night before between two juvenile gangs, but there was no direct evidence of murder, and no witness. Nevertheless, 300 young Latinos were arrested, 23 indicted, and 17 convicted. The defendants were brutally treated while in jail, and racial prejudice was apparent throughout the proceedings. In a pseudo-scientific report to the grand jury, a police lieutenant explained violent crime by Mexicans as a racial characteristic, and the chief of police and the sheriff endorsed the report. The bias in the trial was so blatant and so clearly symptomatic of a larger social injustice that it ultimately led to some improvement in public attitudes. This came in part from the work of a defense committee headed by Carey McWilliams and in part from the verdict of the appellate court, which threw out all the convictions and strongly rebuked the trial judge.

The Sleepy Lagoon case was significant not only because it revealed the depths of xenophobia and racism, but also because it led to what historian Manuel Gonzales has called "the first effective mobilization of the Mexican community in southern California." Helping to mobilize that community were activist Josefina Fierro de Bright and *La Opinión,* the city's largest and most influential Spanish-language newspaper. The Mexican residents of Los Angeles came to perceive that their entire community was on trial, not just those arrested at Sleepy Lagoon.

During this period, some young Latinos were wearing the *zoot suit,* originally as the proper costume for jitterbug dancing but later to attract attention, to show their emancipation from their elders, and to express their group solidarity. Much of the public believed that not only all zoot-suiters but virtually all young Latinos were *pachucos,* or juvenile hoodlums. On June 3, 1943, mobs of white sailors, soldiers, and civilians in downtown Los Angeles began to beat up zoot-suiters and tear off their clothes, and these race riots continued for 6 days until the Navy declared Los Angeles off-limits. Historian Mauricio Mazón, author of *Zoot-Suit Riots* (1984), has interpreted the violence as an act of "symbolic annihilation." Stateside servicemen, far from the actual theaters of war, released their pent-up frustrations by attacking pachucos as ersatz enemies of the nation. Whatever motivated the rioters, their hateful actions left a deep and abiding scar.

The war and postwar periods brought a degree of occupational and geographical mobility that considerably weakened barriers against intermarriage, equality of employment, and housing opportunities. Mexican Americans were not segregated in the armed forces, and many acquired a new experience of integrated living. They volunteered in greater numbers and won more Congressional Medals of Honor, proportionately, than any other ethnic group. After the war, many improved their status by education under the G.I. bill.

By the 1960s, Mexican Americans in California were more heterogeneous and much more urbanized than was commonly supposed. More than 85 percent of them lived in cities; less than 15 percent of those employed were agricultural laborers. During the 1960s many younger Mexican Americans joined a militant new crusade in search of ethnic identity. Reviving the belief of Mexican philosopher José Vasconcelos that people of mixed race would inherit the earth, many Mexican Americans began to call themselves La Raza—"the race" or "the people." Another appellation, also embraced with defiant pride, was *Chicano,* a shortened form of "Mexicano" with the first syllable dropped and the "x" pronounced as "ch" in the fashion of Mexico's Chihuahua Indians. As journalist Rubén Salazar observed, "A Chicano is a Mexican-American with a non-Anglo image of himself." The term "Chicano" was often used to embrace all Spanish-speaking people in the state, although a substantial portion of the Hispanic population was derived from places other than Mexico. In Los Angeles, for instance, 20 percent of all Latinos were descendant from Cuba, Puerto Rico, and Central and South America.

California's Spanish-speaking population was a deeply disadvantaged minority, caught in a vicious cycle of undereducation and underemployment. Of the

Mexican Americans employed in California, about half w
workers, including those in the entrepreneurial and profe
almost every occupational group the earnings of Mexica
lower than the average. In 1976 their median annual incom
$10,000, compared with nearly $15,000 for Anglo-Ameri
families with annual incomes below the official poverty le
percentage for families in general. The school dropout rate
twice that of Anglo students, and more than half of all La .... job market
lacked a high school diploma. Many children had grown up in households where
only Spanish was spoken. In 1976 the state legislature adopted the most ambitious
bilingual education program in the nation to help schools begin to deal more effectively with the language problem. By 1980 about 330,000 students were enrolled
in special bilingual and bicultural classes. Voters in 1986, however, passed an initiative that declared English to be California's official language. Twelve years later,
voters approved an initiative prohibiting bilingual education and mandating instruction in the English language only.

Although Latinos outnumbered blacks in the state by more than two to one,
Mexican Americans had great difficulty in gaining political representation. The
election of Edward R. Roybal to the Los Angeles city council in 1949 broke a long
tradition of Anglo exclusiveness, but during the two decades following his election
to Congress in 1962, no other Mexican American served on the council. During the
administration of Edmund G. Brown, Jr., Latinos were appointed in record numbers to the courts and state agencies but, by 1982, representation in the state legislature was limited to three senators and four members of the assembly.

Several factors contributed to the relative political weakness of the state's largest
minority. Geographical diffusion of the Hispanic population drained off political
strength, and in areas where their numbers were greatest, gerrymandering of election districts often prevented Latinos from exerting what strength they had. Anti-
Latino prejudice remained a barrier. A disproportionate number of Hispanic judges,
for instance, failed to win confirmation at the polls. Perhaps the biggest factor,
however, was low voter participation by the Latino community. In Los Angeles,
where Latinos constituted about 20 percent of the voting-age population, they accounted for only about 5 percent of the voter turnout in most citywide elections.

In the 1980s a major effort was made to arouse the "sleeping giant" of Latino
political power. Voter registration drives were aimed at increasing the Hispanic
presence at the polls. Registered Latino voters numbered about 1 million, but
700,000 eligible voters remained unregistered. Political action groups also encouraged Latino immigrants to apply for naturalization. About one-third of the 2.5 million adult Latinos in California were noncitizens. The number of Hispanic
officeholders grew slowly during the 1980s, but mainly on the local level. By 1986
there were 450 Hispanic elected officials in the state, including city council members Richard Alatorre of Los Angeles and Blanca Alvarado of San Jose. Latinos
suffered setbacks in state politics with the unsuccessful campaign of Mario Obledo
for the Democratic gubernatorial nomination in 1982, and the 1986 defeat of
Supreme Court Justice Cruz Reynoso.

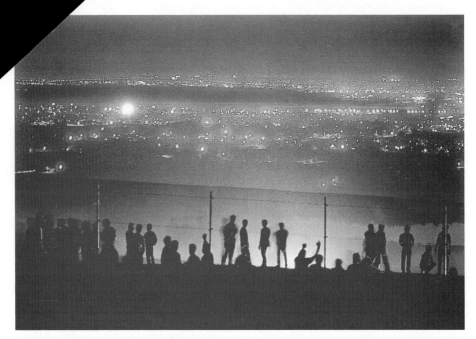

The First View of El Norte. An approaching border patrol vehicle illuminates would-be Mexican immigrants silhouetted against the lights of San Diego. (*Courtesy of photographer Don Bartletti,* Los Angeles Times.)

Illegal immigration of undocumented workers from Mexico continued to swell the Latino population in California and remained an unsolved problem for state and federal officials. By crossing the border, Mexican immigrants could instantly increase their earning power 10 times or more. In the face of this powerful motive, all efforts to curb the flow of illegal immigrants proved ineffective. Estimates of the size of the illegal immigrant population in the state ranged from 750,000 to 1.5 million. Their impact on the state also remained unclear. Some studies indicated that the illegal aliens cost the state and federal government millions of dollars through their use of public services; other observers maintained that they contributed revenues far in excess of the cost of services they received. About 4 percent of the illegal aliens made claims on the welfare system in 1980, whereas nearly 75 percent paid income and social security taxes, and all paid sales taxes. In 1985 a Rand Corporation study termed "a myth" the belief that the large number of Mexican immigrants in California was hurting the state's economy. According to the Rand report, Mexican workers actually stimulated economic growth by keeping wage levels in the state competitive.

Employers throughout California wondered how their enterprises would manage under a new, more restrictive immigration law passed by Congress in 1986. The law imposed stiff penalties on employers who knowingly hired illegal aliens and provided for a substantial increase in the number of agents patrolling the nation's border with Mexico.

Women

California has an ambiguous record in the history of thought, writing, and action relating to the place of women in society. The late-nineteenth-century feminist movement was well represented in California by such energetic advocates of women's rights as Charlotte Perkins Gilman, author of *Women and Economics* (1898), and Laura De Force Gordon, the pioneer California journalist, lawyer, and suffragist. San Francisco novelist Gertrude Atherton, both in her personal life and in her writing, was in constant rebellion against domesticity and the subjection to the male that she believed it involved. Born in 1857, Atherton had the misfortune of being widowed at an early age when her husband died at sea and his body was returned preserved in a barrel of rum. Her liberated fiction included local histories, sensational novels, treatises on women's rights, and an account of the sexual rejuvenation of older women.

In the next generation, the novelist Kathleen Norris, 23 years younger than Atherton, held opposite views about the social role of women and had far greater influence in spreading her views. Norris considered motherhood and the family the heart of any successful and happy woman's life, and this was the message of most of her nearly 80 books of phenomenally popular fiction, beginning in 1911 with *Mother,* an instant best-seller. In the 1930s her novels and short stories made her the highest-paid woman in the world. Her own success was implicit evidence that a woman could have both a career and a family, but she once wrote that "the whole basis of my entire life is Family. I don't care about anything else."

Although California had been one of the early states to grant women the vote, in 1911, California women were rarely successful in obtaining elective office. At first it appeared that it would be otherwise, for in 1918 four women were elected to the state assembly. Yet during the next 50 years, only 10 other women were elected to the lower house and none to the state senate. Women in the California congressional delegation usually numbered only one or two. Representative Florence Kahn was elected in 1925 to her late husband's seat in the House, where she continued to represent San Francisco and to maintain his vigorous advocacy of military preparedness until 1936, and Representative Helen Gahagan Douglas served in Congress from 1945 until her defeat by Richard Nixon in the senatorial election of 1950. As late as 1975, California ranked 48th among the states in the percentage of state elective offices held by women.

The nationwide women's movement of the 1960s and 1970s finally made itself felt in California state elections in 1976, when the number of women in the legislature doubled from three to six, including Rose A. Vuich of Dinuba, the first woman ever elected to the California senate. By 1992, 22 of the legislature's 120 members were women, the highest number in state history. Also, two women held statewide office—Secretary of State March Fong Eu and Treasurer Kathleen Brown—and Democrats Dianne Feinstein and Barbara Boxer were elected to the United States Senate.

On the local level, the number of women elected to public office increased remarkably during the 1970s and 1980s. Dianne Feinstein was president of the San Francisco Board of Supervisors in 1978 when Mayor George Moscone and

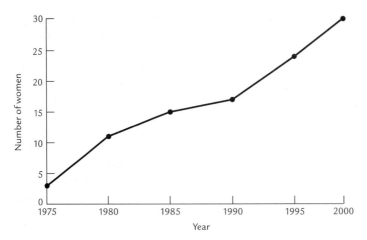

Women in the California legislature, 1975–2000. (*Based on data in the California Journal.*)

Supervisor Harvey Milk were assassinated in their city hall offices. Feinstein was selected by her fellow supervisors to serve out the term of the slain mayor, and in 1979 she became the first woman to be elected the city's chief executive. The election attracted national attention because of the role of San Francisco's large homosexual population, estimated to constitute 20 percent of the city's electorate. Feinstein successfully appealed for support from homosexual voters, and the support they gave her was an important factor in her victory. San Jose city councilwoman Janet Gray Hayes became the first woman elected mayor of the state's fourth-largest city, and Anne Rudin was elected mayor of Sacramento. By 1986, 64 of the state's 296 county supervisors—22 percent—were women. Women were in the majority on boards in Fresno, Santa Clara, Riverside, and San Francisco counties.

The number of women who have served in high appointive positions in state government has been nearly as meager as that of women who have held elective office. Katherine Philips Edson served as the first executive officer of the Industrial Welfare Commission under Governor Hiram Johnson, and Kate Richards O'Hare Cunningham, a nationally known crusader for prison reform, was appointed assistant director of the department of penology by Governor Culbert L. Olson in 1939. Phoebe Apperson Hearst became the first woman on the Board of Regents of the University of California in 1897 and served until her death in 1919. Others on the board included Dorothy Buffum Chandler, wife of *Los Angeles Times* publisher Norman Chandler, who served from 1954 to 1968 and was elected by her colleagues as vice chairwoman; Catherine Campbell Hearst, a regent from 1956 until her resignation in 1976; and Vilma S. Martinez, a founder and president of the Mexican-American Legal Defense and Educational Fund, who was appointed to the board in 1976.

It was in the administration of Governor Edmund G. Brown, Jr., that women for the first time moved into top positions of power throughout state government. In his two terms in office, Brown appointed more than 1600 women to various boards and commissions and named women as directors of the departments of agriculture, finance, transportation, veterans affairs, motor vehicles, conservation, and corrections. In February 1977, Rose Elizabeth Bird became the first woman ever appointed to the California Supreme Court—and Governor Brown made her not merely a justice but the chief justice. The following year Bird won confirmation at the polls by an extremely close margin.

Employment opportunities for women gradually expanded in the twentieth century, and an increasing proportion of women sought employment outside the home. World War II was a catalyst for change in the status of California women, just as it was for the state's racial minorities. Government and military officials and leaders of industry exhorted women to take jobs in factories and offices. Rosie the Riveter was the epitome of a woman doing her patriotic duty. About half the women who went to work in the wartime shipyards and aircraft plants had already been in the labor force, usually at lower-skilled and lower-paying jobs. At war's end most of the women workers wanted to continue in the work they were doing, but as male workers returned from the armed forces and as wartime industries cut back production, many women were displaced from their jobs. Nevertheless, the number of women in the workforce continued to increase. In 1950, 30 percent of all California women were working outside the home; by 1977 a majority of California women were in the labor force. Overwhelmingly, women sought employment for economic reasons. Working was a necessity for the many widowed, divorced, and separated women who composed a major part of the female labor force. For other women, work was necessary to support their families or to provide better education or health care for their children. In the years following the war, relatively few California women sought employment merely for personal fulfillment.

In the early 1970s, the National Organization for Women and other women's rights groups conducted a strong campaign for the equal rights amendment (ERA): "Equality of rights under the law shall not be denied or abridged by the United States or by any state on account of sex." Congress approved the ERA by overwhelming votes in both houses in March 1972 and set a 7-year deadline for ratification of the amendment by three-fourths of the nation's state legislatures. In California the assembly approved the ERA less than a month after Congress had officially proposed it, and, following considerable debate, the state senate joined in ratifying it in November 1972. In the states as a whole, however, after an initial spurt of ratifications, strong opposition developed and stalled the process for several years. By the fall of 1978, 35 states had ratified the ERA, three short of the needed three-fourths majority. After a vigorous campaign by the amendment's supporters, Congress extended the deadline to June 30, 1982, but even with this extension the ERA failed to win the needed additional ratifications.

The issue that came to dominate the feminist movement in the 1980s was *comparable worth*. Although women were making inroads into a few occupations with high status and high earnings, the majority of women continued to be employed as clerks and service workers. As more women moved into the labor force, the discrepancy between their wages and those of men actually increased in some fields.

Most women in the workforce remained concentrated at the lower end of the pay scale, earning considerably less money than their male coworkers. Citing these economic inequities, feminists argued that women workers should receive equal pay for doing comparable, but not identical, work to that of men.

The California legislature in 1981 declared that comparable worth should be considered when setting salaries for state employees in female-dominated jobs. Over the next 3 years, several additional comparable-worth bills were passed by the legislature but were vetoed by Republican governor George Deukmejian. The California Comparable Worth Task Force reported in 1985 that the state's labor force remained highly segregated by sex. It also found that for every $1 earned by a male worker in California, a female worker earned only 60 cents. The task force recommended that businesses in the state be required to close the gap by upgrading the pay scale for their women workers and by integrating them into traditionally male-dominated positions.

Selected Bibliography

Several articles in Robert F. Heizer (ed.), *California* (1978), provide information on California Indians in the twentieth century. See also Troy R. Johnson, *The Occupation of Alcatraz Island* (1996); Adam Fortunate Eagle, *Alcatraz!* (1992); Joan Weibel-Orlando, *Indian Country, L.A.* (1993); George H. Phillips, *The Enduring Struggle* (1981); Jack D. Forbes, *Native Americans of California and Nevada* (1969); and Valerie Sherer Mathes, *Helen Hunt Jackson and Her Indian Reform Legacy* (1990). The larger context is provided in James J. Rawls, *Chief Red Fox Is Dead: A History of Native Americans since 1945* (1996), and Donald Fixico, *Termination and Relocation: Federal Indian Policy, 1945–1960* (1986). Kenneth M. Johnson's monograph, *K-344, or The Indians of California v. the United States* (1966), includes information on the broader history of California Indian problems. Heizer (ed.), *The California Indians v. The United States of America* (1978), contains documents from the 1959 Indian Claims Commission ruling. See also Ferdinand F. Fernandez, "Except a California Indian: A Study in Legal Discrimination," *Southern California Quarterly,* L (June 1968), pp. 161–175.

Sucheng Chan's *Asian Californians* (1991) and *Asian Americans* (1991) are useful surveys. The most thorough accounts of the continuing controversy over Japanese American relocation are Yásuko I. Takezawa, *Breaking the Silence* (1995); Leslie T. Hatamiya, *Righting a Wrong* (1993); and Roger Daniels et al., *Japanese Americans: From Relocation to Redress* (1986). General studies are David J. O'Brien and Stephen S. Fugita, *Japanese American Ethnicity* (1991), and Robert A. Wilson and Bill Hosokawa, *East to America* (1980). Works on the Chinese Americans include Shien Woo Kung, *Chinese in American Life* (1962), and Rose Hum Lee, *The Chinese in the United States of America* (1960). See also H. Brett Melendy, *Asians in America: Filipinos, Koreans, and East Indians* (1977); Tricia Knoll, *Becoming Americans* (1982); Lorraine Crouchett, *Filipinos in California* (1982); Fred Cordova, *Filipinos* (1983); Eui-Young Yu et al. (eds.), *Koreans in Los Angeles* (1982); Chan (ed.), *Hmong Means Free* (1994); and Kitty W. Shek and Arthur G. Auble (eds.), *Cambodians in California* (1996).

For historical background on the wartime and postwar black migration, see Rudolph Lapp, *Afro-Americans in California* (1987); Douglas Henry Daniels, *Pioneer Urbanites*

(1980); Shirley Ann Wilson Moore, *To Place Our Deeds: The African American Community in Richmond, California, 1910–1930* (2000); and Lawrence B. de Graaf, "The City of Black Angels: Emergence of the Los Angeles Ghetto, 1890–1930," *Pacific Historical Review,* XXXIX (August 1970), pp. 323–352.

On the migration and its problems, see Gretchen Lemke-Santangelo, *Abiding Courage* (1996); Dolores Nason McBroome, *Parallel Communities* (1993); Albert S. Broussard, *Black San Francisco* (1993); and Charles Wollenberg, "Black vs. Navy Blue: The Mare Island Mutiny Court-Martial," *California History,* LVIII (Spring 1979), pp. 62–75, and *"James vs. Marinship:* Trouble on the New Black Frontier," ibid., LX (Fall 1981), pp. 262–279. On the housing issue, see Raymond E. Wolfinger and Fred E. Greenstein, "The Repeal of Fair Housing in California," *American Political Science Review,* LXII (September 1968), pp. 753–769.

The controversy over school integration is described in Wollenberg, *All Deliberate Speed* (1976); Irving G. Hendrick, *The Education of Non-whites in California* (1977); and Lillian Rubin, *Busing and Backlash* (1972).

A useful guide to work on Mexican Americans is Armando Valdez et al., *The State of Chicano Research in Family, Labor and Migration Studies* (1983). General surveys of Chicano history include Manuel Gonzales, *Mexicanos* (1999); Mario T. Garcia, *Mexican Americans* (1991); Albert Camarillo, *Chicanos in California* (1984); and Carey McWilliams, *North from Mexico* (1949). More specialized studies appear in Camarillo, *Chicanos in a Changing Society* (1979), which focuses on the Mexican American community in Santa Barbara; Richard Griswold del Castillo, *The Los Angeles Barrio, 1850–1890* (1980), and *La Familia* (1984); Hans Johnson, *Undocumented Immigration to California, 1980–1993* (1996); Edward J. Escobar, *Race, Police, and the Making of a Political Identity* (1999); David G. Gutiérrez, *Walls and Mirrors* (1995); Ricardo Romo, *East Los Angeles* (1983); Mauricio Mazón, *The Zoot-Suit Riots* (1984); Francisco Balderrama, *In Defense of La Raza* (1982); and Rudolfo F. Acuña, *A Community under Siege* (1985).

Anthologies on racial problems in California are Daniels and Spencer C. Olin, Jr. (eds.), *Racism in California* (1972); George E. Frakes and Curtis B. Solberg (eds.), *Minorities in California History* (1971); and Wollenberg (ed.), *Ethnic Conflict in California History* (1970). Thoughtful essays on the need for a multiethnic history of California include Wollenberg, "A Usable History for a Multicultural State," *California History,* LXIV (Summer 1985), pp. 202–209, and Martin Ridge, "Bilingualism, Biculturalism: California's New Past," *Southern California Quarterly,* LXVI (Spring 1984), pp. 47–60.

On the history of California women, see the special issues of *California History,* LXXII (Spring 1993); *Pacific Historical Review,* LXI (November 1992); *Pacific Historian,* XXVIII (Fall 1984); and *Journal of the West,* XXI (April 1982). The many biographies of California women include Emily Wortis Leider, *California's Daughter: Gertrude Atherton* (1991); Mary A. Hill, *Charlotte Perkins Gilman* (1980); and Charlotte S. McClure, *Gerturde Atherton* (1976). On political activity, see Jacqueline R. Braitman, "Elizabeth Snyder and the Role of Women in the Postwar Resurgence of California's Democratic Party," *Pacific Historical Review,* LXII (May 1993), pp. 197–220, and Jean M. Smith, "The Voting Women of San Diego, 1920," *Journal of San Diego History,* XXVI (Spring 1980), pp. 133–154. On the status of women workers, see Sheila Tropp Lichtman, "Women at Work, 1941–1945," Ph.D. thesis, University of California, Davis (1981). The battle over the ERA is described in Margaret I. Miller and Helene Linker, "Equal Rights Campaigns in California and Utah," *Society,* VI (May/June 1974), pp. 40–53. Joan M. Jensen and Gloria Ricci Lothrop, *California Women: A History* (1987), provides a useful introduction to the subject.

A Season of Discontent

The social history of California in the 1960s is a study in contrasts. In the prosperous early years of the decade, California became the most populous state in the Union, culminating more than a century of phenomenal growth.

The 1960s were also years of unprecedented social ferment. Beginning at Berkeley in 1964, college campuses around the state were rocked by a series of student strikes and protest demonstrations. Many young people, alienated from a society they regarded as corrupt and decadent, turned to drugs and adopted unconventional styles of dress and behavior. The unpopular Vietnam War added immensely to the sense of youthful alienation and became the focus of a nationwide antiwar movement. The Watts riot of 1965 was evidence of another kind of discontent, and the following year the radical Black Panther party was organized in Oakland.

By the decade's end, the population growth of California had sharply declined. Changed economic conditions as well as a kind of malaise, which affected the state and its image, contributed to a dramatic slowdown of migration to the state. In the 1970s the historic pattern of growth reasserted itself, but even then the rate of growth remained below that of previous decades.

The Growth Rate: Peak and Slowdown

Through the first half of the 1960s, economic opportunity continued to combine with the amenities of mild climate, scenic beauty, and California's romantic reputation to attract new residents from other states at the rate of almost 1000 a day. (See Color Plate 16.) These newcomers made up nearly two-thirds of a total annual population increase of 600,000 at the peak in 1963. When California passed New York and became the most populous state late in 1962, Governor Edmund G. Brown proclaimed a 4-day celebration—"California First Days"—and called for "the biggest party the state has ever seen." Communities across the state staged local celebrations, and at Truckee an official delegation ceremoniously welcomed the latest carload of newcomers as they crossed the state line. Not everyone viewed California's rise to preeminence as an occasion for celebration. Californian Earl Warren, then United States chief justice, warned: "I would not celebrate with fireworks or dancing in the streets. Mere numbers do not mean happiness."

The growth of California's population was urban—or rather suburban—and was greatest in the southern part of the state. By the mid-1970s more than 90 percent of

The 1970 census confirmed that California was the most populous state in the union. This prescient cartoon by Newton Pratt in the *Sacramento Bee* illustrates some of the problems of preeminence. (*Courtesy of the* Sacramento Bee.)

the people of California lived in the 17 areas that the Census Bureau listed as "metropolitan," and thus California was the nation's most urbanized as well as most populous state. Los Angeles–Long Beach had about 33 percent of the state's population, San Francisco–Oakland about 15 percent, and San Diego 8 percent. Los Angeles County was the most populous county in the nation, and the city of Los Angeles was second only to New York as a center of industrial employment. Orange and San Diego counties grew phenomenally, and part of the migration to them came from Los Angeles. The population of San Francisco declined slightly but steadily, and in the Bay Area, as in southern California, the growth came in the surrounding communities rather than in the central city. San Francisco remained a major financial center, as the permanent site of the Federal Reserve bank of the district, but the increasing ratio of population in favor of southern California—more than two-thirds of the state's people lived south of the Tehachapis—led to the shift of such agencies as the regional headquarters of the Securities and Exchange Commission and the region's stock exchange from San Francisco to Los Angeles.

An important element in the growth of population and wealth in California in the 1950s and 1960s was the tremendous expansion of the aerospace industry, mostly financed by the federal government. Large numbers of immigrants from Mexico and African Americans from the rural south continued to arrive in California during these years, but far more attention was paid to the coming of thousands of highly skilled and highly paid aerospace engineers and scientists. Beginning in 1969, however, federal spending on aerospace was drastically cut, and this coincided with the onset of a long period of economic slowdown, including a major nationwide recession in 1969 to 1970 and an even worse one in 1973 to 1975. Moreover, this period of relative depression in the economy had a cruelly unfamiliar and unwelcome aspect—it was simultaneously a period of severe and continuous inflation.

This strange combination was largely a result of the peculiar economic policies of the federal government during the Vietnam War. The social and psychological consequences of that conflict, as well as its economic consequences, were very different from those of World War II. Pearl Harbor had united the nation, but the war in Southeast Asia became one of the most bitterly divisive issues in American history. In the years before America was plunged into World War II, the country had gone to great lengths to try to avoid an inevitable involvement; in the case of Vietnam many felt that the United States had gone far out of its way to engage in a futile conflict of which the necessity and even the morality were doubtful at best, and the costs tragic and apparently wasted. At the beginning of World War II, the American economy was still in the depression and still operating at a fraction of its productive capacity; it badly needed the injection of huge government expenditures, made psychologically and politically acceptable by unquestioned military demands. During World War II, federal price and wage controls and huge wartime taxes kept some brakes on inflation. At the beginning of major involvement in Southeast Asia, on the other hand, the American economy was already operating close to capacity, and during the great buildup of American forces in Vietnam between 1965 and 1968, involving vast expenditures for the undeclared war, the federal government failed to apply wartime economic controls, and avoided substantial increases in taxes. The result was a massive inflation and overheating of the economy, with dangerously high percentage rates of price increases, compounded from year to year.

In an attempt to halt the inflation process, the Nixon administration in 1969 began drastic cuts in federal spending, and the Federal Reserve Board made a series of increases in interest rates. These actions, though they failed to stop the inflation, led to the first recession in 10 years, and the worst and longest one in 30 years. The stock market fell dramatically. Unemployment rose sharply throughout the nation, but California suffered more than the rest of the country because so much of its manufacturing depended on federal spending.

The remarkable economic expansion and population growth of the early 1960s were reversed by the end of the decade. Though the state's population reached about 20 million in 1970, giving it five more seats in Congress, the increase during that year was less than 1 percent. This was the lowest annual percentage increase on record, and for the first time in its entire history the state's population grew at a slower rate than did that of the nation as a whole. Natural increase, which had almost always formed the smaller part of the state's growth, had suddenly become by far the largest part. Net migration in 1970 was only 27,000 compared with 356,000 in 1963, the peak year of the previous decade. These were the official figures of the state department of finance. Some unofficial estimates maintained that 25,000 more persons actually *left* the state in 1970 than came into it.

The abrupt slowdown in California's growth rate was caused in part by depressed economic conditions, the product of continuing inflation and recession, and also by a fundamental deterioration of the popular image of the state. The traditional picture of California as the land of opportunity, sunshine, and romance was overshadowed by images of a state beset by high unemployment, crowded suburbs, a polluted atmosphere, and campus and racial unrest. A rash of books and articles, with such titles as *How to Kill a Golden State, Anti-California,* and *California: The Vanishing Dream,* either mourned or celebrated the alleged demise of the California dream. Although these popular commentaries often suggested corrective measures, they did little to attract newcomers to the state.

Transportation

Transportation was one of the many fields in which California's broader economic and population trends were reflected. The state's "love affair with the automobile" continued. There were three registered automobiles in California for every four persons of driving age, by far the largest ratio in the world. A vast network of freeways spread over the length and breadth of the state, and most communities welcomed their arrival, though the engineers of the division of highways sometimes showed limited imagination in their design. But in San Francisco a major "freeway revolt" began in 1959 when the new Embarcadero Freeway cut off the view of the lower half of the Ferry Building as seen from Market Street. The public outcry forced the state engineers to leave the freeway half finished, instead of carrying out their plan to extend it all the way around the Embarcadero and the Marina. (Following the disastrous Loma Prieta earthquake of 1989, the offending freeway was eventually torn down.) In 1964, when the state authorities proposed a freeway through a part of Golden Gate Park, the revolt flared again, after folksinger Malvina Reynolds composed a stirring protest song called "The Cement Octopus." Such intransigence made San Francisco the despair of both state and federal highway planners, who called the city the worst highway bottleneck in America.

The absence of another form of modernization, that of the port facilities of San Francisco, was more clearly disastrous for the city. In 1960 San Francisco still handled all the foreign imports of the Bay Area. By 1975 it had lost most of its seagoing traffic, largely to the port of Oakland, where the voters had approved bonds to build the massive cranes required for loading and unloading *containers,* truck-size steel or aluminum boxes lifted from a ship directly onto a truck chassis or railroad flatcar.

The railroads continued to prosper from the hauling of freight, but their passenger traffic steadily declined. They often begged the state public utilities commission to approve the discontinuance or drastic reduction of their passenger service, but the commission turned down most of these requests. The railroads were often accused of making their passenger trains and schedules as unattractive and inconvenient as possible, in the hope that they would eventually be permitted to discontinue entirely the unprofitable business of carrying passengers in competition with automobiles, buses, and airplanes. California's air transportation industry meanwhile doubled its volume in the 1960s, and the air lane between Los Angeles and San Francisco became the most traveled in the world.

While San Francisco was rebelling against freeways, it took the lead in planning an electrified rapid transit system that would have the great advantage of reducing not only traffic congestion but also air pollution from motor vehicle exhausts. In 1962 the voters of San Francisco, Alameda, and Contra Costa counties approved the formation of the Bay Area Rapid Transit (BART) District and the building of a rail network that would connect the cities and suburbs of the East Bay with the stations of a subway under Market Street in downtown San Francisco. BART carried its first passengers in 1972 using an automated, computerized operating system, no conductors, and only a single attendant on each train. It was the first all-new transit system to be built in the United States in 60 years, and in spite of many technical difficulties it was ultimately rated as one of the best.

In Los Angeles, on the other hand, most of the voters and taxpayers showed their determination to cling to the privilege of doing all their traveling throughout the sprawling metropolis in their private automobiles. Los Angeles had 1000 miles of freeways and 10,000 miles of cars. On an average day, more than 350,000 cars and trucks passed one point near the civic center, at the junction of six freeways, where the interchange resembled the mechanism of a giant watch. Except for the very poor, nearly everyone between the ages of 15 and 85 had an automobile. The affluent majority repeatedly refused to subsidize a public rapid transit system, but it often showed considerable enthusiasm for elaborate transit studies and reports. A

Southern California Rapid Transit District did come into existence, on paper, but for years it could do no more than operate a fleet of traffic-bound buses. It was not until 1980 that Los Angeles voters approved a sales tax increase to finance construction and operation of a new rail rapid transit system.

Reapportionment

The population boom of the 1950s and early 1960s also led to increased demands for reform of the state's system of political representation. With the continued growth of the suburban parts of the metropolitan areas, especially those in southern California, the archaic federal system of representation in the California state senate became more and more obviously inequitable. Los Angeles County, with a population of 6,036,771 in the 1960 census, was the most populous legislative district in the United States, yet it had the same number of votes in the state senate as the Alpine-Mono-Inyo district, with 14,294 people: one vote. A resident of Alpine, Mono, or Inyo County cast a vote worth 422 times as much as the vote of a resident of Los Angeles County. This was by far the widest disparity in any state. One-quarter of the population elected three-quarters of the California state senators. A majority of the senators could be elected by 10.7 percent of the California voters.

Initiative proposals to modify the "little federal" system and reapportion the California senate were rejected at the polls in 1928, 1948, 1960, and 1962. Most

The "one man, one vote" ruling of the Supreme Court and the consequent reapportionment of the state senate led to a revival in 1965 of the proposal to split California into two states. (*Courtesy of the* Sacramento Bee.)

'This'll Serve The Supreme Court And Its Reapportionment Right!'

voters clung to the hazy and misleading idea that what was appropriate for the federal government must be appropriate for the states. But the United States Supreme Court ruled in *Reynolds v. Sims,* on June 15, 1964, that one person's vote must be worth as much as another's in the election of state legislators. The equal protection clause of the Fourteenth Amendment, said the Court, required that seats in both houses of a state legislature be apportioned on a population basis. The so-called federal analogy was discarded as fallacious and inapplicable. Counties, the Court pointed out, were merely political subdivisions created by the state governments, not sovereign entities like the states themselves. Chief Justice Earl Warren was one of the prime movers in the adoption of this "one man, one vote" doctrine, even though as governor of California he had been one of those who had opposed reapportionment of its state senate. The northern members of the California senate, many of whom would lose their seats, engaged in a series of desperate maneuvers in the attempt to escape reapportionment. Senator Joseph A. Rattigan of Santa Rosa asked whether a proposal for armed insurrection would be in order, but in 1965 the legislature approved a new apportionment law that included no deviations of more than 15 percent in the populations of the new senatorial districts. Consequently, in the election of 1966, under the new plan of apportionment, the control of the state senate passed to southern California, which had elected a majority of the assembly members since the 1930s.

In 1965, the last year under the federal system, a large group of state senators from northern California revived a proposal that had been made periodically since the 1850s. This was a plan to divide the state at the Tehachapi Mountains, and this latest version of it would have included the counties of Santa Barbara and Kern within the northern state, giving only seven counties to the southern one. But polls showed that more than two-thirds of the voters, even in the north, were opposed to any plan for state division.

Education

In the years of headlong growth and general prosperity that followed World War II, California's public schools remained impoverished. The state spent more than 40 percent of its budget for education, and its per capita expenditures for public schools were among the highest in the country—but these figures were grossly misleading because California's school-age population grew twice as fast as its general population. Between 1950 and 1960, the total number of people in the state increased by roughly 50 percent, whereas public school enrollment grew by more than 100 percent. An unprecedentedly large proportion of the people who were migrating to California were young married couples, able and inclined to produce numerous children. The schools were chronically short of money, of classroom space, of teachers—of everything, in fact, except pupils.

The annual tidal waves of postwar babies that flooded into the public schools in the 1950s began to inundate the colleges and universities in the following decade, and the state responded by greatly expanding its system of public higher education.

In 1960 the legislature adopted the Master Plan for Higher Education to prepare for the massive enrollment growth anticipated during the 1960s. The master
plan defined the mission of the various segments of the state's system of higher
education.

California's state college system traced its origin to 1862, when a 2-year normal
school was established in San Francisco. This was moved to San Jose in 1870.
Other such schools were later established elsewhere in the state. After their programs had been lengthened to 4 years, they were promoted to the rank of teachers'
colleges in 1921 and designated as general state colleges in 1935. After adding
graduate instruction, most of them were renamed "state universities" in 1971. Later,
the entire system became known as the California State University, or CSU. Its primary function was to provide undergraduate and graduate education through the
master's degree.

The beginnings of 2-year junior colleges stemmed from the passage of a state
law in 1907 authorizing the governing boards of city, district, or county high
schools to establish post-high-school courses. Fresno instituted the first public junior college in the United States in 1910, and California has since led all the states
in the establishment and support of such institutions. By midcentury they had
begun to be called "city colleges" or "community colleges," though state policy
prevented them from expanding their programs to 4 years. The mission of the community colleges was to prepare students for transfer to a 4-year college, to award
them an associate of arts or science degree, or to train them for employment in a
vocational or technical program. The community colleges numbered more than
100 by 1980.

The general campuses of the University of California increased to eight. At Los
Angeles a normal school had become the University of California, Southern
Branch, in 1919. This had become UCLA in 1931, and by the 1960s its student
body was larger than the one at Berkeley. Santa Barbara State College became the
University of California, Santa Barbara, in 1944. In the late 1940s, colleges of letters and science were established at Davis and at Riverside in connection with what
had originally been branches of the university-wide college of agriculture. After
1960 new general campuses of the university were established at Santa Cruz,
Irvine, and San Diego. Under the master plan, the university was entrusted with the
responsibility of conducting advanced research and awarding doctoral degrees in
addition to providing undergraduate education.

In the early 1970s, it seemed as though higher education had overexpanded. The
postwar baby boom continued through the 1950s, but the reduction in birthrate following the introduction of oral contraceptives in 1960 and the decline in migration
to the state in the late 1960s undercut earlier projections of growth in college enrollment. Funds for public education were slashed at all levels. The state's universities and 2-year community colleges were able to balance their budgets only by
assigning a scandalously large share of their teaching loads to part-time teachers,
to whom they paid low hourly wages. There was a surplus of trained teachers, as
well as many other people with college and university training, who suddenly found
themselves overqualified and underemployed.

Campus Turmoil

American college students of the 1950s had been called "the silent generation." Those who reached college age in the 1950s had been born in the 1930s, and when these "depression babies" became young adults, they were too driven by anxiety about material success to be interested in any form of political or social dissent. Students took virtually no part, for example, in the University of California loyalty oath controversy.

The college students of the middle and later 1960s, on the other hand, were part of the great wave of postwar babies, born and reared in relative affluence, but in such numbers that they badly overcrowded the public schools and the colleges and were often discontented with the crowding. Some of them discovered that their massive numbers could be a form of power.

Stirrings of student unrest in California had appeared as early as May 1960 when a crowd of college students, protesting their exclusion from a hearing of the House Un-American Activities Committee in the San Francisco city hall, jammed the rotunda by sitting down in the balcony. The police washed them down the stairs with fire hoses and drove them from the building with clubs. At about the same time, black college students in the southern states began to attack the racial segregation of lunch counters with the tactic of the *sit-in*. This tactic had been used for a short time in 1937, in a different context, by some of the relatively radical new CIO unions; it took the form of the sit-down strike, in which striking workers occupied the property of the employer, but organized labor had soon abandoned the sit-down, not only because it was ruled illegal but also because it alienated the public. In the early 1960s, however, the federal courts ruled that the racial segregation of lunch counters was unconstitutional and therefore that those who had participated in the lunch counter sit-ins were merely demanding their constitutional rights and could not be validly arrested.

Several students from the University of California at Berkeley had spent their summers in civil rights activities in the deep south, and when they returned to the campus in the fall of 1964, they organized sit-ins and other demonstrations to protest racial discrimination by Bay Area businesses. In September the university administration announced that a sidewalk area at the southern entrance to the campus—an area previously thought to belong to the city of Berkeley and thus to be beyond university control—was university property and ordered all student groups to stop using the area for setting up tables, recruiting members, or otherwise organizing for off-campus political activity. The groups affected by the university's order included student civil rights organizations, as well as groups ranging in their political philosophy from the far left to the far right. When the administration attempted to enforce its new order, students organized the Free Speech Movement (FSM), called a student strike, and used the civil rights tactic of mass civil disobedience against the university.

The university charter law of 1868 and the state constitution of 1879 (Article IX, section 9) had sought to keep the state university free from "political or sectarian influence," and the regents had long chosen to interpret that phrase as forbidding any political advocacy on a university campus. This had never been the true meaning of the provision. The full sentence forbade "political or sectarian influence *in the appointment of [the university's] regents and the administration of its affairs*" [italics inserted]. Every governor of California with the possible exception of Earl Warren had flatly violated this provision by appointing regents for political reasons. But the regents, like the governors, preferred to ignore this aspect of the matter. Apparently they also chose to ignore the advice of their own attorneys that their rules against political speech and advocacy on campus were in violation of the United States Supreme Court's decision in *Edwards v. South Carolina* in 1963. This ruling stated that "student speakers may even advocate violations of the law provided such advocacy does not constitute a clear and present danger . . ." and that "much of the conduct that the public finds objectionable is constitutionally protected."

Thus the student rebellion at Berkeley in its beginnings was truly a free speech movement against unconstitutional restrictions, and in this particular sense it was successful. Following the disciplining of several students who defied the administration's order restricting political activity, crowds of students occupied the campus administration building. In December 1964 the largest sit-in occurred at Sproul Hall, and Governor Brown ordered state and local police to intervene. In the largest mass arrest in the state's history, more than 700 persons, mostly students, were dragged or carried from the building. Less than a week after the Sproul Hall arrests, the Berkeley faculty passed resolutions that the university should not regulate the content of political advocacy, but should regulate only the time, place, and manner of it in order to prevent interference with normal university functions, and the university administration agreed to liberalize its rules governing student political activity.

At first the Berkeley student rebels relied on methods that were nonviolent, even though they did involve a kind of mass force, but the young radical leaders of the movement became overconfident. In a speech from the steps of Sproul Hall, FSM leader Mario Savio promised his followers that he could protect them from going to jail or from any other form of punishment. The apparent success of the tactics of sitting-in and going limp when arrested made the students feel invincible and invulnerable. The courts soon ruled, however, that occupying a university building was merely a form of illegal trespass and that going limp was merely a form of resisting arrest. In their mass trial in Berkeley in 1965, 578 of them were found guilty of trespassing, and many of resisting arrest. When these hundreds of students were sentenced to jail, many became disenchanted and embittered. The sense of newness and magic began to go out of the movement, and a feeling of frustration and desperation took its place. The idea of nonviolence was soon lost in a welter of confrontation and disruption, and a drift toward violence and vandalism set in. Some student rebels made a mockery of the name of the Free Speech Movement and began to deny the right of free speech to anyone but themselves by shouting down any speaker who disagreed with them. This was a tragedy, not only for the young people themselves but also for a society that cried out for improvement and that badly needed the freshness of youthful idealism.

The Free Speech Movement of 1964 gave Berkeley a considerable reputation as the cradle of student revolt in America, and in the subsequent years this reputation attracted many young radicals, some of them students and others former students, to the university campus and to parts of Berkeley and Oakland to the south of it. Protest against the escalation of the war in Vietnam and a continuing crusade against racism at home were now the major channels of youthful rebellion.

In October 1967 a major draft riot occurred after a crowd of antiwar demonstrators, trying to shut down the Oakland induction center, were routed by police who sprayed them with a temporarily blinding chemical known as Mace. The new vogue of student power spread across the country. In April 1968 hundreds of students staged a sit-in at Columbia University, and when it was broken up by police, many violently resisted arrest. In August, during the Democratic national convention in Chicago, there was a violent confrontation between police and the mass of young militants who had gathered in an effort to pressure the convention into taking a stand against the Vietnam War and into nominating Senator Eugene McCarthy. Prominent among the leaders of the Chicago demonstrations were two Californians: Tom Hayden, a leader of the radical Students for a Democratic Society, and Jerry Rubin, once a graduate student in sociology at Berkeley but now a full-time "revolutionary." Combining his political activities with the use of drugs, which he advocated as an aid to revolution, Rubin was addicted to the politics of absurdity. Earlier he had confronted the House Un-American Activities Committee dressed in a rented Revolutionary War uniform, and had made outrageous statements urging junior high school students to prepare to kill their parents and burn their school libraries.

Late in 1968 radical students at San Francisco State demanded the creation of a black studies department run exclusively by blacks. This was the most important of a series of "non-negotiable demands," some of which had been drafted by a Third World Liberation Front including Latin American and Asian American radical students. To gain acceptance of their demands, the student leaders began a long strike characterized by Maoist rhetoric, violent disruption of classes, vandalism, and personal assault. The large tactical squad of the San Francisco police, specially trained for campus riot duty, finally broke the strike with mass maneuvers and arrests.

Before this uprising was over, a similar movement was launched at Berkeley, early in 1969, with a strike to demand an autonomous "third world college." Though this demand was not granted, the campus did establish a department of ethnic studies. Next came the disastrous affair of People's Park, in May 1969. This began when Berkeley's radical young street people tried to appropriate a block of university-owned land near Telegraph Avenue as a park for their own use. When the university fenced the block, a mob gathered to try to destroy the fence, and there was a riot in which sheriff's deputies responded to the throwing of rocks by firing shotguns. One young bystander, watching from a rooftop on Telegraph Avenue, was killed and another was blinded. This tragedy frightened, enraged, and radicalized thousands of young people throughout the region and produced such a massive movement to "take the park" that a force of the National Guard was sent

Helmeted members of the National Guard and the police stand guard before the ivy-covered walls of the chancellor's residence on the Berkeley campus during the 1969 People's Park controversy. (*Photograph by Lou de la Torre.*)

to protect it. A National Guard helicopter broke up a disorderly crowd on the campus by spraying the whole area with tear gas, which drifted into dozens of classrooms and even into the campus hospital.

By this time, Berkeley was only one of many American university towns with large groups of rebellious and violence-prone young people. There was repeated violence and arson at Stanford. The University of California at Santa Barbara had long been thought of as a quietly conservative campus, but in February 1970 its student residential community of Isla Vista exploded in a series of riots in which the branch of the Bank of America was burned and a student was killed when a deputy's gun discharged accidentally. Mexican American college students and others in southern California formed the Chicano Moratorium Committee to oppose the Vietnam War and to protest the disproportionate loss of Latino lives in the conflict. The committee organized a series of protest marches in Los Angeles in 1970, the largest of which was a gathering of 30,000 protesters at Laguna Park. The demonstration began peacefully but ended in violence. Three Mexican Americans were killed, including *Los Angeles Times* reporter Rubén Salazar.

Student rebellion reached a nationwide climax in May 1970 after a detachment of the Ohio National Guard shot and killed four young people on the campus of Kent State University, following the burning of the ROTC building in protest against the spreading of the war in Southeast Asia to Cambodia. For the rest of the spring term, many American campuses experienced various degrees of disruption. At Berkeley, thousands of students and a few faculty members tried to "reconstitute" the campus as a center for public argumentation against the war and tried to stop all other campus activity until the war was ended.

The Hippie Movement

The college student radicalism of the 1960s was at first quite separate from the hippie movement, but gradually the two phenomena became interrelated. The word "hip" has been defined as "to be in the know, particularly about the drug underworld." The word "hippie" was derived from Norman Mailer's term "hipster." The appeal of the hippie mystique to young people in the 1960s had many aspects, including social protest and normal feelings of rebellion characteristic of adolescence. But many young adherents of the hippie movement were motivated by deep personal maladjustment and alienation. Craving love, joy, and self-realization, many of them believed that such needs could be satisfied by drugs, especially when taken in the company of other young people with similar feelings. They often described their movement as a subculture or counterculture, and sometimes quite candidly as a drug culture. Its culture included electronically amplified rock music, psychedelic art, the doctrines of astrology and Krishna consciousness, and communal social relationships analogous with those of Gypsies or of certain American Indian tribes.

An essential factor in the spread of the hippie movement was the popularization of the new drug lysergic acid diethylamide, or LSD. This drug was first synthesized by a Swiss chemist in 1938. In the early 1960s, Dr. Timothy Leary, a lecturer on clinical psychology at Harvard and the holder of a Ph.D. in psychology from the University of California at Berkeley, was one of a group engaged in experiments with several drugs, including LSD, which they described as psychedelic or consciousness-expanding. Their critics insisted that LSD was more accurately described as mind-distorting and hallucinogenic and that its effects on different individuals were dangerously unpredictable, a kind of "chemical Russian roulette." Colors intensified and changed, shape and spatial relations were distorted, and inanimate objects seemed to pulsate and to assume great emotional significance. To some the experience was deeply moving, exhilarating, and self-revealing—an episode of "cosmic oneness" or an "exploration of inner space." But to others it brought panic, bizarre and suicidal behavior, and temporary or even permanent psychosis. The frequency of the hippies' use of LSD varied considerably, but many of them used marijuana almost every day when they could obtain it.

In 1966 the news media began to give the hippies massive publicity and often described them as "flower children" or "the love generation." In 1967 when the movement reached its peak, there were probably about 200,000 hippies in the nation, and millions of other Americans, young and old, were sympathetic to the movement. The largest colony was in the Haight-Ashbury district of San Francisco, scene of the nationally publicized Summer of Love in 1967. Other large concentrations of hippies could be found in the Telegraph Avenue area south of the university campus in Berkeley; in Los Angeles on the Sunset Strip and along Fairfax Avenue in West Hollywood; and in Greenwich Village in New York. Smaller enclaves sprang up in almost every major American city, and there were various rural communes, notably in California, New Mexico, and Colorado.

Hippie leaders maintained that they were seeking to establish a new communal freedom from individual anxieties and to remove themselves from a decadent society full of war and oppression into a utopia of peace and love. It was more than coincidental that the years in which the hippie movement attracted its greatest following were also the years of the great expansion of American armed forces in Vietnam. Many young Americans believed that their country's participation in the war in Southeast Asia was morally indefensible, and their hatred of the war was a major factor in their feelings of alienation from the whole prevailing system of society.

Black Radicalism

About the time when student radicals had shifted their main attention to opposing the Vietnam War, and away from the black civil rights movement, that movement itself had taken a new and radical turn. In 1966 Stokley Carmichael became the new head of the Student Nonviolent Coordinating Committee. He soon turned it into a movement of violent nonstudents, ordered all whites to get out of it, and raised the cry of "black power." In the autumn of 1966, the Black Panther Party for Self-Defense was founded in Oakland by two young black militants, Huey P. Newton and Bobby G. Seale. They had met as students at the old Grove Street campus of Merritt College, a community college drawing many of its students from predominantly black areas in west and north Oakland. Newton and Seale were influenced by the writings of Malcolm X and Frantz Fanon, and later by those of Marx, Lenin, Mao Tse-tung, Ho Chi Minh, and Che Guevara. But their strongest feeling, growing out of their personal experience, was a hatred of the frequently prejudiced and cruel treatment of African Americans by white police. The black panther was originally the ballot emblem of a black civil rights party organized in Alabama in 1965. Newton liked the name and adopted it because, he said, the panther was reputed never to make an unprovoked attack, but to defend itself ferociously. Newton and Seale established a system of patrol cars; carrying law books and guns, they trailed police cars through the Oakland slums to protect the constitutional rights of African Americans.

One of the new party's first and most important converts was Eldridge Cleaver, a vigorously articulate black man who had twice been in prison. His first term, beginning when he was 18, had been spent in the California state prison at Soledad for possession of marijuana. After his release, according to his widely read memoir *Soul on Ice,* he was burning with resentment and had turned to the raping of white women as a symbolic act of "insurrection," intended "to send waves of consternation throughout the white race." This brought him another and longer term in prison, during which he came to repudiate the act of rape and to regard his own resort to it as a symptom of the "dehumanization" that he had suffered; however, he resolved to fight by more effective means against the social system that he felt had brutalized and degraded black people like himself.

In prison Cleaver had become an admirer of the Black Muslim leader Malcolm X, who was assassinated in 1965. Early in 1967, the widow of Malcolm X made a visit to San Francisco, and Cleaver, recently released on parole, wanted to meet her. A squad of Black Panthers appeared at the airport and acted as her bodyguards while she was in the city. They wore paramilitary black uniforms and black berets and carried guns. The sight of them was an exhilarating experience for Cleaver, and he threw himself into the cause of the new party. He became its minister of information. Seale was chairman, and Newton was minister of defense and later supreme commander.

Intense fear and hostility between police and Panthers soon led to many tragic shooting affrays. On October 28, 1967, gunfire erupted after an Oakland police car stopped an automobile driven by Huey Newton. One officer was killed; another policeman and Newton were wounded. On April 6, 1968, also in Oakland, there was more shooting in which two policemen were wounded, a young Panther was killed, and Eldridge Cleaver was wounded and arrested. Newton was tried in the summer of 1968 and convicted of manslaughter, but the conviction was reversed on appeal, and two later trials ended in hung juries. Cleaver was released on bail, became the candidate of the Peace and Freedom party for the presidency of the United States, and chose Jerry Rubin as his running mate. Shortly afterward, a higher court ordered Cleaver's parole revoked, and rather than return to prison, he jumped bail and fled to Algeria.

Though their beliefs and tactics were radical, the Panthers did not share the extreme separatism of the black *cultural nationalist* groups and ridiculed their advocacy of wearing African styles of dress and studying Swahili and other aspects of African culture. In January 1969, during an argument over such issues at a meeting of the Black Students Union at UCLA, two young leaders of the Black Panther movement in Los Angeles were shot and killed by members of a cultural nationalist faction, in a dispute partly fomented by undercover agents of the FBI. Black radicalism was further divided and weakened when a bitter quarrel developed between Cleaver, who issued periodic calls for revolutionary guerrilla warfare from his exile in Algeria, and Newton, who favored much more moderate tactics including free breakfasts for children, a free medical clinic, and free bus transportation for relatives of prisoners on visiting days.

The Decline of Radicalism

By the fall of 1970, the volcano of student rebellion had become dormant, if not extinct. By 1971 even radical students at Berkeley began to speak of "the old New Left of the 1960s" and to debate why the movement died. Foremost among the reasons for the decline in student radicalism was the gradual winding down of the Vietnam War. Other factors were the extreme political reaction of taxpaying voters against the disruptive tactics of the student demonstrators, the dampening effects of the economic recession, the coming of the 18-year-old vote, and the growth of interest among young people in the possibilities of "working within the system." Mass disruption on the campus was an idea whose time had come and gone.

Throughout the 1970s the mood on college campuses in California and across the nation grew steadily more conservative. A survey of students entering Berkeley in 1980 revealed a marked contrast to the attitudes of students polled 8 years earlier. The proportion of students who described themselves as "middle-of-the-road" politically increased from 33 to 45 percent, whereas those who said they were conservative rose from 10 to 17 percent. Those who identified themselves as liberal declined from 50 to 37 percent, and those who said they were far left dropped from 7 to 2 percent. Faced with greater economic uncertainty after graduation, a growing number of students in the 1970s chose majors in business and engineering rather than in the social sciences or liberal arts, and when asked about the most important objective in their life, they expressed the desire to be well-off financially. The resumption of draft registration in 1980 led to a flurry of antidraft rallies on campuses throughout the state, but some observers speculated that the new antidraft movement was related more to the rise of careerism on campus than to any widespread political or moral opposition to military service. Today's college students, cynics charged, were opposed to the draft because it would delay their entry into the job market.

A few of the leaders of the radical movement were still in the news during the 1970s but were no longer very radical. Eldridge Cleaver returned from exile in 1976 to surrender himself for trial, explaining that he had acquired a new and more favorable view of the United States after several years of unpleasant experiences elsewhere. Jerry Rubin complained that reporters, who occasionally still interviewed him, treated him "like a museum piece"; by 1980 he had become a research analyst for a New York investment firm. Bobby Seale and Tom Hayden became unsuccessful though quite conventional political candidates for mayor of Oakland and United States senator, respectively. Moreover, John Tunney's Senate seat was lost in 1976 not to Tom Hayden in the Democratic primary but rather to the Republican nominee, S. I. Hayakawa, who had become an outstanding symbol of resistance to student radicalism when he was president of San Francisco State University.

Although the radical era ended in public rejection, it left some positive and permanent aftereffects. The decade of protest had generated a greater awareness of the rights of racial minorities, and the liberalization of public attitudes had resulted in some legislative reforms. Possession of small amounts of marijuana, for example, had been reduced from a felony to a misdemeanor comparable to a traffic citation, and state laws forbidding various sexual activities between consenting adults were repealed. Hayden rebounded from his 1976 defeat to found a grassroots political organization, the Campaign for Economic Democracy, which won passage of rent control ordinances and elected progressive candidates in cities across the state. Hayden himself later won election to the state assembly as a liberal Democrat from Santa Monica. Furthermore, many young people who had been part of the movement in the 1960s carried their earlier values with them as they entered the professions, assumed greater responsibilities, and began the task of rearing a new generation of Californians.

Selected Bibliography

Economic and population trends may be followed in the *California Statistical Abstract* and the *Economic Report of the Governor* prepared by the state Department of Finance, both annual publications. On developments up to the 1950s, see Margaret S. Gordon, *Employment Expansion and Population Growth, the California Experience, 1900–1950* (1954), and Warren S. Thompson, *Growth and Changes in California's Population* (1955). James J. Rawls, "Visions and Revisions," *The Wilson Quarterly*, IV (Summer 1980), pp. 57–65, describes the deterioration of the popular image of California in the late 1960s and early 1970s.

Several major works trace the rise of southern California. *Los Angeles and Its Environs in the Twentieth Century* (1973), edited by Doyce B. Nunis, Jr., is a valuable guide to materials. See also Kevin Starr, *Material Dreams* (1990); Mike Davis, *City of Quartz* (1990); Andrew Rolle, *Los Angeles* (1982); John Halpern, *Los Angeles* (1979); John Caughey and LaRee Caughey (eds.), *Los Angeles* (1977); and Christopher Rand, *Los Angeles* (1967). Other metropolitan areas are treated in Robert W. Cherny and William Issel, *San Francisco* (1981); Charles Wollenberg, *Golden Gate Metropolis* (1985); Richard F. Pourade, *City of the Dream: The History of San Diego* (1977); Christian L. Larsen, *Growth and Government in Sacramento* (1966); and Beth Bagwell, *Oakland* (1982). On reapportionment, see Bruce E. Cain, *The Reapportionment Puzzle* (1986).

Material on the history and problems of the public schools may be found in John A. Douglass, *The California Idea and American Higher Education* (2001); Irving G. Hendrick, *California Education* (1980); Roy W. Cloud, *Education in California* (1952); and Merton E. Hill, *The Junior College Movement in California, 1907–1948* (1949). The best of the institutional histories are Edith R. Mirrielees, *Stanford* (1959), and Verne A. Stadtman, *The University of California, 1868–1968* (1970).

Landon Y. Jones's *Great Expectations: America and the Baby Boom Generation* (1980) is a portrait of the generation that reached maturity in the 1960s. On campus radicalism, see Gerard J. DeGroot, "The Limits of Moral Protest," *Pacific Historical Review*, LXIV (February 1995), pp. 95–119; David Lance Goins, *The Free Speech Movement* (1993); W. J. Rorabaugh, *Berkeley at War* (1989); Seymour M. Lipset and Sheldon S. Wolin (eds.), *The Berkeley Student Revolt* (1965); Michael V. Miller and Susan Gilmore (eds.), *Revolution at Berkeley* (1965); and Irwin Unger, *The Movement* (1974). On the hippie phenomenon, see Timothy Miller, *The Hippies and American Values* (1991); Gene Anthony, *The Summer of Love* (1980); Theodore Roszak, *The Making of a Counter Culture* (1969); and Lewis Yablonsky, *The Hippie Trip* (1968), a sociological study.

Important works on black radicalism include Eldridge Cleaver, *Soul on Ice* (1968); Bobby Seale, *Seize the Time: The Story of the Black Panther Party and Huey P. Newton* (1970); Philip S. Foner (ed.), *The Black Panthers Speak* (1970); and Bruce Michael Taylor, "Black Radicalism in Southern California, 1950–1982," Ph.D. thesis, University of California, Los Angeles (1983).

CHAPTER 32

Culture and Identity

In the years after World War II, California emerged as a leading cultural region of the United States. Hollywood remained the nation's movie capital and soon became the center for television production as well. Works by California writers, artists, architects, and musicians achieved widespread recognition and often expressed values and attitudes distinctly Californian.

The essence of California's artistic identity was rooted in the state's astounding diversity of land and people, and in its energizing sense of freedom from prior tradition and constraint. As the cultural life of California matured, it came to be identified with a distinctive flair for openness and irreverence. Playwright David Henry Hwang rightly decribed California as a "fascinating crucible in which the future of America can be seen." And feminist artist Judy Chicago, reflecting on her own career, commented: "It was my coming up as a young artist in Southern California that gave me the freedom to dream that I could create a new approach to art history. I don't think there's a chance in hell that I could have done it in New York. Absolutely not. There was an openness here to new ideas that was very, very essential."

Literature

A remarkable group of poets gathered in San Francisco in the late 1940s. Several of them, notably Robert Duncan and William Everson, had been conscientious objectors during the war and were attracted to San Francisco by the circle of pacifists and philosophical anarchists that formed there. The opposition of these poets to all government, and particularly to war, which they regarded as government at its worst, had an important influence on the intellectual atmosphere of the San Francisco Bay area for many years to come. Their poetry often manifested what Everson called "the repudiation of received forms," a conscious rejection of established literary standards of composition. In several articles in national magazines, the

437

older poet Kenneth Rexroth did much to publicize "the San Francisco Renaissance" as a name for this regional movement of innovative and experimental poetry.

In the mid-1950s the cultural libertarianism of San Francisco attracted another group of writers, particularly from the New York area. Self-styled the "beat generation," they began to achieve notoriety in 1956 with the publication of Jack Kerouac's exuberant and formless novel *On the Road* and Allen Ginsberg's startling *Howl and Other Poems*. The beat writers were a somewhat different group from the poets of the San Francisco Renaissance, though they were often lumped together. They were even more extreme in rebelling against the prevailing norms of society and government and also against the established poetic and literary forms. Kerouac announced in a television interview that "beat," a word of his own coinage, meant "beatific." When the Russians put the first Sputnik into orbit, the San Francisco columnist Herb Caen dubbed the beat generation the "beatniks," and the derisive nickname stuck.

Ginsberg's poems were first published in England, and much of their original fame resulted from their seizure by the San Francisco customs office on the ground that they were obscene. They were then published in San Francisco by Lawrence Ferlinghetti, poet and proprietor of the City Lights Bookshop, a center for many writers and artists. Ferlinghetti was tried and acquitted on a charge of publishing an obscene book, and the publicity of this trial did much to ensure popular interest in the beats and their writings. Kerouac's novels and Ferlinghetti's poems were relatively gentle and benevolent, but Ginsberg's poetry, though it had a kind of Whitmanesque power, was intensely morbid. His "Howl" consisted of one continuous sentence nearly 2000 words long and was filled with references to drugs, tragically unhappy sexual encounters, madness, and suicide, all blamed on the corruption of the existing form of society. In many poems and speeches, Ginsberg inveighed against materialism, technology, the war machine—"all the forces that have assaulted the individual human spirit."

In the 1960s a new generation of California writers established themselves as major figures in contemporary American literature. In some ways their work was an extension of the literary style and concerns of the beat generation, but it also reflected the turbulence of their own times. The impulse toward experimentalism, evident earlier in the poetry of Ginsberg and the runaway prose of Kerouac, was manifest in the complex layering of voices in the novels of Ken Kesey, and the surreal imagery of Richard Brautigan. Kesey, born in Colorado in 1935, studied creative writing at Stanford University and worked briefly in the Veteran's Hospital at nearby Menlo Park. His comic, macabre first novel, *One Flew over the Cuckoo's Nest* (1962), is set in a mental ward and powerfully portrays the struggle of the individual against the overwhelming forces of conformity in modern society. Kesey adopted a lifestyle as unconventional as his prose, becoming a cult hero in the 1960s as he toured the country with a busload of followers known as the Merry Pranksters. Brautigan moved to the San Francisco Bay area in the 1950s from his native Washington and first received widespread attention with his unorthodox and disturbing book *Trout Fishing in America* (1967). Like some modern-day Leatherstocking, the narrator of *Trout Fishing* longs for the restoration of frontier innocence and agrarian simplicity, but finds that such qualities are beyond recall in the age of technology and commerce.

Since the beginnings of the state's literature, serious California writers have provided a counterpoint to the prevailing myth of California as the land of boundless opportunity, success, and romance. The failure of this myth became a major preoccupation for the writers of the 1930s, finding its most powerful expression in the works of Nathanael West and John Steinbeck. The later generations of California writers also used the California dream as a background or a foil for their fiction. Much of the appeal of their work, as James D. Houston has pointed out, derived "from the fact that the dream is always there—if only to be betrayed—the ongoing western promise of the Big Romance, the Second Chance, which is a given in the environment, as potent and as insistent as the coastline."

One of the most important figures among the new California writers was novelist-essayist Joan Didion. Born and reared in Sacramento, Didion, in 1963, published her first novel, *Run River,* an evocative story of a rancher's daughter in California who, under the accumulation of a multitude of small pressures, goes insane. The novel is suffused with a pervasive sense of loss, the decline of a "certain pride," and the disappearance of old, familiar ways in the author's native Sacramento Valley. During the next several years, Didion wrote a series of essays, collected as *Slouching towards Bethlehem* (1968), that expanded her vision of California in decline. In "Notes from a Native Daughter," Didion described the dramatic early history of Sacramento and its gradual evolution into the comfortable, rich farm town she knew as a girl. "In that gentle sleep Sacramento dreamed until perhaps 1950," she wrote, "when something happened. What happened was that Sacramento woke to the fact that the outside world was moving in, fast and hard. At the moment of its waking Sacramento lost, for better or for worse, its character. . . ." Didion made

Joan Didion in the living room of her Malibu home in 1977. (*Photograph by Mary Lloyd Estrin. Courtesy of Simon & Schuster.*)

plain that she was talking about more than just her hometown, "for Sacramento *is* California, and California is a place in which a boom mentality and a sense of Chekhovian loss meet in uneasy suspension."

Didion also wrote about those who had come from "the outside world" to California, seeking and often not finding that which had eluded them somewhere else. In "Some Dreamers of the Golden Dream," she told the pathetic story of a desperate woman, convicted of the murder of her husband, who lived in the San Bernardino Valley. "Of course she came from somewhere else, came off the prairie in search of something she had seen in a movie or heard on the radio, for this is a Southern California story." In the title essay, "Slouching towards Bethlehem," Didion provided a firsthand look at the Haight-Ashbury district of San Francisco in the spring of 1967. With an ear finely tuned to the rhetoric of the drug culture, she described with precision the sense of anomie and rootlessness of the young people drifting into San Francisco for the much heralded "summer of love." Didion's later essays and novels also conveyed a sense of loss, of disintegration, not just in California but in all of contemporary society.

An alternative vision of California informed the work of writer Gerald Haslam. Both Didion and Haslam were natives of the Central Valley, born just a year apart, but their sensibilities were radically different. Whereas Didion distanced herself from her California roots, Haslam celebrated his regional identity, making it the source of his greatest insight and power. Haslam became the leading spokesman for what he called "the other California," the small towns and rural areas of the state's interior. In half a dozen books of essays and short stories, Haslam wrote about the oil-rig workers, Mexican laborers, and poor white farmers of his native Kern County. His style, said Carey McWilliams, was "country music set to prose."

Haslam's first collection of short stories, *Okies* (1973), contained scenes that were reminiscent of John Steinbeck. There was a hint too of the naturalism of Frank Norris in Haslam's portrayal of the forces of poverty and hopelessness. Yet Haslam's vision was essentially optimistic. In an essay called "Writing about Home," published in *Coming of Age in California* (1990), Haslam acknowledged the disintegrating forces of modernism and offered the antidote of regionalism "for with it may come rootedness, tradition and values." His novel *Straight White Male* (2000) celebrated the world of the Central Valley offspring of the Dust Bowl migrants of the 1930s, secure in their comfortable status as middle-class Californians but "never far from their humble roots." When asked by critics why he continued to write about the region of his birth, Haslam replied: "In this site can be found all the great subjects, all the grand dramas, and they are not only themes of my stories and essays, but in a sense they are the settings, too: place and people and passion inseparable as the terrain of the heart. And the heart is our primary locale."

The new generation of California writers also included several African American, Native American, Latino, and Asian American authors whose work added a richness and distinctive texture to the recent literature of the state. In the early 1970s, black novelists Al Young and Ishmael Reed began publishing in Berkeley the *Yardbird Reader,* a journal dedicated to the promotion of a diverse, multicultural American literature. Reed, a native of Tennessee, regarded California as the natural place for such an enterprise because here was America's first "truly world state," a state that had produced "a colorful gumbo culture." Reed called his own writing "neo-hoodooism," a blend of black magic, African imagery, and contemporary African American life. The complex, unrestrained style of his novels placed Reed squarely in the tradition of California's experimental literature. As the central character in Reed's *Yellow Back Radio Broke-Down* (1969) observes, "No one says a novel has to be one thing. It can be anything it wants to be, a vaudeville show, the six o'clock news, the mumblings of wild men saddled by demons." Like many other writings of his generation, Reed's work was a response to the dissension and chaos of recent California history. In *The Last Days of Louisiana Red* (1974), a novel set in Berkeley in the 1960s, Reed offered a thinly veiled parody of the Black Panther party and the once-fashionable rhetoric and violence of such organizations.

Native American writers showed a similar willingness to critique their own media-blessed spokespersons while aiming their sharpest barbs at those who would relegate Indian people to the world of collectible artifacts and colorful ancient times. Gerald Vizenor, a professor of Native American literature at Berkeley, lampooned contemporary Indian activists who attempted to fulfill white fantasies of resurrected mythic warriors. In *The Trickster of Liberty* (1988), Vizenor offered a devastating portrait of an "urban pantribal radical" who bore a striking resemblance to the American Indian Movement's outspoken leader, Dennis Banks. Other California Indian writers, such as Darryl Babe Wilson, explored the lives of those who were seeking to preserve the knowledge of traditional culture within the context of contemporary society. In a short story titled "Diamond Island: Alcatraz," Wilson wrote: "Perhaps a generation approaching will be more aware, more excited with tradition and custom and less satisfied with being off balance somewhere between the world of the 'white man' and the world of the 'Indian,' and will seek this knowledge."

In 1959 José Antonio Villareal published *Pocho,* the first novel about Mexican American life written by a Mexican American. Son of immigrant parents, Villareal was born in the Imperial Valley and worked as a youth in California's orchards and fields. *Pocho* chronicled the hardships of Mexican immigrants who came to the United States following the revolution of 1910. It focused on the disintegration of the Rubio family in the Santa Clara Valley and on the dilemma of young Richard Rubio, torn between the traditional Mexican values of his parents and the new way of life he finds in California.

The most important figure in the emergence of a Mexican American literature was Luis Valdez, a playwright and director born in Delano in 1940. After graduation from San Jose State, Valdez returned to Delano in 1965 and founded El Teatro Campesino. Combining ancient Mexican myths, bilingual dialogue, and a concern for contemporary political issues, El Teatro toured the state's agricultural labor camps and became the dramatic voice of the farm worker movement. The highly imaginative and inventive plays of Valdez had an appeal far beyond the farm workers for whom they were originally written. In 1978 Valdez's most ambitious work, *Zoot Suit,* premiered in Los Angeles and later made a brief run on Broadway. The play, inspired by the Los Angeles Sleepy Lagoon murder case of 1942, was made into a film in 1981 starring Edward James Olmos. Valdez's later works included

A scene from Luis Valdez's 1981 film *Zoot Suit,* starring Edward James Olmos as El Pachuco. (Copyright © 1981 by Universal City Studios, Inc. Courtesy of MCA Publishing Rights, a Division of MCA Inc. All rights reserved.)

Bandido (1981), a play about "Tiburcio Vasquez, Notorious California Bandit"; *Los Corridos* (1982), a series of playlets based on traditional Mexican folk ballads; and *I Don't Have to Show You No Stinkin' Badges* (1986), a tragicomic view of an upwardly mobile Mexican American family in Los Angeles.

Reflecting the constant movement of people into California, a recurring theme in the state's literature has been the interplay of a character's present with a past lived somewhere else. (See Color Plate 13.) This theme, evident in the work of the new Mexican American writers, was also a major concern of Maxine Hong Kingston, daughter of immigrants from China who came to the United States in the 1930s. Kingston was born in Stockton in 1940 and grew up with a keen interest in the stories and legends of her family's life in China. In *The Woman Warrior* (1976), a book subtitled *Memoirs of a Girlhood among Ghosts,* Kingston explained: "Those of us in the first American generations have had to figure out how the invisible world the emigrants built around our childhoods fits in solid America." Kingston's narrative explored both her childhood memories of growing up in the family laundry in Stockton and the customs, traditions, and fables of village life in China. In *China Men* (1980) Kingston took this exploration even further, contemplating the nature of exile and the effects of discrimination on earlier generations of Chinese immigrants. Her *Tripmaster Monkey* (1989) portrayed the challenges facing Chinese Americans who attempt to balance the demands of assimilation with the imperatives of tradition. Likewise, the theme of Amy Tan's *The Joy Luck Club* (1989), a collection of stories of four Chinese immigrant mothers and their American-born daughters, is the impact of past generations on the present. Tan was born in Oakland in 1952, the only daughter of Chinese immigrants, and recalled vividly the conflicting demands of her parents: "They wanted us to have American circumstances and Chinese character." Her second book, *The Kitchen God's Wife* (1991), was based on her mother's harrowing experiences in China and escape to the United States in 1949. In *The Hundred Secret Senses* (1995), Tan explored the world of nineteenth-century China and twentieth-century California through the all-seeing eyes of a young woman who navigates her way between cultures and epochs.

Similar concerns distinguished the work of Japanese American writers during this period. A common source of dramatic tension in their work was the contrast between contemporary California and a remembered or imagined life in Japan. Among the many books to deal with the experience of relocation during World War II, the most successful was *Farewell to Manzanar* (1973), written by Jeanne Wakatsuki Houston and her husband, James D. Houston. *Farewell to Manzanar* tells the story of the Wakatsukis, an industrious southern California family resettled in 1942 at the Manzanar relocation camp in Owens Valley. The Wakatsukis face their hardships with dignity and resourcefulness, but disintegrate as a family unit. "I felt the miserable sense of loss," Jeanne Wakatsuki Houston recalled, "that comes when the center has collapsed and everything seems to be flying apart around you." David Mas Masumoto's *Silent Strength* (1985) and *Country Voices* (1987) present moving portraits of the effects of relocation on a small farming town in Fresno County. Masumoto, born after the war, recalled the silence that later surrounded the story of his own family's relocation: "A silence felt by my family and carried through the years; a silence that teaches yet I do not fully understand." The tension between acculturation and tradition, evident in Villareal's *Pocho* and Kingston's *Woman Warrior,* was thus heightened for Japanese Americans by the tragedy of relocation.

California has always been a fertile ground for the imagination. The latest generation of California writers, continuing in the tradition of Frank Norris and John Steinbeck, has created from California's recent past a literature redolent of the region but whose power and diversity are part of the larger American culture.

Painting and Sculpture

Two of the most significant art movements in California since the end of World War II were *abstract expressionism* in the San Francisco Bay area in the late 1940s and the *L.A. look* of southern California in the 1960s. These two movements were part of larger currents in the development of modern art, but were also shaped by the distinct artistic environments of northern and southern California. Their order of occurrence was evidence of the growing importance of Los Angeles in the state's cultural history.

In the early 1930s, the California art scene was vitalized by the visit of the German-born painter Hans Hofmann, often called the dean of abstract expressionism. Hofmann, whose abstract paintings exhibited bold thrusts of vibrant color, was a visiting instructor at Berkeley and the Chouinard Art Institute in Los Angeles. His influence was especially strong in the Bay Area where in the late 1940s the California School of Fine Arts (later renamed the San Francisco Art Institute) invited Clyfford Still and Mark Rothko, two of the nation's leading abstract expressionists, to join the faculty. Still's paintings were characterized by large, ragged patches of dissonant color, while Rothko produced forceful rectangular shapes, blurred at the edges, painted in a more limited color range. The work of Still, Rothko, and the generation of artists they influenced marked the golden age of San Francisco painting.

By the mid-1950s, abstract expressionism in the Bay Area had begun to decline. Many of the students of Clyfford Still followed him to New York, where abstract expressionism was gaining acceptance, and the work of those left behind became increasingly imitative. Out of this decline came a movement away from total abstraction and back to a style of painting that represented figures or elements of the landscape. The most important of the so-called Bay Area figurative painters were David Park and Richard Diebenkorn, both of whom taught at the California School of Fine Arts. Park led the movement to representation with his richly colored paintings emphasizing the human form, whereas Diebenkorn remained essentially an abstract expressionist until 1955, after which he turned slowly to landscapes, figures, and still life. His colors, as one critic observed, were "essentially tonal, rooted in the California landscape."

It was also in the 1950s that the California beat generation made a distinct contribution to the evolution of modern art, the assemblage. The art of assemblage, a kind of sculpture created from bits of cast-off materials from everyday life, was a reaction against "high-brow" art just as the writing of Kerouac and Ginsberg represented a rejection of established literary standards. Constructed from old furniture, clothing, tin cans, license plates, store mannequins, wire, and string, the completed three-dimensional assemblages were often a statement of horror or anguish at the materialism and corruption of modern industrial society.

Out of the assemblage tradition came what was known as *funk art,* a hybrid of painting and sculpture constructed from such materials as leather, clay, steel, and vinyl. The term "funk" apparently was borrowed from the vocabulary of jazz or blues musicians to whom "funky" meant a heavy beat, an earthy, sensual sound. Correspondingly, the constructions of such funk artists as Robert Arneson often were biomorphic forms with ribald or scatological connotations. Arneson's most controversial work was a ceramic bust of George Moscone, the mayor of San Francisco who was assassinated in 1978. The bust had an unnaturally long neck and was placed on a pedestal carved with graphic references to Moscone's life and death. Among the references was the word "Twinkies," a reminder of the defense argument that the judgment of Moscone's assassin had been impaired by his consumption of highly sugared cakes. The bust was unveiled at the George Moscone Convention Center in 1981 but was removed after heated protests. The *San Francisco*

Portrait of George. Robert Arneson's controversial ceramic bust of assassinated San Francisco mayor George Moscone. (*Courtesy of the artist. Photograph copyright M. Lee Fatherree, 1992.*)

Examiner suggested that the bust should be "deposited out of public view—perhaps in the Bay, at the deepest place."

It was clear that the momentum in California art was shifting south. Abstract expressionism continued to be the dominant style of painting in Los Angeles in the 1950s, but by the end of the decade a distinctive regional variation had emerged. Among the paintings of Los Angeles artist Craig Kauffman in 1957 and 1958 were several works in which forms appeared sharply outlined in silhouette. Los Angeles painter Billy Al Bengston commented that Kauffman "was the first southern California artist *ever* to paint an original painting." In 1959 the Los Angeles County Museum opened an exhibition of four California painters whose work emphasized an austere form of composition marked by geometric forms clearly, distinctly delineated. A Los Angeles critic christened the new style "hard edge," a term that accurately suggested the abrupt boundaries between shapes and colors in the new paintings. The exhibit at the county museum traveled to London, and hard edge abstraction provided Los Angeles with its first international success as a center for modern art.

One of the chief concerns of the hard edge painters was to achieve an immaculate finish to their work. By an extraordinarily even application of paint and by limiting their colors to two or three saturated hues, the hard edge abstractionists were able to create paintings with a remarkable optical shimmer. Critic Peter Plagens saw in these qualities a reflection of the aesthetic climate of Los Angeles.

"Hard Edge arose out of Los Angeles's desert air, youthful cleanliness, spatial expanse, architectural tradition . . . and, most vaguely and most importantly, out of optimism."

In the mid-1960s a group of Los Angeles artists and sculptors, most notably Ed Ruscha, Billy Al Bengston, John McCracken, and Larry Bell, carried the concern for precision and impeccability of surface to an extreme. Their work achieved international recognition as the California finish fetish or, more commonly, the L.A. look. The objects they created were as lustrous as the glossy surface of a highly polished automobile or a new fiberglass surfboard. Among such sculptors the preferred materials were neon, stainless steel, and polyester resin or other new forms of plastic. Larry Bell, a sculptor born in Chicago in 1939 and educated at the Chouinard Art Institute, mastered the complicated procedures and expensive technology necessary to work the new materials and produced in the 1960s a series of mirrorlike cubes of chrome and glass. The inspiration for the cubes of Larry Bell seemed to be the "glass box" office buildings of downtown Los Angeles. Their materials were drawn from the local aerospace industry, and their concern with the surface of things, the facade, mirrored the influence of Hollywood. Even more than hard edge abstraction, the L.A. look was a product of the singular atmosphere of southern California.

One of the major international art movements of the 1960s was *pop art,* a movement that both ridiculed and celebrated the affluent consumer society. Pop art flourished in southern California and, like abstract expressionism in the previous decade, took on there a distinctive regional quality. Los Angeles pop artists regarded impeccable craftsmanship as crucial to their work, and they took great pains to produce art of a highly polished, finished quality. Pop art in Los Angeles, in other words, had the characteristic L.A. look. It was also distinguished by a mildness, subtlety, and benevolence that was lacking in the more strident pop art produced elsewhere.

Typical of the easygoing, nonmilitant pop artists working in southern California in the 1960s was Edward Ruscha. Born in Omaha in 1937 and reared in Oklahoma City, Ruscha moved to Los Angeles and attended Chouinard from 1956 to 1960. One of his best-known works was *Hollywood* (1968), a series of prints depicting the large sheet-metal letters in the Hollywood hills. The popular culture of Los Angeles was a major inspiration for the work of Ruscha, but his attitude toward that culture was ambiguous. One critic saw in the work of Ruscha a "mock worship of California's earthly paradise," and yet there was also in his work a kind of affectionate regard for Los Angeles and its environs. It remained for the viewer to decide whether the pastel sky of *Hollywood,* created by Ruscha out of Pepto-Bismol and caviar, was a tribute to the beauty of a Los Angeles sunset or a reminder of the unpleasant effects of smog.

Less ambiguous were the so-called Chicano murals that appeared on the concrete walls of Los Angeles storm drains and freeway overpasses in the 1970s. The murals often featured crowded scenes of contemporary Latino life, painted on an imposing scale with bold lines and primary colors. Among the most successful muralists were Los Four: Carlos Almaraz, Gilbert Luján, Frank Romero, and Beto de la Rocha.

Hollywood, a silk-screen print by Edward Ruscha. (*Gift of the Phoenix Collection of Graphic Art, San Francisco. Courtesy of the University Art Museum, University of California, Berkeley.*)

Almaraz traveled frequently to Mexico and saw firsthand the works of such master muralists as José Orozco and Diego Rivera. His intent was to adapt this grand tradition to the dramatization of such contemporary issues as the struggle of California's farm workers. "I paint and draw what I see and what I feel," Almaraz commented, "and reflect much of my Mexican background in this process." Similar concerns were evident in the work of Rupert Garcia. His series of dramatic posters illustrated a wide range of political and social issues. Each poster powerfully conveyed a specific mood, alternating between militant, melancholic, and majestic.

Among the important artists working in Los Angeles in the 1970s and 1980s was D. J. Hall. Her paintings often commented on the youth-obsessed middle-class women of southern California. Her style was akin to that of photo-realism, yet her canvases were marked by a tone at once more subtle and evocative. Her work presented a surface reality of youth and glamour, yet beneath that surface lurked the repressed dread of mortality and decay. In *Juice* (1982) Hall presents women of uncertain age in a blue-green swimming pool, their limbs grotesquely foreshortened and foreshadowing the coming of shriveled skin and withered limbs. Her *Good and Plenty* (1985) suggests the superficiality of aging devotees of southern California's cult of youth.

Probing beneath the surface of things became an obsession of Los Angeles artists in the 1990s. Their thesis was a familiar one: just below the sunny facade of southern California lay a stratum of alienation, murder, and apocalyptic fantasies. Artist Chris Burden produced a work called *Medusa's Head* (1992) consisting of a 7-ton lump of dyed concrete and rocks hanging by a chain and symbolizing (perhaps) the degrading forces of modernization. Burden's work was included in a retrospective of 1990s art displayed at the Los Angeles Museum of Contemporary Art (MOCA). One bemused New York critic dismissed the entire collection as a monument to perpetual adolescence: "America invented it; Los Angeles glorifies it; and MOCA is its Louvre."

California curators and collectors regarded such dismissive assessments as pathetic expressions of regional ignorance and jealousy. One California art critic

Good and Plenty, a painting by D. J. Hall. In the full-size canvas, a miniature California landscape is visible in the metallized sunglasses worn by the woman on the right. (*Courtesy of the artist and the Los Angeles Municipal Art Gallery.*)

patiently explained that New Yorkers simply "don't know the history of California art, and until they do, they won't understand its depth and give it the credit it deserves." To document that history, several of the state's leading art museums mounted major retrospectives in the late 1990s and early 2000s. Among the most memorable were Stanford University's "Pacific Arcadia: Images of California, 1600–1915" and the Los Angeles County Museum of Art's monumental exhibition "Made in California: Art, Image, and Identity, 1900–2000."

California art in recent decades has been dominated as much by institutions as by individuals. In 1968 the University Art Museum in Berkeley opened its new $3 million building, designed by Mario J. Ciampi, which included a special gallery for the large Hans Hofmann collection recently donated to the university by the artist. The following year the Oakland Museum opened its extraordinary new complex, a museum dedicated exclusively to the history, art, and natural history of California. Its art gallery featured a retrospective of California art, from the watercolors of visiting artists during the Spanish period, through the landscapes of

William Keith and Albert Bierstadt, to the reflective cubes of Larry Bell. A splendid new home for the San Francisco Museum of Modern Art opened in 1995, a building hailed by one critic as "an extraordinary work of Modernist art in its own right." The museum was part of Yerba Buena Gardens, an extravagant new 87-acre center for the visual and performing arts.

Meanwhile, in southern California the Los Angeles County Museum of Art in 1965 was installed in magnificent new quarters on Wilshire Boulevard, adjacent to the La Brea tar pits, and in its first year it attracted a larger attendance than any other museum in the west. In 1971 the California Institute of the Arts, known popularly as Cal Arts, opened its new campus in the San Fernando Valley. Incorporating the Chouinard Art Institute and the Los Angeles Conservatory of Music, Cal Arts became a major educational institution for the visual and performing arts. Its new campus was in large part a monument to the generosity of the family of Walt Disney, who contributed some $30 million to the institute.

Two other wealthy southern Californians made important contributions to the arts in the late twentieth century. In 1974 the Pasadena Art Museum, whose new buildings had opened in 1969 as a showcase for contemporary art, became the Norton Simon Museum. Simon, a business executive with headquarters in Los Angeles, had created one of the largest collections of paintings and sculpture assembled by an individual in modern times. The same year the J. Paul Getty Museum opened its new quarters near Pacific Palisades. The museum, modeled on a Roman villa, drew mixed reviews, for it included reproductions as well as authentic art among its displays of Greek and Roman antiquities, paintings, sculpture, and furniture. When Getty died in 1976, he left the bulk of his estate to the museum, making it the richest museum in the United States. The Getty Trust, valued at $4 billion, opened in 1997 its gleaming new Getty Center on a hilltop in the Brentwood section of Los Angeles. The center, designed by architect Richard Meier, was faced with a million square feet of travertine taken from the same quarry in Italy that had supplied the stones for the Coliseum in Rome and the colonnade of Saint Peter's Basilica.

Architecture

The suburban growth of California's population following World War II spawned several distinctive forms of commercial and domestic architecture. At the center of the new suburban communities, dispersed widely by the spreading freeway system, were *shopping centers,* clusters of stores designed exclusively for the automobile-borne shopper. The orientation of these stores toward their expansive parking lots, rather than toward the main street, was a major break with past traditions of commercial architecture. By the 1960s shopping centers had been transformed into *shopping malls,* large self-contained units centered on an enclosed mall, which contained an array of small shops and one or more major department stores.

The houses that filled the new suburban tracts in the late 1940s and 1950s were almost all variations of a single style, the California ranch house. The roots of this ubiquitous style lay in the California bungalow of the early twentieth century, and like the bungalow the new ranch-style homes typically were single-floor

An aerial view of the Getty Center in the foothills of the Santa Monica Mountains. (*Photo by John Stephens/© The J. Paul Getty Trust.*)

dwellings, low in profile, with an informal arrangement of living spaces. Both styles were distinctly Californian in their emphasis on the close relation between indoor and outdoor living. The ranch-style homes were characterized by picture windows, sliding glass doors, terraces, patios, and, in the wealthier suburbs, swimming pools. Like the California bungalow, the California ranch was widely copied and came to be accepted as an important regional contribution to American domestic architecture.

Along the windswept cliffs of the Sonoma County coastline, a planned community of homes and condominiums known as Sea Ranch initiated in the 1960s yet another California style. Architects Charles Moore and William Turnbull in effect turned the California ranch house on end to create an elongated vertical box, sheathed in wooden siding and covered by a shedlike roof. Because the coastal winds were so strong, the Sea Ranch buildings were designed without overhanging eaves. The resulting vertical shed-roof box became the latest California export. As the cost of single-family homes rose to unbelievable heights, clusters of shed-roof box apartments and condominiums began to dot the landscape from coast to coast. Roof gardens, balconies, and hot tubs succeeded terraces, patios, and pools, and the California ideal of the indoor-outdoor house lived on.

Whereas the suburbs of California proved to be centers of major architectural innovation in the mid-twentieth century, California cities tended to follow rather than initiate trends in architectural design. The dominant style for commercial and institutional buildings since the end of World War II was the International style, in which the structural skeleton of a building was often enclosed by a "curtain wall" of nonsupporting glass and metal panels. The impression of the typical International style building was one of machinelike precision and anonymity, and skylines of cities across the state in the 1950s and 1960s came to be dominated by monuments to the high-rise aesthetic of internationalism.

Inevitably a reaction set in to the boring, unbearable monotony of the new buildings. California architects began to display the same spirit of innovation and experimentation in their urban design as had been evident in the state's earlier domestic architecture. Architectural historian David Gebhard has suggested that a distinctive "lack of intellectual intent" among contemporary California architects came to give their work "a lightness and at times tinselly quality of make-believe which has more to do with Disneyland and Magic Mountain than it does with the traditional values of Modern architecture." Gebhard found a remarkable playfulness in the California architects' arbitrary use of such geometric shapes as circles, cones, and pyramids. San Francisco's Transamerica Pyramid (1972), designed by Los Angeles architect William Pereira, was a monumental and often unappreciated example of this whimsical quality of California design. Further evidence of architectural innovation was Daniel Libeskind's startling new Jewish Museum (2003), designed in the shape of the Hebrew word *chai,* or "life," projecting from Willis Polk's 1907 red-brick South of Market power station. In Golden Gate Park, a sleek new home for the M. H. de Young Museum was scheduled to open in 2005; its designers were chosen because of their reputation for creativity and innovation. Architect Jon Jerde, who grew up in Long Beach, maintained that the spirit of innovation was even furthur advanced among the architects of southern California. They were on the cutting edge of experimentation, freed from the ossified traditions that bound designers elsewhere. "L.A. is a teenager," Jerde proudly proclaimed. "It's a punk city. You can do anything you want around here. There's creative freedom, not only for artists and architects but for everybody. . . . You can begin to look at tomorrow here."

Music

By midcentury, California had become a world center for the composition and performance of the most advanced forms of contemporary music. In large measure the musical prominence of California was a product of the immigration to the state of leading European composers during the years before World War II.

The first and probably most influential of the Europeans to settle in California was Arnold Schoenberg, developer of the revolutionary twelve-tone technique of composition. Schoenberg had been a professor of music in Berlin until deposed by the Nazis because of his unconventional music and Jewish origins. In 1933 he immigrated to the United States and decided to settle permanently in Los Angeles, where he was appointed to the faculty of the University of Southern California in 1935 and later became a professor at UCLA. In 1940 Schoenberg was joined in southern California by Igor Stravinsky, the most important composer of the twentieth century. Stravinsky's music, like that of Schoenberg, was highly controversial and represented a radical departure from traditional forms of composition. He remained in Hollywood until 1969 and composed there major works for orchestra and chorus. Meanwhile, in northern California, Darius Milhaud, the foremost French composer since Maurice Ravel, joined the faculty of Mills College in Oakland after fleeing Nazi-occupied France. Following the war, Milhaud remained at Mills and also served as a professor of composition at the Paris Conservatory.

Schoenberg and Milhaud, through their teaching, directly influenced a generation of California composers and musicians. Most prominent among the twentieth-century composers born and educated in California was Los Angeles native John Cage. Like many of his contemporaries, Cage believed that the music of the western world was at a dead end and that composers henceforth must seek new sounds, new media, and indeed a new language of musical expression. In search of such a language, Cage studied composition under Schoenberg but soon moved beyond the twelve-tone technique to the use of electronic equipment, tape recordings, noisemakers, and assorted unconventional percussion instruments. His "Third Construction in Metal" (1941) was scored for rattles, drums, tin cans, cowbells, and a lion's roar.

The performance of contemporary music, often subject to skepticism and even hostility from concertgoers, was encouraged in California by several key individuals and institutions. In 1945 a group of young composers around Roger Sessions, then a professor of music at Berkeley, organized the Composers' Forum, which for years sponsored a concert series featuring the work of Stravinsky, Schoenberg, and other contemporary composers. Under the direction of Pierre Monteux, the San Francisco Symphony Orchestra in the 1940s also became a major force in popularizing the music of modern composers.

The San Francisco Symphony continued to flourish under the leadership of the noted Austrian conductor Josef Krips during the 1960s and Seiji Ozawa in the early 1970s. Ozawa, born in China of Japanese parents, invariably conducted the classics as well as the most advanced contemporary music from memory—a remarkable feat. Replacing Ozawa in 1977 was the Dutch conductor Edo de Waart, under whose direction the San Francisco Symphony moved to its new quarters at the $31 million Louise M. Davies Symphony Hall in 1980. Davies Hall, together with the accompanying addition to the War Memorial Opera House and construction of the Zellerbach rehearsal hall, brought to completion the San Francisco Performing Arts Center begun nearly 50 years earlier.

As in all things cultural, the recent history of California music also reflected the rise of southern California. The traditional dominance of San Francisco had first been challenged by the creation of the Los Angeles Philharmonic Orchestra in 1919, which, under the direction of conductor Otto Klemperer in the 1930s, rose to first rank. From 1961 to 1978, the Los Angeles Philharmonic was under the direction of Zubin Mehta, a brilliant and glamorous conductor born in Bombay in 1936. During Mehta's tenure the Philharmonic finally obtained a permanent year-round home. Since the 1920s the summer concerts of the Los Angeles orchestra had been performed in the spectacular Hollywood Bowl, but the winter concerts were confined to an unsatisfactory leased auditorium. Los Angeles voters had repeatedly rejected bond issues for a municipally owned center for the performing arts. Dorothy Buffum Chandler worked almost single-handedly to secure enough private contributions to make possible a new complex of buildings for music and drama at the civic center. The largest of these structures, the Dorothy Chandler Pavilion, opened in 1964. Thirty years later the "cultural corridor" along Grand Avenue was completed with the opening of the Walt Disney Concert Hall, the new home of the Los Angeles Philharmonic. Meanwhile, a major counterpoint to the Los Angeles complex opened in Orange County, the dramatic new Performing Arts Center in Costa Mesa.

Both northern and southern California participated in the premiere of an experimental work for orchestra and chorus in 2001. *El Niño* was written by John Adams, composer-in-residence of the San Francisco Symphony, and directed by Kent Nagano, principal conductor of the Los Angeles Opera. Hailed by critics as boldly innovative, the work narrates the familiar Christmas story and celebrates more generally the miracle of birth itself. A third of the text is in Spanish, reflecting the California origins of *El Niño*. As John Adams explained, "the intensity and genuineness of Latin American art and culture is one of the great gifts one receives by living in California."

In the years following World War II, California also played a major role in the development of American popular music. In the 1940s much of the impetus for traditionalist jazz came from the state, and in the 1950s California was the center of the so-called west coast jazz movement. The band of Stan Kenton, a native of Kansas reared near Los Angeles, served as an important training ground for other California musicians. Pianist and composer Dave Brubeck organized a quartet in northern California that quickly rose to the top among modern jazz bands in the United States. Born in Concord in 1920, Brubeck had studied composition under Milhaud and Schoenberg.

If California can be said to have had an indigenous music in the twentieth century, it would have to be rock. Although regarded by musicologists as being of little or no musical importance, rock music nevertheless was an important part of recent California history. The recording industry generated thousands of jobs and millions of dollars of income for Californians, and rock lyrics reinforced widely held conceptions about life in the Golden State. Images of romance and sexual liberation were at the heart of Scott McKenzie's "If You're Going to San Francisco" and Tupac Shakur's "California Love." The Rivieras' "California Sun" and Tony Toni Tone's "It Never Rains in Southern California" were paeans to the California climate. Recordings such as the Mamas and the Papas' "California Dreaming" and the Pet Shop Boys' "Go West" unabashedly celebrated the California dream, while a darker vision pervaded the lyrics of R.E.M.'s "I Remember California," the Dead Kennedys' "California Über Alles," and the Red Hot Chili Peppers' "Californication."

During the 1960s, California groups initiated several new rock styles that had an enormous impact on national and international popular music. The California sound first appeared in the music of a group appropriately styled the Beach Boys, formed in 1961 in the suburbs of Los Angeles. Through their energetic melodies and cheerful repetitions, the Beach Boys effectively captured the bright simplicity of life on the southern California beaches in the early 1960s. Wholesome, tanned, and vigorous, the Beach Boys appeared in concert to be the very embodiment of California outdoor living. The lyrics of "Surfin' Safari" and "California Girls" insisted that life among the dunes and surf was carefree and that romantic opportunity was bountiful. A sense of easy mobility and love of speed was reflected in a score of recordings such as "Little Deuce Coupe" and "This Car of Mine."

Beginning in 1964, American young people were introduced to more sophisticated musical technique and melodic intricacy by a series of English rock bands. First, of course, came the Beatles, followed closely by Mick Jagger and the Rolling Stones. The first indications of an American response to the English invasion of popular music came from California. The new Los Angeles sound, pioneered by a southern California group known as the Byrds, was essentially a combination of folk and rock music. The mix appealed to earlier devotees of hard rock and folk music and had the advantage of an American twang of country harmony. The popularity of Los Angeles folk rock was soon overshadowed by the appearance in San Francisco of the startling and highly controversial acid rock. Originally intended to reproduce the distorted hearing of a person under the influence of LSD, acid rock was characterized by hyperamplification, bizarre electronic effects, and exotic imagery in its lyrics. When acid rock was performed at one of the city's auditoriums, such as the Fillmore or Avalon ballrooms, the illusion of an LSD experience was further heightened by light shows designed to reproduce the visual distortion induced by the drug.

The proliferation of rock bands in San Francisco in 1966 and 1967 was a measure of the tremendous influx of young people into the city. Some of the bands, such as Quicksilver Messenger Service and the Grateful Dead, were immensely popular among residents of the Haight-Ashbury district but did not achieve immediate commercial success. The first San Francisco band to establish a national following was the Jefferson Airplane, whose music was a blend of jazz, folk, blues, and "surrealistic tinkering." With the recording of such hits as "Embryonic Journey" and "White Rabbit," the band became a national sensation. Radio stations across the country broadcast the intonations of lead vocalist Grace Slick that "one pill makes you larger, and one pill makes you small."

In rapid succession California had spawned surf rock, folk rock, and acid rock. California was the center of the youth movement of the 1960s, and the music of the decade reflected this preeminence. Rock was a galvanizing force for young Californians, shaping and recording their ebullient history. It was appropriate, therefore, that a California musical event should become a symbol for the end of the decade and for the demise of the counterculture. At the conclusion of their 1969 American tour, the Rolling Stones sought to hold a free concert in San Francisco's Golden Gate Park. The city refused to grant permission, and the concert was rescheduled for the Altamont Raceway in Alameda County. There, on December 6, 1969, more than 300,000 young people attended the performance, an event marred by violence. The Rolling Stones had recruited members of the Hell's Angels motorcycle gang to provide "security" for the band, and in the process the gang administered numerous beatings and stabbed one boy to death as he tried to reach the stage.

Altamont, combined with the death by drug overdose of rock superstars Jimi Hendrix and Janis Joplin the following year, triggered a change in the attitude of many young people toward drugs and signaled a sobering reevaluation of the future of the now-aging youth movement. One of the most popular rock lyrics of the early 1960s had celebrated the decade as "the dawning of the age of Aquarius," and one observer now remarked that the age of Aquarius had ended with the flash of a knife at Altamont. The student newspaper at the University of California at Berkeley described the tragedy of Altamont as "the end of a decade of dreams; the beginning of a decade of facing the realities of the human condition."

Selected Bibliography

Anthologies of recent California literature include Jack Hicks et al. (eds.), *The Literature of California* (2002); Gerald Haslam (ed.), *Many Californias* (1991); Haslam and James D. Houston (eds.), *California Heartland* (1979); Houston (ed.), *West Coast Fiction* (1979); and Ishmael Reed (ed.), *Calafia* (1979). Lawrence Ferlinghetti's *Literary California* (1980) is a lively survey by a central figure of the beat generation. See also Richard Candida Smith, *Utopia and Dissent* (1995); John A. Maynard, *Venice West* (1991); David Wyatt, *The Fall into Eden* (1986); Michael Davidson, *The San Francisco Renaissance* (1989); Houston, "The New Anatomy of California," *California History,* LXIII (Summer 1984), pp. 256–259; William Everson, *Archetype West* (1976); Thomas Parkinson (ed.), *A Casebook on the Beats* (1961); and Dennis McNally, *Desolate Angel: Jack Kerouac* (1980). Mark Royden Winchell, *Joan Didion* (1980), presents an analysis of the author's early works. On the work of Luis Valdez, see Yolanda Broyle Gonzalez, *El Teatro Campesino* (1994). See also Greg Sarris (ed.), *The Sounds of Rattles and Clappers: A Collection of New California Indian Writing* (1994).

The best survey of modern California painting and sculpture is Peter Plagens, *Sunshine Muse* (1974). The northern California scene is described in Thomas Albright, *Art in the San Francisco Bay Area, 1945–1980* (1985). On specific movements, see Susan Landauer, *The San Francisco School of Abstract Expressionism* (1994); Peter Selz, *Funk* (1967); and Marcia Tucker, *"Bad" Painting* (1978). The emergence of Los Angeles is described in Anne Bartlett Ayres, "Los Angeles Modernism and the Assemblage Tradition, 1948–1962," Ph.D. thesis, University of Southern California (1983); and Nan R. Piene, "L.A. Trip," *Art in America,* LVIII (March 1970), pp. 138–141. Marcia R. McGrath's *Edward Ruscha, Books, Prints* (1972) is a catalog from an exhibition at the University of California, Santa Cruz.

The indispensable guides to contemporary California architecture are Sally Woodbridge, *California Architecture* (1988); David Gebhard et al., *A Guide to Architecture in San Fran-*

cisco and Northern California (1973); and Gebhard and Robert Winter, *A Guide to Architecture in Los Angeles and Southern California* (1977). Important interpretations include Gebhard and Susan King, *A View of California Architecture: 1960–1976* (1976), and Reyner Banham, *Los Angeles* (1971).

A valuable resource for the history of California music is Stephen M. Fry (ed.), *California's Musical Wealth* (1988). On the L.A. music scene, see Dorothy Lamb Crawford, *Evenings On and Off the Roof* (1995). Useful guides to popular music include Jim Miller (ed.), *The Rolling Stone Illustrated History of Rock and Roll* (1976; rev. ed., 1980); Jack McDonough, *San Francisco Rock* (1985); and Anthony Fawcett, *California Rock, California Sound* (1979). Richard Aquila, "Images of the American West in Rock Music," *Western Historical Quarterly,* XI (October 1980), pp. 415–432, includes an analysis of California imagery, as does Heather Mayne, "The Wild, Wild West: Images of California in Contemporary Rock Music," *California History,* LXXXIX (Spring 2000), pp. 70–75.

CHAPTER 33

Recent California Politics

The recent decades of California's political history have been shaped by conflicting pressures generated by the phenomenal growth and increased diversity of the state's population. The Democratic party remained the state's majority party, but voters continued to divide their loyalties by often electing Republican governors and Democratic majorities to the state legislature. Meanwhile, leaders of both parties had to contend with a rising tide of voter discontent, skepticism, and a steady disengagement from the whole political process. These and other matters are the subject of this chapter; furthur consideration of individual issues appears in the chapters that follow.

The Conservative Revival

The most visible result of the turmoil of the 1960s was a new wave of political conservatism in state and national affairs. Beset by rapid increases in the cost of living, voters became increasingly restive under the burden of taxation and resentful of the growth of government. Political candidates appealed to the conservative mood of the voters by offering to restore "law and order," cut welfare and other unwanted government programs, and lower taxes.

Ronald Reagan was among those who benefited most from the conservative revival. Reagan was a convert to conservatism. As a student at a small college in Illinois, the state of his birth, he had been one of the leaders of a strike against a drastic cut in the college's budget, a strike so successful that it forced the resignation of the president who had proposed the cut. Reagan came to Hollywood in 1937, where he not only became a successful actor, but also served as president of the Screen Actors Guild. In these early years his political views were those of a liberal Democrat. His name was once omitted from a list of supporters of Helen Gahagan Douglas because he was considered too far left. But later he became a

Democrat for Eisenhower and a Democrat for Nixon, and finally changed his registration to Republican in 1962.

Reagan acquired a 305-acre ranch in the Malibu hills for the breeding of thoroughbred horses. The rise in the value of the land, and a series of large increases in the taxes on it, coincided with a change in Reagan's political philosophy. He became strongly hostile toward taxation and toward the growth of governmental activities that required tax support. During the same period, in the 1950s and early 1960s, the General Electric Company employed him to appear regularly on the television programs it sponsored and also to make speeches to its employees and to civic groups. These addresses lauded private enterprise and were increasingly critical of government.

During the presidential campaign of 1964, Reagan delivered a nationwide television speech in support of Barry Goldwater. Although the speech could not save Goldwater's doomed candidacy, it demonstrated beyond doubt the effectiveness of Reagan as a political campaigner. Following the Republican debacle in the November election, some conservatives expressed the wish that Reagan had been the candidate instead of Goldwater.

Among those attracted to Reagan were a group of wealthy southern California Republicans who formed the nucleus of a movement to make him the next governor of California. In 1965 Reagan met with members of this group, and after expressing some reluctance to become a candidate, he agreed to enter the Republican primary the following year. Reagan won the Republican nomination with considerable ease and in the general election faced Edmund G. Brown, the Democratic incumbent who was seeking a third term.

During the gubernatorial campaign of 1966, the disorderly demonstrations at Berkeley and elsewhere continued to receive great attention from the news media. Although Governor Brown had taken a hard line in dealing with the Free Speech Movement, Reagan now used to his own advantage the issue of campus unrest and pledged that if elected he would clean up the "mess at Berkeley." Reagan also claimed that 8 years as governor were enough for any incumbent and that Brown did not deserve a third term.

Another major factor in the gubernatorial campaign was the white backlash against black demands for residential desegregation and job equality. These issues shattered the coalition between organized labor and racial minority groups that had been essential to Brown's victories in 1958 and 1962. Reagan, in his campaign speeches, repeatedly expressed his opposition to the open-housing Rumford Act of 1963 but insisted that in doing so he was defending the right of private property, not indulging in racial bigotry. This stand won him the votes of many white Democrats, including labor union members and their families. Reagan's attacks on the rising costs of government also won some defectors from the Democratic ranks. Many members of labor unions, and of the lower and middle classes in general, had been enjoying rising incomes and were experiencing a new resentment against taxation. In the election on November 8, 1966, Reagan defeated Brown by 3,742,913 to 2,749,174, a margin just short of a million votes.

In his inaugural address, delivered on January 5, 1967, Governor Ronald Reagan outlined the central idea of his administration: "The cost of California's government is too high. It adversely affects our business climate. . . . We are going to squeeze and cut and trim until we reduce the cost of government." Speaking as a self-styled citizen-politician who had never before held a public office, Reagan thus made a powerful appeal to the popular mood of hostility toward government and taxation. "The time has come," Reagan declared, "to run a check to see if all the services government provides were in answer to demands or were just goodies dreamed up for our supposed betterment."

Reagan's political and social philosophy was a stunning reversal of the ideas of such governors as Earl Warren and Edmund G. Brown, who had believed that government services should have a major, direct, and positive role in the state's development. As governor, Reagan soon learned that an actual reduction in the total budget of a huge and growing state was virtually impossible. Most of the state government's annual expenditures were mandated by law. The largest of the state services whose budgets could be reduced at the governor's discretion were in the fields of mental health and higher education, and in these sensitive and vulnerable areas

Governor Ronald Reagan is sworn in by California Supreme Court Justice Marshall F. McComb in the specially decorated capitol rotunda shortly after midnight, January 2, 1967. Reagan's left hand is on the Bible of Father Junípero Serra, which is held by California Senate Chaplain Wilbur Choy. In the background are statues of Queen Isabella and Christopher Columbus. (© *Bettman/Corbis.*)

Reagan made drastic cuts. He slashed funding for the state department of mental health, cutting substantially its staff and effectiveness. Reagan also reduced funding for the state's colleges and universities, and proposed significant increases in tuition to make up part of the difference. These measures, he said, "would help get rid of undesirables. Those there to agitate and not to study might think twice before they pay tuition." Reagan's cuts in mental health were generally regarded as the greatest mistake of his first year in office, but his hard-line education policies won him widespread approval.

In one of his campaign speeches, Reagan had said that he was "sick at what has happened at Berkeley. Sick at the sit-ins, the teach-ins, the walkouts. When I am elected governor I will organize a throw-out, and Clark Kerr will head that list." Reagan was not, however, solely responsible for the dismissal of University of California president Kerr, although it occurred at the first regents' meeting that he attended as governor, early in 1967. Most of the regents had been dissatisfied with Kerr's handling of student disruptions since the Sproul Hall sit-in of December 1964. The dismissal of Kerr sent shock waves throughout the national academic community, where it was angrily denounced as an anti-intellectual assault on academic freedom.

Reagan's Democratic challenger in the 1970 gubernatorial election, Assembly Speaker Jesse Unruh, tried to blame Reagan for the continuation of campus disorders, but the voters doubted Unruh's claim that he could have dealt with unruly students more effectively. The hostile reaction of most California voters to the radicalism of the student new left contributed heavily to Reagan's reelection victory over Unruh.

Early in his second term, Governor Reagan renewed and intensified his calls for "reform" of the welfare system, which to him meant primarily reduction of its cost. He called it "a cancer eating at our vitals." Democratic leaders in the legislature were skeptical that massive cuts in welfare could be achieved. They pointed out that Reagan's hopes of removing many people from the welfare rolls by requiring them to work would be limited by the fact that only about 1 percent of the recipients were able-bodied adult males, whereas the mass of them were mothers, children, the blind, the disabled, or the aged. Reagan and the Democratic legislators eventually worked out a compromise measure that was intended to reduce the cost of the state's welfare system by about $200 million.

When Reagan submitted his annual budget in January 1971, he insisted that the state's expenses for the next fiscal year could be met without increasing taxes if welfare costs were further reduced, cost-of-living increases denied to state employees, and various other state expenses cut to the barest minimum. Yet in spite of these austerities, Reagan was forced to sign a bill increasing state taxes by $500 million. The bulk of the new revenues came in the form of an income withholding tax, effective on January 1, 1972. Of the 38 states with income taxes, California had been the only one that did not provide for withholding; Reagan had long promised never to approve it, and after signing the bill, he told reporters that he had been "dragged kicking and screaming" to the desk where he did so.

In 1973 Reagan sought to embody the essence of his conservative philosophy in a sweeping tax reduction measure. His proposal would have forced the gradual reduction of state spending over a period of years and required a two-thirds vote rather than a simple majority of the legislature to adopt a new tax or increase an existing one. Drafted by one of Reagan's special task forces, the measure was 5000 words long and very complex. In an unguarded moment, Reagan confessed to a reporter that he himself did not fully understand the language of it. When the plan went to the voters as Proposition 1 in November 1973, it was decisively rejected. The voters thus handed the governor a stinging personal defeat.

All Reagan's promises of massive tax reductions proved impossible to carry out. The state budgets he signed increased every year, from $5 billion for 1967–68 to $10.2 billion for 1974–75.

In 1976 Ronald Reagan launched an all-out campaign for the Republican nomination for president. As Hiram Johnson had once dreamed of "Californianizing the nation" by taking to Washington the progressive program that he felt he had created in California, so Reagan hoped to take his conservative crusade all the way to the White House. The odds against him were heavy. The incumbent president, Gerald Ford, was also seeking the Republican nomination. Ford had assumed the presidency two years earlier, following the resignation of Richard Nixon during the Watergate scandal. At the 1976 Republican convention, Reagan came within about 100 delegate votes of winning the nomination away from the incumbent president who was seeking it—something that had not happened since 1884 when Chester A. Arthur lost to James G. Blaine.

Many observers concluded that Reagan's career in major public office was over, but Reagan and his advisers began at once laying the groundwork for yet another campaign for the presidency.

The Era of Limits and Beyond

Ronald Reagan's effective use of the third-term issue in 1966 against Edmund G. Brown had made it practically impossible for Reagan himself to seek a third term as California governor in 1974. For the first time since 1958, the incumbent governor chose not to run for reelection, and the wide-open contest attracted 29 candidates, each of whom strove to achieve greater name recognition. In this crowded field, the Californian whose name already had the highest statewide recognition was Edmund G. Brown, Jr., son of the former governor.

Known from youth as "Jerry," the younger Brown launched his statewide political career in 1970 with a successful campaign for secretary of state. In 1974 he became the principal sponsor of an initiative known as the Political Reform Act, which called for the strict disclosure of campaign contributions and the creation of a Fair Political Practices Commission. During the 1974 gubernatorial campaign, the Watergate scandal dominated the headlines and Jerry Brown's name was linked with the most popular issue of the day, political reform. Brown won the Democratic primary, and the Political Reform Act was overwhelmingly approved by the voters. Brown's margin of victory in the general election was less than 178,000 votes out of more than 6 million cast, making the race the closest gubernatorial contest in California since 1920.

Governor Edmund G. Brown congratu-
lates his son (and future governor) Jerry
Brown at the 1960 commencement
exercises of the University of California,
Berkeley. (*Courtesy of the California
Historical Society.*)

Through largely symbolic actions, Brown appealed to the strain of antigovern-
ment sentiment potent among voters in the aftermath of Watergate. He denounced
the new governor's mansion, built for Reagan with gifts of money from his wealthy
supporters, as "that Taj Mahal" and chose instead to live in a modest apartment. In
contrast to Reagan's official Cadillac, Brown went about in a blue Plymouth sedan.
On a more substantial level, Brown's policies toward government spending and
taxation were consistently conservative. At the beginning of his first term, he
pledged that he would approve no new taxes or general tax increases, and he recommended reducing proposed increases in state funds for higher education and social welfare programs. "The first test of all of us," Brown counseled the legislature,
"is to live within realistic limits."

The most important accomplishment of Brown's first term was enactment of the
landmark Agricultural Relations Act of 1975. The new law, which created the Agricultural Labor Relations Board (ALRB) to oversee union elections by the state's
farm workers, was a personal triumph for the governor and his secretary of agriculture, Rose Elizabeth Bird. But representatives from the state's agricultural districts
became angered when Brown appointed a majority of labor-oriented members to
the ALRB and the board adopted policies that the growers opposed.

Brown also came under powerful attack for creating an "adverse business climate." Through his appointments to such agencies as the Air Resources Board
and Energy Commission, Brown oversaw vigorous enforcement of environmental
protection standards and withheld licensing of large-scale power plant facilities.
Business leaders charged that Brown was stifling economic development. Stung
by criticism that the "era of limits" was antibusiness, Brown began speaking of
the "era of possibilities."

The one very evident problem that Jerry Brown failed to solve during his first term was the need for tax reform. The overriding issue in the 1978 elections proved to be an initiative to reduce property taxes; it appeared on the June primary ballot as Proposition 13. Brown campaigned vigorously against the initiative, but it passed by a landslide margin of nearly 2 million votes. Brown now had a choice. He could continue to oppose Proposition 13 and probably lose the general election, or he could reverse his position and win. Brown quickly became an enthusiastic supporter of the initiative. "I've been talking about limits since I got here," he proudly announced, "and now [Proposition 13] has given me new tools." Brown's enthusiasm following the initiative's passage was sufficient to convince voters that it was he, and not his Republican opponent, who would best be able to implement it. In November 1978 Brown was reelected by more than 1.3 million votes.

Brown began his second term in office with a call for further retrenchment in state government. His inaugural address in January was so reminiscent of that of Reagan in 1967—"We are going to squeeze and cut and trim until we reduce the cost of government"—that one political commentator saw it as the beginning of "Ronald Reagan's third term." Brown's inaugural message also signaled his intention to challenge Jimmy Carter, the Democratic incumbent, for the presidency in 1980 by mounting a campaign to cut federal taxes and goverment spending. From the beginning, Brown's campaign was beset by financial problems, and his record in the 1980 presidential primaries was one of dismal failure.

In comparison with Brown's disastrous 1980 campaign for the presidency, Ronald Reagan's was a model of efficiency. Reagan easily won the Republican nomination and scored an upset victory over Jimmy Carter in the general election. In personnel and policy, the new Reagan presidency bore many similarities to Reagan's years as California governor. His efforts to reduce the state budget and cut taxes in California were duplicated on the national level when he won congressional approval of his "program for economic recovery." At the center of the program was a major reduction in virtually every area of the federal budget except defense. Just as Reagan's philosophy as California governor had stood in sharp contrast to that of his predecessor, his federal economic policy marked a dramatic reversal of nearly half a century of expanding government involvement in the nation's social welfare.

The reputation of a president or a governor is often defined in crisis. Passage of Proposition 13 in 1978 marked the beginning of a massive reduction in government revenues and presented Governor Jerry Brown, the legislature, and the people of California with a crisis of major proportions.

The roots of the tax revolt lay in several separate but related developments. First, inflation had deeply eroded the real income of California taxpayers. The cost of government was the one price that consumers had the power to vote down. Second, because state and local taxes were steadily increasing at rates greater than the general inflation rate, taxes were absorbing an increasing share of personal income. Third, although the cost of government was steadily rising, the level of satisfaction with government services was declining. Dissatisfaction was especially strong among middle-income taxpayers who believed that in recent years government spending had shifted from programs that directly benefited them, such as those for streets and highways, to programs such as welfare that benefited only a few. The anger of California taxpayers also was fueled by the growth of a multibillion-dollar surplus in the state treasury, labeled "obscene" by the sponsors of the tax-cutting initiative.

Proposition 13 provided that property taxes should be limited to 1 percent of a property's assessed value. This meant an average reduction in property taxes of about 57 percent and a reduction in annual property tax revenues for cities, counties, school districts, and other units of local government of about $7 billion. The assessed value of all property would be rolled back to its 1975 level and could rise from that figure by only 2 percent per year. Property would be reassessed only when sold or improved. Furthermore, state and local governments were forbidden to increase property taxes. The legislature or local voters could raise other taxes, but only by a two-thirds vote rather than by the previous simple majority.

One immediate effect of Proposition 13 was a decline in the state's per capita tax burden, falling from one of the nation's highest to about average among the states. Homeowners were gratified that their property taxes were more than cut in half. The greatest beneficiaries of the initiative, however, were the owners of large business properties. The *Wall Street Journal* estimated that in the first year after its passage, Proposition 13 saved Southern Pacific $20 million in taxes and Standard Oil of California about $47 million. Homeowners had supported Proposition 13 as a means to reduce their property taxes, yet in every year after its adoption they came to bear an ever-greater share of the total property tax burden. Because residential properties tended to change hands more often than business properties and because under Proposition 13 property could be reassessed only when it was sold, property taxes on residences increased at rates greater than those on businesses. By the early 2000s, California's per-capita tax burden had risen back to eighth among the states.

Among the harmful effects of Proposition 13 was a growing deterioration of the state's infrastructure, the network of publicly financed services necessary for a society to function. As state and local governments were forced to cut back on spending, budgets for the maintenance and repair of roads, bridges, sewers, water mains, and public buildings were often deferred or severely reduced. California quickly fell to 49th among the states in spending for new streets and highways. In the first 5 years after Proposition 13 was enacted, California also fell from 17th to 35th among the states in per-pupil spending for public education. By 1986 California ranked dead last in its teacher-student ratio, with more students per teacher than any other state in the nation.

Proposition 13 also produced a redistribution of revenue and power among the levels of government. Within the state there was a fundamental centralization of power, one of the most far-reaching structural changes in any governmental system in the United States since the New Deal. In the aftermath of the victory of Proposition 13, the legislature passed emergency measures to bail out local governments by providing them with financial aid from the state surplus. Units of local government— cities, counties, school districts, community colleges—became dependent on the state for a larger proportion of their operating budget and thus came under increased state control. The bailout legislation, distributing state funds to local governments, permitted state intrusion into areas that previously had been local domain.

The distribution of bailout funds steadily depleted the surplus in the state treasury. After the enactment of Proposition 13 in 1978, the state began spending annually about a billion dollars more than it collected in tax revenues. Finally, in 1981, Governor Brown made the fateful announcement: "The surplus is gone. The cupboard is bare." The governor ordered immediate cuts in the budgets of most state departments, including the colleges and universities, and warned that California cities and counties would have to "tighten their belts in the face of a new fiscal austerity." With the surplus exhausted, California governments at last faced the awful dilemma of sharply reducing existing programs or raising new taxes.

In the midst of the state's worst fiscal crisis since the depression, Californians went to the polls to elect a new governor in 1982. Jerry Brown's popularity was at a low ebb. He wisely decided not to seek a third term but ran instead (and unsuccessfully) for the United States Senate. The California gubernatorial election of 1982 attracted widespread interest, in part because one of the major candidates was black. Tom Bradley, the popular mayor of Los Angeles, easily won the Democratic nomination. Attorney General George Deukmejian emerged as the Republican nominee and went on to defeat Bradley in one of the closest elections in California history. Deukmejian's plurality of 0.68 percent of the vote was the smallest of any incoming governor since 1886. The election was so close that an early morning edition of the *San Francisco Chronicle*—in a gaffe reminiscent of the *Chicago Tribune*'s famous "Dewey Defeats Truman" headline of 1948—proclaimed "First Black Elected Governor."

The narrowness of Deukmejian's victory was reflected in the outcome of other contests in the 1982 election. Democrats won election to each of the remaining statewide partisan offices, including lieutenant governor, and they strengthened their domination of the state's legislature and congressional delegation. The results of many of the races in 1982 were determined a year earlier by the Democratic-controlled legislature's redrawing of legislative and congressional district lines. With good reason, Republicans had denounced the reapportionment plan as an "outrageous gerrymander."

The issue that soon came to dominate the Deukmejian administration was the state's worsening financial crisis. Deukmejian presented the legislature with a plan to make drastic cuts in state spending, including reductions in health and welfare programs and in aid to local governments. The Democratic-controlled legislature opposed the governor's plan and argued instead for a tax increase to protect existing programs. As the legislature debated the governor's plan, the financial crisis intensified. For the first time since the depression, the state was forced to pay some of its bills with *registered warrants* instead of cashable checks. The warrants in effect were IOUs from the state.

California's financial crisis passed, temporarily, as the state and national economies rebounded in the mid-1980s. Increased revenues poured into the state treasury, a tax increase was avoided, and the state once again began to accumulate a surplus. Voters in 1984 enthusiastically approved an initiative to establish a state-run lottery; a third of the lottery's revenues was reserved for the state's cash-starved schools. Deukmejian's popularity increased as California's financial condition improved, and in 1986 the incumbent governor began his campaign for reelection with a commanding lead in public opinion polls. His Democratic opponent, once again, was Mayor Tom Bradley of Los Angeles. Bradley had scored an impressive victory in 1985, becoming the first mayor in the city's history to be elected to a fourth term.

Overshadowing the other issues in the 1986 election was the battle over the reconfirmation of Supreme Court chief justice Rose Elizabeth Bird, a bitter contest that one political analyst called "the war of the Rose." Bird's consistent opposition to the death penalty aroused a vehement response from a host of conservative organizations, and she became a detested symbol for all those who believed that the courts had become too lenient on criminals. During the gubernatorial campaign, George Deukmejian vigorously denounced Bird, whereas Tom Bradley unsuccessfully tried to sidestep the issue. Deukmejian easily defeated Bradley in the general election. The voters also overwhelmingly rejected the reconfirmation of Chief Justice Rose Bird, along with two other associate justices who had been appointed by Jerry Brown. The rejection of the three incumbent justices was the first such defeat since the state adopted the confirmation process more than 50 years earlier.

The criminal justice system proved to be one of the few areas of state government in which George Deukmejian achieved substantial change. He appointed conservative judges to all levels of the state judiciary, including the Supreme Court, and signed dozens of laws that toughened the sentencing of convicted criminals. During his administration 15 new prisons were constructed, the budget for the Department of Corrections more than quadrupled, and the number of Californians behind bars increased 250 percent.

Governor Deukmejian also took great pride in his improvement of the state's business climate. He reduced the budget of state agencies such as the California Coastal Commission, the Agricultural Labor Relations Board, the Consumer Affairs Department, and the Public Employment Relations Board. Deukmejian filled such agencies with appointees who shared his pro-business ideology. Critics charged that the Republican governor had systematically neutered some of the state's toughest watchdog agencies, stripping workers and consumers of protections they had enjoyed for many years.

The impact of Deukmejian's economic policy was far from certain. The state's economy, like that of the nation, continued to expand during most of his tenure. As revenues flowed into the state treasury, Deukmejian boasted that he had "brought California from IOU to A-OK." But that assertion proved to be a vulnerable claim on which to stake his legacy. Near the end of his second term, the national and state economy again entered a prolonged recession. Deukmejian spent his last year in office scrambling to avoid blame for California's sagging economy—an economy that he earlier claimed had benefited from his pro-business policies. In the end, Deukmejian left office with a state deficit twice as large as the one he had inherited from Jerry Brown.

The Politics of Resentment

Californians grew increasingly disenchanted with George Deukmejian during his second term; polls showed a steady deterioration in his standing with voters. Many Republicans hoped that Deukmejian, in spite of his declining popularity, could be persuaded to seek a third term in 1990. But Deukmejian declined to run, convinced that he had "kept his promises" and accomplished all that was on his limited agenda. Party leaders, including George H. W. Bush and Ronald Reagan, then successfully urged United States senator Pete Wilson to enter the race for governor. Wilson and his Democratic opponent, former San Francisco mayor Dianne Feinstein, each took a remarkably similar stand on several key issues. Both favored the death penalty, abortion rights, and more vigorous protection of the environment. Wilson's great advantage in the general election was his access to superior financial resources. When the final ballots were counted, Wilson defeated Feinstein by a vote of 3,763,151 to 3,497,875.

In November 1990, the voters of California also approved one of the most far-reaching institutional changes ever adopted by the citizens of any state. Known as Proposition 140, the measure rivaled in importance Proposition 13, the tax-cutting initiative of 1978. Proposition 140 was a constitutional amendment that set limits on the number of terms state lawmakers could serve. Members of the assembly were limited to three terms, or 6 years, whereas state senators and most other constitutional officers were limited to two terms, or 8 years. The measure also cut the

"I'm just too busy to pick or prune!"
(*Cartoon by Dennis Renault. Courtesy of the* Sacramento Bee.)

Governors Pete Wilson and George Deukmejian meet the press to discuss the gubernatorial transition in 1991. (*Courtesy of the Governor's Office.*)

operating budget of the state legislature by nearly 40 percent. The passage of Proposition 140 sent shock waves through the nation; soon term-limit proposals were appearing on ballots in other states as well.

The support for Proposition 140 was a measure of widespread voter dissatisfaction with the workings of state government. Many Californians had become convinced that the state legislature was dominated by powerful special interests and was hopelessly out of touch with the concerns of average citizens. Certain that it was futile to try to defeat incumbents individually, voters decided that it was best to throw them out en masse through the passage of the term-limitation initiative.

Another sign of voter dissatisfaction with the political process was the dramatic decline in voter turnout. The number of Californians voting in the mid-1980s was actually *less* than the number who voted 20 years earlier, even though the state had gained 6 million eligible voters. Whereas in 1972 nearly 50 percent of all eligible voters cast a ballot, in 1990 voter participation had dropped to a mere 28 percent. Thus it was that a record low turnout of California voters approved term limits for their elected officials. Pollster Mervin Field sagely observed that the voters, as they left the political process, had tossed "a grenade back over their shoulders."

The enormity of the economic challenge facing the new governor in 1991 was soon apparent in the projections for the coming fiscal year. Whereas George

Deukmejian had faced a projected deficit of $1.5 billion in his first year in office, Pete Wilson was confronted with a projected deficit of $14.3 billion. This was a staggering figure, an amount larger than the entire budgets of all but two of the other states.

The gap between revenues and expenditures was caused by a number of factors, chief of which was the deepening impact of the recession of the early 1990s. As major sectors of the California economy continued to slump, the flow of tax revenues into the state treasury slowed dramatically. In hammering out a new budget for California, Wilson and the legislature faced some difficult choices. It soon became apparent that the projected deficit could not be overcome by either raising revenues or curtailing expenditures. The solution lay in doing *both* at the same time. So it was that the state budget for 1991 included the largest tax increase in the history of California, totaling more than $7 billion in income and sales tax hikes, as well as increases in vehicle registration fees and the highest student fees ever. The budget also included a 4 percent reduction in monthly grants to recipients of Aid to Families with Dependent Children (AFDC), the first such cut in state history.

California continued to face deficits of several billion dollars each year throughout the recession of the early 1990s. The workings of the state government often were imperiled by months of gridlock and partisan debate during what seemed like never-ending legislative battles over the budget. The Democratic-controlled legislature and the Republican governor also locked horns over reapportionment of the state's legislative and congressional districts. Eventually the squabbling was settled when the state supreme court appointed a three-member panel of "special masters" to redraw the district lines without regard to partisan considerations.

Meanwhile, the recession of the early 1990s proved to be the worst in 60 years and voters were looking for someone to blame. Incumbent officeholders across the nation bore the brunt of electoral discontent in the 1992 election. At the top of the ticket was incumbent Republican president George H. W. Bush. His bid for re-election was foiled by Bill Clinton, the first Democratic presidential candidate to carry California since the election of Lyndon Johnson in 1964. Anti-incumbent sentiment also helped elect two California Democrats to the United States Senate, Dianne Feinstein and Barbara Boxer. California thus became the first state in the nation to be represented simultaneously by two female senators.

Pete Wilson entered the race for reelection in 1994 as the most unpopular governor in the history of California, with an approval rating at an abysmal 15 percent. The Democratic nominee was Kathleen Brown, daughter of one former governor (Edmund G. Brown) and sister of another (Jerry Brown). Brown's campaign was fraught with tactical errors and a muddled sense of direction, whereas Wilson ran the campaign of his life. The governor proved especially adept at turning discontent with the economy to his advantage. Aired throughout the campaign was a television spot showing shadowy images of illegal aliens crossing the border into California from Mexico. The commercial's sound track was reminiscent of a 1950s horror movie. It intoned ominously, "They keep coming. . . ." Wilson's message was clear: Don't blame me for the state's economic problems, blame *them.*

The nomination and election of Dianne Feinstein and Barbara Boxer to the United States Senate prompted this ironic comment in 1992. (*Cartoon by Steve Greenberg. Courtesy of the* California Journal.)

On the ballot in 1994 was a highly controversial initiative, Proposition 187, that proposed denying nonemergency medical care, public education, and other social services to undocumented residents. Kathleen Brown passionately denounced the measure as racist and xenophobic; Pete Wilson made it the centerpiece of his campaign. On election day, Proposition 187 was approved by a wide majority of California voters and Wilson scored the most impressive come-from-behind victory in state history. For the first time in 25 years, Republicans were elected to a majority in the state assembly.

Wilson's victory was based largely on his effective use of illegal immigration as a *wedge issue,* one that polarized the electorate and was framed in demogogic terms of *us* versus *them.* Wilson solidified his own base of support by skillfully pitching his campaign toward older, white, suburban voters who resented the increasing ethnic diversity of the state. Political observer Garry Wills credited Wilson with being a master of the politics of resentment. "That resentment," wrote Wills, "is easily triggered by someone who came to the state after them, or just before."

The newly elected Republican majority in the state assembly brought to an end the reign of Democratic assembly speaker Willie L. Brown, Jr., but only after a tortuous melodrama of epic proportions. The lower house of the legislature was engulfed in a year of political intrigue before the Republican majority was able to elect its candidate of choice to the coveted speakership. Even this victory was short-lived. Democrats regained control of the assembly in 1996 and promptly elected one of their own, Cruz Bustamante, as the new speaker. Bustamante, a Fresno Democrat, was the first Latino to serve in the post. The labyrinthine battle in the assembly confirmed the impression of many Californians that their state government was utterly ineffective and irrelevant. Editorial cartoonist Paul Duginski captured the cynical mood of the electorate with a cartoon showing a California-shaped canoe plummeting over a waterfall, while on board a Democratic donkey and Republican elephant flailed away at each other with paddles.

The departure of Willie Brown from the assembly, after 30 years in office, was the most visible sign of the impact of term limits. Proponents hoped that term limits would usher in an era of reform, making legislators more responsive to their constituents. As term limits steadily took their toll on veteran lawmakers, however, it became apparent that the legislature was losing much of its institutional memory. The rapid turnover of officeholders increased, rather than diminished, the role of special interests and professional legislative staffs. Lobbyists had no term limits; they were now in a better position than ever before to supply the expertise needed by short-term lawmakers wrestling with a host of complex issues of public policy.

Governor Pete Wilson, buoyed by his reelection victory, made an unsuccessful bid for the Republican presidential nomination in 1996. Wilson hoped that his anti-illegal-immigrant message would appeal to voters across the nation, but his campaign failed to catch fire. Following a tough speech denouncing undocumented aliens, delivered in front of the Statue of Liberty, Wilson was condemned by the *New York Times* in a scathing editorial titled "An Insult to Miss Liberty." Back in his home state, Wilson was roundly criticized for breaking a pledge to serve out his second term as governor before seeking higher office.

In the midst of his ill-fated presidential campaign, Wilson launched a much-publicized attack on *affirmative action,* the practice of taking race and gender into account in employment, education, and other areas of public life in order to counteract the effects of past discrimination. At a raucous meeting of the University of California board of regents in 1995, Wilson led the vote to end affirmative action in all university admissions, hiring, and contracting. He also gave his support to an anti-affirmative-action initiative, approved by voters in November 1996 as Proposition 209. The initiative prohibited state and local governments from granting preferential treatment to any individual on the basis of race, sex, color, ethnicity, or national origin. Wilson seized upon Proposition 209 as the latest wedge issue, hoping it would boost his flagging bid for the presidency just as Proposition 187 had jump-started his gubernatorial campaign. The steady improvement of the national and state economy, however, undercut the visceral appeal of opposition to both illegal immigration and affirmative action.

As Pete Wilson's second term drew to a close, he could take satisfaction in his stewardship of the state's economy. During his tenure as chief executive, California replaced all the jobs it had lost during the recession of the early 1990s and added a million more. With increased revenues pouring into the state treasury, Wilson won high praise from the state's business community by sponsoring a billion-dollar tax cut to spur further economic growth. Yet Wilson's legacy was tarnished

Governor Pete Wilson fueled the growing opposition to illegal immigrants in his 1994 campaign for reelection. (*Cartoon © copyright 1993 by Paul Duginski.*)

by his use of the politics of resentment at a critical time of transition in California history. "Wilson will be remembered as the governor who presided over the last moments of California as a white majority state," observed Jim Schultz, director of the Democracy Center in San Francisco. "And [Californians] will remember that he managed that transition for what it would gain him among white suburban voters." With obvious regret, a Republican supporter predicted that Pete Wilson "will not be remembered so much for his positive achievements—which are considerable—but for being the architect of racially polarizing and divisive issues."

The Politics of Moderation

California voters in 1998 participated in the state's first-ever blanket primary, created by an initiative 2 years earlier. The new system allowed registered voters to vote in primary elections for any candidate in any party. Previously, voters could cast ballots only for primary candidates who were in their own party. Backers of the initiative hoped that a blanket primary would enhance the success of moderate candidates and increase voter participation. Like California's earlier experiment with cross-filing, sponsored by the progressives, the blanket primary also was an assault on the power of official political party organizations. As expected, the blanket primary led to widespread crossover voting, with nearly a quarter of Republican voters in 1998 casting ballots in the Democratic primary. Eighteen months later, however, the United States Supreme Court declared the blanket primary to be unconstitutional on the ground that it prevented party organizations from controlling the process by which their candidates were chosen.

The 1998 primary also was notable for a couple of high-profile initiatives on the ballot. Proposition 226 was a direct threat to the political muscle of organized labor. It proposed requiring unions to secure signed agreements from each member before union dues could be spent on political campaigns. The campaign in favor of the initiative was chaired by Pete Wilson, angered by union opposition to his pro-business policies. Organized labor viewed the proposal in apocalyptic terms and mobilized a successful effort to defeat it. The other highly charged issue on the ballot was Proposition 227, which called for the dismantling of the state's bilingual education programs. Critics denounced the measure as yet another wedge issue—as odious as Propositions 187 and 209—but the initiative received majority support at the polls.

The two gubernatorial candidates who emerged victorious from the primary were Republicans Dan Lungren and Democrat Gray Davis. Both were rather colorless career politicians who had served in a variety of other elected offices. One observer characterized the 1998 race as "the tortoise versus the tortoise." Lungren was a former congressman who coauthored an abortion-banning Human Life Amendment and opposed reparations for Japanese Americans interned during World War II. He later served as attorney general in the Wilson administration. Davis began his career as chief of staff for Governor Jerry Brown and served terms as assemblyman from Los Angeles, state controller, and lieutenant governor. When the *San Jose Mercury News* described Davis as "perhaps the best-trained governor-in-waiting California has ever produced," he replied: "Perhaps?!! I mean, how many offices do I have to hold?"

Democrats swept the general election in November 1998. They increased their majorities in both houses of the legislature and won all but two statewide offices. Democrat Cruz Bustamante, the former speaker of the assembly, was elected lieutenant governor, thereby becoming the first Latino to win statewide office since 1871. Democratic senator Barbara Boxer easily defeated her Republican challenger, and Gray Davis won 58 percent of the vote to defeat Dan Lungren.

Several factors contributed to the Democratic victory. On the national scene, the presidency of Bill Clinton was mired in a steamy sex scandal involving a White House intern. But California voters apparently decided that the Democratic president's sexual misconduct was less offensive than the inquisitorial tactics of the Republicans who were pressing for his impeachment. Closer to home, Democrats were able to capitalize on the backlash against Republican Pete Wilson and the divisive issues he had championed. Proposition 226 aroused organized labor to a level of political action not seen since 1958. In that year the Republican gubernatorial candidate had endorsed an anti-union initiative, thus incurring the wrath of organized labor and handing the election to Democrat Edmund G. Brown. Forty years later, another Democrat benefited from a similarly revitalized labor movement. "Proposition 226," said Gray Davis, "is my secret weapon." Wilson's assault on illegal immigration and affirmative action also had stirred deep-seated anger among minority voters who cast their ballots in record numbers for Democratic candidates. Gray Davis, meanwhile, effectively painted Dan Lungren as an extremist and presented himself as a cautious middle-of-the-road moderate.

The politics of moderation became the guiding principle of the Davis administration. The new governor sought to govern from the center, seeking workable compromises and avoiding ideological extremes. "I suspect voters are not looking for rigid ideology when they vote for governors," Davis observed. "They want someone who will get things done."

The moderation of Gray Davis was first put to the test in his handling of the simmering issue of Proposition 187. Shortly after its passage, the initiative was declared unconstitutional by a federal court. Governor Wilson then appealed the decision. Davis now faced the choice of continuing the appeal and alienating his Latino supporters, or dropping the appeal and alienating the majority of the electorate. Davis avoided either choice by having the issue decided by mediation. "The obvious interpretation," carped Pete Wilson, "is that he is trying to have it both ways." Precisely. But it was thereby that Davis effectively defused the most divisive issue in recent memory. The mediators eventually concurred that the initiative was unconstitutional.

Davis emerged from the controversy with an enhanced reputation as a consumate compromiser. That reputation was singed, however, by a round of public sniping between the governor and the lieutenant governor. Cruz Bustamante publicly denounced Davis for keeping Proposition 187 alive through mediation. The governor then responded by cutting the budget for the office of the lieutenant governor and stripping Bustamante's staff of parking spaces in the capitol garage. Such pettiness became the fodder for satire on late-night talk shows.

Relations between Gray Davis and the Democratic-controlled legislature also were marked by a surprising degree of contention. Things got off to a rocky start when Davis remarked that the role of the legislature was "to implement my vision." But the source of contention was not the governor's arrogance; it was a fundamental difference in temperament. After 16 years of Republican governors, the Democratic leaders of the legislature were impatient for a sea change in policy. Davis, ever the moderate, preferred a more measured and incremental approach.

The temperamental difference between the governor and the legislative leaders was especially manifest in the annual battles over the state budget. The surging economy of the late 1990s generated record revenues, filling the state treasury with a substantial surplus. Whereas Pete Wilson had faced a budget deficit of $11 billion at the midpoint of his first term, Gray Davis reached the same point in 2000 with a surplus of $12 billion. Legislative leaders pushed for large and permanent increases in funding for social welfare programs, but Davis preferred smaller increases coupled with one-time-only expenditures and the retention of healthy reserves. The governor defended his cautious approach by warning (wisely, as it turned out) that a downturn in the economy would quickly reduce state revenues and deplete the surplus. He once described himself as a man perpetually "waiting for the other shoe to drop."

In spite of his caution, Gray Davis scored a number of impressive legislative victories. Among his proudest achievements was educational reform. Shortly after his inauguration, Davis declared that education was the "first, second, and third priority" of his administration. He took the lead in winning passage of legislation to boost student performance on standardized exams, toughen curriculum standards, and require an exit exam for all high school graduates. His early annual budgets substantially increased funding for education, bringing the state's per-pupil spending close to the national average.

Davis also won passage in 1999 of what he called the "the toughest gun-control package in the nation." Included in the legislation was a comprehensive ban on military-style semiautomatic weapons and tight restrictions on the production and sale of cheap handguns known as "Saturday night specials." Republican opponents in the legislature were surprised at the vigor with which the governor pushed his proposals. Recalling Davis's reputation for bland innocuousness, one legislator mused, "Sharks are gray too, aren't they?" The gun-control achievement of Gray Davis led *Time* magazine to crown him "The Most Fearless Governor in America."

Most of Davis's accomplishments, however, were circumscribed by his penchant for compromise and caution and incrementalism. Early in his first term, Democratic leaders of the legislature presented the governor with more than 60 bills aimed at reforming the state's health maintenance organizations (HMOs). Davis balked at the flow of bills and signed only a select few. It was a classic Davis compromise, splitting the difference between patients' rights activists and the health care industry. Davis negotiated similar compromises in a host of other policy arenas, ranging from transportation and organized labor to the environment and energy.

The elections of 2000 indicated considerable satisfaction with the prevailing Democratic leadership of the state. The date of the primary was permanently changed from June to early March, allowing California voters to participate in Super Tuesday, the largest day of primary voting in the nation's history. The front-runners for the presidential nomination—Democrat Al Gore and Republican George W. Bush—both carried California. Among the state propositions to receive majority support were an initiative banning same-sex marriages and a constitutional amendment allowing Indian tribes to offer Nevada-style gambling on tribally owned lands. The presidential election in November was marred by contested ballots in Florida, but eventually Bush was certified the winner. Even though Gore virtually ignored California, he easily won the state's 54 electoral votes. Democratic Senator Dianne Feinstein trounced her Republican challenger, and Democrats once again increased their majorities in both houses of the state legislature and in the state's congressional delegation. Only one Republican, Secretary of State Bill Jones, remained in statewide office.

Surveying the wreckage, Republican leaders acknowledged that the Grand Old Party in the Golden State was in danger of extinction. The wedge issues of yesterday had become the liabilities of today. The vast majority of California Latinos (and other minority voters) were estranged from the GOP. Disgruntled Republicans recognized the seriousness of the problem. "Those of us fossilized Republicans have to realize that the state has changed dramatically over the past 20 years," advised one veteran Republican strategist. "We need to look at the demographics, work on outreach, and overcome some stereotypes." The party's stand on such issues as gun control and abortion had placed it outside the California mainstream. While more than 70 percent of California voters believed that the government should not interfere with a woman's access to abortion, the state Republican party chair told a religious magazine that "killing babies" was the GOP's "issue of the century." A Republican consultant was horrified. "Abortion is eating our party alive," he said. "It is an issue that divides us internally and has driven away votes on the outside."

Other issues soon emerged that had a dramatic impact on the state's political landscape. The most acute crisis to hit California during the early years of the Davis adminstration involved the supply and pricing of electricity. The crisis arose after state energy policy was fundamentally restructured—based on a deregulation plan approved by the legislature during the governorship of Republican Pete Wilson. (See Chapter 34.) As the situation worsened in the winter and spring of 2001, Davis's approval rating plummeted. The Democratic governor recognized that his administration would likely be remembered for how well it handled the crisis: "This is my moment to provide leadership." Davis's Republican critics agreed completely. "The reason we are at this crisis today," thundered one Republican assemblyman, "is because of the governor's lack of action and lack of leadership." Secretary of State Bill Jones, declaring his candidacy for the Republican nomina-

Governor Gray Davis urges the California Energy Commission to approve construction of new power plants in 2001. (© AP/Wide World Photos.)

tion for governor in 2002, derided Davis for his handling of the crisis. Davis responded by reminding his critics how it all began: "This deregulation disaster was authored by a Republican legislator, passed by a Republican assembly, signed into law by a Republican governor, and implemented with undue haste by a Republican Public Utilities Commission."

The electric energy crisis soon was overshadowed by the devastating terrorist attack on the United States on September 11, 2001. Hijackers seized four California-bound commercial jetliners and crashed two of them into the twin towers of the World Trade Center in New York City. Thousands of American lives were lost. Authorities quickly identified the hijackers as members of a terrorist organization with cells in the Middle East and elsewhere around the world.

The attack, viewed by many as "another Pearl Harbor," had a profound impact on the nation and the state. Security and public safety became matters of intense concern, and California politics reflected the fundamental change in mood. "Our whole world changed after September 11," said Governor Davis. "There's no higher priority than keeping Californians safe." Most Californians supported the subsequent military campaign directed against the terrorists, but many also shared the sentiments of veteran political consultant Stuart Spencer, who wisely counseled: "We have to honestly ask why people hate us to the point they become terrorists, then attack the root causes of terrorism." When Davis received "credible evidence" of a terrorist threat to the state's suspension bridges, he issued a public warning and ordered National Guardsmen to stand watch. When critics charged the governor with overreacting, he replied (characteristically): "I'm going to err on the side of caution." Indeed, the cautious nature of the governor now was paying rich political dividends. His approval rating once again began to rise. Political analyst Mark Baldassare, who earlier had excoriated the governor for a lack of vision, noted that Californians "have a very positive reaction to how their political leadership is handling one of the greatest crises the nation has ever faced."

The terrorist attack also contributed to the steepest decline in state revenues since the end of World War II. As consumer confidence fell, the state and nation slipped back into recession in 2001. Governor Davis announced that the state surplus (a surplus he had guarded with care) was now depleted. He projected a budget shortfall for 2002 of more than $14 billion and ordered an immediate statewide hiring freeze.

The slumping economy, coupled with the electric energy crisis, encouraged the political rivals of Davis. Richard Riordan, the former mayor of Los Angeles, entered the race for the Republican gubernatorial nomination in 2002 by declaring his intention to lift "the dark cloud [that] has settled over our state." Wealthy Los Angeles businessman Bill Simon, the successful aspirant for the GOP nomination, attacked the "failed leadership" of Davis and proclaimed himself a leader "worthy of renewing the California dream." Davis, meanwhile, enjoyed the advantages of incumbency in the aftermath of the terrorist attack and won high marks for his newfound zeal for public security.

Amid the continuing turmoil of day-to-day California politics, many careful observers at the beginning of the twenty-first century were disturbed by signs that the

A DAY OF INFAMY

Los Angeles Times cartoonist Michael Ramirez compares the terrorist attack on the twin towers of the World Trade Center to the bombing of Pearl Harbor. (*2001 © Copley News Service.*)

state's entire political process was becoming dysfunctional. Chief among the concerns was the pervasive and potentially corrupting role of money. The cost of campaigning in California had become extraordinarily expensive; statewide races routinely cost $40 million, and even legislative district races easily cost in excess of $1 million. Candidates from among the super rich had become a regular part of the California scene. Among the most prominent "checkbook candidates," able to finance campaigns from their own personal wealth, were multimillionaire challengers to both Dianne Feinstein and Gray Davis. Once in office, successful candidates had to spend an inordinate amount of time and effort fund-raising for their next campaign. Gray Davis led the way, collecting a record-breaking $25 million in just his first two years in office.

Efforts at campaign finance reform were less than successful. The Political Reform Act, sponsored by Jerry Brown in 1974, required disclosure of campaign finances but failed to limit the size of contributions. Voters in 1996 approved an initiative imposing strict limits on campaign contributions, but the measure was overturned by federal courts as a restriction on speech. In 2000 the legislature placed on the ballot a much ballyhooed campaign finance reform initiative, Proposition 34, which passed with 60 percent of the vote. The initiative limited the amount of money individual candidates could raise, but it put no restrictions on how much political parties could raise before transferring funds to the candidates. It also set campaign expenditure limits but defined them as "voluntary." Most observers agreed that the measure was likely to have little effect in curbing the role of money in political campaigns. Indeed, California's system of campaign finance remained one of the least regulated in the nation.

The power of money also was evident in the dramatic increase in the number and importance of lobbyists in the state capital. With their role in the legislative process enhanced by term limits, lobbyists became ever bolder in the formulation of public policy. More than a thousand registered lobbyists were at work in Sacremento in 2000, a 50 percent increase in less than a quarter century. Expending $100 million annually in campaign contributions, and many millions more on other activities, lobbyists came under fire for having undue influence in state government. The Field Poll in 1999 found that more than two-thirds of Californians believed that elected officials were more influenced by special interests than by the voting public.

Distrusting their elected representatives, Californians turned increasingly to the initiative process to decide major issues. Although the initiative had been around since the progressive era, more than half of all propositions approved by Californians were passed since the 1970s. "I think the initiative process is out of control," concluded political scientist David Magleby. "The numbers exceed the ability of all but a few voters to gather the necessary information to make informed choices." Peter Schrag, author of *Paradise Lost: California's Experience, America's Future* (1998), regarded the rise of ballot propositions as symptomatic of widespread voter disenchantment: "During the two decades since the passage of [Proposition] 13, California has been in a nearly constant revolt against representative government."

More disturbing than the numerical increase of initiatives was the role of special interests in determining their outcome. As envisioned by the progressives, the initiative was to be a bulwark against the corrupting power of money in the legislative process. But the skyrocketing costs of mounting a successful initiative campaign opened the door to special interests. David S. Broder, author of *Democracy Derailed: Initiative Campaigns and the Power of Money* (2000), concluded that the initiative process had been subverted irretrievably from its original purpose. What began as "a weapon against special-interest influence," he warned, "has become a favored tool of interest groups and millionaires with their own political and personal agendas." Recognizing that money alone did not guarantee electoral success, an editorial in the *Sacramento Bee* concurred: "Never before has money played so large a part in determining what gets on the ballot; never before has that money distorted the issues so greatly."

As California entered the twenty-first century, many residents found themselves alienated and disengaged from the political process. Voter turnout remained at abysmally low levels (suggesting the more appropriate term might be "voter turnoff"). Fewer Californians were bothering to register to vote, and among those who did register, fewer were bothering to vote. Likewise, both major parties experienced a decline in rates of voter affiliation. The media contributed to the disengagement by their penchant for negative reporting. Good political journalism, explained Riverside publisher Marcia McQuern, had become synonymous with exposing wrongdoing by corrupt public officials. Such reporting "fuels the public's cynicism about government and politicians." Most troubling of all was the nonparticipation of young Californians. Commenting on the views of her own Gen X, Donna Frisby of Santa Monica observed: "This generation doesn't distinguish the system from the politicians, whom they see as corrupt and evil." Another cynical 21-year-old nonvoter was convinced that politicians were "all bought and paid for and could care less about the people." In defense of her nonparticipation, she said: "Why bother when they're not listening?"

The tragedy was that California needed all the help it could get to solve the very real problems it confronted in the new century. A great deal had changed since the ascendancy of Ronald Reagan in the mid-1960s. Yet many of the fundamental challenges facing California remained the same. Californians still were wrestling with basic issues of identity and equity, trying to achieve stability in an era of rapid change—and the nation continued to look to California for political and social leadership.

Selected Bibliography

A comprehensive history of recent California politics remains unwritten. The broader contours are suggested in Mark Baldassare, *California in the New Millennium* (2000); Ken DeBow and John C. Syer, *Power and Politics in California* (2000); David G. Lawrence, *California: The Politics of Diversity* (2000); Peter Schrag, *Paradise Lost* (1998); and Gerald Lubenow, *Governing California* (1998). Earlier surveys appear in Jackson K. Putnam, *Modern California Politics, 1917–1980* (1980); Gladwin Hill, *Dancing Bear* (1968); and Royce D. Delmatier et al., *The Rumble of California Politics* (1970). *California Journal,* beginning in January 1970, is an indispensable digest of state government and politics.

The careers of Edmund G. Brown and Ronald Reagan are analyzed in Gary G. Hamilton and Nicole Woolsey Biggart, *Governor Reagan, Governor Brown* (1984). Specialized studies include Gerard J. DeGroot, "Ronald Reagan and Student Unrest in California," *Pacific Historical Review,* LXV (February 1996), pp. 107–129, and Garin Burbank, "Governor Reagan's Only Defeat," *California History,* LXXII (Winter 1993/1994), pp. 360–373. Totton J. Anderson and Eugene C. Lee, in "The 1966 Election in California," *Western Political Quarterly,* XX (June 1967), pp. 535–554, deal with Reagan's first election. Ronald Reagan, *Where's the Rest of Me?* (1965), is an autobiography as told to Richard Hubler. Dissenting views may be found in Edmund G. Brown, Sr., *Reagan and Reality* (1970) and *Ronald Reagan, the Political Chameleon* (1976). Biographical studies include Joseph Lewis (1968), Hedrick Smith et al. (1980), William Boyarsky (1981), Rowland Evans and Robert Novak (1981), and Lou Cannon (1982).

Jerry Brown has been the subject of several books: Ed Salzman (1976), John C. Bollens and G. Robert Williams (1978), J. D. Lorenz (1978), Robert Pack (1978), and Orville Schell (1978). See especially Roger Rapoport, *California Dreaming: The Political Odyssey of Pat and Jerry Brown* (1982).

Tax Revolt Digest, published monthly by the *California Journal* from November 1978 to October 1979, contains a wealth of information on the tax revolt in California and elsewhere. The best introductions to the subject are Michael A. Shires, *Patterns in California Government Revenues since Proposition 13* (1999); Shires (ed.), *Has Proposition 13 Delivered?* (1998); John J. Kirlin, *The Impacts of Proposition 13 upon California Governments* (1979); George G. Kaufman and Kenneth T. Roseus (eds.), *The Property Tax Revolt* (1981); and Valerie Raymond, *Surviving Proposition 13* (1988).

In contrast to his immediate predecessors, George Deukmejian has not attracted much attention from biographers. Larry Liebert offers a perceptive analysis of the Deukmejian governorship in "The Duke's Recipe for Success," *California Journal,* XVI (April 1985), pp. 141–144. Deukmejian offers his own views in an interview published in ibid., XV (January 1984), pp. 7–10. On the importance of the Rose Bird issue, see Preble Stolz, *Judging Judges: The Investigation of Rose Bird and the California Supreme Court* (1981).

Gerald C. Lubenow (ed.), *California Votes* (1991, 1995, 1999), are invaluable resources on three successive gubernatorial campaigns. The beginnings of the Pete Wilson administration are described in Richard Zeiger, "Pete Wilson Inherits a State in Disarray," *California Journal,* XXI (December 1990), pp. 560–563, and "Pete Wilson," ibid., XXII (December 1991), pp. 541–546. The later years are analyzed in Steve Scott, "Wilson vs. Labor," ibid., XXIX (February 1998), pp. 14–23, and Block, "The Wilson Legacy," ibid., XXIX (November 1998), pp. 6–11. On the Davis administration, see the articles in ibid., XXIX (October 1998), and XXXI (August 2000). Steve Scott offers a particularly useful analysis in "Which Shade of Gray?" ibid., XXX (January 1999), pp. 10–14. See also Block, "The Republican Bust of 1998," ibid., XXIX (December 1998), pp. 6–7. Block's analysis of the impact of the terrorist attack is particularly insightful; see ibid., XXXII (November 2001), pp. 8–19. On the intrigue in the assembly, see Richard A. Clucas, *Willie Brown and the California Assembly* (1995), and James Richardson, *Willie Brown* (1996). The intersection of ethnicity and politics is the subject of Bruce Cain, Jack Citrin, and Cara Wong, *Ethnic Context, Race Relations, and California Politics* (2000), and Michael B. Preston et al., *Racial and Ethnic Politics in California* (1998). Other important studies include Bruce E. Cain and Roger Noll, *Constitutional Reform in California* (1995); Eugene Smolensky et al., *Welfare Reform in California* (1992); and Dan Walters and Jay Michael, *The Third House: Money and Power in Sacramento* (2003). For an analysis of the controversies surrounding reapportionment, see Cain, *The Reapportionment Puzzle* (1986). The pivotal role of ballot initiatives is the subject of David S. Broder, *Democracy Derailed: Initiative Campaigns and the Power of Money* (2000); Thomas E. Cronin, *Direct Democracy* (1989); and David D. Schmidt, *Citizen Lawmakers* (1989).

The annual editions of *California Policy Choices,* edited by John J. Kirlin and David R. Winkler, contain essays identifying "meaningful choices for Californians."

CHAPTER 34

The Environment and Energy

One of the major themes in California history since at least the progressive era has been controversy over the use and preservation of the state's natural resources. The controversy intensified in the decades following the observance of Earth Day, a nationwide demonstration in 1970 to dramatize environmental concerns. New groups joined forces with older conservation organizations such as the Sierra Club to lobby for the protection of California's land, air, and water. The environmental protection movement scored a series of impressive victories, both in the state legislature and through the initiative process. The opponents of the environmentalists, however, argued that environmental legislation retarded economic development by harming the state's business climate. A fierce struggle between the forces of economic development and environmental protection was waged on many fronts.

On the thirtieth anniversary of Earth Day, more than two-thirds of all Californians remained "greatly concerned" about threats to the environment. Latinos, the largest group of new Californians, were more likely than others to favor the toughening of environmental safeguards. Most promising of all was the emergence in the early 2000s of a new understanding that environmental protection and economic growth are not mutually exclusive. The research office of the California senate, in a report titled *The Myth of Jobs vs. Resources,* concluded that on all economic measures "states with stronger environmental policies out-perform states with weaker policies."

Regional Protection

The first important victory for the environmental protection movement came in 1965 with the establishment by the state legislature of the San Francisco Bay Conservation and Development Commission (BCDC). Uncontrolled filling of the bay during the previous century reduced its size by 40 percent, and conservationists warned that without effective controls the bay would eventually become little more

Members of the Costanoan-Rumsen Carmel tribe dance to celebrate the restoration of wetlands at former Crissy Field on San Francisco Bay, November 9, 1999. (*Photo by Liz Hafalia. Courtesy of the* San Francisco Chronicle.)

than a river. The new BCDC regulated all developments in a 100-foot-wide band around the bay shoreline and provided a useful model for the creation of other regional agencies in the state. During its first 35 years of operation, the commision achieved a net gain of 1700 acres of surface water for the bay. The breaching of dikes around the bay's periphery restored hundreds of acres of wetlands drained more than a century earlier.

The BCDC was unable, however, to solve all of the bay's problems. Upstream diversions continued to diminish the flow of freshwater into the bay, and wastewater from irrigated lands in the interior carried huge loads of fertilizers, pesticides, and other toxic substances into the bay each year. As a result, the bay wildlife population continued to suffer a precipitous decline. The state Water Resources Control Board in 1995 found high levels of cancer-causing pollutants in the bay's resident harbor seal population and in eight species of fish. The survival of native plants and animals also was threatened by the invasion of exotic species introduced into the bay by the flushing of contaminated ballast water from visiting ships. A federal report labeled San Francisco Bay "the most invaded aquatic ecosystem in North America."

More emotional fuel was added to the environmental movement early in 1969 when an offshore well of the Union Oil Company sprang a leak in the Santa Barbara Channel and smeared hundreds of square miles of ocean and 30 miles of beaches with oil. Dozens of species of shorebirds, marine mammals, and fish were adversely affected. In 1970 the state legislature, acting partly in response to the

Santa Barbara oil spill, passed the California Endangered Species Act (CESA) to protect animal and plant species facing extinction, and the California Environmental Quality Act (CEQA). The CEQA required that an environmental impact report be submitted to appropriate public agencies for approval prior to the commencement of any project that "could have a significant effect on the environment." Under terms of the act, environmentalists brought suit to halt or modify scores of environmentally damaging projects. The California Chamber of Commerce denounced the act as harmful to the state's economy. The Santa Barbara oil spill also ignited a long-standing controversy over the further development of offshore oil resources. Whenever the federal government attempted to lease new offshore tracts to private companies to drill for oil and gas, California environmentalists argued that further development was a needless threat to the fragile ecosystem of the coast.

Californians in growing numbers were becoming convinced that the scenic regions of the state needed special protection from private development. In 1976 the legislature established the California Coastal Commission to govern development of California's coastline and to preserve reasonable public access to it. The commission, which enjoyed the enthusiastic support of Democratic governor Jerry Brown, denied permits for several large developments and often required substantial modifications in the proposals it did approve. Business leaders soon charged that the commission was guilty of "bureaucratic and environmental zeal." The commission subsequently reversed direction under Republican governors George Deukmejian and Pete Wilson, approving the construction of several large coastal hotels and housing projects.

Supporters of coastal protection scored a major victory with the election of Democratic governor Gray Davis in 1998. One of Davis's first acts as governor was to order the Coastal Commission to oppose future oil drilling on offshore federal leases. The commission also tackled the problem of *nonpoint pollution,* the accumulation of pollutants discharged from a variety of sources. Southern California beaches during the 1990s experienced a thousand beach closures a year—70 percent due to elevated bacterial levels caused by the discharge of inadequately treated sewage. In 2000 the Coastal Commission adopted the most comprehensive nonpoint pollution prevention program of any state in the nation.

The Tahoe Regional Planning Agency (TRPA), jointly operated by California and Nevada and authorized by Congress in 1967, tried to combat both the pollution of Lake Tahoe's pure, blue waters by sewage and the threatened destruction of the beauty of its surroundings by excessive and hasty construction, but for years the effectiveness of the agency was undercut by inadequate funding. By the early 2000s, the lake was losing water clarity at the rate of 1 foot per year. Governor Davis, a supporter of the campaign to "Keep Tahoe Blue," increased funding for the TRPA to protect environmentally sensitive lands around the lake. Democratic attorney general Bill Lockyer, on his first full day in office, joined a suit to ban from the lake jet skis, powered by heavily polluting two-stroke engines. Lockyer took the action, he said, to demonstrate that "environmental quality is part of our law enforcement duty."

Controversy also centered on California's parklands and wilderness areas. Use of California's state parks grew eightfold between 1970 and 2000, while funding for park maintenance and repairs declined sharply during the adminstrations of

Deukmejian and Wilson. Reversing decades of decline, Governor Davis allocated additional funds for deferred park maintenance and supported the largest-ever state park bond measure. Davis's head of state parks, Rusty Areias, adopted a strategic vision from the Iroquois Confederacy: "In our every deliberation, we must consider the impact of our decisions on the next seven generations." At the federal level, environmentalists achieved one of their major goals in 1994 when Congress passed the California Desert Protection Act, the largest wilderness protection measure in the history of the continental United States. Sponsored by Democratic senator Dianne Feinstein, the act created two new national parks and extended federal protection over 7.6 million acres of desert lands. A Sierra Club spokesperson praised the act as "the sunrise for desert protection and the sunset for desert abuse."

Among the most spectacular lands under federal protection in California was the Yosemite Valley, which by 2010 was expected to be visited by more than 6 million people a year. On summer weekends the valley, only 1 mile wide and 7 miles long, was overburdened with visitors who trampled lush meadows and filled the roadways with bumper-to-bumper traffic. The National Park Service came under conflicting pressures from environmental organizations to "deurbanize" the valley and from the park concessionaire to maintain adequate services and conveniences for visitors. In 1980 the park service unveiled a master plan to reduce overnight accommodations and to restrict the number of private vehicles allowed into the valley. Congress failed, however, to appropriate adequate funding for the plan, and few of its provisions were implemented. Prospects for the park brightened in 1997 when federal officials announced a new Yosemite Valley Implementation Plan to eliminate several roads, bridges, and more than 2000 parking spaces for day-use visitors. The Sierra Club applauded the plan, hoping it would ensure "the park's ecosystems are maintained for this and future generations." (See Color Plate 17.)

One of the most intense environmental battles in the past decade or so was fought over the few remaining stands of old-growth California redwoods. Environmental activists descended on logging towns in the Redwood Summer of 1990 and attempted to block the cutting of the virgin trees, only 5 percent of which remained after a century and a half of virtually unrestricted timber harvesting. The disruptive tactics of the activists failed to slow the logging operations, but they succeeded in increasing public awareness of the issue. In 1996, after a decade of controversy, an agreement was reached to protect the Headwaters Forest of old-growth redwoods in Humboldt County. The *New York Times* praised the agreement as "the most ambitious public-private effort so far to protect an entire ecosystem," but activist Julia Butterfly Hill (who spent 2 years living atop a threatened redwood tree) criticized the plan for being too little too late.

Biodiversity

Environmentalists expressed growing concern in the early 2000s about threats to California's once-thriving biological diversity. California had more native species at risk than any other state. Twenty percent of the state's native animal species were classified as endangered or threatened, and one-quarter of all endangered

A political cartoon comments on plans to save the Headwaters Forest after destruction of 95 percent of the old-growth California redwoods. (*Cartoon by Steve Greenberg. Courtesy of the California Journal.*)

plant species in the United States were located in California. Habitat destruction had taken a heavy toll. California wetlands, once extending over 5 million acres, were reduced by 90 percent during two centuries of "reclamation." The swampy marshlands and sloughs near Los Banos in Merced County once hosted wildlife as rich as the Serengeti Plain of Africa. Millions of waterfowl filled the sky. By the early twenty-first century, the wildlife population had been greatly reduced; species that formerly had been common were extinct or remained only as rarities.

Agriculture, logging, and the damming of inland rivers caused a precipitous decline in chinook salmon, steelhead trout, and other fish. Runs of anadromous species on the Eel River fell to less than 5 percent of their historic highs; even the official state fish, the brilliantly colored golden trout, neared extinction. Along the Pacific coast, reductions in lingcod and rockfish reached disastrous levels. "We think the ocean is so vast that we can't exterminate its fish," commented policy analyst Kate Wing, "but that's precisely what we're doing." Gill-net fishing and routine oil spills endangered deep-diving seabirds as well as California sea lions, harbor seals, and elephant seals. A mysterious increase in the number of dead whales washing up on California beaches prompted marine biologists to speculate that "something is askew in the ocean environment."

Even the smallest of species showed signs of distress. Several types of California butterflies and other insects were in steep decline, caused perhaps by the accumulation of pollutants and pesticides at threshold levels. Frogs and other amphibians virtually disappeared from entire water systems. "You can hike the Sierra for days and weeks and not see a frog anywhere," reported a researcher from the University of California, Santa Barbara. Describing the polluted San Joaquin River as a "witch's brew" of toxins, environmentalist Bill Jennings warned: "A world not safe for frogs and butterflies won't be safe for children."

As with all things environmental, the protection of endangered species was subject to shifting political currents. Republican governor Pete Wilson in 1993 called for the relaxation of a wide range of environmental regulations to foster the creation of "jobs, jobs, jobs." Among the regulations under assault was the landmark California Endangered Species Act. In 1995 the governor announced his intention to drop all currently listed species within 5 years and to require more stringent standards of endangerment before relisting. Defenders of the CESA were outraged. "We are losing species and habitats so fast it is almost mind-boggling," said Peter Moyle of the University of California, Davis. A lobbyist for the Sierra Club charged Wilson with caving in to the state's agribusiness and timber interests: "This provides opportunities for the governor's supporters to mow down more endangered species." Environmentalists expressed similar concerns when the administration of Republican George W. Bush announced its intention to weaken key federal protections of endangered species. Democratic congressman George Miller accused the Bush administration of sacrificing endangered species for the benefit of its wealthiest "clients." An attorney for the Center for Biological Diversity noted that Bush's policies would cause critical delays and thus doom additional species: "Every day we delay increases the possibility of extinction."

One of the bright spots in the ongoing controversy over biodiversity was a cooperative venture between environmentalists and California rice growers. By changing their farming practices, rice growers in the Sacramento Valley were able to provide 90,000 acres of winter habitat for waterfowl such as the magnificent snow goose and sandhill crane. The migrating populations of waterfowl through the valley slowly recovered, reaching their highest levels in more than 20 years in 1996.

Californians renewed their commitment to preserving the state's biodiversity in the early 2000s. Voters in 2000 supported two of the largest conservation bond measures ever approved in the nation's history. "The public's approval of these bonds," said a spokesperson for the Nature Conservancy, "makes our task of protecting the state's biological diversity much more feasible." Under Governor Gray Davis, the Resources Agency launched an ambitious project to combine state-of-the-art mapping with habitat assessment techniques. The Davis administration also imposed strict limits on logging along the state's fish-bearing streams to protect endangered habitat. Not surprisingly, timber industry leaders warned that the new limits would cause "severe financial hardships."

Growth Control

The environmental movement, although its roots lay deep in California history, represented a radical reversal of traditional values. Throughout the state's history, growth had been thought of as the greatest good, but the environmentalists denounced unrestricted growth as a menace to the quality of life. Beginning with a Petaluma ordinance in 1973 limiting construction of new residential units within the city to 500 per year, communities across the state took steps to limit their population growth. Builders criticized the Petaluma measure as a "no-growth" plan and challenged its constitutionality, but in 1976 the United States Supreme Court upheld the ordinance. During the next two decades, California voters approved more than 1500 slow-growth measures.

The growth-control movement was under constant attack from prodevelopment forces. Critics charged the movement was "elitist," dominated by wealthy residents who wanted to protect their own property values by stopping further construction. In the late 1980s, developers mounted a major counteroffensive against the movement to restrict growth. They amassed huge war chests and adopted sophisticated techniques to defeat local growth-control initiatives. The prodevelopment forces in Orange County in 1988 spent $2.2 million to defeat a local growth-control initiative, overpowering their opponents, who spent less than $100,000. It was the most expensive county initiative campaign in California history. "They bought themselves a landslide," commented the coauthor of the initiative. "It just shows you how much power that much money can generate."

The recession and attendant slowdown in population increase in the early 1990s temporarily reduced the intensity of the growth-control issue. As the California economy rebounded later in the decade, local communities became divided once again between progrowth and antigrowth forces. Affluent enclaves on the west side of Los Angeles, for instance, remained fiercely antigrowth, whereas poorer neighborhoods in the eastern and southern parts of the city were desperate for development. Encouraged by the economic boom of the late 1990s, progrowth forces scored victories from Ventura to Glendora, from Tracy to Monterey. The flight of families from the congested San Francisco Bay area, however, gave new life to the antigrowth movement in the San Joaquin Valley and foothills of the Sierra. Growth control became the number one issue throughout northern and central California, where "rural heritage initiatives" won widespread support. "People are sick of standing by and watching greenbelts and open space paved over," commented one antigrowth activist.

Eventually, many Californians concluded that effective growth control could be achieved only by statewide or regional planning. It was apparent that such growth-related problems as urban sprawl, air pollution, and crowded freeways could never be solved by local governments. State leaders began calling for a comprehensive statewide plan for managing population growth. Echoing sentiments that first had been expressed a generation earlier, urban planner Amy Liu observed in 1999 that growth control is "no longer a regional issue but is now a state and national issue; it's resonating with a lot more people."

Air Pollution

Air pollution was the most obvious menace to the quality of the California environment. Smog began to produce a sharp decrease in visibility and painful irritations of nose and eyes in Los Angeles in 1943, and by the 1960s this condition had become so chronic that on bad days the city vanished. When, as often happened, the air in and over the Los Angeles basin became stagnant and a temperature inversion occurred, the rays of the sun reacted photochemically with various waste products in the air to produce new and still more dangerous pollutants. The result was not merely a blight on the beauty of the region and a cause of sharp discomfort but also a menace to health and a source of costly damage to several crops. The growing of leafy vegetables in the Los Angeles basin virtually ceased.

The San Francisco Bay area, like the Los Angeles basin, had a bowl-like shape, and smog began to be a severe problem in the bay region also. Los Angeles created an air pollution control district in 1947, and the San Francisco Bay counties formed a similar district in 1955. These agencies had some success in persuading or compelling industrial plants to reduce the emission of noxious wastes, often by installing expensive equipment. Yet the smog grew steadily worse. It became apparent that the chief offender was the automobile, with its output of hydrocarbons, oxides of nitrogen, and toxic carbon monoxide.

The state legislature in 1960 passed the first automobile antismog law in the nation, requiring the installation of various smog-control devices in motor vehicle engines.To meet federal air-quality standards, the legislature in 1982 required car owners to have their vehicles inspected every other year. Cars that met strict emission standards would be certified, whereas those that failed would have to be repaired. The law applied to each of the state's populated air basins, including the San Francisco Bay area and much of southern California.

In 1991 the state Air Resources Board (ARB) approved the most sweeping vehicle emissions standards in the world, including the first-ever requirement for the mass production of electric cars. The new standards mandated that 10 percent of all new cars sold in California produce *zero* emissions by 2003. Electric cars were the only vehicles that could meet this absolute standard. The major automakers fought the requirement, arguing that electric vehicles were too costly to manufacture and that consumer demand was too low. The ARB in 2001 agreed to modify its standards, requiring only 2 percent of new cars be zero-emission vehicles and another 8 percent be vehicles with extremely low emissions. The 8 percent goal could be met by cars with methanol-powered fuel cells or gasoline-electric hybrid motors. "It's about reducing pollution," said filmmaker Francis Ford Coppola, a satisfied electric car owner. "It's about a wild new technology."

The state ARB also adopted the world's stiffest gasoline rules, intended to cut smog-forming emissions by an additional one-third. To meet the new standards, oil refiners reformulated their gasoline to make it burn more cleanly. The reformulated gasoline, introduced in the mid-1990s, contained a substance known as MTBE (methyl tertiary butyl ether). A suspected carcinogen, MTBE soon began contaminating California groundwater. More than 3500 sites were polluted statewide, with the heaviest concentrations in Los Angeles and Orange counties. Governor Gray Davis responded by ordering the removal of MTBE from all gasoline products by the end of 2002.

The combined effect of state and federal regulations was a steady improvement in California air quality. The San Francisco Bay area in 1995 became the nation's largest metropolitan area to achieve federal air-quality standards. Annual exposure to smog in the Los Angeles basin, the most seriously polluted region in the country, decreased 50 percent between 1980 and 2000. Air pollution worsened, however, in inland communities that were even more vulnerable to smog than the coastal areas. Medium-size cities in the Central Valley, such as Bakersfield and Fresno, had smog problems rivaling those of New York and Chicago.

In spite of decades of progress, 90 percent of all Californians in 2000 still breathed unhealthy air on some days. Especially disturbing was the proliferation of heavy polluters. Diesel-fueled trucks and cars made up only 2 percent of the vehicles on California's roadways, but they produced more than half the cancer-causing particles inhaled deep into the lungs. The Sierra Club labeled the newly popular sport utility vehicles (SUVs) the "cars from hell" because they produced 47 percent more air pollution than average cars. Meanwhile, consumer products—such as hair sprays, deodorants, and household cleansers—were releasing more pollutants each day than the combined emissions of all the state's refineries and gas stations. In 2000 the state ARB launched a campaign to reduce smog-forming chemicals in consumer products by more than half within the next 5 years.

Scientists warned that air pollution was causing devastating changes to the earth's atmosphere and climate. When airborne pollutants reach the upper atmosphere, they damage the protective ozone layer that shields the earth from the sun's harmful ultraviolet rays. Increased exposure to ultraviolet radiation produces an elevated risk of skin cancer. The pollutants also create a blanket of gases over the earth, trapping the reflected heat from the sun like a greenhouse and thus contributing to global warming. Environmentalists were outraged when President George W. Bush, shortly after his election in 2000, rejected the 1997 Kyoto treaty on global warming. The president argued that reducing the emission of greenhouse gases, as mandated by the treaty, would hurt the nation's economy. He also confounded environmentalists by breaking a campaign pledge to curtail power-plant emissions of the largest single contributor to global warming. "Bush is turning his back not only on his campaign promise," commented a senior researcher with the Natural Resources Defense Council, "but on the world's scientists, who warn this problem is more serious than we previously thought." Climatologists predicted that California's average winter temperatures would rise significantly by 2030, causing severe droughts, outbreaks of exotic diseases, and the inundation of coastal areas. "Many of the places we know and love in California are vulnerable to a changing climate," warned a biologist at Stanford University. "A variety of changes are coming, and many will have profound ecological and economic consequences."

Water Resources

The long-standing controversy over the use and distribution of the state's water resources was renewed in the late 1970s as the legislature considered authorization of the Peripheral Canal, a 43-mile-long channel around the periphery of San Francisco Bay that would connect the Sacramento River directly with the existing California Aqueduct. By being drawn from the Sacramento, rather than from the southern end of the Sacramento–San Joaquin River Delta, the annual supply of water delivered by the aqueduct to southern California could be increased by at least 700,000 acre-feet.

Support for the Peripheral Canal was virtually unanimous throughout southern California. Opposition to the canal was led by environmental groups and others in northern California who believed that the massive diversion of freshwater supplies from the delta would harm San Francisco Bay and delta water quality. The issue was a matter of grave concern because the delta supplied two-thirds of the state's drinking water. One Bay Area assembly member warned: "Please, southerners, don't think you can rob our water and destroy our ecosystem, because there will be a civil war in this state if you do. The aqueduct will be blown up. National Guardsmen will be shot." In 1980 the legislature passed a bill authorizing construction of the canal, but a coalition of environmentalists and northern California public officials drafted a referendum to block its construction. When the referendum appeared on the ballot, in June 1982, the canal was rejected statewide by a vote of 62 percent.

An important step toward resolving the decades-long controversy between northern and southern California water interests was taken in 1986 when Congress approved a new policy of cooperation between federal and state water agencies. The federal government promised to use the huge resources of its Central Valley Project (CVP) to protect the water quality of the delta and San Francisco Bay. The state, for its part, agreed to allow up to 1 million acre-feet of surplus water from the federal system to flow through the California Aqueduct to southern California and the Central Valley. Further progress came in 1992 when Congress passed the Central Valley Project Improvement Act, the first basic reshaping of the CVP since its creation in 1935. Under terms of the act, about a tenth of the CVP's water was reallocated to protect fisheries and endangered habitats. The act also permitted transfers of project water anywhere in the state, allowing rural water districts to sell a portion of their allocations to the cities.

By the early 2000s, the water quality of the Sacramento–San Joaquin River Delta—in spite of important legislative reforms—had deteriorated to the lowest level in more than two decades. The delta was suffocating from the continued drainage of agricultural wastewater, saltwater intrusion, and freshwater diversions. "The overarching impression," said the head of the state's Resources Agency, "is of an ecosystem in decline." State and federal agencies, water users, and environmentalists formed a coalition known as Cal-Fed to address (once again) the issue of delta water quality. In 2000 the coalition announced a bold new plan to meet the state's growing water needs while restoring the delta after decades of degradation. The plan called for the largest habitat and ecosystem restoration in the nation's history. Secretary of the Interior Bruce Babbitt praised the plan for setting "a precedent for how our nation can balance environmental protection and economic growth." The California Farm Bureau Federation promptly filed suit to block the plan, claiming it threatened a million acres of farmland by promoting "habitat sprawl."

Meanwhile, other battles over the state's water resources continued. A campaign to save Mono Lake pitted the National Audubon Society and a host of environmental groups against the city of Los Angeles. Described by Mark Twain as "one of the

"You watch the birds in their arrivals, departures, and intricate ceremonies and stalking grace, and you take comfort and joy from such order and cyclical permanence. It is hard to watch this spectacle crumble to dust." (*Lee Vining, courtesy of the Mono Lake Committee, California.*)

strangest freaks of nature to be found in any land," Mono Lake was the primary breeding ground for 90 percent of the California gull population and an important stopover for millions of migratory birds. Since the early 1940s, Los Angeles had been tapping the streams flowing into Mono Lake, causing its water level to drop by more than 40 vertical feet and its surface area to diminish by one-third. As the lake shrank, its chemical content changed drastically, thus reducing the supply of brine shrimp necessary for the survival of the nesting gulls and their chicks. A University of California biologist reported in 1982 that only 5000 California gulls were hatched at Mono Lake that year, compared with more than 35,000 just 4 years earlier. In 1983 environmentalists scored a major victory when the state supreme court ruled that water could not be taken from a lake or other natural source without consideration of the possible harm to the source itself. The court's doctrine of *source protection* was a repudiation of Los Angeles's long-held exclusive right to take water from the Mono Lake basin. Eleven years later the state's Water Resources Control Board ordered the Los Angeles Department of Water and Power (LADWP) to restore waterfowl habitats lost due to the decline of the lake's water level. It also restricted further water exports from the basin until the lake had stabilized at about 25 feet below its pre-diversion level.

A similar battle was waged over the preservation of the free-flowing waters of the rivers of northern California. Environmentalists lost their fight to protect a 9-mile stretch of white-water rapids along the upper Stanislaus River, but in 1984

Congress placed a similar portion of the Tuolumne under federal protection as a "wild and scenic" river. The following year, the Supreme Court upheld similar federal protection for large stretches of the Klamath, Trinity, Smith, and Eel rivers, all on the northwest coast, and the lower American River near Sacramento. The Court's ruling protected the rivers from dam building and logging. The Environmental Defense Fund hailed the Court's action as a "tremendous victory," whereas representatives of various water agencies and the state's timber industry complained that the ruling would have "dire economic consequences."

Water experts in the early 2000s warned that California faced a new era of "permanent drought" because its demand for water was rapidly outstripping the supply. By 2010, unless the state reduced its overall demand or reallocated its available supply, water shortages would occur 9 years out of 10. The state Department of Water Resources estimated that by 2020 California could experience a water shortfall equivalent to the combined needs of all the residents of Los Angeles and San Diego. "We've lived an illusion, creating an environment we could not support," said one water expert. "California has always been a semiarid environment, and that means we are naturally in a state of shortage. That is how we must learn to live."

Pesticides and Toxic Wastes

The use of pesticides and the disposal of toxic wastes in California became matters of intense controversy in recent decades. Each year California growers were applying more than 120 million pounds of pesticides, nearly one-third of the total used in the United States, to increase the yield and enhance the appearance of California farm produce. Because residues from the pesticides posed a danger to human health, state and federal agencies established minimum levels of tolerance and began a residue inspection program. Environmentalists charged these steps were inadequate, and in 1978 the administration of Democratic governor Jerry Brown instituted new regulations that subjected pesticides to stricter health and environmental tests, required manufacturers to provide more information on possible hazards, and established new requirements for the issuance of pesticide permits.

César Chávez, leader of the United Farm Workers (UFW), fasted for 36 days in 1988 to protest the continued use of pesticides that he claimed endangered agricultural workers as well as consumers. UFW officials attributed an unusually high number of birth defects and cancer deaths among farm worker children to the use of pesticides. The following year the legislature expanded the state's food-testing program, requiring farmers to keep detailed records of pesticide usage, and instituted a more vigorous system of assessment to measure the health effects of pesticide residues, especially on children. The number of pesticide-related illnesses steadily declined, but nearly a thousand cases a year still were being reported in the early 2000s.

Pesticide residues also posed a threat to California wildlife. In 1980 the Kesterson National Wildlife Refuge began receiving thousands of acre-feet of drainage water from irrigated farmlands in the San Joaquin Valley. Within a few years, gross abnormalities, deformities, and mutations were widespread among the refuge's wildlife population. Studies revealed that the wastewater flowing into the refuge contained high concentrations of salts from chemical fertilizers, pesticide residues, and the naturally occurring poison selenium. In 1985 the Interior Department ordered a halt to the flow of wastewater into Kesterson. Part of the refuge was ultimately declared a toxic dump, and hundreds of acres of poisoned ponds were filled with dirt. The manager of the refuge in 1991 pronounced the area "an environmental wasteland."

Even small amounts of agricultural chemicals could have a devastating impact on wildlife. In 1998 the United States Geological Service announced that pesticide concentrations in the San Joaquin River were among the highest in the nation. The pesticides killed invertebrates—mostly insects and tiny shrimp—critical for spawning salmon, steelhead trout, and striped bass. Pesticides also accumulated in riverbed sediments and in the tissues of fish and clams.

In response to growing consumer demand for chemical-free food products, state and federal legislation promoted what came to be called organic farming. Congress passed the Organic Foods Production Act in 1990 to boost organics from 2 to 10 percent of total agricultural production. The state legislature established its own innovative program at the University of California, Davis, to encourage the state's farmers to "go organic." The director of the program predicted that the day was fast approaching when there would be more reasons for California farmers to stop using pesticides than to continue using them. Peach grower David Mas Masumoto, one of California's 750 certified organic farmers, discovered that consumers were eager to buy his produce even though it lacked the cosmetic appeal of chemically enhanced products. "Organic customers don't buy with their eyes," Masumoto explained, "they buy with their taste buds in mind."

For decades the dumping of toxic substances from industrial and chemical plants in California went uncontrolled and largely unnoticed. By the mid-1980s, 26.5 million truckloads of toxic wastes were being produced in California each year—about one truckload per person. As the wastes began to leach into the surrounding soil and water supply and to release noxious fumes into the atmosphere, they became serious health hazards. One such dump in Fullerton, site of a newly completed housing project, was found to be emitting toxic vapors from chemicals capable of causing cancer and damaging the liver, respiratory tract, and central nervous system. California environmentalists soon won legislation creating some of the nation's strictest regulations for the treating and disposing of toxic wastes. Consequently, California industries began shipping their wastes to nearby (and less regulated) states. Between 1986 and 1990, the number of tons of toxics exported from the Golden State increased by more than 900 percent.

Federal and state agencies succeeded in cleaning up dozens of toxic-waste dump sites, but critics questioned the effectiveness of the cleanup operations and pointed out that many of the sites were small and insignificant. Los Angeles, Contra Costa, Alameda, Santa Clara, and Orange counties remained in the top 1 percent of the nation's hazardous-waste counties. "I'm not impressed with California's performance," concluded one federal official. "We've discovered that even a progressive state like California is doing a worse job at toxic cleanup than the federal government." Meanwhile, the federal government's own Superfund program to clean up the most seriously polluted sites was in nearly complete disarray, a victim of political indecision and fiscal gridlock. The major difficulties were the enormous costs involved and the uncertainty of who was to pay for the cleanup. Government researchers estimated that removing all the toxic substances from the 10,000 known dump sites in the nation would cost in excess of $1 trillion.

The decommissioning of the state's military bases in the aftermath of the cold war compounded the problem of toxic hazards. Remaining on the former bases were contaminants that had accumulated for decades. Of highest priority were hundreds of sites of unexploded ordnance. The Department of Toxic Substances Control removed from Monterey County's Fort Ord more than 100,000 rounds of various sizes and types of munitions.

California voters passed a major toxic-control initiative in 1986. Known as Proposition 65, the initiative required the state to maintain a list of chemicals known to cause cancer and birth defects. Each year thereafter, through the early 2000s, the state supplemented the list with additional toxins. The initiative also required businesses to warn consumers of possible exposure to toxic chemicals and prohibited their discharge into potential supplies of drinking water. Within 5 years of the initiative's passage, the state's Environmental Protection Agency (EPA) reported that 85 percent of the companies surveyed had reduced or eliminated some form of toxic exposure. "In its first 5 years, Proposition 65 produced 100 years of progress," commented an attorney for the Environmental Defense Fund.

Renewable Energy

California was hard hit by an energy crisis in the mid-1970s and again in the early 2000s. The first crisis was caused by a sudden rise in the cost of imported crude oil, leading to sharp increases in the price of gasoline and petroleum-generated electricity. Rising prices, coupled with growing concerns about pollution, led California to adopt a sweeping program of energy conservation measures and to develop a wide range of renewable energy technologies, Renewable energy is produced by low-polluting resources that do not run out or are quickly renewed through natural processes.

The California Energy Commission, formed in 1975, set maximum energy consumption limits for new household appliances sold in the state and established the nation's most stringent energy conservation standards for new residential and commercial buildings. The commission achieved substantial energy savings by requiring insulation in the walls, floors, and ceilings of all new construction, and by promoting the use of low-intensity lighting and double-paned windows. The energy efficiency of new appliances also improved remarkably. The amount of electricity needed to run an "energy saver" 1999 model refrigerator was less than a third of that needed to power a typical 1977 model. By 2000 the new energy standards had saved more than $16 million in energy costs; the savings were

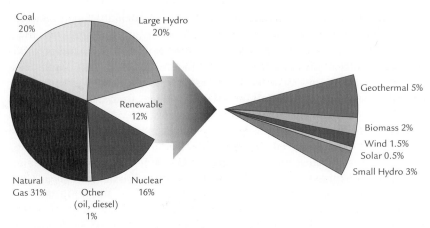

California sources for the generation of electricity, 2001. The state leads the nation in the development of renewable sources. (*Based on data from the California Energy Commission.*)

expected to exceed $43 billion by 2011, supplying three-quarters of the state's expected electricity needs.

California's major alternative energy sources were solar, wind, geothermal, biomass, and cogeneration. With an average of 270 days of sunshine a year, the state had more than 40 percent of the total United States solar collector capacity. The winds off the Pacific coastline represented an enormous energy potential, and the volatile geology of the state provided California with the nation's largest geothermal resources. Renewable energy sources supplied about 12 percent of California's total energy needs in the early 2000s, making the state's electrical power mix the most diverse in the nation.

The nation's first solar thermal power project began generating electricity in 1982. Called Solar One, the project was built for Southern California Edison in the Mojave Desert near Barstow. The power project consisted of 1800 giant *heliostats,* or mirrors, which reflected sunlight onto a central boiler-receiver atop a 300-foot tower. The receiver produced superheated steam, which was used to generate electricity. Additional power was generated by Solar Two, dedicated in 1996, and by a nearby plant that focused solar radiation on a heat transfer fluid in a horizontal tube. Farther north, in the San Joaquin Valley, an even more ambitious solar project used huge photovoltaic collectors to convert sunlight directly into electricity. The Energy Commission estimated that California sunlight could produce enough electricity to meet the state's entire electrical power needs. In spite of its enormous potential, solar energy was producing less than 1 percent of the state's total electricity in the early 2000s.

California's wind energy potential also far exceeded its development. During the early 1980s, the world's largest collection of windmills was built near Livermore in eastern Alameda County. Nearly 2000 wind turbines were installed at Altamont Pass in 10 strikingly different configurations. The windmills produced more than enough power to meet the electricity needs of all the households in the

Livermore area. Over the next two decades, more than 13,000 wind turbine genera-tors were installed throughout the state in such places as San Gorgonio Pass near Palm Springs and in the Tehachapi Mountains southeast of Bakersfield, making California far and away the wind-power capital of the world. Altogether these wind turbines produced about 1.5 percent of the state's electrical power, representing 30 percent of the world's supply of wind-generated electricity.

In 1960 the nation's first commercial geothermal power plant began operations at The Geysers in Sonoma County, where superheated steam released at the earth's surface was fed to turbines to generate electricity. California soon had 15 geother-mal plants in operation with a total output of more than 900 megawatts of power, representing enough electricity to meet the needs of a city nearly the size of San Francisco. (One megawatt equals 1000 kilowatts, enough power to supply the elec-tricity needs of about 1000 residential customers.) Geothermal resources elsewhere in California—notably in the Imperial Valley, along the eastern Sierra, and in the northeastern part of the state—boosted the total geothermal energy potential of the state to 15,000 megawatts. By the early 2000s, geothermal plants were producing about 5 percent of California's electrical power, representing 40 percent of the world's geothermally generated electricity.

Another important renewable energy source was biomass, the generation of elec-tricity from organic residues obtained from harvesting agricultural and forestry crops. Rather than being dumped into already overburdened landfills, the residues (such as forest slash) could be used as fuel in power plants. At their peak, biomass facilities generated more than 2 percent of the state's total electricity production. Additional power was provided by cogeneration, the use of waste heat, steam, or gases from an industrial plant for the generation of electricity. Used in Europe for decades, cogeneration only recently attracted much attention in the United States. To encourage its development, the California Public Utilities Commission (PUC) ordered the state's utilities to offer incentives to their large industrial customers so that they could profitably produce their own electricity.

California's commitment to the development of alternative sources of energy led to a remarkable change in the pattern of energy production. In 1977 California relied on petroleum for about 50 percent of its electricity generation. Three years later only 16 percent of the state's electricity came from this nonrenewable source, and by the early 2000s the proportion had been reduced to less than 1 percent.

Nuclear Power

The most controversial energy source was nuclear power. Energy planners in the early 1960s blithely predicted that by the end of the century, nuclear power would be able to supply half the nation's energy needs and would be "too cheap to meter." Forty years later that prospect had virtually disappeared.

The nation's first licensed commercial nuclear reactor began operations in 1957 at Vallecitos in Alameda County. The plant was shut down in 1977 by the federal Nuclear Regulatory Commission (NRC) after discovery of a nearby fault, making

'Someday, son, this will all be yours. And your son's. And your sons's son's. And your son's son's son's. And his son's. And his . . .'

Concern over the safe disposal of radioactive wastes from nuclear power plants inspired this 1974 editorial cartoon by Dennis Renault in the *Sacramento Bee*. (*Courtesy of the* Sacramento Bee.)

it vulnerable to earthquakes. In 1963 the Pacific Gas and Electric Company (PG&E) activated a second California reactor at Humboldt Bay. The Humboldt plant was plagued by malfunctions and frequent shutdowns after it was found to be releasing excessive amounts of radioactive vapors. It was closed in 1976 for failure to meet seismic safety standards, and 7 years later PG&E announced the plant's permanent shutdown. The first large-scale nuclear facility in California, the San Onofre plant located halfway between Los Angeles and San Diego, began operations in 1968 and by 1980 was providing Southern California Edison with 4 percent of its energy supply. In northern California the Rancho Seco plant near Sacramento went on-line in 1975, but a series of breakdowns kept it from operating at full capacity. The Rancho Seco facility, owned by the Sacramento Municipal Utility District, earned a reputation for being the nation's least reliable nuclear plant and eventually was shut down by a vote of the people.

Opposition to nuclear power arose out of concern for the safe disposal of radioactive wastes produced by the plants, which remain potentially lethal for thousands of years. Opponents also feared the disastrous consequences of an accident at a nuclear plant. In 1976 the legislature prohibited the California Energy Commission from authorizing construction of any further nuclear plants until the federal government had approved "a documented technology for the disposal of

The Diablo Canyon nuclear power plant. (*Courtesy of Pacific Gas and Electric Company.*)

high-level nuclear waste." Already authorized was the massive 2200-megawatt nuclear plant built for PG&E at Diablo Canyon near San Luis Obispo. Construction of the Diablo Canyon plant began in 1969 and was nearly complete when PG&E reported the discovery of a major offshore earthquake fault. After extensive new buttresses and other safeguards were added, the first unit of the facility began producing electricity in 1985. The following year—more than 17 years after construction began—the entire plant went into full production.

Public opposition, and the enormous costs involved, seemed to have doomed the nuclear power industry. By the early 2000s, no American utility had proposed construction of a new nuclear plant for a quarter of a century. In California only the San Onofre and Diablo Canyon plants remained in operation; together they supplied about 16 percent of the state's electricity. Attitudes toward nuclear power, however, began to shift (at least temporarily) during the electric energy crisis. Whereas in 1984 two-thirds of all Californians had opposed nuclear power, nearly 60 percent favored the construction of new nuclear plants in 2001.

Petroleum Dependency

California made substantial progress in the development of alternative sources of energy for the production of electricity, but still unsolved was the state's dependence on petroleum as a fuel for transportation. Petroleum, of course, is a finite resource. Once it is used up, it cannot be replaced.

The proportion of California's total energy needs that were met by petroleum was one-fourth higher than that of the nation as a whole. California's higher level of oil dependency was due mainly to the state's huge transportation system, which

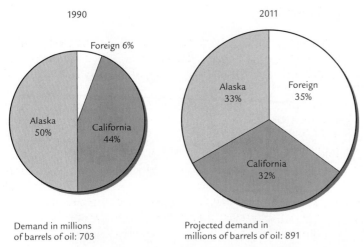

1990

2011

Foreign 6%

Alaska
50%

California
44%

Alaska
33%

Foreign
35%

California
32%

Demand in millions
of barrels of oil: 703

Projected demand in
millions of barrels of oil: 891

California's growing dependence on foreign sources of petroleum. (*Based on data
from the California Energy Commission.*)

was over 99 percent reliant on oil. It was readily apparent that the use of petroleum
could be reduced by increasing the efficiency of the transportation system and by
developing alternative transportation fuels. In response to the energy crisis of the
mid-1970s, the California Department of Transportation promoted a variety of
projects—ride sharing, park-and-ride lots, exclusive bus and carpool lanes—to increase the energy efficiency of the state's highway system. Federal and state regulators mandated greater fuel efficiency for new vehicles and encouraged drivers to
moderate their speed. Cars that averaged 25 miles per gallon (mpg) at 70 miles per
hour (mph) could get 30 mpg at 55 mph. The California Energy Commission also
began studying a variety of alternative transportation fuels, including methanol,
ethanol, gasohol, natural gas, propane, and synthetic fuels. It found that methanol
was the most promising alternative. Methanol was cleaner burning than other fuels
and could be produced from biomass, natural gas, oil, or coal. The Energy Commission, in cooperation with private industry, put more than 6500 methanol-fueled
vehicles into public and private transportation fleets. The Golden Gate Transit District, Yosemite National Park, and Federal Express introduced methanol-fueled vehicles for regular use. And major automakers—including Ford, General Motors,
and Volkswagen—developed prototype methanol-powered cars.

In spite of such gains, California's dependence on petroleum for transportation
remained undiminished, and its reliance on foreign sources steadily increased. The
Persian Gulf crisis in 1991 and the war in Afghanistan a decade later demonstrated
the importance of reducing the nation's reliance on a vital resource from such a
volatile region as the Middle East. The California Energy Commission reported
that the state's reliance on foreign sources of petroleum rose from 6 percent in
1990 to 22 percent in 1999 and predicted that it would rise to 35 percent by 2011.
The chairperson of the commission issued a dire warning: "The general public
doesn't realize the relatively precarious nature of the energy supplies we rely on."

The Electric Energy Crisis

The abundance of inexpensive supplies of fossil fuels in the 1980s and 1990s lulled many Californians into assuming the energy crisis was over. That assumption was challenged in the early 2000s with the onset of a crisis in the supply and pricing of electricity.

The latest crisis was precipitated by the state legislature's restructuring of state energy policy in 1996. Prior to restructuring, providers of electricity in California had been regulated by the Public Utilities Commission as "natural monopolies." Three investor-owned utilities—Pacific Gas and Electric, Southern California Edison, and San Diego Gas and Electric—supplied about 85 percent of the state's electricity. Under the old system, the utilities operated their own power plants and transmission lines. The PUC granted the utilities the exclusive right to sell electricity within their regions at rates that guaranteed a return to their investors above the costs of production. The utilities, lacking sufficient incentives to improve efficiency or reduce costs, steadily raised their PUC-approved rates. By the mid-1990s, Californians were paying rates 50 percent higher than the national average.

The utilities and their large industrial customers, along with out-of-state power generators and marketers, joined forces to demand a change in state energy policy. The resulting restructuring plan—massively complex and little understood—was unanimously approved by the legislature in 1996.

The restructuring plan required the utilities to divest themselves of most of their electricity-generating power plants. The legislature expected that increased competition among independent power producers would lower wholesale electricity prices and consumers' utility bills by as much as 25 percent. Beginning in 1998, retail electricity rates were frozen at 1996 levels, where they were scheduled to remain for several years. The plan also created two new state agencies. The Independent System Operator (ISO) was to regulate the flow of electricity through the statewide grid of transmission lines. The Power Exchange (PX) would act as a commodities market from which the big three utilities were required to purchase their electric power.

Problems with the plan first became apparent in the summer of 2000 when the temporary rate freeze was removed in San Diego. Customers of the San Diego Gas and Electric Company, expecting rates to drop, were startled to find their utility bills suddenly tripled. Maureen O'Connor, the former mayor of San Diego, urged the legislature to scrap the restructuring plan. "We already have the train wreck in San Diego," she warned her fellow Californians. "It's coming your way next."

What apparently had been unforeseen by the legislature was a sharp rise in the wholesale electricity rates charged by the companies that had bought power plants from the state's utilities. The power companies—headquartered in Texas, North Carolina, Georgia, and other states—increased the wholesale price of electricity from $30 per megawatt hour to more than $400. The profits of the power generators and marketers surged accordingly, more than quadrupling within a single year. Governor Gray Davis denounced the "out-of-state profiteers" for price gouging. One California consumer advocate declared that the increased rates represented the greatest "transfer of wealth from people in this state to those outside the state in

"Get in, Tom—we're goin' to Oklahoma. Hear tell they got 'lectricity."

California's electric energy crisis was viewed with amusement on the pages of the *New Yorker* in 2001. (© *The* New Yorker *Collection 2001, by Tom Hachtman, from cartoonbank.com. All rights reserved.*)

history." A spokesperson for the power industry invoked classical economics to defend the price rise: "In a free market, people will charge whatever the market will bear."

The state's two largest utilities were caught in a bind. Both PG&E and Southern California Edison remained subject to the state-mandated freeze on the retail prices they could charge their customers. The power generators, meanwhile, were charging the utilities dramatically higher wholesale prices. Crushed by the yawning disparity between wholesale and retail rates, the utilities accumulated billions of dollars of debt, lost their creditworthiness, defaulted on payments to their suppliers, and eventually were unable to purchase enough electricity to meet their customers' needs. In early 2001, for the first time ever, the entire state was hit by rolling blackouts. Blocks of the statewide power grid were shut down, leaving more than a million customers temporarily without electricity.

Leaders of state government responded to the crisis in a variety of ways. Governor Gray Davis began by challenging Californians to reduce their overall demand for electricity. Consumers responded by purchasing water-heater blankets, fluorescent bulbs, window insulation kits, and other energy-saving products. Electricity use fell by more than 10 percent, exceeding the goal set by the governor. To encourage the expanded development of renewable energy sources, the legislature established a fund of $540 million to support new and emerging energy technologies. The governor signed additional legislation to support expanded renewable energy development by $135 million a year through 2012.

Governor Davis and the legislature realized, however, that conservation and the development of renewable energy sources alone were not sufficient to meet the immediate crisis. Using emergency powers, the governor in 2001 streamlined the approval process for the accelerated building of dozens of new power plants. No major new plants had been built in California for a decade or more, yet each year electricity demand had increased as the state's population and economy expanded. Said Davis: "I am determined to get as much power on-line as humanly possible."

The state government also took action to aid the ailing utility companies. Governor Davis began buying electricity daily on behalf of the cash-starved utilities. He also signed long-term contracts with power companies for enough electricity to meet the needs of 9 million residential customers. The contracts, valued at $43 billion, were hailed by the governor as "the bedrock of a long-term energy solution." To finance the purchases, the legislature approved a bond issue, the largest sale of its kind in the nation's history. The PUC in 2001 unanimously approved an average 40 percent increase in the retail prices the utilities could charge their customers. The rate increase, tiered to encourage conservation, was the biggest ever approved. "These are extraordinary moments in California history," said one commissioner, "and extraordinary moments demand extraordinary courage." Chanting protesters responded with cries of "Hell no, we won't pay."

In 2001 Governor Davis also signed an agreement with Southern California Edison to buy its transmission lines, thus providing the utility with an infusion of cash and a restoration of its credit. In exchange, the utility agreed to provide low-cost power to its customers for the next 10 years. Davis failed in his efforts to sign a similar agreement with PG&E. The northern California utility, having funneled hundreds of millions of dollars to its parent company, chose to declare bankruptcy. The announcement came just hours after PG&E awarded its top managers $50 million in bonuses and raises. "PG&E's management is suffering from two afflictions," declared an outraged governor, "denial and greed."

State and federal regulatory agencies soon launched a series of investigations of the electric power generators. The PUC charged the generators with illegally manipulating prices by deliberately withholding electricity. The Federal Energy Regulatory Agency (FERC) probed charges of price gouging by the generators and imposed sweeping price ceilings on wholesale energy prices. The price caps were supported by Democratic senator Dianne Feinstein and Governor Davis; they were vigorously opposed by the power generators as unwise and counterproductive. Davis also demanded that the FERC order a refund to California of $9 billion in overcharges. The generators, Davis charged, "have taken advantage of the market, gamed the system, and ripped people off."

For some observers the electric energy crisis was damning evidence of the power of money in the political process. Windfall profits were being reaped by the very same interests that had supported the restructuring legislation that precipitated the crisis. Attention soon focused on Enron Corporation, a huge Texas-based energy marketing firm. Enron was one of the loudest voices calling for restructuring in 1996 and later raked in enormous profits as wholesale energy prices skyrocketed. Following the spectacular collapse of Enron, state and federal officials began investigating charges that the company had conspired to drive up prices by manipulating the California energy market. "Enron's fingerprints are all over all the dysfunctional parts of the market," commented an aide to the chair of the state legislative committee on deregulation. "The energy crisis story in California raises a national issue, not only because of the challenge of meeting the crisis itself," observed the president of Common Cause in 2001, "but because it's a classic example of the influence, or the potential influence, of money in politics."

By the beginning of 2002, the crisis seemed to have passed. California's electricity needs were being met by new power plants that had come on-line and by the long-term contracts signed by the governor (contracts that critics charged had locked the state into buying too much power at too high a price). Californians also continued to practice energy conservation. "The days of the blackouts are over," declared energy expert Peter Navarro of the University of California, Irvine. "We have an embarrassment of power riches."

Others were not so sure. They warned that supplying future energy needs remained one of the gravest challenges of the twenty-first century. Alistair W. McCrone, petroleum geologist and president of Humboldt State University, believed that the state's recent electricity supply and price problems were but the beginning of crises "on a much wider and larger scale." What had happened in California was the harbinger of a global energy crisis to come. Worldwide energy production, based on the burning of petroleum and other fossil fuels, would begin to decline around the year 2010. The decline would start slowly and then accelerate with growing swiftness. United States Energy Secretary Spencer Abraham concurred: "America faces a major energy crisis over the next two decades. The failure to meet this challenge will threaten our nation's prosperity, compromise our nation's security, and literally alter the way we live our lives."

Selected Bibliography

Among the finest books on contemporary environmental issues are Robert Dawson and Gray Brechin, *Farewell Promised Land* (1999), a devastating portrait; Carolyn Merchant (ed.), *Green versus Gold* (1998), a collection of sources; Mike Davis, *Ecology of Fear* (1998), a nightmare vision; Carl G. Thelander (ed.), *California on the Edge* (1994); and Tim Palmer (ed.), *California's Threatened Environment* (1993). Also useful is Bern Kreissman, *California: An Environmental Atlas and Guide* (1991). For historical background, see Raymond F. Dasmann, *The Destruction of California* (1965), *California's Changing Environment* (1981), and "Environmental History," an edition of the *Pacific Historical Review,* XLI (August 1972). One of the best case studies is Alfred Runte, *Yosemite: The Embattled*

Wilderness (1991). For a critique of the environmental movement, see Bernard J. Frieden, *The Environmental Hustle* (1979).

The coastal issue is examined in Stanley Scott (ed.), *Coastal Conservation* (1981), and John Woolfenden, *Big Sur* (1981). On the issues of land use and conservation, see Stephanie S. Pincetl, *Transforming California* (1999), and Frank Wheat, *California Desert Miracle: The Fight for Desert Parks and Wilderness* (1999). See also David E. Dowall, *The Suburban Squeeze* (1986), and Rob Kling, Spencer Olin, and Mark Poster (eds.), *Postsuburban California* (1991).

Competition for California Water (1982), edited by Ernest A. Englebert, is a symposium on alternative solutions to the state's future water needs. *The California Water Atlas* (1980), edited by William Kahrl, is a monumental collection of maps and text illustrating the development of state water resources; the definitive study is Norris Hundley, Jr., *The Great Thirst: Californians and Water* (1992). See also the sources on California water cited in Chapter 24. The best account of the controversies over Lake Tahoe and Mono Lake are Douglas Strong, *Tahoe: An Environmental History* (1984), and John Hart, *Storm over Mono* (1996). State and federal efforts to reduce smog may be followed in James E. Krier and Edmund Ursin, *Pollution and Policy* (1977).

James C. Williams provides historical background to the energy issue in *Energy and the Making of Modern California* (1997). Raymond Vernon, *The Oil Crisis* (1976), contains a discussion of the national and international aspects of the escalation of OPEC (Organization of Oil Exporting Countries) prices, and several articles in *California Journal*, XXXII (January 2001), discuss the electric power crisis of the early 2000s. On the controversy over nuclear power, see Thomas Raymond Wellock, *Critical Masses: Opposition to Nuclear Power in California, 1958–1975* (1998), and John W. Gofman and Arthur Tamplin, *Poisoned Power* (1971). The energy potential of conservation and renewable resources is described in Robert W. Righter, "Wind Energy in California," *California History,* LXXIII (Summer 1994), pp. 142–155; Robert Stobaugh and Daniel Yergin (eds.), *Energy Future* (1979); and Jennifer K. Hollon, *Solar Energy for California's Residential Sector* (1980). For a full assessment of public policy affecting California energy use, see the biennial report of the California Energy Commission.

CHAPTER 35

The New California Economy

California's economic growth in recent decades has been phenomenal. The state leads the nation in the most advanced technological fields, including electronics, computers, multimedia, aerospace, and bioengineering. It has emerged as the global center of the New Economy in which information, goods, and services are accessible worldwide via the Internet. It also remains the nation's leading agricultural state, number one travel destination, and home of the entertainment industry. If California were an independent nation, it would be one of the world's major economic powers, ranking sixth in gross domestic product.

The Sunbelt Shift

The remarkable growth of the California economy has been a part of one of the greatest population shifts in American history. Since World War II, the southern and western regions of the country have grown much more rapidly than the northeast and midwest. The population of what came to be called the Sunbelt more than doubled between 1940 and 1980, whereas the population of the so-called Frostbelt increased by less than half.

The most commonly used indicators for economic growth are gross product, employment, and income. California's annual gross product, the value of all goods and services produced in the state, doubled between 1960 and 1985. Fifteen years later, California was producing one-eighth of the country's goods and services; its trillion-dollar economy exceeded the gross product of all but five nations. Employment in California also grew rapidly. Between 1950 and 1980, while older regions of the country were suffering from structural unemployment, California's labor force grew by 250 percent. The state lost jobs during the recession of the early 1990s but gained them all back—and a million and a half more—by the end of the decade. Economic forecasters in 2000 predicted that California would post a 25 percent gain in jobs by

2010, compared to a national growth of less than 15 percent. As California entered the twenty-first century, its major metropolitan centers continued to generate more employment opportunities than those of any other state. The booming Los Angeles basin emerged as the world's twelfth largest economy. Twenty-five of the nation's fastest-growing companies were in California, compared to just five each in New York and Massachusetts. "I don't think there's any question that New York simply isn't the dominant city," concluded an economist at Chase Manhattan Bank. "The whole point is, there's a shift away from New York and to Los Angeles."

The economic indicator that best represented the welfare of the average Californian was personal income. Following the dramatic increase in per capita income during World War II, Californians continued to earn more than most of their fellow Americans. By 1959 California ranked third among the states in per capita income. During the economic boom of the late 1990s, household income in the technology-rich San Francisco Bay area zoomed to nearly 50 percent above the national average. Sunbelt denizens of the New Economy—enjoying a steady increase in disposable income and a rising standard of living—became the envy of the nation. Stephen Levy, cofounder of the Center for Continuing Study of the California Economy, remained optimistic even as the state and nation slipped back into recession in 2001, ending the longest economic expansion on record. "California is ideally positioned for the next few years," commented Levy. "We believe that the state will continue to outpace the nation in jobs, income, and spending."

The Pacific Rim

Californians found themselves beneficiaries of another, even more far-reaching shift in the national economy. In 1977 the Pacific Rim overtook Europe as the leading trading partner of the United States. The 28 nations bordering the Pacific emerged as the most dynamic economic region in the world.

California had established itself as a major partner in trans-Pacific trade in the years before World War II. Standard Oil of California led the way by opening Japan as a market for the state's petroleum exports. This profitable trade was interrupted by the war but was reestablished as part of the American postwar reconstruction of Japan. Even before the war's end, California entrepreneurs were looking to the rebuilding of the shattered economies of East Asia. Henry Kaiser, speaking before the San Francisco Chamber of Commerce, declared in July 1945: "I accept the judgment of the experts who proclaim that the Pacific Basin will be the theatre where civilization makes its next great advance. . . . I am ready to accept the forecast that the Orient will be one of our best customers, even as we will be one of theirs."

The driving force in the rise of the Pacific Rim was the economic vitality of the nations of East Asia. Japan, at the center of the emerging Asian industrial complex, developed the most productive workforce and industrial plant in the world. South Korea, Taiwan, and Hong Kong outperformed the economies of virtually every major European country.

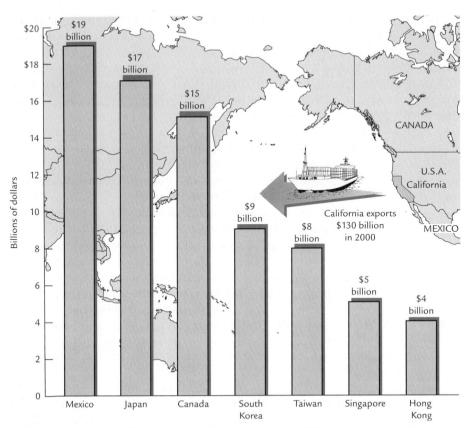

California's top seven Pacific Rim markets. (*Based on data from the Office of Economic Research, California Trade and Commerce Agency.*)

This shift in the global economy was viewed with considerable apprehension in the world's traditional economic centers—from London and Paris to Boston and New York. In California, however, the view was much more sanguine. "Our future is with the Pacific Basin," observed the director of the California Office of International Trade. "Sixty percent of humanity lives there, over forty percent of all world trade. We're right in the middle of it. If the Basin prospers, we prosper."

In the mid-1990s, Los Angeles overtook New York as America's premier gateway for foreign trade. Forty percent of all United States trade with the Pacific Rim passed through California's ports. Exports to Asia slumped near the decade's end, during a severe downturn in the Asian economy, but soon rebounded. By 2000 California accounted for more than 20 percent of the nation's total foreign trade, up from just 10 percent two decades earlier. Chief among the state's exports were electronic components and computer equipment, as well as advanced services such as engineering and financial consulting. The recession and the terrorist attacks of September 2001 led to another temporary dip in California's foreign trade. Especially hard hit were exports to Asian countries that assembled California-made components into finished products.

State and local officials soon took positive steps to encourage stronger commercial ties with the Pacific Rim. Delegations from San Francisco, Oakland, and Los Angeles visited Tokyo, Beijing, Manila, and other Asian cities. New trade links and sister-city agreements were signed. The California Trade and Commerce Agency sent missions to various Asian capitals to promote trade and investment, and the University of California established at its San Diego campus a new teaching and degree program for Pacific Rim studies.

California trade with the nations of the Pacific Rim also was boosted by the North American Free Trade Agreement (NAFTA), approved by Congress in 1993. NAFTA allowed the tariff-free exchange of goods, services, and investments among the United States, Canada, and Mexico. Over the next decade, trade with Mexico and Canada increased dramatically; by 1999 Mexico had surpassed Japan as California's number one trading partner. About three-quarters of the new trade was with Mexican *maquiladoras,* foreign-owned factories that principally exist to manufacture goods for the United States market. As hundreds of American-owned factories sprang up along the border, San Diego and Tijuana became the world's largest center for the manufacture of televisions, producing also many of the VCRs and cellular phones sold in the United States. Journalists dubbed the region "the Gringo Archipelago" and "San Dijuana." Critics charged that maquiladoras were taking jobs away from American workers, violating Mexican workers' rights, and increasing pollution. Lon Hatamiya, director of the California Trade and Commerce Agency, was more positive. "Maquiladoras," he said, "are a tremendous opportunity for California."

The future of trade with the Pacific Rim brightened in the early 2000s with the normalization of trade relations with China, the world's most populous nation. The United States Senate granted China "permanent normal trade relations" in 2000, and the following year China joined the World Trade Organization (WTO). Normalization was opposed by human rights activitists, anticommunists, and some unions and environmentalists. But the prospect of increased trade with China was greeted with enthusiasm by California manufacturers and agribusinesses. "This is truly a landmark achievement," said a spokesperson for one of the state's largest corporations. "By opening, once and for all, the vast Chinese market, we've opened broad new doorways of opportunity for exports and investments."

California's foreign trade doubled during the 1990s, with annual exports rising to $130 billion by 2000. The nations of the Pacific Rim continued to be the state's leading trade partners and were expected to experience the world's highest rates of economic development through the early 2000s. The phenomenal growth of foreign trade, especially with the dynamic nations of the Pacific Rim, became one of the mainstays of California's New Economy.

The Post-Industrial Revolution

California's economy in the twentieth century not only expanded dramatically but also underwent a basic transformation in terms of the kind of work being performed to earn a living.

Social scientists divide economies into three sectors or stages of development. The primary sector includes jobs that produce the basic raw materials needed for living. Jobs in agriculture, mining, forestry, and fishing are considered part of this sector. The primary sector is the basis of all pre-industrial societies. The secondary sector, which encompasses manufacturing and construction, is the foundation of an industrial society. The, tertiary, or third, sector of the economy is composed mainly of jobs in the service fields. Service jobs include health care, wholesale and retail trade, finance, insurance, real estate, government, transportation, communication, and utilities. The service fields expand as technological improvements in both the primary and secondary sectors increase productivity and enable workers to move on to other areas of employment. The rise of the service sector has been called the *post-industrial revolution,* a twentieth-century phenomenon as fundamental as the nineteenth-century shift from an agricultural to an industrial economy.

The national economy became post-industrial sometime around 1956, when for the first time more than half the nation's workers were employed in service industries. California reached this crossover point far earlier. By the 1920s, over half of all Californians in the workforce were employed in the service sector. The tertiary sector grew to nearly 70 percent by 1970, far outdistancing the secondary sector, which accounted for only 27 percent of the labor force, and the primary sector, which had fallen to about 3 percent.

In spite of the predominance of the service industries, it would be premature to conclude that manufacturing was no longer an important part of the California economy. Ever since 1974, California has led the nation in employment in manufacturing and has remained the number one industrial state, leading in almost every general manufacturing category.

But manufacturing in California was changing fundamentally. Small firms creating consumer goods dependent on design and style were replacing large manufacturers of heavy industrial products. The trend was especially evident in southern California, where creative entrepreneurs carved out niches in textiles, apparel, furniture, and toys. Los Angeles emerged as a leader in women's fashion. The "southern California look" in casual apparel was sought eagerly by style-conscious consumers around the world.

The nature of work in California's New Economy was being transformed in other ways. In the old economy, traditional employment meant holding a single, full-time job year-round. Only about a third of the state's labor force fit that pattern by the early twenty-first century. Instead, vast numbers of Californians held part-time jobs, telecommuted, or were employed as independent contractors. The rate of job turnover also was on the rise. Forty percent of California workers, traditional or otherwise, had been at their current jobs for under 3 years. "California is on the leading edge of change in the workforce," commented Laura Trupin, a senior researcher at the University of California, San Francisco.

High Technology

The key factor in the economic transformation of California has been technological innovation. Technology was the driving force of the post-industrial revolution, just as it had been for the earlier transformation of the nation from an agricultural to an industrial society.

Technology in California has been bolstered by successive waves of foreign-aid-style support from the federal government. The massive federal spending in the state during World War II continued after the war, and thus Washington helped finance the postwar economic expansion of California just as it did that of Japan and Germany. The influx of federal aid tended to concentrate in California the most sophisticated technologies as well as a high level of technical expertise.

In the decades since the end of World War II, the center of much of California's high-tech industry has been the Santa Clara Valley. Once known as the Valley of Heart's Delight, this 25-mile stretch of the San Francisco peninsula was rechristened in the early 1970s as Silicon Valley. The valley was generating 20 percent of all the high-tech jobs in the United States by 1980. Twenty years later it was the undisputed capital of the global New Economy. Los Angeles, Orange, and San Diego counties also emerged as major high-tech centers.

The California electronics industry began early in the twentieth century. In 1909 Stanford University president David Starr Jordon invested $500 in a company sponsoring the pioneering work of a local Palo Alto engineer, Lee de Forest. Three years later de Forest perfected the vacuum tube, a key invention in the evolution of modern electronics. The vacuum tube became the basis for future developments in radio, television, tape recorders, and early computers. Another local inventor, Philo Farnsworth, developed a technique for the electronic projection of pictures. Farnsworth achieved the first successful television transmission in 1927.

The person most responsible for the development of Silicon Valley was Frederick Terman, a professor of electrical engineering at Stanford. Terman became disturbed that his students often had to leave the state in order to find jobs as engineers. He began to encourage his graduates to form their own companies near the university. Two of Terman's brightest young students, William Hewlett and David Packard, acted on his suggestion and formed an electronics company in a Palo Alto garage. From this humble beginning in 1938 came one of the world's largest and most successful electronics firms. In 1946 Frederick Terman became the dean of the Stanford engineering school. He proposed that the university lease some of its vast real estate holdings to local industries. The proposal was accepted, and in 1951 Stanford Industrial (later Research) Park was created. The sleek, campuslike facilities of the park set a precedent for Silicon Valley industrial architecture.

Another important step in the evolution of California's high-tech industry was the formation of the Shockley Transistor Company in Palo Alto in 1956. Stanford professor William Shockley, whose discredited views on race and intelligence would later spark great controversy, discovered the principle that made possible the transistor. Transistors were far more efficient and long-lasting than vacuum tubes, and they represented a quantum leap forward in miniaturization. Transistors soon became the basis for a new generation of compact calculators, radios, televisions, and other electronic devices. The Shockley laboratories also experimented with the use of silicon as a semiconductor of electricity. Silicon, a common ingredient in beach sand, is the earth's most abundant element after oxygen. When mixed with minute bits of other chemicals, silicon could transmit on-off electrical signals—the basis of all modern computers—at incredible speeds. In a process that would repeat itself many times in the years ahead, eight of Shockley's top engineers left the company in 1957 to form their own firm. The new company, Fairchild Semiconductor, became the valley's first viable semiconductor company.

The most significant technological breakthrough in the history of electronics was the introduction in 1959 of the integrated circuit, commonly known as "the chip." Made of silicon and measuring a mere quarter inch on a side, the earliest chips could hold more than a million electronic components. The microprocessor, or "computer on a chip," was a marvel of seemingly infinite capacity; the number of components that could be crammed onto a given area of silicon doubled every 18 to 24 months. This was the technical basis for the exponential increase in power and memory of an endless stream of upgraded computer products. By the early 2000s, the typical personal computer had more processing power than those of entire corporations or governments a few decades earlier.

Demand for the latest marvels of California's technological wizardry was worldwide. High-tech products accounted for more than half the state's total exports by the end of the twentieth century; leading the way were computer components, including software, keyboards, disk drives, and specialized workstations. The normalization of trade relations with China presented California's high-tech firms with a virtually unlimited potential market. Whereas nearly 60 percent of Americans had personal computers in 2000, only one-tenth of 1 percent of China's 1.3 billion citizens were similarly provisioned. The president of the American Electronics Association was ecstatic. China, he noted, was "a country hell-bent on becoming more technologically advanced."

California also emerged as the world's biotechnology capital. Biochemists at Stanford University in the early 1980s discovered key enzymes that allowed foreign genes to be spliced into other cells. This discovery paved the way for the first bioengineered drugs and gave birth to the biotech industry. Eventually, about a third of all genetic engineering companies were headquartered in California, far more than in any other state. The largest biotech cluster was in the San Francisco Bay area, followed by Los Angeles and Orange counties. Biotechnology achieved a major breakthrough in 2000 when geneticists completed a preliminary mapping of the human genome, the complex genetic code that influences every aspect of human development. Entrepreneurs filed patents to prove they were the first to discover particular genes, thereby winning the right to monopolize drugs or therapies later derived from the genes. "The year 2000 will be viewed as the beginning of the genetic revolution," observed one Bay Area scientist.

The success of California's high-tech industry rested on a unique combination of factors. Foremost was the contribution of the state's colleges and universities. California's leading institutions of higher education—including Stanford University, the University of California, and the California Institute of Technology—established themselves as centers for the most advanced work in the natural sciences, mathematics, chemistry, physics, and engineering. The universities provided the ideas and the technical knowledge necessary for technological innovation.

A second factor in the rise of California high technology was the ready availability of capital. Not only was the federal government pumping billions of dollars into the state each year for research and development, but local financial institutions were also eager to invest in the high-tech boom.

The growth of high technology also depended on the personal ambition of thousands of hard-driving California entrepreneurs. Often young and from modest backgrounds, the successful high-tech entrepreneurs combined sophisticated technical knowledge with sharp business skills. Steven Jobs and Stephen Wozniak, cofounders of Apple Computer, were typical of this new breed of business executive. Jobs and Wozniak built their first computer in a Los Altos garage in 1976. Within 5 years, Apple Computer occupied more than 20 buildings in Silicon Valley and had assembly plants around the world. Commenting on the wealth and lifestyle of California's new high-tech elite, *Fortune* magazine observed that Silicon Valley seemed to be "mass-producing millionaires."

High technology was not only producing California millionaires, it was also creating a new set of problems for the state. Electronics, especially the production of semiconductors, required a labor force that was markedly different from that of traditional manufacturing. At the top were highly skilled technical and professional workers. Compared with other industries, these workers were more numerous and better paid. The actual production work, however, required large numbers of low-skilled workers. Wages for these workers were below average for manufacturing. Many earned barely more than the minimum wage. Furthermore, the opportunity for advancement for these workers was less than in traditional industries.

For many years, the high-tech industry was viewed as a clean, light, "sunrise" industry as compared with the heavy, dirty smokestack industries of the past. This image was challenged in 1981 when officials in South San Jose discovered that more than 50,000 gallons of highly toxic solvents and other waste chemicals had leaked into the local water supply. The chemicals had come from an underground storage tank at a nearby manufacturing plant owned by Fairchild Semiconductor. Local residents blamed the leak for an unusually high incidence of birth defects, miscarriages, and liver and kidney diseases. In subsequent investigations, at least 120 other sites were identified where toxic solvents were leaking from underground tanks. One Silicon Valley investigator warned, "We're sitting on a toxic timebomb." By 1986, Santa Clara County had earned the dubious honor of having more federal toxic cleanup sites than any other county in the nation.

High-tech companies also were identified as sources of air pollution. Although most of the smog was belched from the automobiles of electronics workers driving to and from their jobs, semiconductor firms also were emitting tons of fumes and toxic gases into the air each day through hidden vents. The air quality of Santa Clara County was consistently ranked as the worst in the Bay Area.

The rapid growth of the high-tech industry exposed California to the danger of the "Detroit syndrome," so called for that city's reliance on automobile manufacturing, as Silicon Valley and other areas in the state became almost totally dependent on the electronics industry. The danger of such overreliance became apparent during the recessions of the early 1990s and early 2000s as layoffs, plant closings, mandatory vacations, and salary cuts were announced almost daily at semiconductor and computer-related companies. Following the terrorist attacks of 2001, the high-tech industry scrambled to recoup some of its losses by marketing state-of-the-art security gear to consumers beset by terrorism-generated anxieties.

The Internet Revolution

California's high-tech industry experienced a dizzying round of rapid growth with the advent of the Internet in the late 1990s.

The latest technology was truly revolutionary. Information and products from anywhere in the world were instantly accessible via the Internet. Known first as "the information superhighway," the Internet soon became the indispensable marketplace for e-commerce (business conducted electronically). By 2001 more than half of all American adults were Internet users. With the proliferation of home and business computers, dot-com entrepreneurs hastened to meet the seemingly insatiable demand for on-line goods and services available 24/7/365 (24 hours a day, 7 days a week, 365 days a year).

The explosion of e-commerce was the new California gold rush. Eager dot-commers rushed to stake their claims on the World Wide Web. Speed was of the essence. Internet startup companies raced to get the FMA (first-mover advantage), to do it FBC (faster, bigger, cheaper), and to GBF (get big fast). The dream of every fledgling startup was the initial public offering (IPO), the conversion of a company from private to public ownership, selling its shares on the stock market and making its founders rich enough to retire for life.

The on-line New Economy was fueled by an unprecedented increase in investment capital. More than $1 billion *a week* flowed into startups in 2000, with San Francisco Bay area firms capturing a third of the nation's total. Internet companies received 84 percent of the new capital, compared to just 41 percent 2 years earlier. On-line marketing doubled annually during the late 1990s; global e-commerce transactions were expected to reach $6 trillion by 2004. In the words of one self-satisfied venture capitalist, the Internet represented "the largest legal creation of wealth in the history of the planet!"

Silicon Valley was at the heart of the Internet revolution, but its boundaries expanded to include other Bay Area locations. The spread of telecommunications transformed parts of Sonoma County into "Telecom Valley"; San Francisco was home not only to many of the largest investment banks but also to "Multimedia Gulch"; other venture capitalists were concentrated in San Mateo County. Pervading everything was a culture that rewarded risk-taking and fast-paced innovation. "At its core," commented journalist Joe Garofoli, "the Silicon Valley boom is a confluence of smart and driven people turned on by the intellectual buzz of inventing and reinventing the world and themselves."

That buzz, however, began to sputter in the early 2000s. The rapid growth of the Internet fueled a binge of spending on computers and software by dot-com startups and by traditional businesses gearing up for e-commerce. "The Internet bubble drove spending ever higher," noted one economist. "Capital spending got ahead of itself." With inventories at all-time highs, the corporate demand for high-tech products contracted rapidly. Consumer demand also declined as customers became temporarily satiated by their ingestion of all the latest technological gizmos. "What's left to buy," asked *Time* magazine, "when you already have your SUV, your DVD, and your MP3?"

Evidence of an economic slowdown was registered on the tech-dominated NASDAQ stock exchange, where equity prices plummeted. The flow of venture capital into Internet-related companies slowed precipitously, high-tech industry leaders (such as Cisco Systems, Intel, and 3Com) laid off tens of thousands of workers, and hundreds of dot-coms in the San Francisco Bay area failed. Southern California, with its more diversified economy, was less affected by the downturn. "In the wake of the dot-com collapse, the south has emerged as the sturdier pillar of the state's economy," the *Los Angeles Times* exulted in 2001. "Southern California is playing the steady tortoise to the Bay Area's exhausted hare."

The woes of the high-tech sector were compounded by the electric energy crisis and the terrorist attack of the early 2000s. The bursting of the dot-com bubble led to some predictable overreactions. The *New York Times* ran a headline proclaiming "California's Golden Dream Goes Dark," and an editorial writer for the *Wall Street Journal* professed to have watched with "amazement, amusement, and horror" as California was reduced "from the nation's most prosperous state to a Third World country." Meanwhile, Michael J. Mandel, author of *The Coming Internet Depression* (2000), predicted a deep and sinister collapse.

Apparently forgotten by many euphoric dot-commers of the late 1990s was the undeniable fact that the high-tech sector always has been susceptible to cycles of expansion and contraction. The rapid deceleration of the early 2000s was hardly surprising after a period of explosive growth. "In the life of every innovation there is a boom phase," explained UCLA senior economist Tom Lieser in 2001. "This is an adjustment phase that may last as long as two years. No one doubts the strength of demand in the long run." Even with the fading of many of the quirkier ideas for e-commerce (such as the selling of pet food on-line), the Internet remained fundamentally sound and continued to generate waves of innovation. A new generation of high-tech products and services, marketable by and for the Internet, was moving steadily through the pipeline. "The technological revolution is still in its infancy," noted *Business Week,* "and several huge advances are just starting to take shape." Market strategist Alfred Goldman offered an important corrective to the purveyors of gloom-and-doom: "Ninety percent of dot-coms will never be heard from again. But that doesn't mean the Internet is dead. It is a vibrant part of our economy."

The Arsenal of America

One of the most significant factors in the California economy after World War II was the growth of the state's defense industry. At the war's end, many observers wondered if the California economy could adjust to peace. The state's industrial leaders, however, were determined not to lose the momentum generated by the wartime boom. The technological advances made during the war—in aerodynamics, electronics, radar, and other fields—provided the basis for California's domination of the postwar defense industry.

As tensions with the Soviet Union increased during the cold war, the United States entered into its first sustained peacetime defense boom. By the late 1940s, California's aircraft producers were benefiting from a new wave of military spending. California firms won 55 percent of all the Pentagon's airplane contracts in 1948, twice their percentage during the war. Defense spending accounted for more than half the state's economic growth between 1947 and 1957.

During the 1960s, the rivalry between the two superpowers led to a race to be the first nation to place a person on the moon. Each country also sought to acquire a supply of missiles large enough to guarantee its security against the other. California's aircraft industry, transformed now into "aerospace," played a leading role in these new forms of international rivalry. In 1965 nearly 500,000 Californians—about one-third of the total number employed in manufacturing—were working in the various branches of the aerospace industry, including the production of aircraft, missiles, electronic equipment, and related instruments.

Southern California became the nation's leading center of aerodynamic research, partly because much of the aircraft industry was already concentrated there and partly because the empty spaces of the Mojave Desert to the north and east of Los Angeles were ideal for aerospace testing and experimentation. The concentration of scientific talent at the California Institute of Technology and the Jet Propulsion Laboratory, both in Pasadena, also played a major role in the region's burgeoning aerospace industry.

During the 1980s, under the Reagan presidency, the aerospace industry entered a new era of prosperity. Between 1980 and 1984, the value of prime contracts awarded by the Department of Defense to California firms more than doubled. The defense industry became the state's largest source of revenue, generating $28.5 billion in income. California firms in 1985 received about one-fifth of the nation's total defense budget—more than the combined total of the state's three nearest competitors.

Throughout the Reagan era of defense spending, southern California maintained its dominant position. Los Angeles County remained the nation's top location for weapons development, followed by Orange, San Diego, Santa Barbara, and San Bernardino counties. In northern California, Santa Clara County received the lion's share of defense spending. Only six states received more military dollars than Silicon Valley. The town of Sunnyvale, home of the Lockheed Missile and Space Company, won a larger portion of the national defense budget than 29 states.

The nation's defense came to be based on what was called the Triad, an interlocking network of three kinds of weapons: missiles launched from under the sea, strategic bombers, and ground-launched missiles. California was the center for production of two of the three legs of the Triad. Lockheed built all the ballistic missiles for the Polaris, Poseidon, and Trident submarines. Likewise, the latest generations of strategic bombers were developed in the state. Rockwell International, at

El Segundo, was awarded a $20 billion contract in 1981 to build 100 B-1 bombers for the Strategic Air Command, and the Los Angeles–based Northrop Corporation became the prime contractor for developing the advanced-technology Stealth bomber. California also made a major contribution to the third leg of the Triad, missiles launched from the ground.

Not all of the federal money spent in California for weapons came from the Department of Defense. About a third of the research and development budget of the Department of Energy was allocated to the University of California for its operation of the Lawrence Livermore National Laboratory. This laboratory and its sister UC lab in New Mexico, the Los Alamos National Laboratory, were responsible for the development of all the nation's nuclear weapons. California also received more than a third of the funds distributed by the National Aeronautics and Space Administration (NASA). Much of the NASA allocation was for the space shuttle program, about 30 percent of which was believed to be targeted for military purposes.

California led the nation as well in the variety of nuclear weapons located at the more than 100 military installations in the state. Strategic bombers were based at Mather, Castle, and March Air Force bases. San Diego, home to more military personnel than any other city in the nation, contained both a major naval base and an air station. In addition, California contained three important storage facilities for nuclear warheads. The largest of these, the Concord Naval Weapons Station, occupied a 12,000-acre site within a few miles of residential neighborhoods in suburban Contra Costa County. Hundreds of nuclear weapons, some with the explosive power of 1 million tons of TNT, were stockpiled at the station.

With unexpected suddenness, an astonishing series of international events in the late 1980s and early 1990s signaled the end of the cold war rivalry between the United States and the Soviet Union. The Berlin Wall, the most infamous symbol of the cold war division of Europe, came down in November of 1989 and was followed less than a year later by the reunification of West and East Germany. In early 1991 the Warsaw Pact was officially dissolved, and by year's end the Soviet Union had been transformed into a commonwealth of independent states. These monumental events had a profound effect on American defense policy because about 70 percent of United States defense spending had been aimed at protection against a Soviet threat. With that threat removed, or considerably reduced, cutbacks in defense spending were inevitable.

The most visible manifestation of the defense "build-down" was the closure or substantial reduction of more than 300 military bases across the country. Forty of the bases were in California, far more than in any other state. Included in four rounds of base closures between 1988 and 1995 were San Francisco's Presidio Army Base, Moffett Field Naval Air Station, Hunters Point Naval Shipyard, Vallejo's Mare Island Naval Shipyard, Long Beach Naval Station, Castle Air Force Base near Merced, Irvine's El Toro Marine Corps Air Station, and Monterey County's Fort Ord. Each of the state's nuclear weapons storage facilities also closed, including the one at the Concord Naval Weapons Station.

The base closures were part of an overall plan to reduce defense spending by 25 percent between 1990 and 1997. Congress agreed to troop reductions that brought

American troop levels down to their lowest level since 1948. Production of major weapons systems, such as the Trident submarine, was terminated; others were scaled back by a third or more. The defense cutbacks sent shock waves through the California economy. The base closures meant the loss of more than 50,000 civilian jobs in the state. Tens of thousands of other jobs were impacted. Major layoffs were announced by such stalwarts as McDonnell Douglas, Hughes, Lockheed, and Aerojet. Overall employment in the state's aerospace industry dropped from 370,000 in 1987 to an estimated 189,000 by 1994. Annual defense contracts awarded to California firms plummeted from $60 billion to less than $35 billion.

The decline of defense spending was the single most important factor in the recession of the early 1990s. Ever since World War II, California's economy had relied on the steady infusion of defense dollars. Suddenly, that flow was drastically reduced.

The California aerospace industry rebounded modestly in the early 2000s. Following the terrorist attacks of 2001, the *Los Angeles Times* predicted the state and nation would soon experience "the biggest military buildup in years." Economists also expected that federal military spending would rise as aging weapons systems were refurbished and replaced. Anticipating future expansion, the Boeing Company became the state's largest private employer with its acquisition of McDonnell Douglas and Rockwell International. Meanwhile, former defense contractors succeeded in converting a portion of their enormous productive capacities to peacetime use, providing (among other things) a new generation of low-orbiting satellites for telecommunications. The conversion of the state's closed military bases to civilian use also proved to have some unexpected positive consequences. Sacramento County transformed a portion of Mather Air Force Base into a family housing complex, and the California State University established a new campus at Fort Ord.

In spite of these modest gains, California's recovery from the 1990s recession was extraordinary because it was achieved *without* a resumption of massive military spending. The growth in international trade, high technology, tourism, and the entertainment industry more than made up for the losses in aerospace and defense. "This is a recovery like no other," observed Joel Kotkin of Pepperdine University. "The fundamental economic mix has changed hugely, and it's the kind of change that is positioning the state extremely well for the twenty-first century."

Tourism

The only sector of the California economy able to rival the defense industry during the heyday of the cold war was tourism. And the continuing strength of the tourist industry helped pull the state out of the post-cold-war recession of the early 1990s. California remained the nation's top travel destination, ranking first among the 50 states in travel expenditures. Travelers in 2000 spent $75 billion in the state, providing jobs for more than a million Californians.

California had been a favorite vacation spot since the late nineteenth century. The term "tourism" was coined in the state to describe the growing travel industry spawned by the railroad and by the success of such resort hotels as the Del Monte near Monterey and San Diego's elegant Hotel Del Coronado. Tourist attractions in California were as various as the diverse interests of the visitors themselves. The five national parks—Yosemite, Sequoia, Redwood, Lassen, and Kings Canyon—remained perennial favorites, as did the countless other scenic attractions throughout the state.

California's top attractions in recent years were almost all commercial enterprises. Heading the list was Disneyland, the nation's premier amusement park, which opened amid the orange groves of Anaheim in 1955. Within a year nearly 4 million people visited the park; by the early 2000s annual attendance had more than tripled. The success of Disneyland was due in part to its successful re-creation of small-town America and its celebration of such traditional values as free enterprise and individual liberty. The other leading commercial attractions (in order of annual attendance) were Universal Studios, Knott's Berry Farm, Sea World, and Six Flags Magic Mountain. Visitors to Universal Studios could ride a Disneyesque tram though parting seas, past killer sharks, over a collapsing bridge, around space creatures, and into a roaring avalanche. Walter Knott set up his fruit stand in Buena Park, southeast of Los Angeles, in 1920, and later expanded his operations to include a restaurant, gift shop, and amusement park. Sea World opened in 1964 in San Diego's Mission Bay Park, providing visitors a chance to see performing whales, dolphins, and sea lions. Magic Mountain premiered such rides as Déjà Vu, a super-boomerang roller coaster that carried thrill seekers forward and backward over twisting, looping inverted steel tracks.

Northern California also had its commercial attractions, most notably Six Flags Marine World in Vallejo and Paramount's Great America in Santa Clara, but the chief travel destination in the north was the city of San Francisco. Tourism became San Francisco's leading industry, prompting one critic to dub the city "Disneyland North." In addition to such long-standing favorites as Chinatown and North Beach, tourists flocked to the Cannery and the old Ghirardelli chocolate factory, two of the many structures in the city that were converted into tourist attractions. The appeal of Fisherman's Wharf was expanded southward to Pier 39 to include a collection of tourist-oriented shops constructed along the waterfront. The fishing industry itself, meanwhile, virtually disappeared from the wharf. "They are turning Fisherman's Wharf into a carnival," complained one of the area's few remaining fishermen.

The growth of disposable income during the substantial boom of the late 1990s boosted travel spending in California to new heights. The state captured 10 percent of the nation's tourist dollars and more than a quarter of all spending by foreign visitors. California tourism, however, was hard hit by a temporary decline in domestic and international travel following the 2001 terrorist attacks in New York and Washington, D.C. Airlines, hotels, and related industries sharply cut back their workforce. The Los Angeles Convention and Visitors Bureau projected that Los Angeles County alone would lose $2 billion in spending by tourists.

New and expanded attractions nevertheless strengthened the state's competitive advantage among domestic and foreign visitors. Downtown sports facilities opened in San Francisco and Los Angeles, and a new ballpark was planned for the San

Major tourist attractions in California. (*Based on data from the Division of Tourism, California Trade and Commerce Agency.*)

Diego Padres. Long Beach completed its new Aquarium of the Pacific, a worthy rival to the Monterey Bay Aquarium. San Diego and Orange counties launched major expansions of their convention centers. Magic Mountain introduced Goliath, a thrill ride with a near vertical zero-gravity drop, and Marine World offered Medusa, the tallest, fastest, and longest roller coaster in northern California. Meanwhile,

The entrance to Disney's California Adventure. Featured at the park is *Golden Dreams,* a film that tells "the history of the people whose hopes, dreams, and hard work made California what it is today." (*Copyright © Disney Enterprises, Inc.*)

the proprietor of the state's leading tourist attraction, Disneyland, built a second theme park adjacent to the first in Anaheim. The new park, called Disney's California Adventure, represented a $1.4 billion investment and opened in 2001. Barry Braverman, executive producer of Walt Disney Imagineering, explained that the new park was a celebration of "the special magic of the California dream. Our goal is to immerse guests in compelling stories, evocative places, and fantastic adventures that will bring the California dream to life."

Entertainment

California has been the entertainment capital of the world since the golden age of Hollywood, and in recent years the entertainment industry has played an increasingly important role in the state's economy.

The number of Californians working in the motion picture industry increased by 70 percent between 1990 and 2000. Indeed, the vigorous growth of the entertainment industry was one of the prime factors in California's recovery from the recession of the early 1990s. By mid-decade more than twice as many Californians were employed in the making of motion pictures than in the making of missiles, and the average entertainment worker was earning $10,000 more than a worker in the defense industry. Economists described this dramatic shift between defense and

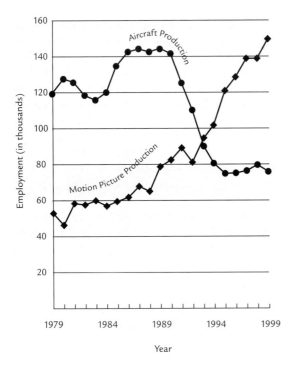

The number of southern Californians working in the film industry grew so rapidly that it far exceeded the number making aircraft. (*Based on data from the Center for the Continuing Study of the California Economy.*)

entertainment as an economic transformation comparable to the gold rush. *Fortune* magazine heralded the news with an article headlined "It's Glitz Not Guns behind California's Comeback."

Evidence of the transformation was not hard to find. San Francisco's Treasure Island Naval Station became a model for the conversion of surplus military bases into sound stages for the production of motion pictures. Several major films—including Disney's animated feature *James and the Giant Peach* and Warner Brothers' thriller *Copycat*—were filmed at the base prior to its closure in 1997. San Bernardino's decommissioned Norton Air Force Base became the setting for Paramount's action film *Congo*. The perfect metaphor for the defense-to-entertainment metamorphosis was the proposed transformation of a portion of the San Francisco Presidio into a sleek new $250 million movie-making center. Proposed by filmmaker George Lucas, the Digital Arts Center would occupy 23 acres of the former army base.

California's dominance of the entertainment industry was astounding. By the late 1990s, the state's major studios and independent filmmakers were producing more than 80 percent of all feature films made in the United States, pumping $28 billion into the state's economy. The state also dominated the exploding worldwide videotape market; exports of California-made videos more than quadrupled in the 1990s. Likewise, almost 90 percent of all television series and other prime-time shows were being made in California. "Whether you want to be an actor, or a writer for films and television, or a producer—you still have to come to California," commented one award-winning Hollywood screenwriter.

Also flourishing in California were festivals celebrating the ethnic diversity of the entertainment industry. Best known was the international film and video festival sponsored by Oakland's Black Filmmakers Hall of Fame. Dedicated to "empowering future generations to excel in film, video, and television," the Hall of Fame offered year-round symposia, workshops, and lectures. The San Francisco International Asian American Film Festival, founded in 1982, soon became the largest of its kind in the world. "Much of what is happening in the Asian world is best expressed in video and film," said festival programmer Paul Yi. "These are the media that give people a chance to see commonalities around the world."

After decades of decentralization, the entertainment industry experienced a new burst of consolidation in the 1980s and 1990s. Typical was the expansion and revitalization of the Disney company. Under the direction of CEO Michael Eisner, Disney revived its animation and live-action production through the acquisition of Touchstone and Hollywood Pictures. It also captured a healthy share of the home video market by rationing the rerelease of Disney classics. Disney stores opened in malls across the nation, and new Disney theme parks blossomed in Europe and Asia. In 1995 Disney acquired the ABC television network, thus becoming the largest entertainment conglomerate in America.

Not all the expansion of the entertainment industry was in southern California. Filmmakers George Lucas and Francis Ford Coppola established their Zoetrope Studios in San Francisco in the late 1960s. A decade later, Lucas began building Skywalker Ranch in the rolling hills of Marin County and opened his Industrial Light and Magic (ILM) special effects unit in nearby San Rafael. Skywalker Ranch became the most technically advanced filmmaking enterprise in the world, complete with state-of-the-art video editing equipment and other postproduction facilities. From the Lucas film studios came half a dozen of the highest-grossing movies ever made, including subsequent episodes of the fabulously successful *Star Wars* saga that ushered in a new era of special effects.

The most rapidly growing sector of the entertainment industry was what came to be called "Siliwood," the joining of the high-tech multimedia wizardry of Silicon Valley with the movie-making magic of Hollywood. The hottest new technology was digital imaging, first used by ILM designers in 1988 to create a shimmering, snakelike figure for an underwater movie called *The Abyss*. This first on-screen digital character was soon followed by computer-generated robots in *Terminator 2,* full-size dinosaurs in *Jurassic Park,* and dead presidents in *Forrest Gump.* In 1996 a computer graphics company, owned by Apple Computer cofounder Steven Jobs, won a special Academy Award for *Toy Story,* the first entirely computer-animated full-length feature film. "Computers are going to be as ubiquitous in the entertainment industry as they are in the business world," predicted the president of Silicon Graphics.

Producing computer-generated special effects was only one application of multimedia technology. Surfers of the Internet and players of CD-ROM computer games also relied on multimedia, as did businesspeople in far-flung locations who teleconferenced with colleagues without leaving their offices. Multimedia jobs required a unique combination of computer literacy and entertainment creativity;

Computer artists at George Lucas's Industrial Light and Magic studios used 3-D graphics to position a ferocious Tyrannosaurus Rex in *Jurassic Park* (1993). (*Copyright © by Universal City Studios, Inc. Courtesy of MCA Publishing Rights, a Division of MCA Inc. All rights reserved. Courtesy also of the* San Francisco Chronicle.)

workers who possessed both commanded some of the highest wages in the entertainment industry. California in 2000 had more than 630 multimedia firms, far more than any other state.

Local and state officials initiated a broad range of policies to support the burgeoning entertainment industry. In 1995 Los Angeles created the Entertainment Industry Development Corporation to speed the permit-granting process for local filmmakers and to assist them in gaining access to desired locations. Ten years earlier the state legislature created the California Film Commission (CFC) to retain, attract, and promote film production in the state. One of the CFC's most successful services was to collect and catalog more than 300,000 photographs of potential California locations for the shooting of films. The CFC began digitalizing its images in the 1990s with the help of NASA and the Jet Propulsion Laboratory in Pasadena. "The goal of the CFC," said the chair of the commission, "is to promote a better understanding that the motion picture industry provides a unique and significant contribution to the economy of California."

Agriculture

Perhaps the most striking feature of California's contemporary economy was its diversity. Even as the state led the nation in such fields as high technology, tourism, and entertainment, it remained the leading agricultural state. With less than 3 percent of United States farmland within its borders, California produced more than 50 percent of the country's fruits and vegetables. California continued to lead the nation in the production of milk, butter, beef cattle, strawberries, tomatoes, turkeys, and more than 60 other farm commodities, producing all of the nation's commercially grown almonds, artichokes, dates, figs, olives, pistachios, and prunes. California also gained the dubious distinction of being the country's leading producer of marijuana, reckoned by some to be the state's largest cash crop. By 2000 California's agricultural cornucopia was pouring more than $26 billion into the state's economy, providing jobs for 400,000 workers.

Modern California agriculture was still shaped by earlier trends, but it also faced some new and difficult challenges. Consolidation continued to reduce the number of farming units and to increase their average size. Between 1940 and 1980 the number of farms in the state was cut in half, and their average size more than doubled. Over 70 percent of California's farm income went to less than 15 percent of the farms, most of which were owned by large corporations.

Thousands of commmercial family farms remained in operation in California, but in the general trend toward consolidation and mechanization many small farmers were squeezed out. Hard hit by soaring fuel prices, increased foreign competition, and rising costs of production, San Joaquin Valley farmers in 2000 formed the Coalition to Save the Family Farm. "The small farmer problem is really scary, a sad situation," said Gloria Palacios, a former operator of a small farm near Fresno.

To improve their chances for survival, California's small farmers turned increasingly to high technology. Nearly half the state's farmers in 2000 were wired to the Internet, many of whom were selling their produce directly to consumers via e-commerce or gathering data for crop planning. Teleconferencing became a regular part of farm life, and the California Farm Bureau added interactive functionality to its Web site to facilitate on-line meetings.

Meanwhile, California's supply of prime agricultural land was threatened by urban development. By the 1990s, such land was being lost to housing developments, shopping centers, and freeways at the rate of more than 50,000 acres per year. The problem was especially evident in the Central Valley, ranked by the American Farmland Trust in 2000 as "the single most threatened agricultural region in the United States." Most of the urban growth was caused by refugees from the coastal metropolitan areas who were attracted to the Central Valley by its relatively inexpensive housing and lower cost of living. The conversion of so much valuable farmland into tracts of suburban housing, in the words of a former Sierra Club president and Kern County resident, was "a crime and a tragedy."

Another unresolved problem in California agriculture was the status of the state's farm workers. The creation of the Agricultural Labor Relations Board (ALRB) in 1975 raised hopes that the status of California's agricultural workers would be permanently improved. Farm workers did make major gains during the late 1970s when Democratic governor Jerry Brown appointed a prolabor majority to the ALRB. Many of these gains were reversed as Brown's Republican successors staffed the board with representatives of the growers and reduced its funding. The influence of César Chávez and the United Farm Workers (UFW) also declined in the 1980s; union membership fell from more than 70,000 in the 1970s to less than 20,000 in 1993. The UFW experienced a modest renaissance in the late 1990s and early 2000s, acquiring additional members and signing new contracts with some of the state's largest growers.

Employers of agricultural labor turned increasingly to the use of farm-labor contractors. The subsequent decline in wages, benefits, and working conditions for California's agricultural workers amounted to a counterrevolution in the fields. In 1990 a federal investigation revealed that only 40 percent of the harvesters in the San Joaquin Valley had toilets or hand-washing facilities available at the job sites. Incidents of hepatitis and related health problems were on the rise; compensation was rarely above the minimum wage. Conditions in some areas were comparable to what they had been during the depression a half century earlier.

California farmers also faced the challenge of increased foreign competition as trade barriers around the world were reduced. Growers of specialty crops—such as broccoli, cauliflower, asparagus, and tomatoes—encountered particularly strong competition from Mexican farmers following congressional approval of the North American Free Trade Agreement (NAFTA) in 1993. NAFTA tended to benefit, however, the state's beef and dairy industries as well as its growers of apples, pears, and nuts. Foreign ownership of key components of California's agricultural industry steadily increased. A Japanese conglomerate bought the state's only cotton mill, and dozens of California's premium wineries were foreign-owned, mostly by Europeans. Almaden, Beaulieu, Buena Vista, Inglenook, and Christian Brothers vineyards were all owned by British corporations, and in 2000 Beringer Brothers was purchased by Australia's Foster Brewing Company.

Exports of California agricultural products became increasingly important in recent decades. In the early 2000s, more than half the state's cotton, rice, and wheat was being sold abroad. Annual exports of California food products exceeded $12 billion, with more than half the state's agricultural exports being shipped to the nations of the Pacific Rim.

As California entered the twenty-first century, its economy had been transformed. Traditional industries, such as defense and aerospace, had declined and new ones had risen to take their place. During the longest sustained boom since World War II, California found itself at the vital center of the global New Economy of high technology and e-commerce. But economists cautioned that the state's continued prosperity was threatened by the very growth it had produced. "This growing prosperity attracts even more new residents to California and increases pressures on land, the environment, and quality of life," explained Stephen Levy. "This is the paradox of a strong economy." Practitioners of the New Economy, added Levy, demanded "good schools, clean air and water, efficient transportation, excellent public services, and great recreational and cultural amenities—in short, a high quality of life." The state's future prosperity absolutely *depended* on Californians taking bold action to protect the environment and improve basic services. If such action was not taken, warned Levy, "we won't have this economy."

Selected Bibliography

The literature on the Sunbelt is extensive. The term was coined by political strategist Kevin Phillips in his 1969 book *The Emerging Republican Majority.* More recent studies include Richard M. Bernard and Bradley Rice (eds.), *Sunbelt Cities* (1983), and Peter Wiley and Robert Gottlieb, *Empires in the Sun* (1982). For a dissenting view, see Clyde E. Browning and Wil Gesler, "Sun Belt–Frost Belt: A Case of Sloppy Regionalizing," *Professional Geographer,* XXXI (February 1979), pp. 66–74.

The best available survey of California's contemporary economy is *California Economic Growth* (2000), published by the Center for the Continuing Study of the California Economy. See also the excellent surveys in Dan Walters, *The New California* (1992), and Joel Kotkin and Paul Grabowicz, *California, Inc.* (1982). A useful compilation of statistics is available in *California: An Economic Profile* (1995) and *Facts on the Pacific Rim* (1985), publications of the California Department of Commerce, Office of Economic Research. On international trade, see Jon D. Haveman, *California's Vested Interest in U.S. Trade Liberalization Initiatives* (2001), and Abraham F. Lowenthal and Katrina Burgess (eds.), *The California-Mexico Connection* (1994).

The classic work on post-industrialism is Daniel Bell, *The Coming of Post-Industrial Society* (1973). On California, see Todd R. LaPorte and C. Abrams, "Alternative Patterns of Postindustria: The California Experience," in Leon Lindberg (ed.), *Politics and the Future of Industrial Society* (1975); LaPorte and Ted K. Bradshaw, *Advanced Industrial California* (1977); and Michael B. Teitz, "The California Economy: Changing Structure and Policy Responses," in John J. Kirlin and Donald R. Winkler (eds.), *California Policy Choices* (1984). See also Rob Kling, Spencer Olin, and Mark Poster (eds.), *Postsuburban California* (1991).

On the rise of California's high-tech industry, see several articles on the New Economy in *California Journal,* XXXII (February 2001); the special issue of ibid., XXXI (July 2000); and AnnaLee Saxenian, *Silicon Valley's New Immigrant Entrepreneurs* (1999). Older studies include Dirk Hanson, *The New Alchemists: Silicon Valley and the Microelectronics Revolution* (1982), and T. R. Reid, *The Chip* (1985). Useful short histories of Silicon Valley appear in Charles Wollenberg, *Golden Gate Metropolis* (1985), and Moira Johnson, "Silicon Valley," *National Geographic* (October 1982), pp. 459–477. For a dark view of the future, see Michael J. Mandel, *The Coming Internet Depression* (2000).

Analyses of the defense industry in California appear in Ehud Yonay, "The Anatomy of U.S. Defense," *California,* X (October 1985), pp. 91, 146–148; David Phinney, "Deploying Defense Dollars," *Bay Area Business Magazine* (March 1986), pp. 14–19, 50; J. S. Taub, "Defense Dollars," *California Journal,* XVIII (June 1987), pp. 274–277; and two publications from the California Department of Economic and Business Development, Office of Economic Policy, *The Aerospace Industry in California* (1981) and *The Effect of Increased Military Spending on California* (1982). Particularly useful is Patrick Lloyd Hatcher, *Economic Earthquakes: Converting Defense Cuts to Economic Opportunities* (1994).

The California Department of Commerce, Office of Tourism, compiles an annual statistical analysis of tourism in the state, *California Travel: Its Economic Impact.* See also

Hal K. Rothman, "Stumbling toward the Millennium," *California History,* LXXVII (Fall 1998), pp. 140–155; Michael Vinson, *Motoring Tourists and the Scenic West* (1989); and John F. Sears, *Sacred Places: American Tourist Attractions* (1989).

The literature on the entertainment industry is abundant. See, for instance, the California Production Special Issue of *The Hollywood Reporter* (November 3–5, 1995); Benedicte Raybaud and Danielle Starkey, "California's Film Industry Beats the Recession," *California Journal,* XXIV (January 1993), pp. 37–38; and the biographies of entertainment moguls in ibid., XXVI (December 1995), pp. 17–18.

Stephen Johnson, Gerald Haslam, and Robert Dawson, *The Great Central Valley* (1992), explores the natural and social history of California's agricultural heartland. Contemporary agricultural problems are analyzed in Jerome B. Siebert, "Agriculture," *California Journal,* XXI (January 1990), pp. 41–46, and Al Sokolow, "Urbanizing California's Farmlands," ibid., XXI (November 1990), pp. 535–538.

CHAPTER 36

Contemporary California Society

As California entered the twenty-first century, it remained the land of opportunity for an endless stream of newcomers from across the nation and around the world. Demographers predicted that the number of Californians would swell to more than 50 million by the year 2020. This burgeoning population put a tremendous strain on the state's infrastructure, including such basic services as transportation, education, health care, and the criminal justice system. Meanwhile, evidence mounted of a growing polarization of California society into a privileged upper class and an exploding underclass of frustrated Californians dependent on a system of inadequate and deteriorating public services. The Public Policy Institute of California reported in 1999 that in recent decades the income gap between the top fifth and bottom fifth of the population had widened more in California than in any other state.

Transportation

One of the most visible and agonizing consequences of population growth was the growing congestion of the state's more than 166,000 miles of streets and highways. The problem was particularly severe in major metropolitan areas, where freeways filled daily with bumper-to-bumper traffic. At peak commute hours the average speed on urban freeways in 1990 was 23 miles per hour. The average speed was expected to drop to 15 miles per hour soon after the turn of the century. In 1999 the Metropolitan Traffic Commission predicted that traffic delays in the San Francisco Bay area would increase by 249 percent by 2020. The psychological and economic consequences of such a calamity were awesome. "Traffic congestion is one of the most frustrating experiences people go through every day," observed a spokesperson for the California Chamber of Commerce.

The underlying cause of the congestion was readily apparent. During the last two decades of the twentieth century, the number of California motorists increased by about 50 percent whereas the capacity of the state highway system grew by only 7 percent.

The major barrier to achieving a solution to the state's transportation problem was the enormous cost involved. Building new freeways where they were needed most, in congested urban areas, had become prohibitively expensive. Construction of the Century Freeway in Los Angeles cost the state over $100 million a mile. While the expense of new construction soared, the willingness of Californians to pay for transportation improvements lagged far behind. The state gasoline tax, the main source of revenue for freeway construction, was among the lowest in the nation. In terms of per capita spending on highways, California slipped to dead last among the 50 states.

The state legislature in 1989 enacted an innovative plan to authorize private firms to build new highways and to collect tolls from the motorists who used them. Orange County's Foothill Tollway, the first toll road built in California since the depression, opened in the mid-1990s. Supporters of the toll-road concept believed that it offered a unique opportunity for the private sector to help solve a critical problem. Critics charged that toll roads represented an unwelcome privatization of the state's infrastructure, leading eventually to "a two-tiered transit system with the affluent motoring along well-kept tollways and the poor bumping along from pothole to pothole."

The first signs of a new willingness of voters to support needed improvements in the public transportation system came in 1990 with the approval of a ballot initiative that doubled the state's gasoline tax. It was the largest single increase since the tax was first enacted in 1923. Revenue from the increased tax was used for an $18.5 billion program of new highway and railroad construction, the largest single transportation investment in state history. Voters also approved two bond measures that outlined specific road-building, mass transit, and railroad construction projects.

The revitalization of rail transportation was reminiscent of an earlier era. Nearly all intercity travel in California had been by rail as late as 1920; 50 years later rail passenger service had virtually disappeared. The new rail system envisioned for the state included a high-speed rail corridor linking the urban centers of northern and southern California. The new bullet trains would travel at speeds up to 220 miles per hour, shuttling passengers between Los Angeles and San Francisco in just 2½ hours. Governor Gray Davis initially viewed the project with skepticism, calling it a "Buck Rogers idea." Recalling the skeptical reception received by railroad dreamer Theodore Judah 150 years earlier, the deputy director of the California High Speed Rail Authority was not discouraged. "Having people say we're nuts is probably a compliment to us," he replied. "We have history on our side." (Prospects for the bullet trains brightened after the terrorist attacks of 2001 temporarily crippled the airline industry.)

The bond measures approved in 1990 also included funds for improving local commuter rail projects throughout the state. Improvements were slated for the Bay Area Rapid Transit system (BART) and the San Diego and San Jose trolleys, and construction was planned for new commuter rail lines in the Los Angeles basin. In 1993 a new 4-mile subway, dubbed the Metro Red Line, began carrying passengers in downtown Los Angeles. Beset by massive cost overruns and allegations of corruption, the $6 billion subway system eventually extended from Union Station to Westlake/MacArthur Park. Meanwhile, nearly 200 miles of Metrolink commuter rail lines connected the city center with outlying communities in Orange, San Bernardino, Ventura, and Riverside counties. Spanning about 20 miles, the Metro Green Line carried passengers from Norwalk to Marine/Redondo. The Metro Blue Line, an electric light-rail trolley, began operating between Los Angeles and Long Beach. The Blue Line was the first interurban rail line in the Los Angeles basin since 1961 when the last of the Pacific Electric's Red Car rail lines were torn up to make way for the freeways. The new light-rail line followed almost exactly the route of the last Pacific Electric line.

The sustained economic boom of the late 1990s increased congestion in each of California's major urban areas and led to a new round of measures to improve the state's overburdened transportation system.

Some of the worst congestion was in and around Silicon Valley. South Bay commuters spent 4 to 5 hours a day traveling to and from their homes in far-flung suburbs. The *San Francisco Chronicle* warned that "traffic gridlock is one of the greatest threats to the future of a region that has been an engine of prosperity for the global economy." Local governments and high-tech businesses responded by supporting an extension of BART to Santa Clara County and sponsoring a new commuter rail line between Stockton and San Jose. The Altamont Commuter Express, equipped with laptop hookups and an espresso bar, whisked passengers (in the words of one inspired journalist) "from cow chips to computer chips." Congestion on the bridges across San Francisco Bay was eased somewhat with the introduction of electronic toll-collection devices. As vehicles sped through FasTrak tollbooths, a small transponder attached to their windshields allowed tolls to be collected from a pre-paid account.

Traffic conditions also worsened in the San Diego area. The explosion of maquiladoras along the Mexican border clogged local roadways and led to an accident rate five times the statewide average. The light-rail San Diego Trolley, carrying commuters to the border, increased its annual ridership by 30 percent.

Meanwhile, congestion on the freeways of the Los Angeles basin reached crisis proportions. Some observers despaired. "If you were born in L.A., as I was," said one former assemblyman, "you never expected transportation to be good." Others placed their hope in a new technology called Intelligent Vehicle Highway Systems (IVHS). Regarded as the core of the surface transportation system of the future, IVHS technology allowed traffic managers to operate freeways more efficiently by using integrated applications of computers and telecommunications. The first successful IVHS project encompassed one of the busiest commuter corridors in the nation, the Santa Monica, Harbor, and San Diego freeways.

In 2000 Governor Davis proposed a $5 billion plan to reduce congestion in selected bottlenecks throughout the state. The plan included proposals for new freeway lanes, many of which would be high-occupancy vehicle (HOV) lanes for carpools, vanpools, and low-emission buses. A new busway—a buses-only roadway—would link the San Fernando Valley with the Metro line in North Hollywood.

Critics complained that the governor's plan failed to identify adequate funding for the proposed improvements. One observer said it amounted to "throwing a nickel at problems that cost a dollar." Looking ahead to the year 2010, the Center for the Continuing Study of the California Economy estimated that the total cost for needed improvements to the state's transportation infrastructure was more than $100 billion.

Education

The relentless growth of California's population put enormous pressures on the state's already overburdened system of public education. Enrollment in elementary and secondary schools exceeded 6 million students in the academic year 2001–2002. Demographers predicted the total school-age population of California would nearly double by the year 2020, meaning that the state would have to build 12 new classrooms *every day* to keep pace with the increase in students.

California's school-age population also was becoming increasingly diverse. Whereas only one-quarter of the students in the state's schools were members of ethnic minorities in 1970, 30 years later more than 60 percent were minority students and one out of every four had only limited proficiency in English. The primary language of students in Los Angeles schools included 80 languages other than English. The largest number spoke Spanish, followed by Armenian, Korean, Cantonese, Tagalog, Vietnamese, Russian, and Farsi. The state's child poverty rate also was increasing. By 2001 a quarter of California's children were living in poverty—a rate even higher than that of Russia. Michael W. Kirst, a professor in the School of Education at Stanford University, has commented that schools increasingly must educate students whose backgrounds and experiences they were not designed to accommodate and whose needs they historically have not served well.

The changing ethnic makeup of California's public schools. (*Based on data from the California Department of Education.*)

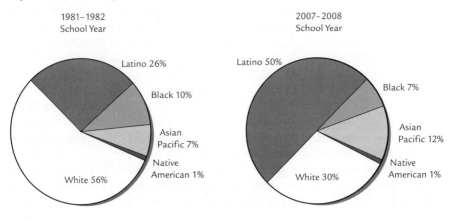

1981–1982
School Year

Latino 26%
Black 10%
Asian Pacific 7%
Native American 1%
White 56%

2007–2008
School Year

Latino 50%
Black 7%
Asian Pacific 12%
Native American 1%
White 30%

JOHNNY AT HOME

JOHNNY AT SCHOOL

Concern over the lack of advanced educational technology inspired this editorial cartoon by Christopher van Overloop. In 1995 California ranked fiftieth among the states in the availability of computers in public school classrooms. (*Reprinted from the* California Journal *with permission, April 1993.*)

Meeting the needs of children was especially difficult in an era when public schools were constrained by tight fiscal limits. Following the passage of Proposition 13 in 1978, California's system of public education began to suffer from slow starvation. Schools became grossly underfunded and scandalously overcrowded. By 1992 California ranked forty-second among the states in per-pupil spending and highest in student-teacher ratio. Peter Schrag, author of *Paradise Lost: California's Experience, America's Future* (1998), observed: "California's public schools, which had been among the most generously funded in the nation, began a path of decline from which they have never recovered."

In addition to having the highest student-teacher ratio in the nation, California's schools ranked last in providing counselors and librarians. More than a third of the state's schools had no guidance counselors, and nearly 90 percent lacked professional librarians. California schools spent only a tenth of the national average on new library book acquisitions; by 2000 the average copyright date of nonfiction books on the state's school library shelves was 1972.

Almost beyond belief was the lack of advanced educational technology in the public schools of California. The state's high-tech industry led the nation in the production of multimedia interactive educational software, and yet California's classrooms had fewer computers per student than any other state. California schools lagged in the availability of CD-ROM or laser disc players, and few of the state's classrooms were wired for access to the Internet. Nor were California's teachers being adequately trained in the use of educational technology. "I go to the schools of California and teachers don't even have access to the most basic technologies," reported Superintendent of Public Instruction Delaine Eastin. "There is nothing in this state that looks like the 1950s except the schools."

The most disturbing evidence of educational decline was the dismal performance of California students on nationwide exams. In 1995 the reading comprehension scores of California's fourth-graders were the lowest in the nation, tied with the fourth-graders of Mississippi. Less then 20 percent of California's eighth-graders in 1998 were proficient at writing coherent paragraphs free of spelling and grammatical errors. For the twelfth year in a row, California's high school seniors in 2000 scored lower than the national average on the Scholastic Aptitude Test (SAT). The following year, the state's fourth- and eighth-graders ranked last on a standardized national science exam. Meanwhile, the gap between scores of white and minority students widened after narrowing earlier. "This is a depressing reversal of gains made over the previous two decades," commented African American scholar Michael Nettles. The president of the organization that sponsored the SAT warned of a growing division "between a small class of an educational elite and an underclass of students academically ill-prepared for the demands of college or the workplace."

The economic consequences of low student achievement were soon evident. In 1991 less than half of all job applicants in California were able to demonstrate satisfactory mathematical or verbal abilities on entry-level exams. Stephen Levy, director of the Center for the Continuing Study of the California Economy, warned that the state's economic future was in peril unless dramatic improvements were made in public education. Levy argued that a highly skilled and well-educated workforce was absolutely essential if California was to remain competitive in the twenty-first century. The *Economist* agreed: "The state's shabby and dangerous schools look less and less like breeding grounds for the biotechnologists and virtual-reality script-writers of the future."

Not surprisingly, educational reform became a major political issue. In 1983 the legislature passed the most comprehensive school reform law in state history, mandating more than 80 separate changes. The law established tougher curriculum standards and new graduation requirements. Five years later, voters approved Proposition 98, guaranteeing the schools no less than 40 percent of the state's annual budget. Stung by criticism that California's classrooms remained the most crowded in the nation, state lawmakers in 1996 provided additional funds for reducing class size for kindergarten through third grade. The reform was based on the simplest of notions: smaller classes would allow teachers to spend more time with individual students and thus improve the quality of education. The reduction of class size, however, created an instant shortage of qualified teachers. One in every seven California classroom teachers by 2001 was not properly credentialed. The unqualified teachers were concentrated in schools serving primarily minority and low-income students—thus exacerbating inequities in student performance. One state educator warned that reducing class size "will do us very little good if the teachers aren't qualified."

The most controversial changes of recent years was the dismantling of the state's program of bilingual education, created to meet the needs of students whose primary language was not English. Opponents of bilingual education complained that it was failing to prepare students quickly enough for immersion in "an English-language culture." Defenders of the program charged its critics with xenophobia and nativism. In June 1998, California voters overwhelmingly approved Proposition 227, an initiative that prohibited bilingual education (except where specific exemptions were granted) and mandated public school instruction in the English language only.

The pace of educational reform quickened following the election of Governor Gray Davis in 1998. Appearing on the November ballot was Proposition 1A, an initiative authorizing the largest bond issue in state history. Approved by a whopping 63 percent of the voters, the $9.2 billion bond provided funds to build new schools, repair aging facilities, and upgrade classrooms with Internet connections. The new governor supported the bond measure and stated unequivocally that education was the number one priority of his administration. In his first address to the legislature, Davis proposed a package of reforms "to improve the reading skills of our children, to enhance the quality of our teachers, and to institute tough standards of performance and accountability for each of our 8000 schools."

The centerpiece of the Davis educational agenda was the Public Schools Accountability Act of 1999. Aimed at boosting the performance of students on standardized exams, the act provided cash incentives to teachers whose students showed significant improvement. The reform produced immediate results. Within a year, teachers in more than two-thirds of the state's schools had met academic improvement targets. This good news was marred, however, by charges that some teachers had falsified their students' exams to qualify for the cash rewards. Davis also won passage in 1999 of tougher high school graduation requirements. Beginning in 2004, no student could graduate without passing a newly created High School Exit Exam (HSEE).

In his 2000 budget, Governor Davis offered California schools their largest-ever increase in state funding. After years of falling further behind other states, California's per-pupil spending rose close to the national average. Acquiring additional funding was eased by the passage of an initiative in November 2000 that eliminated the requirement of a two-thirds majority for the passage of local school bonds. The initiative was supported by Silicon Valley entrepreneurs who were convinced that improving California's schools was imperative if the state was to meet its future needs for a skilled workforce.

Decades of inadequate funding and an unrelenting growth in enrollment also threatened the ability of the state to fulfill its Master Plan for Higher Education. Adopted in 1960, the master plan promised a place at one of the state's public colleges or universities for "all who have the capacity and willingness to profit by a college education." Clark Kerr, the chief architect of the plan, warned in 1991 that its promise was being broken.

Enrollment pressures continued to mount in the early 2000s as campuses were inundated by the college-age children of baby boomers and by waves of new immigrants. Dubbed "Tidal Wave II," the surge in enrollment was expected to reach 2.7 million by 2010, an increase of more than 35 percent in a single decade. "This is the largest number of students that any state, any time, any place, has faced," commented the executive director of the California Postsecondary Education Commission. "This is a tremendous challenge for the colleges and universities of California."

The entry point to higher education for many Californians was the state's more than 100 community colleges. Their enrollment was expected to soar to over 2 million by the year 2010, meaning an additional 25 to 30 new colleges would be required to meet the increased demand. The existing colleges became crowded with frustrated and discouraged students who were unable to get the classes they needed. As one disgruntled student observed, admission to a California community college amounted only to "a license to hunt for classes."

Like every other segment of public education, the community colleges' basic problem was a lack of money. Their fiscal difficulties began with the passage of Proposition 13 in 1978 that shifted funding from local college districts to the state. The adoption of Proposition 98 in 1988 provided community colleges with additional state funds, but also set a cap, or limit, on state-financed enrollment. Once the colleges reached their limit, state financing ended even though the schools had to continue to accept students. Lacking sufficient funds to hire additional full-time instructors, the community colleges turned increasingly to part-time faculty. By 2001 about two-thirds of community college instructors were part-timers, earning 31 percent less than full-timers with an equivalent course load. "They are truly the working poor of California's educational system," observed the leader of the California Federation of Teachers, "and in the wealthiest state in the nation, that is a disgrace."

Similar pressures affected the multicampus California State University (CSU) system. Budget deficits and soaring enrollments eroded the system's ability to fulfill its obligation under the master plan to admit the top one-third of the state's graduating high school seniors. The CSU chancellor predicted in 2000 that enrollment in the system would increase by more than one-third over the next decade, requiring the construction of 10 new campuses the size of Hayward State. Unable to afford the cost of construction, CSU responded by establishing several off-campus "learning centers" in cities such as El Centro, Stockton, Ventura, Palm Desert, and Pleasant Hill. The university trustees in 1989 approved the conversion of one such center, at San Marcos in northern San Diego County, into the state's twentieth CSU campus. Two additional campuses were added in 1995, CSU Monterey Bay on the grounds of the deactivated army base at Fort Ord and CSU Maritime Academy in Vallejo; in 2002 the learning center in Ventura became the system's twenty-third campus, CSU Channel Islands. To expand the overall capacity of the system, the colleges also began offering more on-line courses and increasing the number of summer school classes.

California State University prided itself on being one of the nation's most ethnically diverse systems of higher education. Its total minority enrollment was 52 percent in 2000, more than twice the national average for 4-year public institutions. Yet the challenges facing minority students were daunting. While only 28 percent of white freshmen failed the CSU entry math exam in 1998, 80 percent of African American freshmen and 72 percent of Latino freshmen failed. The dropout rate among black and Latino students also was high; fewer than 40 percent who enrolled at CSU graduated. One state legislator cautioned that such trends would lead eventually to "de facto educational, economic, and social apartheid."

Meanwhile, enrollment at the nine campuses of the University of California (UC) also continued to grow at a remarkable rate. The master plan provided that the university select its entering freshmen from the top one-eighth of the state's high school graduates. But the pool of eligible students was growing faster than the system's capacity to educate them. "The analogy is to a hospital," observed one UC official. "We're in effect being asked to admit students for whom there are no beds." Total UC enrollment was expected to grow by an additional 63,000 students between 2000 and 2010.

University of California president Richard Atkinson in 1999 approved several creative approaches to mitigating the enrollment crunch: cash rebates for students who graduated early, expanded off-campus and study-abroad programs, and increased on-line classes. "There is no one answer to the tidal wave of students," agreed the executive director of the California Postsecondary Educational Commission. "We need a variety of reponses." Meanwhile, the legislature authorized construction of a tenth university campus in Merced County. Scheduled to open in 2004, UC Merced was opposed by environmentalists who claimed the proposed site threatened the largest "vernal pool grassland environment anywhere in the world."

One of the most promising trends in higher education in recent decades was the increased enrollment of minority students at the University of California. The university's affirmative action recruitment policy led to a dramatic increase in the admission of underrepresented minorities throughout the 1970s and 1980s. Minority enrollment was threatened in 1995, however, by the decision of the university regents to end affirmative action in all admissions, hiring, and contracting. The following year, California voters completed the assault on affirmative action by approving Proposition 209. (See Chapter 33.) "Proposition 209 and the regents' directive succeeded in turning the clock back 30 years," observed legal scholars Richard Delgado and Jean Stefanic. Enrollment of African American and Latino undergraduates at UC Berkeley and UCLA plummeted by more than 50 percent in a 1-year period. (Minority enrollment at other campuses remained about the same or showed increases.) Enrollment of blacks and Latinos at the university's medical schools and law schools also declined sharply, and the systemwide hiring of female faculty fell dramatically. Jerome Karabel, author of *The Rise and Fall of Affirmative Action at the University of California* (1999), concluded that these declines constituted "the sharpest reversal in opportunities for underrepresented minorities in the history of American higher education." The regents, in a largely symbolic action, rescinded their ban on affirmative action in 2001. The university president, meanwhile, announced his intention to make UC admissions more democratic (and more closely keyed to the high school curriculum) by abandoning the use of the SAT.

Improving the quality of undergraduate education was another major challenge facing the state's colleges and universities. In 1990 the Carnegie Foundation for the

Advancement of Teaching reported that undergraduate instruction was being short-changed at many institutions of higher education where instructors were evaluated almost entirely on the basis of their scholarly research and publication. Ten years later, President John L. Hennessey of Stanford University announced the largest initiative to enhance undergraduate education ever undertaken by any university. Support for improving undergraduate education also came from the University of California. Historian Page Smith, founding provost of the Santa Cruz campus, decried the emphasis on faculty research at the expense of quality instruction. Smith added that most academic research was "pedestrian work" that was read only by a handful and "need not and should not be done." Meanwhile, Berkeley sociologist Neil Smelser reported that the concept of scholarship was slowly expanding at several UC campuses to include increased recognition of the value of teaching.

Health Care

The health care system of California utilizes the most sophisticated technologies and advanced medical treatment programs in the world. Yet it also has left a large and growing number of Californians with limited access to even the most basic medical services. Dr. Kenneth Kizer, director of the California Department of Health Services, diagnosed the state's health care crisis as a "paradox of medical want amidst medical plenty."

California's system of health care was a complex mix of private and public institutions, and included a wide range of services funded by federal, state, and local governments. Ever since the mid-1960s, the federal government's Medicare program had provided aid to the elderly for medical care. Medicaid extended that assistance to those in need, such as the blind and disabled, who were too young to receive Medicare benefits. California's own Medi-Cal system administered the federal programs and contracted with doctors and hospitals to provide medical services to those who qualified for assistance.

The problems confronting the health care system were as complex as the system itself. First in importance was the growing number of residents without health insurance. More than 7 million Californians were uninsured in 2000, and their ranks were swelling at the rate of 50,000 *per month*. Most of the uninsured were members of working families, many of whom had low-paying jobs in agriculture or the service sector. Their employers failed to provide them with private health insurance, and yet they failed to qualify for Medi-Cal. Members of ethnic minorities were the most likely to be uninsured. Forty percent of Latinos and 23 percent of African Americans lacked health insurance, compared to just 15 percent of whites.

Unable to afford routine health care, the uninsured tended to seek treatment only when their conditions became acute. Emergency rooms, required by state law to admit anyone with a medical emergency, became the primary health care providers for millions of Californians. The chairperson of the California Assembly Health Committee remarked that emergency rooms were becoming repositories of the proof that the state's health care system was not working.

Escalating medical costs and reduced levels of government support, however, led 19 financially strapped California hospitals to close their emergency rooms between 1997 and 2000. Reductions in service in Los Angeles more than doubled the response time required for a critically injured person to be taken by ambulance to an emergency room. The crisis in health care was thus a matter of life and death. "People who feel very comfortable and protected right now because they have insurance," warned one UCLA professor of public health, "could end up in the morgue because that hospital emergency room that they simply assumed would be there for them has its doors locked."

California health-rights activists called for a system of universal health insurance, but state leaders offered only modest reforms. The state legislature in 1993 established the Health Insurance Plan of California (HIPC), an experiment in collective purchasing that offered small businesses affordable insurance for their workers. Four years later, state officials launched California Healthy Families, a program to provide low-income families with government-subsidized insurance for their children. Dozens of other health care proposals, however, failed to win legislative approval. Reformers were disappointed that Governor Gray Davis did not show the same enthusiasm for health care as he did for education. When asked about health care shortly after his election, Davis responded bluntly: "That ain't my agenda." The director of the UCLA Center for Health Policy Research speculated that reform of the health care system would win more support from state leaders if its beneficiaries were other than low-income families. "But these are people who don't have strong political voices," he noted, "and unfortunately they are the ones who are at highest risk."

About half of all Californians with health insurance received their medical services through managed-care health maintenance organizations (HMOs), systems of doctors and hospitals that provide health services to enrolled members for a predetermined annual fee. Because such organizations generally provided medical services at lower rates, the state legislature required that all Medi-Cal patients be enrolled in managed-care systems by 1996. One health-rights activist viewed the new requirement as "a sea change in California's system of providing health-care services to the poor."

Membership in health maintenance organizations grew rapidly, but complaints against the HMOs also increased. Doctors found themselves caught between caring for their patients and staying within reimbursement limits set by the HMOs. Critics charged that these limits encouraged doctors to delay care, avoid expensive tests, and refuse referrals to specialists. In 1996 the legislature established a Managed Health Care Improvement Task Force, headed by an Oxnard attorney whose sister had died after an HMO had denied a bone marrow transplant to combat her metastasized breast cancer. Three years later, Governor Davis signed legislation permitting Californians to sue their HMOs for punitive damages.

The most controversial health care issue in recent years was acquired immunodeficiency syndrome, better known as AIDS. The disease appeared in California in June 1981, when five young homosexuals in Los Angeles were diagnosed as having a rare type of pneumonia found only in people with deficient immune systems.

Almost simultaneously, epidemiologists discovered the same disease in five homosexuals in San Francisco. A breakthrough in treating the disease came 3 years later when scientists succeeded in isolating the human immunodeficiency virus (HIV) that causes AIDS. The virus attacks a person's immune system, leaving the body vulnerable to a host of opportunistic infections and cancers.

By the twentieth anniversary of the onset of the AIDS epidemic, more than 115,000 Californians had been stricken with the disease and 60 percent of those had died. Homosexuals and intravenous drug users continued to account for nearly 80 percent of all AIDS victims. Thirty-three thousand San Franciscans were HIV-positive, more per capita than in any other major American city. In southern California, only the seaside town of Laguna Beach had a higher rate of infection than San Francisco. Long fashionable as a gay tourist mecca, this popular resort community was hard hit by the disease. Randy Shilts, author of an early history of the AIDS epidemic, caught the irony of such devastation in an idyllic setting. "The reality of AIDS is so contrary," Shilts observed, "to the Southern California ethos of youth and beauty."

California led the nation in committing its resources to the fight against AIDS. The state developed a computerized AIDS registry, mandated universal blood-donor screening, and established a highly successful program for voluntary, anonymous HIV testing. State-sponsored prevention programs and a safe-sex ethic slowly reduced the overall rate of HIV infection. The late 1990s and early 2000s, however, witnessed an alarming increase in the rate of infection. Seventy percent of the new cases were African Americans and Latinos. "For young gay men of color," reported the director of the White House Office of National AIDS Policy, "the epidemic is getting worse, not better." Also alarming was the rate of infection among youth between the ages of 13 and 19, and AIDS remained the leading cause of death among American males between the ages of 25 and 44. "I don't think most young people really understand it," said a spokesperson for the National Association of People with AIDS. "We have to be clear: If you get HIV in your 20s, you will die by [the time you are] around 40 years old."

The AIDS epidemic, of course, was not limited to California or the United States. It soon became the fastest-growing disease in the world, taking an especially heavy toll in the developing countries of Africa. Thirty-four million people woldwide had been stricken by 2000, with 10,000 new infections each day. The president of the World Health Organization declared that AIDS was "the world's first truly global epidemic, and it calls for a global response." He warned that the epidemic was "still gaining momentum and its major impact is yet to come."

Criminal Justice

Another issue of grave concern to Californians in recent decades was the rising crime rate. The rate of violent crime more than doubled in the 1960s and continued to spiral upward in the following two decades before stabilizing and beginning to decline in the 1990s. California voters demanded that their elected officials take vigorous action to ensure public safety.

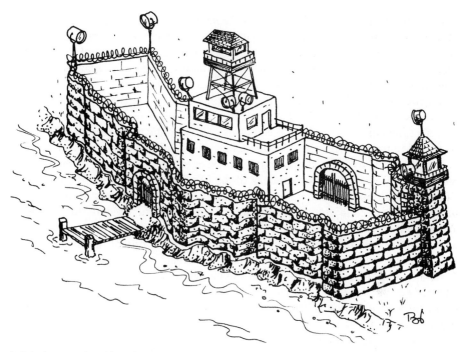

Political cartoonist Rob Wilson comments on the dramatic increase in the rate of incarceration and the construction of new prisons in California. (*Courtesy of the* California Journal.)

The growing concern about crime led to several fundamental changes in California's criminal justice system. The most dramatic change came in 1977 when the state legislature reinstated the death penalty. California's first execution in a quarter century took place in 1992. Soon the process became routine as an average of one condemned inmate each year was put to death by lethal injection; by 2000 more than 570 inmates were awaiting their turn on San Quentin's death row.

The legislature altered another important part of the criminal justice system in 1977 when it changed the way prison terms were set. Formerly, a state parole board had decided when prisoners were rehabilitated and ready to return to society. The legislature abandoned this practice in 1977 in favor of setting fixed sentences for specific crimes. Punishment, not rehabilitation, became the primary function of imprisonment. In subsequent years, the legislature regularly increased the length of prison terms and required mandatory sentences for a host of criminal offenses. The toughest of the new measures was the "three strikes and you're out" law of 1994; it ordered judges to send repeat felony offenders to prison for 25 years to life, even if their last offense was relatively minor and nonviolent.

The results of the new sentencing policies were soon apparent. The state's prison population increased more than fivefold between 1984 and 1999. To house this exploding population, the Department of Corrections opened an additional 21 state prisons. The new prisons, however, were unable to keep pace with the growth in the number of inmates. By 2000 the state prisons were at 200 percent of capacity.

Likewise, more than two-thirds of the state's county jails exceeded their capacity. California also incarcerated a higher percentage of its juveniles for longer periods of time than any other state in the nation. Barry Krisberg, president of the National Council on Crime and Delinquency, reported that California's incarceration rate was the highest in the world.

Whether the state's tougher sentencing policies and increased rate of incarceration caused a reduction in crime became a matter of widespread public debate. The overall crime rate in California decreased steadily through the 1990s, proof to many that locking up more criminals had reduced crime. Others were not so sure. "It's quite impossible to authoritatively suggest what causes short-term changes in the crime rate," cautioned the former dean of the UC Berkeley School of Criminology. Another expert noted that demographic factors in California had a greater impact on the crime rate than did incarceration. The state's rate of violent crime followed more closely the declining proportion of young males in the population—those most likely to commit crimes—than it did the increasing rate of imprisonment. As California's population aged, its crime rate diminished.

Meanwhile, the correctional officers in charge of the state's prison population came under fire for alleged misconduct. A series of articles in the *Los Angeles Times* chronicled abuses at Pelican Bay, a new maximum-security prison near Crescent City. The charged abuses included officers sanctioning inmate attacks on convicted child molesters. Guards at Corcoran State Prison were accused of staging "gladiator fights" among inmates who were then shot when the fighting got out of control. Investigators ruled that two-thirds of the shootings at Corcoran were unjustified. Overall, more inmates were shot by officers in California's prisons than in the rest of the nation's prisons combined.

Critics also complained that a disproportionate share of the state's fiscal resources was being spent on corrections. More prison guards were hired in the 1990s than all other state employees combined, and the annual allocation for the Department of Corrections was the fastest-growing portion of the state budget. The superintendent of public instruction protested that California was building "Cadillac prisons and jalopy schools."

The spiraling costs of California's prisons led to a renewed search for more cost-effective means of reducing crime. Attorney General Bill Lockyer was especially concerned that California had the nation's highest recidivism (relapse) rate among its prison population. "We know the typical prisoner reads at a third- or fourth-grade level," he commented, "has very few employable skills, often is mentally ill, and has drug or alcohol histories that are serious." Lockyer advocated expanding prevention and treatment programs as a way of reducing long-term prison costs. San Jose State University criminology professor Michael Rustigan concurred that the best way to reduce the rate of violent crime was early intervention aimed at prevention.

Nowhere was the preventative approach needed more than in the fight against drug abuse. Drug-related crimes accounted for more than half of all the felonies committed in California, and 80 percent of the state's prison inmates were substance abusers. In addition to crimes committed by those under the influence,

drug-related offenses included crimes committed to finance the habit, crimes resulting from competition among drug dealers, and illicit drug manufacturing and
trafficking. California led the nation in the number of clandestine drug labs producing methamphetamines and was the primary point of entry for cocaine from
abroad. California drug gangs, centered in Los Angeles, distributed their deadly
merchandise across the nation. One leading drug expert warned that California had
became a "world-class" center for the manufacturing and distribution of drugs. "If
California were a nation," he observed, "it would be the largest, most important
polity among all the world's nations in terms of illicit drugs."

Efforts to combat the drug problem included a mix of federal and state programs, spending over a billion dollars a year. California voters in 2000 approved
an initiative to send first- and second-time nonviolent drug offenders into treatment
instead of prison. The measure represented a radical overhaul of the state's antidrug policies. "California has a reputation as a tough-on-crime state," said one of the
initiative's sponsors, "and now I think we're showing we can be smart on crime too."

A highly successful antidrug education program in the schools and in the media
contributed to a decline in drug use among young and middle-class users. There
was no decline, however, among the growing underclass of Californians. The California Department of Justice reported that drug use among the state's poor was "intensifying at levels never seen before anywhere in the world." As with many other
aspects of recent social history, California's pattern of drug abuse was divided
along lines of social class. The outlook for the future was bleak. "The drug problem is expected to continue in rapacious severity at the poorer end of the social
structure," observed Steven White, district attorney for Sacramento County. "What
we're likely to see is an economic demarcation line. Those above the line will use
drugs less; those below will continue as now, and may fall even farther into the
chasm cut by drugs."

The New Californians

The United States Census reported that the population of California in 2000 was
more than 33.8 million. Demographers predicted that the state would grow to 50
million within two decades.

The most striking quality of California's burgeoning population was its ethnic
diversity. More than half the state's population growth in the 1980s and 1990s was
from foreign immigration, primarily from Asia and Latin America. By 2000 one
out of four Californians was foreign-born. Much of the remaining growth was due
to the high birthrate among those who had recently arrived. Ethnic minorities made
up only one-third of the state's population in 1980, but 20 years later they constituted more than half. California also led the nation in the number of persons who
identified themselves as members of more than one race. Among the country's top
10 cities with the highest proportion of mixed-race residents, 5 were in California
(Glendale, Hayward, Stockton, Vallejo, and Sacramento). David Rieff, author of
Los Angeles: Capital of the Third World (1992), reported that the state's largest

city was home not only to more Mexicans than any other city except Mexico City but also to more Koreans than any other city except Seoul and to more Filipinos than any other city but Manila.

Los Angeles also had the distinction of being home to one of the nation's largest populations of Native Americans. Although there were no distinct Indian neighborhoods in the city, a network of social and economic institutions provided the Indian people of Los Angeles with feelings of tradition and community. The 2000 census reported that more than 628,000 Indians lived throughout California, more than in any other state. Projections to the year 2020 indicated that Native Americans would continue to make up between 1 and 2 percent of California's overall population.

Native people remained active in a wide range of activities to revive and preserve traditional languages and cultures. Community-based groups flourished throughout the state, matching elders who were fluent in traditional languages with younger tribal members who were eager to learn. "The only way we'll stay alive as a people," observed Nancy Richardson Riley (Karuk), "is if we practice and live our culture."

Native Americans also actively sought to have artifacts and human remains returned, or "repatriated," from museum collections. When northern California tribal leaders learned that the brain of Ishi had languished for more than 80 years in storage at the Smithsonian Institution, they requested that it be returned. Eventually, the brain was presented to Pit River elders who buried it, along with Ishi's cremated remains, near Mount Lassen in the summer of 2000.

The Native American issue that captured the greatest public attention in the late twentieth century was legalized gambling. In the early 1990s, California tribes began operating casinos that soon were generating more than $1 billion in annual revenues. Life on some (but by no means all) reservations was transformed as gaming revenues led to dramatic improvements in housing, education, and health care. Faced with opposition from Republican governor Pete Wilson, the gaming tribes placed on the November 1998 ballot an initiative, Proposition 5, that mandated state approval of tribal casinos.

The battle over Proposition 5 proved to be the most expensive initiative campaign in the nation's history. The gaming tribes spent $70 million in support of the initiative; the owners of Nevada casinos spent nearly half as much in opposition. Proposition 5 passed overwhelmingly, but within months the state supreme court ruled it unconstitutional. The gaming tribes then launched a successful campaign to win passage of a constitutional amendment containing the essence of Proposition 5. Democratic governor Gray Davis signed agreements with about half the state's tribes, recognizing their right to operate casinos on tribally owned lands. Harrah's and other gambling interests immediately joined with the tribes to build new Nevada-style casinos featuring video slot machines and house-banked card games. Annual revenues from the casinos were expected to reach $4.4 billion by 2004.

To protect their newfound prosperity, the California gaming tribes became major players in state politics. They formed political action committees and contributed millions of dollars to Davis and other candidates for local and state offices. One

Mark Macarro, chair of the Pechanga Luiseño Band of Mission Indians, was the spokesperson for Proposition 5 in television spots aired throughout the 1998 campaign. (*Courtesy of Winner/ Wagner & Mandabach Campaigns, Santa Monica.*)

observer calculated that the gaming tribes were contributing more money to political campaigns than any other interest group in the state. The advent of high-stakes Indian gambling not only transformed the lives of thousands of native people, it also had a profound impact on California politics.

The ethnic group experiencing the least growth in recent decades was the category identified by the Census Bureau as "non-Hispanic whites." The Anglo population actually *declined* by more than a million during the 1990s, having the lowest birthrate and the highest rate of *out-migration.* The Anglos' overall proportion in the population fell from two-thirds in 1980 to less than half by the turn of the century. The shrinking proportion of non-Hispanic whites was even more startling among the state's younger residents. Whereas Anglos constituted 47 percent of the general popluation in 2000, their proportion among residents under the age of 18 was a mere 35 percent. "What it all means," commented one demographer, "is that bigger changes are still to come."

One of the most salient characteristics of the Anglo population was its relatively high rate of political participation. But as the non-Hispanic white population declined, its dominance within the electorate steadily diminished. While Anglos comprised more than 80 percent of the voters in 1994, they accounted for less than 65 percent 4 years later. Nevertheless, non-Hispanic whites continued to hold the lion's share of elective offices in the state. Of the 120 members of the state legislature in 2000, only 23 were Latino, 4 African American, and 2 Asian. As California's minority population achieved majority status, it presented the state with a fundamental challenge. "It will test whether we can peacefully change," observed a spokesperson for California Tomorrow, "from a European-dominated society with minorities to a world society where everybody is a minority."

This challenge was already being faced in the schools of California, where no one ethnic group had been in the majority since 1988. Anglo students struggled to find ways to fit into a society increasingly defined in multicultural terms. Non-Hispanic whites at Anaheim High School stirred widespread controversy in 1992 by organizing a club for "European Americans." Critics feared that the club was racist, but the Anglo students argued successfully that the club was analogous to other campus organizations such as the Asian Club, the Black Students Union, and the Mexican American Engineering Society. Meanwhile, in 1992 the Berkeley campus of the University of California began requiring all its first-year students to take a class on "American cultures." The requisite cultures to be included were Native American, African American, Latin American, Asian American, and European American.

The Census Bureau reported that African Americans held steady at about 7 percent of the state's population in 2000, having grown only modestly during the past decade. The areas of greatest growth were in the suburban neighborhoods of Riverside, Vallejo, Fresno, and Sacramento, rather than in the established black communities of Los Angeles, San Francisco, and Oakland. "Blacks are moving out of cities for the same reasons as whites," explained geographer James Johnson. "They want better housing and they want to get away from the negative things in the cities like gangs and poor schools."

Wherever African Americans resided, they continued to confront barriers of prejudice and discrimination. "There is more negative prejudice against blacks than against any other group," reported UCLA political scientist David Sears in 1998. African Americans in 2000 remained twice as likely as other Californians to report discrimination on the job. Acknowledging a widespread pattern of prejudice against black employees, a San Francisco jury rendered a multimillion-dollar punitive judgment against the nation's largest wholesale bakery. The pattern of discrimination included tolerating racial slurs, denying promotions, and assigning menial jobs on the basis of race. "This shouldn't be happening in the 21st century," commented the jury foreman.

The continuing racial divide in California was powerfully evident in an outbreak of violence in the spring of 1992, following the acquittal of four white Los Angeles police officers accused of beating black motorist Rodney King. Five days of violence, centered in South Central Los Angeles, destroyed property valued at more than $1 billion and left at least 54 people dead. King's plaintive words were later widely reported: "People, I just want to say . . . can we all get along? Can we get along?" In terms of loss of life and destruction of property, the violence was far more devastating than the Watts riot of 1965. The underlying causes of both civil disturbances were the same; indeed, conditions in South Central had actually grown worse during the intervening quarter century. Whereas 27 percent of the area's families lived in poverty in 1965, over 30 percent were impoverished in 1992. The major change was the ethnic identity of the residents. South Central was about 80 percent African American in 1965, whereas by 1992 more than half its residents were Latino. Of the more than 17,000 people arrested during the riot, two-thirds were unemployed. Some South Central community leaders described the violence as a "revolt of the poor" and pointed out that black and Latino Californians were twice as likely to live in poverty as Anglo Californians and that their average income was one-third less. Jeffrey Lustig, director of the Center for California Studies, captured the larger significance of what was happening: "California is now a two-tiered society filled with rage."

The declining proportion of African Americans in the state's urban cores led to an unexpected diminishing of black political power. Journalist A. G. Block com-

Willie L. Brown, Jr., was elected mayor of San Francisco in 1995 after serving more than two decades as speaker of the assembly. (*Courtesy of the Office of the Mayor.*)

mented in 1998 that black Californians were "on the verge of being marginalized politically, economically, and socially." The slippage was most evident in Los Angeles, where Mayor Tom Bradley, an African American, decided not to seek re-election in 1993 after an unprecedented five terms as leader of the nation's second-largest city. The city's black population dipped from 14 percent in 1990 to just 11 percent in 2000. With no African Amercian candidate in the race for mayor in 2001, black voters supported the successful candidacy of James Hahn. Son of a county supervisor who long had represented a heavily black district, Hahn was dubbed the "surrogate black candidate." The most prominent black leader in the state remained Willie L. Brown, Jr., elected San Francisco's first African American mayor in 1995 after serving as assembly speaker longer than anyone in the history of California. Yet the political influence of black San Franciscans was steadily being eclipsed by that of Asian and Latino voters. "We as black people are used to being the number one minority," commented San Francisco attorney Eva Paterson. "We're going to have to deal with new realities."

Among those new realities were such dramatic reversals as the University of California's decision to dismantle affirmative action in 1995 and passage the following year of the anti–affirmative action initiative, Proposition 209. Enrollment of blacks and Latinos at UC professional schools plummeted; only one African American first-year student enrolled at Berkeley's Boalt Hall School of Law in the fall of 1997. "We must be more aggressive and we must be less patient," said the leader of the Oakland branch of the National Association for the Advancement of Colored People (NAACP). "This rap generation is not going to be a patient group of people singing 'We Shall Overcome.'"

The fastest-growing ethnic group in California was the category described by the Census Bureau as "Asian or Pacific Islander." California's Asian American population grew by more than a third during the 1990s; by 2000 about 11 percent of California's population was of Asian descent, and 40 percent of all Asians in the United States lived in California. The influx of Asians was encouraged by the Immigration Reform Act of 1990, which substantially raised the annual number of immigrants allowed into the United States and tripled the number of openings for skilled workers. The composition of California's Asian American community was transformed by the continuing arrival of educated professionals with marketable skills from the Philippines, Korea, Hong Kong, and Taiwan. To meet the growing demand for additional skilled workers, Congress in 2000 agreed to nearly double the number of temporary visas for skilled high-tech workers. Most of the new workers came from India and China.

The growing diversity within the Asian American community manifested itself in a variety of ways. By the 1990s nearly three-quarters of all Asian Americans were immigrants, whereas 20 years earlier less than half were foreign-born. The newcomers to California came from more than 30 separate cultures. The single largest Asian group continued to be Filipinos, followed by Chinese, Japanese, Koreans, Vietnamese, Cambodians, and Laotians. To encompass also those who came from Guam, Tonga, and other islands of the Pacific, many came to prefer the term "Asian Pacific Americans."

Asian Americans continued to gain additional political power, but their dispersal throughout the state undercut their strength. San Francisco was an exception. By 2000 Asian Americans held top positions in city government, including the chief of police and three spots on the Board of Supervisors. "In the last half of the 1990s," observed David Lee of the Chinese American Voter Education Committee, "Asians have made more gains than they have in 150 years in San Francisco." Asian Americans tended to be considerably more conservative than other minorities, and they often supported candidates who appealed to their interests as homeowners and operators of small businesses. The highest-ranking Asian American officeholder was Republican Ming Chin, son of a Chinese immigrant potato farmer, appointed to the state supreme court in 1996. Former congressman Norman Mineta, who spent part of his boyhood in a wartime relocation camp, became the first American of Asian descent to serve in a president's cabinet when Democrat Bill Clinton appointed him secretary of commerce in 2000. The following year, Republican George W. Bush named Mineta to the post of secretary of transportation.

One of the areas in which Asian Americans continued to excel was higher education. In the fall of 1991, Asian American students became the largest ethnic group among freshmen at the Berkeley and Los Angeles campuses of the University of California. Nearly all of the Asian Americans were admitted on the basis of their academic merit; half had straight-A averages in high school. "Asian success is a tribute to their hard work and the fact they took difficult courses and made an extra effort," commented one UC regent. Berkeley chancellor Chang-Lin Tien agreed, pointing out that Asian American high school graduates were more than twice as likely as their white counterparts to meet the UC's tough admissions requirements. The high level of educational and economic achievement of Asian Americans led some demographers to see them as part of "an Anglo-Asian overclass that will dominate California's two-tier society of the 21st century."

The remarkable success of Asian Americans was clouded by an increase in ethnic hostilities during the prolonged recession of the early 1990s. "Fears of the old 'yellow peril' are still alive and well," warned Japanese American historian Nadine Hata. China's detention of the crew of a downed American spy plane in 2001 led to a flurry of anti-Chinese political cartoons laden with outrageous ethnic stereotypes. A national poll the same year revealed that one in four Americans had "strong negative attitudes" toward Chinese Americans. "We always knew there was negativity out there," commented Henry Tang, "but we were startled at the magnitude."

Ethnic tensions increased further following the terrorist attacks of September 11, 2001. Living in California were more than a million Muslims, including 250,000 whose roots lay in the Middle East. Federal authorities arrested and detained hundreds of individuals of Middle Eastern descent; the State Department tightened visa applications for 26 Arab and Muslim nations. Harassment and despicable hate crimes directed against Arab Americans and Muslim Americans were reported across the nation, including arson attacks in San Jose, beatings in Los Angeles, the shooting of Yemeni shopkeepers in Fresno and Tulare counties, and the vandalizing of Afghan and Iranian businesses in San Francisco. President George W. Bush issued a stern rebuke: "No one should be singled out for unfair treatment or unkind words because of their ethnic background or religious faith."

The largest number of new Californians in recent decades were Latinos, most of whom were of Mexican origin. The state's Latino population grew by more than 3 million during the 1990s; by 2000 one out of every three Californians was Latino. Heralding the arrival of "the Latino Century," demographers estimated that by 2020 Latinos would compose the largest ethnic group in the state, and by midcentury they would constitute the majority. Latino Californians tended to be younger than the general population, and their birthrate was nearly twice that of non-Latinos.

Los Angeles County continued to be the center of the state's Hispanic population; the number of Latinos living in the county was expected to more than double between 1990 and 2020, increasing from 3.3 million to 7.5 million. But Latino residents were also moving in record numbers from the crowded neighborhoods of East Los Angeles into the northern reaches of the San Fernando Valley. The Latino population in the Central Valley was also growing rapidly. More than 40 percent of the residents of Fresno, Merced, and Tulare counties were Latino and Asian. "This valley is the richest multiethnic rural environment in the nation, if not the world," observed Central Valley native Gerald Haslam.

Education remained one of the greatest challenges facing the state's Hispanic population. About 45 percent of Latinos in the workforce had less than a high school education, compared with 8 percent of non-Latinos, and the dropout rate of Latino students was three times higher than that of Anglo students. The passage of Proposition 227 in 1998 dismantled the state's bilingual education system, but Latino Californians remained determined to overcome the language barrier. "By the third generation, they have replaced Spanish with English," observed Arturo Vargas of the National Association of Latino Elected and Appointed Officials. "People are struggling to be part of this society, not be separate from it."

Although a substantial Hispanic middle class was emerging, sustained by more than 650,000 Latino-owned businesses, the median income of Latinos remained far below that of other Californians. Nearly 23 percent of Latino families in 2001 lived in poverty, compared to just 8 percent of non-Hispanic whites. Hispanic workers, with limited education and low skill levels, remained concentrated in low-wage jobs. "We are in the workforce," noted Sonia Perez of the National Conference of La Raza. "The problem is, we are moving in and getting stuck." With the lowest rates of computer ownership and Internet access, Latinos also found themselves on the downside of the "digital divide." "We live in a fractured state," one high-tech CEO observed. "People are divided by income, language, and access to information." Researchers at the University of California, San Francisco, confirmed in 2000 that although Latinos were being employed in record numbers, they were not sharing equally in the state's economic boom. "There are a lot of indications that we're moving towards a more polarized society," concluded UCSF researcher Laura Trupin, "and the divide continues to be defined by race and ethnicity in the year 2000."

The spectacular growth of California's immigrant population became an intensely debated political issue in the 1990s. Republican governor Pete Wilson's enthusiastic support of Proposition 187, overwhelmingly approved by voters in 1994, ignited a firestorm of opposition from Latinos. (See Chapter 33.) The initiative provoked one of the largest protest demonstrations in the history of Los Angeles and led to an unprecedented level of Latino political activity throughout the state. One million Hispanic Californians registered to vote in the latter half of the 1990s. Whereas Latino voters had represented only 10 percent of the electorate in 1990, they accounted for 16 percent in 2000. Gregory Rodriguez, a researcher at Pepperdine University, credited Pete Wilson and Proposition 187 with finally awakening the "sleeping giant" of Latino political power: "Pete Wilson will be known in the future as the 'father' of Latino California. He's done what thousands of activists could never have done."

Also helping mobilize the Latino community were Spanish-language newspapers such as *La Opinión*. Headed by Monica Lozano, whose grandfather founded the paper in Los Angeles during the 1920s, *La Opinión* had a readership of nearly half a million. Lozano said that her goal was not just to report the news but also to educate her Latino readership in the basics of the American political and economic systems.

Monica Lozano, president and chief operating officer of Los Angeles–based *La Opinión,* the largest Spanish-language daily newspaper in the United States. (*Courtesy of* La Opinión.)

Emerging in the late 1990s and early 2000s was a new generation of Latino leaders, skilled at building coalitions and dedicated to the politics of ethnic transcendence. Christened by political satirist Lalo Lopez as "Generation Mex," the new leaders remained loyal to their ethnic heritage but also embraced broader issues. Typical of the new generation was Fresno Democrat Cruz Bustamante, elected in 1996 as the first Hispanic speaker of the assembly. Two years later he became lieutenant governor, the first Latino to serve in statewide office in the twentieth century. In the days after the terrorist attacks of September 11, 2001, Bustamante rallied his fellow Californians with a stirring speech: "Let those who would seek to destroy us see our numbers, feel our commitment, know our resolve . . . that we will never allow evil to prevail. Not in our day, and not in our time. Not in our community. Not in our California. Not in our country."

Succeeding Bustamante as speaker of the assembly was Los Angeles Democrat Antonio Villaraigosa, a master in the art of crossover appeal. Upon assuming the speakership, Villaraigosa announced his determination to reinvigorate the California dream by improving the lives of all Californians. "I'm a Latino and I'm proud of that," he told the *Los Angeles Times,* "but I'm also an American and I'm proud of that, too." Following his unsuccessful bid to become the first Latino mayor of Los Angeles since 1872, Villaraigosa's prospects remained bright. Meanwhile, Rocky Delgadillo was elected Los Angeles city attorney in 2001. Delgadillo, a Harvard-educated centrist Democrat, won a majority of support from Latinos, African Americans, and Asians as well as from white conservatives, independents, and Republicans. "There will be a Latino mayor," commented one political observer, "who could just as easily be a conservative—or a Republican."

The new generation of leaders offered the hope that California, at long last, might overcome its bitter legacy of ethnic and racial hostilities. That legacy formed the essential backdrop to the Census Bureau's historic announcement in 2001 that California's minority population was now in the majority. The bureau predicted that an additional 8 million immigrants would come to California by the year 2020 and Latinos then would outnumber non-Hispanic whites. "No other industrial nation, let alone state, has ever experienced such a dramatic alteration of its ethnic composition," commented demographer Leon Bouvier. "There will be no place in the state that is not touched by immigration and these racial and ethnic changes," added Mark Baldassare, author of *California in the New Millennium* (2000). "We will be inventing a new kind of society."

The single most important challenge facing Californians in that new society of the new millennium was adjusting to the state's growing diversity. (See Color Plate 18.) "We Californians have the opportunity, the necessity, the responsibility to realize our great challenge," declared Democratic senator John Vasconcellos, "the promise of a multicultural democracy in the global economy." The challenge is to appreciate the strengths that come from diversity, to celebrate the differences as well as the shared experiences of this diverse population. "Let's put it this way," said Arturo Vargas. "If California cannot shape a true multicultural society, then the whole country is doomed." Or to put it in more positive terms, if California *can* meet the challenge of diversity, then the whole nation may be illumined by the brilliance of its example.

Selected Bibliography

The best interpretive surveys of the forces shaping contemporary California are Mark Baldassare, *California in the New Millennium: The Changing Social and Political Landscape* (2000); Peter Schrag, *Paradise Lost: California's Experience, America's Future* (1998); and Dan Walters, *The New California: Facing the 21st Century* (1992).

On transportation issues, see David E. Dowall, *California's Infrastructure Policy for the 21st Century* (2000); Michael Neuman and Jan Whittington, *Building California's Future* (2000); and various monthly bulletins and annual reports from the California Department of Transportation.

Useful guides to current issues in educational policy are the California Department of Education's annual *Fact Book.* See also Robert K. Fullinwider, *Public Education in a Multicultural Society* (1996), and Julian R. Betts, *The Changing Role of Education in the California Labor Market* (2000).

On the battle over affirmative action, see Richard Delgado and Jean Stefanic, "California's Racial History and Constitutional Rationales for Race-Conscious Decision Making in Higher Education," *UCLA Law Review,* XL (August 2000), pp. 1521–1614; Lydia Chavez, *The Color Bind: California's Battle to End Affirmative Action* (1998); and Jerome Karabel, *The Rise and Fall of Affirmative Action at the University of California* (1999).

The crisis in health care is described in E. Kathleen Adams et al., *Medi-Cal and Managed Care* (2000); Emelyn Rodriguez, "Health Care Epidemic Deepens," *California Journal,* XXXI (May 2000), pp. 10–17; and Tom Philp, "Whither Health Care Reform?" ibid., XXX (September 1999), pp. 8–19. On the AIDS epidemic, see *California HIV/AIDS Update,* a monthly digest of statistical information published by the Department of Health Services, Office of AIDS, and Randy Shilts, *And the Band Played On: Politics, People, and the AIDS Epidemic* (1987).

On the soaring rate of incarceration and the construction of new prisons, see *Crime in California* (1994), published by the Office of the Legislative Analyst, and Kristina Emanuels, "Prisons," *California Journal,* XX (December 1989), pp. 507–509. For a view from the inside, see *Corrections: Public Safety, Public Service* (1991) and *CDC Facts* (1992), publications of the California Department of Corrections.

Major studies of the changing nature of California's population, in addition to those cited for Chapter 30, include Belinda I. Reyes (ed.), *A Portrait of Race and Ethnicity in California* (2001); Zoltan Hajnal and Baldassare, *Finding Common Ground: Racial and Ethnic Attitudes in California* (2001); Deborah Reed, *California's Rising Income Inequality* (1999); Michael B. Preston et al., *Racial and Ethnic Politics in California* (1998); Dale Maharidge, *The Coming White Minority* (1996); David Rieff, *Los Angeles: Capital of the Third World* (1992); and Leon Bouvier, *Fifty Million Californians: Inevitable?* (1991). On the new Latino leadership, see Gregory Rodriguez, "Antonio Villaraigosa," *California Journal,* XXIV (March 1998), pp. 10, 55–56, and "The Latino Century" special issue, ibid., XXXI (January 2000).

Subject and Author Index

Note: Entries in SMALL CAPS are the names of authors listed in the Selected Bibliographies at the end of each chapter.

abortion, 476
Abraham, Spencer, 504
ABRAMS, C., 527
abstract expressionism, 442–44
Achik, Long, 148
ACUÑA, RUDOLFO, 419
ADAMIC, LOUIS, 253, 342
ADAMS, E. KATHLEEN, 553
ADAMS, GRAHAM, JR., 253
ADAMS, JOHN, 453
admission as a state (1850), 116, 117, 122
aerospace industry, 422, 506, 515–18
affirmative action, 471–72, 537, 548
African Americans:
   constitution of 1849 and, 118–19, 122
   filmmakers, 523
   health care, 539
   higher education, 536, 548
   literature by, 440–41
   oppression of, 155–56
   original settlers include, 42
   during Spanish period, 42
   in twentieth century, 358, 406–7, 433, 471–72,
      536, 545–49
   during World War II, 358
   (*see also names of individuals*)
agricultural labor, 68, 155, 157, 249, 250,
      328–29, 387, 390–91, 402–3, 525
Agricultural Labor Relations Act (1975), 397,
      462–63

Agricultural Labor Relations Board (ALRB),
      397, 462–63, 525
Agricultural Workers Organizing Committee,
      393–94
agriculture, 6, 7, 11–13, 109–10, 201–5, 386–87,
      462, 463, 494, 510
AIDS (acquired immunodeficiency syndrome),
      539–40
aircraft industry, 7, 359–61, 515–18
air pollution, 8–9, 446, 488–90, 513
Air Resource Board, 489
AKIN, WILLIAM E., 338
Alatorre, Richard, 413
ALBERTS, S. S., 352
Albrier, Frances, 357
ALBRIGHT, THOMAS, 455
Alcatraz Island, Indian occupation of
      (1969–1971), 402, 441
Alemany, Joseph S., 167
Alien Land Law (1913), 276–78, 404
All–American Canal, 317, 319
ALLEN, ARTHUR P., 367
Allen, Lawrence, 336
Allen, Willis, 336
Allensworth, Allen, 275
Allensworth (town), 275
ALLSWANG, JOHN M., 282
ALMAGUER, TOMÁS, 158, 253
Almaraz, Carlos, 446
ALMQUIST, A. F., 158

Alta California (newspaper), 133, 161, 165
Altamont Pass:
  rock concert at (1969), 455
  wind turbines at, 496–97
Alvarado, Blanca, 413
Alvarado, Juan Bautista, 59, 64–65, 78–79, 146
ALVAREZ, DAVID, 168
AMBROSE, STEPHEN, 178
American Civil Liberties Union (ACLU), 333
"American Cultures" (course requirement), 546
American Federation of Labor (AFL), 242, 248,
  389, 393
American Indian Historical Society, 401
American Legion, 361
American Medical Association (AMA), 372–73
American party, 124–25
"American Plan" for open shop, 290
Ames, John J, 162
Anderson, Gilbert M. ("Broncho Billy"),
  303–4
ANDERSON, HENRY P., 398
ANDERSON, MARION K., 20
ANDERSON, TOTTON J., 480
ANKLI, ROBERT E., 213
ANSWELL, MARTIN R., 308
ANTHONY, GENE, 436
Anti–Saloon League, 272
Anza, Juan Bautista de, 40–41
Apple Computer Company, 513, 523
Aquarium of the Pacific (Long Beach), 520
AQUILA, RICHARD, 456
Arbuckle, Roscoe ("Fatty"), 308
ARCHIBALD, KATHERINE, 367
ARCHIBALD, ROBERT, 57
architecture, 77, 225–26, 349–52, 449–51
Areias, Rusty, 485
Argonaut (San Francisco magazine), 216
Argüello, Concepción, 54
Aronson, Max, 303
art, 223–26, 348, 443–49
Asian Indians, 249, 250
Asing, Norman, 148
Asisara, Lorenzo (Ohlone), 63
Assembling California (book), 2
Associated Farmers of California, 343, 388–89
Atherton, Gertrude, 415
ATHERTON, GERTRUDE, 190
Atkinson, Richard, 537
AUBLE, ARTHUR G., 418
Austin, Mary, 4
Australia, 8, 133
Automobile Club of Southern California, 301
automobiles, 300–303, 423–25, 488–90, 499,
  529–31

Ayala, Juan Miguel de, 41
AYERS, ANNE BARTLETT, 455
Ayers, Thomas, 223
AZUMA, EIICHIRO, 338

B-1 bomber, 517
Babbitt, Bruce, 491
Bacall, Lauren, 376
BACHUS, EDWARD J., 214
BAGWELL, BETH, 436
BAILEY, PAUL, 114
BAIRD, NEWTON D., 352
Baker, Edward D., 126–27
BAKKEN, GORDON M., 139
BAKKER, ELNA, 9
Baldassare, Mark, 478, 552
BALDASSARE, MARK, 480, 553
BALDERRAMA, FRANCISCO, 338, 419
Bancroft, George, 85, 88
Bancroft, Hubert Howe, 131, 146, 220–22, 224
BANCROFT, HUBERT HOWE, 57, 70, 85, 114, 137,
  220, 224, 229
Bandini, Juan, 59
Bandini, Maria, 76
BANHAM, REYNER, 353, 456
Bank of America (formerly Bank of Italy), 293,
  387, 431
Bank of California, 187–88
Banking, 110
Banking industry, 110–11, 237, 267–68, 293
Banks, Dennis, 441
Banning, Phineas, 110
BANNON, JOHN FRANCIS, 38
BARBOUR, MICHAEL, 9
BARCLAY, THOMAS S., 295
Bard, Thomas R., 297, 400
BARD, THOMAS R., 308
BARKER, CHARLES A., 128, 229
BARNHART, EDWARD N., 367
BARNHART, JACQUELINE BAKER, 168
BARRETT, EDWARD L., JR., 385
BARTH, GUNTHER, 158, 199, 230
Bartleson, John, 79, 80
Bartlett, Washington Allon, 99
Bartolomea (Gabrielino), 50–51
Bassett, J.M., 233
BATCHELOR, L. D., 214
BATES, JACK W., 240
BATMAN, RICHARD D., 81, 295
BAUER, JACK K., 96
BAUER, JOHN E., 214
Baxter, Leone, 372, 363
Bay Area figurative painters, 444
Bay Area Rapid Transit (BART), 424, 513, 514

Beach Boys, 454
Beale, Edward F., 101, 151–52, 159
Bean, Lowell John, 15
BEAN, LOWELL JOHN, 20
BEAN, WALTON, 264, 339
Bear Flag Revolt (1846), 89–91
BEAR, MARKELL C., 385
BEARD, ESTLE, 159
Beasley, Delilah, 326
BEASLEY, DELILAH, 159
"beatniks," 438, 440
BECK, WARREN A., 9
BECKER, JULES, 114, 200
BECKER, ROBERT H., 114, 158
BEEBE, ROSE MARIE, 70
BEILHARZ, EDWIN A., 56
BELDEN, JOSIAH, 82
BELL, DANIEL, 527
BELL, GEOFFREY, 309
Bell, Larry, 446, 449
Bell, Theodore A., 261, 264
Bellamy, Edward, 239, 259
BEMIS, GEORGE W., 295
BENDETSEN, KARL R., 367
Bengston, Billy Al, 445, 446
BENNETT, MELBA BERRY, 352
BENNION, SHERILYN COX, 230
BENSON, IVAN, 168
BENSON, JACKSON J., 352
BENSON, TODD, 158
Benton, Thomas Hart, 85, 87, 88
Berkeley, George, 227
BERKOWITZ, MADELON, 283
BERNARD, RICHARD M., 527
BERWICK, ARNOLD, 253
Better America Federation, Los Angeles, 290–91
BETTS, JULIAN R., 552
Biddle, Francis, 363
Bidwell, John, 79–80
BIDWELL, JOHN, 82
BIEBER, RALPH P., 114
Bierce, Ambrose, 216–17, 235
Bierstadt, Albert, 223, 449
Big Four, 171–77, 180–84, 232
BIGGART, NICOLE WOOLSEY, 395, 480
Bigler, John, 124, 148, 163
Bilingual Education Act, 550
Billings, Warren K., 286, 337
BINGHAM, EDWIN, 230
biodiversity, 11, 485–87
Biograph (film company), 304
biomass (renewable energy source), 497
biotechnology, 512
Bird, Rose Elizabeth, 417, 462, 466

Birth of a Nation (film), 306
BLACKBURN, THOMAS C., 20
BLACKFORD, MANSEL G., 264, 282
Black Panther party, 420, 433, 441
blacks (see African Americans)
blanket primary, 472
BLEW, ROBERT W., 139
Block, A. G., 546
"bloody Thursday" (1934), 331
BOBB, BERNARD E., 56
Boeing Company, 518
Boessenecker, John, 131
BOESSENECKER, JOHN, 139
Bogart, Humphrey, 376
BOLLENS, JOHN C., 480
BOLTON, HERBERT EUGENE, 38–39, 56
BONADIO, FELICE A., 295
BONFILS, WINFRED BLACK, 352
Bonneville, Benjamin, 75
BOOKSPAN, SHELLEY, 140
Booth, Newton, 239
Borica, Diego de, 53, 71
BOSWELL, F. E., 139
BOSWORTH, ALLAN R., 367
BOTTLES, SCOTT LEE, 309
Bouchard, Hippolyte de, 56, 76
Boulder Canyon Project, 316–19
boundaries, state, 119–20
Bouvier, Leon, 552
BOUVIER, LEON, 553
Boxer, Barbara, 415, 469, 473
BOYARSKY, WILLIAM, 480
braceros (agricultural laborers), 390, 392, 396
Bradley, Thomas:
   gubernatorial candidate, 465, 466
   mayor of Los Angeles, 410, 465, 594
BRADSHAW, TED K., 527
Braitman, Jacqueline R., 275
BRAITMAN, JACQUELINE R., 282, 419
BRANCH, EDGAR M., 168
Branciforte, Villa de, 53
Brannan, Samuel, 98–99, 132–34, 160, 206
Brautigan, Richard, 438
Braverman, Barry, 521
BRECHIN, GRAY, 504
Breen, Margaret, 81
Breen, Patrick, 81
BRETNOR, HELEN HARDING, 168
Bridges, Harry R., 331–33
BRIGGS, DONALD C., 128
BRILLIANT, ASHLEIGH E., 309
BRISSENDEN, PAUL F., 253
bristlecone pine (Pinus longaeva), 4
Broder, David S., 479

BRODER, DAVID S., 481
Broderick, David C., 123–24, 125, 136
BROUSSARD, ALBERT S., 419
BROWN, ALAN K., 39
Brown, Edmund G., Jr. ("Jerry"):
  background, 461
  governor, 461–63, 465, 466, 478, 493, 526
  presidential candidate, 397, 413, 416–17
  senatorial candidate, 465
Brown, Edmund G., Sr. ("Pat"), 337, 379–81,
  420, 429, 458, 461–62, 473
BROWN, EDMUND G., SR., 480
BROWN, JAMES LORIN, 190, 229
Brown, Kathleen, 415, 469, 470
Brown, Richard Maxwell, 131
BROWN, RICHARD MAXWELL, 139
Brown, Willie L., Jr., 410, 470, 471, 547
Browne, J. Ross, 155
BROWNE, J. ROSS, 128
BROWNING, CLYDE E., 527
BROWNING, ROBERT E., 39
Brubeck, Dave, 453
BRUCE, JOHN ROBERTS, 168, 230
Bryant & Sturgis (Boston firm), 72
Bryce, James, 231
BRYCE, JAMES, 200
BUCHANAN, A. RUSSELL, 128, 140
Buchanan, James, 86
Budd, James H., 236
Bull Moose (Progressive) party, 269, 278–82
BULLOCK, PAUL, 253, 385
BULLOUGH, WILLIAM A., 240
BURBANK, GARIN, 480
Burbank, Luther, 386
BURCHELL, R. A., 200
Burden, Chris, 447
Bureau of Reclamation, U.S., 321
BURGESS, KATERINA, 527
BURGESS, SHERWOOD D., 115
BURKE, ROBERT E., 295, 339
Burke, Yvonne Brathwaite, 410
Burlingame, Anson, 188, 191
Burlingame Treaty (1868), 180, 191
Burnett, Peter H., 121, 156
Burnham, Daniel Hudson, 349
BURNS, EDWARD M., 230
BURNS, JOHN F., 128
Burns, William J., 248, 257
BURNS, WILLIAM J., 253
Bush, George H. W., 467, 469
Bush, George W., 475, 487, 490, 548, 549
Bustamante, Cruz, 471, 473, 474, 551
Butler, Anthony, 83–84
Butterfield, John, 169

BYNUM, LINDLEY, 81

Cabrillo, Juan Rodríguez, 22–24
Caen, Herb, 438
Cage, John, 452
Cahuenga Pass, battles of (1831 and 1845), 62,
  66, 127
CAIN, BRUCE E., 295, 436, 480, 481
Cal–Fed (water policy coalition), 491
Calhoun, Patrick, 258
California Coastal Commission, 466, 484
California Colored Convention, 156
California Democratic Council (CDC), 373, 383
California Department of Corrections, 466
California Department of Health Services,
  538–39
California Department of Justice, 543
California Desert Protection Act (1970), 485
California dream (popular image of the state),
  345, 423, 438–40
California Endangered Species Act (1970), 484,
  487
California Energy Commission, 462, 495–96,
  498, 500
California Environmental Quality Act (1970),
  484–85
California Farm Bureau, 525
California Film Commission (CFC), 524
California Fruit Growers' Exchange, 204
California Indian Education Association, 402
California Indian Rural Health Board, 402
California Institute of Technology (Cal Tech),
  512, 516
California Institute of the Arts (Cal Arts), 449
California Medical Association (CMA), 374
Californian (newspaper), 160
California Packing Corporation (CalPac), 387,
  389
California ranch house (architectural style),
  449–50
California Real Estate Association, 407
California Republican Assembly (CRA), 373
California School of Fine Arts, 444
"California sound" (popular music style),
  454–55
California Star (newspaper), 98, 100, 160
California State Automobile Association, 301
California State University (CSU), 427, 536–37
California Steam Navigation Company, 175, 182
California Water Resource Control Board, 492
CAMARILLO, ALBERT, 338, 404
Cameron, George T., 347
Caminetti, Anthony J., 208, 273
Campaign for Economic Democracy, 435

campaign management firms, 370–73
Campaigns, Inc., 372–73
CAMPBELL, LEON G., 57
Canby, E. R. S., 154
Canfield, Charles A., 297
Cannery and Agricultural Workers' Industrial
    Union (CAWIU), 330
CANNON, LOU, 480
capital punishment, issue of, 380, 466, 467
CARDWELL, KENNETH H., 353
Carmichael, Stokely, 433
CARNER-RIBALTA, JOSEP, 39
CARNEY, FRANCIS, 385
CAROSSO, VINCENT P., 213
CARPENTER, FREDERICK I., 352
Carpentier, Horace W., 180
CARRANCO, LYNWOOD, 159
Carrillo, José Antonio, 59, 62, 93, 118
Carrillo, Josefa, 76
Carson, James H., 100
Carson, Kit, 93
Carter, James, 156
CARTER, ROBERT W., 114
CARUSO, A. BROOKE, 96
Casey, James P., 136
CASTAÑEDA, ANTONIA I., 57
Castillo, Edward D. (Cahuilla/Luiseño), 19
CASTILLO, EDWARD D., 57, 70
Castro, José, 59, 64, 66, 86, 88, 89
CAUGHEY, JOHN WALTON, 114, 115, 140, 158,
    165, 229, 352, 436
CAUGHEY, LAREE, 352, 436
CD–ROM, 523, 533
Center for California Studies, 546
Center for the Continuing Study of the California
    Economy, 534
Central Pacific Railroad, 170, 177
Central Valley Improvement Act (1992), 491
Central Valley Project, 321–23, 491
CEPLAIR, LARRY, 385
CERMEÑO, SEBASTIÁN RODRÍGUEZ, 27
Chabot, Anthony, 108
Chaffey, George, 209–10, 316
CHAMBERS, CLARKE A., 338
Chan, Sucheng, 11
CHAN, SUCHENG, 150, 158, 199, 200, 418
Chandler, Dorothy Buffum, 416, 453
Chandler, Harry, 317, 346, 359
Chandler, Norman, 416
CHANDLER, ROBERT J., 128
CHANEY, LINDSAY, 352
Chaplin, Charlie, 304
CHAPMAN, CHARLES E., 39
Chapman, Joseph, 76

CHARTKOFF, JOSEPH L., 19
CHARTKOFF, KERRY KONA, 19
Chávez, César, 393–94, 396, 493, 526
CHAVEZ, LYDIA, 553
CHEN, YONG, 158
CHERNY, ROBERT W., 200, 253, 264, 295, 339,
    426
Chew, Lew, 192
Chicago, Judy, 437
Chicano Moratorium Committee, 431
Chicanos (see Latinos)
Chico, Mariano, 64
Chilenos, 133, 142
Chinese:
    discrimination against in gold rush, 108,
        147–50
    exclusion of, 197–99, 405
    immigration, 191–97
    literature by, 442–43
    political movements against, 191–99
    railroad construction work by, 176–78
    in twentieth century, 405, 548–49
    (see also names of individuals)
Chinn, Ming, 540
CHIU, PING, 199
Chouinard Art Institute, 348, 444, 446, 449
Chouinard, Nelbert, 349
Chun–chuen, Lai, 148
Chupu (Chumash deity), p. 46
CHURCHILL, CHARLES B., 81
CITRIN, JACK, 481
Civil War, California and, 126–27
Clappe, Louise Amelia Knapp Smith ("Dame
    Shirley"), 161
CLARK, GEORGE T., 178
CLARK, HARRY, 229
CLARK, THOMAS R., 383
CLARKE, DWIGHT L., 96
Cleaver, Eldridge, 433–34
CLEAVER, ELDRIDGE, 436
CLELAND, ROBERT GLASS, 70, 81, 96, 115, 213
Clemens, Samuel L. ("Mark Twain"), 164–65
CLEMENTS, KENDRICK A., 323
Cleveland, Richard, 72
CLEVELAND, RICHARD, 81
climate, 7–9
Clinton, Bill, 469, 473, 548
clipper ships, 102
CLODIUS, ALBERT H., 265
CLOUD, BARBARA, 168
CLOUD, ROY W., 436
CLOUGH, CHARLES, 397
CLUCAS, RICHARD, 481
CLYMAN, JAMES, 81

coal, 169, 297–98

Coast Range, 2, 5, 7

"code talkers," 358

COFFMAN, YAYLOR, 353

cogeneration of electricity, 496–97

COHEN, MICHAEL P., 323

COLEMAN, CHARLES M., 324

Coleman, William Tell, 110, 133–38, 194

colleges and universities, 166–67, 226–29,
    426–34, 535–38
    (*see also specific colleges and universities*)

Coloma, gold discovery at (1848), 97–98

Colorado River Aqueduct, 319–21

Colton letters, 232

Colton, David D., 226, 232, 238

Colton, Ellen M., 233

Colton, Walter, 116–17, 160

COLTON, WALTER, 128

Columbia Pictures, 308

communism, 288–90, 330, 331, 335, 342–43,
    375–79, 381–84

Communist Labor party, 288

community colleges, 427, 536–37

COMPANYS, FERNANDO B., 38

computers, 511–15, 523–24, 533

Comstock Lode, 164, 186–88

Concord Naval Weapons Station, 517

CONDON, EMMET, 264

CONKLING, MARGARET B., 178

CONKLING, ROSCOE P., 178

CONLIN, JOSEPH R., 114, 253

CONN, STETSON, 367

CONRAT, MAISIE, 367

CONRAT, RICHARD, 368

conservation and use of natural resources,
    310–13, 482–504

Consolidated Virginia (mine), 188

constitutions:
    1849, 118–21
    1879, 196–98, 428

Contra Costa Canal, 321–22

Contract and Finance Company, 177, 182

COOK, SHERBURNE F., 20, 57, 159

Coolbrith, Ina, 166

Coolidge, Calvin, 291

COOLIDGE, MARY ROBERTS, 199

Cooper, Gary, 376–77

Cooper, John, 77

Coppola, Francis Ford, 489, 505

Cora, Charles, 136–37

CORD, STEVEN, 229

CORDOVA, FRED, 418

Corley, James H., 377

Cornelius (Tuolumne), 150

CORNFORD, DANIEL, 200, 252, 367

Cortes, Hernán, 21

Costansó, Miguel, 35, 36

COSTELLO, WILLIAM, 385

COSTO, JEANNETTE HENRY, 57

Costo, Rupert (Cahuilla), 401

COSTO, RUPERT, 57

COTTLE, REX L., 398

COUGHLIN, MAGDALEN, 81

COWAN, ROBERT G., 128

CRAWFORD, DOROTHY LAMB, 456

Crédit Mobilier, 177

Creel, George, 334

CRESAP, DEAN R., 384

Crespí, Juan, 34–36

Criminal Syndicalism Act (1919), 288–90

Crocker Art Gallery, 223–24

Crocker, Charles, 171, 173, 175–77, 195, 224

Crocker, Edwin Bryant, 174, 223

Crocker, William H., 281

CRONIN, THOMAS E., 481

Crosby, Harry, 29

CROSBY, HARRY W., 39

cross-filing, 269, 291, 380, 472

CROSS, IRA B., 115, 200, 252

CROUCHETT, LORRAINE J., 295, 398, 418

Crow, Walter J., 186

Cullinan, Eustace, 321

CULTON, DONALD R., 265

Cunningham, Imogen (photographer), 347

Cunningham, Kate Richards O'Hare, 416

CUTTER, DONALD C., 38, 57

Cypriano (Awal), 150

D-Q University, 402

DAGGETT, EMERSON, 190

Daggett, Rollin M., 161

DAGGETT, STUART, 178, 240

DAKIN, SUSANNA BRYANT, 70

"Dame Shirley" (Louise Amelia Knapp Smith
    Clappe), 161

Dana, Richard Henry, 68, 72–73, 76, 130, 243

DANA, RICHARD HENRY, 81

Dana, William Goodwin, 76

DANIEL, CLETUS E., 253, 397

DANIELS, DOUGLAS HENRY, 158, 418

DANIELS, ROGER, 283, 295, 367, 368, 418, 419

Darrow, Clarence, 248

DARROW, CLARENCE, 253

Darwin, Charles, 219, 228

DAS, R. K., 397

Dasmann, Raymond, 112

DASMANN, RAYMOND F., 114, 504

DAVENPORT, F. M., 283

Davenport, Homer, 235, 236
DAVIDSON, MICHAEL, 455
Davies, Louise M., Symphony Hall, 452
Davis, Arthur Powell, 316–17
Davis, Gray:
  background, 473
  environmental issues, 484, 487, 489
  electric energy crisis, 476, 501–3
  governor, 473–78, 530, 531, 535, 544
  health care, 539
  terrorist attacks (2001), 477
  transportation, 530, 531
DAVIS, MARGARET LESLIE, 308, 323
DAVIS, MIKE, 214, 436, 504
DAVIS, RONALD L., 353
DAWSON, ROBERT, 504, 528
"Dear Pard" letters, 233
death penalty (see capital punishment)
DEBOW, KEN, 480
Debs, Eugene Victor, 285
Decker, Peter, 131
DECKER, PETER R., 139
DEFALLA, PAUL M., 200
defense industry, 354–61, 422–23, 515–18
de Forest, Lee, 511
DEGRAAF, LAWRENCE B., 159, 419
DEGROOT, GERHARD J., 436, 480
de la Guerra, María, 93
Delano, Alonzo, 162
de la Rocha, Beto, 446
Delgadillo, Rocky, 552
DELGADO, JAMES P., 114
Delgado, Richard, 537
DELGADO, RICHARD, 553
Dellums, Ronald V., 410
DELMATIER, ROYCE D., 129, 338, 480
Del Monte (fruit & vegetable label), 387
deMille, Cecil B., 305, 307
DENEVI, DON, 39
de Pérez, Eulalia Arrila, 45
Derby, George H. ("John Phoenix"), 162
Deukmejian, George:
  attorney general, 410, 465
  governor, 418, 465–67, 469, 484
Deverell, William, 231, 266
DEVERELL, WILLIAM F., 240, 266, 282
DE VOTO, BERNARD, 96
DeWitt, John L., 362–64
DEWITT, JOHN L., 367
de Young, Charles, 198, 222
de Young, M. H., Memorial Museum, 222, 237,
  347, 451
Diablo Canyon (nuclear power plant), 497–99
DICK, BERNARD F., 309

Dickson, Edward A., 260, 261
DICKSON, EDWARD A., 283
Didion, Joan, 439–40
Diebenkorn, Richard, 444
Dies, Martin, 375
"Digger" (pejorative), 12
DiGiorgio Corporation, 387, 394
DILLON, RICHARD, 82, 158
Direct Legislation League, 260
direct primary, 262
Disney, Walt, 376, 449, 521, 523
Disneyland, 519, 521
Disney's California Adventure (theme park), 521
DISTASI, LAWRENCE, 367
Dodge, Grenville M., 177
Doheny, Edward L., 297–300
DONLEY, MICHAEL W., 9
Donner party (1845–1846), 80–81
Dorr, Ebenezer, 71
DOTI, LYNNE P., 115
Douglas, Donald, 359–61
Douglas, Helen Gahagan, 377, 415, 457
DOUGLASS, JOHN A., 436
DOWALL, DAVID E., 504, 552
DOWLING, PATRICK J., 200
Downey, Sheridan, 336
DOWNEY, SHERIDAN, 324
Drake, Francis, 25–26
Drought, 343, 491–93
DUBOFSKY, MELVIN, 253
DUE, JOHN F., 214
Duginski, Paul, 471
DUMKE, GLENN S., 214
DUNBAR, ANDREW J., 324
Duncan, Robert, 437
DUNNE, JOHN GREGORY, 398
Durán, Narcisco, 64, 74
DURRENBERGER, ROBERT D., 9
Durst, Ralph, 252, 275
Dust Bowl migration (1930s), 342–43, 348, 389,
  440
DUTKA, BARRY, 114
Dwinelle, John W., 227
Dymally, Mervyn, 410

EAGLE, ADAM FORTUNATE, 418
Earl, Edwin T., 260, 284, 315
Earth Day (1970), 482
Earthquakes, 2–3, 256–57, 424
Eastin, Delaine, 534
Eaton, Fred, 314–16
Echeandía, José Maria, 61–62, 74–75
E Clampus Vitus (fraternal organization), 113
Edison, Thomas A., and movies, 303–4

Edson, Katherine Philips, 272, 275, 416
education:
    before 1846, 69
    since 1900, 426–27, 532–38, 549–50
    to 1900, 166–67, 226–29
    bilingual, 413, 473, 535, 549
    campus turmoil, 427–32
    constitution of 1849 and, 119
    impact of Proposition 13 on, 464
    increased funding for, 466
    reform of, 474–75
    segregation in, 156, 167, 276, 278, 406–7
    student attitudes, 433–34
    (*see also* colleges and universities)
Edwards v. South Carolina (1963) (free speech
    on college campuses), 429
EGAN, FEROL, 96, 190
Eisenhower, Dwight David, 374, 382–83, 458
Eisner, Michael, 523
El Congreso del Puebo de Habla Española, 410
electric cars, 489
electric energy crisis, 478, 496, 501–4
electronics industry, 510–14, 518
Elk Hills (naval oil reserve), 299, 300
ELLIOTT, ARLENE, 367
ELLISON, JOSEPH, 128
Ellison, William Henry, 126
ELLISON, WILLIAM H., 81, 128, 140, 158
El Niño (opera), 453
ELSASSER, ALBERT B., 19
EMANUELS, KRISTINA, 553
End Poverty in California (EPIC), 333
energy crisis, 477, 478, 495–504
ENGELBERT, ERNEST A., 505
Engelhardt, Zephyrin, 50
ENGELHARDT, ZEPHYRIN, 39
ENGH, MICHAEL, 168
ENGLANDER, SUSAN, 282
ENGLUND, STEVEN, 385
ENGSTRAND, IRIS H. W., 39, 96
entertainment industry, 7, 303–8, 506, 521–27
environment, concern for, 112, 155, 310–13,
    482–95
Enviromental Defense Fund, 495
Environmental Protection Agency (EPA), 495
Equal Rights Amendment (ERA), 417
ESCOBAR, EDWARD J., 419
Eshleman, John M., 267, 281
ESPIRITU, YEN LE, 295
Essanay Film Manufacturing Company, 303–4
Estanislao (Lakisamni Yokuts), 60
ETHINGTON, PHILLIP J., 139
Eu, March Fong, 405, 415
EVANS, CERINDA, W., 178

EVANS, ROWLAND, 480
EVERETT, MILES C., 265
Everson, William, 437
EVERSON, WILLIAM, 455
EWERS, JOHN C., 81
"excess land law," (see Newlands Reclamation
    Act)

Fages, Pedro, 36, 37, 40, 54
Fair, James G., 188
Fairchild Semiconductor Company, 512
Fair Political Practices Commission, 461
Fall, Albert B., 300
FARAGHER, JOHN MACK, 114
Farnham, Eliza, 112
Farnsworth, Philo, 511
FARRELLY, DAVID, 339
FATOUT, PAUL, 229
FAULHABER, CHARLES B., 229
FAWCETT, ANTHONY, 456
Feather River Project, 381
"Federal Plan" of reapportionment (1926), 294
FEINMAN, RONALD L., 338
Feinstein, Dianne, 415–16, 467, 469, 475, 478,
    495, 503
Ferlinghetti, Lawrence, 438
FERLINGHETTI, LAWRENCE, 455
FERNANDEZ, FERDINAND F., 418
FERRIER, WILLIAM WARREN, 220
FERRIS, DAVID F., 168
Fickert, Charles M., 287
Field, Mervin, 468
Field, Stephen J., 192, 238, 288
Fierro de Bright, Josefina, 410, 412
Figueroa, José, 62, 64, 69
Filipino Farm Labor Union, 393
Filipinos, 249, 292, 393, 405, 548 (*see also*
    names of individuals)
Fillmore, Millard, 123
FINDLEY, JAMES C., 283
FISHER, J. A., 159
Fixico, Donald, 400
FIXICO, DONALD, 418
flag of California, 89–90
Flint, Timothy, 75
Flood, James C., 188, 189
Flores, José Mariá, 92, 94
FOGELSON, ROBERT M., 214, 309
Foltz, Clara Shortridge, 270
FONER, PHILIP S., 436
FONTANA, BERNARD L., 56
Fontana, Mark J., 387
Forbes, Alexander, 84
FORBES, JACK D., 39, 418

FORD, BONNIE L., 168
Ford, Gerald R., 461
Ford, Henry, 300
Ford, Richard ("Blackie"), 252
Ford, Tirey L., 258
foreign miners' license tax (1850), 142
foreign miners' license tax (1852), 148
FOSTER, MARK S., 324, 367
Foster, Stephen C., mayor of Los Angeles, 135
FOWLER, HARLAN D., 178
FOX, JOHN, 96
FOX, STEPHEN, 323
Fox, William, 305
FRADKIN, PHILIP L., 9, 324
FRAKES, GEORGE E., 419
FRANKIEL, SANDRA S., 168
FRANKLIN, WILLIAM E., 128, 159
FRANKS, KENNY A., 308
free speech movements, 251
    at Berkeley, 428–32, 458–61
Frémont, Jessie Benton, 88, 144, 163
Frémont, John Charles, 73, 80, 86–94, 121,
    144–46
FRENCH, WARREN, 229, 352
Fresno Republican (newspaper), 261
Friant Dam and Friant–Kern Canal, 321
FRIEDERICKS, WILLIAM B., 214
FRIEDMAN, LAWRENCE M., 139
FRONTENROSE, JOSEPH J., 352
FROST, RICHARD H., 294
FRY, STEPHEN M., 353, 456
FUGITA, STEPHEN S., 418
FULLINWIDER, ROBERT K., 552
FULTON, A. R., 309
funding bill, 234–36
funk art, 444
Furuseth, Andrew, 244

GALARZA, ERNESTO, 397, 398
Gale, William A., 72
GALLAWAY, SARA ESSA, 282
Gálvez, José de, 31, 35, 44
GALVIN, JOHN, 56
GARCIA, MARIO T., 158, 419
García Richard, 395
GARCÍA, RICHARD A., 158, 398
Garcia, Rupert, 447
GARDNER, DAVID P., 385
Garland, Judy, 376
Garra, Antonio (Cupeño), 153
GATES, PAUL W., 115, 158, 190
GAY, THERESSA, 114
GAYDOWSKI, J. D., 338
Gayley, Charles Mills, 228

GEARY, GERALD J., 70
Gebhard, David, 451
GEBHARD, DAVID, 353, 456
GEIGER, MAYNARD, 39
general strike, San Francisco (1934), 330–33
GENEROUS, TOM, 129
GENINI, RONALD, 253
GENTRY, CURT, 294
geography of California, 1–9
geologic origins of California, 1–4
George, Henry, 215–16, 259
GEORGE, HENRY, 190, 229
geothermal power, 496, 497
GERHARD, PETER, 56
German Americans, 364 (see also names of
    individuals)
Getty, J. Paul, Museum, 449
Ghirardelli chocolate factory, 245, 519
Giannini, Amedeo Peter, 293, 387
Giannini, Lawrence Mario, 375, 378
GIBSON, JAMES R., 57
GIFFORD, BARRY, 352
GILBERT, BENJAMIN F., 129, 338
GILBERT, BILL, 81
Gilbert, George S., 296
Gill, Irving, 349–52
Gillespie, Archibald, 88, 91, 92
Gillett, James N., 260–61
Gilman, Charlotte Perkins, 415
Gilmore, Earl B., 302
GILMORE, GLADYS, 385
GILMORE, N. RAY, 398
GILMORE, SUSAN, 436
Gilroy, John, 76
Ginsberg, Allen, 438, 444
GIOVINCO, JOSEPH P., 295
GIRDNER, AUDRIE, 368
Gitelson, Alfred, 408
GLASSCOCK, C. B., 190
Glenn, Hugh J., 201
GLEYE, PAUL, 353
GOFMAN, JOHN W., 505
GOINS, DAVID LANCE, 436
gold discovery:
    at Coloma (1848), 4, 7, 97–98
    at Placerita Creek (1842), 98
Golden Era (literary weekly), 161, 163
Goldman, Alfred, 515
GOLDMAN, MARION S., 190
gold rush, 97–114
Goldwater, Barry, 384, 458
Goldwyn, Samuel, 305
Gompers, Samuel, 248
GONZALES, GILBERT G., 397

Gonzales, Manuel, 95, 135, 412
GONZALES, MANUEL, 95, 139, 419
GONZALES, YOLANDA BROYLE, 455
González, Michael, 68
GONZÁLEZ, MICHAEL J., 57, 70
Good Government League, Los Angeles, 259–60
Goodhue, Bertram, 351
GOODMAN, DAVID, 114
Goodyear Tire and Rubber Company, 319
GORDON, JOHN D., 139
Gordon, Laura de Force, 270, 415
GORDON, MARGARET S., 436
GORDON, MARY, 114
Gore, Al, 475
GOTTLIEB, ROBERT, 352, 527
GRABOWICZ, PAUL, 527
GRAEBNER, NORMAN A., 95–96
graft prosecution, San Francisco, 256–59
Graham, Isaac, 64, 79
GRAHAM, MARY, 397
GRANT, CAMPBELL, 20
GRASSMAN, CURTIS E., 240
GREBLER, LEO, 397
Greed (movie), 306
Green, Thomas Jefferson, 118, 121–22, 142
Greene, Charles, 350
Greene, Henry, 350
GREENSTEIN, FRED E., 419
GREENSTEIN, PAUL, 294
GREENWOOD, ROBERT, 352
GREGORY, JAMES NOBLE, 397
GRENIER, JUDSON A., 339
Griffith, David Wark, 304, 306
GRIFFITHS, DAVID B., 240
Grigsby, John, 80, 89
GRISWOLD, ROBERT L., 168
GRISWOLD DEL CASTILLO, RICHARD, 96, 398, 419
GRIVAS, THEODORE, 128
GRODZINS, MORTON, 367
Guadalupe Hidalgo, Treaty of (1848), 83, 95,
    142–43
GUARNERI, CARL, 168
GUERIN-GONZALES, CAMILLE, 338
GUEST, FRANCIS F., 57
GULLETT, GAYLE ANN, 282
Gum San (Gold Mountain), 147
gun control, 475, 476
GUNNING, TOM, 309
GUSTAFSON, JANIE L., 39
GUTIÉRREZ, DAVID G., 419
Gutierrez, Nicolas, 64
GUTIÉRREZ, RAMON A., 20, 57, 70
Gwin, William M., 118, 123–25, 145, 150
GYORY, ANTHONY, 200

Haas, Lisbeth, 52, 57, 145
HAAS, LISBETH, 158
HAAS, YNEZ D., 9
HACKEL, STEPHEN W., 57
Hackel, Steven, 45
HAFEN, LEROY R., 81, 171
HAGUE, HARLAN, 58, 81, 96
Hahn, James, 547
Haight, Raymond L., 336
Haight-Ashbury district, San Francisco, 432,
    440, 454
HAJNAL, ZOLTAN, 553
Haldeman, H. R., 383
Hale, Edward Everett, 21
HALE, EDWARD EVERETT, 38
Hall, D. J., 447
Halleck, Henry W., 120, 143
Hallidie, Andrew L., 210
HALPERN, JOHN, 436
Hamilton, Alexander, 87
HAMILTON, GARY G., 385, 480
"Ham 'n' Eggs" (pension plan), 336–37
HAMMOND, GEORGE P., 81
HAMMOND, PHILLIP E., 168
HANNA, WARREN L., 38
HANSEN, GLADYS, 264
HANSEN, HUGH G., 324
HANSEN, WOODROW JAMES, 70, 128
HANSON, DIRK, 527
Haraszthy, Agoston, 203
HARDESTY, DONALD L., 82
HARDY, OSGOOD, 213
HARLOW, NEAL, 95
Harriman, Edward H., 212, 258, 262
Harriman, Job, 255
HARRIS, LEON, 339
HART, JAMES D., 38, 230
HART, JOHN, 505
Hart, Mills D., 186
Hart, Sallie, 270
Harte, Bret, 55, 152, 153, 161, 163–64
Hartnell, William E. P., 65, 69, 72
HARVEY, RICHARD B., 385
Haskell, Burnette G., 243–44, 312
Haslam, Gerald, 440, 550
HASLAM, GERALD, 167, 352, 455, 528
HASSELSTROM, LINDA M., 81
Hastings, Lansford W., 80, 101, 104
Hata, Nadine, 549
HATAMIYA, LESLIE T., 418
Hatamiya, Lon, 509
HATCHER, PATRICK LLOYD, 527
Hatfield, Charles M. ("rainmaker"), 319–20
HAVEMAN, JON D., 527

HAWGOOD, JOHN A., 82, 96
Hawkins, Augustus, 410
Hayakawa, S. I., 405, 435
HAYDEN, DOLORES, 159
Hayden, Tom, 430, 435
Hayes, Janet Gray, 416
HAYMOND, CREED, 240
Haynes, John Randolph, 259–60
Hays, Will H., 308
Headwaters Forest, 485
health care, 475, 538–40
Health Insurance Plan of California (HPIC), 539
Hearst, Catherine Campbell, 416
Hearst, George, 222
Hearst, Phoebe Apperson, 350, 416
Hearst, William Randolph, 217, 222–23, 235, 261, 291, 332, 345–47
HEIZER, ROBERT F., 19, 57, 158, 418
HELPER, HINTON ROWAN, 114
HENDRICK, IRVING G., 168, 230, 419, 436
Hendrix, Jimi, 455
Heney, Francis J., 257, 262, 278, 281–82
Hennessey, John L., 538
HENNINGS, ROBERT E., 283, 295
HENSTELL, BRUCE, 308
Hepburn, Katharine, 376
HERR, PAMELA, 96
Herrin, William F., 238, 258, 260–61, 264, 267, 371
Hetch Hetchy controversy, 313–14, 318
Hewlett, William, 511
HICHBORN, FRANKLIN, 240, 264, 283
HICKS, JACK, 168, 229, 352, 455
Hidalgo, Miguel de, 56
high technology industry, 510–15, 553
Híjar, José María, 62
Hilgard, Eugene W., 228
Hill, Gladwin, 373
HILL, GLADWIN, 480
Hill, Julia Butterfly, 485
HILL, MARY A., 419
HILL, MERTON E., 436
Hill, Sarah Althea, 239
Hill, Thomas, 223
HILTON, GEORGE, 214
HINDERAKER, IVAN, 339
HINE, ROBERT V., 229, 294
hippie movement, 432–33
Hispanics (*see* Latinos)
Hiss, Alger, 377
Hittell, John S., 147
Hittell, Theodore H., 221
HJALMARSON, BIRGITTA, 230
HOFFMAN, ABRAHAM, 323

Hofmann, Hans, 444–49
HOFSOMMER, DON L., 240
HOLLIDAY, J. S., 114
HOLLON, JENNIFER K., 505
Hollywood, 303–8, 343, 375–77, 446
Holmes, Rachel Hobson (wife of Thomas Larkin), 77
HOLMES, STEVEN J., 323
Holt, Benjamin, 202
Holt Manufacturing Company, 303
HOLTZMAN, ABRAHAM, 338
Homestead Act (1862), 184
homosexuality, 416, 539–40
HONNOLD, DOUGLAS, 353
Hoover Dam, 316, 319
Hoover, Herbert, 228, 317–18, 333
Hopkins, Mark, 171–74, 232
HORNBECK, DAVID, 9, 70
HOSOKAWA, BILL, 368, 418
Hounds (nativist organization), 132–33
housing, racial discrimination in, 197, 406–10, 458
Houston, James D., 439, 443
HOUSTON, JAMES D., 82, 455
Houston, Jeanne Wakasuki, 443
Howard, John Galen, 349, 350
HOWARD, THOMAS FREDERICK, 178
HSU, MADELINE, 158
HUBLER, RICHARD, 480
Huerta, Dolores, 394, 395
Hughes, Charles Evans, 281
HUGHES, EDNA MILTON, 230, 353
Humboldt State University, 504
Humphrey, Isaac, 105
HUNDLEY, NORRIS, JR., 283, 323, 324, 505
HUNGERFORD, EDWARD, 178
HUNT, AURORA, 129
HUNT, ROCKWELL D., 82
Hunt, Timothy Dwight, 167
Huntington Beach oil field, 298
Huntington, Collis P., 171–73, 211, 221–32, 236, 239
Huntington, Henry E., 211–13, 301, 315
Huntington Library and Art Gallery, 211, 349
HURTADO, ALBERT L., 57, 159
HUSTON, LUTHER A., 385
HUTCHINSON, W. H., 308
HUTCHISON, C. ALAN, 70
HUTCHISON, CLAUDE B., 213
Hutchison, James M., 161
Huxley, Aldous, 345
Hwang, David Henry, 437
hydraulic mining, 112

hydroelectric power, 316–22
HYSLOP, RICHARD S., 9

ICHIOKA, YUJI, 283
Ide, William B., 80, 89–90
IGLER, DAVID, 190
IGLI, INA RAE, 168
IGNOFFO, MARY J., 128
Imperial Canal, 209–18, 316
Imperial Irrigation District, 317
Independence League (1906), 261
Independent Taxpayers party, 239
Indian Claims Commission Act (1946), 400
Indians:
    aboriginal, 1, 10–11
    impact of missions on, 48–53
    oppression of, 148–57
    population of, 13, 52, 164, 400–402
    reservations for, 150–52
    resistance to missions, 45–48
    role of women, 12, 16–17
    Spain's policies toward, 28–32, 48–53
    spirituality of, 13–14, 17
    in twentieth century, 399–406, 544–45
    in World War II, 358
    writers, 441
    (see also names of individuals)
Indo-Chinese refugees, 404–6, 548
Industrial Accident Board, 273
Industrial Association of San Francisco, 290, 389
Industrial Welfare Commission, 275
Industrial Workers of the World (IWW), 250–52, 288, 290, 330
INGLIS, RUTH A., 309
initiative, 260, 262, 268, 479 (see also specific propositions)
International Longshoremen's Association (ILA), 331
Internet revolution, 514–15, 525
Irish Americans, 177, 192 (see also names of individuals)
IRONS, PETER, 367
Ishi (Yahi), 154, 544
ISSEL, WILLIAM, 253, 264, 295, 436
Italian Americans, 364 (see also names of individuals)
Itliong, Larry, 393, 394

Jackson, Andrew, 83, 85
JACKSON, DONALD, 96, 114
Jackson, Helen Hunt, 394
Jackson, Robert H., 366
JACKSON, ROBERT H., 57
JACKSON, W. TURRENTINE, 178

James v. Marinship Corporation (1945) (blacks in labor unions), 409
Japanese:
    agitation and legislation against, 275–80
    literature by, 443
    recent history of, 402–6, 548–52
    "relocation" of, 361–67, 402–3
    trade and investments by, 507–9
    women, in California, 277
    (see also names of individuals)
Jayme, Luís, 42, 46
jazz movement, west coast, 453
Jeffers, Robinson, 340–42
Jefferson Airplane, 454
JELINEK, LAWRENCE J., 115, 397
JENKINS, J. CRAIG, 398
Jenkins, John, 133
Jennings, Bill, 487
JENSEN, JAMES M., 115
JENSEN, JOAN M., 419
Jerde, Jon, 451
Jesús, José (Siakumne), 150
Jobs, Steven, 513, 523
John Birch Society, 382–83
John Paul II (Pope), 52
JOHNSON, CAROLYN, 229
JOHNSON, DAVID ALAN, 128
Johnson, Grove L., 263, 277
JOHNSON, HANS, 419
Johnson, Hiram Warren:
    governor, 252, 262, 263, 264, 268, 269, 273, 359, 380, 416
    prosecutor, 263
    senator, 280–82, 291–92, 317, 354, 461
JOHNSON, JAMES W., 385
Johnson, J. Neely, 125, 137
JOHNSON, KENNETH M., 96, 418
JOHNSON, KRISTEN, 82
Johnson, Lyndon B., 384, 469
JOHNSON, MARILYNN S., 367
JOHNSON, MOIRA, 527
Johnson, Robert Underwood, 312
JOHNSON, STEPHEN, 528
JOHNSON, SUSAN LEE, 114
JOHNSON, TROY R., 418
Jones, Bill, 475, 476
JONES, HELEN H., 178
JONES, HOLWAY R., 323
JONES, LANDON Y., 436
Jones, Thomas ap Catesby, 84, 92
Jones, William Carey, 144
Joplin, Janis, 455
Jordan, David Starr, 206, 228, 400, 511
JOSHI, S. T., 229

journalism, 160–63, 222–23, 237, 346–47
Juanita (Josepha Segovia), lynched at
    Downieville (1851), 135
Juarez, José (Chauchila), 153
Judah, Theodore D., 170–76, 218, 530

KAGEL, JOHN, 339
Kahn, Florence Prag, 415
KAHRL, WILLIAM L., 323, 505
Kaiser, Henry J., 356–59, 507
Kaiser Permanente (HMO), 539
Kalloch, Isaac S., 198
Kan, Andrew, 193
KAPPEL, TIM, 352
Karabel, Jerome, 537
KARABEL, JEROME, 553
KARMAN, JAMES, 352
KATCHER, LEO, 385
KATZ, SHERRY J., 282
KAUER, RALPH, 200
KAUFMAN, GEORGE G., 480
KAVANAGH, JAMES, 9
Kaweah colony, 244, 312
KAZIN, MICHAEL, 253
Kearney, Denis, 194–95, 242
Kearny, Stephen Watts, 93–94
Keith, William, 224, 230, 449
Kelley, "General" Charles T., 286
KELLEY, ROBERT, 115, 214, 217, 317, 324
Kelly, Gene, 376
KELSEY, HARRY, 38
KEMBLE, EDWARD C., 168
KEMBLE, JOHN H., 190
Kemperer, Otto, 453
Kennedy, Kate, 227
KENS, PAUL, 240
Kent, Elizabeth Thacker, 272
Kent State University, 431
Kent, William, 272, 291
Kenton, Stan, 453
Kern County Water District, 491
Kerouac, Jack, 438, 444
Kerr, Clark, 460, 535
Kesey, Ken, 438
Kesterson National Wildlife Refuge, 493–94
Key System (interurban rail network), 211
Kientipoos ("Captain Jack"), 154
KIMES, MAYMIE B., 323
KIMES, WILLIAM E., 323
Kimmel, Husband E., 362
Kin, Huie, 193
KING, GEBHARD, 456
King, Rodney, 546
KING, SUSAN, 456

King, T. Butler, 118
King, Thomas Starr, 127
King of William, James, 136–37
Kings Canyon National Park, 312
Kingston, Maxine Hong, 442
Kino, Eusebio, 31
KIRKER, HAROLD, 230, 353
KIRLIN, JOHN J., 480, 481, 527
Kirst, Michael, 532
KISER, GEORGE C., 397
KISER, MARTHA WOODY, 397
KITANO, HARRY H., 368
Kittredge, Charmian (second wife of Jack
    London), 219
Kizer, Kenneth, 538
KLEINSORGE, PAUL L., 324
KLING, ROB, 504, 527
KNIGHT, ARTHUR, 309
Knight, Goodwin J., 375, 379, 381
KNIGHT, ROBERT E. L., 253
Knight, William, 89
Knights of Labor, 243
KNOLES, GEORGE H., 339
KNOLL, TRICIA, 418
Knott, Walter, 519
Knotts Berry Farm, 519
Knowland, Joseph R., 285
Knowland, William F., 379–80, 384
Know-Nothing movement, 124–25
KOPPES, CLAYTON R., 324
Koreans, 405, 548
Korematsu v. United States (1944) (Japanese
    relocation), 366
Kotkin, Joel, 518
KOTKIN, JOEL, 527
KOWALEWSKI, MICHAEL, 168
KREISMAN, BERN, 504
KRIER, JAMES E., 505
Kroeber, Alfred L., 154
KROEBER, THEODORA, 19, 158
KRONINGER, ROBERT H., 240
Ku Klux Klan, 306
KUNG, SHIEN WOO, 418
KURUTZ, GARY F., 114, 214
KURUTZ, KD, 214
Kuster, Una Call (wife of Robinson Jeffers),
    340–41

L. A. look (art movement), 443–44, 445–46
LABOR, EARLE, 229
LA BOTZ, DAN, 308
La Follette, Robert M., Jr., 380, 390
LAMBERT, PAUL F., 308
LANDERER, SUSAN, 455

Land grants:
  Mexican, 66–68, 142–47
  to railroads, 174, 180–82, 183–86
  to states, 120, 185
land ownership:
  Japanese denied right to, 278
  monopoly in, 184–86
  single tax proposed for, 215–16
Lane, Franklin K., 314
LANG, JULIAN, 9
Lange, Dorothea (photographer), 344, 348–49, 365
LANGE, DOROTHEA, 367, 368, 397
LANGUM, DAVID J., 81, 82, 96
La Opinión (newspaper), 412, 550
La Pérouse, Comte Jean François de, 48, 49, 85
LA PÉROUSE, JEAN FRANÇOIS GALAUP DE, 57
LAPORTE, TODD R., 527
LAPP, RUDOLPH M., 158, 418
LARIMORE, JOHN A., 190
Larkin, Thomas Oliver, 77, 80, 85–86, 88, 143, 225
LARROWE, CHARLES P., 339
LARSEN, CHARLES E., 339
LARSEN, CHRISTIAN L., 436
LARSEN, GRACE H., 283
Lasky, Jesse L., 305
Lassen, Peter, 104
Lasuén, Fermín Francisco de, 48, 57
Latinos:
  after 1940, 413–18, 482, 536, 549–52
  as farm laborers, 390–97, 526
  during gold–rush era, 141–42
  emerging middle class, 550
  higher education, 536
  land grant controversy, 142–47
  literature by, 441
  during Mexican period, 58–69
  paintings by, 447
  political leadership, 551–52
  in World War II, 358
  (*see also names of individuals*)
LAVENDER, DAVID S., 178, 190
LAWRENCE, DAVID G., 480
Lawrence Livermore National Laboratory, 517
LAYNE, J. GREGG, 265
LAYTON, EDWIN, 295
LAZOROWITZ, ARLENE, 295
LEADER, LEONARD, 338, 339
League of Nations, 291
Leary, Timothy, 432
Le Conte, Joseph, 227
Lee, Archy, case of (1858), 156
Lee, David, 548

LEE, EUGENE C., 384, 480
LEE, LAWRENCE, 214, 352
LEE, ROSE HUM, 418
Leese, Jacob P., 86, 89
LEIDER, EMILY WOTIS, 419
Lelia Byrd (ship), 72
LEMKE, NANCY, 38
LEMKE-SANTANGELO, GRETCHEN, 419
LENNON, NIGEY, 168, 294
LEPORE, HERBERT P., 283
Levering Act (1950) (loyalty oath), 379
LEVI, STEPHEN C., 295
LEVY, JOANN, 114
Levy, Stephen, 507, 527, 534
LEWIS, DAVID RICH, 114
LEWIS, HENRY T., 20
LEWIS, JOSEPH, 480
LEWIS, OSCAR, 114, 129, 178, 190, 240, 352
LEWIS, SAMUEL L., 338
Lewis, Sinclair, 344
Libeskind, Daniel, 451
LICHTMAN, SHEILA TROPP, 419
LIEBERT, LARRY, 480
LIEBMAN, ELLEN, 397
LILLARD, RICHARD G., 214
LIMERICK, PATRICIA NELSON, 158
LINCOLN, A., 283
Lincoln, Abraham, 126, 173
Lincoln-Roosevelt League, 260–64, 272
LINDBERG, LEON, 527
Lindbergh, Charles A., 359
LINKER, HELENE, 419
LIPSET, SEYMOUR MARTIN, 436
LISCA, PETER, 352
Lissner, Meyer, 260, 261
LISTER, ROGER CHARLES, 115, 282
literature, 160–67, 215–17, 340–49, 437–43
LITTLEFIELD, DOUGLAS R., 214
Liu, Amy, 488
Llano del Rio (utopian colony), 285
lobbyists, 370–71, 471–79
Lockheed Company, 359, 516, 518
LOCKLEAR, WILLIAM R., 200
Lockyer, Bill, 484, 542
Loew, Marcus, 305
Loew's (film company), 308
LOFTIS, ANNE, 352, 368
Loma Prieta earthquake (1989), 424
London, Jack, 166, 218–19, 284, 286
LONDON, JOAN, 229, 386
Lonergan, Thomas, 257
LONG, EDWARD R., 385
LONGSTRETH, RICHARD, 353
Long Valley, reservoir in, 314

Lopez, Lalo, 551
LORENZ, J. D., 480
Lorenzano, Apolinaria, 68, 145
Los Angeles:
  aircraft industry in, 359–61, 522
  air pollution in, 488–90
  architecture, 351–52
  art and music in, 223, 348–49, 444–49,
    451–55
  automobile in, 300–303
  busing controversy, 408–9
  climate of, 7–8
  economy, 506, 507, 508, 510, 512, 515
  electric railways, 210–13
  founding, 44
  freeways, 424
  geologic origins of, 3
  good government movement, 259–60
  harbor fight, 233–34
  labor in, 245–48
  land grant controversy, 146
  Latino leaders, 550–52
  Mexican Americans in, 413, 441, 549, 552
  movie industry, 303, 308
  Native Americans in twentieth century, 544
  oil discoveries, 296–300
  population growth, 408
  railroad connection, 181–82
  rapid transit, 529–32
  Rodney King riot, 546–47
  water supplies, 314–16, 319–20
  Watts riot, 407–8, 420, 546
Los Angeles Better America Federation, 290
Los Angeles Board of Realtors, 406
Los Angeles Bureau of Power and Light, 318
Los Angeles Conservatory of Music, 449
Los Angeles County Museum, 445, 448
Los Angeles Department of Water and Power
    (LADWP), 492
Los Angeles Examiner (newspaper), 315, 347
Los Angeles Express (newspaper), 260
Los Angeles Friday Morning Club, 271
Los Angeles Merchants and Manufacturers'
    Association, 247, 285, 290
Los Angeles Museum of Contemporary Art, 447
Los Angeles Philharmonic Orchestra, 452, 453
Los Angeles sound (popular music style), 454
Los Angeles Star (newspaper), 152
Los Angeles Times (newspaper), 223, 234,
    246–48, 260, 281, 302, 315, 317, 382, 416,
    515, 542, 552
Los Angeles Unified School District, and busing
    controversy, 408
Lotah, Kate (Chumash), 402

LOTCHIN, ROGER W., 140, 367
LOTHROP, GLORIA RICCI, 419
lottery, 466
Loughead, Allen, 359
Loughead, Malcom, 359
Love, Harry, 163
LOWENTHALL, ABRAHAM F., 527
LOWER, RICHARD, 265
LOWITT, RICHARD C., 295, 323, 338
loyalty oaths, 378–79, 427
Lozano, Monica, 550, 552–53
LUBENOW, GERALD C., 480, 481
Lucas, George, 522, 523
Luckie, Kate (Wintun), 155
Luján, Gilbert, 446
Lummis, Charles F., 206, 400
LUNDY, ROBERT D., 229
Lungren, Dan, 473, 474
Lustig, Jeffrey, 546
Lux, Charles, 185, 209
Lux v. Haggin (1886) (water rights), 209
LYDON, SANDY, 158, 199
LYMAN, GEORGE D., 82, 190
LYMAN, STANFORD M., 158
lynching, 326 (*see also vigilance committees*)
lysergic acid diethylamide (LSD), 432, 454

Mackay, John W., 188, 189
MACLACHLAN, COLIN M., 38
Maddern, Bessie (first wife of Jack London), 219
MAFFLY-KIPP, LAURIE F., 168
Magleby, David, 479
MAGLIARI, MICHAEL, 190, 240
MAHARIDGE, DALE, 553
MAINO, JEANETTE G., 82
MAJKA, LINDA, 398
MAJKA, THEODORE, 398
MAKINSON, RANDELL, L., 353
Malaspina, Alejandro, 48
Mandel, Michael J., 515
MANDEL, MICHAEL J., 527
Manifest Destiny, 87–88
Manila galleons, 26–27
MANN, RALPH, 115
Manrique, Miguel, 41
Manzanar (relocation camp), 364–66, 443
maquiladoras, 509, 531
MARBERRY, M. M., 168
MARCHAND, ERNEST L., 229
MARGOLIN, MALCOLM, 20, 57
Market Street Railroad Company, 235
MARKHOLT, OTTILIE, 339
MARKS, PAULA MITCHELL, 114
MARRYAT, FRANK, 114

Marsh, John, 77–78, 80
Marshall, James Wilson, 97–98
Marshall, Robert Bradford, and plan for Central
    Valley Project, 321
MARTI, WERNER H., 96
Martin, Glenn L., 359
Martinez, Vilma S., 416
Marwedel, Emma, 227
Mason, Bridget ("Biddy"), 157
Mason, Richard B., 98, 100, 101, 117, 143
MASON, WILLIAM MARVIN, 57
Master Plan for Higher Education (1960), 380,
    426–27, 535
Masuda, Mary, 366
Masumoto, David Mas, 443, 494
MATHER, R. E., 139
MATHES, VALERIE SHERER, 159, 418
MATHES, W. MICHAEL, 38, 56
MATSON, FLOYD W., 367
Matsui, Robert, 405
Matteson, Edward E., 108
MATTHEWS, GLENNA, 338
MATTHIESEEN, PETER, 398
MAVITY, NANCY BARR, 338
Maybeck, Bernard, 349–50
Mayer, Louis B., 305, 308, 335, 345, 376
MAYNARD, JOHN A., 455
MAYNE, HEATHER, 456
MAZO, EARL, 385
MAZÓN, MAURICE, 419
Mazón, Mauricio, 412
McAdoo, William Gibbs, 291, 324, 336
McAfee, Ward, 126
MCAFEE, WARD M., 128, 240
MCBRIDE, DENNIE, 324
MCBROOME, DELORES MASON, 419
McCarran-Walter Immigration and Nationality
    Act (1952), 404
McCarthy, Eugene, 430
McCarthy, Joseph R., 377–79
McCarver, M. M., 119
MCCAWLEY, WILLIAM, 20
MCCLAIN, CHARLES J., 199
McClatchy, Charles ("C. K."), 223
McClatchy, James, 143–44, 223
McClatchy, Valentine S., 361
McCloy, John J., 363
MCCLURE, CHARLOTTE S., 419
McClure, S. S., 218
MCCLURG, SUE, 323
McComb, Marshall F., 459
MCCOY, ESTHER, 353
McCrone, Alistair W., 504
McCulloch, Hugh, 72

McDonnell Douglas, 518
MCDONOUGH, JACK, 456
McDougal, John., 121, 126, 152
McDougall, James A., 173
MCELRATH, JOSEPH R., 229
MCGINTY, BRIAN, 213, 338
MCGOWAN, JOSEPH A., 213
MCGRATH, MARCIA R., 455
McGrath, Roger D., 131
MCGRATH, ROGER D., 139
MCGREEVY, JOHN T., 240
MCHENRY, DEAN E., 384
McKay, Donald, 102
MCKEE, IRVING, 229, 265
McKinney, Joseph, 144
McManigal, Ortie, 248
MCNALLY, DENNIS, 455
McNamara, Eugene, 85
McNamara, James B., 248, 285, 287
McNamara, John J., 248, 285, 287
McPhee, John, 2
MCPHEE, JOHN, 9
McPherson, Aimee Semple, 327
McQuern, Marcia, 479
McWilliams, Carey, 242, 386, 389, 390, 440
MCWILLIAMS, CAREY, 190, 214, 253, 324, 339,
    385, 397, 411, 419
Medi-Cal (health plan), 538
Mehta, Zubin, 453
Meier, Richard, 449
MELENDY, H. BRETT, 295, 338, 418
MELTON, ALICE K., 352
Menken, Adah Isaacs, 166, 187
MERCER, LLOYD, 190
MERCHANT, CAROLYN, 504
Merchants' and Manufacturers' Association
    of Los Angeles, 247, 285, 290
Merchants' and Manufacturers' Association
    of Stockton, 285
MERK, FREDERICK, 96
MERRIAM, C. HART, 9
Merriam, Frank, 327, 331, 334–38
Merritt, Ezekiel, 89
Metcalf, Victor H., 276
Methanol (alternative fuel), 500
Metro–Goldwyn–Mayer (MGM), 305, 306, 308,
    335
Metropolitan Water District of Southern
    California, 319–21
Mexicans and Mexican Americans (see Latinos)
Mexican War (1846–1848), 83, 86, 90–95
MICHAEL, JAY, 481
Micheltorena, Manuel, 66, 84–85, 86, 146
MIDDLETON, WILLIAM D., 214

Midway, battle of (1942), 364
Migrant Mother (photograph), 348
MILES, DIONE, 253
Milhaud, Darius, 452, 453
militia, 121–23, 137, 152
MILLER, CRANE S., 9
MILLER, DARLIS A., 129
Miller, George, 487
MILLER, GRACE L., 253, 265
Miller, Henry, 185, 209
MILLER, JIM, 456
Miller, Joaquin, 163, 165–66
MILLER, MARGARET I., 419
MILLER, M. CATHERINE, 190, 214
MILLER, MICHAEL V., 436
MILLER, RICHARD CONNELLY, 230, 253
MILLER, ROBERT RYAL, 70
MILLER, SALLY M., 323, 367
MILLER, STUART C., 158, 199
MILLER, TIMOTHY, 436
MILLER, WILLIS H., 240
Milliken, Randall, 46
MILLIKEN, RANDALL, 57
Mills, Cyrus T. (founder of Mills College), 229
Mills, James R., 379
Mineta, Norman, 405, 548
minimum wage, 262, 273–74
MIRANDA, GLORIA E., 70
MIRRIELEES, EDITH R., 436
missions, 27–56, 58–64
MITCHELL, DON, 397
MITCHELL, GREGG, 339
Modoc War (1872–1873), 153–54
MOELLER, BEVERLY B., 324
Mofras, Eugène Duflot de, 85
MOHOLY, NOEL F., 39
MOLEY, RAYMOND, 309
Mono Lake, 491
Monroy, Douglas, 68
MONROY, DOUGLAS, 70, 338
Montalvo, Garcí Ordoñez de, 21–22
Monterey:
    constitutional convention at, 117–21
    European discovery, 27–28
    founding, 37
    impact of base closures on, 517
"Monterey style" (architecture), 77
Monteux, Pierre, 452
MONTGOMERY, GAYLE B., 385
MONZINGO, OBERT, 129
Mooney, Thomas J., 286–87, 337
Moore, Charles, 450
MOORE, MARIAN, 339
Moore, Shirley Ann Wilson, 155

MOORE, SHIRLEY ANN WILSON, 144, 367, 419
MOORE, TRUMAN E., 398
MOORE, WINSTON, 339
MOORHEAD, MAX L., 57
Moraga, Gabriel, 54
Moraga, José, 42–43, 54
MORATTO, M. J., 19
MOREFIELD, R. H., 158
Morena, Luisa, 330, 410
MORGADO, MARTIN J., 39
Morgan, Dale L. 74
MORGAN, DALE L., 81
Morgan, Julia, 346–47, 350
Morina, Louisa, 330, 410
Mormons, 99–100
Moscone, George, assassination of, 415–16, 444
MOSES, VINCENT, 214
mother lode, 104
Moulder, Andrew Jackson, 167
MOURE, NANCY DUSTIN WALL, 230, 353
movies, 7, 303–8, 521–26
MOWRY, GEORGE E., 240, 265, 282
Moyle, Peter, 487
MOYNIHAN, RUTH B., 114
MTBE (methyl tertiary butyl ether), 489–90
Muir, John, 310–14
MULHOLLAND, CATHERINE, 324
Mulholland, William, 314, 317
MULLEN, KEVIN J., 139
MULLINS, WILLIAM H., 338
Murieta, Joaquín, 163, 166
Murphy, Frank, 366
Murray, Hugh C., 148
music, 225, 451–55
Mussel Slough, battle of (1880), 186, 218
MYERS, SANDRA, 114
MYERS, WILLIAM A., 324

NADEAU, REMI A., 190, 214, 323
Nagano, Kent, 353
Nahl, Charles Christian, 223
Nash, Gerald D., 109
NASH, GERALD D., 114, 190, 213, 240, 283, 295, 367
National Association of Colored People (NAACP), 275, 548
National Association of Manufacturers, 290
National Conference of La Raza, 550
National Farm Workers Association, 393–94
Nationalist party, 239
National Industrial Recovery Act (1933), 330
National Organization for Women (NOW), 417
National resources, conservation and use of, 310–15, 482–95

Native Sons of the Golden West, 361
Navarro, Peter, 504
Neagle, David, 239
negroes (*see* African Americans)
NELSON, BRUCE, 339
NELSON, BYRON, 159
Nemos, William, 220
Nettles, Michael, 534
NEUMAN, MICHAEL, 552
Neutra, Richard, 352
NEUTRA, W. DIONE, 353
Neve, Felipe de, 44
NEVINS, ALLAN, 96
New Deal, 264, 338, 464
Newlands Reclamation Act (1902), 322–23
new left movement, 427–35
Newton, Huey P., 433, 434
Neyland, John Francis, 267, 289, 332, 378
NIGEL, GUNTHER W., 230
Nixon, Richard M.:
    congressman, 376–77
    gubernatorial candidate, 382–83
    president, 423
    presidential candidate, 382–83, 395
    senator, 377
    vice president, 382–83
    Watergate crisis, 461
NIXON, RICHARD M., 385
Noble, Robert, 328
NOLL, ROGER, 481
Norris, Frank, 202, 217–18, 306, 440, 443
Norris, Kathleen, 415
NORRIS, R. M., 9
North American Free Trade Agreement
    (NAFTA), 509, 526
North, J. W., 204
Northrop, John K., and Northrop Corporation,
    359, 361, 517
NOVAK, ROBERT, 480
NOW (National Organization for Women), 417
nuclear power, 497–99
Nuclear Regulatory Commission (NRC), 497
nuclear weapons, 516–18
NUNIS, DOYCE B., JR., 56, 81–82, 140, 230, 436

Oak, Henry L., 220
OAK, HENRY L., 57, 70
Oakland:
    black radicalism in, 433–34
    film festival in, 523
    founding of, 146
    health care in, 539
    homicides in, 542
    impact of Proposition 13 on, 464

    port facilities, 424
    waterfront monopoly, 180–82
Oakland Museum of California, 448
Oakland Transcript (newspaper), 215
Oakland Tribune (newspaper), 370
Oakland Waterfront Company, 180
Obledo, Mario, 413
O'BRIEN, DAVID J., 418
O'Brien, William S., 188, 189
Occidental and Oriental Steamship Company,
    183
O'CONNELL, JAY, 253
O'CONNOR, COLLEEN M., 385
O'Connor, Maureen, 501
O'CONNOR, RICHARD, 168, 229
"Octopus" (railroad monopoly), 182, 218
O'Donnell, Charles C., 197
OGDEN, ADELE, 81
O'Hare, Kate Richards, 416
oil industry, 6, 296–300, 484, 494–95, 499–500
Okamoto, Toki, 278
O'KEEFE, TIMOTHY J., 264
OKUBO, MINE, 368
"Old Block" (Alonzo Delano), 162–63
OLDER, CORA B., 230
Older, Fremont, 257–58, 288
OLDER, FREMONT, 264
OLIN, SPENCER C., JR., 240, 265, 282, 419, 504,
    527
Olmos, Edward James, 441
OLMSTEAD, ALAN L., 213
Olmsted, Frederick Law, 310
OLMSTED, ROGER, 140
Olson, Culbert L., 336–38, 362, 374, 390, 416
OLSON, KEITH W., 265
O'MEARA, JAMES, 128
ONG, PAUL M., 178
open shop, "American Plan" for, 246–49, 290
Ophir (mine), 189
Orange County, bankruptcy crisis in, 469
Orange County Performing Arts Center, 453
Organic Foods Production Act (1990), 494
Oroville Dam, 381
Orozco, José, 447
ORSI, RICHARD J., 20, 57, 70, 114, 115, 128, 158,
    178, 214 240, 397
OSBORNE, THOMAS J., 213
Osio, Antonio María, 31, 46
OSIO, ANTONIO MARÍA, 70
OSTRANDER, GILMAN M., 295
Otis Art Institute, 348
Otis, Harrison Gray, 223, 234, 237, 246–48, 251,
    259–60, 281, 284, 285, 315, 317, 347, 348
Otter (ship), 71

OTTLEY, ALLAN R., 82
Overland Monthly (literary magazine), 164, 166, 219
OWENS, KENNETH, N., 82
Owens Valley-Los Angeles Aqueduct, 314–16
Oxnard, Henry, 203
Oxnard, Robert, 203
Ozawa, Seiji, 45

Pacheco, Romualdo, 62
Pacific Electric Railway Company, 213, 315, 513
Pacific flyway, 6
Pacific Gas and Electric Company (PG&E), 256, 286, 318, 321–22, 389, 402, 498, 501, 502, 503
Pacific Mail Steamship Company, 175, 182
Pacific Railroad Act (1862), 173
Pacific rim, 501–10, 526
PACK, ROBERT, 480
Packard, David, 511
Padilla, Genaro, 89, 96
Padrés, José Mariá, 61–62
Palace Hotel, 189
Palace of Fine Arts, San Francisco, 350
Palacios, Gloria, 525
Palmer, A. Mitchell, 288
PALMER, TIM, 504
Palóu, Francisco, 34, 48
Panama Pacific Exposition, San Diego (1915), 350, 351
Panama Pacific International Exposition (PPIE), San Francisco (1913), 279, 350
Panto, Jose (Kumeyaay), 153
Paramount Pictures, 307, 308
PARINS, JAMES W., 168
PARKER, CARLETON H., 253
Parker, Walter, 261
PARKHURST, DONALD B., 309
PARKINSON, THOMAS, 455
Parrish, Essie (Pomo), 28
Parsons, James J., 7
PARSONS, JAMES J., 9
Pasadena Art Museum, 449
PATERSON, THOMAS G., 294
Pattie, James Ohio, 75
PAUL, RODMAN, 114, 115, 213
PAYNE, WALTER A., 213
PAYSON, GEORGE, 114
PEFFER, GEORGE ANTHONY, 199
"People's Park," Berkeley, 430
People's party, San Francisco, 139
People's (Populist) party, 239–40
People v. Hall (1854) (exclusion of Chinese testimony), 148

Pepperdine University, 550
Peralta, Luís, 146
Peralta, Vicente, 146
PERCIVAL, ROBERT V., 139
Pereira, William, 451
PEREZ, CRISOSTOMO N., 70
Pérez, Eulalia Arrila de, 45
Perez, Sonia, 550
Peripheral Canal controversy, 490–91
PERRY, JOHN, 229
PERRY, LOUIS B., 253
PERRY, RICHARD S., 253
Persian Gulf war (1991), 500
pesticides, 493–95
Petaluma, growth control ordinance of (1973), 488
PETERSEN, ERIC F., 240, 241
PETERSON, MARTIN S., 168
PETERSON, RICHARD H., 129, 158, 352
petroleum (*see* oil industry)
Phelan, James D., 255, 257, 277, 313–14
PHELPS, ROBERT, 253
PHILBRICK, HOWARD R., 384
Phillips, George, 61, 153
PHILLIPS, GEORGE H., 57, 158, 159, 418
PHILLIPS, KEVIN, 527
PHILP, TOM, 553
PHINNEY, DAVID, 527
"Phoenix, John" (George H. Derby), 162
photography, 349
Pickford, Mary, 306
"pick handle brigade" (1877), 194
Pico, Andrés, 93–95, 126–27
Pico, Pío, 59, 65–66, 86, 92, 143
PIENE, NAN R., 455
PINCETL, STEPHANIE S., 323, 504
Pinus longaeva (bristlecone pine), 4
PISANI, DONALD J., 214, 324, 397
PITCHELL, ROBERT J., 384, 385
PITT, LEONARD M., 158
Pittman, Tarea Hall, 357
PIZER, DONALD, 229
Placerita Creek, gold discovery at (1842), 98
Plagens, Peter, 445
PLAGENS, PETER, 455
plate tectonics, 1–3
Pleistocene epoch, 3, 10
Plessy v. Ferguson (1896) (school segregation), 408
Political Reform Act (1974), 461, 478
POLK, DORA B., 38
Polk, James K., 85–86, 88, 91–92, 94, 101
Polk, Willis, 349, 451
POLLACK, JACK HARRISON, 385

POLOS, NICHOLAS C., 168
POMEROY, EARL S., 129
Pony Express, 169–70
Poole, Alonzo W., 186
pop art, 446
Populist movement, 239
Port Chicago Naval Magazine, 355
Portolá, Gaspar de, 31, 35, 36–37
POSNER, RUSSELL M., 96, 295
POSTER, MARK, 504, 527
post-industrial revolution, 509–10
POURADE, RICHARD F., 436
POWDERMAKER, HORTENSE, 309
POWELL, LAWRENCE CLARK, 229, 352
POWER, ROBERT H., 38
power:
   cogeneration, 497
   geothermal, 496, 497
   hydroelectric, 316–19, 321
   nuclear, 497–99
   solar, 496
   wind, 496–97
Prat, Pedro, 35
Preparedness Day parade and bombing (1916), 286
PRESCOTT, GERALD L., 175
Preston, John W., 400
PRESTON, MICHAEL B., 481, 553
Preston, William, 11
PRIESTLEY, HERBERT I., 39
prisons, 466, 540–43
PRITCHARD, R. L., 385
Progressive party, 269, 279–80, 291–93
prohibition, 271, 291–92
Proposition 1 (1973) (Reagan tax initiative), 461, 535
Proposition 5 (1998) (Indian gaming), 544
Proposition 13 (1978) (property tax reduction), 463–67, 536
Proposition 14 (1964) (rejection of "fair housing" law), 407
Proposition 18 (1958) ("right to work"), 379–80
Proposition 34 (2000) (campaign finance), 478
Proposition 65 (1986) (toxic control), 495
Proposition 98 (1988) (educational funding), 534, 536
Proposition 140 (1990) (term limits), 467–68
Proposition 187 (1994) (undocumented aliens), 470, 471, 473–74, 550
Proposition 209 (1996) (affirmative action), 471, 473, 537
Proposition 226 (1998) (organized labor), 473
Proposition 227 (1998) (bilingual education), 473, 535, 550

Public Policy Institute of California (PPIC), 529
Public Schools Accountability Act (1999), 535
Public Utilities Commission, 477, 497, 501, 503
PUTNAM, JACKSON K., 295, 338, 339, 384, 480

Quinn, Arthur, 25
QUINN, ARTHUR, 38, 128
QUINT, HOWARD, 294
QUINTARD, TAYLOR, 159

racial discrimination in housing, 197, 406–10
Radio-Keith-Orpheum (RKO), 308
RAE, JOHN B., 367
RAFFERTY, JUDITH ROSENBERG, 230, 282
Rafferty, Max, 409–10
railroad, 169–77, 180–85, 196–98, 210, 226–40
railroad regulation, 197, 264
Ralston, William Chapman, 187–89
RAMIEREZ, SALVADOR A., 240
Rancho Seco (nuclear power plant), 498
RAND, CHRISTOPHER, 436
RAPHAEL, RAY, 159
RAPOPORT, ROGER, 385, 480
Rattigan, Joseph A., 426
RAWLS, JAMES J., 20, 114, 158, 385, 418, 436
RAYBAND, BENEDICTE, 528
RAYMOND, VALERIE, 480
Reagan, Ronald:
   background, 372, 376, 457–58
   governor, 395, 397, 408, 457–61, 463, 480
   president, 463, 516
   presidential candidate, 463
reapportionment of state legislature, 293, 425–26, 469
recall, 260, 261, 268
Reclamation Act (1902), 322–23
Reclamation Reform Act (1982), 323
REDFERN, ROD, 9
Red Light Abatement Act (1913), 272
Redwood National Park, 485, 519
REED, DEBORAH, 553
Reed, Ishmael, 440–41
REED, ISHMAEL, 455
Reed, James, 81
referendum, 260, 268
refugees:
   Indo-Chinese, 405, 548
   Vietnamese, 405, 548
Reid, Hugo, 50
REID, JOHN P., 114
REID, T. R., 527
REIS, ELIZABETH, 253
REISLER, MARK, 397
REISNER, MARC, 324

relocation camps:
  Mazanar, 364–67, 443
  Tule Lake, 364–66
  (*see also* Japanese)
renewable energy resources, 495–97
RENSHAW, PATRICK, 253, 348
reservations for Indians, 150–51, 399
restructuring (energy policy), 581
REUTHER, WALTER, 214
Rexroth, Kenneth, 438
REYES, BELINDA I., 553
Reyes, Francisco, 45
Reyes, Inocencia, 93
Reynolds v. Sims (1964) ("one man, one vote"),
  426
Reynosa, Cruz, 413
Rezanov, Nikolai Petrovich, 54–55
RHODENHAMEL, JOSEPHINE D., 168
RICE, BRADLEY, 527
RICE, WILLIAM B., 168
Richardson, Friend W., 292–93
RICHARDSON, JAMES, 481
Richardson, William A., 99
Richardson, William H., 136
Richfield Oil Corporation, 299
RICHMOND, AL, 294
Ricketts, Edward F., 344
Ridge, John Rollin ("Yellow Bird"), 163
RIDGE, MARTIN, 419
Rieff, David, 525
RIEFF, DAVID, 553
RIGHTER, ROBERT W., 229, 505
"Right to Work," 247, 380
Riles, Wilson, 409–10
Riley, Bennet, 117–18
Riley, Nancy Richardson, 544
Riordan, Richard, 487
RISCHIN, MOSES, 338
Rivera y Moncada, Fernando, 35–36, 38, 42, 47
RIVERS, WILLIAM, 353
Roberts, Fred, 326
ROBERTS, GARY L., 240
Roberts, Owen J., and report on Pearl Harbor,
  362
Robinson, Alfred, 76, 79, 81
ROBINSON, ALFRED, 81
ROBINSON, JUDITH, 230, 352
ROBINSON, W. W., 158, 324
RODRIGUEZ, EMELYN, 553
Rodriguez, Gregory, 550
RODRIGUEZ, GREGORY, 553
RODRIGUEZ, JOSÉ, 353
RODRIGUEZ, RAYMOND, 338
ROGERS, FRED B., 96

Rogers, Will, 291
ROGIN, MICHAEL P., 240, 338
Rohrbough, Malcolm, 113
ROHRBOUGH, MALCOLM, 114
ROLFE, LIONEL, 294
ROLLE, ANDREW, 96, 230, 436
Rolling Stones, 455
Rolph, James, Jr. ("Sunny Jim"), 293, 325–26
Romo, Ricardo, 410
ROMO, RICARDO, 419
Roney, Frank, 243
Roosevelt, Franklin D., 318–319, 332–34, 338,
  360, 363, 405
Roosevelt, James, 374
Roosevelt, Theodore:
  and California progressives, 257, 262, 263,
    266, 276
  and conservation, 311–12, 315, 319
  and Japan, 277
RORABAUGH, W. J., 436
ROSE, ALICE M., 265
ROSENBAUM, FRED, 168
ROSENUS, ALAN, 70
ROSEUS, KENNETH T., 480
Rossi, Angelo, 331
Rosten, Leo, 305
ROSTEN, LEO C., 309
ROSZAK, THEODORE, 436
Rothko, Mark, 444
ROTHMAN, HAL K., 528
ROWE, LEONARD C., 385
Rowell, Chester H., 251, 261
Rowland, John, 80
ROWLEY, WILLIAM D., 324
Roybal, Edward R., 413
Royce, Josiah, 59, 113, 131, 138, 222
ROYCE, JOSIAH, 114, 139
RUBENS, LISA, 294
RUBIN, DAVID, 353
Rubin, Jerry, 430, 433, 434
RUBIN, LILLIAN, 419
Ruef, Abraham, 245, 254–59, 260, 261, 313
RUIZ, VICKI, 338, 385
Rumford Act (1963) (open housing law), 407–8,
  458
RUNTE, ALFRED, 214, 323, 504
Ruscha, Edward, 446
RUSCO, ELMER R., 384
RUSSELL, T. C., 57
Russians, 54–55
Rustigan, Michael, 542
Ryan, Arbella ("Belle Cora"), 136
Ryan, T. Claude, 359

saber-toothed cat (*Smilodon californicus*), 4
Sacramento:
   architecture in, 451
   education in, 167
   exploration of, 53–54
   founding of, 78–79
   geologic origins of, 6
   in gold rush, 100
   Johnson family in, 262–63
   land title troubles in, 143
   location of state capital, 121
   newspapers in, 223
   nuclear power plant near, 498
   railroad founded at, 169–73
   recent elections in, 416
Sacramento Bee (newspaper), 223, 351, 479
Sacramento Municipal Utilities District, 322
Sacramento Valley Railroad, 170
Salazar, Rubén, 412, 431
SALOUTOS, THEODORE, 397
Salton Sea, 316
SALZMAN, ED, 480
SALYER, LUCY E., 200
Samish, Arthur H., 370–72
SAMISH, ARTHUR H., 384
San Andreas Fault, 2–3
San Diego:
   aircraft industry in, 359–60
   electric energy crisis, 501–3
   European discovery of, 23–24
   founding of, 7, 35–36
   higher education in, 536
   labor relations in, 251
   native resistance at, 45
   nuclear power for, 498
   population growth of, 422
   transportation in, 531
   water for, 320–21
San Diego Gas and Electric Company, 501
San Diego Padres, 520
San Francisco:
   air pollution in, 489
   culture in, 160–63
   earthquake and fire (1906), 256–57
   European discovery of, 36
   "freeway revolt," 423–24
   geologic origins of, 5–6
   "golden age" of painting in, 443–44
   graft prosecution, 256–59, 261–64
   labor relations in, 191–96, 242–46, 273,
       285–88, 330–33
   Loma Prieta earthquake (1989), 424
   naming (from Yerba Buena), 99
   population growth of, 422

   recent economic development of, 507, 519
   tourism in, 519
   vigilance committees, 132–39
   waterfront control, 180
   water supply of, 313–16
   Workingmen's party activities in, 193–96, 248
San Francisco Art Institute, 444
San Francisco Bay Conservation and Develop-
       ment Commission (BCDC), 482–83
San Francisco Bulletin (newspaper), 136, 161,
       180, 222, 251, 257, 267
San Francisco Call (newspaper), 161
San Francisco Chronicle (newspaper), 198, 222,
       347, 531
San Francisco Examiner (newspaper), 223, 235,
       347
San Francisco Franchise League, 155
San Francisco General Strike (1934), 330–33
San Francisco Museum of Art, 348
San Francisco News (newspaper), 343
San Francisco News Letter (newspaper), 216
San Francisco Opera, 349, 452
San Francisco Performing Arts Center, 452
"San Francisco Renaissance" (poetry
       movement), 438
San Francisco State University, 405, 430
San Francisco Symphony Orchestra, 452–53
San Joaquin valley, 6
San Jose:
   first state capital, 121
   founding of, 44
   lynching in, 326
   mayoral election in, 416
San Jose State University, 441, 542
San Onofre (nuclear power plant), 498
San Pasqual, battle of (1846), 93
Sanborn, Henry, 389
Sánchez, George I., 410
Sánchez, Jose Bernado, 74
SÁNCHEZ, JOSEPH P., 57
SANDMEYER, ELMER C., 199
Sandos, James, 51, 153
SANDOS, JAMES A., 57, 158
San Simeon, Hearst's "castle" at, 346–47, 350
Santa Barbara:
   architecture of, 451
   campus turmoil in, 431
   geologic origins of, 5
   native cultures of, 14, 17, 18, 19
   oil spill at, 484
Santa Barbara News–Press (newspaper), 382
Santa Clara Valley, 330
Santa Fe Railroad, 207
SANTOS, ROBERT L., 114

Sargent, Aaron A., 173, 233, 271
Sargent, Ellen Clark, 271
Saroyan, William, 344–45
SARRIS, GREG, 455
SAUDER, ROBERT A., 323
SAUNDERS, RICHARD, 229
Savio, Mario, 429
Saxenian, AnnaLee, 527
SAXTON, ALEXANDER P., 158, 199, 252, 282
Scannell, David, 137
SCHAFFER, RONALD, 282
SCHARLIN, CRAIG, 398
SCHARNHORST, GARY, 168
SCHELL, ORVILLE, 480
Schenley Industries, 387, 394
SCHERER, JAMES A. B., 140
SCHIESL, MARTIN J., 265, 367, 385
SCHLESINGER, ARTHUR M., JR., 338
SCHLISSEL, LILLIAN, 114
SCHMIDT, DAVID D., 282, 481
Schmitz, Eugene E., 250, 258–59, 277
SCHNEIDER, BETTY V. H., 367
Schoenberg, Arnold, 452
SCHOENHERR, ALLEN A., 9
SCHONEBERGER, WILLIAM A., 367
Schrag, Peter, 479, 533
SCHRAG, PETER, 480
SCHREPFER, SUSAN, 323
SCHULTZ, CHARLES R., 114
SCHULTZ, DAVID E., 229
Schultz, Jim, 472
SCHUPARRA, KURT, 384
SCHURZ, WILLIAM L., 38
SCHUTZ, JOHN A., 56
SCHWANTES, CARLOS A., 294
SCHWARTZ, BERNARD, 385
SCHWARTZ, HARVEY, 339
SCHWEIKART, LARRY, 115
SCOBIE, INGRID W., 385
Scott, Howard, 328
Scott, James, 31
SCOTT, STANLEY, 504
SCOTT, STEVE, 481
Scott, Thomas A., 296–97
Screen Actors Guild, 376, 457
Screen Cartoonists Guild, 376
SCRUGGS, OTEY M., 398
SDS (Students for a Democratic Society), 430
Seale, Bobby, 433, 435
SEALE, BOBBY, 436
seal of the state, 120–21
Sea Ranch (housing development in Sonoma County), 450
Sears, David, 546

SEARS, JOHN F., 309
secularization of the missions, 29–30, 58–64
SEGAL, MORLEY, 338
Segovia, Josefa (Juanita), lynched at Downieville (1851), 135
Selig, William (film producer), 203–304
SELVIN, DAVID F., 252, 339
SELZ, PETER, 455
Selznick, Lewis J., 305
Semple, Robert, 89, 128, 160
Senkewicz, Robert, 131
SENKEWICZ, ROBERT M., 70, 139
Sequoia giganteum (Sierra redwood), 6, 312
Sequoia National Park, 244, 312, 519
Sequoia sempervirens (coast redwood), 6
Sequoya League, 400
Serra, Junípero, 32–34, 48–52
SETTLE, MARY, 178
SETTLE, RAYMOND W., 178
Severance, Caroline Maria, 272
SEVERN, BILL, 385
SHAFFER, RALPH E., 294
Shakur, Tupac, 453
Shaler, William, 72
SHALER, WILLIAM, 81
SHANKS, ROSALIE, 253
Shannon, William E., 119
Sharon, William, 188–89, 238
Shasta Dam, 321–22
SHEBL, JAMES, 82
SHEK, KITTY W., 418
Shelley v. Kraemer (1948) (fair housing), 406
Shell Oil Company, 299
Sherman, William Tecumseh, 137
SHIDELER, JAMES H. 397
Shilts, Randy, 540
SHILTS, RANDY, 553
Shima, George, 277
SHINN, CHARLES H., 114, 139
Shipbuilding industry, 355–57
SHIRES, MICHAEL A., 480
"Shirley letters," 162
Shockley, William, 511
Short, Walter C., 362
SHOVER, JOHN L., 240, 338
SHOVER, MICHAEL, 200
Shuler, Robert P., 327–28
SHUMSKY, NEIL L., 200
SIEBERT, JEROME B., 528
Sierra Club, 312, 313, 482, 485, 487, 525
Sierra National Forest, 315
Signal Hill (oil field), 299
Silicon Valley, 510–15, 531
Silliman, Benjamin, Jr., 296–97

silver, 2, 164, 186–89
SIMMONS, JEROLD, 385
Simmons, William, 15
SIMMONS, WILLIAM, 19
Simon, Bill, 478
Simpson, George, 84
SINCLAIR, ANDREW, 229
Sinclair, Harry F., 300
Sinclair, Upton, 289, 333–34, 337, 372
Single Tax, 215–16
Sitton, Tom, 266
SITTON, TOM, 264, 282
Six Companies (Chinese), 192
Six Flags Magic Mountain (amusement park),
    519
Six Flags Marine World (amusement park), 519
slavery, 123, 155–56
"Sleepy Lagoon" murder trial (1942), 411–12,
    441
Slidell, John, 85, 91
Sloat, John Drake, 92
SLOBODEK, MITCHELL, 253
SMART, NINIAN, 168
Smelser, Neil, 538
Smilodon californicus (saber-toothed cat), 4
Smith, Francis Marion ("Borax"), 211
SMITH, GENE A., 96
Smith, Gladys (Mary Pickford), 306
SMITH, HEDRICK, 480
SMITH, HENRY NASH, 168
SMITH, JEAN M., 419
Smith, Jedediah Strong, 73–75
SMITH, MICHAEL, 323
Smith, Page, 538
Smith, Paul C., 347
SMITH, RICHARD CANDIDA, 455
SMITH, WALLACE, 190, 213
SMITH-BARANZINI, MARLENE, 114, 168
smog, 488–90, 513
SMOLENSKY, EUGENE, 481
socialism, 239–40, 242, 318
    rise and fall of movement, 284–86, 288–90
    of Upton Sinclair, 333–35
Social Security Act (1935), 336–38
SOKOLOW, AL, 528
solar energy, 495–96
SOLBERG, CURTIS B., 419
SONNENBURG, PAUL, 367
Southern California Edison Company, 496, 501,
    503
Southern California Rapid Transit District,
    425
Southern Pacific Land Company, 186, 299,
    464

Southern Pacific Railroad Company, 182–84,
    206, 231–40, 261–64, 266–72, 299, 301,
    388, 453
special interests (political influence), 479
SPENCE, MARY LEE, 96
Spencer, Herbert, 219
Spencer, Stuart, 477
Spoor, George K., 303
Spreckels, Claus, 203
Spreckels, John D., 237, 251
Spreckels, Rudolph, 257
Spring Valley Water Company, San Francisco,
    318
Sproul, Robert Gordon, 378, 403
Sproul Hall, student demonstration at (1964),
    428–29, 445
SQUIRES, RADCLIFF, 352
Stackpole, Ralph, 224
STADTMAN, VERNE A., 230, 436
Standard Oil Company, 298–99
STANDART, M. COLETTE, 158
Stanford, Jane Lathrop, 228, 229
Stanford, Leland, 127, 171, 174, 175, 177, 180,
    221, 224, 228, 232
Stanford University, 228, 229, 437, 438, 448,
    517, 532, 538
STANGER, FRANK M., 39
STANLEY, GERALD, 128
STARKEY, DANIELLE, 528
Starr, Kevin, 30, 141, 158
STARR, KEVIN, 158, 167, 214, 229, 308, 338, 367,
    436
ST. CLAIR, DAVID J., 115
Stearns, Abel, 76, 86, 206
Stefanic, Jean, 537
STEFANIC, JEAN, 553
Steffins, Lincoln, 258, 261
STEIN, WALTER J., 397
Steinbeck, John, 342–44, 389, 439, 443
Stephens, Henry Morse, 228
Stephens, William D., 281, 288
STERLING, GEORGE, 352
STEVENS, JOSEPH E., 324
Stevenson, Adlai E., 373, 376–77
Stevenson, J. D., 117, 132
STEWART, GEORGE R., 82, 114, 139, 168, 385
Still, Clyfford, 444
Stilwell, Joseph W., 366
STIMSON, GRACE H., 253, 294
Stimson, Henry L., 363
Stimson, Marshall, 260
STOBAUGH, ROBERT, 505
Stockton, Robert F., 92–93, 94
STOLL, STEVEN, 214

STOLZ, PREBLE, 481
STONE, IRVING, 82, 96, 229, 385
Storke, Thomas M., 382
ST. PIERRE, BRIAN, 352
Stravinsky, Igor, 452
Strobridge, J. H., 176
Stroheim, Erich von, 306
Strong, Daniel W., 170–71
STRONG, DOUGLAS, 505
Stuart, James, 134
Studebaker, John, 110
Students for a Democratic Society (SDS), 430
SUGDEN, JOHN, 38
Suhr, Herman, 252
SULLIVAN, CHARLES L., 213
Sullivan, Louis H., 351
sunbelt, 506–7
Sunkist Growers, Inc., 203–5, 304
Sutro, Adolph, 188, 235
Sutter, John A., 78–79, 81, 89, 97–98
SUVs (sport utility vehicles), 490
SWAN, HOWARD, 353
SWANBERG, W. A., 230, 352
sweathouse, 13–14, 52
Swett, John, 167
Swing, Phil, and Boulder Canyon Project, 317
SWISHER, CARL B., 200
SYER, JOHN C., 480

Tac, Pablo (Luiseño), 46, 51–52
TAFT, PHILIP, 252
Taft, Robert A., 374
Taft-Hartley Labor Relations Act (1947), 379
Tahoe Regional Planning Agency (TRPA), 484
Takaki, Ronald, 199
TAKAKI, RONALD, 199
TAKEZAWA, YUSUKO J., 418
TAMPLIN, RTHUR, 505
Tan, Amy, 443
Tang, Fung, 149
Tang, Henry, 549
TANIGUCHI, NANCY J., 158
Tape, Mamie, 199
TAPER, BERNARD, 168
Tator, Nettie, 271
TAUB, J. S., 527
taxation, 118, 126, 215–16, 267, 301, 326, 458,
    463–65, 469, 530
TAYLOR, BRUCE MICHAEL, 430
TAYLOR, PAUL S., 253, 324, 397
TAYLOR, RONALD B., 398
Taylor, Zachary, 91, 117–18
Teague, Charles C., 204
TEAGUE, CHARLES, 214

Teapot Dome (naval oil reserve), 300
technocracy, 328
TEITZ, MICHAEL B., 527
Tejon reservation, 152
television, 308, 437, 511
Temescal (see Sweathouse)
TENBROEK, JACOBUS, 367
Tenney, Jack B., 377
Terman, Frederick, 511
terrorist attacks (September 11, 2001), 477–78,
    508, 518, 519, 530, 549, 551
Terry, David S., 125, 137, 238
testimony law (1850), 156
Texas Company (Texaco), 299
THELANDER, CARL G., 504
THELIN, JOHN R., 230
Thieriot, Charles de Young, 347
THOMAS, BOB, 384
THOMAS, DOROTHY S., 368
THOMAS, LATELY, 338
THOMPSON, CARL D., 324
THOMPSON, GERALD, 159
Thompson, Waddy, 84
THOMPSON, WARREN S., 214, 436
THORPE, JAMES, 214
THROWER, NORMAN J. 38
Thursday's Child (racing yacht), 102
Tien, Chang-Lin, 549
TIKHMENEV, P. A., 57
Tolman, Edward C., 378
Tolman v. Underhill (1952) (loyalty oath case),
    378
TONG, BENSON, 199
Tourism, 205–8, 302–4, 518–21
Townsend, Francis E., and Townsend Plan, 328,
    336
toxic wastes, 493–95, 513
Toypurina (shaman), 51
transportation, 169–78, 180–84, 206–13,
    300–303, 423–24, 499–500, 529–32
Trask, Bonnie, 390
TRASK, BONNIE, 397
TREADWELL, EDWARD F., 190
Treaty of Guadalupe Hidalgo (1848), 83, 95,
    117, 143
TREUTLEIN, THEODORE E., 56
Truman, Harry S, 311, 382, 390, 391, 465
Trupin, Laura, 510, 550
TSAI, SHIH-SHAN, 199
TUCKER, MARCIA, 455
Tule Lake (relocation camp), 366
Tunney, John, 435
Turnbull, William, 450
TURNER, FREDERICK, 323

Turner, Frederick Jackson, 184
TUTOROW, NORMAN E., 129, 178, 190
Twain, Mark, 164–65, 491
Twentieth Century-Fox, 308, 343
TYGIEL, JULES, 252, 264, 308
Tyler, John, 84

UMBECK, JOHN, 114
UNGER, IRWIN, 436
Union Labor party of San Francisco, 245,
    254–59
Union Oil Company, 297, 319, 483
Union Pacific, 174, 176, 182
United Artists, 308
United Cannery, Agricultural, Packing and Allied
    Workers of America (UCAPAWA), 330
United Farm Workers (UFW), 394–95, 483,
    526
United Negro Labor Committee, 357
United Railroads of San Francisco, 256, 258,
    286
Universal Pictures, 308
Universal Studios, 519
University of California, 120, 227, 347, 377,
    387, 427, 512, 517, 537–38
University of California, Berkeley, 271, 219,
    227, 286, 373, 379, 428–32, 452, 460, 537,
    548, 549
University of California, Davis, 387, 427, 494
University of California, Irvine, 427, 504
University of California, Los Angeles (UCLA),
    427, 452, 515, 537, 539, 546
University of California, Riverside, 427
University of California, San Diego, 427, 509
University of California, San Francisco, 510, 550
University of California, Santa Barbara, 427,
    431, 487
University of California, Santa Cruz, 427, 538
UNO, EDISON, 368
Unruh, Jesse, 406, 460
UNRUH, JOHN D., JR., 82
Unruh Civil Rights Act (1959), 406
URSIN, EDMUND, 505
Utopian Society, 328

VALDEZ, ARMANDO, 419
VALDEZ, DENNIS NORDÍN, 397
Valdez, Luis, 441
Vallecitos (nuclear power plant), 497
Vallejo, Mariano Guadalupe, 59, 60, 63, 65, 69,
    78, 86, 89, 118, 121
Vallejo, Rosalía, 90
Van Buren, Martin, 83
Vancouver, George, 52–53

VANE, SYLVIA BRAKKE, 20
Van Ness, James, 137
VAN NOSTRAND, JEANNE, 230
VAN NUYS, FRANK W., 283
VAN VALEN, NELSON, 295
Vargas, Arturo, 550, 552
Vasconcellos, John, 552
Vasconcelos, José, 412
Vasquez, Tiburcio, 442
VAUGHT, DAVID, 397
VELIE, LESTER, 384
VERGE, ARTHUR C., 367
VERNON, RAYMOND, 505
Victor, Frances Fuller, 220
Victoria (*see* Bartolomea)
Victoria, Manuel, 61–62
VIEHE, FREDERICK WILLIAM III, 264, 309
Vietnamese refugees, 406, 548
Vietnam War, 406, 420, 422
vigilance committees, 130–39, 141, 252, 286,
    326, 331, 343
Vignes, Jean Louis, 203
VILLANUEVA, LILIA V., 398
Villaraigosa, Antonio, 551
Villareal, José Antonio, 441
VINSON, MICHAEL, 528
Virginia City Territorial Enterprise (newspaper),
    164–65
Vizcaíno, Sebastian, 27
Vizenor, Gerald, 441
VON BRETON, HARIETTE, 352
Voorhis, Jerry, 358, 376
Vuich, Rose A., 415

Wa, Har, 148
WADSWORTH, GINGER, 353
wage, minimum, 262, 274
WAGNER, HENRY R., 38
WALKER, FRANKLIN, 167, 229
Walker, Joseph Reddeford, 75
Wallace, A. J., 272
WALSH, JAMES P., 200, 264
Walt Disney Concert Hall (Los Angeles), 453
Walt Disney Imagineering (WDI), 521
WALTERS, DAN, 481, 527, 552
WALTERS, DONALD E., 240
WALTON, JOHN, 323
Wanzer, Lucy Marcia Field, 271
Ward v. Flood (1874) (school segregation), 156
WARD, ESTOLV E., 294
Warner, Jack, 376
Warner, J. J., 86
Warner Brothers, 308
War Relocation Authority (WRA), 364, 402

Warren, Earl:
  attorney general, 361, 362
  Chief Justice, 374, 379, 408, 421, 426
  governor, 373–75, 378
Wasp (magazine), 183, 196, 217
Watergate scandal, 461–62
Waterman, Thomas T., 154
Waters, Frank, and Hoover Dam, 318
Waters, Maxine, 410
Water supplies and projects, 9, 208–10, 310–23,
    380–81, 482, 489–90
WATSON, DOUGLAS S., 39
Watts riot (1965), 407, 420
WEATHERSON, MICHAEL ALLEN, 265
WEAVER, JOHN D., 385
WEBB, R. W., 9
Webb, Ulysses S., 278, 361
WEBBER, H. J., 214
Weber, David, 46
WEBER, DAVID J., 56, 57, 70, 81
WEBER, DEBRA, 338
WEBER, FRANCIS J., 57
Webster, Daniel, 84, 123
WEIBEL-ORLANDO, JOAN, 418
Weinstock, Harris, 273
WEINTRAUB, HYMAN G., 253
WEITZE, KAREN J., 353
Welch, Robert, 382
welfare, 460–61, 463, 469
Weller, John B., 135, 150
WELLOCK, THOMAS RAYMOND, 505
Wells, Fargo & Company, 111, 175
west coast jazz movement, 453
West, Nathanael, 345, 439
wetlands, 14, 483
WHEAT, CARL I., 178
WHEAT, FRANK, 504
Wheatland riot (1913), 252
Wheeler, Benjamin Ide, 228
WHEELER, B. GORDON, 159
WHIPPLE, MARY ANN, 19
Whitaker, Clem, 372–73
WHITE, G. EDWARD, 385
WHITE, GERALD T., 308
WHITE, RICHARD, 158
WHITEHEAD, RICHARD S., 57
WHITEMAN, LUTHER, 338
Whitney, Asa, 170
Whitney, Charlotte Anita, 288–90, 378
WHITTEN, WOODROW C., 253, 294
WHITTINGTON, JAN, 552
Wiggin, Kate Douglas, 227
WILEY, PETER, 527
WILKINS, THURMAN, 323

WILLIAMS, DAVID A., 128
WILLIAMS, G. ROBERT, 480
WILLIAMS, JAMES C., 505
WILLIAMS, MARY FLOYD, 139
WILLIAMS, R. HAL, 240
Wills, Garry, 470
Wilmot Proviso (1846), 117, 123
Wilshire, Gaylord, 284
Wilshire's Magazine, 284
Wilson, Benjamin D., 80
Wilson, Darryl Babe, 441
WILSON, JAMES Q., 385
Wilson, J. Stitt, 264, 285–86
Wilson, Pete:
  as governor, 467–72, 474, 484, 487, 544,
      550
  as gubernatorial candidate, 467–69
  as presidential candidate, 471
  as senator, 467
WILSON, ROBERT A., 418
WILSON, TERRY P., 158
Wilson, Woodrow, 278, 287, 306
WINCHELL, MARK ROYDEN, 455
wind power, 496–97
Wing, Kate, 486
WINKLER, DAVID R., 481
WINKLER, DONALD R., 527
WINKLER, JOHN K., 230
WINTER, ROBERT, 455
WINTHER, OSCAR O., 178
WOLF, DONALD E., 374
WOLFE, LINNIE MARCH, 323
WOLFINGER, RAYMOND E., 419
Wolfskill, William, 203
WOLIN, SHELDON S., 436
WOLLENBERG, CHARLES, 367, 397, 419, 436,
      527
WOLT, IRENE, 352
women:
  appointment of, 416–17
  "comparable worth" issue and, 418
  constitution of 1849 and, 120
  discrimination against in professions, 227
  electoral politics, 415–16, 470
  employment patterns, 416–17
  equal rights amendment (ERA), 417
  farm laborers, 396
  during gold rush, 112–13
  higher education, status in, 228–29
  impact of Chinese exclusion on, 198–99
  labor movement and, 245, 330
  during Mexican War, 93
  minimum wage for, 273–75
  native cultures, role in, 12, 14, 17

Spanish & Mexican periods, activities in, 30, 45, 50, 54, 68–69
   suffrage for, 269–72
   during World War II, 358, 359
   (*see also names of individuals*)
Women's Christian Temperance Union (WCTU), 271
WONG, CARA, 481
Woo, Michael, 405
WOOD, RAYMOND F., 168
WOODBRIDGE, SALLY B., 230, 455
Woods, "Gusher Charlie," 298
Wool, John E., 137–38
WOOLFENDEN, JOHN, 504
WOOLSEY, RONALD C., 128
workers' compensation, 262, 273, 396
Workingmen's party of California, 193–98, 242
Workman, William, 80
World War I, 250, 285, 286, 288, 341
World War II, 308, 354–67, 515–18
World Wide Web, 514
WORSTER, DONALD, 214, 324
Wozniak, Stephen, 513
Wright, Frank Lloyd, 351
WRIGHT, LOUIS B., 168
Wright Irrigation Act (1887), 209
WYATT, DAVID, 352, 455

YABLONSKY, LEWIS, 436
"Yellow Bird" (John Rollin Ridge), 163
YENNE, BILL, 178, 240
Yerba Buena, 99–100
YERGIN, DANIEL, 505
Yi, Paul, 523
YONAY, EHUD, 527
Yosemite:
   creation of, 3
   European-American discovery of, 75
   national park, 310–13, 485, 500, 519
Young, Al, 440
Young, Brigham, 99
Young, Clement C., 289, 292–93
YOUNG, JOHN P., 230
YU, EUI-YOUNG, 418
Yuma massacre (1781), 46–48
YUNG, JUDY, 199

Zalvidea, José María, 50, 74
Zamarano, Agustín, 62, 160
Zanuck, Darryl, 343
ZEIGER, RICHARD, 481
ZIMMERMAN, TOM, 339
Zola, Émile, 217
ZOLLINGER, JAMES P., 82
"zoot suit" riots (1942), 410–11, 441
Zukor, Adolph, 305

Appendix
Select Websites on California History

 www.californiahistoricalsociety.org is an inviting portal to the abundant resources of the California Historical Society. Founded in 1871, the society is the state's official historical society. Its San Francisco galleries and research library offer art, artifacts, publications, and statewide educational activities on California history. The Website provides a comprehensive overview of the society's collections, programs, exhibitions, publications and a reciprocal access membership program. The friendly navigation system allows visitors to experience current and past exhibitions, purchase books and items from the museum store, support CHS through membership, explore the collections, download free instructional materials, and schedule school tours.

 The site is also home to **California History Online,** an educational, online exhibit covering a timeline of more than 300 years of California history, from the first Californians, to the Spanish colonial frontier, and into the twenty-first century. It includes key events, personalities, and anecdotes from California's past and is illustrated with 400 images from the California Historical Society's fine Arts and Research Collections.

The official site for the eighth edition of *California: An Interpretive History* is **www.mhhe.com/rawls8**. It includes student quizzes and interactive exercises for each chapter, Web links, and map exercises. Instructors may download from the site dozens of historical images to create Power Point classroom presentations.

Recommended Links for Historical Research on California

The following list, compiled by the staff of the California Historical Society, describes some useful links for researchers and students of California history.

http://bancroft.berkeley.edu

The Bancroft Library   The Bancroft Library is a collection of printed and manuscript material relating to the history of western North America, from the western Great Plains to the Pacific Ocean, and from Alaska to Panama. The greatest concentration of material relates to two areas—California and the west coast, and Mexico and Central America—and has been collected intensively to the present. In addition to books and manuscripts, the Bancroft Library includes maps, newspapers, photographs and other pictorial documentation, microfilm of original documents in private hands and in foreign archives, and other materials. The site provides information on accessing the collections, research programs, news, events, exhibitions, and publications.

www.cdlib.org

California Digital Library (CDL)   A co-library of the campuses of the University of California, the California Digital Library was founded in 1997 by University of California President Richard Atkinson. CDL provides access to the following digital resources: the Online Archive of California, Counting California, the MELVYL catalog, the California Periodicals Database, thousands of electronic journals, dozens of journals abstracting and indexing the databases, and specialized and reference resources.

www.library.ucsb.edu/speccoll/cema

California Ethnic and Multicultural Archives (CEMA)   The California Ethnic and Multicultural Archives are located in the Donald C. Davidson Library at the University of California, Santa Barbara. CEMA is a permanent program offering collections of primary research materials that document the cultural and political experiences of African Americans, Asian Americans, Latinos, and Native Americans in California. The site provides information on the collections as well as exhibits, catalogs, essays, and related archives and Websites.

www.cimcc.indian.com

California Indian Museum and Cultural Center   At this museum, Native Americans of California portray California Indian history and culture from an Indian perspective. The facility also encourages the present-day renaissance of California Indian culture. The site provides links to resources on California history, California Indian maps and lists of tribes, recommended reading and resources, and online articles.

www.missionsofcalifornia.org

California Missions Foundation   The foundation is dedicated to preserving the history of the California missions. The site provides historical background on each mission as well as a comprehensive chronological timeline of mission history.

www.library.ca.gov

California State Library   The California State Library makes available directly or through local public libraries a variety of services to all Californians. Resources include California historical documents, records of state legislation, books in Braille and recorded formats, English-language literacy programs, and public access to the Internet. The state library is also the main research library for the state government, providing reference and information services to all state government agencies and specialized nonpartisan research services to the legislature, governor's office, and other state constitutional officers. The site includes a catalog, research tools, and a list of library services and products.

http://bss.sfsu.edu/calstudies

California Studies Program   The Website of the California Studies Program at San Francisco State University provides access to many California history online resources including the California Studies Online Syllabi project (CSOS), a compilation and distribution of syllabi and bibliographies for California-related university and college courses.

www2.h-net.msu.edu/~cal

H-California   H-California is an international electronic discussion group for scholars and teachers of historical demography. The site provides historians and others interested in researching and analyzing California with a forum for discussing new (and old) theories, methods, and findings. H-California offers a wide range of experts for consultation. It is one of the networks of H-NET, published by the University of Illinois, Chicago, and Michigan State University.

www.heydaybooks.com

Heyday Books   Heyday Books is dedicated to producing books about California and is the publishing partner for the California Historical Society Press. Founded in 1974, Heyday has maintained a highly respected list of titles covering California history and culture, natural history, literature, poetry, regional guides, and California Native American life.

www.huntington.org

The Huntington Library, Art Collections, and Botanical Gardens   Founded in 1919, the Huntington is an oasis of art and culture set amid 150 acres of gardens. Three art galleries and a library showcase magnificent collections of paintings, sculptures, rare books, manuscripts, and decorative arts. Of special interest is the Huntington Library's extensive collection of Californiana. The Website offers several online exhibits as well as information on using the library's collections, attending conferences and lectures, and obtaining fellowships.

www.learncalifornia.org

LearnCalifornia.org   LearnCalifornia.org offers direct access to the collections of the California State Archives. Established in 1850, the state's public archives are the oldest non-constitutional function of California government. The site provides resources for teachers, students, and researchers, including access to other online resources and historical writing on various California topics. "This Day in California History" is a special feature on the site's homepage.

www.museumca.org

Oakland Museum of California   The Oakland Museum is dedicated to the art, history, and natural sciences of California. Its comprehensive permanent exhibits on three floors portray California's natural wonders, events, eras, and people who have shaped the state. The Website offers several online exhibits and curricula, including dozens of images and pages of narration.

www.ca.gov

Welcome to California   The official site for the state of California provides historical resources on the land, culture, people, public policy, and laws of the Golden State.